BOOK OF CANADIAN WINNERS & HEROES

Prudential's

BOOK OF
CANADIAN
WINNERS
&HEROES

BY BRENNA BROWN
EDITOR: JEREMY BROWN
ASSISTANT EDITOR: FAY MATTHEWS

A PRENTICE-HALL/NEWCASTLE BOOK

ACKNOWLEDGEMENTS

Many people contributed time and skill to the assemblage of the text. Fay Matthews Garcia organized the initial thrust, sending out thousands of letters to institutions and associations, then collecting and collating the information. Caryn Smith and Tracy Hamilton continued the quest. Cathy Munro worked assiduously refining the original material. Richard Thornton, with ineffable good humour, worked particularly on the arts section. Susan Barrable, a paradigm, marshalled schedules. Ellen Vanstone laboured often around the clock copy editing the final manuscript. Brant Cowie designed it, Glenn Ireland, Scott Phipps and crew of Q Composition set the type, and Ron Hearnden of Gagné Printers arranged the printing. Then there were the hundreds of respondents who checked their files and submitted their winners to us. Peter Bruton of Prudential was endlessly patient and supportive. They all helped make it possible, including Dean Kelley, the demon driver. To us, each is a winner.

Produced by
Newcastle Publishing Limited
30 Howland Avenue
Toronto, Ontario   M5R 3B3

Published by
Prentice-Hall Canada Inc.
1870 Birchmount Road
Scarborough, Ontario   M1P 2J7

Printed and bound in Canada

CANADIAN CATALOGUING IN PUBLICATION DATA
Main entry under title:
Prudential book of Canadian winners and heroes

ISBN 0-13-731695-X (bound). – ISBN 0-13-731679-8 (pbk.)

1. Canada – Biography.   2. Heroes – Canada – Biography.
3. Success – Canada – Biography.   I. Brown, Jeremy,
1932-

FC25.P78
F1005.P78   920'.071   C83-098062-8

Contents

Terry Fox running down Toronto's University Ave., flanked by Darryl Sittler, r, and Jonathan Brown

Introduction

It all started on an airplane flying between Toronto and Montreal. I saw an old friend, Peter Bruton, in the third-to-last row of the Nordair flight. I hadn't seen him for 10 years, but previous to that we had been colleagues on the old *Toronto Telegram*.

Bruton is with the Prudential Insurance Company of America, Canadian Operations, as director of public affairs. During the flight, we agreed to meet. When we did, Bruton expressed the thought that he was fed up with the phenomena of Canadians running themselves down. "A common pastime," he said, "and it really annoys me. I don't think people have the slightest idea of just how many winners there are in this country . . . normal, average unacknowledged Canadians whose individual and combined accomplishments should be a source of considerable national pride."

Thence was born PRUDENTIAL'S BOOK OF CANADIAN WINNERS AND HEROES. It started off with just "winners" in the title. But after the kind of endless meetings that go into a project such as this, we agreed we had to expand and broaden the goal. There are a lot people who didn't have the chance to win a VC, trophy, medal, certificate or award, yet who contributed mightily to the achievements of mankind. There are a number of stories to be told of high achievement that couldn't be contained in a simple list of certified bemedalled winners. Therefore we examined the history of Canada to find those who might not have been officially recognized in a conventional fashion, but who, by any other criterion, would merit recognition.

The bulk of the book is composed of the winners and heroes of today. By no stretch of the imagination could the work be considered complete, either in terms of contemporary winners or winners of the past. There are just too many. What we have tried to do is reflect some of the achievements of Canadians from the early 15th century to today. If the reader feels outraged by an ommission, he or she should know that our initial flood of material could have produced 1,000 pages of text or a separate book for every area of endeavour.

The country drew a remarkable number of adventurers, explorers, entrepreneurs, proselytizers and zealots. Some of them were thugs, mugs, yeggs, or picaroons. Others were totally selfless in the devotion to their cause. I think of the nurses in the early days of Quebec, whose record of achievement against byzantine odds should shake the foundations of the complacent.

We have the modern heroes, ranging from Terry Fox to Wayne Gretzky, to the nameless members of the selection committee of the Gairdner Foundation, who unerringly select scientists who later go on to win the Nobel Prize. Frankly, producing this book has been great fun. We have found people, who, in Brenna's words, "march through their lives, doing what they do very well, illuminating the way for the rest of us." We have omitted the names of thousands of winners. Either we didn't have them, or couldn't find them, or didn't have the room for them. But we *did* find an enormous number. Some of the awards may seem self-serving; but on the whole, we believe the contents of this book show beyond a scintilla of a doubt that there is a large cadre of people in many fields of endeavour who have not only sought the very best, but have achieved it.

In our preliminary enquiries, one of our group asked a librarian for source material on winners. The librarian riposted that "Canada has no winners." We hope this book gives lie to that statement. Without being maudlin, Canada has a heroic share of both winners, and heroes.

There is one final winner. Her name is Brenna Brown, the person who wrote the entire text, researched the historical anecdotes and produced what follows.

Jeremy Brown
Toronto, June 1983

Winners and Heroes

The writers have exercised their option to present their own personal list of winners and heroes. The list is highly arbitrary, highly personal and arguable. But is their's.

J. Lyman MacInnis. A scrappy goal tender from Prince Edward Island, MacInnis dropped out of high school to persue hockey. When he wanted to enrol in accounting, the registrar at the Ontario Institute of Chartered Accountants said he would never be admitted. In 1982/83, MacInnis was president of the Institute, a partner in a major international accounting firm, advisor to Anne Murray, a best selling author, a daily commentator on Canada's largest radio station, the drollest wit this side of the Sahara, a dreadful punster with an encyclopedia memory of the best moments of hockey, and the feistiest professional negotiator the writers' know.

Thérèse Casgrain, a native of Montreal, was the force behind social reforms in Canada that promoted justice and equality. She was a champion of women's rights and a supporter of national unity. Throughout her life she chose to defend the cause of disadvantaged members of society, to denounce social injustice and to lend a voice to those who had no voice.

In 1970 she became the first member of the NDP to be named to the Senate, where she sat as an independent. She was a companion of the Order of Canada, an officer of the Order of the British Empire and received the Woman of the Century award from the Council of Jewish Women of Canada.

Thérèse Casgrain died in 1982, at the age of 85. The government of Canada is commemorating her name by creating a new national award.

Wayne Gretzky's list of honours should be writ on litmus paper. The centre for the Edmonton Oilers is perhaps the best player of Canadian hockey in the world, and continues to re-write the National Hockey League's book of records. He has won money, trophies, rings, cars and the bric-a-brac of sports stardom. It would take a separate book to list the honours. He has been lionized in the United States as well as Canada, and is well beyond being a mere millionaire. And he carries his fame gracefully.

Anne Murray, of Springhill, N.S., is carrying her distinctively iridescent voice and playful, self-depreciating charm to world stardom in the pop music field. Her records are sold around the world, and her tours continent-wide annd internationally sell out. Her television specials consistently draw top ratings and her record of philanthropy is substantial.

What a glorious moment when the U.S. space shuttle Challenger sent back a picture of Canada's remote manipulator arm extended in space, shaped like the number 7, dispatching satellites to space and retrieving packages. The National

Aeronautics and Space Administration awarded Public Service medals to **John MacNaughton**, vice-president, **Terry Ussher**, director of programs, and **Claus Wagner-Bartak**, v-p and general manager, of Spar Aerospace of Toronto, designers of the *Canàdarm*. A giant step for Canada. Arm in Arm with NASA.

Terry Fox is a special case. The cancer-stricken youth electrified all but the most jaded Canadians with his own one-legged run across Canada, truncated at Thunder Bay by a second round of cancer, this round fatal. His purity of purpose engendered an emotional response never before experienced in Canada. He is perhaps the truest hero of this book.

Bob Mossman of the weekly newspaper, The Bulletin, published in Bridgewater, N.S., received the 1982 premier award for best editorial writing from the Canadian Community Newspapers Association. He said it well:

Terry Fox deserves an editorial that really can't be written.

You always lose something in transferring a feeling, or life itself into words, because words really are just man-made labels. They are not life, and they are not feelings.

There are times when television has its place. Television showed us Terry Fox. Shortly after we were introduced to him, and the nightly news clips of his Marathon of Hope progress started to be televised our affinity with hin began to grow. It grew to the point that many of us began to accept our tears as a natural part of the film clip we were viewing. We were simply saying: "How can you do that. Here I am with all of my limbs. And you're doing that, and I'm sitting here. This is not right. By God, at least I can cry."

The tears probably helped him. Terry Fox was pure spirit. He gave up any lasting concern for his body long before he began his marathon in St. John's in April of 1980. To him it was just a machine. He put it in the best shape possible, and the spirit took over, and drove that damn machine.

Terry possessed a quality that everyone naturally envies. He was one-pointed in a good sense. Being one-pointed in a good sense is an attribute that few of us have. The world would be a much better place if more people were like Terry Fox. Like Albert Schweitzer, or Mother Teresa, or Martin Luther King Junior. Canada has had only a small number of selfless giants. Such people are not hatched out of political worlds. In fact they very often avoid the political maze. Their route is more direct, and in many cases they just don't have the patience "to play the game."

People who are guided by rightful inspiration in this world very often lay aside considerations held sacred by the majority. Whether or not an action on our part will be painful is always a major consideration. Terry Fox, from what he went through in running half way across the country, must have considered pain almost a non-priority on his list of considerations.

Terry's sense of determination is still for the most part of a mystery to us. Certainly he was angry at cancer, and being awakened to the high cost of treatment and research, through his own experience with the disease, decided to launch himself, in an effort to literally beat cancer into the ground. The worthiness of his cause is unquestionable. Cancer is an indiscriminate killer. It strikes at any age and shatters the happiness of families all over the world.

We may never know the exact nature of Terry's inner self that prompted his crusade. In just four and a half months Terry's profile went from very low, to very high, as stations around the world began to televise his marathon progress. Perhaps his actions tells us enough. God, he was determined. We couldn't watch him without almost feeling his pain. We couldn't watch him without internally pleading for him to stop. But Terry wouldn't.

I don't think he ever did — stop. The machine halted temporarily in Thunder Bay, but not the spirit. The machine gave out completely on Sunday, June 28 in British Columbia. But not the spirit. It's just impossible to destroy the spirit.

Terry Fox was trying to tell us that. Let's never forget it.

Written by editor Bob Mossman.

WINNERS AND HEROES YOU SHOULD KNOW

Here is a list of Canadians, living or dead, who have achieved distinction here or abroad in virtually every field of endeavour. You should know 90 per cent of them: **Marius Barbeau**, folklorist and anthropologist, **Margaret Atwood**, novelist, **Mario Bernardi**, conductor, **Billy Bishop**, war hero, **Dr. George Fisher Brown**, population research, **William Boyd**, pathologist, **Leonard Brockington**, orator laureate, **Jack Bush**, painter, **Emily Carr**, painter, **Adrienne Clarkson**, TV/diplomacy, **Father Coady**, educator, **Toller Cranston**, ice skater/artist, **Thomas S. Cullen**, gynacologist, **Robertson Davies**, author/educator, **Yvon Deschamps**, actor, **Paul Desmaris**, financier, **Ben Dunkleman**, war hero/industrialist, **Cyrus Eaton**, industrialist/philanthropist, **Arthur Erickson**, architect, **John Kenneth Galbraith**, economist, **Gratien Gelinas**, actor/teacher, **Donald Gordon**, industrialist/builder, **Glenn Gould**, pianist, **Gerhard Herzberg**, Nobel laureate, **Bruce Hutchinson**, author, **Lotta Hitchmanova**, humanitarian, **Claude Jutra**, film director, **Karen Kain**, ballet dancer, **William Hutt**, actor, **Don Daynard**, broadcaster, **James Houston,** Eskimo art expert/author, **Stephen Leacock**, humourist, **Roy Thomson** , media millionaire, **Cardinal Leger**, **Jean-Paul Lemieux**, painter, **Margaraet Laurence**, author, **Monique Leyrac**, singer, **Hugh MacLennan**, author, **Ernest MacMillan**, conductor, **Vincent Massey**, culture/diplomacy/former governor-general, **Norman McLaren**, wizard film maker, **Marshall McLuhan**, communications guru, **A.G.L. McNaughton**, scientist/soldier, **Eugene Forsey**, political savant, former senator, **Grattan O'Leary**, journalist, **Ferguson Jenkins**, baseball, **Northrop Frye**, literary/social critic, **Lester Pearson**, **Wilder Penfield**, neurosurgeon, **William Osler**, **Jean Paul Riopelle**, painter, **Barbara Ann Scott**, skater, **Gordon Robertson**, mandarin, **Charles Saunders**, wheat king, **Frank R. Scott,** educator and poet, **Hans Selye**, understanding stress, **Terry Shortt**, ornithologist and painter, **E.P. Taylor**, financier and industrialist, **Healy Willan**, composer and organist, **J.S. Woodsworth**, CCF founder, **Saul Bellow,** author, **Norman Bethune**, doctor, **Andrew Bonar Law**, British prime minister, **Emily Murphy**, first woman magistrate in British Empire, and **Bryan Williams**, Vancouver lawyer.

HERE IS A LIST OF CANADIAN-BORN ENTERTAINMENT FIGURES:

Mary Anglin, Dan Ackroyd, Beverly Adams, Paul Almond, Paul Anka, Robert Ayres, Johnny Alesworth, Frank Peppiatt, Robert Beatty, Ben Barzman, Lloyd Bochner, Bernie Braden and Barbara Kelly, Genevieve Bujold, Raymond Burr, Rod Cameron, Jack Carson, Paul Carpenter, Susan Clark, John Colicos, Hume Cronyn, Suzanna Cloutier, Kate Nelligan, Sidney Olcott, Patricia Owens, Louis B. Mayer, Albert (Cubby) Brocoli, Jack Warner, Mary Pickford, Christopher Plummer, Donald Sutherland, Walter Pigeon, Beatrice Lilly, Harold Russell, Toby Robbins, Donnelly Rhodes, Craig Russell, Cecelia Parker, Barbara Perkins, Lee Patterson, Ben Piazza, Gordon Pinsent, Alvin Rakoff, Kate Reid, Percy Rodrigues, Robert (Robin) MacNeil,

Giselle MacKenzie, David Manners, Fletcher Markle, Paul Massi, Lois Maxell, Douglass Montgomery, Lionel Murton, Howie Mandel, Raymond Massey, Larry Mann, Silvio Narizzano, Leslie Nielsen, Nick Mancusso, Berton Churchill, Yvonne De Carlo, Colleen Dewhurst, Marie Dressler, Douglass Dumbrille, Fifi D'Orsay, Paul Dupuis, Robert Farnon, Rockliffe Fellowes, Deanna Dursin, Don Francks, Glenn Ford, Sidney J. Furie, Chief Dan George, Lorne Greene, Hughie Green, Kathleen Howard, Victoria Hopper, Arthur Hiller, Arthur Hill, Harvey Hart, John Ireland, Saul Ilson, Robert Ito, Norman Jewison, Lou Jacobi, Harmon Jones, Peter Jennings, Ruby Keeler, Peter Kastner, Margot Kidder, Alexander Knox, Ted Kotcheff, Carla Lehman, Gene Lockhart, Raymond Lovell, Wilfred Ducas, Fay Wray, Harry Saltzman, Norma Shearer, Douglas Shearer, Joanna Shimkus, Jay Silverheels, Ned Sparks, Helen Shaver, Rosie Shuster, Wayne and Shuster, Bernie Slade, William Shatner, Michael Sarrazin, William Stevenson, Alexandra Stewart, Eric Till, Shannon Tweed, Stephen Young, Lucille Watson, Al Hamel, Alex Trebeck, Monty Hall, Joyce Davidson, Anne Murray, Gordon Lightfoot, Bruce Cockburn, Joni Mitchell, Oscar Peterson, Edward Johnson, Teresa Stratas, Jon Vickers, Guy Lombardo, Anna Russel, Art Linkletter, Lynn Seymour, Neil Young, Buffy Sainte-Marie. The Guess Who, Ronnie Hawkins, Loverboy, Rush, April Wine, Maynard Ferguson, Liona Boyd, The Canadian Brass, Maureen Forrester, Michael Bawtree, Suzanne Mess, Marg Kimball, John Fisher, Salli Terri, George London.

General Awards

ORDER OF CANADA

The Order of Canada was established as the centrepiece of our system of honours on July 1, 1967, Canada's Centennial year. It pays tribute to those who exemplify the highest qualities of citizenship and whose contributions enrich the lives of all of us. The three levels of merit are Companion, Officer and Member.

The Queen of Canada is the Sovereign of the Order, who, through the Governor-General, annually presents the awards. Non-Canadians may be appointed honorary members.

1983 **Companion**
Christopher Pratt, St. Catharines, Nfld., was made an Officer of the Order of Canada in 1973. An internationally renowned painter and printmaker, he is a member of the Royal Canadian Academy of Arts and the Canadian Society of Graphic Arts.
OFFICERS:
Sonja I. Bata, Toronto a director of Bata Ltd. and of Alcan Aluminum Ltd.; **Peter J.C. Bentley**, Vancouver, head of Canadian Forest Products Ltd.; medical researcher **Dr. John M. Bowman**, Winnipeg; **Debbie Brill**, high jumper; **David Broadfoot**, comedian; engineer and educator **Angus A. Bruneau**, St. John's; **Dr. G. Everett Chalmers**, Fredericton, former public servant and provincial Cabinet minister; law professor **Roger Contois**, Montreal; **David M. Culver**, Montreal, head of Alcan Aluminum, **Richard J. Doyle**, editor-in-chief, *The Globe & Mail*; oil exploration pioneer **John Patrick (Jack) Gallagher**, Calgary,

chairman of Dome Petroleum; diplomat **Klaus Goldschlag**, Ambassador to West Germany; ballerina **Evelyn Anne Hart**, Winnipeg; **Naim Kattan**, Ottawa, novelist, playwright and senior official of the Canada Council; entertainer **Jean Lapointe**, Montreal; **Sister Denise Lefebvre**, Montreal, nursing educator; singer **Mary Morrison**, Toronto; **Helen J. Morton**, Ottawa, architect of federal employment policy for the handicapped; mining researcher **Garnet T. Page**, Calgary; engineer **Chris Ritchie**, Calgary, chairman of Monenco Ltd.; synchronized simming instructor **Donalda M. Smith**, Vancouver; engineer **Robert James Uffen**, Kingston, Ont., former federal science advisor who has served on two Ontario royal commissions; and **R. Howard Webster**, honorary chairman, *The Globe & Mail*.
MEMBERS:
Businessman **Lanfranco Amato**, Toronto; conservationist **C.M. Anahareo** of Heffley Creek, B.C.; theologian **Eric W. Balcom**, Port Dufferin, N.S.; speed skater **Gaetan Boucher**, St. Hubert, Que.; patients' rights activist **Claude Brunet**, Montreal; children's singer **Raffi Cavoukian**, Toronto; Charlottetown community worker **Evelyn MacEwan Cudmore**; **Rev. Joseph Doherty**, a missionary in Chile; educator and rights activist **Muriel Duckworth**, Halifax; businessman and community worker **Maxwell Enkin**, Toronto; educator **Eugenie Fillier**, Roddickton, Nfld.; musician **Marguerite Fournier**, Prince Albert, Sask.; accountant and hospital board executive **Duncan J. Gordon**, Toronto; **Margherita Austin Howe**, a Niagara-

on-the-Lake environmentalist; social worker **Anne Kalias**, Moorefield, Ont.; judo champion **Yuzuru (Jim) Kojima**, Richmond, B.C.; **Edmond E. Landry**, mayor of Grand-Anse, N.B., and a long-time community leader; health and recreation worker **Rev. Ronald Landry**, Riviere-du-Loup; **Rev. Lucien Larre**, Montreal, Director of a home for troubled teen-agers; industrialist **Jacob Lowy**, Montreal, president of Lowy Investment Corp.; **Sister Geraldine MacNamara**, group home founder in Winnipeg; Quebec union activist **Romeo Mathieu**, Montreal; community worker **Robert Donald McAllister**, Azilda, Ont.; logging and sawmill executive **Alton Morse**, Chapleau, Ont.; musician and educator **Mary Elizabeth Munn**, Calgary; **E. Peter W. Nash**, Toronto, educator and Jesuit leader; singer and native activist **Alanis Obomsawin**, Montreal; Quebec graphic artist **Pierre Ouvrard**; community worker **Mary Adapowska Panaro**, Winnipeg; educator **Rene Paquette**, Laval, Que.; **Edward A. Pickering**, former head of the Toronto Symphony and a force behind the new Roy Thomson Hall; **Stephen R. Ramsankar**, a prominent Edmonton community worker; health care expert **Dr. James Rankine**, Kelowna, B.C.; native rights activist **Mildred Redmond,** Toronto; sports medicine expert **Dr. Ian L. Reid**, Selkirk, Man.; **Col. John Redmond Roche**, Montreal, a National Parole Board commissioner and lawyer, businessman-aviator **Walter R. Ross**, Lethbridge, Alta.; social worker **Rev. Roger Roy**, Montreal; arts co-operative manager and Justice of the Peace **Terrence Ryan**, Cape Dorset, NWT.; **Gustav A. Schousboe**, King's Corner, N.B., community worker and farm group organizer; **Elsa H. Stewart** and **R. Arthur Stewart**, Pakenham, Ont., farmers and municipal activists; **Edith E. Temple**, St. Anne de Bellevue, Que., patient care volunteer; historian **Lewis H. Thomas**, Regina; engineer and community worker **M.A. (Mickey) Thomas**, Vancouver, retired lumber executive; and hospital board director **Godfrey H. Tullidge**, Vancouver.

DECORATIONS FOR BRAVERY

Government of Canada

Decorations for bravery, established in 1972, include the Cross of Valour, the Star of Courage and the Medal of Bravery. On the advice of the Queen's Privy Council for Canada, the Governor-General presents the awards for acts of the most conspicuous courage in circumstances of extreme peril in the interest of Canada. Canadians or non-Canadians, in or outside Canada, may receive an award.

Cross of Valour

The Cross of Valour is this nation's highest decoration for bravery and has been awarded only twelve times since the decoration was established in 1972.

1982 **Anna Lang**, Hampton, N.B. In the early afternoon of September 9, 1980, Anna Lang rescued two passengers from a submerged car she had just escaped from herself.

At the entry of the Hammond River Bridge a fuel tanker hit Lang's car and rammed it through the railing into the river. The tanker then fell into the river and exploded. Despite a concussion, rapidly spreading fire, and the threat of further explosions, Lang swam to shore, removed her heavy clothing, and returned to the submerged car. She reached her passengers through a wall of fire on the surface of the water and with much difficulty dragged Lana Walsh and her four-year-old son Jaye a safe distance from the inferno. Despite extensive burns, she continued with both toward shore until two young men came to assist. The two young men, Jackie Chaisson and Eric Sparks, received Stars of Courage.

Stars of Courage

1982 **Edward Button**, 17, Toronto, Ont., (posthumous award). Edward Button died after saving his brother Patrick's life during a fire at their home in 1980. He carried Patrick to the window of their bedroom, pushed him into the roof but was unable to escape himself.

Benoit Chabot, Malartic, Que., rescued three co-workers left stranded by a fast-moving mud slide at the Balmoral Mine in 1980. He skillfully managed to drive a scoop tram through the mud directly to the three miners who jumped on the back of the tram which he then drove to safety.

George Smith, Petersfield, Man. Immediately following an accident that occurred in May, 1980, George Smith, in spite of a heart condition, ran to the car he had just collided with and pulled Ronald Grieve out of the window of the burning vehicle before the car was destroyed by fire.

James Wadden, Cleveland, Richmond County, N.S. Early on January 30, 1981, James Wadden ran to help his neighbour, Lloyd Hill, who was trapped in a burning house. After two attempts he finally managed to enter the house and brought Hill out (Hill did not survive).

William George Ivany, 16, Sunnyside, Nfld. Ivany was playing hockey on the ice in the harbour at Sunnyside when he saw Lisa Snook, who had been skating by herself, fall through the ice. Despite the extreme danger, he stretched on to the thin ice and pulled her to safety.

Roy Flake, London, Ont. Despite very poor health, Flake rescued an 8-year-old boy from a fire in his building. He dragged the boy to safety while hardly able to see anything in the thick smoke.

Constables Bruce Norman, Oshawa, Ont., and **Charles Reed**, Toronto, Ont., entered a flaming house to rescue a fire victim. When Reed fell and struck his head, Norman heard the cries and re-entered the house, now completely engulfed by flames, to lead both to safety.

Thomas Warren, Manitouwadge, Ont., succeeded in pulling two people from a burning car despite the danger of explosion in July, 1980.

Captain Keith Gathercole, Master Corporal Steve Gledhill and **Corporal Craig Seager**, Comox, B.C., executed a daring helicopter rescue of six people trapped in the flooding Cheakamus River.

Ron Doxtater and his son Mark, of Ottawa, Ont., rescued two bird hunters whose canoe capsized in the dangerous waters of the St. Lawrence, near Morrisburg, Ont., in November, 1980. Father and son paddled to rescue the two men and brought them to shore, almost losing them in the icy waters.

Lieutenant Michael J. Maxwell, Ottawa, Ont., tried in vain to save E.A. Knechtel from being struck by a fast-moving train in Algonquin Park in 1980. Without concern for his own safety, Maxwell ran into the path of the oncoming locomotive. Knechtel was killed and Lieutenant Maxwell suffered severe injuries when they were struck by the train.

Dale Cameron Schive, Edmonton, Alta. Hearing a seven-year-old girl screaming inside a burning house, Schive entered through a bedroom window but was forced back by thick smoke. Schive re-entered the room wearing a scuba mask, crawled along the floor, found the victim and rescued her.

1983 **Firefighter Randall Bush**, Keswick, Ont., (posthumous award). Bush died March 25, 1981, after he fell through ice on Lake Simcoe, Ont., trying to rescue Charles Clarke, who also died in the incident.

Armed forces **Private Roger Chiasson**, Petawawa, Ont., crossed a minefield, risking direct fire, to rescue a fellow soldier who had left his post while on peacekeeping duty in Cyprus.

George Cross, Thunder Bay, Ont., was wheelsman of the vessel *M.V. Ralph-Misener* who rescued three injured men from a fire aboard the vessel.

Jim Fehr, Hague District, Sask., rescued a woman after her canoe overturned in the South Saskatchewan River.

David Frazee, West Vancouver, B.C., rescued a crewman trapped in a fishing vessel that capsized outside Victoria harbour.

Doreen Hewitt, Ottawa, Ont., risked her life by helping a taxi driver who was being held at gunpoint by a passenger. Before police arrived, the passenger had jumped from the cab wielding a knife and stabbed her.

Tugboat **captain Andrew Rae**, Lower Sackville, N.S., saved a man whose boat was sinking off Labrador.

Fire Department Captain **James Worrall** and firefighter **Ronald Rowe**, Dunnville, Ont., rescued two people after their sailboat overturned on Lake Erie.

David Wood of Calgary, Alta., disarmed a man who had killed a waitress and wounded another patron in a restaurant.

Medals of Bravery

1982   **Roger Guay**, Clarenceville, Que.
Constable Donald Clark, Bradford, Ont.
Frank Armstrong and **William Doran**, Newmarket, Ont.
Edward Earl Bowman and **Lorne Albert Simpson**, Roseneath, Ont.
William Bier, Selkirk, Ont.
Wayne Whitbread, Terrace, B.C.
James Arthur Catto, Mississauga, Ont.
Paul Prysiazniuk, St. Catharines, Ont.
Thomas Tedesco, Lasalle, Ont.
Fire Chief **Gerald Jurgens**, Eatonia, Sask.
Cory McCallum, 10, Pinehouse, Sask.
George Tschida, Kelowna, B.C.
Michel Bilodeau, Roxboro, Que.
Gaétan Fortin, Hemmingford, Que.
Paul Butcher and **Steve Ditmore**, London, Ont.
David Churm, Frank Czukar and **James Redwood**, Hamilton, Ont.

Constable James Smith, Dundas, Ont., and **Ron Wakley**, Waterdown, Ont.
Gordon Clark, Lantzville, B.C.
Darlene Doskas, 10, **Kenny Doskas**, 9, **Rolland Picard**, 12, Verdun, Que.
Antonio Rosati, 16, Montreal, Que.
Bruce Humphrey, Coaldale, Alta.
Fire Chief **Robert Kibbons**, Edmonton, Alta.
Dr. Timothy Birkhead, Sheffield, England.
Erick P. Greene, Halifax, N.S.
Robert C. Forbes II, Yarmouth County, N.S.
Jean Grandmaison, Val D'Or, Que.
Glynn Richard Green, Fonthill, Ont.
Rod Anderson and **Peter Dean**, Tobermory, Ont.
James Kilworth, Miller Lake, Ont.
Patric Ryan, Muskoka Lake, Ont.
Mildred Byrne, Michael Hilton and **Dorothy Hughes**, Lethbridge, Alta.

1983   **Roy Asselstein**, Dunnville, Ont.
Kevin Augustine, Big Cove, N.B.
Darla Davenport, Brantford, Ont. and her mother,
Jean Bailey, Kingsville, Ont.
Frank Baine, Dundas, Ont.
Gerald Kool, Mississauga, Ont.
Michael Burke, Halifax, N.S.
Richard Cliche, North Hatley, Que.

CANADA'S PEACEMAKER

Rt. Hon. Lester Bowles Pearson, PC, CC, OBE (1897-1972), former prime minister of Canada, was a world statesman and Nobel Prize winner.

After serving in the First World War he completed his studies at the universities of Toronto and Oxford and then taught history at the U. of T. In 1928 he began his career with the federal government and rose to become Secretary of State for External Affairs.

He won the Nobel Peace Prize in 1957 for his efforts to end the military intervention of Britain and France in the Suez Crisis. He became prime minister of Canada in 1963.

"Canada can always take a disinter-

ested stand, in the sense that she can do what is right irrespective of what anybody else does. This is easier for us because we have no national interests that are continually under examination or challenge at the United Nations. So we do not need to feel superior or smugly virtuous.

"We have also to remember that in cases of doubt as to what is right or wrong — and most international issues involve doubt in this sense — we have always to take into consideration the importance of co-operating with friends. We should never break with them unless we are absolutely sure we are right. On the other hand, if we follow the United Kingdom or the United States automatically, any influence we have with them or in the international community would soon disappear."

Lester Pearson, *Karsh Canadians*,
Yousuf Karsh,
University of Toronto Press

PEARSON PEACE MEDAL

United Nations Association in Canada

The Pearson Medal honours that Canadian who, through voluntary and other efforts, has personally contributed to those causes for which Lester Pearson stood: aid to the developing world, mediation between those confronting one another with arms, succour to refugees and others in need, and peaceful change through world law and world organization.

The medal is presented by the Governor-General. The august group of previous winners includes: Paul-Emile Cardinal Leger in 1979; J. King Gordon in 1980 and Lt. Gen. E.L.M. Burns in 1981.

1982   Hugh Llewellyn Keenleyside, Victoria, B.C. Dr. Keenleyside joined the department of External Affairs in 1929

and opened the first Canadian mission in Japan the following year. He served in External Affairs and Mines and Resources until 1950. From 1950 to 1962 he served Canada and the world at the United Nations, first as Director-General of the UN Technical Assistance Administration and then as Under Secretary-General of the UN for Public Administration.

ONE OF THE FIRST CANADIAN HEROES

Canadians have been heard to say that there are no Canadian heroes. Perhaps Canadians don't know enough of this country's history, in particular the story of Adam des Ormeaux Dollard.

Dollard was a Frenchman who was just 23 when he came to Canada in 1657 as an officer in the garrison at Ville-Marie (Montreal.)

The little settlement had suffered for years from Iroquois attacks and once again was under threat.

Dollard, with 16 men, set out for the Ottawa River hoping to turn the approaching attackers aside. They were joined by 40 Huron and four Algonkin Indians, between Ville-Marie and the Long Sault.

At Long Sault they were attacked by about 300 Iroquois. Dollard's party took possession of an Algonkin fort and fought off the attack for five days. When 500 more Iroquois arrived, however, all of the Hurons except the chief Annaotaha switched sides.

Still Dollard and his companions fought on. It was another three days before they were finally overrun. The five survivors were put to death by the Iroquois.

Dollard's mission succeeded, however, when the attackers, perhaps daunted by such spirited defence, turned away from Ville-Marie and the settlement was, once again, saved.

ROYAL BANK AWARD

Royal Bank of Canada

Rev. George-Henri Levesque, OP, was named recipient of the $100,000 Royal Bank Award in June, 1982.

Now retired, Father Levesque founded the faculty of social sciences at Laval University and was founder and chief rector of National University in Rwanda, Africa.

The 80-year-old Dominican priest planned to use part of his prize money for a student loan fund at the National University.

ORDER OF ST. JOHN

Priory of Canada of the Most Venerable Order of the Hospital of St. John of Jerusalem

The Order of St. John is best known for its work through the St. John Ambulance Association and Brigade. The order began as an ancient nursing order of knights who cared for the wounded in battle. Today it is an honour society which awards various degrees of membership to individuals who have distinguished themselves through outstanding service to their community and country.

The following Members of the Order of St. John were invested in their grade in the Order in 1982.

KNIGHT/CHEVALIER
His Honour the Honourable George F.G. Stanley, Fredericton, N.B.
L. Col. James P.C. MacPherson, Kingston, Ont.
L. Col. John T. Stubbs, Sault Ste. Marie, Ont.
David Charles Raven, St. Thomas, Ont. (received posthumously by **Catherine Raven**)
DAME
Dr. Helen K. Mussallem, Ottawa, Ont.
COMMANDER/COMMANDEUR
Col. Lorne E. Barclay, Ottawa, Ont.
Elaine Laurin, Toronto, Ont.
R. Gordon MacPherson, Burlington, Ont.

L. Col. Harriet J. Sloan, Ottawa, Ont.
OFFICER/OFFICIER
Col. Jean J. Benoit, Ottawa, Ont.
Ronald Coell, Dartmouth, N.S.
Col. William R. Coleman, Ottawa, Ont.
Ivy L. Cunnington, Ottawa, Ont.
Kenneth B. Harding, Thornhill, Ont.
Sydney M. Hermant, Toronto, Ont.
The Hon. F. Walter Hyndman, Cornwall, P.E.I.
Arthur T. Jenkyns, Calgary, Alta.
The Hon. John Angus MacLean, Belle River, P.E.I.
Dr. Peter Ransford, Victoria, B.C.
Ruth L. Stanley, Fredericton, N.B.

Another 76 Canadians were invested as Serving Brother or Serving Sister.

LIFE SAVING MEDALS

Order of St. John

The Priory Council of the Order of St. John awards the medals to Canadians for courage in a life-threatening rescue.

1982   **Silver Medal Awards**
Montague John Vialoux, 40, a hotel manager near Traverse Bay, Man., for rescuing one woman from a burning house trailer and attempting, in vain, to rescue another.
Wendall Wayne Froese, 22, a student in Saskatoon, Sask., for entering a smoke-filled house to rescue a woman who was later revived by mouth-to-mouth resuscitation.
Thomas Warren, 65, a miner, Manitouwadge, Ont., for rescuing two injured passengers from a burning car despite the risk of explosion.
George Fisher, 45, a store proprietor, Sioux Narrows, Ont., for assisting in the rescue of two passengers from a burning car.

1982   **Bronze Medal Awards**
Constable Terrance Arbuckle Cameron, 28, of the RCMP at Thompson, Man., for rescuing Band Constable Moses Beardy who had crashed through thin ice on his snowmobile. Cameron dismounted from his own snowmobile and extended one of his

gauntlets which Beardy was able to grasp. Cameron, towing Beardy backwards stumbled and twice went through the ice but was able to recover before he submerged. His persistence paid off and eventually he got Beardy to safe ice and out of the water.

1983 Meritorious certificates-risk of life
Leopa Akpalialuk, Pangnirtung, N.W.T.
James Richard Cheeseman, Pasadena, Nfld.
Mary Eleanor Gilbert, Oromocto, N.B.
Robert Hartt, Gagetown, N.B.
Livee Kulluaalik, Pangnirtung, N.W.T.
Garth Crookedneck, Pierceland, Sask.
Joelee Mike, Pangnirtung, N.W.T.
James Murray, Cape Tormentine, N.B.
George Prior, Grand Bank, Nfld.

1983 Meritorious certificates-non-risk of life
Eric Arsenault, Miscouche, P.E.I.
Nick Benyk, Sherridon, Man.
Edward Beaubien, Winnipeg, Man.
Wayne Brinkman, Nakusp, B.C.
Shawn Cody, Pitt Meadows, B.C.
Ernie Collette, Stony Plain, Alta.
Bea Lillian Cook, Fredericton, N.B.
Eric Craig Danielson, Victoria, B.C.
William Demchuk, Cranbrook, B.C.
Constable P.C. Easton, (RCMP), Port Alberni, B.C.
Helen Mary Flynn, Sherwood, P.E.I.
Jo Degeus, Pitt Meadows, B.C.
Constable J.F.R. Guay, RCMP Victoria, B.C.
Constable John Halsey, CP Police, Chamblay, Que.
Ivan Joseph Hinks, Stephenville, Nfld.
Rae-Lene Lorenzo, Port Alberni, B.C.
Lynda Lyons, West Vancouver, B.C.
Constable A.D. MacIntyre, RCMP Drumheller, Alta.
Constable V.A. Massey, RCMP Victoria, B.C.
Gary E. Miller, Lunenburg, N.S.
Barry Dean Moffatt, Drumheller, Alta.
Ray Miles, Victoria, B.C.
James Albert Monaghan, Edmonton, Alta.
John Nicholson, Surrey, B.C.

Harry Thomas Nolie, Okanagan Falls, B.C.
Sally Petryk, Surrey, B.C.
George Pyne, Weyburn, Sask.
Alvin Joseph Paul, Stephenville, Nfld.
Donald R. Rhodenhizer, Winsloe, P.E.I.
Ivan Joseph Peter Richard, Cornwall, P.E.I.
Lou Roelofsen, Surrey, B.C.
Gerald T. Sheppard, Cardigan, P.E.I.
Dewar R. Sherren, Bunbury, P.E.I.
Jackie Vanoosten, Surrey, B.C.
Constable Heather Varey, RCMP Victoria, B.C.
Brian D. Williams, Bridgewater, N.S.

FOUR CANADIANS JOIN ELITE GROUP

The Albert Einstein College of Medicine of Yeshiva University in New Yok awarded Honorary Doctorates of Humane Letters to four Canadians in the spring of 1983. The convocation, in Toronto, was held outside of the United States for the first time.

Receiving the degrees were: William Davis, premier of Ontario; Nathan Starr, president of Acklands Ltd.; Abraham Lieff, former justice of the Ontario Supreme Court, and Donald Carr, a partner of the law firm of Goodman and Carr.

The college has, in other years, honoured such people as Albert Einstein and Robert Kennedy.

CANADA COUNCIL MEDAL

Canada Council

The Canada Council Medal was awarded from 1961 to 1968. It honoured persons in the humanities, social sciences, or fine arts, for a significant contribution over a period of years. In June of 1982, on the 25th anniversary of the Council, a special presentation of the medal was made to honour those members of the first Canada Council who are still active, and the founding director and associate director of the Council.

The medal is a bronze disc four inches across and was designed by Dora de Pedery Hunt.

1982 Special Canada Council Medal Presentation
Rev. Père **George-Henri Lévesque**, Montreal, Que.
Jules Bazin, Montreal, Que.
Francis Leddy, Windsor, Ont.
Frank MacKinnon, Calgary, Alta.
Norman McKenzie, Vancouver, B.C.
Andrée Paradis, Outremont, Que.
David H. Walker, St. Andrews, N.B.
Elena Wait, Toronto, Ont.
Albert W. Trueman, founding director, Toronto, Ont.
Eugène Bussière, associate director, Deux Montagnes, Que.

BENE MERENTI DE PATRIA

La Société Saint-Jean Baptiste de Montréal

Prizes which are given to French-Canadians for outstanding achievements in the humane sciences and the arts that serve the French-Canadian people. The prize consists of the medal Bene Merenti de Patria and a cash award of $1,500.

1982 Prix de Littérature Duvernay
Jean-Ethier Blais
Prix de musique Calixa-Lavallée
Marie-Thérèse Paquin
Prix de Sciences Humaines Esdras-Minville
Jacques Grand'maison
Prix de Sport et d'Athletisme Maurice-Richard
Serge Arsenault
Prix de Journalisme Olivar-Asselin
Marcel Pépin
Prix des Arts Plastiques Philippe-Hébert
Micheline Beauchemin
Prix de Théâtre Victor-Morin
Michèle Rassignol

"WE SHOULD HOLD FAST"

"**Strangers have surrounded us whom it is our pleasure to call foreigners; they have taken into their hands most of the rule, they have gathered to themselves much of the wealth; but in this land of Quebec nothing has changed. Nor shall anything change, for we are the pledge of it. Concerning ourselves and our destiny but one duty have we clearly understood: that we should hold fast, should endure.**
Louis Hémon, *Maria Chapdelaine*, published in 1921

THE PERSONS AWARDS

Status of Women Canada

The award recognizes outstanding contributions made towards improving the status of women in Canada and was initiated in 1979 to celebrate the 50th anniversary of the Persons Case.

On October 18, 1929, women in Canada and the British Empire won the legal right to be recognized as persons thus giving Canadian women the right to become senators. This victory was won through the efforts of the "famous five" Western Canada women, Emily Murphy, Louise McKinney, Nellie McClung, Dr. Irene Parlby and Henrietta Muir Edwards who signed the petition requesting an amendment to the British North America Act to grant women "person's" status.

The Governor-General presents an engraved medal to five persons during an annual ceremony at Government House, held as close to October 18 as possible.

1982 **Nancy Adams**, Saskatoon, Sask.
Sarah Binns, Toronto, Ont.
Hilda Hellaby, Whitehorse, Yukon
Liliane Labelle, Montreal, Que.
Edith McLeod, Thunder Bay, Ont.

MARIAN PORTER PRIZE

Canadian Research Institute for the Advancement of Women

The $50 prize is given annually for the best feminist article published in an anthology or periodical. The prize awards academic excellence, originality of evidence and theme and the importance of the issue to women.

1982 **Marta Danylewycz**, Toronto, Ont.

MURIEL DUCKWORTH AWARD

Given to the woman feminist who, through her work, research or actions, contributes to peace or social justice in Canada in the areas of humanities, science, law, arts or media.

An especially designed scroll and $50 were awarded in 1982.

1982 **Kay Macpherson**, Toronto, Ont.

HONORARY MEMBERSHIP

Canadian Research Institute for the Advancement of Women

A lifetime honorary membership is given to an outstanding feminist who has done research work which contributes to the advancement of women.

1981 **Sylvia Gelber**, Ottawa, Ont.
1982 **Jeanne Lapointe**, Ste. Foy, Que.

WOMEN OF DISTINCTION

Young Women's Christian Association

Bronze Aggie's, named for the YMCA founder in Canada, Agnes Amelia Blizard are presented to six winners for their achievements in their own field and for their contribution to the advancement of women.

1983 **Dormer Ellis**, Business/Professions/Labour. An engineer with degrees in social sciences and education, she works with literacy centres, assists the International Conference of Women Engineers and helps other women engineers.

Shelagh Wilkinson, Health/Education. She teaches women's studies and English. She has made a significant contribution by founding *Canadian Women's Studies*, a journal with impact on educational institutions and governments.

Ruth Budd, Arts and Letters. The Toronto Symphony's first woman bass player, she has been a successful campaigner for day care as a tax deduction and an ardent fighter for better conditions for Canadian musicians.

Thora McIlroy Mills, Community Service Award. McIlroy has been a force in improving the lives of diabetics. She helped clothe thousands of European children during the Second World War; has raised money for countless community groups and sought to assist Canadian Indian Girls. She is past president of the Ontario Council for Women.

Michele Landsberg, Communications. A committed feminist, she is an ardent advocate of children's rights. A columnist for the *Toronto Star* she has written a book, *Women and Children First*.

Doris Anderson, Public Affairs/Public Service. As editor of *Chatelaine*, she changed the format from strictly food and fashion to include features on feminist issues. She led the fight for women's rights in the new Canadian Charter while she was chairman of the advisory Council on the Status of Women in Canada.

TERRY FOX HUMANITARIAN AWARD PROGRAM

Government of Canada

There were 18 winners out of 1,992 eligible applicants for the first Terry Fox Humanitarian Awards. The program gives renewable scholarships of up to $3,000 annually to post-graduate students displaying humanitarianism and good citizenship.

Terry Fox himself set the criteria for the awards. The successful applicant must display courage, humanitarianism, compassion and magnanimity, while the student pursues academic, extracurricular, amateur sports, fitness and health, and voluntary community activities. Academic excellence is not a major criterion. Though the requirements are stiff, the selection committee hopes to present more awards each year.

1982 **John O'Donnell**, 20, Antigonish, N.S.
R. Bruce Aylward, 20, St. John's
John Herbert, 28, Charlottetown

Frances Murphy, 21, Westmount, Que.
Louise Vitou, 20, Montreal.
Tom Silletta, 24, Montreal
Joanne Terry Bouw, 19, St. Catharines, Ont.
Adrienne Lemay, 19, Red Rock, Ont.
Nancy Griffin, 19, Toronto
Mario Demarinis, 19, North Gower, Ont.
David Patrick, 21, Ottawa
Cameron Clokie, 20, Toronto
Grant Darby, 19, Hamilton
Halldor Bjarnason, 19, Winnipeg
Laura Davies, 20, Saskatoon
Anita Flash, 21, Yorkton, Sask.
Diane Walker, 18, Burnaby, B.C.
Maria Denholme, 18, Vancouver, B.C.

The Arts

GENERAL AWARDS

DIPLÔME D'HONNEUR
Canadian Conference of the Arts

An award to honour Canada's artists who have made an exceptional contribution to the encouragement of the arts in Canada.

It is presented by the Governor General, and consists of a framed diploma and a talisman created by the West Coast craftsman Bill Reid, cast in sterling silver.

1983 **Anita Aarons**, sulptor and director of the Art Gallery at Harbourfront, Toronto, Ont.
Pierretee Alarie, OC, and Leopold Simoneau, OC, the husband and wife duo of singers and educators of Opera Piccolo Canada.
Dr. Llyell Gustin, music educator.
Arnold Spohr, artistic director of the Royal Winnipeg Ballet.

Recipients of the Diplôme d'honneur 1954 — 1982

1954 **Vincent Massey**, *Chairman, Massey-Lévesque Commission*
1956 **Tom Patterson**, *founder, Stratford Festival*
1957 **Jean Bruchési**, *author and patron of the arts*
1958 **Walter Herbert**, *founder, Canada Foundation*
1959 **Senator Donald Cameron**, *founder, Banff School of Fine Arts*
1960 **Hon. Brooke Claxton**, *first Chairman of the Canada Council*

1961 **Thea Koerner**, *patron of the arts*
1962 **William A. Riddell**, *Chairman, Saskatchewan Arts Board*
1965 **Albert Trueman**, *first Director of the Canada Council*
1968 **Marius Barbeau**, *Quebec folklorist and anthropologist*
1969 **Alan Jarvis**, *Director, National Gallery*
1970 **Wilfrid Pelletier**, *orchestra conductor*
1971 **Peter Dwyer**, *Director, the Canada Council*
1972 **Alain Grandbois**, *poet*
1973 **Donald Wetmore**, *pioneer in arts development in Nova Scotia*
1974 **Erik Bruhn**, *choreographer / teacher, National Ballet*
Floyd S. Chalmers, *patron of the arts*
Esse W. Ljungh, *Head of CBC Radio Drama*
Mariette Rousseau-Vermette, *tapestry artist*
1975 **Ludmilla Chiriaeff**, *founder, Les Grands Ballets Canadiens*
S.C. Echkardt Gramatté, *composer*
Tanya Moiseiwitsch, *set and costume designer*
Oscar Peterson, *jazz pianist*
Robert Weaver, *story editor, CBC Radio Drama*
Moncrieff Williamson, *art curator*
1976 **Glenn Gould**, *pianist*
Florence James, *pioneer in prairie theatre development*
Félix Leclerc, *chansonnier and poet*
Félix-Antoine Savard, *writer*
1977 **Ernest Lindner**, *visual artist*
Alfred Pellan, *visual artist*
Barbara Pentland, *composer*
1978 **Gilles Lefebvre**, *founder, Jeunesses Musicales of Canada*

Barker Fairley, *writer, visual artist and poet*

Norman McLaren, *film animator*

Norma Springford, *drama teacher*

1979 **Arthur Gelber**, *patron of the arts*

Bill Reid, *visual artist and craftsman*

Yvonne Hubert, *pianist and teacher*

1980 **Père Émile Legault**, *founder, Théâtre du Nouveau Monde*

Maureen Forrester, *singer*

Gabrielle Roy, *author*

1981 **Maxwell Bates**, *painter*

Robert Fulford, *writer and arts critic*

Antonine Maillet, *author and playwright*

Hon. Pauline McGibbon, *patron of the arts*

1982 **Betty Oliphant**, *founder, National Ballet School*

Louis Archambault, *sculptor*

G. Hamilton Southam, *first Director General, National Arts Centre*

Mario Bernardi, *founding Musical Director, N.A.C. Orchestra*

for outstanding contributions to the arts, humanities or social sciences. They rank among the highest Canadian awards in the field of culture and carry a $25,000 purse.

1982 **Alan C. Cairns**, Political Scientist, U. of British Columbia, a teacher, scholar, thinker and advisor to government.

Louis-Edmond Hamelin, geographer, Trois-Rivieres, Que. Hamelin has revealed us to ourselves as a Northern People through his work in the Canadian North.

Jack McClelland, publisher, Toronto, for his enormous dedication to the cause of Canadian writing and publishing.

Gilles Vigneault, singer, who has renewed and deepened our vision of Quebec, especially by his use of myths about the faraway land of Natashquan.

CANADA'S FIRST CULTURAL HERO

The French poet and lawyer Marc Lescarbot was a member of the colonists' settlement at Port Royale, N.S. While there he wrote twelve poems, *Les muses de la Nouvelle France*, which were subsequently published in Paris in 1609. He also wrote and presented a play in the form of a masque, loaned out books from his library and began teaching classes attended by the Micmac Indians. Later in France he wrote an account of a mass baptism of Indians, and his main work, *Histoire de la Nouvelle-France*, an account of French explorations in the Americas and a study comparing the natives of North and South America with other peoples of the world.

MOLSON PRIZES

The Canada Council

Established in 1963, the prizes are awarded annually to Canadian citizens

EARLY ENTERTAINMENT

The first circus to tour Canada was Rickett's which journeyed from London, England, complete with wild animals and clowns. Its premiere performance in the Americas was in Quebec in 1798.

The world's first Wild West Show was staged at Niagara Falls, Ont., on August 28, 1872. The main attraction was none other than Wild Bill Hickock, who commanded a ticket price of 50 cents.

NATIONAL THEATRE SCHOOL AWARD

An annual award to a student chosen by the faculty of the National Theatre School who shows promise and has need of financial assistance. The student may be enrolled in any course at the school.

1982 **Jean-Yves Ahern**, Montreal, Que.

ACTOR WINS HONOURS

Internationally acclaimed actor Donald Sutherland was recently made an Honorary Doctor of Letters at Saint Mary's University in Halifax. Sutherland was born in Saint John, N.S., but spent most of his years as a teenager in Bridgewater near Halifax.

PAULINE McGIBBON AWARD

Colleen Blake, production manager, of Toronto's Young People's Theatre, received the 1983 Pauline McGibbon Award of $5,000. Pauline McGibbon, former Lieutenant-Governor of Ontario, has been a strong supporter of the arts in Canada.

BOX OFFICE BOATS

The first play in North America was performed at Port Royal, N.S., on November 14, 1606. Entitled *The Theatre of Neptune*, the play welcomed Poutrincourt the governor home from an exploratory voyage. Appropriately, the action took place on the water as the performers sailed out in small boats to meet the governor's ship.

DORA MAVOR MOORE AWARDS

The Dora statue, designed by Canadian sculptor and painter John Romano, is presented annually in recognition of outstanding accomplishments in Toronto theatre performance and production.

1982   Outstanding new play: **Tamara**, by John Krizanc
Outstanding new revue or musical: **Rock and Roll**, by John Gray
Outstanding production of a play: **Tamara**, produced by Tamara International (originally created by Necessary Angel Theatre Company)
Outstanding production of a revue or musical: **Man of La Mancha**, produced by Errant Productions
Outstanding direction of a play: **Richard Rose** for *Tamara*
Outstanding direction of a revue or musical: **John Gray** for *Rock and Roll*
Outstanding musical direction: **Bob Ashley** for *Piaf — Her Songs, Her Loves*
Outstanding performance by a male (revue or musical): **Charles Page Fletcher** in *Rock and Roll*
Outstanding performance by a female (revue or musical): **Kathy Michael McGlynn** in *Piaf — Her Songs, Her Loves*
Outstanding performance by a male in a leading role (play): **John Evans** in *True West*
Outstanding performance by a female in a leading role (play): **Rosemary Dunsmore** in *Straight Ahead/Blind Dancers*
Outstanding performance by a male in a featured role (play): **Gregory Ellwand** in *Night and Day*
Outstanding performance by a female in a featured role (play): **Mary Ann McDonald** in *The Al Cornell Story*
Outstanding set design of a revue or musical: **Antonin Dimitrov** for *Man of La Mancha*
Outstanding costume design of a revue or musical: **Olga Dimitrov** for *Man of La Mancha*
Outstanding lighting design of a revue or musical: **Nick Cernovitch** for *Rock and Roll*
Outstanding set design of a play: **Dorian L. Clark** for *Tamara*
Outstanding costume design of a play: **Linda Muir** for *Tamara*
Outstanding lighting design of a play: **Harry Frehner** for *Dreaming and Duelling*
The Brenda Donahue award: **Mallory Gilbert**

MIGHTY OAKS FROM LITTLE ACORNS

In 1951, Tom Patterson, a small-town Ontario businessman, approached a somewhat suspicious Stratford city council with a request for funds. He wanted to visit New York and enlist the aid of Laurence Olivier in fostering a theatrical dream. On the advice of his mother, Patterson asked for $100 to finance the trip. The council, in an excess of generosity, voted him $125— which somehow enabled him to lasso Alec Guinness and Tyrone Guthrie and create, against all odds, the Stratford Shakespearean Festival.

CMC MEDAL
Canadian Music Council

Commissioned in 1971 from Quebec sculptor Charles Daudelin, the medal is presented annually to honour musicians for outstanding service to Canadian musical life.

1983　**Roland Brunelle**, CSV, Joliette, Que., is a music educator who has devoted a lifetime to string teaching. Among his former pupils is the exceptional young violinist, Angèle Dubeau.
Maureen Forrester, CC, D Mus., one of the world's leading contraltos, is well known as Canada's musical ambassador to the world. A great supporter of young artists, she also believes strongly in Canadian composers and regularly programs their works.
Ruby Mercer, D Mus, has for many years been the cheerful "voice of opera" in Canada for countless CBC listeners. Editor and founder of *Opera Canada* magazine, she also founded the Canadian Opera Children's Chorus and wrote a biography of tenor Edward Johnson.

ROBERT FLEMING AWARD FOR YOUNG COMPOSERS
Canadian Music Council

An award of $1,000 is made annually to an outstanding graduating student in composition.

1982　**Richard Gibson**, Moncton, N.B.

THE CONSTANCY OF MORALITY

The Bishop of Quebec, in 1694, was Jean Baptiste de la Croix de Chevrieres de Saint-Vallier. He was a rather autocratic reformer who was often at odds with the governor of Quebec, le Comte de Frontenac. In January 1694, some plays including Molière's Tartuffe, were presented for the citizens of Quebec under the auspices of the Governor. The Bishop denounced the plays as immoral.

JULES LÉGER PRIZE FOR NEW CHAMBER MUSIC
Canadian Music Council

Created in 1978 to encourage composition for chamber ensembles, the annual prize is a trophy designed by Montreal sculptor Louis Archambault and $5,000 cash.

1981　**John Rea**, Montreal, Que., for *Compossession*.
1982　**Walter Boudreau**, Montreal, Que., for *Odessée au soleil* for eight brass instruments.

FORBES WAS FIRST

Beth Forbes, a second-year medical student at the University of Western Ontario, led the university band and became the first drum majorette in all of Canada in 1937.

PRESIDENT'S TROPHY
Kiwanis Festival

The two-week-long annual Kiwanis Festival is the largest competitive event of its kind in the world.

1983　**Ronald Chambers**, cellist and third-year student in faculty of music at U. of Toronto.

INTERNATIONAL STEPPING STONE CANADIAN COMPETITIONS

The annual prize was established in 1971 to familiarize young Canadian musicians with the demands of international competition and to help the most promising among them to further their careers.

1982

$3,000 **Douglas Finch**, pianist, Toronto, Ont.
Marc-Andre Hamelin, pianist, Montreal, Que.

$1,500 **Johanne Perron**, cellist, Chicoutimi, Que.
Anne-Elise Keefer, flutist, London, Ont.

STRAINS OF STRATAS

Teresa Stratas, born in Toronto in 1938, was the first woman to sing the title role of *Lulu* (Berg) in its first complete version at the Paris Opera on May 28, 1979. Pierre Boulez was the conductor.

Stratas sings Violetta in the hit film *La Traviata* directed by Zeffirelli.

FOURTH ANNUAL BLACK MUSIC AWARDS

The Canadian Black Music Awards, held in Toronto, honoured the following in 1983:

Top guitar player: **David Bendeth**
Top bass player: **Leroy Sibbles**
Top keyboard player: **Jackie Mittoo**
Top drummer: **Carl Otway**
Top steel band: **Tradewinds**
Top funk group: **Sweet Ecstasy**
Top calypso: **Protector**
Top funk producers:**Carl Otway** and **Carl Harvey**
Top reggae producer: **R. Zee Jackson**
Top dance single: **Pull Our Love Together**
(Sweet Ecstasy)
Top reggae single: **Gypsy Girl** (Leroy Brown)
Top album: **Evidence** (Leroy Sibbles), tied with **Chariots of Fire** (Demo Cates)
Top female vocalist: **Arlene Duncan**
Top male vocalist: **Leroy Sibbles**
Performer of the year: **Leroy Sibbles**
Top reggae group: **Messenjah**
Top reggae album:**Rock You High** (Messenjah)
Newcomer of the Year: **Messenjah**
Canadian black music hall of fame:
Stranger Cole, Wayne St. John, Leroy Sibbles

COUNCIL HITS QUARTER CENTURY

The Canada Council celebrated its 25th anniversary in 1983. By the end of its 1982/83 fiscal year it had distributed more than $53.5-million in grants to arts organizations and individual artists.

SYLVIA GELBER FOUNDATION AWARD

Canada Council

The award of $5,000 is presented annually to an outstanding performer of classical music under the age of 30.

1982   **Angèle Dubeau**, violinist, Quebec, Que.

HEALEY WILLAN PRIZE FOR AMATEUR CHOIRS

Canada Council

The $2,000 prize was established in 1980 to honour Willan's contributions to the musical life of Canada: compositions for choirs; training choral groups; and successful efforts to interest Canadian composers and conductors to write and perform choral music.

1981   **The Donovan Chorale**
1982   No prize awarded

MANAGING OPERA STAR

Edward Johnson from Guelph, Ont., is the only man to have been a leading international opera star and subsequently general manager of a leading international opera company. Johnson became head of the Metropolitan Opera in New York in 1935. The University of Toronto's faculty of music building and its library were named in his honour.

CREATIVE ARTS AWARD

Canadian Federation of University Women

Established in 1969, the award is $1,000 and a commission for an original chamber work.

1981 **John Winiarz**, St. Boniface, Man.
1982 **Anthony Genge**, Victoria, B.C.

ORIGINAL ORGAN

Rev. Charles A. Martin played the first organ in Canada, imported from France in 1659 by Bishop Laval. Before it arrived, the only instruments used for church music had been two violins.

11TH ANNUAL CANADIAN STAGE BAND FESTIVAL

1983 **Senior stage band**
Harry Ainlay Band, Edmonton, Alta.
Fort Richmond Collegiate, Winnipeg, Man.
Don Mills Collegiate, North York, Ont.
Senior jazz combo
Nemesis Fusion, North York, Ont.
Triple Image, Qualicum, B.C.
Harry Ainlay, Edmonton, Alta.
Intermediate stage band
Magee Secondary School, Vancouver, B.C.
Mount Douglas S. S., Victoria, B.C.

Summerland Swingphonics, Summerland, B.C.

OLDEST HYMNIST

Fred Young, 81, the oldest surviving member of the Salvation Army Band in Toronto, has played hymns on street corners every Sunday since 1913.

COMPETITION FOR YOUNG COMPOSERS

CBC National Radio

The biennial awards were conceived by the English and French service Radio Music departments, together with the Canada Council. Additional funds are provided by the Arts Councils of Quebec, Ontario, Manitoba, Saskatchewan and British Columbia. The aim is to promote composition of original concert music by Canadians and to ensure performance of these works.

Electronic Music:
First prize: none awarded.
Second prize and $3,000 each: **Bernard Gagnon**, Montreal, Que., for *Gwendolyne Descendue*.
Alain Thibault, Montreal, Que., for *Sonergie*.
Compositions requiring up to twelve performers:
Denys Bouliane, Quebec, Que., for *Jeu de Société*.
John Winiarz, Manitoba, for *Nightflower*.

The grand prize winner and recipient of an additional $5,000 was **Denys Bouliane**, Quebec, Que.

COMPETITION FOR AMATEUR CHOIRS

CBC National Radio

The biennial competition was instituted in 1975 to further the development of amateur choral music in Canada. Cash prizes of $1,000 and a trophy are awarded for the top choir in each of seven categories.

Children's choirs
Toronto Children's Chorus, directed by Jean Ashworth-Gam
Ottawa Board of Education Central Choir, directed by Barbara Clark
Youth choirs
No first prize awarded
Lutheran Collegiate Bible Institute Concert Choir, directed by Gerald Langner, Outlook, Sask.
Adult mixed choirs
Donovan Chorale, Montreal, Que., directed by John and Bernadette Donovan
U. of Guelph Choir, Guelph, Ont., directed by Gerald Neufeld.
Adult mixed chamber choirs
Guelph Chamber Choir, Guelph, Ont., directed by Gerald Neufeld
Ensemble Vocale de l'Université de Montréal, Montreal, Que., directed by Jean-Francois Senart
Traditional and ethno-cultural choirs
Vesnivka Ukrainian Girls' Choir, Toronto, Ont., directed by Halyna Kuitka Kondracki
Merezhi Vocal Ensemble, Edmonton, Alta., directed by Sergei Eremenko
Contemporary choral music
No first prize award
Powell River Youth Choir, Powell River, B.C., directed by Don James

TALENT COMPETITION
CBC National Radio

Established in 1959, the competition offers $22,500 to winners in five categories. A grand prize of $5,000 is awarded to the overall winner. First prize in each category receives $2,500 and a scholarship to either the Banff School of Fine Arts or the Orford Arts Centre in Quebec.

1983   Jon Kimura Parker, pianist, Vancouver, B.C.
       Amira Acre, pianist, Dollard-des-Ormeaux, Que.
       Debra Parker, vocalist, Sanford, Man.
       Iraina Neufeld, vocalist, Waterloo, Ont.

The Hoebig-Moroz Trio, Vancouver, B.C.

Grand prize winner was Jon Kimura Parker, Vancouver, B.C.

FIRST CAROL

Jesus, He is Born, also known as the *Huron Christmas Carol*, is considered to be Canada's first Christmas carol. It was written in the Huron language by Father Jean deBrebeuf about the year 1641.

HEINZ UNGER AWARD

The annual award of $1,000 is to assist promising young Canadian conductors. Contestants are required to conduct the University of Toronto faculty of music's repertory orchestra.

1982   James Wegg, Toronto, Ont.
1983   Claude Lapalme and Daniel Swift, Quebec

JUNO AWARDS
Canadian Academy of Recording Arts & Sciences

The awards were established in 1970 as the Maple Leaf Awards, but were renamed in honour of Pierre Juneau, then head of the CRTC. Eventually the spelling was changed to Juno, after the chief goddess of the Roman pantheon. The 23-inch-tall acrylic statue was designed by Stan Klees, one of the original organizers of the awards.

About 900 people, most of whom work in the music industry, vote for the Juno winners, and the nominees in nearly all categories are determined by sales of their recordings.

1983   Best children's album: **When You Dream a Dream**, Bob Schneider
       International album of the year: **Business As Usual**, Men at Work

Anne Murray, Grammies, Junos, gold, platinum and gross rating points

Producer of the year: **Bill Henderson, Brian McLeod** (Chilliwack)
Recording engineer of the year: **Bob Rock** (Payolas)
Country group: **The Good Brothers**
Country male vocalist: **Eddie Eastman**
Country female vocalist: **Anne Murray**
Most promising group: **Payolas**
Most promising male vocalist: **Kim Mitchell**
Most promising female vocalist: **Lydia Taylor**
Best jazz album: **I Didn't Know About You**, Fraser MacPherson, Oliver Gannon
Best album graphics: **Dean Motter** (Metal on Metal, by Anvil)
Album of the year: **Get Lucky**, Loverboy
Single of the year: **Eyes of a Stranger**, Payolas
Hall of Fame Award: **Glenn Gould**
Instrumental artist: **Liona Boyd**
Best classical album: **Bach's Goldberg Variations**, Glenn Gould
Group of the year: **Loverboy**
Female vocalist: **Carole Pope**
Composer of the year: **Bob Rock, Paul Hyde**, Eyes of a Stranger (Payolas)
International single of the year: **Eye of the Tiger**, Survivor

SUCCESSFUL SINGER

Canadian singer Terry Jacks of Vancouver, B.C., sold more records than anyone else in the world in 1974. His *Seasons in the Sun* sold 11 million copies and is still number five on the all-time international best-seller list.

He is the only Canadian to have produced two number-one hits on U.S. charts and he won seven Juno awards in such capacities as writer, producer and vocalist, and as part of a group.

Jacks has even made his mark in fiction: he is mentioned in Stephen King's *The Shining*.

WEST COAST MUSIC AWARDS

1982   Outstanding group: **Chilliwack**
Album of the year: **Chilliwack**
Producers of the year: **Brian McLeod** and **Bill Henderson**, Chilliwack
Guitarist of the year **Brian McLeod**
Bassist of the year: **Ab Bryant**
Vocalist of the year: **Bryan Adams**
Most promising act: **Bryan Adams**
Best jazz act: **Tom Keenlyside**
Best reed or bass player: **Tom Keenlyside**
Best single of the year: **Payolas**, for *Eyes of a Stranger*

BIGGEST BOX OFFICE

The Stratford Festival's biggest box office success in 1982 was the Gilbert and Sullivan operetta *The Mikado*, **staged by Brian McDonald.**

ACADEMY OF COUNTRY MUSIC ENTERTAINMENT AWARDS

1982   Vocal group of the year: **The Family Brown**
Album of the year: **Raised on Country Music** (The Family Brown)
Single of the year; **Some Never Stand a Chance** (The Family Brown)
Song of the year: **Some Never Stand a Chance** (Barry Brown, Songwriter)
Female vocalist of the year: **Carroll Baker**
Newcomer of the year: **Ruth Ann**
Entertainer of the year: **The Family Brown**

COUNTRY MUSIC NEWS FAN AWARDS

1983   Performers of the year: **The Family Brown**
Single of the year: **Raised on Country Music** (The Family Brown)
Album of the year: **Raised on Country Music** (The Family Brown)
Male vocalist of the year: **Carisse**

Female vocalist of the year: **Marie Bottreel**
Country music group of the year: **The Family Brown**

"ANNE" PLAYS ANNUALLY

The heroine of *Anne of Green Gables*, by Lucy Maud Montgomery, has become one of the most famous characters in Canadian literature. The musical based on the book has played Osaka, New York, London and Canadian centres, as well as being featured for two months every year since 1965 at the Charlottetown Festival in P.E.I.

DU MAURIER SEARCH FOR THE STARS

Amateur and professional Canadian performing artists are eligible to apply for an audition. Between 700 and 800 applicants audition in eight Canadian cities. Eighteen semifinalists are chosen and, in addition to receiving a $2,000 bursary, each is featured in a series of prime-time *Search for the Stars* specials aired by the CBC. Six final winners receive a further bursary of $5,000 each and are featured on a final CBC *Search for the Stars* special.

1982 **Gianetta Baril**, 21, harpist, Edmonton, Alta.
Cecile Frenette, 28, vocalist, Montreal, Que.
Jodi Glassman, 26, musical theatre performer, Toronto, Ont.
Chantal Juillet, 21, classical violinist, Vaudreuil, Que.
Cornelia Boucher-MacLeod, 33, country and western singer, Arichat, Cape Breton, N.S.
Cosimo Natola, 23, singer/pianist, Burnaby, B.C.
1983 **The Gerald Danovitch Saxophone Quartet** (Gerald Danovitch, Peter G. Freeman, Abe Kestenberg and Nancy Newman), Montreal, Que.

Duo Victoria, Classical Piano Duo comprising Robert Tweten and Kevin Fitz-Gerald, Victoria, B.C.
Gregory Fehr, 28, popular singer/guitarist from Regina, Sask.
Olga Gross, 20, classical pianist, Montreal, Que.
Sophie Rolland, 21, classical cellist, Montreal, Que.
Lucie Roy, 22, popular singer/composer, Charlesbourg, Que.

CHART CHAMPION

A Canadian band holds the all-time record on the top-100 chart in Australia. It's Toronto's Rough Trade whose *All Touch* has been on the charts longer than any Beatles or BeeGees tune

WILLIAM HAROLD MOON AWARD

Performing Rights Organization of Canada

For the musician who has generated the greatest international interest in Canadian music in the previous calendar year.

1974 **R. Murray Schafer**
1975 **Randy Bachman**
1976 **Harry Somers**
1977 **Hagood Hardy**
1978 **Serge Garant**
1979 **The Irish Rovers**
1980 **Frank Mills**
1981 **Moe Koffman**
1982 **Robert Aitken**

CANADIAN THEME

At L'Aquila, Italy, the annual international festival of music and architecture was devoted entirely to Canada in 1982.

BALDWIN PIANO AND ORGAN FESTIVAL

The festival, established in 1978, features competitors selected from preliminary and regional competitions across Canada. Junior winners receive $500, seniors $1,000.

1982 **Junior** (16 and under)
Classical piano: **Cary Chow**, 12, Victoria, B.C.
Popular organ: **Jim Virginillo**, 15, Lethbridge, Alta.
Classical organ: **John Charron**, 16, Windsor, Ont.
Senior
Classical piano: **Esther Charron**, 18, Quebec, Que.
Popular organ: **David Nelson**, 19, Toronto, Ont.
Classical organ: **Rosemary Puling**, 22, London, Ont.

CHAUVEAU MEDAL

Royal Society of Canada

The award honours Pierre J.O. Chauveau (1820-1890), writer, orator and educator. Chauveau was the second president of the Royal Society and the first premier of Quebec, from 1867 to 1872. He was Speaker of the Senate in 1874.

The award is presented for distinguished contribution to knowledge in the humanities other than Canadian literature and Canadian history.

1983 Professor Balachandra Rajan, department of English, U. of Western Ontario. Rajan is a literary critic and scholar of international reputation in the study of Milton and the English Literary Renaissance and is also an eminent interpreter of Yeats and Eliot. In addition to authoring scholarly books and articles, he has written two novels and reviewed books on Milton for the *Times Literary Supplement* since 1966.

LORNE PIERCE MEDAL

Royal Society of Canada

For an achievement in imaginative or critical literature.

1982 **Dr. Malcolm Ross**, Dalhousie U., Halifax, N.S., for services to Canadian literature, both as professor and as initiator of the New Canadian Library Series (McClelland and Stewart) in 1958.

GOVERNOR-GENERAL'S LITERARY AWARDS

The Canada Council

Prizes are presented to eight winners by Governor-General Edward Schreyer.

1983 English Fiction: **Guy Vanderhaeghe** for *Man Descending* (Macmillan)
Poetry: **Phyllis Webb** for *The Vision Tree: Selected Poems* (Talonbooks)
Drama: **John Gray** for *Billy Bishop goes to War, a play by John Gray with Eric Peterson* (Talonbooks)
Nonfiction: **Christopher Moore** for *Louisbourg Portraits: Life in an Eighteenth-Century Garrison Town* (Macmillan)
French Fiction: **Roger Fournier** for *Le Cercle des arènes* (Albin Michel)
Poetry: **Michel Savard** for *Forages* (Editions du Noroit)
Theatre: **Rejean Ducharme** for *H A ha! ...* (Editions Lacombe)
Nonfiction: **Maurice Lageux** for *Le marxisme des années soixante: une saison dans l'histoire de la pensée critique* (Hurtubise HMH)

WRITERS WHO HAVE WON TWO OR MORE GOVERNOR-GENERAL'S LITERARY AWARDS

N.J. Berill 1953, 1955
Pierre Berton 1956, 1958, 1971
Gérard Bessette 1965, 1971
Earle Birney 1942, 1945
Marie-Claire Blais 1968, 1979
George Bowering 1969, 1980
J.M.S. Careless 1953, 1963

Donald G. Creighton   1952, 1955
R. MacGregor Dawson   1947, 1949
Réjean Ducharme   1966, 1973, 1983
Robert Finch   1946, 1961
Gwethalyn Graham   1938, 1944
John F. Hayes   1951, 1953
Anne Hébert   1960, 1975
Bruce Hutchison   1942, 1952, 1957
Margaret Laurence   1966, 1974
Douglas Le Pan   1953, 1964
Dorothy Livesay   1944, 1947
A.R.M. Lower   1946, 1954
Hugh MacLennan   1945, 1948, 1949, 1954, 1959
Edgar McInnes   1942, 1944
Brian Moore   1960, 1975
Alice Munro   1968, 1978
Michael Ondaatje   1970, 1979
Fernand Ouellet   1970, 1976
Pierre Perrault   1964, 1975
E.J. Pratt   1937, 1940, 1952
Thomas H. Raddall   1943, 1948, 1957
James Reaney   1949, 1958, 1962
Mordecai Richler   1968, 1971
Gabrielle Roy   1947, 1957, 1977
Laura G. Salverson   1937, 1939
David Walker   1952, 1953
Marjorie Wilkins Campbell   1950, 1954
Kerry Wood   1955, 1957

WINS FRENCH PRIZE

Dr. McAllister Johnson has been awarded the Prix Bernier by the Academie des Beaux-Arts, Institut de France, for his catalogue for the exhibition French Royal Academy of Painting and Sculpture Engraved Reception Pieces, 1672-1789. Dr. Johnson is the first person living outside of France to have received the Prix Bernier.

CANADA-SCOTLAND WRITERS-IN-RESIDENCE EXCHANGE

Canada Council

1983   Canadian writer and critic **Fred Cogswell** goes to the University of Edinburgh while Scottish writer Ron Butlin will fill the position at the University of New Brunswick at Fredericton,

N.B. Cogswell receives 7,000 pounds sterling plus all travelling expenses from the Scottish Arts Council.

CANADA-AUSTRALIA LITERARY PRIZE

Canada Council

1983   Australian novelist and playwright **Barry Oakley** will receive a trip to Canada and cash award of $3,000. The prize is designed to make Canadians and Australians familiar with each other's writers. It is awarded annually to an Australian and a Canadian alternately, based on the author's complete works. There are no restrictions on genre.

TRANSLATION PRIZE

Canada Council

Two prizes of $5,000 each are awarded for translations from French to English and English to French.

1982   **Ray Ellenwood**, Toronto, Ont., for *Entrails* (Coach House), a translation of *Les entrailles* by Claude Gauvreau.
Ivan Steenhout, Montreal, Que., for *John A. Macdonald* (Les Editions de l'Homme), a translation of Donald Creighton's two-volume work, *John A. Macdonald: The Young Politician* and *John A. Macdonald: The Old Chieftain.*

CHILDREN'S LITERATURE PRIZES

Canada Council

Two awards of $5,000 each are made to writers of outstanding books for young readers in English and French categories.

1982   **Monica Hughes**, Edmonton, Alta., for *The Guardian of Isis* (Hamish Hamilton)
Susan Martel, Montreal, Que., for *Nos amis robots* (Editions Heritage)

Lori Asseton-Smith, 1983 Miss Teen
Canada

R.M. Thomson, best supporting actor
Genie for *If You Could See What I See*

Rae Dawn Chong, best actress Genie
for *Quest For Fire*

Pierre Berton, various literary prizes

KUDOS FOR KOGAWA

Toronto writer Joy Kogawa received an American Book Award in 1983 for her historical novel *Obasan*, which deals with the internment and dispersion of West-Coast Japanese-Canadians during and after the Second World War. Kogawa is the first Canadian to win the award. In announcing the award the foundation said that *Obasan* "shows us again that it is possible for the omissions and errors of history to be corrected by great writers and great literature."

BEEFEATER CLUB PRIZE FOR LITERATURE

Beefeater Club of the Incorporated Ancient Order of the Beefeater

A coveted prize, which has hitherto been awarded only to British or American authors, it is given for book-length works which involve both Great Britain and the United States.

1982 $10,000 **Pierre Berton**, Kleinburg, Ont., for his two-volume work *The Invasion of Canada* and *Flames Across the Border* (McClelland & Stewart, 1980, 1981). The Beefeater Club said that it "bent the rules" to give the prize to Berton, a Canadian, because the works were of such excellence.

Berton also won the 1981 Canadian Authors Award and the 1982 Canadian Booksellers Award for the volumes.

ESSAYS EXCEL

The American Library Association chose *The Celtic Consciousness* by Robert O'Driscoll of Toronto, Ont., as outstanding academic book of the year. The volume of essays on 3,000 years of the Celtic continuum is the most extensive exploration of the civilization ever written. The book examines the myths, music, history, literature, folklore, art and archaeology of the Celtic civilization, now regarded as the oldest in Europe.

ALBERTA WRITING-FOR-YOUTH COMPETITION

A prize of $1,500 is awarded biennially for the best manuscript, fiction or non-fiction, by an Alberta author for young readers.

1981 **Monica Hughes** for *Hunter in the Dark*.

CBC LITERARY COMPETITION

A total of $18,000 is given to award winners in three categories. Winning entries are broadcast on CBC Radio's *Anthology* series.

1982 Short Story
Michael Ondaatje, Toronto, Ont., for *The Passions of Lalla*
Nancy Bauer, Fredericton, N.B., for *Prologue*
Anton Baer, Whitehorse, N.W.T., for *Germany, 1946*
Poetry
Roo Borson, Toronto, Ont., for *Summer's Drug*
Elfreida Read, Vancouver, B.C., for *Growing up in China*
David Day, residing in London, England, for *Nine Lost Animals*
Drama (Comedy)
No first prize awarded
Larry Snyder, Toronto, Ont., for *A Taste of the Sweet Apple*
Lynn Kirk, Regina, Sask., for *Woman of Merit*
Drama (Adventure)
Rachel Wyatt, Toronto, Ont., for *Jupiter's Feet: A Love Story*
Glynis Whiting, Edmonton, Alta., for *The Darkened Room*

Warren Graves, Edmonton, Alta., for
The Miklos Incident
Children's Story
Alice Tomlinson, Victoria, B.C., for
The Hen's Castle
Mary Alice and **John Downie**, Kingston, Ont., for *The Bright Paddle*
Peter Garvey, Bramalea, Ont., for
King Albert's Mines

LIFE STORY HELPED WIN FREEDOM

Uncle Tom's Cabin, a novel by Harriet Beecher Stowe, was published in 1850. The success of the book was amazing: 500,000 copies were sold in the U.S. alone within five years. An indictment of slavery, the book evoked fierce militant anti-slavery sentiment in the northern states and became a factor in precipitating the American Civil War.

Beecher's book was based on the life of Josiah Henson, whom she met at Dresden, Ont. Henson had been born a slave but rose to be overseer on his master's plantation in Kentucky. He was, as well, an ordained Methodist Episcopalian minister. He fled to Canada with his wife and four little children in 1830, after discovering that his family was to be separated. He settled at Dawn, Upper Canada (near present day Dresden), where he was one of the founders of the fugitive-slave settlement and pastor of the Methodist church. In later life he travelled, and was received at the White House and by Queen Victoria.

SEAL BOOKS FIRST NOVEL COMPETITION

The prize is $10,000 plus a $40,000 nonreturnable advance on royalties. The winning novel is published in hardcover by McClelland & Stewart in Canada. A year later it is published by Bantam (USA) and Corgi (UK) in paperback.

The six-year-old annual award was shared by two winners for the first time in 1983.

1983   David Kendal, Toronto, Ont., for
Lazaro
Jonathan Webb, Toronto, Ont., for
Pluck

FIRST NOVELIST

The first novel written in Canada was the *History of Emily Montague* by Frances Brooke. She was the wife of the chaplain of the garrison at Quebec who served between 1763 and 1768, and the book gives detailed sketches of life in Quebec during that period.

BOOK OF THE YEAR FOR CHILDREN

The competition, established in 1946, annually awards a gold metal for an outstanding children's book written by a Canadian.

1982   Janet Lunn, Toronto, Ont., for *The Root Cellar* (Lester & Orpen Dennys)

AIR CANADA AWARD

A general award which does not cite a particular work is made to a promising young writer. The prize is two return tickets to any Air Canada destination.

1982   Gail Hamilton, Toronto, Ont.

CANADIANS FAMOUS ABROAD

Morley Callaghan has a Russian literary agent. Margaret Atwood's novels have been translated into 14 languages, including Welsh. Alice Munro has a letter from a man in Inner Mongolia wanting to translate one of her stories into Chinese. Irving Layton was first nominated for the Nobel Prize for literature by a group of Italian admirers.

LITERARY AWARDS

Canadian Authors Association

A $5,000 cash prize and a silver medal are awarded for outstanding works published in the previous calendar year.

1982 Fiction: **Joy Kogawa**, Ottawa, Ont., for *Obasan* (Lester & Orpen Dennys).
Nonfiction: **Claude Bissell**, Toronto, Ont., for *The Young Vincent Massey* (U of T Press).
Poetry: **Gary Geddes**, Ottawa, Ont., for *The Acid Test* (Turnstone).
Drama: **Allan Stratton**, Toronto, Ont., for *Rexy* (Playwright's Press).

VICKY METCALF AWARD

Canadian Authors Association

1982
$1,000 **Janet Lunn**, Toronto, Ont., for the book *The Root Cellar* (Lester & Orpen Dennys)
$500 **Barbara Greenwood**, Toronto, Ont., for the short story "A Major Resolution" from the anthology *Contexts* (Nelson).

READING RECORD

The world's longest poetry reading, featuring 150 versifiers who held forth for 75 hours nonstop, took place in 1976 to mark the closure of a Toronto coffeehouse called the Bohemian Embassy. The club, a launching pad for many now-famous entertainers, suffered from the fact that Bell Canada's Yellow Pages persisted in listing it under "foreign consulates."

GERALD LAMPERT MEMORIAL AWARD

League of Canadian Poets

A prize of $300 is presented to the best new Canadian writers. The annual award alternates between prose and poetry.

1982 **Edna Alford**, Livelock, Sask., for *A Sleep Full of Dreams* (Oolichan), **Abraham Boyarsky**, Montreal, Que., for *Shreiber* (General).

PAT LOWTHER MEMORIAL AWARD

League of Canadian Poets

A hand-lettered scroll and $300 are awarded annually for the best book of poetry written by a Canadian woman.

1982 **Rona Murray**, Victoria, B.C., for *Journey* (Sono Nis).

ALBERTA NONFICTION AWARD

The prize of $1,500 cash is for the best book of general nonfiction written in English by a resident of Alberta.

1982 **Ann Gomer Sunahara** for *The Politics of Racism* (Lorimer). The book examines the politics behind the internment of Japanese Canadians during the Second World War.

MARIE MORIN

One of the first Canadian-born nuns, Morin also had a book published in the 20th century.

Marie Morin was born at Quebec in 1649 and entered the Hotel-Dieu de Montreal in 1662. She is noted because she wrote the story of the founding of her order, of the endowment of the hospital, of its early difficulties and of its development. After her death other nuns continued the story.

The collection of writings was published in 1921 under the title *Annales de l'Hotel-Dieu de Montreal* **by the Historical Society of Montreal.**

EATON'S B.C. BOOK AWARD

Eaton's buys $2,000 worth of the winning book and donates copies to B.C. school libraries. The B.C. Ministry of Education buys enough additional copies to ensure that every secondary school library in the province receives one.

1982 **Hugh Brody**, for *Maps and Dreams* (Douglas and McIntyre). Brody's winning book combines descriptions of the daily lives of the Beaver Indians with the author's commentary on the history, politics and social conditions of northeastern B.C.

FIRST NOVEL AWARD

Books in Canada

A cash prize of $15,000 is awarded for the best first novel by a Canadian published in English in the previous calendar year.

1982 **W.P. Kinsella**, Calgary, Alta., for *Shoeless Joe* (Thomas Allen and Son).

FIRST DICTIONARY

The first Canadian dictionary, a French-Huron compendium, was compiled by a Recollet missionary, Rev. J. LeCaron.

STEPHEN LEACOCK MEMORIAL MEDAL FOR HUMOUR

Stephen Leacock Association with the Hudson's Bay Company

The award was established in 1947 to encourage the writing and publishing of humorous works in Canada. The silver medal, created by Emanuel Hahn, and $2,000 cash from the Hudson's Bay Company are presented annually in Orillia, Ont.

1983 **Morley Torgov**, Toronto, Ont., for *The Outside Chance of Maximilian Glick* (Lester & Orpen Dennys). The story describes the culture shock occasioned by the arrival of a new rabbi — who always has wanted to be a stand-up comedian — in a small city, based on Torgov's own birthplace of Sault Ste. Marie. Torgov also received the Leacock medal in 1974 for *A Good Place To Come From*.

DUVERNAY AWARD

Societé Saint-Jean-Baptiste de Montréal

1982 **Jean Ethier-Blais**, for the body of his works as a literary critic, essayist and novelist.

EARLY ALPHABET

An Illustrated Comic Alphabet **of 1859 is thought to be the first Canadian picture book published.**

CHALMERS CANADIAN PLAYWRIGHT AWARD

Ontario Arts Council

$5,000 is presented to a Canadian playwright for an outstanding play produced in the Toronto area during the previous year.

1982 **Anne Chislett**, Victoria, B.C., for *Quiet in The Land*. *Quiet in the Land* recounts the struggle between a father and a son in southwestern Ontario's Amish community during the First World War. Two awards of $1,500 were also made to John Lazarus and Joa Lazarus for *Dreaming and Duelling* and to Tom Walmsley for *White Boys*.

MYSTERY WINS

Toronto writer Larry Morse won the Mystery Writers of America Edgar

Award for his thriller *The Old Dick*. Published in paperback by Avon Books, *The Old Dick* is about a private eye who comes out of cranky retirement to solve one last case in Los Angeles.

CITY OF TORONTO BOOK AWARDS

A $5,000 prize is awarded annually to a literary work about Toronto published the previous year.

1983   **Michael Bliss**, Toronto, Ont., for *The Discovery of Insulin*.
Lucy Booth Martyn, Toronto, Ont., for *The Face of Early Toronto: An Archival Record 1803-1936*.
1982   **Claude Bissell**, Toronto, Ont., for *The Young Vincent Massey* (U of T Press).
Marian Engel, Toronto, Ont. for *Lunatic Villas* (McClelland and Stewart).

FIRST CANADIAN TYPEFACE

Carl Dair, who designed the Cartier typeface, was the first Canadian to design a typeface for body text.

IODE BOOK AWARD

The annual award is for the best children's book written or illustrated by a Canadian resident in Toronto and environs and published by a Canadian publisher within the preceding year. The prize is a scroll and a $1,000 cash award.

1982   **Bernice Thurman Hunter**, Toronto, Ont., for *That Scatterbrain Booky* (Scholastic).

RECORD BID

Macmillan of Canada optioned the Canadian paperback rights for Alice Munro's fourth collection of short stories, *Moons of Jupiter*, for a record $45,000 in 1982. The Penguin bid is considered the highest amount ever paid for short stories in Canada.

JOHN A. MACDONALD PRIZE

Canadian Historical Association

$5,000 is awarded annually for a nonfiction work of Canadian history deemed to have made the most significant contribution to an understanding of the Canadian past.

1982   **Paul-Andre Linteau**, U. of Quebec, Montreal, for *Maisonneuve: Comment des promoteurs fabriquent une ville, 1883-1918* (Boreal Express publications).

WALLACE K. FERGUSON PRIZE

Canadian Historical Association

A prize of $2,000 is awarded for outstanding work in a field of history other than Canadian, published in a two-year period.

1982   **Christopher R. Friedrichs**, for *Urban Society In An Age of War: Nordlingen, 1580-1720* (Princeton University Press).

FIRST COPYRIGHT

The first copyright issued in Canada was to *A Canadian Spelling Book*, granted in 1841.

WRITER'S QUARTERLY EDITOR'S PRIZE

The *Writer's Quarterly* founded and established the Cross-Canada Writer's Workshop in 1978. The first of its kind in the world, the workshop was established to bring writers from across Canada together by mail.

Winning entries in poetry and short fiction are published in Cross-Canada *Writer's Quarterly*.

1983 Poetry
James Falcone, Bedford, N.S., for *Final Entry*.
Tsigane, Niagara-On-The-Lake, Ont., for *Washed Up On The Grau du Roi, Provence*.
Short Fiction
Johanne Caulfield, Laval des Rapides, Que., for *The Last Rose*.
Gary Eikenberry, Dartmouth, N.S., for *Mr. Deacon*.

PRINTING PREMIERE

The first book printed in Canada was published in Quebec in 1765 under the title *Catechisme du Diocese de Sens*.

NOVA SCOTIA CULTURAL LIFE AWARD

Writers Federation of Nova Scotia

The award was created in 1980 to recognize outstanding volunteer service to the cultural growth of the province.

1982 **Joyce Barkhouse**, Woodville, N.S., has published poems, stories and articles mostly for children. In 1980 she co-authored the children's novel *Anna's Pet* (Lorimer) with her niece, Margaret Atwood.

EARLY FLICKERS

The world's first propaganda film was cranked out in 1903, when Sir Clifford Sifton talked the CPR into bankrolling a movie extolling the virtues of the West to prospective European immigrants.

Canada's first motion picture theatre was opened in 1906 by Ernest Ouimet, in a converted Montreal dance hall. His programs featured a uniformed orchestra and a singer who entertained between 20-minute reels.

The first Canadian feature-length film was a 1914 dramatization of Henry Longfellow's *Evangeline*.

GENIE AWARDS

Canada's own version of the Oscar is presented to winners in feature film, short and documentary categories.

1983 Best motion picture: **The Grey Fox**
Best performance by an actor in a leading role: **Donald Sutherland** in *Threshold*
Best performance by an actress in a leading role: **Rae Dawn Chong** in *Quest For Fire*
Best performance by an actor in a supporting role: **R.H. Thomson** in *If You Could See What I Hear*
Best performance by an actress in a supporting role: **Jackie Burroughs** in *The Grey Fox*
Best performance by a foreign actor: **Richard Farnsworth** in *The Grey Fox*
Best performance by a foreign actress: **Glynnis O'Connor** in *Melanie*
Best achievement in art direction: **Bill Brodie** for *The Grey Fox*
Best achievement in costume design: **John Hay** for *Quest for Fire*
Best achievement in cinematography: **Michel Brault** for *Threshold*
Best achievement in direction: **Phillip Borsos** for *The Grey Fox*
Best achievement in film editing: **Yves Langlois** for *Quest For Fire*
Best achievement in sound editing: **Ken Heeley-Ray, Martin Ashbee, David Evans, Kevin Ward** for *Quest For Fire*
Best music score: **Michael Conway Baker** for *The Grey Fox*
Best original song: **Burton Cummings** for *Save My Soul* in *Melanie*
Best original screenplay: **John Hunter** for *The Grey Fox*
Best screenplay adapted from another medium: **Richard Paluck** for *Melanie*
Best achievement in overall sound: **Ken Heeley-Ray, Joe Grimaldi, Austin Grimaldi, Claude Hazanavicius, Don White** for *Quest For Fire*

Genie winners for *The Grey Fox*: l to r, Michael Baker (best music score), Phillip Boros (best director), Peter O'Brian (producer/best picture), Bill Brodie (best art direction), Richard Farnsworth (best foreign actor), Jackie Burroughs (best supporting actress), John Hunter (best original screenplay)

Terri Nash, director, *If You Love This Planet*

Dr. Helen Caldicott, writer, for the Oscar-winning film *If You Love This Planet*

Best theatrical short: **Bernadette Payeur** for *Elvis Gratton*
Best theatrical documentary: **Bill Brind**, **Robert Fortier**, **Adam Symansky** for *The Devil at Your Heels*

The Academy's special annual award, the Air Canada Award, was presented to Fin Quinn for outstanding contributions to the business of film-making in Canada.

THEY LOVED *HATE*

The Concordia University annual student film festival presented 38 entries from 14 film schools across the country. The winning film, *Hate*, by producer-director Trevor Harris from Toronto's Ryerson Institute, was the outstanding documentary and received the unanimous acclaim of both jury and audience.

CANADIAN INDEPENDENT SHORT FILM SHOWCASE COMPETITION

Canada Council

Winning short films are released to commercial movie houses across Canada in collaboration with the Canadian Motion Picture Distributors' Association. Established in 1982, to encourage new sources of film production by providing technical, marketing and promotional services for those films sponsored by the showcase, prizes of $3,000 per winning film are awarded.

1982 *Brushstrokes*, by **Sylvie Fefer**, Burnaby, B.C.
(Animation) A comical look at what happens when one tries to stray from the norm.
La Cage Ronde, by **Claude Lavoie**, Montreal, Que.
(Experimental) Based on a poem by Jacques Prevert, the film parallels human relationships with the taming of a wild bird.

Suit of Many Crayons, by **Kevin McCracken**, Vancouver, B.C.
(Animation) A humorous look at life through a child's crayon drawings.
Kelekis, by **Barry Lank**, Winnipeg, Man.
(Documentary) The 50th anniversary of Winnipeg's famous hotdog and chip restaurant.
Butterfly, by **Dieter Mueller**, Vancouver, B.C.
(Animation) A quick look at a man's habit at a cocktail party.
Oh Sean, by **Heidi Slomkvist**, **Genni Selby**, **Jay Cestnik** and **Gerard Paquette**, Toronto, Ont.
(Animation) A glimpse into the wondrous imagination of a child, an imagination that can turn the most mundane into a great adventure.
Hawkesville to Wallenstien, by **Richard Kerr**, Toronto, Ont.
(Documentary) A black and white pictorial of the Mennonite area of Waterloo County.
Bay St. Tap, by **John Barclay** and **Tony Sloan**, Toronto, Ont.
(Narrative) An interesting twist to a rainy day on Bay Street in Toronto.

CINEMA SHORTS

A Canadian documentary about immigrant farmworkers in the Fraser Valley has won second prize in the Leipzig film festival in East Germany. *A Time To Rise* won the Silver Dove award in November 1982. The Festival theme was films for peace in the world.

Nick Mancuso won the best actor award at the Houston, Texas, International Film Festival, 1982. He also received awards for the same role in Italy, as well as a Canadian Genie.

A War Story won top honours at the eighth annual Alberta Film and Television Awards. Produced by the National Film Board, and directed by Anne

Wheeler, the film was given the award for best direction and musical score.

The opening episode of a television series called *Masters of the Performing Arts* took first prize in the performing arts category at the American Film Festival, 1982. The show featured Maureen Forrester and was directed by Tony and Norman Campbell.

Imagine the Sound won the Silver Hugo Award for the best feature-length documentary in the 1981 Chicago Film Festival. The Canadian film was directed by Ron Mann.

Dar Robinson was paid $100,000 for the 1,100-foot leap he made from the CN Tower in Toronto in November 1979 for *High Point*. His parachute opened only 300 feet above the ground.

BIJOU AWARDS

Academy of Canadian Cinema and the Canadian Film and Television Association

The awards celebrate outstanding achievements in short film and television production in Canada, both public and private.

1983   Television drama under 30 minutes
Michael MacMillan, Seaton McLean, Janice Platt for *The Olden Days Coat* (Atlantis Films Ltd.)
Television drama over 30 minutes
Bill Gough for *War Brides* (CBC)
Documentary under 30 minutes
Wolf Koenig for *Nose & Tina* (NFB)
Documentary over 30 minutes
The Grierson Award/Le Prix Grierson
Stephen Low for *Challenger: An Industrial Romance* (NFB)
Television variety / music
Trevor Evans for *Air Farce* (CBC)
Instructional
Peter Jones for *Estuary* (NFB)
Sales, promotion, public relations

Lloyd Walton for *Snow* (Ontario Provincial Parks)
Animation
Jerry Krepakevich for *Getting Started* (NFB)
Commercial
Patti Grech for *Energy Efficiency — Imperial Oil* (Rabko Television Productions)
Audio-video non-portable, 1-7 projector programs
Multiple Images Inc. for *Modulighting*
Audio-video non-portable, 8-18 projector programs
Norman Nattrass for *The Green Network* (K.J. Communications Ltd.)
Best independent production
Ira Levy and **Peter Williamson** for *The Breakthrough* (Lauron Productions)
Outstanding performance by an actor
Chuck Shamata for *Running Man*
Outstanding performance by an actress
Lally Cadeau for *You've Come A Long Way, Katie*
Outstanding art direction
Barbara McLean for *War Brides*
Outstanding cinematography in a dramatic production
Vic Sarin, csc for *War Brides*
Outstanding cinematography in a documentary production
Robert Fresco for *Steady As She Goes*
Outstanding direction in a dramatic production
Donald Brittain for *Running Man*
Outstanding direction in a documentary production
Norma Bailey for *Nose & Tina*
Outstanding editing in a dramatic production
Myrtle Virgo for *War Brides*
Outstanding editing in a documentary production
Harvey Zlaterits, Barry Gilmore for *The Hawk*
Outstanding original music score
Larry Crosley for *The Lost Pharaoh*
Outstanding non-dramatic script
Michel Gérard for *The Canadian Establishment — 10 Toronto Street*
Outstanding screenplay
Roger Lemelin, Gilles Carle for *Les Plouffe*
Outstanding sound

Ed Chong for *Running Man*
Outstanding visual effects
Colin Chilvers for *Innertube — R.C. Cola*
Nielsen-Ferns International First Production Award
Wayne Arron for *Exposure* (Exposure Productions)
The Chetwynd Award
PFA Labs, President: Fred Lemmin

TOLLER TOPS

Toller Cranston's *Strawberry Ice* CBC TV dance fantasy special won the top TV network entertainment prize in 1982 at the San Francisco Film Festival, beating out 30 entries from around the world.

CBC TELEFEST COMPETITION

The award recognizes promising young film and video producers.

1983 *Get Happy*, by Humber College's **Paul Sarossy**, was best short film. It's a black comedy that uses the Judy Garland song as a soundtrack.
Truth or Dare, by Humber's **Ivan McDonald**, was best long TV show. It's a love-triangle play about a young woman's revenge.
Call, by Ryerson's **Kevin Dimitroff**, was best video short. It's a video rock show.
Tale Wind, by Sheridan College's **Greg Gibbons**, was best animation entry. It took viewers on a quick world tour through the eyes of a leaf blowing in the wind.
Paternity Blues, by York University's **John Podolak**, won as best long film and also took the Director's Award as best overall entry. The film is a comedy about a young man on the brink of matrimony who is thinking of murdering his bride-to-be.

ACADEMY AWARDS

Canadian productions won three Oscars, including one for a documentary film labelled by U.S. authorities as political propaganda, at the 55th Academy Awards in 1983.

The award for documentary short subject went to *If You Love This Planet* by the National Film Board of Canada. The U.S. Justice department had labelled the anti-nuclear film (and two others made in Canada) as propaganda.

Just Another Missing Kid, made for the CBC's public affairs program *the fifth estate*, won in the documentary feature category. It is the first time CBC's English language division picked up an Oscar. (The French language network won the previous year for *Crac*.)

Quest For Fire, a Canadian co-production with France, won for best make-up. Sarah Monzani and Michele Burke had used a number of complicated techniques to make actors look like prehistoric people.

Before winning an Academy award, Terri Nash's film about nuclear disarmament, *If You Love This Planet*, won a Special Award presented by the World Peace Council at the 25th International Leipzig Documentary and Short Film Festival in Leipzig, East Germany.

GOLDEN SHEAF AWARDS

Yorkton Short Film and Video Festival

North America's oldest continuous short-film festival is held each fall at Yorkton, Saskatchewan.

VIDEO
Best video of the festival: **The Catch**, CKND-TV, Winnipeg
Best in human condition category: **We Won't Let Him Die**, CFAC Lethbridge Television
Best in human dynamic category: **Colony Trek**, CBC Television, Saskatoon
Best in spontaneous human category: **B.C. — A Special Christmas**, Cinera Productions Ltd., Toronto

Best in commercial promotional/vignette category: **A Meewasin Moment: I Remember Saskatoon**, Meewasin Valley Authority, Saskatoon

CRAFT AWARDS

Best director: **Allan Kroker**, *The Catch*, CKND-TV, Winnipeg

Best performer: **Louisette Dussault**, *Joe*, Videography Inc., Montreal

Best videography: **John Wilson, Norman Alin, Wally Donaldson**, This Land — Rideau Journey, CBC, Toronto

Best picture editing: **Richard Wells**, *The Shroud of Turin*, CBC, Toronto

Best sound editing: **Dave Hillis**, *Othello in 5, 4, 3*, Provincial Educational Media Centre, Richmond, B.C.

People's choice award: **The Accident**, Infocus Productions, Toronto

Special jury award: **The Electronic Web**, CBC, Toronto

B.C. — A Special Christmas, Cinera Productions Ltd., Toronto

Certificates of merit: **Noel Buys a Suit**, CBC, Children's Television, Toronto

Game Plan, ACCESS Alberta, Edmonton

FILM

Best film of the festival: **P4W: Prison for Women**, Holly Dale/Janis Cole, Toronto

Best in human condition category: **P4W Prison for Women**, Holly Dale/Janis Cole, Toronto

Best in human dynamic category: **Breaking Through — The Story of Norman & Tom**, National Institute on Mental Retardation, Downsview

Best in spontaneous human category: **Steady As She Goes**, NFB., Montreal

CRAFT AWARDS

Best director: **Veronika Soul**, *End Game in Paris*, NFB., Montreal

Best performer: **Ron Cook**, *A Time To Be Brave*, The Film Works, Toronto

Best cinematography: **Nesya Shapiro**, *P4W: Prison for Women*, Janis Cole/Holly Dale, Toronto

Best picture editing: **Veronika Soul**, *End Game In Paris*, NFB., Montreal

Best sound editing: **Jackie Newell**, *End Game In Paris*, NFB., Montreal

Best children's production: **Distant Islands**, NFB., Montreal

Nettie Kryski Canadian Heritage Award: **Ted Baryluk's Grocery**, NFB., Winnipeg

Special jury awards: **Quallunaani**, One Six Productions, Toronto

Life Another Way, Hamilton-Brown Film Productions, Toronto

Certificates of merit: **Good Monday Morning**, Laura Sky, Toronto

The Battle of Beech Hall, Christopher Wilson, Toronto

If You Love This Planet, NFB., Montreal

WINNING AT FOREIGN FESTIVALS

Two of the major winners of the Atlanta Annual Independent Film and Video Festival in 1981 were Canadian artists Teri Chmilar, Guelph, Ont., for *Sudz*, a 33-minute humorous documentary about the laundromats of southwestern Ontario, and Ardele Lister, Calgary, Alta., for *Split* a 21-minute narrative work about a 16-year-old punk girl at odds with her family and with society. *Split* also won a major award at the fourth annual Tokyo Video Festival and has been chosen for inclusion in the Ithaca Film Festival, which will tour to video centres in the United States, Canada, Europe and Japan.

Micronesia: The Winds of Change, produced by Toronto's Rosebud Films, won the special Jury Gold Prize at the Houston International Film Festival in 1983. The hour-long film, which chronicles the rapid social changes in the Pacific area of Micronesia, was directed by Peter Rowe.

Producer Daniel Bertolino and composer Osvaldo Montes of Montreal were awarded the Grand Prix Audiovisuel Européen by the Paris-based Academie du disque français for their album *Indian Legends of Canada*.

Rushes, a film by Benoit Meek, took the first Grand Prix at the international

Super-8 Festival in Caracas, and a selection of nine Quebec films received one of the five Grand Prix at the Brussels Festival for Universality of Language.

Quebec film critics voted *Le Confort et l'indifference*, a National Film Board production about the province's referendum on independence, Quebec's best feature-length film of 1982. Director Denys Arcand accepted the L.E. Ouimet-Molson prize given by the critics' association and a cash award of $5,000 donated by Molson Breweries.

JACQUELINE LEMIEUX PRIZE

Canada Council

The $1,000 prize is awarded to winners of the Canada Council grants in two annual competitions for individuals in dance.

1981   Robert Desrosiers
        Roxanne D'Orleans Juste
1982   Daniel Leveille
        Amelia Itcush

CRITICS IMPRESSED

Napoli, the National Ballet of Canada's first full-length work in five years, won cheers from leading New York Dance critics visiting Toronto. It was created by Danish choreographer August Bournonville and restaged by company dancer Peter Schaufuss.

"*Napoli*," said *New York Times* critic Anna Kisselgoff, "promises to be the National Ballet's sleeper." The *New York Post*'s Clive Barnes said, "The dancing was possibly the best I have ever seen by the Canadians."

JEAN A. CHALMERS AWARD IN CHOREOGRAPHY

Ontario Arts Council

The annual $5,000 prize is presented at the Dance in Canada banquet.

1982   Edouard D. Lock

STAR STEP-DANCER

Lori-Lynne Boston of Etobicoke, Ont., is the step-dancing champion of North America. She won top prize at the National Traditional Old Timers' Fiddlers Contest in Vermont. Step-dancing is similar to tap dancing, but puts more emphasis on the quick and snappy use of the toes.

CLIFFORD E. LEE CHOREOGRAPHY AWARD

Clifford E. Lee Foundation and the Banff Centre

The award, established in 1978, includes a cash prize of $3,000 and a summer residency at the Banff School of Fine Arts.

1982   **Stefanie Ballard**, associate artistic director, Winnipeg's Contemporary Dancers.

VICTORY BALL

The first ball in Canada was given by Chartier de Lotbiniere, Lieutenant du Roi at Quebec in 1667, as a victory celebration following the successful repulsion of an Iroquois attack.

NATIONAL BALLET SCHOOL AWARD

Students chosen by the faculty of the National Ballet School who show promise and have need of financial assistance are awarded $300 each annually.

1982   **Jaqueline Cousineau**, Toronto, Ont.
        Michael Okamura, Toronto, Ont.

HER LOWEST SCORED HIGHEST

The lowest height for a flaming bar under which a limbo dancer has passed is 6 $^1/_8$ inches off the floor at Port of Spain Pavilion, Toronto, June 24, 1973 by Marlene Raymond, 15. Strictly no part of the body other than the sole or side of the foot should touch the ground, though brushing the shoulder blade does not usually result in disqualification.

FIFTH ANNUAL DANCE ONTARIO AWARD

1983   Patricia Beatty, David Earle and Peter Randazzo, co-founders and artistic directors, Toronto Dance Theatre.

HEROINE OF THE DANCE

In 1950, Mrs. F.J. Mulqueen, Mrs. J.D. Woods and Mrs. R.B. Whitehead, all of Toronto, sent Stewart James, who was holidaying in London, to see Ninette de Valois, director of the Sadler's Wells, to help find the right person to form a national dance company in Canada. The answer from Dame de Valois, "Celia Franca, if you can get her."

De Valois' assessment of Franca's character was profound; for who else but Miss Franca would have had the strength of character, the resourcefulness, and the patience to build a professional national ballet company in a country where dance was in its infancy and where most men thought dance "sissyfied."

Thanks to her, her colleagues and the young people whose vision she inspired, ballet in Canada has become an art form that Canadians from coast to coast love and enjoy. The National Ballet of Canada, which she created and nurtured, is today one of the foremost ballet companies in the world.

GOVERNOR-GENERAL'S MEDAL FOR ARCHITECTURE

Awarded in recognition of outstanding achievement in the field of Canadian architecture.

1983   Arthur Erikson, Architects, Vancouver, B.C., for the Museum of Anthropology, Vancouver, B.C.
Boudrias, Boudreau, St. Jean, Longeuil, Que., for Usine de Pompage d'eau brute.
Bruno Freschi, Architect, Vancouver, B.C., for "Ping Pong One."
DuBois Plumb and Associates, Toronto, Ont., for "The Oaklands."
J.H. Cook, Architects, Calgary, Alta., for the Corporate Head Office of NOVA, Calgary, Alta.
James Cheng, Architect, Vancouver, B.C., for Willow Court, Willow Arbor and Heather Terrace.
Jim Strasman, Architect, Toronto, Ont., for the Wondrich Residence.
Jodoin Lamarre Pratt, Montreal, Que., for Chapelle de Sacre-Coeur, Montreal.
Russell Vandiver, Architects, Vancouver, B.C., for the Multi-Tennant Research Building, Vancouver, B.C.

ARCHITECTS PICKED TO DESIGN MUSEUM

Edmonton architect Douglas Cardinal and the Montreal firm of Tetrault, Parent, Languedoc have been chosen by the federal cabinet to design the new National Museum of Man. The museum, to be built at Parc Laurier in Hull across the river from Ottawa, is scheduled for completion late in 1987.

RAIC GOLD MEDAL

Royal Architectural Institute of Canada

For great contribution to the architectural profession. The award recognizes achievement in architecture, or science and letters relating to architecture and the arts.

1982/83 Ralph Erskine, Sweden, for architecture responsive to the climate, notably the high North.

RAIC ALLIED ARTS MEDAL

Royal Architectural Institute of Canada

A silver medal is awarded for outstanding achievement in arts allied to architecture.

1982 Henry Kalen, (architectural photographer, Winnipeg, Man.).
1983 Alfred Pellan, painter and pioneering Quebec modernist, Quebec.

SAFDIE AWARDED NATIONAL GALLERY DESIGN

Moshe Safdie, the Montreal-based architect who created the world famous Habitat for Expo '67, has been chosen, along with Toronto architect John C. Parkin, to design Canada's first permanent National Gallery.

The gallery has been housed "temporarily" for the past 22 years in an Ottawa office building.

The site of the new gallery is on the edge of Nepean Point Park and overlooks Parliament and the river. The gallery is expected to be finished in late 1987.

GABRIELLE LEGER MEDAL

Heritage Canada Foundation

For outstanding work in architectural conservation in Canada.

1982 Colin J.G. Molson, Montreal, Que., for his more than 25 years of dedicated work to preserve Canada's architectural and historical heritage.

Long before most others, he recognized the need to preserve fine old buildings and thus he purchased properties to save them from the wrecker's ball and "progress."

LIEUTENANT GOVERNOR'S MEDAL

Heritage Canada Foundation

For outstanding work by an individual or group in architectural conservation in a province.

1982 Dr. John H. Archer, Regina, Sask., for his work in the preservation of Saskatchewan's heritage, particularly for encouraging property legislation and for making the general public more aware of heritage issues.

HEAVY HOMES

Sod houses were often the first homes of many early prairie settlers. A typical sod home used 50 tons of sod units in construction.

CREDIT FONCIER AWARD

Heritage Canada Foundation

For the best restoration of a building of historical or architectural importance. The annual award of $20,000 is divided equally between the architect and developer.

1982 Canadian Income Properties and Karas Corporation, London, Ont., for the Selby, an old shoe factory which has been restored and converted to office and retail space.
Ken Hampson and Norman Spatz, Montreal, Que., for the "popliger," a 1920s abandoned luxury apartment building which has been restored and is now a co-operative condominium.

Roy Thomson Hall, Exterior and interior

ACCESS AWARD

City of Toronto

Created in 1982, the Access award is bestowed upon a person, group or organization which has made a significant contribution toward improving the quality of life for the city's disabled residents.

The first award was for **Roy Thomson Hall**, designed to fit the needs of the disabled as well as the able of Toronto. Special attention was paid to the blind, hearing-impaired and those in wheelchairs.

GROWING PANES

The first glass windows in Canada were fitted in 1689 into the home of the high-ranking Longueuil family who lived in Montreal.

FIRST ARTS AND CRAFT SCHOOL IN CANADA

Bishop Laval founded Canada's first School of Arts and Crafts at Saint-Joachim in the vicinity of Sainte-Anne de Beaupré in 1668.

Laval believed that the colony in New France should be self-sufficient and that it needed its own craftsmen to further its development.

The school was an extension of the Quebec seminary. Students usually remained in the school until they were 18. Along with classical studies, they were also taught cabinet-making, sculpture, painting, gilding for the church decoration, carpentry and masonry. There were also classes in tailoring, shoemaking, tool-making, locksmithing and roofing.

Attached to the school was a model farm where agricultural instruction was given, and architecture studies were added a few years later. The school was set up to give practical instruction, with students working under the teachers' direction on actual projects.

Most of the wood decorations and some of the paintings of the chapel at Sainte-Anne which can be seen today are likely the work of those students.

CANADIAN ART HEROES

Tom Thomson (1877-1917). His paintings of Northern Ontario (long a part of every Canadian schoolchild's education) make him famous. But his story, that of the artist and the solitary visionary at home in the wilds, and his mysterious death at Canoe Lake (in Ontario's Algonquin Park) in July 1917 make him an irresistible legend.

Jack Bush (1909-1977). His reputation has continued to grow in Canada and abroad since his death in 1977. Exhibitions of his work continue to be mounted in the U.S. The NFB has produced a film on his life and work and the Robert McLaughlin Gallery in Oshawa mounted a 10-museum tour in 1981 featuring not only his work, but also that of 13 younger Canadian modernists variously affected by his life and his art.

WHO'S WHO OF CANADIAN ART

If the Order of Canada, which is given to outstanding Canadians, is a measure, then the following list represents Canada's outstanding painters and sculptors.

There are three levels of the Order — Member, Order of Canada (CM), for outstanding regional contribution Officer, Order of Canada (OC), for outstanding national contribution Companion, Order of Canada (CC), for outstanding national and international contribution

Painters (in alphabetical order)
Aba Bayefsky, CM (1979)
A.J. Casson, OC (1979)
George C. Clutesie, CM (1973)
Alex Coleville, OC (1967), CC (1981)
Charles T. Comfort, OC (1972)
Jacques de Tonnancour, OC (1979)
Corinne Dupuis-Maillet, CM (1973)
Kenneth Forbes, OC (1967)
Yves Gaucher, CM (1980)
Violet Amy Gillett, CM (1976)
Illingworth Kerr, CM (1982)
Roy Kiyooka, OC (1978)
J. Fenwick Landsdown, OC (1976)
Jean-Paul Lemieux, CC (1968)
Ernest Lindner, OC (1979)
Kenneth Lochhead, OC (1970)
Guido Molinari, OC (1971)
Norval Morrisseau, CM (1978)
Will Ogilvie, CM (1979)
Alfred Pellan, CC (1967)
Christopher Pratt, OC (1973)
Jean-Paul Riopelle, CC (1979)
Carl Fellman Schaffer, CM (1978)
Jack Shadbolt, OC (1972)
Michael Snow, OC (1981)
Phillip Surrey, CM (1982)
Claude Tousignant, OC (1976)
Harold Town, OC (1968)
Joseph Arthur Villeneuve, CM (1972)
Joyce Wieland, OC (1982)

Sculptors (The Plastic Arts)
Louis Archambault, OC (1968)
Jean Julien Bourgault, OC (1970)
Sylvia Daoust, CM (1976)
Dora de Pedery-Hunt, OC (1974)
Rufus Ezra Moodie, CM (1976)

LOTS OF SNOW — AND RONALDS

William Ronald, a founding member of Painters 11 and a still-active abstract-expressionist, claims to have more works in Canadian and American galleries and institutions than any other Canadian artist.

His work is represented at 47 American institutions including the Museum of Modern Art, the Guggenheim and the Whitney Museum, all in New York,

and in 22 Canadian institutions, including the National Gallery, the Art Gallery of Ontario, Montreal Museum of Fine Arts, the Canada Council Collection and the Canada Council Art Bank.

The longest Curriculum Vitae in *Contemporary Canadian Art* (versatility division) is that of Michael Snow. His listing of achievements, awards, exhibitions, appointments and performances as painter, sculptor, film-maker, photographer, musician and teacher here in Canada as well as in the U.S. and Europe is truly breathtaking.

Leafing through it one day in the early 1970s, fellow artist and musician Gerald McAdam was stunned at the number of entries. Handing the c.v. back to Snow, however, he coolly remarked, "Make a nice Christmas card."

AMELIA FRANCES HOWARD-GIBBON ILLUSTRATOR'S AWARD

Established in 1971, the award is presented annually with a gold medal.

1982 Heather Woodall, Vancouver, B.C., for *Ytek and the Arctic Orchid: An Inuit Legend*, by Garnet Hewitt (Douglas and McIntyre).

U OF T BENEFITS FROM ART ENDOWMENTS

An endowment of historic and artistic significance was left to the University of Toronto in 1981. Dr. Lillian Malcove Ormos, Winnipeg-bred and until her death one of New York City's leading Freudian psychoanalysts, left her entire collection of 500 works to the University.

The collection of Medieval Christian art is housed at St. Michael's College, Pontifical Institute of Medieval Studies. The Malcove Collection, as it is known, was insured for $6-million at the time of it's owner's death.

In 1982, Jules and Fay Loeb of Toronto endowed, for $1-million, a Fay Loeb Chair in Canadian Art at the University of Toronto. It is intended "to provide a foundation for academic development, research and graduate studies in Canadian Art."

At the same time the Loebs presented the university with their collection of 200 Canadian historical and contemporary artworks, conservatively valued at $4-million. The Loeb home in Toronto, also given to the university, will house the collection and serve as a resource centre.

The total value of the endowment is estimated at between $5-million and $10-million.

VANTAGE ARTS ACADEMY AWARDS

R.J.R. MacDonald Inc.

The awards were established by the tobacco firm to promote theatre arts in Canada.

1983 $25,000 **Actor's Fund of Canada**
The Actor's Fund will use the grant in its work to assist destitute and ill performers.
$20,000 Centaur Theatre, Montreal
The award was accepted by Centaur director, Maurice Podbrey, "on behalf of the beleaguered English community of Montreal."

PRICEY PAINTING

The greatest price paid for a Canadian painting at a public auction was $240,000. The painting was *South Shore, Baffin Island*, 32 inches by 40 ¼ inches, ca 1930, by the late Lawren Harris. The work by the Group of Seven artist was hammered down in May 1981 at Sotheby, Parke, Bernet, Auctioneers, in Toronto.

WORLD CHAMPIONSHIP WILDFOWL CARVING CHAMPIONSHIPS

Ward Foundation, USA

Held in Salsbury, Maryland, the 1982 World Wildfowl Carving Competitions drew over 800 entrants and 2,000 decorative bird carvings.

As 20,000 people watched, novice, amateur and professional carvers gave their best to win the World Carving Crown and a piece of the $50,000 prize money.

Pat Godin of Brantford, Ont., won first place in the World Decorative Lifesize Competition and collected $18,000 for his artistry and skill. Pat, a two-time champ, is a muscular waterfowl biologist who trained at Manitoba's Delta Waterfowl Research Station. Now 29, he was the youngest world champion ever at age 23.

TALK LEADS TO NEW ART FORM

(A story related by Toronto art critic Barrie Hale)
One winter night in 1957, James Houston, who had lived in and travelled the Arctic since 1948, sat with his friend Oshaweetok, a famous Inuit hunter and carver. Oshaweetok had been studying two packs of the same brand of cigarettes and comparing the sailor's head trademark on one, with the identical picture on the other. Finally he remarked that it must be a wearying occupation, this business of painting one sailor's head after another, each identical to the last, pack after pack.

Houston tried, in vain, to explain in Inuit the offset printing process. Finally he picked up an ivory walrus tusk with a surface engraved with designs by Oshaweetok. He coated the surface with thick, black residue from a bottle of ink that had been frozen and thawed many times. Then he carefully laid a sheet of toilet tissue on the inky surface, rubbed it lightly, and pulled off a printed image of Oshaweetok's design.

Oshaweetok took a look and said, "We could do that."

The first Inuit prints were produced in the summer of 1958 and shown at the Stratford Festival in Ontario where they were an immediate success. In 1959, the first catalogued edition of Cape Dorset prints appeared. There has been one each year since and Inuit prints are eagerly sought by art collectors the world over.

SAIDYE BRONFMAN AWARD FOR EXCELLENCE IN THE CRAFTS

Established in 1977, the annual award of $15,000 is for excellence over a significant period of time. Consideration is also given to innovation in relationship to traditional methods.

1982 **Micheline Beauchemin**, OC, RCA, Les Grondines, Que. Beauchemin, well-known tapestry artist and one of Canada's finest craftsmen, studied weaving and stained glass in Montreal, France and Japan.

THE CANADIAN AVANT-GARDE

Prior to the First World War, the Salon d'Automne in Paris was the international showcase for advanced art of the day. Three Canadian painters had their work exhibited there.

W.H. Clapp (1879-1954)
J.W. Morrice (1871-1945)
Emily Carr (1871-1945)

They were Canadian painters who dared to break from the traditional schools of Canadian printing.

TOP DESIGNERS

Members of the Associated Designers of Canada will be represented at the 1983 Prague Quadrennial, the most important theatre design competition in the world. The national jury selected eight designers, each represented by a single production.

Mary Kerr for *Desert Song*, Shaw Festival
James Plaxton for *Too Good To Be True*, Shaw Festival
Daphne Dare for *Farther West*, Theatre Calgary
Lawrence Schafer for *Hey Marilyn*, Edmonton Citadel Theatre
Meredith Caron for *Saga of the Wet Hens*, Tarragon Theatre, Toronto
Roy Robitschek for *Endgame*, Neptune Theatre, Halifax
Susan Benson for *The Woman*, Stratford Festival
John Ferguson for *The Visit*, Stratford Festival

QUICK SKETCHES

When Susan Festeryga became an apprentice engraver at the Canadian Mint it was a victory both for women and for the physically disabled. The 26-year-old Bradford, Ont., resident is the first female engraving apprentice hired by the mint since it was built in 1908. She has worn a hearing aid since she was an infant.

David Lloyd Blackwood was commissioned by the Uffizi Gallery in Florence, Italy, to do a selfportrait in pencil. The commission consists of an etching accompanied by the working drawing.

The Ring House Gallery received an Award of Excellence for Brochure Design from the Art Museum Association Publication Competition (San Francisco)

for its exhibition brochure "O! Osiris, Live Forever!" The design work was done by Terrance Zacharko, a visual communications student at the University of Alberta.

The world's smallest paintings are the work of British Columbia's Gerard Legare, who exerts himself in oils on pinheads as tiny as $1/_{32}$ inch across.

A portrait of Sir Martin Frobisher, by the Dutch painter Cornelius Ketel, was commissioned in 1577 by the Cathay Company. It was given in 1674 to Oxford University and hangs today in the Bodleian Library.

Donald Sutherland, Genie awards, best actor

Teresa Stratas in La Traviata

Commerce & Industry

BUSINESS

CANADIAN BUSINESS HALL OF FAME

Junior Achievement of Canada

The Canadian Business Hall of Fame was established in 1979 to honour Canadians who have made outstanding contributions to the development of the private enterprise system in Canada. It honours leaders both living and from the past; those currently occupying active executive positions do not qualify — the book on them is still open.

1983 **Robert Carlton Scrivener** (born 1914), retired chairman of Bell Canada and of Northern Telecom, whose leadership and foresight transformed those corporations into an international communications equipment giant and a world leader in electronic technology, respectively.

When he graduated from the University of Toronto in 1937, he remembers, his father's advice was: "Whatever you do, do it better than anyone else. And in five years you'll be identified as a comer."

Sam Steinberg, OC (1905-1978), shaped a small family grocery business into Steinberg Inc., a diversified Canadian corporation. Steinberg said that the secret of his success was "a matter of anticipating people's needs and responding at once with the best products and services at the best price."

Steinberg was a small boy when his family arrived from Hungary. After school, he and his brothers and sisters helped in the small grocery store his mother opened in 1917 in Montreal.

By the age of 14, food retailing had become his career and at 25 he assumed the presidency of the firm that had grown into a small eight-store chain. Today the company he developed operates a chain of supermarkets, food warehouses, limited-line food outlets, convenience stores, department stores, restaurants and large distribution and manufacturing centres. A real estate subsidiary has interests in more than 40 shopping centres and a U.S. subsidiary operates 20 large supermarket-department stores in Arizona. Consolidated sales of Steinberg Inc., and its subsidiaries totalled more than $3.3-billion in 1982 and the company employed 32,000 persons.

A founder and co-chairman of the Canadian Council of Christians and Jews, Sam Steinberg also helped to develop hospitals and homes for the aged. The year before his death in 1978, he was inducted as an Officer of the Order of Canada.

Leon J. Koerner (1892-1972), who revolutionized the forest industry in British Columbia by utilizing hemlock, which he marketed as Alaska Pine, was a philanthropist and patron of the arts and learning.

Koerner fled Czechoslovakia and Hitler in 1938. With his brothers Otto and Walter he established the Alaska Pine Company in B.C. in 1939. His firm revolutionized the industry by using cutting and drying so precisely to specifications that the product was soon competing successfully with the best Scandinavian white wood in world trade. As well, Koerner and his brothers helped to bring improved labour relations and working conditions to the forest industry in B.C.

In 1955 he established a foundation which provides grants and scholarships for the arts throughout B.C. and he built a new faculty club and graduate student centre at UBC.

Izaak Walton Killam (1885-1955), who built a financial empire by developing pulp and paper and hydro electric power companies from Newfoundland to British Columbia.

Killam, who has been called the "mystery man of Canadian finance" was born in Yarmouth, N.S. He joined Royal Securities as a salesman in 1904 and 10 years later his employer, Lord Beaverbrook, made him company president. By 1929 he had his own company which provided management of public utility undertakings. He nurtured B.C. Pulp and Paper and International Power through their infancies, and expanded Calgary Power. He launched Ottawa Valley Power Company and regenerated light and power companies in all the Atlantic provinces, and then risked his fortune by opening Mersey Paper, a newsprint development at Liverpool, N.S.

When Killam's wife died 10 years after his death in 1955 she had more than doubled her $40-million inheritance, and her will carried out her husband's wishes to assist the arts, sciences and education in Canada.

The Canada Council was launched in 1957 from inheritance taxes on Killam's estate, universities and institutions across the country received millions of dollars and the Izaak Walton Killam Hospital for Children in Halifax has become a leading facility for the health care of children and for the study of children's diseases.

T.A. St-Germain (1874-1956) spearheaded the dynamic growth of a small Quebec insurance firm, Le Groupe Commerce, into one of Canada's leading general insurance firms.

Born in Saint-Aimé, Théophile-Alex began working at age 13, in a Rhode Island cotton spinning mill. He was an apprentice blacksmith at age 17, and after working his way to ownership of his own forge, sold his business to become a railroad telegraph operator and station master. When the local railway he worked for closed in 1903, St-Germain turned to selling insurance for Great-West Life and in 1907, at age 33, joined with five partners to establish a mutual insurance company in Saint-Hyacinthe.

As manager of the firm, St-Germain criss-crossed the province, offering business protection at lower rates than competing Montreal insurance firms.

The company Mutuelle du Commerce took over three more insurance companies through the next decade, two of which were destined to become the Canadian Mercantile and the other, the Canadian National. The business extended from coast to coast in the 1940s but in the 1960s it consolidated within Quebec.

Timothy Eaton (1834-1907), who revolutionized the retailing business by selling merchandise for cash at a fixed price, backed by the pledge "goods satisfactory or money refunded," to build one of North America's largest department stores.

"A square deal for those we sell to, those we buy from and those who work for us." This saying, a favourite of Timothy Eaton, reflects the philosophy of the Irish immigrant who revolutionized merchandising and developed one of Canada's most successful retailing empires.

His dream began to become reality when he opened a tiny dry goods store in Toronto, in 1869, thirteen years after coming to Canada.

He shocked his competitors by selling for cash at a fixed price, eliminating extended credit and bartering. He guaranteed satisfaction, put full-page ads in newspapers and pioneered shopping by mail through the Eaton's catalogue. He was generous and considerate to his staff, who worked shorter hours than was general in the trade at the time.

Eaton's remains a family enterprise and the stores across the country that bear his name are a memorial to his success.

WINNING SALES

Merchants in Toronto's Eaton Centre were, on the whole, happy in September 1982. Sales for the first six months in the shopping mall were 13½ per cent ahead of a year earlier on a sales-per-square-foot basis. That was the highest sales-per-square-foot showing by any regional shopping centre in North America. There are 300 merchants in the centre.

LAUREATES OF THE HALL OF FAME

1979 J. Armand Bombardier
David Dunkelman
K.C. Irving
Frederick C. Mannix
Hart Massey
Sir Donald Alexander Smith
1980 Alphonse Desjardins
Sir Joseph Flavelle
Sir Herbert Samuel Holt
H.R. MacMillan
Frank M. McMahon
W. Garfield Weston
1981 Senator Pat Burns
J.-Louis Levesque
Grant McConachie
John Molson
James Armstrong Richardson
Muriel Sprague Richardson
Rt. Hon. Lord Thomson of Fleet
1982 L.L.G. (Poldi) Bentley
Edmund C. Bovey
Henry Birks
Samuel Bronfman

CANADA VICTORIOUS IN CAR WARS

For the first time since 1972, according to Statistics Canada, this country can boast of an overall surplus in automotive trade with the United States.

A greater demand for larger cars which are made at Canadian plants, gave Canada a $2.9-billion surplus in auto trade with the U.S. last year, up from a $1.7-billion deficit in 1981.

THE FINANCIAL POST 50 INDUSTRIALS

(Taken from *The Financial Post* 500 Industrials list.)
Companies are ranked by sales. Revenue figures represent thousands.

1	Canadian Pacific Ltd. (Montreal)	12,336,266
2	General Motors of Canada Ltd. (Oshawa)	10,416,050
3	Imperial Oil Ltd. (Toronto)	8,185,000
4	George Weston Ltd. (Toronto)	7,428,609
5	Bell Canada (Montreal)	7,389,900
6	Ford Motor Co. of Canada (Oakville, Ont.)	7,206,600
7	Alcan Aluminium Ltd. (Montreal)	5,968,622
8	Shell Canada Ltd. (Toronto)	4,751,000
9	Gulf Canada Ltd. (Toronto)	4,583,000
10	Texaco Canada Inc. (Toronto)	4,375,332
11	Canadian National Railway (Montreal)	4,285,821
12	Hudson's Bay Co. (Winnipeg)	4,172,442
13	TransCanada PipeLines Ltd. (Calgary)	3,404,897
14	Provigo Inc. (Montreal)	3,293,960
15	Massey-Ferguson Ltd. (Toronto)	3,175,031
16	Ontario Hydro (Toronto)	3,161,508
17	Canada Development Corp. (Vancouver)	3,136,351
18	Simpsons-Sears Ltd. (Toronto)	3,129,625
19	Noranda Mines Ltd. (Toronto)	3,030,394
20	Canada Safeway Ltd. (Winnipeg)	3,006,302

21	**Hiram Walker Resources Ltd.**	
	(Toronto)	2,945,334
22	**Canada Packers Ltd.** (Toronto)	2,943,099
23	**International Thomson Organisation Ltd.**	
	(Toronto)	2,867,566
24	**Total Petroleum** (North America) Ltd.	
	(Calgary)	2,854,265
25	**Hydro-Quebec** (Montreal)	2,809,000
26	**Steinberg Inc.** (Montreal)	2,806,409
27	**Nova Corp.** (Calgary)	2,669,551
28	**PetroCanada** (Calgary)	2,646,365
29	**Dominion Stores Ltd.**	
	(Toronto)	2,594,337
30	**T. Eaton Co.** (Toronto)	2,500,000
31	**Chrysler Canada Ltd.**	
	(Windsor)	2,480,600
32	**Inco Ltd.** (Toronto)	2,261,222
33	**Air Canada** (Montreal)	2,258,231
34	**Moore Corp.** (Toronto)	2,252,997
35	**Dome Petroleum Ltd.**	
	(Calgary)	2,238,800
36	**MacMillan Bloedel Ltd.**	
	(Vancouver)	2,209,670
37	**Stelco Inc.** (Toronto)	2,173,775
38	**Genstar Ltd.** (Vancouver)	2,145,922
39	**Seagram Co.** (Montreal)	2,127,279
40	**Saskatchewan Wheat Pool**	
	(Regina)	1,941,433
41	**Oshawa Group Ltd.** (Toronto)	1,896,569
42	**IBM Canada Ltd.** (Toronto)	1,845,000
43	**Alberta & Southern Gas Co.**	
	(Calgary)	1,767,668
44	**Dofasco Inc.** (Hamilton)	1,767,509
45	**Domtar Inc.** (Montreal)	1,764,744
46	**Abitibi-Price Inc.** (Toronto)	1,763,385
47	**Canadian General Electric Co.**	
	(Toronto)	1,700,102
48	**Crown Investments Corp. of**	
	Saskatchewan (Regina)	1,676,414
49	**F.W. Woolworth Co.** (Toronto)	1,675,984
50	**BP Canada Inc.** (Toronto)	1,593,986

WORKFORCE GROWTH ASTOUNDING IN ONE DECADE

The Canadian workforce grew by an astonishing 40 per cent to more than 12 million people during the years 1971-1981 according to Statistics Canada.

LONGER LIFESPAN

The average lifespan for women in North America has increased by a year to 75 years, according to a 1983 group mortality table prepared for insurance company actuaries. According to the 1983 table, the average lifespan for men is 69 years.

VEUVE CLICQUOT AWARD FOR THE CANADIAN BUSINESSWOMAN OF THE YEAR

House of Veuve Clicquot-Ponsardin and Schenley Canada

The award was initiated in France in 1974 and is now presented annually in several countries. 1982 was the first year the award was presented in Canada.

Madame Clicquot, widowed in 1805 at 28, defied convention and overcame almost impossible odds when she took over her late husband's champagne business and built it into an innovative and successful company.

The winner must possess four qualities as demonstrated by Madam Clicquot herself: an enterprising spirit, acceptance of responsibility, the ability to wield power and success in her field.

The winner is flown to France and inducted into Le Cercle des Amis de la Veuve in a ceremony in Reims. A vine stock is named in her honour and she receives a silver reproduction of the tastevin used by Madame Clicquot as well as a case of vintage La Grande Dame. Each year thereafter, the winner receives a bottle of Veuve Clicquot champagne on her birthday.

1982 **Wendy B. McDonald**, president, B.C. Bearing Engineers Ltd. MacDonald managed her husband's two-man machine shop when he was overseas during the Second World War. When he died a few years later, she decided to keep the company alive herself.

Under her direction it has grown to 30 branches in western Canada and five in the U.S. and has sales of more than $35-million a year.

She is a trustee of the B.C. Hall of Fame, a director of the Vancouver Economic Advisory Council and a director of the Vancouver Whitecaps.

Now 60, she is a mother of 10 (five adopted) and a grandmother of 20. She believes "you have to want to work hard. No matter what advantages you start with, if you can't deliver they won't matter."

BIGGEST CANADIAN BUSINESS GIFT — WHAT A PRIZE

The Hudson's Bay Company is Canada's oldest business enterprise.

The "Governor and Company of Adventurers trading into Hudson's Bay," otherwise known as the Hudson's Bay Company, received a charter from King Charles II of England on May 2, 1670. The chartering of commercial companies by the Crown had been a method of English trade and territorial expansion for a century. The East India Company was another such example of British commercial enterprise of the period.

It is questionable whether the royal mind could have envisaged the magnitude of the grant he was bestowing. The charter gave the company rights to "sole trade and commerce" of an area which would comprise 38.7 per cent of present-day Canada. It included, in terms of current geography, the provinces of Ontario and Quebec north of the Laurentian watershed and west of the Labrador boundary, all of Manitoba, most of Saskatchewan, the southern half of Alberta and a large part of the Northwest Territories — in all, 1,468,000 square miles.

The 13 courtiers and merchants who were the principal investors in the company could not, in their most vivid imaginings, have conceived of the wilderness, the winters, the wildlife, the peoples, or the future of the vast land that had been put under their control. They were excited by the prospect of profit from the "colonies" and were interested in settlement only to the extent that it was necessary to remove the goods they required. In a little more than a decade, the company had built five forts (four on James Bay and one on the west shore of Hudson Bay) at mouths of rivers that were easily travelled by the Indians on whom the Company depended to trap furs.

The Company was not unchallenged. The French tried determinedly to drive them from the North until 1713, and later there were attacks from fur-trading rivals. The Company managed to pay dividends until 1690. Through the next 27 years it paid none, but its shareholders hung in and were later rewarded for their steadfastness.

As the fur trade became established in the coastal areas, local animals became scarce. Company employees were sent out to explore and penetrate the continent in search of fresh sources of supply.

After the union with the North West Company, a rival fur-trading company, in 1821, the empire which the company ruled included all of modern Canada except the Great Lakes basin and the Atlantic provinces.

By the 1800s the pressure to settle the West was growing. Canada was laying claim to the territories that had been under the Company's rule. Throughout the century the company gradually surrendered its holdings. The principal feature of the surrender agreement worked out in 1868 was that the country under control of the Company would revert to the Crown and then be transferred to Canada, for which Canada would compensate the Company 300,000 pounds and one-twentieth part of the land in any township settled within the fertile belt (bounded on the south by the U.S. border, the west by the Rockies, the north by the North Saskatchewan River, the east by Lake Winnipeg, Lake of the Woods and the waters connecting them).

The final transfer of lands from the Company was completed in 1925.

SIR GEORGE SIMPSON — "THE LITTLE EMPEROR"

George Simpson was the governor-in-chief of the Hudson's Bay Company from 1825 until his death in 1860. Known as the "Little Emperor," he ruled over all the Company territory with an "iron will and a bland manner." Completely devoted to the Company, he worked energetically and tirelessly for its profit. He brought order to the Company's affairs, made a series of inspection trips throughout the entire domain, encouraged exploration, developed trade on the West Coast and managed the fur trade with the sense of a conservation-minded farmer: resting areas that were in danger of being over-trapped, for example. During his tenure the Red River Settlement developed into a colony (the first of any consequence in western Canada), Fort Victoria was built and a crown colony was established on Vancouver Island. Simpson was knighted by Queen Victoria in 1841. He died at the age of 73, just a few days after entertaining the Prince of Wales (Edward VII) at his summer home.

JUNIOR ACHIEVEMENT COMPANY OF THE YEAR

Junior Achievement of Canada

Junior Achievement is an international, nonprofit organization dedicated to teaching young people about business.

More than 7,000 teenagers in 67 Canadian centres are actively involved in JA's "learn-by-doing" program.

1982 **Richco Company**, Richmond, B.C.; president, Johnson Cheng (age 17). Formed in October 1981 under the guidance of a CP Air advisor team, the 20 students organized their company and capitalized it by selling 144 $1 shares. They decided to manufacture and sell ceramic tile clocks.

The company reached the break-even point by mid-December and was dissolved in April 1982. It returned a profit of $6.90 on a $1 investment to its shareholders.

The judges commended Richco for the selection of product, the efficiency of production and sales, for detailed minutes and the presentation of the company annual report as well as the active participation of personnel.

NATIONAL JA AWARD FOR BEST ANNUAL REPORT

Junior Achievement of Canada

Selected from among 400 JA companies operating in Canada in 1982.

1982 **MASH**, Halifax, N.S.; president, Scott Lewin (age 18). The judges were impressed with the MASH (Maritime Apple Serviette Holder) annual report because it was clear and concise with a well-written president's report. The judges approved the use of a covering letter to shareholders which included an analysis chart, and stated that the cost of the report was appropriate to the company's profitability.

The company manufactured a wood apple-shaped serviette holder and at liquidation returned the shareholders' investment and a 25 per cent dividend.

SALES SKYROCKET

The Canadian Real Estate Association reported in March 1983 that sales of

homes through multiple listing services were way up from a year earlier. March sales were 32 per cent higher than March sales in 1982.

Sales in Vancouver and Kamloops more than doubled and sales in Victoria were up 75 per cent over the corresponding period a year earlier. Sales in Calgary dropped, but they were higher in Edmonton. Sault Ste. Marie sales declined, but
Toronto sales were up by more than 50 per cent. Substantial increases were also reported in Montreal and Quebec City and throughout the Atlantic region.

INSURANCE BENEFITS

In 1915, Geoffrey Carson took out two insurance policies with riders covering the hazards of war. The policies named William Cole, Carson's cousin, as beneficiary.

Carson died in 1918, as a result of mustard gas poisoning from the First World War.

In 1980, Cole's daughter, Bea Hunter, found one of the old policies in her mother's personal effects. She took the policy to Prudential's Edmonton office where the company's unclaimed equities division uncovered the second policy. Together, they were worth a face value of $1,180 plus more than $12,000 accumulated interest.

The 65-year-old Prudential Insurance Company of America policy paid $13,300 to pensioner William Cole, now 92, of Edmonton. Cole, who depended on his Canada Pension Plan for living expenses, avoided the next cold winter in Edmonton by taking a trip to Phoenix, Arizona.

GOVERNOR-GENERAL'S MEDAL AND CICA AWARDS

Canadian Institute of Chartered Accountants

Awarded to graduating Chartered Accountants who received the highest marks in the Uniform Final Examinations.

GOVERNOR-GENERAL'S MEDAL
Edmond Gunn Prize of the CICA

1983 $500 Jennifer Dettiol, Clarkson Gordon, Vancouver, B.C.

CICA SILVER MEDAL
Founders' Prize

1983 $300 Cindy Jean Serkes, Clarkson Gordon, Winnipeg, Man.

CICA BRONZE
Founders' Prize

1983 $200 Eric Brassard, Malette, Benoit, Boulanger, Roundeau & Associés, Québec

---

FIRST VENTURE CAPITALISTS IN CANADIAN ENTERPRISE

Bristol, England, shipowners, notably John Jay and Thomas Croft, were funding expeditions in search of a new world even before Columbus embarked upon his famous voyage.

They provided the capital for Cabot's 1497 expedition. Later John Jay and The Company of Adventurers into the New Found Land sent expeditions from 1501 until 1505.

HIGHEST STANDING IN FINANCE ANNUAL STUDENT AWARD

Financial Executives Institute of Canada

A medal is awarded to students in Canadian universities who have achieved the highest average standing in the finance course, bachelor level, of the

BUSINESS HALL OF FAME INDUCTEES

Timothy Eaton

Sam Steinberg

Robert Scrivener

Izaak Walton Killam

Leon J. Koerner

T. A. St-Germain

graduating year of business administration.

1982 Gold Medal Winner in Finance
Susan Boyce, U. of Alberta, who achieved a perfect mark in 39 out of 40 courses.

Silver Medalists
Stefano Caraghan, McGill U.
Frederic Fairon, l'Ecole des Hautes Etudes Commerciales
Eric Fortier, Concordia
Nicole Giroux, U. du Quebec à Montreal
Mayna P. Anam, U. of Toronto
Lorraine McIntosh, York U.
Steven R. Hawkins, McMaster U.
Karen Maureen Lee, U. of Calgary
Jill Allison, Simon Fraser U.
Scott Brunsdon, U. of British Columbia
Cheri Wilson, B.C. Institute of Technology

LARGEST PARTY

Dofasco Inc., of Hamilton, Ont. is Canada's largest steel company and is one of the largest nonunion companies in North America. Each year the company holds a Christmas party that is the largest in the Commonwealth.

There were 38,000 guests at the 1981 yule bash and all the children attending received gifts. About 14,000 presents were handed out to youngsters under 17 years of age and 120 tons of canned goods were distributed. The party was held in a rented warehouse larger than two football fields.

The first such event was held in 1937 when the company employed fewer than 300 workers. No alcohol is served at the shindig, because the party is mainly for children.

GOLD MEDAL OF THE INSTITUTE

Institute of Canadian Bankers

The awards are offered to employees of Canadian Chartered Banks who have completed university-level courses offered by the institute.

1982 GOLD MEDAL (for receiving 10 honours credits in 10 courses)
Stephen Cozier, Toronto, Ont.
Gordon Paterson, Toronto, Ont.

SILVER MEDAL (for receiving 8 or 9 honours credits in 10 courses)
Paul Brownell, Ottawa, Ont.
James E. Campbell, Toronto, Ont.
Richard E. Chadwick, Vancouver, B.C.
Christine Laycock, Toronto, Ont.
Stephen J. White, Toronto, Ont.
Diane Wright, Toronto, Ont.

PILING UP PROFITS

The Government-owned Bank of Canada was the most profitable business in the nation in 1982. It showed a profit of $1.87-billion, up 1.3 per cent from a year earlier. The profit, paid to the receiver-general, helped to reduce the government's huge deficit.

Much of the Bank's profit accrued from interest it received from the reserves it holds for private sector banks. The reserves were $6.43-billion at the end of 1982, and because few of the large banks are expected to collapse, the profits amount to an effective tax on the industry.

HONORARY FELLOWS

Institute of Canadian Bankers

Honorary fellowships are bestowed on leading Canadian bankers, senior government officials, businessmen, and educators to mark their unique role in the economy and society.

1983 **W. Earle McLaughlin**, former chairman of the Board, Royal Bank of Canada, in recognition of his dedication to the banking industry during a career of 44 years and for his achievements in Canadian society. During his years as chief spokesman of the Royal Bank, he became known as a leading corporate commentator upon Canada's economic situation and economic policies.

Allen Thomas Lambert, former chairman of the Toronto Dominion Bank. Under Lambert's direction the Toronto-Dominion Centre was built, the first major step in the rejuvenation of Toronto's downtown business district. He also played a significant role in the development of the bank's unique collections of contemporary Canadian art and Eskimo sculpture. He was a member of a group that was instrumental in the founding of York University and he was chairman both of the Advisory Group on Executive Compensation in the Public Service and the Royal Commission on Financial Management and Accountability in the Government of Canada.

DEALERS DELIGHTED

Bond dealers had a super year in 1982. These securities recorded their best gain in more than a quarter century and had a total return of almost 50 per cent. It was the largest rise of any investment in the country, according to a Toronto-based investment house, McLeod Young Weir, Ltd.

However, the investment house cautions, "History continues to tell us bonds are only a good investment in one year out of about five ... and then should not be held for more than one year if capital gain is the important criterion."

EARLY EXCHANGE

Trading in the first Canadian stock exchange began at Quebec City in 1708.

HISTORIC LAST TRADE

One hundred shares of B.C. Resources Investment Corporation were traded at $3.50 a share, at 4 p.m., on May 6, 1983. It was the final trade at the Bay Street home of the Toronto Stock Exchange.

The exchange, one of the world's busiest, has new quarters, complete with high-tech electronics.

The Bay Street building, constructed in 1937 at a cost of $750,000, is noted as a fine example of art deco and for the interior murals painted by Charles Comfort.

At the close of trade, the traders toasted the exchange with champagne, sang Auld Lang Syne and threw reams of papers into the air.

SOME CANADIANS NAMED AS FELLOWS OF THE INSTITUTE OF CANADIAN BANKERS

1969 **Louis Rasminsky**, Past Governor of the Bank of Canada

1970 **R.B. Bryce**, Past Deputy Minister, Department of Finance, Government of Canada

C.F. Elderkin, Past Inspector General of Banks

R.M. MacIntosh, Past Chairman, Board of Governors, Institute of Canadian Bankers Past Executive Vice-President, The Bank of Nova Scotia President, The Canadian Bankers' Association

1973 **J.J. Wettlaufer**, Past member of the Board of Governors, Institute of Canadian Bankers Past Dean, The School of Business Administration, The University of Western Ontario

1976 **Gerald K. Bouey**, Governor, Bank of Canada

1981 **Roger Larose** O.C. Ancien vice-recteur à l'administration, Université de Montréal Past member of the Board of Governors, Institute of Canadian Bankers

SUPER SALARIES

A salary survey filed with the U.S. Securities and Exchange Commission revealed in June 1982 that the incomes of most of Canada's top executives continued to climb in 1981.

Twenty-five companies were surveyed. In 17 companies compensation for senior officers rose, while it dropped in four. The remaining four companies did not reveal figures.

Edgar Bronfman of Seagram's made $1,066,025 in 1981, tops in Canada. Philip Beekman and Harold Fieldsteel, also of Seagram's, earned more than $700-thousand each. CP's Ian Sinclair, A. Jean de Grandpre and W.F. Light of Bell Canada and G.R. Albino of Rio Algom all earned more than $500-thousand.

Canada's securities laws do not require companies to file personal salary information, so compensation data on officers of companies that trade publicly in Canada is not available.

H.L. GASSARD MEMORIAL AWARD

Canadian Securities Institute

A cash prize of $1,000 is presented to the Canadian Securities Course student with the highest final mark.

1982   Sandra G. Benton, Wood Gundy Ltd., Toronto, Ont.

JOHN R. KIMBER MEMORIAL AWARD

Canadian Securities Institute

A cash prize of $1,000 is presented to the Canadian Investment Finance Course Part II candidate employed by a member firm of an institute sponsor who attains the highest standing overall in the final exams.

1982   Michael G. Horrocks, Wood Gundy Ltd., Toronto, Ont.

FLYING HIGH

Claude Taylor, president and chief executive officer of Air Canada, was honoured in the spring of 1983 when he became the first Canadian to receive the Excellence in Communications Leadership Award from the International Association of Business Communicators.

INSURANCE INSTITUTE OF QUEBEC

The Institute is a regional educational body for the general insurance industry in Quebec. It has 3,200 members and awards prizes for academic achievement.

1982   Philippe Duclos
        Andrée Chagnon
        Yves Desforges
        John R. Emory
        Richard St. Louis
        Louis Tessier
        Vincent Frechette

CANADIAN DEVELOPMENT FIRM WINS BIG IN U.S.

Bramalea Ltd. of Toronto is a main partner in a $1-billion commercial development in Dallas, Tex. Construction of the $300-million-plus first phase was begun in mid-December 1982. The completed project will comprise two 70-storey office towers, a hotel and retail space on four city blocks in downtown Dallas. Bramalea also has development projects underway in eastern Canada and in California.

JOHN A. TORY MEDAL

Institute of Chartered Life Underwriters of Canada

The institute was formed in 1906 to unify the thousands of part-time life insurance agents who operate throughout the country. The institute provides programs and training courses which emphasize ethics and professional conduct. The gold medal is awarded to the graduate who has achieved the most outstanding success in writing the examinations leading to the title Chartered Life Underwriter.

1982 **Barbara Lesli Wright**, Kingston, Ont.

LESLIE W. DUNSTALL MEMORIAL MEDALS

Institute of Chartered Life Underwriters of Canada

Silver medals awarded to candidates who have achieved the highest degree in writing CLU examinations in their respective provinces.

1982 **Robert L. Robinet**, Stratford, Ont.
Marc E. Decary, Laval, Que.
Henry M. Reiner, Edmonton, Alta.

SIR WILLIAM FORD COAKER, A UNIFYING FORCE

The first union of fishermen in the Atlantic region was formed at Herring Neck, Notre Dame Bay, Newfoundland, in 1908. The Fishermen's Protective Union (FPU) was developed to counteract the powerful merchant system which had, at the time, great influence on the lives of fishermen. Led by William Coaker, the FPU formed its own company, the Union Trading Company, to provide supplies for fishermen and to market their catch. The company, of which the fishermen were shareholders, provided cash income for the men from the earned profits.

Coaker was a man of accomplishment and wide interest. Concerned with the human condition, he sought to improve the lives of fishermen. He was interested in improving education and work-ing conditions. He had an electricity plant built at Port Union. He invented the first device to artificially dry fish, and he tried to help sealers and loggers as well. He formed the Union Party, which played a critical role in Newfoundland politics for a number of years.

The first fishermen's union, the FPU was all but a memory at the time of Confederation with Canada in 1949. The Newfoundland Fishermen, Food and Allied Workers Union (NFFAWU), formed under the guidance of Father Desmond McGrath, is the voice of Newfoundland fishermen today.

DISTINGUISHED SERVICE TO HUMANITY AWARDS

Canadian Labour Congress

"What we desire for ourselves we wish for all. To this end may we take our share of the world's work and the world's great struggles" — J.S. Woodsworth. The Canadian Labour Congress presents a small sculpture to the Canadian who best captures the spirit of the above sentiment, expressed by a founder of the CCF and former leader of the Canadian labour movement.

1982 **Grace MacInnis.** The former NDP Member of the House of Commons was known as an advocate of social reform. First elected to the House in 1965, she championed consumer affairs and women's rights. She was named one of the 15 most important women in the world by the French magazine *Marie-Claire*. She was the only Canadian on the list.
Stanley Knowles. The NDP member has long been respected as "the conscience of the House." A master of parliamentary rules and procedures, he steered the house through seeming impasses on a number of occasions, acting as intermediary between the main parties and finding parliamentary

procedures which would allow a party to escape gracefully from a difficult situation. A strong spokesman for the CCF and the NDP, he was first elected to the House in 1942 and held his seat in all but one election since.

CLASSIC BEARS FOR BUSINESS

Peter Nygard, the 40-year-old, Finnish-born owner of Tan Jay International Ltd., of Winnipeg, is now the biggest manufacturer of women's clothing in Canada. He took over an $800,000-a-year business in 1968 and transformed it into an international operation which grossed around $70-million in 1982.

His approach was to avoid fashion trends and to supply conservative classic styles for women in the over-25 market. He expects his company's market share to continue to grow as the general population ages.

The world's busiest shoemaker is Tom Bata of Bata Shoes. With a head office in Toronto, his 100 companies operate more than 100 shoe factories, manage 5,000 retail outlets and sell 240 million pairs of shoes each year. Annual sales generated by the Bata organization were about $2-billion in 1981.

Philip Kives, the son of Turkish Jews who emigrated to Hoffer, Sask., began his ascendancy in the business world when he sold food slicers and dicers in the 1950s.

The founder and president of K-Tel International now directs, with two brothers and a cousin, an operation which by 1982 was grossing more than $150-million a year with franchises in 34 countries.

K-Tel used hard-sell television ads to promote its products. Using the telephone and charge cards, people bought such products as greatest-hit records and the Miracle lint brush by the millions. The Winnipeg-based company now has interests in the entertainment business, oil and gas, as well as commercial real estate.

Dylex Ltd.'s name is an acronym devised by Winnipeg businessman James Kay. His company is now the largest specialty retailer in the nation.

The company owns or has interest in a number of chain retail outlets. It went into shopping centres in 1967. Since 1976 sales have soared 123 per cent to $549.13-million at the end of the 1982 fiscal year.

The year was 1884. George Weston, an 18-year-old apprentice baker, bought a bread delivery route in Toronto.

Forty years later, his son Garfield inherited a chain of Ontario-based bakeries and biscuit factories, as well as his father's savvy. By the mid-1960s, Weston had assembled 225 companies and subsidiaries in North America and built a British-based organization that was nearly as big.

Today the conglomerate of companies reaches into four continents, and owns thousands of shops and supermarkets, and hundreds of bakeries and manufacturing plants, as well as mills and warehouses. Weston companies include Loblaws, the Eddy Paper Co., Donlands Dairy, B.C. Packers, Kelly, Douglas & Co., and the National Tea Co. in the U.S.

Canadian businessman George Sinclair Hanson of Toronto, president of the New Zealand Lamb Co., was named a Member of the Order of the British Empire in 1982. His name appeared on the Queen's Birthday Honours List published in New Zealand. The honour was in recognition of Hanson's work for New Zealand exports and for promoting New Zealand's interests in Canada.

Murray Koffler, founder and chairman of Shoppers Drug Mart, held a giant party in March 1983 for owners, executives, pharmacists and suppliers of the 439-store chain. The party celebrated the more than $1-billion a year in retail sales reached for the first time in 1982.

MONTGOMERY MEMORIAL MEDAL

Canadian Construction Association

A gold medal is given for innovation in construction. Innovations may be in general or trade contracting, specialist work, or in the provision and erection of materials and equipment. The award honours Hugh R. Montgomery, who contributed to developments that would increase the speed and quality of construction practice.

1981 **Blenkhorn and Sawle Ltd.**, for its innovative construction of a stainless-steel, air-supported roof at Dalhousie University.
Les Enterprises Kiewit Sons, Ltd., for an original and economical solution for Hydraulic Sluicing of Overburden at LG-4 Main Dam at James Bay.
1982 **Brittain Steel Ltd.**, for its construction of a steel bridge onshore and then launching the bridge into its final position using innovative rocker girder guides.

ATTENDANCE UP, COSTS DOWN

Kellogg, Imperial Oil Ltd. and the Northern Alberta Building Trades Council began a productivity enhancement program in October 1982 and it's working.

The program, the first of its kind in Canada, is called Productivity Results in Individuals' Desire for Efficiency, or PRIDE. It attempts to motivate workers by improving the environment, promoting teamwork and rewarding achievement.

Absenteeism at Project Alpha, the upgrading of Imperial's Strathcona Refinery, was reported to have dropped from 17 to 5 per cent in the first six months of the program and Kellogg's cost factor (a ratio of actual costs to budget costs) had dropped 50 per cent.

MacMILLAN BLOEDEL WINS FIRST FROM JAPAN

Canada's MacMillan Bloedel Ltd. became the first foreign company to win a paper order for telephone directories from the Nippon Telegraph and Telephone Public Corp. The order, announced in January 1983, is for 5,000 tonnes of special directory paper and is worth about $4-million.

THE TOP 10 LIFE INSURERS

Virtually all of the companies listed below have extensive operations outside Canada. Prudential Insurance is North America's largest life insurer, with net worldwide premium income in 1982 of $11,964,223,000 — more than $5,378,000,000 ahead of the second largest company, Metropolitan Life Insurance Co. The top Canadian life insurer, on the basis of worldwide premium income, is Great-West Life Assurance with $1,765,508,000 in 1982.

The figures on the right represent net Canadian premium income, in thousands.

1	**Sun Life Assurance Co. of Canada** (Toronto)	1,024,436
2	**Great-West Life Assurance Co.** (Winnipeg)	877,124
3	**Mutual Life Assurance Co. of Canada** (Waterloo, Ont.)	754,773
4	**London Life Insurance Co.** (London, Ont.)	697,713
5	**Confederation Life Insurance Co.** (Toronto)	643,764

6 Canada Life Assurance Co.
   (Toronto)   643,728
7 Manufacturers Life Insurance Co.
   (Toronto)   485,544
8 Prudential Insurance Co. of America
   (Toronto)   370,985
9 Metropolitan Life Insurance Co.
   (Ottawa)   367,207
10 Standard Life Assurance Co.
   (Montreal)   342,416

FATHERS OF THE B.C. SALMON-CANNING INDUSTRY

Alexander Loggie, James Wise, David S. Hennessy and Alexander Ewen entered into partnership in June 1870, opening a fish plant at Annieville, down the Fraser from New Westminster in what is now Surrey Municipality.

Ewen had come from Scotland in 1864 in response to a newspaper ad for a fisheries superintendent. Possibly the only man not attracted to the region by the lure of gold, he brought practical fishing experience. He worked for a former Cariboo gold miner before entering the partnership.

The other partners were also practical fishermen, without knowledge of canning. They turned to James Knowles, master canmaker, who fitted the cans for the processed fish. Canning was then a laborious hand process. Each body was measured separately on a sheet of tin plate. The tin was hand cut with shears, turned and soldered. The tops and bottoms were measured by compass before they were cut and soldered to the cans.

Fish that were not suitable for canning went into the saltery where barrels were waiting for them.

For five years before his death in 1907 Ewen was president of the British Columbia Packers' Association. Much of the early progress of the industry and its establishment in world markets has been attributed to his efforts.

RESISTING RECESSION

Consumers Distribution Co. Ltd., a Canadian catalogue retail company, had a profit for 1982 that was at least 2.4 times larger than in 1981, despite what its chairman, Jack Tupp, called "an abysmal retailing climate." He credited improved catalogues with wider distribution, upgraded merchandise, aggressive marketing and a successful Christmas season for the good year. The company, which has about 200 showrooms in Canada as well as 110 outlets in the U.S., projected a profit of about $10.9 million or about $1.90 to $2 a share, the second-highest in the company's history behind $12.34-million made in 1978.

SOME WINNERS IN THE CANADIAN LABOUR MOVEMENT

Dennis McDermott, president of the Canadian Labour Congress, is head of the 2-million central labour body. His union life began in 1948 when he started work as an assembler and welder at Massey-Ferguson.

Grace Hartman, national president of the Canadian Union of Public Employees, was the first Canadian woman to be elected as a top union leader, and she is the Canadian member on the executive board of the Public Services International, the first woman to be on the board in the organization's 75-year history.

Robert White is Canadian director and international vice-president of the UAW. He gained national attention in 1983 when he negotiated a Chrysler contract following a strike at Chrysler Canada.

Allen T. Lambert (left), W. Earle McLaughlin at banking awards

Johnson Cheng, 17, Junior achiever of 1982

Canadarm overlooking an upside down world. Photo courtesy NASA

Quirks and Quarks winners: Producer Anita Gordon, host Jay Ingram and associate producer Penny Park

Film-making winners: Seated Michael Bennett, l to r James Murray, Richard Longley, and Allan Bailey

Communications & Transportation

COMMUNICATIONS & TRANSPORTATION

WILLIAM MAXWELL AITKEN, LORD BEAVERBROOK

A Canadian who controlled one of the greatest newspaper empires in the English-speaking world, Lord Beaverbrook also helped Britain survive its darkest hours during the Second World War.

Max Aitken, a clergyman's son, was born in Maple, Ont., in 1879. He studied law at the University of New Brunswick before entering the business world in Montreal. Scrupulous in his financial dealings, he had an eye for buying good companies and then selling them for a profit. He wrote of one deal, "I simply found a situation in existence and pointed out to others the logical development which should flow from it. I did not make situations; I turned them to account."

By 1907 Aitken was a millionaire. He brought about mergers which created the Canada Cement Company and another merger which developed into the Steel Company of Canada. Then, in 1910, he moved to England and entered British politics.

During the First World War he was appointed "Eye-Witness" to the Canadian Expeditionary Force, Canadian Government Representative at the Front and Officer in Charge of Records, responsible for organization and distribution of war films for the British War Office. During the same period, he bought a controlling interest in the London *Daily Express* and built its circulation to more than four million daily. He later founded the *Sunday Express* and purchased the London *Evening Standard*.

During the Second World War he served as Minister of Aircraft Production, Minister of State, Minister of Supply and Lord Privy Seal for Churchill's government. Soon after Churchill became Prime Minister, the Luftwaffe began systematic daily bombing of the British Isles. Initial attacks were made by about 100 bombers but soon the Luftwaffe was putting up nearly 1,000 planes each day with London as the main target.

As Minister of Aircraft Production, Beaverbrook wheedled, cajoled, bullied, wheeled and dealed to make survival possible. Air Chief Marshal Dowding, head of fighter command throughout the Battle of Britain, wrote in *The Times* in 1945: "We had the organization, we had the men, and we had the spirit which could bring us victory in the air, but we had not the supply of machines necessary to withstand the drain of continuous battle. Lord Beaverbrook gave us those machines, and I do not believe that I exaggerate when I say that no other man in England could have done so."

After the war Beaverbrook left active political life and became an "apprentice of Fleet Street." Later he said, "I took more pride in my experience as a journalist than in any other experience I have had in my long and varied life."

When he was created a peer, he chose the title Beaverbrook after a small stream near his childhood home in New Brunswick.

He was Chancellor of the University of New Brunswick from 1947 until 1953 and founded the Beaverbrook Gallery of Art at Fredericton and the Canadian Beaverbrook Foundation before his death in 1964.

NATIONAL AWARDS

Canadian Science Writers' Association

Awards are given annually for the best print science journalism in Canada. Winners receive $1,000.

1983 Science and Technology
Newspapers: **Val Sears**, *Toronto Star*
Magazines: **Claude de Launiere**, *Quebec Science*
Science and Health
Newspapers: **Marilyn Dunlop**, *Toronto Star*
Magazines: **Paul Tisdall**, *Equinox*
Science and Natural Resources
Newspapers: **Gilles Provost**, *Le Devoir*
Magazines: **Adrian Forsyth**, *Equinox*
Science and Society
Print Media: **Lesley Krueger** *Maclean's*
$500 Junior Award (presented to a science journalist with less than two years experience)
Laura Robin, *Ottawa Citizen*

MEXICO BUREAU BEST

The *Globe and Mail*, published in Toronto, won one of the Inter-American Press Association's top awards in 1982.

The IAPA, which represents newspapers in the Western Hemisphere, awarded the Tom Wallace bronze plaque to the *Globe's* Mexico City bureau for bringing readers in Canada new insights into Latin America and the Caribbean. Oakland Ross, a former assistant editor at the *Globe*, is the paper's correspondent in Mexico City. A seasoned reporter, he has reported on the Falkland Islands conflict, covered civil wars in El Salvador and Guatemala as well as reconstruction in Nicaragua, and political upheavals in the Caribbean islands.

ANNUAL OUTDOOR WRITING AWARDS

Canadian National Sportsmen's Show and the Outdoor Writers of Canada

The awards commemorate conservationist Francis H. Kortright and encourage excellence in outdoor writing. Each winner receives a $1,000 prize and an engraved plaque.

1983 Book Division
Robert Scammell, Alberta, for his book *The Outside Story*, a collection of columns he wrote for Alberta newspapers on fishing, hunting and conservation.
Magazine Division
Erich Hoyt, Montreal, Que., for his article "Orca The Killer Whale," which appeared in *Equinox*.
Newspaper Division
Tony Eberts, Aldergrove, B.C., for his story on the Fraser River, "A Giant in Need of Protection," which appeared in the Vancouver *Province*.

FREE PRESS IS HARD WON

A plaque commemorating Francis Collins, parliamentary reporter and publisher of the *Canadian Freeman*, was unveiled in Toronto in 1982.

Freeman was Canada's first professional parliamentary debates reporter. An advocate of a free press, he was jailed in 1828 for his printed attacks on the Family Compact (Upper Canada's Establishment) but was pardoned after a debate in the House of Assembly.

NATIONAL BUSINESS WRITING AWARDS

Royal Bank of Canada and the Toronto Press Club

The awards are presented for outstanding achievement in business journalism. The winners receive a cheque for $1,000.

1983 Distinguished Service Award
Alexander Ross, Toronto, Ont. Sandy Ross is part owner of *Canadian Business* magazine, business columnist for *Toronto Life* magazine and has written three books.
Business News Award
Hyman Solomon, *The Financial Post*, for a series on Canada-U.S. relations.
Investigative Reporting Award
Bill Schiller, *The Windsor Star*, for a story, "Amway's Alleged Plan to Defraud Canada of Millions."
Feature Writing Award
Diane Francis, *The Toronto Star*, for a story on the federal deficit.
Regular Column Award
Andrew Allentuck, Winnipeg, Man., for columns in the *Financial Post Magazine*.

Award for Non-Journalist
Richard Lipsey and **Douglas Purvis**, Queen's University, for columns in the *Financial Post*.
Smaller Publications Category
Gerry Warner, *Kamloops News*, for a series on tenants in Kamloops apartment buildings.
Feature Writing in Smaller Publications Award
Ron Graham, Saskatchewan, for a story on the shutdown by Eldorado Nuclear Ltd. at Uranium City, in *Saturday Night*.

AND A HELLOFA SOFTBALL PITCHER

Martin Wise Goodman started as a reporter for the Toronto Star in 1960, ran two major bureaus (Washington, Ottawa), travelled the world, won a prestigous Nieman Fellowship at Harvard, rose swiftly up the ranks to become president, at the age of 43, of Toronto Star Newspapers Limited, Canada's largest newspaper. At 46, he was struck down by inoperable cancer. He continued working 14-hour days until close to the end. After he died, a fellowship was established for a Canadian journalist at the Nieman Foundation for Journalism at Harvard. In addition, a $380,000 five-mile jogging and cycling trail on Toronto's waterfront was named after him, to salute Goodman's love for athletics and fitness.

KENNETH R. WILSON MEMORIAL AWARDS

Canadian Business Press

The awards are given for editorial and graphic excellence in business and agricultural publications.

1982 Best Editorial
Robert Catherwood, *The Financial Post*
Colin Munsie, *Marketing Magazine*
Best Merchandising Article
Ylvan Buuren, *Canadian Footwear Journal*
Best Industrial Article
George A. Peer, *Heavy Construction News*
Best Industrial Report
Steve F. Gahbauer, James Barnes, *Modern Power & Engineering*
Best Short Article
Ilvan Buuren, *Canadian Footwear Journal*
Best Professional Development Article
Mary Jo Cartwright, *Engineering & Contract Record*
Best General Article
Robert L. Parry, *The Financial Post*
Best Selected, Contributed, Edited or Cooperative Effort
Olev Edur, William Roebuck, *Plant Management & Engineering*
Best Cover
Terry Shoffner, *Metropolitan Toronto Business Journal*
Best Single Article
Faye Bourgeois, Ernie Francis, *Modern Purchasing*
Best Complete Issue
Roy Wilson, *Metropolitan Toronto Business Journal*

CANADA'S OLDEST WEEKLY NEWSPAPER

R.D. Chatterton founded the *Cobourg Star* (Cobourg, Ont.) in 1831. Renamed the *Cobourg Sentinel-Star*, it is the country's oldest weekly.

WATKINS ON THE FRONT

Cathleen Blake Watkins of the *Toronto Mail* was the world's first fully accredited female war correspondent. She covered the Spanish-American War which ended in 1898.

SOUTHAM FELLOWSHIPS FOR JOURNALISTS

Southam Inc.

Awarded annually to encourage improvement in journalism by offering to qualified men and women an opportunity to broaden their knowledge by studying in a university setting for one year. The award underwrites all travel expenses, university fees and two-thirds of the recipient's regular annual salary.

1983 **Murray Campbell**, *The Globe and Mail*
Linda Hossie, *Vancouver Sun*
Wendy Koenig, *Edmonton Journal*
Bill Peterson, *Saskatoon Star Phoenix*
Joann Webb, freelance, formerly of *Harrowsmith* magazine

FIRST PHOTOGRAPH

The *Canadian Illustrated News* was the first periodical in the world to reproduce an actual photograph. In 1869, it contained a photo of Prince Arthur, Queen Victoria's third son.

NATIONAL MAGAZINE AWARDS

National Magazine Awards Foundation

The awards honour excellence in the magazine industry in Canada. Established by the universities of Western Ontario and Laval and by the Canadian Periodical Publishers' Association and Magazines Canada, the gold and silver awards are accompanied by $1,000 and $500 prizes.

1982 The University of Western Ontario President's Medal Awards for General Magazine Articles
Robert Fulford, "Doyle of the Globe," *Saturday Night*.
Gerald LeBlanc, "Les Conducteurs Quebecois: non-coupables," *L'Actualite*.
Toronto Dominion Bank Awards For Humour
Derek Maitland, "High Noons," *Quest*.
Claude Fortier, "Ma Fille Chez MacDonald," *Chatelaine*.
Mutual Life of Canada Awards For Business Writing
Michael Bliss, "The Unconventional Wisdom of John Kenneth Galbraith," *Saturday Night*.
Peter Foster, "The Power of Petrocan," *Saturday Night*.
RBW Awards for Science and Technology
Adrian Forsyth, "Flower Power Reconsidered."
Pierre Sormany, "Les 5 mythes du Cancer," *L'Actualite*.
Molson Awards For Canadian Sports Writing
David Macfarlane, "The Gardens" *Saturday Night*.
Daniel Perusse, "Villeneuve comme dans ... Jacques" *L'Actualite*.
Abitibi-Price Awards For Politics
Ann Charney, "The Radicals at Renee's Heel's," *Today*.
Ron Graham, "Jean Chretien and the Politics of Patriotism," *Saturday Night*.
Canada Packers Awards For Agriculture
Daniel Perusse, "Pour quelques arpents de vert," *L'Actualite*
Donald Cameron, "The Potato Prophet," *enRoute*
McClelland & Stewart Awards For Fiction

Gerald Lynch, "Rita Maguire's Vermilion Dress," *Waves*.
Audrey Thomas, "Real Mothers," *Chatelaine*.
du Maurier Awards For Poetry
Michael Ondaatje, "The Cinnamon Peeler in Brick," *Writing*.
Susan Musgrave, "Three Poems," *Writing*
Brascan Awards For Culture
Georges-Hebert Germain, "Race D'ecrivain," *L'Actualite*.
Harry Bruce, "The Most Important Realist Painter in The Western World," *Atlantic Insight*.
Norcen Awards For Comment
Jean Pare, "Le charme discret de la Bureaucratie," *L'Actualite*.
Rick Salutin, "The Culture Vulture," *This Magazine*.
Air Canada Awards For Travel
Christiane Berthiaume, "Arabie aux pieds d'argile," *L'Actualite*.
Peter Worthington, "A Natural Selection," *Toronto Life*.
A.C. Forrest Memorial Awards For Religious Journalism
Marci McDonald, "The Witness," *City Woman*.
Bharati Mukherjee, "An Invisible Woman," *Saturday Night*.
Consumers' Gas Awards For Food Writing
George Bain, "Salud y Pesetas," *Toronto Life*.
George Bain, "Time in a Bottle," *Toronto Life*.
Dominion Textile Awards For Fashion Features
Sybil Young (producer), **Tim Saunders** (photographer), **Ursula Kaiser** (art director), "Boxed and Beautiful," *Homemaker's*.
David Livingstone, "Iona, Queen of the Jungle," *Toronto Life Fashion*.
Seagrams Awards For Magazine Illustration
James Hill, "Take Me Back To My Backyard," *The Review*.
Hock Tiam Lee, "Who Killed Muriel Cliche?" *Reader's Digest*.
Kodak Canada Awards For Photography

Gillean Proctor, "Summer Takeoff," *City Woman.*
Bert Bell, "Angels," *Toronto Calendar.*
Allan R. Fleming/MacLaren Awards For Art Direction
Louis Fishauf, "Summer Takeoff," *City Woman.*
Jon Eby and Joanna Bain, "Angels," *Toronto Calendar.*
Bomac Batten Awards for Magazine Covers
Michel Pilon (photographer), Stephen Costello (art director), "Raging Berbick," *Quest.*
Ron Tanaka (photographer), Barbara Solowan and James Ireland (art directors), "The Kids Are Not Alright," *Toronto Life.*

Our Little Chamber Concerts, Janette T. Hospital, *Saturday Night.*
Magazines, Personality
Pratt & Pratt, Harry Thurston, *Equinox.*
Magazines, Humour
Bootless Cries, Marni Jackson, *Toronto Life.*
Cover Design, Paperbacks
The Northern Magus, Brant Cowie, Paperjacks, Ltd.
Cover Design, Magazines
Can Textbooks Survive the System?, Ken Rodmell, *Quill & Quire.*
Book of the Year
Kiss Mommy Goodbye, Joy Fielding, New American Library of Canada.
Author of the Year
Richard Gwyn, Paperjacks Ltd.

POPULAR PUBLICATION

Until its demise in 1976, the Eaton's catalogue was Canada's most widely read publication. At one point it ran to 16 million copies a year — enough to form a stack 1,500 miles high.

AUTHOR'S AWARDS

Periodical Distributors of Canada

A total of $5,700 is awarded in prizes to writers and graphic artists in the mass market periodical and paperback book industry.

1982   Paperback Fiction
Fat Woman, Leon Rooke, General Publishing Co. Ltd.
Paperback Non-Fiction
The Northern Magus, Richard Gwyn, Paperjacks Ltd.
Magazines, Public Affairs
Crisis in the Heartland, John Barber, *Financial Post Magazine.*
Magazines, Business/Finance
Quebec's New Revolutionaries, Ramsay Cook, *Saturday Night.*
Magazines, Science/Medicine
Cosmic Crucibles, Terence Dickinson, *Equinox.*
Magazines, Fiction

MARKETING MOXY

Larry Heisey is president of Harlequin Enterprises, the largest paperback publishing firm in the world. A fifth-generation Canadian, the former Proctor and Gamble executive used P & G marketing techniques to develop Harlequin into a company which in 1982 sold 215 million paperbacks in 12 languages in 90 countries.

Most of the books, sold in kiosks and newsstands, are written by women (with the exception of three men who write under feminine *noms de plume*). Heisey's favourites include New Brunswick writer Flora Kidd, who has written 40 novels for Harlequin.

ROY BRITNELL AWARD

Book Publishers' Professional Association

An annual award presented to the Canadian bookseller who has made an outstanding contribution to the business of bookselling and to the community served by that bookseller.

1982   **Charles Burchell,** The Book Room, Halifax, N.S.

THE AMERICAN DREAM

BULLETIN IS BEST

The University of Toronto *Bulletin* was named the best internal university periodical in North America by the Council for Advancement and Support of Education (C.A.S.E.) in 1983.

C.A.S.E. has 2,400 member institutions and 9,000 individual members in Canada and the U.S. It encompasses everyone working in higher education in all areas of institutional relations.

The Toronto paper beat out similar periodicals from the University of Michigan, the University of Southern California, the University of Miami, the University of Chicago and Princeton.

ANNUAL WRITERS' AWARDS

Writers Development Trust and the National Book Festival

1982 Fiona Mee Literary Journalism Award
A $1,000 prize is given on the basis of continued excellence in literary journalism. The award honours the late Fiona Mee, who was publisher of *Quill & Quire*.
Sandra Martin, *The Globe and Mail*, for her paperbacks column in the *Globe* and for her profile of Mordecai Richler which appeared in *Books in Canada*.
Books in Canada First Novel Award
Joy Kogawa, Toronto, for *Obasan* (Lester & Orpen Dennys).
Gerald Lampert Award for Best New Canadian Writer (shared prize)
Abraham Boyarsky, Montreal, for *Schrieber* (General Publishing).
Edna Alford, Livelong, Sask., for *A Sleep Full of Dreams* (Oolichan Books).
Pat Lowther Award, Best Book of Poetry by a Woman
Rona Murray, Victoria, B.C., for *Journey* (Sono Nis Press).

ACCLAIM FOR CARTOON

The *Toronto Sun's* irresistible cartoonist Andy Donato won international acclaim with a cartoon he drew in 1979, depicting the Ayatollah Khomeini receiving the butt end of America's scorn. The cartoon was chosen as the first prize winner of 1980/81 in the editorial category of the International Salon of Cartoons. The cartoon, chosen out of 779 entries, now hangs in the Salon's permanent collection at the Canadian Pavilion in Montreal's Man and His World. Donato received a $1,000 cash prize.

STRIP SUCCESSFUL

Lynn Johnston from Lynn Lake, Man., which she says "is 800 miles north of nowhere," has gained millions of loyal readers throughout North America with her comic strip *For Better of for Worse* since it made its debut in 1979. The strip now appears in more than 250 newspapers and its creator is the only woman cartoonist with a daily forum on family life.

The Superman comic strip was co-created by Torontonian Joe Shuster, (brother of Wayne and Shuster's Frank Shuster) who based his fictional newspaper, the *Daily Planet*, on his workplace, the *Toronto Star*.

NATIONAL NEWSPAPER AWARDS

Toronto Press Club

The annual awards are presented for excellence in Canadian journalism to men and women on the staffs of Canadian daily newspapers and press associations. The winners receive certificates and $1,000 cash prizes.

1983 Spot news reporting: **Christopher Young**, *Southam News*

Column writing: **John Slinger**, *Toronto Star*

Critical writing: **Peter Goddard**, *Toronto Star*

Spot news cartooning: **Blaine**, *Hamilton Spectator*

Feature writing: **Glen Allen**, *Montreal Gazette*

Editorial writing: **Joan Fraser**, *Montreal Gazette*

Enterprise reporting: **Vancouver Sun**

Sports writing: **Michael Farber**, *Montreal Gazette*

Spot news photography: **Robert Taylor**, *Edmonton Sun*

Feature photograph: **Bruno Schlumberger**, *Ottawa Citizen*

Citations of Merit

Feature writing: **Judy Steed**, *The Globe & Mail*

Editorial writing: **John Dafoe**, *Winnipeg Free Press*

WHITE WINS TWICE

Jim White of the *Toronto Star* has been named the best food writer in North America, twice over. He won the Vesta prize, which named him the top food writer in North America among papers with a circulation greater than 400,000, both in 1980 and in 1982. The award is sponsored by the American Meat Institute, although nothing about meat need be mentioned by the newspaper food writers.

White won the awards for excellence in writing, knowledge of nutrition matters and art layout. His 1982 award acknowledged a series on nutrition, for seniors a series on food relating to a month-long tour of China and an article on Canadians' over-use of salt.

PUBLISHING PREMIERES

Canada's first periodical was the *Nova Scotia Magazine and Comprehensive Review of Literature, Politics and News*. Born in 1789, it lived only until 1792.

Canada's first bilingual magazine was *Quebec Magazine*, written half in English and half in French. The first issue was published in 1792, the last in 1794.

Bartholomew Green Jr. brought a printing press to Halifax from Boston in 1751 and opened a printing business. Green died before he could begin his planned newspaper but his former partner came to Halifax and took over the business. Thus, John Bushell became Canada's first journalist, publishing the first edition of the *Halifax Gazette* on March 23, 1752.

Philadelphia printers William Brown and Thomas Gilmore produced the *Quebec Gazette* in 1764, the year after the Treaty of Paris changed New France to British Canada.

The *Royal Gazette and Nova Scotia Intelligencer* was established in Caleton, N.S. (St. John, N.B.), in 1783.

The *Upper Canada Gazette* or *American Oracle* began publishing in 1793 at Newark (Niagara-on-the-Lake) at the instigation of John Graves Simcoe.

The *Montreal Gazette*, first known as *La Gazette due Commerce et Litteraire*, began its long life in 1778.

The early press in the colonies and Canada was generally neutral and non-provocative, due in part to its dependence on government support.

BETTER NEWSPAPERS COMPETITION

Canadian Community Newspapers Association

The awards honour the best of the approximately 550 community newspapers across Canada.

1982 Best All-round Broadsheets
Circulation under 1,999: **Portage La Prairie (Man.)** *Leader*
Circulation under 3,499: **Ladysmith (B.C.)** *Chemainus Chronicle*
Circulation under 4,499: **Acton (Ont.)** *Free Press*
Circulation under 6,499: **Yorkton (Sask.)** *This Week*
Circulation under 9,999: **Milton (Ont.)** *Canadian Champion*
Circulation over 10,000: **Mississauga (Ont.)** *News*
Best All-round Tabloids
Circulation under 1,999: **Mayerthorpe (Alta.)** *Freelancer*
Circulation under 3,499: **Stittsville (Ont.)** *News*
Circulation under 4,999: **Grimsby (Ont.)** *Independent*
Circulation under 9,999: **Fort Saskatchewan (Alta.)** *Record*
Circulation over 10,000 **North York (Ont.)** *Mirror*
Best Advertising Idea Award: **Mississauga (Ont.)** *News*
Best All-round Armed Forces Base Paper: **CFB Esquimalt (B.C.)** *Lookout*
Best local cartoon: **Steve nease,** *Lakeshore Advertiser*/Etobicoke (Ont.) *Guardian*
Best editorial writing: **Bob Mossman,** *The Bulletin, Bridgewater, N.S.*
Community service award: **Mississauga (Ont.)** *News*
Best news story: **Maple Ridge (B.C.)** *Gazette*
Best historical story: **Barry's Bay (Ont.)** *This Week*
Best feature story:**Oakville (Ont.)** *Beaver*
Best newspaper promotion: **Drayton Valley (Alta.)** *Western Review*
Outstanding columnist: **Alex Lay, Ajax Whitby (Ont.)** *News Adviser*

MA MURRAY — LILLOOET'S LEADING LADY

Ma Murray and her husband George Matheson Murray started the *Bridge River-Lillooet News* **in 1933 and the** *Alaska Highway News* **in Fort St. John 10 years later.**

The masthead on the Lillooet weekly read, "Printed in the sagebrush country of Lillooet every Thursday, God willing. Guaranteed a chuckle every week and a belly laugh once a month or your money back. Subscription $4 in Canada, Furriners $5. This week's circulation 1,347 and every bloody one of them paid for."

Using basic vocabulary in her editorials she flung barbs with unerring accuracy against the high and mighty and the jabs were felt all the way to Ottawa. She was sought out by television, especially at election time, for her colourful commentaries.

She was named to the Order of Canada in 1970 and when she sold the Bridge River-Lillooet News in 1973 she said "Sold it for peanuts to be free. You either do a job or get off the pot."

Ma Murray died at the age of 95 in 1982.

THE NELLIES — ACTRA AWARDS

Association of Canadian Television and Radio Artists

The Nellie, a statuette designed by William McElcheran, is presented in 20 categories for outstanding achievement in performance and production of Canadian radio and television.

1983 Earle Grey Award for best acting performance in TV in a leading role
Rosemary Dunsmore for *Blind Faith*, a segment of CBC's *For the Record*.
Andrew Allan Award for the best acting performance in radio
Gerard Parkes for *1,000 Years of the Nights*.
Du Maurier Award for the best new performer in Canadian TV
Allan Katz and **Judith Katz**.
Gordon Sinclair Award for outspoken opinions and integrity in broadcasting

Laurier LaPierre, Independent TV, Vancouver.

Foster Hewitt Award for excellence in sportscasting
Steve Armitage, CBC.

Best acting performance in a supporting role in TV
Budd Knapp for a *Choice of Two*, CBC.

Best variety performance on TV
Toller Cranston for *Strawberry Ice*, CBC.

Best variety performance on radio
Royal Canadian Air Farce, CBC.

Best host/interviewer on TV
Eric Malling, *the fifth estate*, CBC.

Best host/interviewer on radio
Peter Gzowski, *Morningside*, CBC.

Best writer of television drama
Sheldon Chad, *Seeing Things*, CBC.

Best writer for radio drama
Michael Riordan, *Quiet in the Hills*, CBC.

Best writer for television variety
Royal Canadian Air Farce, CBC.

Best writer for television documentary/public affairs
Peter Kent, a segment on the Polish struggle, CBC's *The Journal*.

Best writer for radio documentary/public affairs
Diane Silverman, *How Shall I Live Without You*, CBC.

Best children's television program
On My Own, CBC.

John Drainie Award for distinguished contribution to broadcasting
Lucio Agostini, in acknowledgement of his many accomplishments.

Best radio program of the year
Fruit of the Poisoned Tree, *Scales of Justice* series, CBC.

Best television program of the year
Billy Bishop Goes To War.

AMERICANS CLAIM THE FIRST STATION — WE DISPUTE IT

KDKA Pittsburgh claims that it was the first radio station in the world, broadcasting in the year 1920 with the call letters XWB. But CFCF, Montreal, was there first — in 1919 using the call letters XWA.

RADIO-TV NEWS DIRECTORS AWARDS

Radio-Television News Directors Association of Canada

Winners receive a plaque to honour their achievement.

1983　Radio

Charlie Edwards Award for spot news reporting: CFTR-Toronto, for coverage of the fire at Plaza II.

Sam Ross Award for news commentary: CFPL-London's Ric Wellwood, for his commentary on the death of Ontario's former premier John Robarts.

Television

Charlie Edwards Award for spot news reporting: CITV-Edmonton for the coverage of the kidnapping of Peter Pocklington.

Dan McArthur Award for TV documentary: CKGN-TV (Global) Toronto for *No Regrets*, the story of a couple who adopted 13 handicapped children.

President's Award: William (Bill) Hutton, Selkirk Broadcasting, for an outstanding career in broadcast journalism.

RADIO FIRSTS

Of course you know that Guglielmo Marconi received the first transatlantic wireless message. But where was he when he received it? You were right if you said he was standing on a hill in St. John's Newfoundland. His antenna on the December day in 1901 was a kite with the antenna attached.

While Marconi was struggling with voiceless transmission, Reginald Fessenden, who was born in East Bolton, Que., had developed a theory of sound waves in 1866 that was contrary to Marconi's.

Fessenden saw radio signals as waves moving in ever widening circles. Other scientists thought Fessenden's ideas ridiculous but in 1900 he succeeded in transmitting the first voice message. The message travelled a mile but was clearly heard.

Then on Christmas Eve in 1906 Fessendon amazed operators specially equipped with receivers aboard ships of the United Fruit Company when they heard the first radio broadcast ever made. Fessenden made the announcements, played his violin, sang a verse of a Christmas carol and was the world's first disc jockey when he wound up his phonograph and transmitted a rendition of Handel's *Largo*. He made the broadcast from a small studio and transmitter outside Boston, Mass.

He was noted for several other inventions including a micro-photographic recorder and a height indicator for aircraft. When he died in 1932 he was recognized as one of the world's greatest inventive geniuses.

GOLD RIBBONS OF THE C.A.B.

Canadian Association of Broadcasters

Awards are made to private broadcasters in Canada for achievement, ingenuity and imagination.

Gold Ribbon for Public Affairs

Given to a radio or television station for the most effective picture of matters of public interest and concern, whether they be local, regional or national.

1982   CFRN-TV, Edmonton, Alta.

Gold Ribbon for News

Given to a radio or television station, or group of stations for improved news gathering, news presentation, reliability and enlightenment in news broadcasting.

1982   CFRN-TV, Edmonton, Alta.

Gold Ribbon for Community Service

Honours the radio or television station which has made the greatest charitable or public service contribution to a community.

1982   CKIQ, Kelowna, B.C.

Gold Ribbon for Distinguished Service

Presented for truly outstanding service to Canadian private broadcasting in the previous year.

1982   Gary Hanney, BCTV, Vancouver, B.C.

Gold Ribbon of Canadian Talent Development

Presented to the broadcasting station which has made the greatest contribution to the development of Canadian talent through broadcast exposure in the entertainment field.

1982   CFPL-TV, London, Ont.

Gold Ribbon for Engineering Achievement

Presented for the development of engineering or technical ideas which improve operator techniques in private broadcasting.

1982   CHED Radio, Edmonton, Alta.

FAST TALKER

The world's fastest talking broadcaster is thought to be Gerry Wilmot, who was born in Victoria, 1914 and was a hockey sportscaster following World War II.

RAYMOND CRÉPAULT SCHOLARSHIP

Canadian Association of Broadcasters

The late Raymond A. Crépault, Q.C., a well-known Quebec business man and broadcaster, acquired CJMS, Montreal, in 1954 and opened CJMS-FM, Canada's first French-language privately owned FM station, in 1963. Still later he formed the Radiomutuel Network. The scholarship honours his contribution to broadcasting and his deep commitment, as a French Canadian, to Canadian unity.

The scholarship provides $5,000 to a French-speaking Canadian to study broadcasting skills at a Canadian university or institution.

1982 Johanne St-Arnauld, Université du Québec.

CBC WINS PEABODY

The Peabody Awards, among the most prestigious in North American broadcasting, are presented annually by the University of Georgia's school of journalism and mass communication.

CBC Radio won one of the 29 awards in 1983. The CBC special for *Morningside* was about the year 1905 and was written and narrated by Lister Sinclair, and produced by Alan Guettel. The winning program was entered in the education category.

RUTH HANCOCK SCHOLARSHIPS

Canadian Association of Broadcasters

The scholarship commemorates the late Ruth Hancock who for years worked on behalf of broadcast associations in Canada. The four $1,000 scholarships are to encourage talented, hard-working students to pursue careers in Canadian broadcasting.

1982 **Darryl Perry**, McGill U.
Linda Nelson, Ryerson Polytechnical Institute
Barry Lyn Ens, Lethbridge Community College
Jocelyne DeLa Fontaine, RPI.

RAVE REVIEWS

The CBC received almost unanimous rave reviews and a sizable share of the TV audience when it telecast the Canadian epic series, *Empire, Inc.* A kind of Canadian *Dallas*, the series took nine months to film and cost $3.5-million.

CANPRO 83

CanPro is an annual national festival of locally produced television programs, in which 22 stations compete for 55 national awards.

Canpro Award of Excellence

1983 Best program in the festival
We Won't Let Him Die, **CFAC-TV, Lethbridge, Alta.**

The big winners were:

CFAC-TV, Lethbridge, with the best of show and three additional awards.
CFCN-TV, Calgary, four awards.
CFTM-TV, Montreal, four awards.
CKND-TV, Winnipeg, four awards.
CKTV-TV, Regina, three awards.
CFCF-TV, Montreal, three awards.
CFAC-TV, Calgary, three awards.
CKCO-TV, Kitchener, three awards.

RADIO RECORD

The longest nonstop spoken radio program ever broadcast was on June 16, 1982, when CBC stereo joined Radio Telefis Eireann to broadcast an unedited

Emmy Award winners: The SCTV group, bottom row, l to r, John Candy, Joe Flaherty, Eugene Levy, Andrea Martin, Catherine O'Hara and Dave Thomas

and uninterrupted 30-hour reading of James Joyce's celebrated novel *Ulysses*.

Joyce's account of ordinary Dubliners, who were nobodies until he made them historic, took place on June 16, 1904, since known as "Bloomsday," a reference to the main character, Leopold Bloom.

CHILDREN'S BROADCAST INSTITUTE AWARDS

Children's Broadcast Institute

The Children's Broadcast Institute, in Toronto, Ont., concerns itself with all aspects of television as it relates to children. Every two years the institute holds a competition to select the best Canadian-produced television programs in English or French for children up to 12 years old.

1983 Animation category
The Raccoons on Ice, produced by Gillis-Wiseman Productions.
Independent category
The Kids of DeGrassi Street, produced by Playing With Time, Inc.
Stations category
The Missing Bear Caper, produced by CFCN-TV.
Network category
Going Great, produced by CBC.
Garage Gazette, produced by Access.
Cable Category
Just Kidding, produced by WHTV.

CANADIANS WIN EMMY

The 34th annual Emmys were presented in September 1982 in Hollywood, for the best television programs seen in the U.S.

SCTV, the zany Canadian-produced series, won an Emmy for "writing in a variety or music program." The award was for the *Moral Majority Show*, written by John Candy, Joe Flaherty, Eugene Levy, Andrea Martin, Rick Moranis,

Catherine O'Hara, Dave Thomas, Dick Blasucci, Paul Flaherty, Bob Dolman, John McAndrew, Doug Steckler, Mert Rich, Jeffrey Barron, Michael Short, Christ Cluess, Stuart Kreisman and Brian McConnachie.

How's that for a group of hosers, eh?

ANIK AWARDS/COMITÉ DES PRIX ANIK

Canadian Broadcasting Corporation

The Prix Anik Awards are presented for excellence in CBC television regional and network English or French programming.

One program, *Strawberry Ice*, broke all previous records in the history of the competition by winning a total of six Anik Awards.

1982 **Le temps d'une paix**, produced by Yvon Trudel, Montreal. A Christmas family drama set in Quebec's Charlevoix county in the 1920s.
Strawberry Ice, freom the Superspecial series, produced by David Acomba. Executive producer, John Dimon (Toronto). A skating spectacular starring Toller Cranston.
Music — Special Mention
Philharmonic Festivities, produced by Armand Baril, Calgary.
Documentary
Spirit Speaking Through, from the Spectrum series, produced by Donnalu Wigmore, Toronto. An arts documentary on the work of seven artists of the Woodland Indians school.
Journalism
Newscentre Evening news, executive producer, Helen Slinger, Vancouver.
Journalism — Special Mention
Ce soir atlantique, produced by Patrice Tremblay, Moncton.
Ce soir regional, produced by Michel Frechette, Rimouski.
Network series (information)
The fifth estate, executive producer Robin Taylor, Toronto.
Network series (entertainment)

Seeing Things, produced by Louis Del Grande and David Barlow, executive producer Robert Allen, Toronto.
Regional series (information)
Edmonton Extra Special, executive producer C.V. (Caryl) Brandt, Edmonton.
Regional series (entertainment)
Switchback, produced by John Nowlan, Halifax.
Regional entertainment series — special mention
Stepping Out, produced by Judith Murray, Montreal.
Photography
Jean-Pierre Lefebvre for "Arioso" from the series *Les Beaux Dimanches*, Montreal.
Documentary camera
Rudolf Kovanic for "Long Point" from the series *The Nature of Things*, Toronto.
Production editing
Claude Meilleur for "Diane Dufresne" from the series *Femme d'aujourd'hui*, Montreal.
Sound editing
Anthony J.R. Lancett, for "Long Point" from the series *The Nature of Things*, Toronto.
Lighting director
John Bryden for "Strawberry Ice" from the series *Superspecial*, Toronto.
Video
Raymond Beley for the VTR editing of "Strawberry Ice" from the series *Superspecial*, Toronto.
Set design
Milton Parcher for "Strawberry Ice" from the series *Superspecial*, Toronto.
Costume design
Frances Dafoe, for "Strawberry ice" from the series *Superspecial*, Toronto.
Outstanding contribution
George Clark for the special effects of "Strawberry Ice" from the series *Superspecial*, Toronto.

BIGGEST AUDIENCE

Nova Scotia singer Anne Murray's Caribbean cruise special, broadcast in the U.S. on the CBS network, drew the biggest audience of the 1983 winter season for a special.

AWARD FOR EXCELLENCE IN BROADCAST SAFETY MESSAGES

Canada Safety Council

An award which recognizes station-created, public-service safety messages.

1982   **CHIQ-FM**, Winnipeg, for a Halloween safety message.

CANADIAN SPORTS AWARDS

Sports Federation of Canada

1982   Sportscaster of the Year
       Robert J. Picken, CBC Radio, Winnipeg, Man.

TVO TOPS

TVO, or the Ontario Educational Communication Authority, is one of the best educational television systems in the world. It produces 450 hours of new programs each year and has won some 10 major international awards each year. Its annual budget is $32-million. TVO was recognized by the federal government in May 1983 when it was awarded $1.2-million under the official languages education program, "in view of the important role played by TV Ontario in areas of education and culture with respect to the interests of the francophone minority." The government gave TVO another $40,000 for the application of new technology in education.

TVO receives most of its operating funds from the provincial government but also seeks funds from corporations and the general public.

SCOTTY HARPER AWARD

Canadian Curling Association

The award, in the form of a plaque and a $500 Canada Savings Bond, commemorates the memory of the late Scotty Harper of the *Winnipeg Free Press*, whose curling reports enlivened that journal for many years.
Best Curling Program on Radio or TV

1982 Bob Irving, Winnipeg, Man.

EDWARD (TED) SAMUELS ROGERS, A RADIO REVOLUTIONARY

Rogers was fascinated by radio as a young boy. He made a battery short wave radio in 1914 that reportedly picked up a broadcast from London, England, announcing the beginning of World War I hostilities, which gave him a scoop on the Toronto press.

His major achievement was the invention of the electric radio. His radio used an alternating-current tube and could be plugged into household current.

He formed Rogers' Majestic Radio Company and established the world's first batteryless radio station with the call letters CFRB, still one of Canada's most successful radio stations.

Rogers was working on television and radar when he died at 39, in 1939.

NATIONAL AWARDS

Canadian Science Writers' Association

Awards are given annually for the best science journalism on radio and television. Winners receive $1,000.

1983 Science and Technology
Television: **The Nature of Things**, CBC, team of James Murray, Allan Bailey, David Suzuki, Richard Long-
ley, Rudolf Kovanic and Michael Bennett.
Radio: **Quirks and Quarks**, CBC Radio, team of Anita Gordon, Jay Ingram, Penny Park and Ron McKeen.
Science and Health
Television: **Science Realité**, Radio Canada, Montreal, team of Jean Remillard and Donald Dodier.
Radio: **Ideas**, CBC Radio, team of Beth Savan and Max Allen.
Science and Natural Resources
Television: Andre Delisle, Tele Metropole, Dorchester, Que.
Radio: **Quirks and Quarks**, CBC Radio, team of Anita Gordon, Jay Ingram, Penny Park and Ron McKeen.

KARI HANNIKAINEN AWARD

Broadcast Executive Society

The Kari is for the best performance or performances in a commercial.

1983 **Rosemary Dunsmore** and **Larry Mann**
Commercial: *Griswald*
Advertiser: TransCanada Telephone System
Agency: Publicite McKim Ltd., Montreal
Production: The Partners, Toronto

HIGH SIGNS

The highest advertising signs are the four Bank of Montreal logos atop the 72-storey 935-foot-tall First Canadian Place building in Toronto. Each sign, built by Claude Neon Industries Ltd., measures 20 feet by 22 feet and was lifted into place by helicopter.

BESSIES

Broadcast Executive Society

Presented annually for excellence in the Canadian television commercials industry.

1983 Gold Bessy

Toboggan
Advertiser: Ontario Milk Marketing Board
Agency: McKim Advertising Ltd.
Production: the Partners, Toronto, Ont.
Silver Bessy
Early Morning
Advertiser: Quaker Oats Co.
Agency: Doyle Dane Bernbach
Production: Sincinkin, Toronto
Bronze Bessy
Toys
Advertiser: Ontario Egg Marketing Board
Agency: Ogilvie & Mather
Productions: Sincinkin, Toronto.

DOING IT WITH FLARE

Radio CFMI spelt out its call sign in 400-foot letters on Grouse Mountain, Vancouver, B.C., on February 14, 1980 with 450 flares visible from 42 miles distant.

SPIESS AWARD

Broadcast Executive Society

The award is for excellence in film production.

1983   Don McLean, The Partners, Toronto.

CONCOURS/GALA — Coq d'or '83

Le Publicité-Club de Montréal

The awards honour French-Canadian creation and originality in advertising.

Coq d'or: **Cossette et Associés Communication Marketing**
Grand prix argent: **Le Group BCP**
Grand prix bronze: **Cockfield Brown Inc**.
Humanitarian Causes
Ministry of Social Affairs, Government of Quebec, for a TV spot, produced by Les Concepteurs Arsenault Paquette Ltée.
Corporate Style Advertising
Radio Quebec, for a TV spot, produced by Studio of Radio Quebec.

Government Advertising
Ministry of Social Affairs, Government of Quebec, for a poster, produced by Young & Rubicam Advertising.
Best Billboard Advertisement
Retail: **Cossette et Associés** for McDonald's Restaurants.
Manufacturing: **Moscovitz & Taylor Advertising** for Pilot Ball Point Pens.
Service Organizations: **Le Groupe BCP** for Air Canada.
Best Magazine Advertising
Retail: **T. Eaton Co. Ltd.** for Eaton's.
Manufacturing: **Agence de Publicité Media Ltd.** for Merck Forstt, Canada, Inc.
Best Newspaper Advertising
Retail: **T. Eaton Co. Ltd**. for Eaton's
Manufacturing: **Cossette et Associés** for Renault, AMC Quebec.
Service Advertising: **Le Groupe BCP** for Air Canada
Best Direct Mail Advertising
Retail: **T. Eaton Co. Ltd.** for Eaton's.
Manufacturing: **Cossette et Associés** for Renault AMC Quebec.
Service Advertising: **Cockfield Brown Inc**. for Bell Canada.
Best Radio Advertising
Retail: **Le Group BCP** for Air Canada.
Manufacturing: **Cossette et Associés** for Renault AMC Quebec.
Service Advertising: **Cockfield Brown Inc**. for Bell Canada.
Best Television Advertising
Retail: **Publicité Martin** for Podium.
Manufacturing: **Cockfield Brown, Inc**. for Molson Breweries Quebec Ltd.
Service Advertising: **McKim Advertising** for Tele Direct Ltd.
Point of Sale Advertising
Retail: **Publicite Martin** for Quebec Liquor Board
Service Advertising: **Le Group BCP** for Air Canada.
Special Campaigns
Retail: **Cossette et Associés** for McDonald's Restaurants.
Manufacturing: **Cockfield Brown Inc**. for National Dairy Council of Canada.
Service Advertising: **McKim Advertising** for Tele Direct.
Other forms of advertising
Retail: **Cossette et Associés** for McDonald's Restaurants.

Manufacturing: **Publicite Caledon**, Ltd. for O'Keefe Breweries.

INTREPID IMBIBERS

The Canadian Club World Adventure Series is the longest-running advertising campaign in history. Since 1946, intrepid travellers have engaged in seemingly inexhaustible varieties of derring-do, preferably in the most exotic locations, and then relaxed with a soothing glass of grog.

SOCIAL RESPONSIBILITY ADVERTISING AWARD

Canadian Advertising Advisory Board

The award is usually presented to advertisers whose messages are attuned to customer needs and reflect current social issues. The 1982 awards were changed, for this year only, to recognize advertising agencies which contribute time and talent to nonprofit and charitable organizations.

1982 Special Mention
Grey Advertising Ltd., Toronto, Ont., for its commitment to assisting the Children's Aid Society of Metro Toronto in its overall communications package, including advertising.
Other Winners
Freeman/Yipp Advertising Ltd., Calgary, Alta., for United Way of Calgary.
Ted Herriott Associates, Mississauga, Ont. for Big Brothers of Canada.
Benton & Bowles Canada Ltd., Toronto, Ont., for Canadian Hemophilia Society.
Cockfield Brown Inc., Montreal, Que., for Centraide.
Ogilvy & Mather Canada Ltd., Toronto, Ont., for World Wildlife Fund.

CANADIAN FIRMS WIN

F.H. Hayhurst and MacLaren Advertising of Toronto won three medals each for

television commercials at the 24th annual International Film and TV Festival of New York in 1981.

NEWSPAPER ADVERTISING AWARDS

Newspaper Advertising Executive Association

Twelve awards are presented annually for the best in newspaper advertising.

1982 Ross Bates Memorial Award
Frank Sorrintino, The Gazette, Montreal, for contribution to the creation of a sales project.
Best in the Business Award
The Standard, St. Catharines, Ont.
Colour Letterpress Over 50,000 (circulation)
Times-Colonist, Victoria, B.C.
Colour Offset Over 50,000
The Edmonton Journal, Edmonton, Alta.
Colour Offset Under 50,000
The Brandon Sun, Brandon, Man.
Colour Letterpress Under 50,000
The Whig-Standard, Kingston, Ont.
Classified Commercial
The Brandon Sun, Brandon, Man.
Classified Private Party
The Edmonton Journal, Edmonton, Alta.
Frequency Sells — 600 lines or less
Kitchener-Waterloo Record, Kitchener, Ont.
Frequency Sells — 600 lines or more
The Edmonton Journal, Edmonton, Alta.
Paper Promotion — Over 50,000 circulation
Winnipeg Free Press, Winnipeg, Man.
Best Special Section
The Beacon Herald, Stratford, Ont.

BEST OF SHOW

A television commercial produced for the Government of Ontario beat out 1,500 entries from the U.S., Europe and Canada when it won the Best of Show at the U.S. Television Commercials Festival in Chicago, 1982.

Label us Able, produced by Camp Advertising and Rabco Production Co. for the Ontario government, in honour of the International Year of the Disabled, also won first prize for film editing and first prize in the public service category. The Canadian commercial was the first to win Best of Show.

Five Canadian advertising agencies brought home awards from the festival in 1983.

1983 **Camp Associates and Rabco Television Productions**, who won best of show, in 1982 took first place in the travel category for *Snowbird*, a 60-second commercial produced for the Ontario Ministry of Tourism and Recreation. **McKim Advertising**, Montreal, received creative excellence awards for three commercials on *The Yellow Pages*, a campaign produced for Bell Canada/Tele Direct. **SMW Advertising**, Toronto, won a creative excellence award for a Yamaha Motor commercial, *Family Business*. **Palmer Bonner Advertising**, Toronto, also won a creative excellence award for *Life at 3-foot-8*, produced for Dad's Cookies by Boardwalk Motion Picture Co. **Anderson Advertising** won for its *Eskimo* commercial produced for Ray-O-Vac Canada by Trio Films, Toronto, and in the Public Utilities category, **McKim,** Montreal won again for *Griswald*, a commercial prepared for Trans Canada Telephone System. it was produced by Partners, Toronto.

ACA GOLD MEDAL AWARD

Association of Canadian Advertisers

The medal is awarded to Canadians for outstanding contribution to advertising in Canada.

1982 **Tom Blakeley**, former president of ACA, for his creative contribution towards making advertising in Canada more ethical, better understood and more respected.

1983 **Don Davis**, former president of ACA, for devotion to education in advertising and for establishing a new foundation for the advertising industry. **Yves Bourassa** and **Paul L'Anglais**, Montreal, for contributing to a better understanding of French heritage and culture by their English colleagues.

MARKETING GOLD AWARDS

Marketing Magazine

Awarded for excellence in Canadian advertising.

1983 Television Commercial
Advertiser: **Ray-O-Vac**
Agency: **Anderson Advertising**
Creative director: **Dieter Kaufmann**
Copy: **Brian Quennell**
Art: **Dieter Kaufmann and Steve Chase**
Radio Commercial
Advertiser: **CN Tower**
Agency: **Jerry Goodis Agency**
Creative director: **Martin Keen**
Copy: **Martin keen**
Campaigns
Advertiser: **CN Tower**
Agency: **Jerry Goodis Agency**
Creative director: **Martin Keen**
Copy: **Martin Keen**
Newspapers
Advertiser: **CN Tower**
Agency: **Jerry Goodis Agency**
Creative director: **Jerry Goodis**
Copy: **Steve Denvir**
Art: **Karen Howe**
Andy Rodgers Memorial Award for Public Service
Advertiser: **Canadian Rehabilitation Council for the Disabled**
Agency: **McCann-Erikson**
Creative director: **Harrison Yates**
Copy: **Harrison Yates**
Art: **Berry Mitchell**

CPRS AWARD OF ATTAINMENT

Canadian Public Relations Society

For outstanding achievement and service to PR. Presented to a member of the society who has made a significant contribution to the status and acceptance of the public relations function, over and above the call of duty.

1983 **Edsel J. Bonnell**, Bonnell Public Relations, St. John's, Nfld.

CPRS SHIELD OF PUBLIC SERVICE

Canadian Public Relations Society

For distinguished and dedicated service in the public interest.

1983 **William J.E. Rees**, Director of Communications, Alberta Housing and Public Works, for his support of the YMCA, the United Way and the church in his community.

CPRS LECTERN

Canadian Public Relations Society

Awarded to the member society with the most remarkable accomplishments.

1983 **Don Hoskins**, immediate past president, The Ottawa Society.

CPRS AWARDS OF EXCELLENCE

Canadian Public Relations Society

The awards honour innovative and outstanding English and French public relations programs by CPRS practitioners.

1983 **Ray Argyle**, Argyle Communications Inc. Toronto, Ont.
François Aubin, Societe d'energie de la Baie James, Montreal, Que.
Judi Gunter, Calgary Public Libraries, Calgary, Alta.
Chris Ladd, West-Can Communications, Edmonton, Alta.
Jean-Pierre Maltais, Iron Ore Co. of Canada, Sépt-Iles, Que.
Diana Matthews, Saskatchewan Western Development Museum, Saskatoon, Sask.
Suzanne Montange, Quebec Safety League, Montreal, Que.
Christine Smith, Alberta Public Affairs Bureau, Edmonton, Alta.

Keith S. Tisshaw, C-I-L., Toronto, Ont.

Honourable Mentions
Peter J. Bruton, Prudential Insurance Company of America, Toronto, Ont.
Jeffrey W. Elliott, Jeffrey Elliott Communications, Toronto, Ont.
Michele Giroux-Beauregard, Brasserie Molson du Quebec, Montreal, Que.
D. Hal Holden, MacMillan Bloedel, Ltd., Vancouver, B.C.
Michael Horton, Burson-Marsteller, Toronto, Ont.
Daniel Larmarre, Burson-Marsteller, Montreal, Que.
Larry W. Rose, Walden Public Relations Ltd., Vancouver, B.C.

COMMUNICATIONS AWARD TO HONOUR McLUHAN

An award honouring Marshall McLuhan, the Canadian who gained international fame describing the probable significance of the technological revolution, will be awarded for the first time in December 1983.

It will be given biennially in recognition of outstanding contributions to the understanding of communications and technology.

The $50,000 prize was established this year by the Canadian Commission for UNESCO and funded by Teleglobe, the crown corporation responsible for international telecommunications and satellite systems.

McLuhan, who died in 1981, was born in Edmonton in 1911. He joined the English department of St. Michael's College at the University of Toronto in 1946. Described as the guru of the electronic age, he fascinated, angered and baffled people as he described the effects he anticipated on the "global village." He told *Playboy* magazine, "We live in a transitional era of profound pain and tragic identity crisis, but the agony of our age is the labour pain of rebirth."

QUEBEC AHEAD IN COMMUNICATIONS SYSTEMS

Anglo-Canadians used to ask, "What does Quebec want?" If they asked now, Quebec should be able to tell them: Quebec now has more academic programs in communications than any other province. Each of the four Montreal universities offers graduate degrees in the field and Quebec's Department of Communications, formed in 1969, was the first such provincial body.

The media study Quebec, and Quebec studies the media, and this is a media world...

AWARD OF VALOUR

National Transportation Week

The awards are presented for exemplary acts of bravery in perilous circumstances.

1982 Capt. A.W. Knight, Halifax, and **crew MV Balder Hudson**
Crew, 423 Helicopter Anti-Submarine Squadron
Crew, 413 Helicopter Transport and Rescue Squadron
The award was for the rescue of 26 men from the "Graveyard of the Atlantic."
When the 18,000-tonne grain-carrier *Euro Princess*, bound from Montreal to the Black Sea, was driven onto the treacherous shoals of Sable Island by a howling winter storm on November 26, 1981, the commanders and crews of two Canadian Forces helicopters and a small supply vessel carried out a dramatic rescue. All three were cited for valour by the National Transportation Week Committee to receive group awards.

The 7,500-tonne *Balder Hudson*, supply ship for the drilling rig *Rowan Juneau*, was the first to reach the stricken carrier and made numerous attempts to get a line aboard and

evacuate the Yugoslavian crew of 26. The 40-foot seas foiled all efforts.

As Captain Alan W. Knight of the *Balder Hudson* radioed the Canadian Coast Guard, the crippled vessel was wrenched free of the sandbar and started to bear down broadside on the towering oil driller. Captain Knight ordered the 12-man *Juneau* crew to abandon rig. But the grain carrier was swept past the rig with only a few hundred feet to spare, and came to a shuddering halt as two sea anchors were dropped, all of its lifeboats and rafts swept away. The *Hudson* fired more rocket lines in vain, then stood by with scramble nets to pick up possible survivors.

At 11 p.m. in pitch darkness, bucking a 60-mile-an-hour wind on its flight from Shearwater, a Sea King of 423 Helicopter Anti-Submarine Squadron hovered over the *Euro Princess* which was now breaking up. Captain Don MacQuarrie was lowered onto the heaving deck and began strapping the helpless and nearly frozen crew members into the lift-collar to be winched aloft and flown to Sable Island.

Moments later a Voyageur helicopter of 413 Transport and Rescue Squadron arrived from Summerside in the teeth of a blinding snowstorm, and winched aboard the remaining 13 men, including the captain, to fly them to Shearwater (Dartmouth).

Meanwhile, Captain Knight and his 12-man crew went on to assist with the evacuation of the oil rig and then the towing of the crippled grain carrier to Halifax, terminating their operation on November 29 — three days after receiving first Mayday.

Captain Knight, 32, also received the Minister's Certificate of Bravery from Admiral A.L. Collier, Commissioner of the Canadian Coast Guard.

The crews of the Canadian Forces helicopter rescue squadrons were: (423 Helicopter Anti-Submarine Squadron) Lieutenant-Commander David Cradduck, 32, Olean, N.Y. (US Navy exchange officer); Captain Donald MacQuarrie, 39, Hamilton, Ont.; Lieutenant David Amberley, 25, Montreal, Que.; Master Corporal Richard L'Archevêque, 29, Dartmouth, N.S.; Master Corporal David Hutchinson, 34, Hampton, N.B.; (413 Transport and Rescue Squadron) Captain Michael Dorey, London, Ont.; Lieutenant Grant Smith, Middleton, N.S.; Sergeant John Day, Vancouver, B.C.; Master Corporal Brian Smith, Moncton, N.B.; Master Corporal Chris Healey, St. John's, Nfld.; Corporal Michael Byrne, Halifax, N.S.

AWARD OF VALOUR WINNERS FROM PREVIOUS YEARS

Leonard Barney, 30, and *John Normore*, 53, fishermen of l'Anse au Loup, Labrador, in their vessels *Blue Charm* and *Northern Transport* rescued 22 seamen from the Portuguese trawler *Maria Teixeria Vilarhino* when it grounded on a reef near the village of Black Tickle, Labrador, in a screaming gale.

When the vessel sent an SOS in the early morning of September 4, 1980, the only people in the area were fishermen. Despite the crashing seas whipped up by 140 km/h winds out of Greenland, Barney and Normore responded immediately and were first on the scene. They were soon joined by other local fishermen, members of the Canadian Marine Rescue Auxiliary, who took another 13 men from the stricken vessel. A helicopter from 103 Rescue Unit, Gander, evacuated the remaining 29 Portuguese seamen later in the day when the tides subsided.

David Frazee, 20, a university student of West Vancouver, was a summer-employed seaman on board the CCGS *Racer* based at Kitsilano when on July 22, 1980, the U.S. fishing vessel *"Sundowner"* capsized off the British Columbia coast with three men trapped inside the fish hold.

Two managed to escape and clung to the overturned hull as the vessel was pulled by hand alongside the *Racer*. The third fisherman could be heard inside the hold shouting and pounding for help. Frazee, although not a qualified diver, and not fully familiar with the *Racer*'s diving gear, volunteered to go to the rescue. When he located the trapped man, Frazee assisted him by removing his mustang floater suit, then gave him his diving mask and led him out of the hold to the surface where he was taken aboard the *Racer* and given first aid treatment.

SIR SAMUEL CUNARD

The son of a Halifax carpenter, Cunard was born in 1787. He was the East India Company agent in Halifax, owned a whaling fleet and operated sailing ships that ran to New England, Bermuda and Newfoundland. As well as mercantile and banking interests, he was a shareholder in the company that launched the wooden paddle-wheeler *Royal William*, one of the early steamships. In 1838 in England, he put together a group of investors, obtained a contract for the North Atlantic mail service and formed the Royal Mail Steam Packet Company, later known as the Cunard Line. The company's first ship, *Britannia*, was built on the Clyde and made her maiden voyage in 1840 with Cunard himself at the helm. She inaugurated regular transatlantic steamship service. Cunard's first iron ship, *Persia*, entered service in 1855 and *China*, his first screw-propelled ship, followed in 1862. The Cunard Line grew into one of the world's greatest shipping companies. The world's largest passenger ships, the *Queen Mary* and the *Queen Elizabeth*, both sailed under the company flag.

Queen Victoria conferred a baronetcy

on Cunard in 1859 in recognition of his contributions to British shipping.

MADE SHIPPING HISTORY IN HIGH ARCTIC

Captain Kenneth G. Milburn, 43, of Saint John, N.B., native of Nottingham, England, established a Canadian record when he sailed the oil tanker *Irving Arctic* to Rea Point, Melville Island, 50 miles due south of the magnetic North Pole in August 1980. The 38,000 dead-weight-ton tanker was the largest Canadian commercial vessel to successfully penetrate that far west into the hazardous Northwest Passage. The ship delivered 100,000 barrels of petroleum products to the Panarctic Oil exploration station.

ENGINE INGENUITY

Benjamin Tibbetts of New Brunswick invented and constructed the compound steam engine in 1842. His engine, which used steam at both high and low pressure, revolutionized steamboat propulsion.

PATRIOTIC PIRATES

During the Napoleonic wars, when Britain was at war with France and Spain, privateering against enemies of the flag was an honourable act of war. The brig *Rover*, sailing out of Liverpool, N.S., was one vessel engaged in such an occupation. In 1800, a squadron of Spanish ships spied the *Rover* as she sailed the Caribbean, and turned tail. The *Rover* gave chase and captured two of the Spanish ships.

ACCOMPLISHED FIRSTS FOR B.C. FERRY FLEET

E.W. Phillips, of Victoria, B.C., has been employed by British Columbia Ferry Corporation since 1961 as senior construction supervisor. Under his direction, the corporation has built or converted acquired vessels to expand the fleet from two vessels to more than 27. The B.C. Ferry fleet is now one of the largest in the world.

Phillips has supervised increases in vehicle capacity on seven major ferries, first by installation of ramps on the car deck and then the lengthening of each ship by 84 feet. Three 50-foot ferries have been lengthened to 70 feet and recently two vessels have been cut and their superstructures more than double elevated to allow the insertion of a second car deck — a first on the North American continent, and the first time in the world where a ship's superstructure has been lifted over its entire length by simultaneous hydraulic jacking.

FIRST LIGHTHOUSE

Canada's first lighthouse was constructed at Louisbourg, the site of the French fortress, and went into operation in April, 1734.

HIGH-SEA HEROICS

Major Arthur Godfrey Peuchen, vice-commodore of the Royal Canadian Yacht Club, was a hero of the *Titanic* sinking in 1912.

Major Peuchen, who left $200,000 worth of stocks and bonds on board the ill-fated ship, heard a woman cry that her half-lowered lifeboat was manned by only one crew member. When Peuchen announced that he was a yachtsman, an officer said "If you're a yachtsman, then slide down that rope and prove it."

Peuchen went down the rope and helped manage the life boat until they were rescued eight hours later.

INVENTIONS BOON TO TRANSPORTATION

J. Geoffrey Johns, president, World Oceans Systems Ltd., Sidney, B.C., has made an outstanding and innovative contribution to transportation, provincially, nationally and internationally.

The St. Lawrence Seaway awarded a development contract to him to install his invention, the Sub-Sea Lighting Navigation System. This system provides markings for deep-draught vessels for conditions of low visibility. Since that time, his company has been approached by oil companies in the North Sea regarding the possible installation of this system to mark the approaches and the tanker turning basins at the supertanker ports.

In British Columbia, transportation agencies have also adopted his inventions. The National Harbours Board approached Johns after the collision between the Japanese freighter and the Second Narrows CN Railway crossing (Vancouver) to prepare a model for an Enclosure Unit Lighting System for the bridge.

The Transport Policy Analysis Branch (Ministry of Transportation and Highways) recently implemented an Optical Strobe Light System designed by Johns by several small airports in the province.

PLAYED MAJOR ROLE IN SAVING $30-MILLION GOVERNMENT VESSEL

David R. Illing, 20, of Victoria, B.C., formerly of Ottawa, and **Shawn D.**

McLaughlin, 24, of Victoria, seamen divers serving on the CCGS *Camsell,* were credited in large measure by their superiors with saving the $30-million vessel from sinking after it was holed by ice in the Beaufort Sea.

At 5 a.m. on September 10, 1978, the *Camsell,* steaming through Requisite Channel, struck a multi-year ice floe on her port side. Within 20 minutes the engine room was flooded waist-high. DC equipment was short-circuited, throwing the main pumps out of action. Seamen Illing and McLaughlin went over the side to determine the extent of damage. They located a crack in the hull and attempted to stop the flow of water by using large pieces of canvas, mattresses and collision mats. The MVS *Broderick* arrived alongside, was able to provide a large cargo pump, and by 16:00 hours the water level was below the engine room deck.

During the early hours of the next day, however, the ice floe came back and tore the collision mats. The water level started to rise. Illing and McLaughlin were sent down to remove the collision mats. They repacked the canvas and were able to reduce the inflow. They were also required to plug the storm valve outlets. With additional pumps being air-dropped by the Department of National Defence, and the transfer of fuel, the ship was brought under control and was readied for towing.

In a period of some 24 hours the youthful divers made numerous descents under most difficult, sometimes hazardous conditions. They had difficulty in staying under water because the breathing apparatus (regulators) were freezing and they had to surface frequently to thaw them out in boiling water before returning to complete repairs.

SUPER SEISMIC SHIP

The first entirely Canadian-designed and built seismic vessel was launched in

May 1983 at Tracy, Que. The ice-strengthened ship, built at a cost of $23-million, will gather geophysical data off Canada's coasts and do research in other parts of the world. The ship was commissioned for Petro-Canada.

FAITHFUL FERRY

The tender *Hiawatha*, the oldest active vessel in the world on the Lloyd's of London registry, was given a $150,000 refit in the spring of 1983.

The 100-passenger, 65-foot *Hiawatha* has been ferrying passengers from the Royal Canadian Yacht club at Toronto Island since 1895.

Built in Toronto, she was a steam-powered vessel until 1944 when her engines were converted to diesel.

WORLD'S FINEST CLIPPER SHIPS

Donald McKay, son of a Nova Scotia shipbuilder, moved to New York in 1827 at the age of 17. There he apprenticed and after 10 years became a master shipwright. His clipper ships were renowned for their speed and beauty. His ship the *Stag Hound* broke the sailing record from Boston to the Equator. He built other ships which were famous in their time, but his greatest achievement was the building of the *Great Republic*. Over 4,500 tons, she was then the world's largest ship.

WORLD'S FASTEST SAILING SHIP

The *Marco Polo* was built at Saint John, N.B. She began a voyage around the world in 1851, sailing from England to Melbourne then returning to England around Cape Horn. The trip each way took 76 days. They were record-breaking crossings, and the *Marco Polo* was renowned as the world's fastest ship.

COMING AND GOING FIRST

The RCMP patrol ship *St. Roch,* under the command of Henry Asbjorn Larsen, patrolled Canada's arctic waters for a number of years. From 1940 to 1944 she sailed through the Northwest Passage. She passed through first from west to east and then made the journey from east to west. She was the first ship to sail the passage both ways. The *St. Roch* under Larsen, also became the first vessel ever to circumnavigate the North American continent when, on a subsequent voyage, she passed through the Panama Canal.

FIRST ATLANTIC STEAMER

Built at Quebec City, the steamer *Royal William* sailed from Pictou, N.S., to London in 1833, thus becoming the first steamship to cross the Atlantic entirely under her own steampower.

She was sold to Spain where she was refitted as the warship *Isabella Secunda*. Under the flag of Spain, she was the first steampowered warship to fire guns.

PIRATES, BOOTY AND PRIZES

Back in 1612, Harbour Grace, Nfld., was declared a safe haven by Peter Easton, an ex-captain of the Royal Navy turned pirate and adventurer. His 40-ship fleet plundered ships and colonists.

He eventually moved to the warm waters of the Mediterranean, acquired a title and enjoyed the fruits of his labours — the first of many who have worked in Canada, then retired to warmer climes.

TAX DODGE DOOMED

The *Columbus*, built in Quebec and launched in 1824, was by far the largest ship of her day. She was 10 times larger than the next largest ship with a deck 301 feet long, a beam of 50½ feet and a depth of 30 feet.

She was the product of an enterprising profit scheme. She was built of squared logs, spiked and chained together, and the plan was to fill her 6,300-ton capacity with valuable cargo, sail her to England, sell her cargo and then break up the ship to sell the ship's timber, which could not be classified as cargo and would not be taxed.

Columbus sailed in 1824 and the voyage to London took seven weeks. Once there she created a sensation. Her cargo was sold, it is said, for a remarkable 50,000 pounds. Her owners became greedy, and against the advice of her owners sent her back to Canada laden with chalk. Her uncaulked timbers opened in heavy seas, the water mixed with the chalk and then clogged the ships pumps and she sank. (The crew was rescued.)

Another, larger ship was built in the same mode but she too met disaster, thus ending the disposable ship scheme.

The insurance companies are said to have paid out $5-million for the loss of the ships.

CPR SAFETY COMPETITION

There were 23.5 per cent fewer lost-time injuries at CP rail in 1982 than in 1981. The number of lost-time injuries was the lowest since the railway began keeping safety statistics in 1945.

The company gave out a total of $32,000 in prize money to winning employee groups in a safety competition.

1982 **Smiths Falls**: the 600 employees of the division won the System Divisional Safety Trophy and $4,000 for the best safety record. Smiths Falls won for the third consecutive year.
Ogden Shops: the main shop safety

trophy was won by Calgary's Ogden Shops for the second consecutive year.

ROADBED AT LOUISBURG

A roadbed dating back to the 1720s, which most likely supported rails for carts pulled by horses, extends from an old gypsum mine to the back of the Mira River at Louisburg on Cape Breton Island.

TRACK STARS

The Samson, now on display in New Glasgow, N.S., was the first locomotive in North America that burned coal and ran on all-iron rails. Built in England in 1838, the Samson probably arrived at Pictou, N.S., in the spring of 1839. The first six-coupled steam engine in British North America, the Samson was one of the largest and most powerful locomotive engines on the continent. She could move a load of 400 tons on level track and pull more than 33 one-ton cars up a steep hill. The Samson pulled coal in regular service for nearly 30 years. in 1903 she was taken, under the ownership of the Baltimore and Ohio Railroad, to the Chicago World Fair. One of a few survivors of the early steam era, the Samson still has most of her original parts.

The Champlain and St. Lawrence Railroad was Canada's first railway. It was designed as an overland link in the water route between Montreal and New York. It stretched between Laprairie on the St. Lawrence River and St. Johns on the Richelieu and replaced a difficult 16½-stage route between boat connections. The line went into operation in July of 1836. Because the line was not in proper ballast, Canada's first steam engine, Dorchester (affectionately known as the kitten), had a tendency to jump track, so horses hauled the passenger cars until the roadbed was completed. Capable of reaching a speed of 30 miles per hour, the little engine burned cordwood, and pulled a tender and open passenger cars.

The Champlain and St. Lawrence Railroad was eventually amalgamated with another railroad. The new company operated under the name of the Montreal and Champlain Railroad until it was absorbed by the Grand Trunk Railway of Canada, and eventually became part of the Canadian National Railway.

RAILWAY DREAMS REALIZED

The provinces of Canada in 1850 had one of the finest internal navigations systems in the world, with a system of canals and harbours that went from the St. Lawrence Gulf to Lake Huron, and which transported people and cargo by barge, sailing ship and steamship.

Railways promised more. Even though there were only 66 miles of operating railroad in British North America in 1850, people began to recognize their potential. Track could be laid almost anywhere. Trains could travel faster even than steamships and they could run in winter when the Canadian rivers and lakes were frozen. Thomas Keefer, a Canadian civil engineer of the day, said, "as a people we may as well attempt to live without books or newspapers, as without railroads ... they are now indispensable." Canadians realized that if they could build railroads, they would no longer be ruled by the topography of the land or the vagaries of the weather. Canada would only be built if railroads were built.

Francis Hincks, then inspector general in the Baldwin-Lafontain administration of 1848-51, steered through a bill which promised government assistance in the building of railroads, and the Canadian Railway boom began. Ten years later,

there were more than 2,000 miles of track in Canada and when the boom ended in about 1920 Canada had more miles of track per capita than any other country.

INSPIRATION OF A NATIONAL IDEA

"What tempted the people of Canada to undertake so gigantic a work as the Canadian Pacific Railway? The difficulties in the way were great, unprecedented, unknown.

"Had they been known beforehand, the task would not have been attempted. We were under the inspiration of a national idea, and went forward.

"We were determined to be something more than a fortuitous collection of provinces.

"That the difficulties were faced and overcome as they emerged, great temptations to halt or retreat being quietly set aside, proves that we, like our neighbours and progenitors, are not easily discouraged.

"Our ultimate destiny will be none the worse because we gave — not unwillingly — and made sacrifices, in order to make ourselves a nation."

Van Horne, *The Century* 1885

SHARP BUILDS SLEEPER

Sam Sharp built the world's first rail sleeping car in 1857, eight years before the American Pullman car began service. Sharp built his car in the shops of the Great Western Railway at Hamilton, Ont.

IF YOU WANT ME ... JUST WHISTLE

Robert E. Swanson, president of Robert E. Swanson & Associates, Vancouver,

British Columbia, has in both his public and private careers made many outstanding contributions to transportation development in Canada.

During 24 years of service with the British Columbia Department of Transport, he held the positions of chief inspector of railways and later chief engineer of transport. He also was largely responsible for the concept of the port at Roberts Bank and the unique role railway access contributed to its development.

Concurrently, privately, his research into whistles and airhorns produced patents of unique quality, which are heard everywhere today, including the diesel train whistle and the "O Canada" train whistle. He has become known as an expert on railway crossing whistles and is consulted at the international level.

CAA LIFESAVING MEDAL

Canadian Automobile Association

Presented annually by the Governor-General to School Safety Patrollers who, while on duty, saved the life of a person in imminent danger.

1983   Cindy Williams, Calgary, Alta.

MAKING TRACKS

Road building began in earnest after the War of 1812 as the population of British North America grew rapidly. All provinces except Newfoundland had systems of trunk roads by 1850. In 1841 Upper Canada claimed 6,000 miles of post roads. The roads were at their best in the winter time when they hard-packed with snow and ice. The rains of spring and fall made most roads impassable and in summer they were dusty and the natural terrain was exposed. Early roads were frequently made by laying logs side by side across the cleared path, thus called corduroy roads.

Regular coach service on main roads existed throughout all the provinces with inns along the way to provide relay horses as well as food and accommodation for travellers.

By 1850 roads began to be graded and surfaced with smooth board, gravel or a macadamized hardtop.

NATIONAL DRIVER OF THE YEAR

Canadian Trucking Association and Mack Truck in Canada

The award is based on the candidate's safety record, long term service and good character. Seven provincial candidates are selected. Each is provincial Driver of the Year and one is selected national Driver.

1982   National Driver of the Year
John Fotty, Manitoba, travelled 2 million miles
Provincial Drivers of the Year
British Columbia: Dennis Roy Kohn, more than 3 million miles
Alberta: Wilhelm (Willy) A. Maier, more than 2,089,000 miles
Saskatchewan: Ostop Slobodian, 3 million miles
Manitoba: Henry J. Demontigny, 3 million miles
Ontario: Russell Moulton, 3 million miles
Quebec: Alexander J. Barton, 2.5 million miles
Maritimes: John S. Strange, more than 3 million miles

HERO OF THE YEAR

Firestone Tire of Canada

Given to a professional truck driver who performs above and beyond the call of duty. The 1982 winner received a certificate, $1,000 cash, an inscribed wristwatch and an all-expenses-paid weekend at the King Edward Hotel in Toronto, and was guest of honour at the Ontario Truck Driver's convention.

1982   **Terry Kennedy**, Barrie, Ont.

TOP DRIVER

Richard G. Johnson, 57, of North Delta, B.C., on May 5 of 1980 completed 30 years of service as a bus driver for Greyhound Lines of Canada Limited, with a perfect safety record — 1.6 million miles without a traffic accident. That would equal some 330 trips over the Trans-Canada Highway from Victoria, B.C. to St. John's, Newfoundland. His private driving record is also unblemished — another half million miles since he cranked up his first Model T in his native Alberta.

Most of his commercial driving since he started with Greyhound has been over the mountainous route from Vancouver to Cache Creek. Then, much of what is now the Trans-Canada was a rutted road through the bush, so narrow, he recalls, that there were places a car and a bus couldn't get past each other — one would have to back up to a pull-off area.

TIME MAGAZINE QUALITY DEALER AWARD

Federation of Automobile Dealer Associations of Canada

The award recognizes a businessman who has served his community through his business, or through civic politics or educational activities.

1982   **Marcel Castonguay**, Rimousky, Que.

MAN OF THE YEAR

National Transportation Week

For contributions in development and improvement of the highway transportation industry.

1982   **Douglas I. Hindmarsh**, vice-president, Reimer Express Lines Ltd., Winnipeg, Man.

FIRST ROAD

Canada's first road was opened in 1734 between Quebec and Montreal.

AWARD OF MERIT

National Transportation Week

1982   **Stanislas Dery,** QC, Sillery, Que., coroner
Since his appointment in June 1976 as coroner for all judicial districts of the Province of Quebec, Coroner Dery has in his findings taken every opportunity to make recommendations that have prompted the adoption of corrective measures. He has promoted and encouraged safety awareness through all levels of government and in the private sector.

AWARD OF VALOUR

National Transportation Week

The awards are presented for exemplary acts of bravery in perilous circumstances.

1982   **Gordon Rasmussen**, Calgary, Alta.
Three young Nova Scotia men owe their lives to Gordon Rasmussen of Calgary, who was quick to act last July when he saw a rubber raft capsize and dump four people into the turbulent Bow River. One man was sucked into the Livingston fish hatchery weir and his body was not recovered for a month.
Rasmussen, 49, a driver for Federal Neon Ltd. and Universal Installation and Crane Rental, was driving his truck on Deerfoot Trail with two co-

workers when he spotted the rafting accident in his rear-view mirror.

Rasmussen, a non-swimmer, plunged into the swirling current without hesitation and with some assistance pulled three men out. One was unconscious. Rasmussen revived him.

He was also winner of the 1982 Firestone National Truck Hero Award.

AWARD OF VALOUR

National Transportation Week

Steven J. Panteluk of Winnipeg, disregarding his own safety, rushed to help the occupants of a passenger car that had burst into flames after crashing at high speed into his trailer.

RCMP Staff Sergeant D.R. Belfry, who nominated Panteluk for a truck hero award, noted that he risked his life in the rescue effort.

He also operates a 300-acre grain farm.

TORONTO FIRSTS

J.J. Wright developed the first electric street car in 1883. It operated at what is now the Canadian National Exhibition and carried passengers about a third of a mile.

Toronto's Transit Commission was the first major North American transit authority to introduce the electric trolley bus in the 1960s.

CANADIAN NATIONAL RODEO CHAMPION

Canadian Urban Transit Association

Twenty-two of the best bus drivers in Canada competed for the National Bus Rodeo Championship. To qualify for the finals each driver had to win a rodeo in his own municipality.

1982 Champion
George Youngson, Mississauga, Ont.,

received 794 points out of a possible 840. A driver with Mississauga Transit, he has a seven-year safe driving record as a bus driver.

1st runner-up
Bob Durrant, Toronto, Ont., has a 10-year safe driving record with the TTC. Durrant is an Olympic Silver Medalist in shooting.

2nd runner-up
Mike Pawlik, Edmonton, Alta.

PERFECTED SNOWMOBILE

Mechanical snow vehicles have been produced by a number of Canadians since the early 1900s, but J. Armand Bombardier of Valcourt, Que., produced a vehicle in 1922 which put him in the forefront of the snowmobile business.

His company produces the Ski-Doo and designs and builds urban transit systems for major cities throughout the world.

The all-terrain vehicle with the low-pressure balloon tires was invented by Manitoban John Gower.

MAD FOR MOTOR BIKES

A total of 106,136 motorcycles were sold in Canada in 1982. It was the third year in a row in which sales exceeded 100,000. Street motorcycles accounted for 61.1 per cent of sales, up from 54.9 per cent of sales in 1981.

JAUNTY ALOUETTE

Alouette 1, Canada's first satellite, went into orbit in 1969. Canada was the fourth country in the world, after the USA, the USSR and Japan, to put a satellite into orbit.

The satellite, designed and built by the Canadian Defence Research Telecommunications Establishment, became

the first in a network of communications satellites that link Canada.

Canada has never had a failure in the satellite program and our country has become a world leader in telecommunications technology.

TELIDON TOPS

Telidon, the videotex technology that has established itself as a world beater, was invented by a Canadian, Herb Bown, in the Communications Research Centre at Shirley Bay (near Ottawa).

Videotex systems use ordinary television sets to display text and graphic information on demand at home, in offices, and in classrooms. Because it uses low-cost receivers, it is hailed as the "everyman's" computer information network.

The original videotex technology was invented in Britain, and France subsequently developed an improved version, but the Canadian technology, Telidon, represents a substantial leap forward with its high definition graphics and economical transmission costs.

In major cities across North America, newspapers, banks, retailers, cable television systems and a host of other information providers are implementing videotex services, a harbinger of the information revolution.

Source: Peter Bowers

LIGHT OF NORTHERN TELECOM

The number two telecommunications company in North America is Canada's Northern Telecom. The company goes head to head in the U.S. with the other telecommunications giants. The company employs 34,500 people in 50 manufacturing centres throughout the world and has 32 facilities in Canada which employ 10,000 people.

Company chairman and former president Walter Light is credited with leading the company into its strong position. In 1973, the year before he was named president, the firm's revenues were $608-million. Last year they were $3-billion and projections for 1985 are $5-billion.

The company was the first in the world to develop a full family of digital multiplex systems known as telephone switches and has invested more than $500-million in research and development for digital products.

The company is also working to develop an effective marriage of the telephone and computer. Its Displayphone was the first of its kind on the market in 1981 and a new model is soon to be marketed.

THE DEFINITIVE WORD

Is the telephone an American or Canadian invention? Both countries claim the inventor, Alexander Graham Bell, as their own.

In a speech to the Empire Club of Canada in 1917, Bell himself answered the question. He explained that the telephone was devised in Brantford (Ont.), but wasn't made until 1875, when it appeared in Boston. The following year, Bell made the world's first long-distance call, in 1876, between Brantford and Paris, Ont., using Hamlet's famous line, "To be, or not to be."

An eclectic scientific genius, he established the Aerial Experiment Association at Baddeck, N.S., in 1907. A member of the group, J.A.D. McCurdy, made the first flight in the British Empire in 1909 with his airplane the *Silver Dart*.

Bell continued to experiment with planes and hydrofoils at his home in Baddeck. He was buried there in 1922.

WIRING THE WORLD TOGETHER

During the years 1851 to 1871, the Montreal Telegraph Company extended its lines from 500 miles to some 20,000 miles, giving it the longest telegraph lines in the country at the time.

The first wires in the country were strung between Toronto, Hamilton, St. Catharines, and Niagara Falls in the year 1847. In the same year a line joined Montreal and Quebec.

The cable ship *Great Eastern*, sailing from Ventura, Ireland, laid cable across the Atlantic floor in two weeks. She docked at Heart's Content, Nfld., on July 27, 1866, and permanent intercontinental communication was initiated.

ADVANCING AVIATION

Air Vice-marshal A. Earl Godfrey, a noted Canadian airman, was the first flyer to pilot a seaplane from Montreal to Vancouver. He made the flight in 1926 in a Douglas MO-2VS and the flight took nine days, including 34 hours and 41 minutes of actual flying time.

In World War I, Godfrey shot down 17 enemy planes and received the Air Force Cross and the Military Cross.

Godfrey was awarded the McKee Trans-Canada Trophy for substantial contribution to the advancement of Canadian aviation in 1976.

TRANS-CANADA (McKEE) TROPHY

Canadian Aeronautics Space Institute

The Trans-Canada Trophy, generally known as the McKee Trophy, is awarded annually for outstanding achievement in the field of air operations. The trophy is the oldest aviation award in Canada, having been established in 1927 by Captain J. Dalzell McKee, whose historic seaplane flight across Canada in company with (then) S/L A.E. Godfrey was accomplished in 1926.

1982   E.N. Ronaasen (posthumously).

Ronaasen was cited for his unstinted dedication to engineering flight test and evaluation in both military and civil aviation. He was involved in performance testing, handling, stores clearance and weapons ballistics tests, acceptance and maintenance flight testing. Ronaasen retired from the Canadian forces in 1974 and was appointed director of flight operations, Trident Aircraft of Vancouver, where he was responsible for the type certification flight testing of the Trigull Amphibian. In 1977 he moved to Canadair Ltd., Montreal, to prepare for the experimental testing of the company's new Challenger business net. In November 1978, he flew in the right hand seat, Mr. D. Adkins in the left, on challenger 1001's maiden flight, and later, in December, they took the aircraft to Mojave. Ronaasen did most of the experimental flight testing of Challengers 1001 and 1002 at Mojave and it was on one of these flights, in 1980, that he gave his life.

SPAR AEROSPACE WINS CONTRACT

Canada's Spar Aerospace, the firm that built the arm for the U.S. space shuttle, has won a $65-million contract to help build a European communications satellite described as one of the most powerful to date.

Spar will build solar-energy panels for a 164-foot-long satellite being built by three members of the European Space Agency for a 1986 launch.

The contract will create 1,200 person-years of work at Spar plants. Spar won out over competitors from West Germany and France.

McCURDY AWARD

Canadian Aeronautics and Space Institute

The McCurdy Award is presented annually for outstanding achievement in the art, science and engineering relating to aeronautics and space. The award was introduced in 1954 by the Institute of Aircraft Technicians, one of the aeronautical groups that amalgamated in that year to found the Canadian Aeronautical Institute (now the CASI).

Air Commodore the Honourable J.A.D. McCurdy, who is commemorated by this award, was one of the first persons to be made an Honorary Fellow of the Institute. He made the first powered flight in Canada, and indeed in the British Empire, in February 1909, when he flew the *Silver Dart* on the ice at Baddeck, N.S. His long and distinguished career was devoted mainly to aviation. A high point was reached in 1947 when he was appointed Lieutenant-Governor of Nova Scotia.

> **J.P. Uffen** for his outstanding contribution to the advancement of the aerospace sciences in Canada. A fellow of the institute, Uffen served with distinction as a radar officer in the RCN during the Second World War and later in the structures laboratory of NRC. He has been with De Havilland Canada for some 30 years and has participated in many government and industry committees, and has been chairman of the Air Industries Association of Canada's Technical Committee and involved in the MOT committee on airworthiness.

F.W. (CASEY) BALDWIN AWARD

Canadian Aeronautics and Space Institute

The F.W. (Casey) Baldwin Award is presented annually for the best paper published in the Canadian Aeronautics and Space Journal during the preceding calendar year. The selection is based on originality of material, the significance in its field, and writing skill.

Baldwin was the first Canadian (and the first British subject) to fly a heavier-than-air machine, which he did in 1908 in the USA. He had an impressive career in development of hydrofoils and devices used in naval and aerial warfare, eventually entering politics in Nova Scotia in 1933.

> **1982** **W. Wiebe** and **R.V. Dainty** for their paper "Fractographic Determination of Fatigue Crack Growth Rates in Aircraft Components."

WOMAN WINS WINGS

Alys Bryant piloted an aircraft in Vancouver in 1913 and became the first woman to fly a plane in Canada.

C.D. HOWE AWARD

Canadian Aeronautics and Space Institute

The C.D. Howe Award is presented annually for achievement in the fields of planning, policy making and overall leadership in Canadian aeronautics and space activities.

Early in his career, the Right Hon. C.D. Howe became an eminent civil engineer. He entered politics in 1935 and was made the first Minister of Transport and set up Trans-Canada Airlines. He continued as a cabinet minister for more than 20 years, facing tasks which included guiding munitions and supply during World War II, reconstruction later, and defence production in the early 1950s.

> **1982** **L.D. Clarke**, chairman of the Board and Chief Executive officer of Spar Aerospace Limited. Clarke has been a force in Canada's aerospace activities for more than 30 years, both in government and industry. He had the foresight and acumen to arrange the purchase of the special products and applied research division of de Havilland Aircraft of Canada Limited in late 1967 and has developed that

company — Spar Aerospace Limited — into one of Canada's largest Canadian-owned aerospace companies, with sales of some $130-million, and employment of 2,000 in 10 locations.

DE HAVILLAND DEVELOPS MODERN FIGHTER

Twenty years of research at de Havilland Aircraft of Canada Ltd., of Toronto, is paying off. A de Havilland concept is the basis of the design for General Dynamic Corp. for a new supersonic fighter, the E-7, that is being evaluated in the US as a 1990s generation fighter. Another application of the research may be a de Havilland production model prototype of the Buffalo military transport.

W. RUPERT TURNBULL LECTURE

Canadian Aeronautics and Space Institute

W. Rupert Turnbull was born in St. John, N.B., in 1870. After his early training as an electrical engineer and with a consulting practice, he began active research in aerodynamics. In a building known as Anderson's Barn he built the first wind tunnel in Canada in 1902 and during the next few years he did some basic scientific work on the behaviour of aerofoils and the efficiency of aircraft design. In 1908 he presented a paper entitled The Efficiency of Aeroplanes, Propellers, Motors, etc., for which he received the Bronze Medal of the Aeronautical Society of Great Britain.

During the First World War he worked in England, where he developed his ideas on variable pitch and built a 28-inch-diameter model of a variable pitch propeller. An improved version was designed and built in 1925 and eventually flown by the RCAF at Camp Borden in 1927. It was the world's first successful variable pitch propeller.

The W. Rupert Turnbull Lecture is delivered annually at a major meeting of the Institute. The lecturer is selected for his association with some significant achievement in the scientific or engineering fields of aeronautics or space research, and for his qualifications to present a paper related to it.

1982   Dr. John S. MacDonald
MacDonald works in the areas of advanced digital systems engineering, remote sensing, and image processing. He is an advisor to the federal government on data handling and satellite technology, and with the Communications Research Advisory board. He serves as a member of the Science Council of Canada, board of trustees of the Discovery Foundation, board of management of B.C. Research, and board of directors of Discovery Parks, and board of directors of Canadian Advanced Technology Association. He is a registered professional engineer, a senior member of the Institute of Electrical and Electronic Engineers, a member of the Canadian Information Processing Society, and an associate fellow of the Canadian Aeronautics and Space Institute.
The title of his lecture was "Advance in Remote Sensing by Satellite."

EXPANDING SERVICES

Air Canada is the first airline in North America to introduce a new wheelchair for disabled passengers. The newly developed chair will allow disabled passengers to move from airport arrival to aircraft seat with greater ease and without changing chairs.

AWARD OF VALOUR

National Transportation Week

HMCS *Fraser* was nearing the end of a five-month tour of duty with the NATO fleet on November 28, 1980, when, during a gale in the English Channel, a distress signal was received from the British fishing vessel *St. Irene*. The ship with 15 crewmen aboard was in imminent danger of sinking.

The commander of the force proceeded to the scene and soon asked for the assistance of HMCS *Fraser's* helicopter. Other helicopters in the NATO fleet could not get airborne because of the howling gale.

The *Fraser's* aircraft was launched with some difficulty by **Captain David J. McCoubrey**, 37, of Winfield, British Columbia, crew commander. Lieutenant (now Captain) **J.J.G.D. Guertin**, 27, of Ste. Rosalie, Que., co-pilot; **Lieutenant S.A. Lawrie**, 26, of Toronto, navigator; and **Sergeant E.R. Schelenz**, 35.

Arriving at the scene they found the fishing vessel listing at 30 degrees and surrounded by ships that had answered her call but were unable to get close in the mountainous seas.

The Canadian rescuers hovered dangerously close to the stricken ship and threw weighted guidelines to the heaving deck. In two trips they removed 12 men to the *Fraser*; boats saved the other three.

NORSEMAN HELPS TAME BUSH

The Norseman, designed and built by Robert Noorduyn in Montreal in 1935, was the world's first true bush aircraft. The Otter and Beaver, designed and built by de Havilland, also became world-famous work planes.

DESIGNERS' SALES SOARING

Dale Kramer of Welland, Ont., and Christophe Heintz of Nobleton, Ont., are two Canadian aircraft designers who are at the forefront of a revolution in aircraft types.

Kramer's Lazair was selected as the most outstanding ultra-light design in North America in 1981 and his company has sold about 750 kits in Canada and the U.S. at about $5,000 each. An ultra-light aircraft does not need to be certified and its pilot is not required to have a pilot's licence.

Heintz has sold about 400 kits of his Zenair TR1-2 at an average of $10,000 each. The Zenair is a home-built aircraft which must conform to engineering criteria and its pilot is required to be licensed. Because it is home built it costs about half the price of a comparable factory-built model. The Zenair has set a number of records for speed and efficiency. The Zenair takes between 600 and 800 hours to be constructed, compared with up to 5,000 hours for some home-built designs.

AWARD OF VALOUR

National Transportation Week

William Bright, 26, **Robert Devey**, 32, and **Joseph Tymchen**, 35, station attendants at the Winnipeg International Airport, at great personal risk saved an Air Canada DC-9 from destruction when fire broke out during refueling operations on the morning of July 15,1979. Forty-seven passengers were safely evacuated.

CROSSING THE ROCKIES

Captain Ernest C. Hoy, who served with the Royal Flying Corps in World War I, flew a Curtis JN4 named Jenny from Richmond, B.C., to Calgary on Aug. 7, 1919, and thus became the first man to fly over the Rockies. Since the aircraft could only climb to 2,134 metres, he had to fly around mountains and through passes criss-crossed with treacherous air currents.

Sheldon Luck made the first night crossing of the range. He and his mechanic Ron Campbell decided to head back to Calgary after flying a charter to Williams Lake, B.C., one day in 1935. Their battery was dead so they were without navigation or instrument panel lights. Campbell lit matches so that the pilot Luck could read the de Havilland Puss Moth's compass.

Luck had an aviation career that spanned almost half a century. He pioneered a north western mail run with Grant McConachie, later president of CP Air. He was a wartime courier pilot for Winston Churchill during the Quebec Conference. He flew more than 57 different types of aircraft from the high Arctic to South America and Africa.

AWARD OF HONOUR

Canadian Air Traffic Control Association

1983 R.D. Scott, Al Collins
On July 21, 1981, a pilot declared an emergency with Ottawa Terminal Control Unit. The pilot reported that his altimeter had just failed and that he was unable to maintain visual contact with the ground. At this point, the Ottawa weather was a ceiling of 400 feet with visibility of one mile. Scott was the terminal controller who responded to the distress call and over the next one hour and two min-

utes worked in close co-ordination with Warrant Officer Collins of the military Precision Approach Radar unit based at Uplands. Using his expertise as a controller, knowledge as a private pilot, and altitude information supplied by Warrant Officer Collins, Scott vectored the aircraft to the final approach course. From that point Warrant Officer Collins assumed control guiding the aircraft to a successful landing.

LUMBERING AIRSHIPS

A project with Canadian participation is underway to develop airships to haul timber out of Canadian forests. The non-rigid dirigible Cyclo-Crane is expected to remove timber efficiently from areas that would be otherwise inaccessible except by helicopter.

The Canadian-built Skyship 500, 164 feet long, 65 feet high, with 10 seats, was flown in April 1983 at Toronto. Its potential includes patrol and rescue missions and cargo transport work.

Its balloon is made of a polyester fabric. It is filled with helium, a fire-extinguishing gas.

The first reported Canadian balloon ascent was made by C.H. Grimley at Ottawa to celebrate the 10th anniversary of Confederation.

Helen Mussallem, winner of the Florence Nightingale Medal

Sciences

HEALTH

THE GAIRDNER FOUNDATION: A WINNING RECORD

The Gairdner Foundation, established in 1957, had by November 1982 presented awards to 154 individuals worldwide. Twenty-four Gairdner Winners have also been Nobel Prize Winners and 23 of the 24 received their Gairdner prizes before they received the Nobel Prize.

The Gairdner review panel and the medical advisory board have proved they can pick winners with the best.

James Arthur Gairdner of Toronto was a successful investor, but at one time had aspirations of becoming a surgeon. His interest in medicine resulted in the establishment of the Foundation and since his death in 1971, the Gairdner family has continued to support the awards.

Former Gairdner Award Winners who have won the Nobel Prize

	Gairdner Award	Nobel
Julius Axelrod, USA	1967	1970
David Baltimore, USA	1974	1975
Paul Berg, USA	1980	1980
Karl S.D. Bergström, Sweden	1972	1982
Baruch S. Blumberg, U.S.A	1975	1976
Francis H.C. Crick, England	1962	1962
Jean Dausset, France	1977	1980
Christian DeDuve, USA	1967	1974
Walter Gilbert, USA	1979	1980
Roger Guillemin, USA	1974	1977
Godfrey N. Hounsfield, England	1976	1979
Charles B. Huggins, USA	1966	1966
H. Gobind Khorana, USA	1980	1968
Luis F. Leloir, Argentina	1966	1970
Marshall W. Nirenberg, USA	1967	1968
George E. Palade, USA	1967	1974
Rodney R. Porter, England	1966	1972
Bengt Samuelsson, Sweden	1981	1982
Frederick Sanger, England	1971	1958
	1979	1980
Andrew V. Schally, USA	1974	1977
George D. Snell, USA	1976	1980
Earl W. Sutherland, USA	1969	1971
Howard M. Temin, USA	1974	1975
Rosalyn S. Yalow, USA	1971	1977

The Gairdner Foundation awards are among the world's most prestigious medical awards. They are presented to draw public, professional and scientific attention to significant achievements in the medical field, as well as improve communication among scientists.

The awards are not grants for the support of future research; their purpose is to recognize achievement and winners are free to make personal use of their awards any way they choose. Winners are invited to present papers on their work at the Gairdner Foundation Lectures in Toronto.

GAIRDNER FOUNDATION INTERNATIONAL AWARD OF MERIT

The award of $25,000 can be given to an individual or group.

1959 **Alfred Blalock**, MD, ScM, LLD. **Helen B. Taussig**, MD, DSc, LLD. Baltimore, Md., USA. For developing an operation for congenital heart lesions, which introduced a new era in cardiac surgery.

1962 **Francis H.C. Crick**, PhD, FRS, Cambridge, England. For his work in molecular biology and genetics.

1963 **Murray L. Barr**, MD, FRS (C), London, Ont. For his work in microanatomy and human cytogenetics.

1964 **Seymour Benzer**, BA, MS, PhD, Lafayette, Ind., USA. For his work in genetics and molecular biology.

1966 **R.R. Porter**, PhD, FRS, London, England. For his achievements in immunochemistry.

1968 **Bruce Chown**, SMMC, BS, MD, DSc, Winnipeg, Man. For his research of human blood groups.

1976 **Godfrey N. Hounsfield**, FRS, MD, DSc, CBE, Middlesex, England. For the pioneer development of computerized tomography.

WIGHTMAN AWARD

The Gairdner Foundation

An award of $25,000 is occasionally given to a Canadian for leadership in medicine and medical science.

1976 **Keith J.R. Wightman**, MD, FRCP (C), FACP, FRCP, MC, FPC, DSc, LLD, Toronto, Ont., for his contributions as an educator, physician and leader of his profession.

1979 **Claude Fortier**, CC, MD, PhD, LLD, FRCP (C), FRSC, Quebec, Que., for his contributions as a scientist, teacher and scientific advisor to governments.

1981 **Louis Siminovitch**, PhD, FRSC, FRS, OC, Toronto, Ont., for his contributions as a geneticist, advisor to government in the area of science policy,

and as a leader in the Canadian academic community.

GAIRDNER FOUNDATION INTERNATIONAL ANNUAL AWARDS

The awards amount to $15,000 each, or $7,500 each for a joint award to two persons.

1982 **Gilbert Ashwell**, MD, Bethesda, Md., USA, for his research into the mechanisms by which carbohydrate markers regulate the recognition and uptake of proteins by cells.

Gunter Blobel, MD, PhD, New York, N.Y., USA, for his research into the ways newly synthesized proteins are transported within cells.

Arvid Carlsson, MD, PhD, Göteborg, Sweden, for his work on amines, particularly dopamine, as neurotransmitters.

Paul Janssen, MD, Beerse, Belgium, for his invention of haloperidol and related drugs useful in the treatment of mental illness.

Manfred M. Mayer, PhD, Baltimore, Md., USA, for his research on the function of complement. (Relates to blood protein.)

CANADIAN WINNERS OF GAIRDNER FOUNDATION INTERNATIONAL AWARDS

1959 **W.G. Bigelow**, MD, MS, FRCS (C), Toronto, Ont., for his work in cardiology and especially for developing the hypothermia method of open heart surgery.

1961 **Alan C. Burton**, MD, London, Ont., for his work in cardiovascular physiology.

1963 **Jacques Genest**, MD, FRCP (C), Montreal, Que., for his research in vascular physiology, and in particular for his studies of the mechanism of hypertension.

1964 **Gordon D.W. Murray**, MD, FRCS (C), FRCS (England), Toronto, Ont., for his contributions in the field of cardiac physiology and pathology, and the development of several important techniques in cardiac surgery.

1965 **Charles P. Leblond**, MD, PhD, DSc, Montreal, Que., for his research in cellular biology.

1967 **D. Harold Copp**, MD, PhD, FRSC, Vancouver, B.C.
Iain MacIntyre, MB, PhD, MCPath., London, England, for their work on the problems of calcium homeostasis.
Peter J. Moloney, OBC, PhD, FRSC, Toronto, Ont., for his contributions to immunology and diabetes.
J. Fraser Mustard, MD, PhD (Cantab.) FRCP (C), Hamilton, Ont., for his work on thrombosis and athero-sclerosis.

1968 **Robert B. Salter**, MDMS, FRCS (C), FACS, Toronto, Ont., for his research on cartilage degeneration, epiphyseal necrosis, torsional deformation of bone and dysplasia of joints in relation to numerous musculoskeletal disorders, especially congenital dislocation of the hip.
E.A. McCulloch, MD, FRCP (C), Toronto, Ont.
J.E. Till, BA, MA, PhD, Toronto, Ont., in recognition of their development of the spleen colony technique for measuring the capacity of primitive normal and neoplastic cells to multiply and differentiate in the body.

1971 **Charles H. Best,** CH, CBE, CC, MD, DSc, FRS, Toronto, Ont., in recognition of his part in the discovery and development of insulin.

1972 **Oleh Hornykiewicz**, MD, Toronto, Ont., for his elucidation of the biochemical lesion in Parkinson's disease, and his other contributions to our knowledge of the physiology of the brain.

1973 **Harold E. Johns**, BSc, MSc, PhD, LLD, FRS, FRS (C), Toronto, Ont., for his pioneer work in the development of cobalt and high energy radiotherapy and for his many contributions to education and research in the fields of clinical physics and biophysics.

1974 **Judah H. Quastel**, CC, PhD, DSc, FRSC, FRS, Vancouver, B.C., in recognition of his contributions in biochemical research.

1975 **John D. Keith**, MDD, FRCP (C), FACC, Toronto, Ont., in recognition of his contributions to our understanding of congenital heart disease.
William T. Mustard, MBE, MD, MS, FRCS (C), FACS, FACC, Toronto, Ont., in recognition of his contributions to cardiovascular surgery.

1977 **Henry G. Friesen**, MD, FRCP (C), Winnipeg, Man., for his contributions to the understanding of the biochemistry physiology and pathophysiology of lactogenic hormones, and in particular for the identification of human prolactin.

1978 **Samuel O. Freedman**, BSc, MDCM, FRCP (C), FACP, FRSC, Montreal, Que.
Phil Gold, BSc, MSc, MDCM, PhD, FRCP (C), FRSC, OC, Montreal, Que., in recognition of their discovery of carcinoembryonic antigen and for studies which elucidated its biological and clinical significance.

1971 **Charles R. Scriver**, MDCM, FRSC, FRCP (C), FCCMG, Montreal, Que., for his research into genetic disease and, in particular, the detection of genetically determined disease in large population groups, and the development of treatment programs for these disorders.

1980 **Irving B. Fritz**, PhD, Toronto, Ont., for his discovery of the role of carnitine in the regulation of fatty acid metabolism.

1981 **Jerry H-C. Wang**, PhD, Winnipeg, Man.
Wai Yiu Cheung, PhD, Memphis, Tenn., USA, for their discovery of calmodulin.

MEDICAL FIRSTS

Canada's first hospital was a "sick bay" or garrison hospital at Port Royal in Acadia, established sometime between 1606-1613. It was staffed by one or two male attendants, probably from the charitable Order of Saint Jean de Dieu.

L'Hotel-Dieu in Quebec was established in August 1639 and was staffed by

the Nursing Sisters from Dieppe, who provided treatment and care to male and female, French or Indian.

McLAUGHLIN MEDAL

Royal Society of Canada

The McLaughlin Medal was established to honour R. Samuel McLaughlin, the great motor car magnate. The Medal and $1,000 is awarded for research in any branch of medical science.

1981 **Dr. Charles R. Scriver**, FRSC, McGill University, Montreal, Que.
He determined that certain human mutations result in the abnormal transport of specific amino acids, and he determined how the amino acids are transported in the kidney and intestinally. He discovered a dozen diseases, and contributed important knowledge to almost every other disorder of amino acid metabolism or transport in man. In genetics he defined the basic defect in a human disorder of phosphate transport, improved its treatment, and is now examining the molecular basis of phosphate transport in mammals.

1982 **Dr. Charles P. Leblond**, FRSC, McGill University, Montreal, Que.
In recognition of his pioneer work in radio-autography, a technique that permits the accurate localization of radioactive elements within cells, tissue and organs. His work converted the science of histology from a descriptive to a dynamic discipline.
Since joining McGill University in 1941 he has written more than 300 articles, trained 102 graduate students, held executive positions in numerous learned societies and been internationally honoured for his work.

SIR WILLIAM OSLER: A LEADER IN MEDICINE

Often called the "father of modern medicine," Osler, the son of an Ontario clergyman was born in a little village north of Toronto in 1849.

He studied at Toronto's School of Medicine, became professor of medicine at McGill and was later one of the four men who made Johns Hopkins Hospital in Baltimore the leading medical teaching centre in North America.

He later became Regius Professor of Medicine at Oxford and his text became the Bible of medicine, translated into French, Spanish, German and Chinese.

Sir William Osler's Bedside Library for Medical Students

"A liberal education may be had at a very slight cost of time and money ... Before going to sleep read for half an hour, and in the morning have a book open on your dressing table.
   I   Old and New Testament
  II   Shakespeare
 III   Montaigne
 IV   Plutarch's Lives
  V   Marcus Aurelius
 VI   Epictetus
VII   Religio Medici
VIII   Don Quixote
 IX   Emerson
  X   Oliver Wendell Holmes — Breakfast-Table Series"

(From Aequanimitas, Sir William Osler, McGraw-Hill)

CANADIAN LIFE AND HEALTH INSURANCE MEDICAL SCHOLARSHIPS

Canadian Life and Health Insurance Association

Two scholarships are given in clinical and epidemiological medical research and teaching, including research in health services, administration and medical care.

Each scholarship is for $75,000 over a three-year period.

1982 **Penny Jennett**, University of Saskatchewan, to research the effectiveness of continuing education in the fields of cardiovascular and cancer medicine. **Dr. Jeffrey E. Kudlow**, University of Toronto, to work in the field of cell biology.

1983 **Dr. Paul Cooper**, the University of Western Ontario, to work on degenerative brain diseases, such as premature senility (Alzheimer's disease) and Parkinson's disease. **Dr. David Cold**, Dalhousie University, is trailblazing in the field of sulphate metabolism, and what happens when sulphates from acid rain enter the food chain.

LONDON, ONT., MAN FIRST TO RECEIVE MIRACLE ARM

Larry Paterson of London, Ont., is the first Canadian to wear a new $30,000 myoelectric artificial arm. It approximates the feel of a natural arm by using small-skin electrodes that magnify electrical signals emitted by an amputee's arm muscles. Paterson lost his arm above the elbow in a factory accident.

CMA MEDAL OF HONOUR

Canadian Medical Association

The Medal of Honour is given to individuals who are not members of the medical profession, but who have contributed to medical research, medical education, health care organization and health education.

1982 **Esther Robins**, Calgary, Alta.
An exemplary model of the thousands of nonmedical volunteers who make a major contribution to health care in Canada.

Robins, an RN and the mother of four daughters, was diagnosed in 1976 as having stage III lymphatic lymphoma. Since that time she has had recurrences of the disease which required chemotherapy.

A founder of Canadian CanSurmount, a Cancer Society patient-support program, she has trained 300 CanSurmount visitors, visited and supported an equal number of cancer patients, and initiated and trained the leadership for programs in five Canadian provinces since 1978. In three years, well over 2,000 cancer patients have been supported through the program.

CMA MEDAL OF SERVICE

1982 **Dr. Robert Orville Jones**, Halifax, N. S.
A psychiatrist of international reputation, Jones established and chaired the department of psychiatry at Dalhousie University for 26 years. He is currently professor emeritus of the department.

He received the Canadian Centennial Medal in 1967 and the Queen's Jubilee Medal in 1977. He was installed as an Officer in the Order of Canada in 1981. He is an honorary fellow of the British Royal College of Psychiatry, and is charter president of the Canadian Psychiatric Association, charter fellow of the American College of Psychiatrists and life fellow of the American Psychiatric Association. He is the only psychiatrist who has held the office of president of the Canadian Medical Association and has held office in Nova Scotia medical and psychiatric associations.

LA MEDAILLE FREDERIC NEWTON GISBORNE STARR

Canadian Medical Association

The highest distinction given by the CMA is for the improvement of medical service in Canada and abroad.

1982 **Dr. Jacques Genest**, Montreal, Que.
Genest is known for his clinical research, especially in Quebec, where

he was responsible for founding the first clinical research laboratory within a hospital environment.

In 1959 he founded the Clinical Research Club of Quebec.

In 1963 he persuaded the Quebec government to establish a foundation for medical research (now known as the Foundation for Health Research in Quebec) and served as its first president.

In 1976 he founded the Centre Bioethique and was co-founder of the Canadian Society for Clinical Research.

JOHN TODD WON PEACE WITH A NEEDLE

Smallpox and measles epidemics during the mid-19th century decimated the Indians of the Pacific Northwest. Those who survived blamed the fatalities on the coming of the Europeans. When the Shuswap Indians threatened the Hudson's Bay Post at Fort Kamloops in 1845, the factor John Todd averted the attack by convincing a number of the Indians to submit to vaccination and showing them how to vaccinate others.

ROYAL COLLEGE OF PHYSICIANS OF CANADA MEDAL

Royal College of Physicians and Surgeons of Canada

The medal is given for original work done by young clinicians and investigators. Recipients must be under 45 and graduates in medicine. The award: a bronze medal, $500 and an invitation to present the winning paper at the annual meeting of the college.

1982 **R.K. Chandra**, professor of pediatric research, Memorial University, St. John's, Nfld.

1983 **Bernard Zinman**, Toronto General Hospital, Toronto, Ont.

ROYAL COLLEGE OF SURGEONS OF CANADA MEDAL

Royal College of Physicians and Surgeons of Canada

Recipients must be under 45 and graduates in medicine. The award: a bronze medal, $500 and an invitation to present the winning paper at the annual meeting of the college.

1982 **Leonard Makowaka**, Department of Surgery, U. of Toronto.

1983 **M.J. Burnstein**, Toronto Western Hospital, Toronto, Ont.

PIONEER SURGEONS

A surgeon named Bonnerme was likely with Champlain in 1608 but died from scurvy in the winter of 1608/09. In 1610, surgeon Boyer of Rouen dressed the wounds received by Champlain in a skirmish with the Iroquois.

Daniel Hay, a surgeon, and Louis Hebert provided medical care to the first settlers in Quebec in 1617. Surgeon Adrien Duchesne settled in Quebec in 1618. His practice eventually extended from Quebec to the post at Trois Rivieres.

Robert Giffard was the first physician at the Hotel-Dieu. He arrived in 1627, and was followed by Jean Madry, Jean Demosny and Timothee Roussel. In all, 22 surgeons and apothecaries are listed in the Quebec registers for 1629 to 1663.

FAMILY PHYSICIAN OF THE YEAR AWARD

College of Family Physicians of Canada

The award is presented annually to a physician who has been in family practice for at least 15 years. The award: $1,000 plus travel costs and accommodation to attend the assembly at which the award is presented.

1982 **Dr. Robin Krause**, Winnipeg, Man.
1983 **Dr. Raymond W. Pennell**, Melfort, Sask.

NADINE ST-PIERRE AWARD

College of Family Physicians of Canada

1983 **Michel Hebert**, Laval U.

FIRST CANADIAN TO UNDERGO DOUBLE TRANSPLANT

Nineteen-year-old Cameron Evans of Kitchener, Ont., suffering ideopathic pulmonary hypertension, underwent surgery at Pittsburgh's Presbyterian University Hospital on January 31, 1983. The only hope for his life was surgery to give him a new heart and lungs. Evans was eating normally just four days after the double transplant, within two weeks he was walking the hospital corridor and six weeks after surgery he was home in Kitchener. Subsequently, he died.

POSTGRADUATE STUDY AWARDS

College of Family Physicians of Canada

Sixteen annual awards of $1,000 each are given for two-week postgraduate study sessions in North American hospitals.

1983 **Donald C. Paterson**, Sorrento, B.C.
H. Irvine, Sundre, Alta.
G. Vanderburgh, Shelburne, Ont.
T. Barnard, Sioux Lookout, Ont.
D. Atkinson, Fort Frances, Ont.
R. Williams, Timmins, Ont.
B. MacFarlane, Markdale, Ont.
Renald Bergeron, Ste. Foy, Que.
W. Johnson, Saint John, N.B.

Clive S. MacDonald, New Waterford, N.S.
Alan Nixon, Vancouver, B.C.
D. Jansen, Edmonton, Alta.
D. Lawee, Toronto, Ont.
D. Hoag, Peterborough, Ont.
Sylvie Stachtchenko, Montreal, Que.
G. Fowlow, Arnold's Cover, Nfld.

EARLY CANADIAN PHYSICIANS HAVE PLANTS NAMED IN THEIR HONOR

Michael Sarrazin, a physician at l'Hôpital Général de Québec in 1685, was renowned for his knowledge of anatomy and his surgical skills, but he gained international recognition through his studies of plant life. He was the first to use the pitcher plant (Sarracenia pupurea canadensis) as a treatment for smallpox.

During the next century another physician-botanist, Dr. Jean Gaultier, discovered the medicinal value of the wintergreen plant (Gaulteria promcumbens).

C.M. HINCKS SCHOLARSHIP IN PSYCHIATRY

College of Family Physicians of Canada

The scholarship named in honour of the late Clarence Hincks, MD, former director of the Canadian Mental Health Association, is given to a College member for two weeks of continued education in psychiatry. The award is for $1,000.

1983 **Eric S. Sigurdson**, Dauphin, Man.

CANADA'S FIRST HEART TRANSPLANT

The Montreal Heart Institute was the first Canadian hospital to perform a heart transplant, in 1968. Other hospitals in Canada to perform heart transplants are the University Hospital in London, Ont., and Notre Dame Hospital in Montreal, Que.

TRAVEL SCHOLARSHIPS — SUSTAINING FUND AWARDS

College of Family Physicians of Canada

Travel scholarships of $2,500 enable a CFPC member to stay for a minimum of three weeks at a study site.

1983 **Pierre J. Durand**, Duplessis, Que.
Jacques Frenette, Ste. Foy, Que.
Richard A. MacLachland, Halifax, N.S.
Jack B. Sniderman, Peterborough, Ont.
Douglas Wilson, Hamilton, Ont.

SUSTAINING FUND, RESEARCH AND DEVELOPMENT AWARDS

College of Family Physicians of Canada

Practice Enrichment Awards enable members to study under the direction of a Canadian university for a minimum of three months in emergency medicine, geriatric medicine, anesthesia, obstetrics and gynecology, sports or occupation medicine. The award is for $3,000.

1983 **Dale G. Johnson**, Pinawa, Man.
Thandanani G. Kumalo, Thompson, Man.

A SURGICAL FIRST

Matthew Ronald Joseph Shuy who was born five weeks prematurely was the beneficiary of the first fetal surgery in Canada.

Doctors at St. Boniface Hospital in Winnipeg performed the successful operation, clearing a bladder blockage by inserting a needle through the mother's abdomen and implanting a catheter. This was done five months before delivery.

The surgeon, Dr. Frank Manning, said that while the operation had been performed before, the youngest fetus to undergo the procedure previously was seven months.

PRACTICE ENRICHMENT AWARDS

College of Family Physicians of Canada

Practice Enrichment Awards enable members to study under the direction of a Canadian university for at least six months on a part-time basis. The award is for $3,000.

1983 **W. Carlyle Phillips**, Halifax, N.S.

CFP RESEARCH AWARD

College of Family Physicians of Canada

$1,000 is awarded for the best article of original research published during the previous year in the *Canadian Family Physician*.

1983 **M. Bass, A. Donner and I. McWinney**, London, Ont.

FIRST CANADIAN TO WIN SURGERY AWARD

Dr. Blair Fearon received the Chevalier Jackson Award which included the "Philadelphia Bowl," a specially designed Wedgwood bowl from the Philadelphia Laryngological Society in 1980. The Society, which is the oldest surgical society in North America, gave the award to Fearon "for his many contributions to laryngology."

Fearon is the first Canadian to be so honoured.

ORTHO LITERARY AWARD

College of Family Physicians of Canada

An annual award is given for the best article by a family physician to appear in the journal of the College during the current year.

1983   Janet Sorbie, Kingston, Ont.

EMILY STOWE WON RIGHT TO BE A DOCTOR

She had to leave the country to do it, but Emily Jennings Stowe persevered against almost impossible odds to become the first woman doctor in Canada. A teacher, who was also the first woman school principal in Canada, she decided after her marriage (in 1856 to physician John Stowe) to study medicine. The University of Toronto turned her away (the college would not admit women until the turn of the century) but Stowe obtained her MD in 1867 from the New York College of Medicine for Women.

She returned to Canada but suffered 13 years of insult and argument before she was granted her licence to practise medicine.

Later when the few women doctors in Toronto were denied hospital privileges, Stowe became one of the founders of the institution known today as the Women's College Hospital in Toronto.

An active feminist, she founded the Dominion Women's Suffrage Association and was its president until her death in 1903. The Association was Canada's first women's suffrage society.

In 1981, she was one of four Canadian feminists commemorated by a special issue of stamps.

ROSS AWARD

Canadian Paediatric Society

The Ross Award, established in 1972, is awarded annually for achievements in the field of Canadian pediatrics.

1981   Albert Royer, Outrement, Que.
1982   Jessie B. Scriver, Montreal, Que.

PIONEERED MEDICAL METHODS

Dr. Nelles Silverthorne, who was still practising at the age of 81 in 1982, is a senior pediatrician at Toronto's Hospital for Sick Children.

Silverthorne, who developed a vaccine for whooping cough in the 1930s, assisted in developing the concept of the oxygen tent and pioneered treatment against meningitis. Naturally, he is opposed to mandatory retirement.

JELLINEK MEMORIAL FUND AWARD

Addiction Research Centre

Established in 1963 in memory of Dr. E.M. Jellinek, an annual cash award of $5,000 and a bronze bust is presented for contributions in alcohol-related fields.

1981   Dr. Wolfgang Schmidt, Toronto, Ont., for his epidemiological research relating to physical health and the consequences of heavy drinking.
1982   Dr. Albert J. Tuyns, Centre International de Recherche sur le Cancer, Lyon, France, for his research in clinical medicine in relation to alcohol and alcoholism.

NATIVE SAVIOURS IN THE NEW WORLD

Cartier and his men, who were wintering at Stadacona (near the site of present-day Quebec City) in 1535, suffered severely from scurvy until the natives supplied the remedy: tea made from the bark and leaves of white cedar.

Indian guides often kept European explorers alive with food such as baked acorns, reindeer moss and tripe de roche. When Alexander Henry (the elder) and his men were close to starvation on a journey to Sault Sainte-Marie in the 1750s, an Indian woman saved them with boiled lichen. Henry wrote that the Indian potato kept traders at Portage la Prairie from starvation.

And John Gyles, writing in 1726, described an effective Indian treatment for frozen feet made from fir balsam.

EDWARD W. BROWNING ACHIEVEMENT AWARDS

New York Community Trust

The Edward W. Browning Achievement Awards are awarded annually for achievement in five major areas: conserving the environment; prevention of disease; alleviation of addiction; spreading the Christian Gospel; improvement of food source.

The Edward W. Browning Achievement Award for the Alleviation of Addiction is given for outstanding contribution to the prevention and treatment of alcoholism or drug abuse.

In 1982 H. David Archibald of Toronto, Ont., received the gold medal and $5,000 cash.

Archibald, who is executive vice-chairman of the Alcohol and Drug Addiction Research Foundation, is at home among the Hill Tribe people in the opium-producing villages of North Thailand, in the offices of the World Health Organization in Geneva and the United Nations Division of Narcotic Drugs in Vienna. The Addiction Research Foundation which he founded is the largest and most comprehensive institution of its kind in the world.

Working through the A.R.F. and W.H.O., Archibald developed a model primary health care program for the villagers of northern Thailand whose lives for centuries had centred on opium. The plan is based on training villagers to become health workers in their own communities.

CANADIAN WINS TOP POST WITH AA

Gordon Patrick of Lyndhurst, Ont., was elected chairman of the General Service Board of Trustees of Alcoholics Anonymous in the spring of 1982.

The first Canadian elected to this post, Patrick has been a trustee of AA since 1975 and is a consultant at the Donwood Institute in Toronto.

GOODHOST AWARD

Canadian Dietetic Association

The winner receives an honorarium of $1,000 and an engraved plaque for contributions to the dietetic profession.

1982 **Dr. Virginia A. Campbell**, Wolfville, N.S. Dean of the School of Home Economics at Acadia University, Campbell's career covered community nutrition, clinical dietetics and education.

DR. CALDWELL WINS A DUEL

The Montreal General Hospital opened in 1819, expanded in 1822 and later became the Medical Faculty of McGill University. The hospital introduced lay nurses to Montreal when it opened, a move that met with much opposition, with critics arguing that the sick should be nursed by Sisters devoted to God and not by "hirelings."

Dr. Caldwell, from the hospital, and Michael O'Sullivan, a member of the

Quebec Legislature, actually fought a duel over the issue.

O'Sullivan, on the side of the Sisters, was no match for the ex-army surgeon, Caldwell. O'Sullivan took three bullet wounds while Caldwell received only one.

None of the wounds were fatal and there is no record of which kind of nurses provided medical care to the combatants.

WILD-LEITZ JUNIOR SCIENTIFIC AWARD

An annual award is given for contributions to pathology. The winner, who must be under 35, receives a plaque and $1,000 and is invited to present a paper.

1983 **Dr. Ross G. Camperon**, department of pathology, U. of Toronto.

DONALD W. PENNER PRIZE

Canadian Association of Pathologists

A $200 prize is given for the best paper presented at the annual meeting of the Canadian Congress of Laboratory Medicine.

1982 **Dr. S.D. Finkelstein**, department of pathology, Toronto Western Hospital, Toronto, Ont.

GREAT-GREAT-GRANDMOTHER HAS SURGERY AT 101

Stavroulas Mandrapilias of Toronto underwent surgery in March 1983 to correct a prolapsed uterus which had been bothering her since the birth of her first child 73 years ago.

Mandrapilias who is now 101 years old, has seven children, 23 grandchildren, 23 great-grandchildren and one great-great-grandchild.

Some believe that the secret of her longevity and good health can be attrib-

uted to her daily glass of homemade red wine.

CANADIAN NURSES ASSOCIATION AWARD

Canadian Nurses Association

The Canadian Nurses Association, formed in 1908, is a federation of 11 associations representing more than 200,000 professional nurses.

The Association honours a member who has made a contribution to health care or gained increased status and public recognition for the nursing profession.

1981 **Dr. Helen K. Mussallem**, Ottawa, Ont.

1982 **Verna Huffman Splane**, Vancouver, B.C.

CANADA'S FIRST NURSE

Canada's first nurse was not a member of a religious order. She was Marie Hubou, widow of Canada's first apothecary, Louis Hebert. She and her family settled in Quebec in 1617, making them Canada's first resident European family. Marie Hubou took what time she could spare from her farm to nurse the sick recommended to her care by the Jesuit Fathers.

ENID GRAHAM MEMORIAL LECTURE

Canadian Physiotherapy Association

The award is named after a pioneer in the development of physiotherapy in Canada. Recipients are invited to deliver a lecture during the Canadian Physiotherapy Association's Annual Congress.

1981 **Helen Gault**, Montreal, Que.
Helen Gault was the first physiotherapist to deliver the Enid Graham Memorial Lecture. She was the director of the School of Physical and Occupa-

tional Therapy at McGill University from 1973 to 1978, the first physiotherapist in Canada to hold such a position. Through her efforts McGill became the first Canadian university to offer a baccalaureate degree in physiotherapy. She also helped to implement a Master of Science degree, applied in medical rehabilitation.

1982 **Marion Leslie**, Toronto, Ont. During her tenure as executive director of the CPA, the Association has increased in size, sophistication and membership services.

NURSING: FROM VOCATION TO PROFESSION

A doctor named Theophilus Mack, convinced that a profession of trained lay nurses was needed to eliminate prejudice against public hospitals, introduced Canada's first Training School for Nurses at St. Catharines, Ont. Two probationers under the tutelage of two Nightingale nurses from England began study at the school in the General and Marine Hospital in 1874. The program proved successful and seven years later the Toronto General Hospital established Canada's second school of nurses training. Mary Agnes Snively was appointed superintendent in 1884, a position which she held for 25 years. A graduate of Bellevue Hospital in New York, she reorganized the school and implemented a modern development plan. By the time she left, the school was respected worldwide and there were 70 schools for nurses in Canada.

CONSTANCE BEATTIE MEMORIAL FUND

The Fund enables members to do postgraduate study in physiotherapy.

1982 **Edith Herman**, Ancaster, Ont., will pursue graduate studies in a program designed for research and exploration

of clinical problems in medical sciences at McMaster University.

1982 **Jane Proctor**, Toronto, Ont., will follow a course of studies in orthopedics and sports medicine in preparation for teaching physiotherapy. She is enrolled in a Master of Science degree program in physical therapy at the University of Alberta.

HANS SELYE, FATHER OF STRESS RESEARCH IN HUMANS

Hans Selye first studied medicine in Prague but came to Canada in 1933, when he was appointed to the staff at McGill.

In 1945 he became professor and director of the Institute of Experimental Medicine and Surgery at the University of Montreal.

Hans Selye was the first to explore seriously the nonspecific damage inflicted upon the human body by the turmoil of living. He helped prove that psychological strain itself could cause dramatic hormonal change which in turn caused physiological symptoms.

ABBOTT AWARD

Canadian Society of Hospital Pharmacists

The award is given for original scholarly papers, significant innovations, or original research in hospital pharmaceutical technology.

1982 **Therese M. Fabian**, Kincardine, Ont., for "Stability and Sterility of Sodium Hypochlorite Solutions."

1983 **Scott Walker**, Sunnybrook Medical Centre, Toronto, Ont., for "The Effect of Solution and Container Types on Cefazolin Stability."

AYERST AWARD

Canadian Society of Hospital Pharmacists

1982 **Robert S. Nakagawa** and Christopher C. Godwin, Vancouver, B.C., for "The Development of a Drug Measurement Service at St. Paul's Hospital."

CANADA'S FIRST HEALTH INSURANCE

Etienne Bouchard began the practice of medicine in 1654. Anticipating health insurance, he made contracts with 37 citizens of the settlement, treating the subscriber and his family for the equivalent of $1 per year.

BRISTOL AWARD

Canadian Society of Hospital Pharmacists

The award is given for original scholarly papers, significant innovation or original research in a clinical pharmacy program.

1982 **Kathleen Gesy**, Saskatoon, Sask., for "Assessment of a Pharmacokinetic Monitoring Service for Gentamicin."
1983 **Marie Pineau**, Montreal, Que., for "Therapeutic Formulary — A New Concept."

BURROUGHS WELCOME AWARD

Canadian Society of Hospital Pharmacists

The award is given for original scholarly papers; significant innovation or original research on administrative practice in hospital pharmacy.

1982 **Guy Paterson**, Saskatoon, Sask., for "Pharmacy Based Data Processing Systems."
1983 **Kevin Hall** and **Maureen Guay**, Winnipeg, Man., for "The Implementation of Comprehensive Pharmacy Services Through the Development of a Critical Care Satellite Pharmacy."

GREY NUNS WAR AGAINST SUFFERING

Marie-Marguerite d'Youville, a young widow, founded the Grey Nuns in Montreal in 1737.

They opened their ranks to all classes of women but the practical nursing was generally done by unmarried or widowed women. Wearing distinctive grey habits they went two by two to nurse the sick. In 1747, they undertook the nursing responsibilities of the General Hospital at Montreal and in 1755 their order was approved by the Bishop. Mother d'Youville and her sisters raised funds to meet heavy debts by taking in paying guests, making tapers and candles and doing needlework. They started a brewery, operated a farm, a tobacco plant and a freight and cartage business for the government. They put tradesmen to work in return for nursing services. In 1756, with France and England at war, they opened a ward for English prisoners of war and offered sanctuary to a number of English soldiers who had escaped from the Indian allies of the French. Following the war they opened a creche for abandoned children. Though Mother d'Youville died in 1771, her work carried on.

The Grey Nuns nursed through the epidemics of the early 19th century and Grey Nuns went west from Montreal to found hospitals at Kingston and Ottawa and beyond. In 1844, four Grey Nuns travelled by canoe to the Red River where they introduced health hygiene to the natives and nursed the sick in their homes. They recorded some 6,000 visits in the first ten years and established a hospital at St. Boniface.

In 1859, three Grey Nuns went by ox cart to Lake Sainte-Anne, 40 miles from

Edmonton, where they founded a mission encompassing an orphanage, hospital and a refuge for the aged and infirm.

They continued their pioneer missions into the 20th century, founding missions and hospitals even in the far north. Today, hospitals across the country are a testament to their heroic work.

McNEIL AWARD

Canadian Society of Hospital Pharmacists

The award is given for original research in professional pharmacy practice in hospitals.

1982 **Ken Michalko**, Ottawa, Ont., for "A Test of the Health Belief Model as a Tool for Identifying Ambulatory Patients with Drug-Related Problems."

1983 **Andrea Cameron**, Toronto, Ont., for "Procedure for the Safe Preparation of Parenteral Antineoplastic Agents."

ORGANON AWARD

Canadian Society of Hospital Pharmacists

The award is given to a hospital pharmacy resident for the best manuscript for publication, based on the resident's major project.

1982 **Reynald Tremblay**, Montreal, Que., for "Service de Pharmacocinetique pour les Aminosides."

1983 **Sharon Matsumoto**, Hamilton, Ont., for "Patterns of Cefoxitin Use in a Teaching Hospital."

The first medical school in Canada was founded in Montreal in 1824. It later became part of McGill University.

PHARMACIA AWARD

Canadian Society of Hospital Pharmacists

The award is given for original scholarly papers, significant innovation or original research on parenteral nutrition in Canada.

1982 **Joseph T. Murphy**, Saskatoon, Sask., for "Development of a TPN Program in a Community Hospital."

ROCHE AWARD

Canadian Society of Hospital Pharmacists

For original scholarly papers, significant innovation or original research on the use of drugs for specific specialties such as pediatric, geriatric, or cardiovascular drugs.

1982 **Mary Ellen Sharp**, Saskatoon, Sask., for "Monitoring Sulfasalazine Therapy in Patients with Chronic Inflammation Bowel Disease."

1983 **Judith A. Soon**, Abbotsford, B.C., for "Development and Assessment of an Ongoing ADR Monitoring Program in Nursing Care Facilities."

SEARLE AWARD

Canadian Society of Hospital Pharmacists

The award is given for original scholarly papers or audio-visual presentations on hospital-based pharmaceutical counselling of patients.

1982 **S. Lynn Corrigan**, Saskatoon, Sask., for "The Effect of Patient Education on the Compliant Use of Lithium Carbonate in Selected Patients with Pipolar or Unipolar Affective Disorders."

1983 **Shirley E. Tenenbaum**, Toronto, Ont., for "Production and Evaluation of a Slide-Tape Presentation on Drug Therapy in Rheumatoid Arthritis for Patient Education."

MODERN CANADIAN NURSES ARE WINNERS

From Canada's early days to the present our nurses have served with imagination, dedication and courage. The nurses represented below are examples of a noble profession.

Helen K. Mussallem, OC, BN, MA, EdD, OStJ, LLD, DSc, FRCN, Ottawa, Ont.

Mussallem was a lieutenant (nursing officer) with the Royal Canadian Army Medical Corps. She served overseas during the Second World War, often under fire. Following the war she held senior posts with the Vancouver General Hospital and the hospital's school of nursing and she undertook more than 30 international assignments for the World Health Organization and the International Council of Nurses. She was executive director of the Canadian Nurses Association of Canada from 1963 to 1981 and was made an Officer of Canada in 1969. She has prepared numerous major publications relating to nursing and to health and has been a member and adviser to many national and international organizations. She has continued this role since her official retirement in 1981. The library of the Canadian Nurses Association in Ottawa was named in her honour and in 1981 she received the Florence Nightingale Medal, one of the highest awards of the International Red Cross.

She is the 28th recipient of the award which was instituted not to crown a career, however deserving of merit, but to reward outstanding acts of devotion and as recognition of exceptional moral and professional qualities. The citation referred to Mussallem as "Canada's most distinguished nurse in her time and generation."

Ethel L.M. Thorpe, OBE, GNRN, Fort Garry, Man.

Ethel Thorpe was a nursing sister during the Second World War. She served in England, France, Iraq, Iran and India. Following the war she worked in China as a hospital matron. Later, in Jamaica she established training for psychiatric nurses. Thorpe came to Canada in 1963 as a nursing consultant for the Sanatorium Board of Manitoba and gained national recognition as a founding member of the Canadian Tuberculosis and Respiratory Disease Association. She also served as national chairman of the Nursing Section of that organization.

In 1981 Thorpe received one of the highest honours conferred by the International Committee of the League of Red Cross Societies when she was awarded the Florence Nightingale Medal.

Verna Huffman Splane, RN, BSc, MPH, LLD, Vancouver, B.C.

Verna Splane's professional life as a staff nurse, administrator, consultant and teacher has centred on community health. She began her career at a Red Cross outpost in Ontario and was from 1947 to 1958 senior nursing counsellor for the Department of National Health and Welfare. Since then she has been advisor and consultant to governments in Canada and to national and international organizations. She has worked for the World Health Organization in the Caribbean, South America and in Africa as well as in Washington and Geneva. In 1973 she was elected vice-president of the International Council of Nurses and was re-elected to that post in 1977. She has been an official representative at the International Council on Social Welfare, the United Nations International Conference on International Women's Year, the United Nations International Conference on Human Settlements, and the International Congress on Social Development.

She has received an award for Outstanding Public Health Nurse from the

University of Michigan, a Canadian Red Cross Citation for contribution to health care for Canadians, the Queen's Silver Jubilee Medal, an honorary LLD from Queen's University, the Canadian Red Cross Society Distinguished Service Award and in 1981 the International Council of Nurses Citation for Service as an Officer and Director.

In 1982 she received the National Award of the Canadian Nurses Association, that organization's highest honour.

Shirley M. Stinson, BScN, MNA, EdD, Edmonton, Alta.

Dr. Stinson is professor, Faculty of Nursing and Division of Health Services Administration at the University of Alberta. Her experience includes public health staff nursing; nursing service administration; health services education; health services research; nursing service and health service administration consultation; interprofessional health education; professional nursing association work and nursing research development.

She has served on many national nursing and health-related committees and is president of the Canadian Nurses Association.

Stinson was the first woman to receive a Senior National Health Scientist Research Award. She is listed in the World's Who's Who of Women. She has won a Gold Key award, a major athletic award, a Silver "A" executive award and a McGugan Prize for contribution to student welfare, all from the University of Alberta. She has received a Canadian Red Cross Fellowship; a Katherine McLaggan Award; a CNF Scholarship and a New York Trust Scholarship.

In 1981 Stinson was honoured by Teacher's College, Columbia University of New York City, when she received the National Education Alumnae Award for professional leadership in organization.

PAST PRESIDENTS' AWARD

Canadian Foundation for the Advancement of Pharmacy

A prize is given to pharmacy students based on scholarship and school involvement.

1982 **Sylvain Meloche**, U. of Montreal.

GRADUATE FELLOWSHIPS IN HOSPITAL PHARMACY

Canadian Foundation for the Advancement of Pharmacy

An award of $500 each is given to assist graduates of Canadian pharmacy schools.

1982 **Jane T. Benson**, Dalhousie U.,
Renette Bertholet, U. of Alberta,
Layton M. Capefoot, U. of Manitoba,
Nancy J. Daniels, Dalhousie U.,
Janice H. Hall, U. of Toronto,
Wendy Lam, Dalhousie U.

E.L. WOODS MEMORIAL PRIZE IN PHARMACY

Canadian Foundation for the Advancement of Pharmacy

The annual competition is open to pharmacy graduates for experimental or laboratory work. The prize is a certificate of merit and $200.

1981 **Marvin J. Friesen**, U. of British Columbia.

NURSE WINS ORDER OF CANADA

Margaret M. Street, BA, MS, RN, Vancouver, B.C.

Street, now an associate professor emerita of Nursing at UBC, obtained a BA and a teaching certificate in Manitoba, her RN from Royal Victoria in Montreal, and then a certificate in teaching and supervision from the McGill School for Graduate Nurses. She held senior staff and teaching posts in major hospitals and from 1961 until her retirement in

1974 was assistant, then associate professor at the University of B.C. School of Nursing. She received the Dr. Walter Stewart Baird Memorial Award from UBC for her outstanding work in the history of health science in 1974 and has received honorary memberships in RN Associations. Following her retirement she wrote a book about another nurse, *Watch Fires on the Mountain: The Life of Ethel Johns*.

Street became a member of the Order of Canada in 1982.

AUBREY A. BROWN MEMORIAL AWARD

Canadian Foundation for the Advancement of Pharmacy

The competition is for pharmacy graduates for the best paper of the library, archives or survey type. The prize is a certificate and $200.

1982   **Enzo N. Turchet**, U. of British Columbia.

FELLOWSHIPS IN PROFESSIONAL PRACTICE

Canadian Foundation for the Advancement of Pharmacy

Fellowships are given to pharmacy graduates presenting study programs in any professional area.

1982   **Helena R. Bardos**, U. of British Columbia
     Marion L. Pearson, UBC

WILDER PENFIELD

World-renowned as a neurologist, Penfield founded the Montreal Neurological Institute, one of the world's most highly regarded centres for brain surgery. He directed the institute from 1934-60 and is known as a pioneer "mapmaker" of the brain.

GOLD MEDAL AWARD

Canadian Society of Laboratory Technologists

The award is for exceptional work in medical laboratory technology.

1982   **Yvonne Goodman Blades**, Edmonton, Alta.
     Sam Thomson, London, Ont.

AWARD OF MERIT

Canadian Society of Laboratory Technologists

1982   **Mabel Graham**, Edmonton, Alta.
     Nancy McBride, Milton, Ont.
     Rose Marie Lowinger, Longueuil, Que.

CANADIANS LEADING DONORS

The Canadian Red Cross operates the world's most successful blood donor system. In contrast with other countries, where blood is purchased and sold, almost a million Canadians have freely given the gift of life since the program officially began in the mid-1940s.

FOUNDERS' FUND AWARDS

Canadian Society of Laboratory Technologists

Winners receive $500 to further education in medical laboratory technology.

1982   F.J. Elliott Memorial Award
     Carolyn Yu, Calgary, Alta.
     Ileen Kemp Parker Award
     Margaret Klassen, Saskatoon, Sask.
     William J. Deadman Memorial Award
     June Rodych, Saskatoon, Sask.

FISHER SCIENTIFIC AWARD

Canadian Society of Laboratory Technologists

The award is given for the best scientific paper in clinical chemistry.

1982 **Saroj Khimdas**, Hospital for Sick Children, Toronto, Ont.

McGILL DOCTOR WON TIME FOR LIVER PATIENTS

Dr. Thomas Chang of Montreal's McGill University initiated a technique in 1971 which buys time for patients suffering liver failure and awaiting a transplant. He designed a charcoal filtering process which filters the patient's blood. The process can be effective in up to 70 per cent of patients whose livers have been poisoned by viral hepatitis or by overdoses of acetaminophen, provided the treatment is carried out early.

DADE AWARD

Canadian Society of Laboratory Technologists

The award is given for the best scientific paper in hematology.

1982 **Josephine Paulumbo**, St. Joseph's Hospital, Hamilton, Ont.

DIFCO SCHOLARSHIP

Canadian Society of Laboratory Technologists

A $1,000 scholarship is given for study in clinical microbiology.

1982 **Richard Jones**, West Park Hospital, Toronto, Ont.

MALLINCKRODT SCHOLARSHIP

Canadian Society of Laboratory Technologists

A $600 scholarship is given for study in radioimmunoassay.

1982 **Greg Denomme**, McMaster U. Medical Centre, Hamilton, Ont.

NURSES AND HEROINES IN EARLY CANADA

The nursing sisters who established hospitals in Quebec changed the course of Canadian history by saving lives amongst settlers and Indians alike.

Marie Guenet de St. Ignace, aged 29, Anne Lecointre de St. Bernard, 26, and Marie Forstier de St. Bonaventure de Jesus, 22, were Augustinian nuns of the Order of Hospitallers of the Mercy of Jesus. Bound to celibacy, poverty, obedience and the care of the sick, they were known as the "Nuns of Dieppe." They came to Quebec in the summer of 1639 to found Canada's first general hospital, l'Hotel-Dieu.

Nuns of the order were required to be from "good families" and have their "reputations intact." They were expected to be "charitable, tender and compassionate; to be straightforward, sweet, humble, docile, courageous, strong and healthy and have, as well, a sense of humour more gay than sombre." On their arrival, they were confronted with crowds of patients and nearly intolerable working conditions. Space, equipment, supplies, food, water and sleep were all in short supply. Because they were in continuous contact with typhus, scurvy and smallpox, they had to spend their nights doing laundry for no one else would touch the linen for fear of contagion. In all they treated some 300 patients between August and May, managed to maintain their religious offices and also learned the languages of the Indians. They lived for months in the poisonous atmosphere of the hospital with courage, serenity and devotion. During the winter, three of the sisters fell ill and in the spring Mother de St. Marie died.

They moved to larger quarters at the Mission at Sillery (now part of Quebec City) in 1640 where they could care for more Indians. Their white habits became so stained that they dyed them in walnut bark and butternut juice.

Iroquois raids in 1644 forced them to move back to Quebec where they built a new hospital and chapel, working with the tradesmen as labourers while continuing to cook and nurse. When they completed the buildings in 1646, they resumed their white habits and the order quickly grew. By 1671 their community was no longer dependent on imported personnel and in 1683, Canadian-born Jeanne-Francoise Juchereau de la Ferte (Sister Saint-Ignace) was elected Superior of l'Hotel-Dieu.

CLINICAL CHEMISTRY AWARD

Canadian Society of Laboratory Technologists

The award is given to the graduate with the highest mark in clinical chemistry in the General Certificate Exams.

1982   **Glenn Robb**, Southern Alberta Institute of Technology.

NEW GRADUATE AWARDS

Canadian Society of Laboratory Technologists

Graduate of the Year Award

The award is for achieving the highest aggregate on the General Certificate Exams

1982   **Katharine Lee**, Algonquin College, Ottawa, Ont.

CYTOTECHNOLOGY AWARD

Canadian Society of Laboratory Technologists

The award is given to a student in an accredited training program who presents the best case study.

1982   **Cheryl Powers**, Toronto Institute of

Medical Technology and the Toronto General Hospital, Toronto, Ont.

EARLY DOCTORS ON THE WEST COAST

William Anderson sailed as ship's doctor with James Cook in 1776-80 on Cook's third and final exploratory voyage of the Pacific North. There was remarkably little illness on the voyage, which Cook attributed to Anderson's skill. Doctors sailing with Captain George Vancouver were Surgeon Cranstoun and later Surgeon Archibald Menzies.

Dr. William Fraser Tolmie arrived at Fort Vancouver as an employee of the Hudson's Bay Company in 1833 and a German doctor, John Sebastian Helmcken, was the surgeon at the Hudson's Bay Post at Fort Victoria in 1850.

WALTER T. STURDY MEMORIAL AWARD

Canadian Chiropractic Association

The award is given to the graduate with the highest overall academic record after four years at the Canadian Memorial Chiropractic College.

1982   **G.H. Kudo**, DC, Montreal, Que.

NOBEL PRIZE FOR THE CANADIAN DISCOVERERS OF INSULIN

The 1923 Nobel Prize in medicine was awarded to Dr. Frederick G. Banting and Dr. J.J.R. Macleod of the University of Toronto for the discovery of insulin. The medical breakthrough, which was achieved at the University of Toronto in 1921, has saved the lives of millions of diabetics throughout the world.

Dr. Banting shared his prize with researcher Dr. Charles H. Best and Macleod with Dr. J.B. Collip.

MALLINCKRODT AWARD OF EXCELLENCE

Canadian Association of Medical Radiation Technologists

The award is presented annually to the graduates who have earned the highest aggregate scores in the CAMRT examinations in any given year and in each of the disciplines.

1982 **Sandra Butternowskie**, RTR, Misericordia Hospital, Winnipeg, Man.
Diane MacLachlan, RTT, A. Maxwell Evans Clinic of the Cancer Control Agency of British Columbia, Vancouver, B.C.
Janet Lynn Bernaerts, RTNM, Mount Sinai Hospital, Toronto, Ont.

CARTWRIGHT AWARD

Canadian Association of Medical Radiation Technologists

The award is presented annually to the highest submission of a technical paper.

1982 **Christopher O'Brien**, RTNM, Montreal General Hospital, Montreal, Que.

MALLETT AWARD

Canadian Association of Medical Radiation Technologists

The award is presented annually by the board of directors for excellence and dedication to the profession.

1982 **Noreen Hammill**, BSRT, Queen Elizabeth Hospital, Charlottetown, P.E.I.

A MEDICAL BREAKTHROUGH

A medical breakthrough developed by Canadian engineer Dr. Robert Tilliar is helping to win the battle against arthritis.

Doctors implant an artificial joint and surround it with a double layer of minute alloy balls that gradually become part of the joint. The new joint is a porous surface of chrome and cobalt. After implantation, blood seeps into the pores and around the alloy balls to form clots. New bone growth attaches to the implant and keeps it in place until mature bone forms.

DEFRIES AWARD

Canadian Public Health Association

A medal, a citation and an honorary life membership in the CPHA are presented for contributions to public health.

1982 **Dr. Vincent Lean Matthews**, Saskatoon, Sask.

ORTHO AWARD

Canadian Public Health Association

The award is for advancing the cause of public health.

1982 **Dr. Otto Schaefer**, Edmonton, Alta.

LIKE FATHER, LIKE SON, LIKE FATHER, LIKE SON, LIKE ...

No fewer than five Mustard brothers emigrated to Canada from France in 1810 and together they have given four generations to the care of the sick in Canada.

Among the fourth-generation Mustards in medicine in Canada are Dr. Robert Mustard, retired chief of surgery, Toronto General Hospital; Dr. William Mustard, OC, MBE, retired cardiac and orthopedic surgeon, Hospital for Sick Children; and their cousin, Dr. James Fraser Mustard, noted for his research in arteriosclerosis.

ARTHRITIS SOCIETY ASSOCIATESHIPS

Arthritis Society

Associateships are awarded to candidates trained for careers in academic rheumatology.

1982/83 **M.E. Adams**, U. of British Columbia
A. Beaulieu, Laval U.
N. Bellamy, U. of Western Ontario
C. Bombardier, U. of Toronto
S. Brandwein, McGill U.
S. Carette, Laval U.
A. Chalmers, UBC
I. Chalmers, U. of Manitoba
J-Y Dansereau, U. of Montreal
J. Dunne, U. of Ottawa
I. Dwosh, Queen's U.
J. Esdaile, McGill
P.M. Ford, Queen's
M. Fritzler, U. of Calgary
D. Gladman, U. of T.
J. Karsh, McGill
W. Kean, McMaster U.
P. Lee, U. of T.
R. Lewkonia, Calgary
K. Oen, Manitoba
J-P Pelletier, Montreal
R.E. Pett, UBC
P. Rooney, McMaster
A. Shore, U. of T.
J. Tennenbaum, U. of T.
J. Verrier-Jones, Dalhousie U.

ASSOCIATESHIPS IN BASIC SCIENCE

Arthritis Society

Associateships in Basic Science are awarded to PhDs investigating problems of human disease.

1982/83 **E. Goidl**, Laval U.
M.D. Grynpas, U. of Toronto
C.A. Izaguirre, U. of Ottawa
G. McCain, U. of Western Ontario
J. Minta, U. of T.
M. Shulman, U. of T.
K. Wong, U. of Alberta

MILLIONS AWARDED BY SOCIETY

The Arthritis Society awarded more than $4.5-million in Manpower Development Awards and Research Awards in 1982/83.

The Society funded associateships, assistantships, fellowships, grants to Rheumatic Disease Control Units and grants for research projects at Canadian medical schools.

FELLOWSHIPS 1982

Canadian Diabetes Association

1982 **Dr. Connie Prosser**, McMaster U.
Andrew Salter, U. of Toronto

DR. NORMAN BETHUNE

The world's first mobile clinic was a battered station wagon, pressed into service during the Spanish-American War by Dr. Norman Bethune, born in Gravenhurst, Ont. Later, Bethune's work in China made him a national hero in that country. His memory is still revered today for the contributions he made to public health.

DR. DAVID GREEN POST-DOCTORAL FELLOWSHIP

Muscular Dystrophy Association of Canada

Named for the MDAC founder, the fellowship is awarded annually to the highest-rated candidate in the category of post-doctoral fellowships.

1982 **H. Matsui**, Biochemistry, U. of Manitoba

INVENTION HELPS CHILDREN

Luigi Tosti, working with the Children's Rehabilitation Centre of Essex County, has designed a low-rise wheelchair that gives handicapped children independent mobility.

The device, called the Chariot, has a brake, flip-away handles and a low extended front end which allows a child to get in and out of the vehicle safely and unassisted. It has seat belts, chain guards and wheel covers.

The wheelchair is sized for children 2 to 14 years old and is being manufactured by Dynamo-Aid Manufacturing Ltd., of Windsor, Ont.

ARTHUR MINDEN PRE-DOCTORAL FELLOWSHIP

Muscular Dystrophy Association of Canada

Named to honour the first president of MDAC, the award is presented annually to the highest-rated candidate in the category of pre-doctoral fellowships.

1982 **L. Garofalo**, Neurology, Montreal General Hospital Research Institute

MILLIONS FOR RESEARCH

The Muscular Dystrophy Association put more than $6-million into patient services, public and professional information and research in 1982. More than half of the $6-million was for research.

INTERNATIONAL GOLD MEDAL FOR EXCELLENCE IN RESEARCH IN THE DISEASE OF ALCOHOLISM

The Raleigh Hills Foundation of Irvine, Calif.

In 1982, **Dr. Harold Kalant** of Toronto won the International Gold Medal for his contribution to knowledge about the effects of alcohol on the brain and in behavioural patterns.

FIGHTING FOR FREEDOM OF SPEECH

Dr. John Fredrickson, formerly of the University of Toronto's department of otolaryngology, has designed an implantable artificial voice box that brings the possibility of clear speech back to throat cancer victims who have lost their larynx.

Research to perfect the quality of the box's voice output is being done at the university's department of speech pathology. The device is battery-operated and just slightly larger than a half-dollar. It has been implanted in four test patients who have given demonstration talks to medical audiences.

RESEARCH AWARDS

Canadian Thyroid Foundation

The Foundation, established in 1980, raised $15,000 in 1982 for a research project led by **Dr. J.R. Wahl** of Queen's University.

KITCHEN INSPIRATION

Dr. Brenda Gallie, an ophthalmologist in Toronto, used a kitchen spoon as a model for a silicon spoon used to remove eye tumors.

Her device, called a cryonucleator, ensures that tumor cells within the eye are contained as doctors remove them.

GRANTS-IN-AID OF RESEARCH

Canadian Foundation for Ileitis and Colitis

The Canadian Foundation for Ileitis and Colitis was founded to promote research to discover the cause and cure for ileitis (Crohn's disease) and chronic ulcerative colitis, two severe chronic debilitating diseases which afflict up to 200,000 Canadians.

1982/83 Dr. T.B. Issekutz, Dalhousie U.
Dr. H.J. Freeman, U. of British Columbia
Drs. S.J. Baker, E. Jacob, C. Delespesse, U. of Manitoba

MEDICAL BOOK PRIZES FOR EXCELLENCE IN GASTROENTEROLOGY

Canadian Foundation for Ileitis and Colitis

1982 Richard H. Hulfluss, U. of Toronto
Indira Fridhandler, U. of Calgary
Francois Corbeil, U. of Laval
Donald Nixon, Queen's U.
Paul Gordon Janke, U. of British Columbia
Paul Deneault, U. of Ottawa
Rob Turnball, U. of Saskatchewan
Hieu Hanh Ngo, U. of Sherbrooke

AMBULANCE AND EMERGENCY SERVICE

The longest recorded carry of a stretcher bearing a body took place in 1979 when two four-man teams from the Canadian Forces Base in Calgary carried a 140-pound person over 120 miles. The trip took 41 hours and 12 minutes.

PRESIDENT'S AWARD

Canadian Association of Optometrists

A biannual award for a significant contribution to optometry in Canada.

1981 Dr. Elwood J. Spearman, Killarney, Man.

LEARNING IN RECORD TIME

Blind and partially blind students at the University of Toronto are substantially reducing their study time by "speed listening." Using audio tapes of their professors' lectures, they speed up the play-back rate. Some students are able to listen to and understand an hour-long tape in 40 minutes.

They have been able to learn to listen and make sense of the garbled words known as the "Donald Duck" effect. A voice compressor attached to the tape recorder dampens the high pitch of the speeded-up tapes and makes speed-listening even easier.

OUTSTANDING CONTRIBUTION AWARD

Canadian Association on Gerontology

The award is given for outstanding contribution to gerontology in Canada, for research, education or service.

1981 Prof. W.F. Forbes, U. of Waterloo.
Forbes, the first recipient of the award, was the founding president of the association.
His main research has been into risk factors which affect the human life span. He is active locally, provincially, nationally and internationally in gerontological interests.

LIVING LONGER

Life expectancy at the time of confederation was just 40 years. Today it is more than 70 years.

CANADIAN DENTAL RESEARCH FUND AWARD

Canadian Dental Association

1981 Dr. J.L. Berger, Windsor, Ont., for his paper "A Study to Investigate the

Effect of Two Different Ligations Systems on Tooth Movement In Macaca Cynomologous."

1982   **Dr. C. Birek**, U. of Toronto., for her paper "Dome Formation by Oral Epithelia in Bitro."

CANADIAN DENTAL RESEARCH FOUNDATION INSTITUTIONAL TROPHY

Canadian Dental Association

1981   **Orthodonture Department** of the Dental Faculty, U. of Toronto
1982   **MRC Group in Periodontal Physiology**, U. of T.

CLARKE PSYCHIATRISTS DISCOVER DEPRESSION-CAUSING GENE

Psychiatric researchers led by Dr. Harvey Stancer of Toronto's Clarke Institute of Psychiatry and a companion group at the University of Rochester Medical Center found a gene in 1981 that they believe contributes to depression.

Their findings could lead to the prevention of a major incapacitating psychiatric illness, as well as help to explain alcoholism, antisocial personalities and other disorders.

R.M. TAYLOR MEDAL

Canadian Cancer Society and the National Cancer Institute of Canada

The medal honours the late Dr. R.M. Taylor, who was for 22 years a senior executive of the Cancer Society and Cancer Institute.

1982   **Dr. Harold E. Johns**, a nuclear physicist and pioneer in the field of radiobiology.

One of the first to recognize the therapeutic potential of cobalt 60, Johns was the prime mover in the design and installation of the first Cobalt Unit in the world in Saskatoon, Sask.

His book, *The Physics of Radiology*, is in its fifth printing and has been translated into Spanish, Chinese and Russian.

Johns retired in 1980 after 24 years as director of physics for the Ontario Cancer Institute.

He has been awarded the Gold Medal of the Canadian Association of Physicists, the Roentgen Award of the British Institute of Radiologists and the Gairdner International Award. He is a fellow of the Royal Society of Canada and an Officer of the Order of Canada.

RESEARCH AWARDS

Canadian Cancer Society and National Cancer Institute of Canada

Awards totalling $22.9-million were awarded in 1982 by the National Cancer Institute of Canada for research into cancer control, prevention, early diagnosis and treatment. Some $2.3-million is allotted to Terry Fox Special Awards from funds raised during the Marathon of Hope. The rest was raised during the Cancer Society's April campaign.

1983   **Dr. H.G. Kirulata**, Memorial U., received $22,606 to develop a test for bladder tumors to detect which superficial tumor will ultimately become invasive.
        Dr. H.B. Younghusband, Memorial U., received $28,279 to study biochemical events involved in gene regulation and cell growth.

COUNCIL GIVES GRANT

Dr. John Roder, associate professor of microbiology, Queen's University, was awarded a $200,000 grant by the National Science and Engineering Research Council in the spring of 1983. Roder

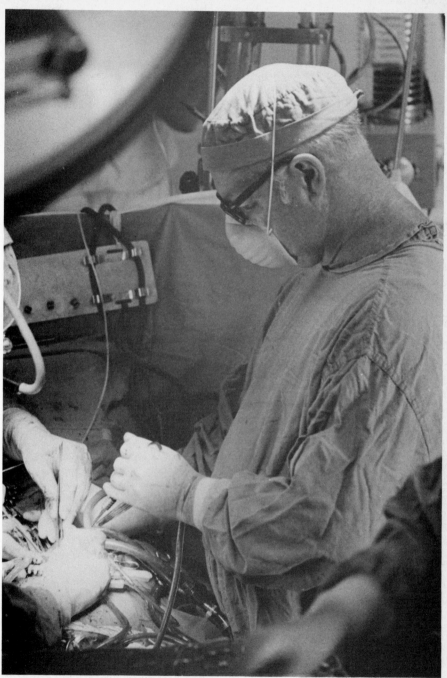

Dr. William T. Mustard, Hospital for Sick Children, Toronto

is developing the technology to make human monoclonal antibodies on a commercial scale.

The human antibodies will be used to fight cancer, auto-immune diseases (diseases where the body's immune system attacks its own tissue rather than foreign substances), leprosy and tetanus.

Dr. R.G. Fenwick, Dalhousie U., received $50,351 to study the molecular analysis of mutation and the effects of carcinogens.

Dr. I.A. Macdonald, Dalhousie U., received a grant to study any significant difference in metabolism between low-risk subjects, control subjects and bowel cancer patients.

Dr. E.W.K. Jay, professor of chemistry at the University of New Brunswick, received $39,186 to research a practical method of producing large-scale commercial quantities of the natural protein interferon for therapeutic use and the production of quantities of pure tumor antigens for biochemical studies.

A MAN OF VISION

Carl Evans of Scarborough, Ont., has developed a contact lens to correct the vision of patients who are both near-sighted and farsighted.

He claims an 85 per cent success rate with people who have these problems. More than 13,000 Canadians are using the lens which he developed in the basement of his office. Most of the beneficiaries are people over 40 who wear bifocals.

The Montreal Cancer Institute, under director Dr. Rene Simard, received $497,450 for basic clinical and operation research.

Dr. P.A. Kelly, McGill U., received $85,987 to study the role of hormones and their receptors on the growth and development of mammary car-

cinom and the effect of prolactin and growth factors on cells derived from human breast cancer biopsies.

Dr. P.P. Major, McGill U., received $34,859 to study the biological properties of human breast cancer-associated antigens.

Dr. C.P. Stanners, McGill U., received $99,394 to study the molecular genetics of surface antigens involved in human cancer.

Drs. S. Hanessian and T. Theophanides, U. of Sherbrooke, received $22,060 to study novel antitumor agents.

Dr. J. Brisson, Laval U., received $65,899 to research the role of diet in the etiology of breast cancer.

Dr. V.M. Whitehead, Montreal Children's Hospital, received $41,488 to continue research into the use of Methotrexate, an antifolate and anticancer agent.

Dr. J. Jolivet, Montreal Cancer Institute, received $58,008, also for the study of Methotrexate as an antitumor agent.

Dr. Mary M. Stevenson, Montreal General Hospital Research Institute, received $48,302 to investigate cellular and biochemical events leading to macrophage (a type of white blood cell) inflammation.

MONTREAL RESEARCHERS MAKE ARTIFICIAL BLOOD

Dr. Thomas Chang and Peter Keipert of McGill University's Artificial Cells and Research Centre have made an important breakthrough in the development of artificial blood derived from human blood. They have managed to link molecules of hemoglobin in middle-sized agglomerates. The hemoglobin itself came from whole blood no longer fresh enough to be used in transfusions.

Their discovery holds promise for a more efficient use of donated blood and for emergency blood transfusions without having to match blood types.

Division of Biological Research, Ontario Cancer Institute, under director Dr. E.A. McCulloch received $1-million to study respiratory cancer mortality among welders in union locals in Toronto, Hamilton, Sarnia and Ottawa.

Dr. I. Broder, Gage Institute, received $71,226.

Dr. M.T. Goldberg, U. of Guelph, received $30,921 to research occupational and lifestyle factors involved in bladder cancer.

Drs. W.R. Inch and **S.F. Prato**, U. of Western Ontario, received $41,357 to develop a technique to predict complications in lung or chest wall tumors.

Dr. U. Ambus, Ontario Cancer Institute, received $10,199 to do a follow-up study of adjuvant therapy for breast cancer in post-menopausal women.

Dr. D.R. McCalla, McMaster U., received $49,536 for research to determine if simple changes in mould-making additives would lower the risk to foundry workers who face an increased risk of lung cancer.

Dr. R.S. Kerbel, director of a research group at Queen's U., received $400,000 to study tumor and host factors in tumor progression.

Dr. S.P. Sielberg, Hospital for Sick Children, Toronto, received $43,067 to devise noninvasive approaches to the diagnosis of possible drug reactions and to counsel patients and families about drug toxicity risk.

Dr. T.P. Conner, Women's College Hospital, Toronto, received $20,841 to evaluate experimental breast scanners and compare their accuracy and efficacy with the traditional x-ray mammography techniques.

TECHNOLOGY VS CANCER

Canadian surgeon Dr. Rudy Falk has pioneered a cancer heat treatment called hyperthermia. The treatment appears to be effective in killing cancer cells and shrinking tumors. Hyperthermia combined with drugs has been used at the Toronto General Hospital to treat several hundred patients.

Falk began using hyperthermia in 1981, employing a bulky machine produced by an American firm. Now, a team of U of T engineers, cancer unit nurses, a medical student trained as an aerospace engineer and doctors have developed a much smaller heat machine.

The new, portable device will allow nurses to visit patients in their homes at their convenience and at considerable less cost than hospital treatment.

A grant of $655,550 went to the **Manitoba Institute of Cell Biology** toward a three-year programme under the administration of Dr. G.J. Goldenberg.

Dr. Harvey Schipper, Manitoba Cancer Treatment and Research Foundation, received $57,899 for a programme to measure the quality of life of cancer patients, especially those in rural clinics serviced by general practitioners.

Dr. S. Shaleve, Manitoba Cancer Treatment and Research Foundation, received $51,927 to investigate the physical basis of diaphanography, or transillumination, the passage of light through the body tissues for purposes of examination.

Dr. R.C. Warrington, department of biochemistry, U. of Saskatchewan, received $31,905 to study growth-control mechanisms which are operative in cultured normal mammalian cells.

Dr. M.J. Robins, U. of Alberta, received $63,361 toward design, synthesis and biological evaluation of possible anticancer agents and the development of procedures for the synthesis of known antitumor drugs.

Dr. E.A. Turley, U. of Calgary, received $7,775 to investigate mechanisms controlling cell movement.

A research group led by **Dr. H.F. Stich**, B.C. Cancer Research Centre, received $499,930 to research environmental carcinogenesis.

Dr. C.J. Eaves and a research team at

the Cancer Research Group at the Terry Fox laboratory received $340,000 for a programme in hematology/oncology.

Dr. J.T. Emerman, U. of British Columbia, received $15,172 for a study of hormone and drug interations in breast carcinoma therapy.

Dr. F.A. Salinas, Cancer Control Agency of B.C., received $36,609 to investigate the clinical significance of immune complexes and associated antigens in breast cancer.

Dr. A.M. Churg, Cancer Control Agency of B.C., received $15,172 to examine patients with a history of asbestos exposure to collect information about exposure to asbestos and other fine fibrous mineral dusts.

Toronto's Sick Children's Hospital which opened on March 23, 1875, was the first hospital in Canada devoted entirely to the care and cure of children. It is still Canada's foremost children's hospital and has received worldwide acclaim for its standards of hospital practice and for the medical breakthroughs that have occurred there.

HOSPITAL FOR SICK CHILDREN VICTORIES

A School of Nursing was established in 1886, just 12 years after Canada's first nursing school was founded. The School of Nursing is the oldest school operated by a children's hospital in North America.

In 1899 an orthopedic shop was instituted in the hospital to provide splints, braces and specially designed prosthetic appliances. In 1972 a "Toronto Splint" developed at the hospital was depicted on an Australian postage stamp.

The hospital began to pasteurize milk as early as 1908 and hospital officials were instrumental in getting the government to make pasteurization mandatory after 1938.

In 1910 a tuberculosis pavilion was opened. Sick Children's was one of the first institutions in the world to realize the value of sunlight and use it extensively.

A nutritional research laboratory was opened in 1918 and work began which led to the development of cereals for infants and national content standards for agricultural products.

In 1921 Dr. Bruce Robertson developed the first exchange transfusions at the hospital, to reduce infant mortality although at that time the Rh blood factor was unknown.

In 1922 Dr. W.E. Gallie developed living tissue sutures at the hospital.

A School of Mothercraft was established at the institution in 1927, heading a movement that subsequently spread throughout Canada.

Drs. Brown, Tisdall and Drake, seeking ways to cut infant mortality, developed the first baby biscuits. Known as McCormicks Sunwheat Biscuits, they contained foods high in nutritional value, and had all the vitamins. In 1931 they brought out Pablum — from the latin word pabulum, meaning food — a precooked cereal for infants, which changed infant feeding the world over. Their work also led to the vitamin enrichment of breads and dairy products. Later Drake and Tisdall each won the Order of the British Empire for their work establishing Red Cross prisoner-of-war parcels during the Second World War.

Dr. G. Hamblin designed the first neonatal transport incubator in 1930 when he placed a mattress on a hot water tank in a wooden box. During the polio epidemic in 1937 the workshops of the hospital produced more than 30 iron lungs and hospital staff organized temporary treatment centres which cared for more than 300 stricken children.

In 1930 Dr. N. Silverthorne developed a vaccine for whooping cough which continues to be used.

In 1941, working in cooperation with the Dominion Department of Agriculture and Health, hospital researchers established standards for Canada Approved white flour and bread. They also carried out studies used by the government to design diets for the Armed forces. The Red Cross also made use of the studies when assembling prisoner-of-war parcels.

The independent Research Institute was established in 1957 as a separate division within the hospital. The laboratory is world renowned and the hundreds of research projects are supported by a $3-million annual budget. One of the laboratory's major successes was the development of a procedure to cut the time to diagnose whooping cough from five days to 30 minutes.

Dr. R.B. Salter developed an operation in 1957 for the treatment of congenital dislocation of the hip. Known as the Salter operation, the procedure permits children to walk and live normal lives and is used worldwide.

Dr. W.T. Mustard, working at the Sick Children's Hospital, perfected an operation in 1964 to correct congenital transposition of the great vessels of the heart. The "blue baby operation" has saved the lives of countless children.

A team led by Dr. B. Shandling successfully completed the first separation of conjoined (Siamese) twins in Canada in 1971.

Drs. A.M. Albisser and B.S. Leibel developed the first artificial pancreas at the Hospital in 1973.

The first treatment of scoliosis (curvature of the spine) by means of implanted electronic muscle stimulator was developed in 1974 by Dr. W. Bobechko.

In 1976 the hospital installed a "whole body" C.T. Scanner and the first bone marrow transplant program in Canada was initiated. In the same year, Dr. Alan Conn introduced new treatment for near drowning victims.

A surgical team led by Dr. Ian Munro has won worldwide fame for craniofacial surgery. They are noted for reshaping and rebuilding the faces, jaws and heads of deformed children.

Patient trials of "open loop" or preprogrammed continuous intraverons insulin infusion were begun in 1980 and in 1982 a super stability system was introduced to correct scoliosis, eliminating the need for post-operative body casts that were previously worn for up to six months by post-op patients.

LOWERING THEIR VOICES

Researchers at the University of British Columbia have invented a device which may enable those with even severe hearing difficulties to hear. The invention works on the premise that most people afflicted by deafness, even those with middle ear nerve damage, are able to hear at very low frequencies.

The hearing aid, a small square device, compresses the high tones of speech into bass rumbles that become audible to the wearer.

DOCTORS AT U OF T PROVE NAPOLEON WASN'T MURDERED

With a sample of Napoleon Bonaparte's hair and the University of Toronto's Slowpoke Reactor Facility, Toronto doctors have concluded that Napoleon died of natural causes. Their "neutron activation analysis" detected only normal levels of arsenic in the hair sample. The research counters a French theory that the French emperor died from an overdose of arsenic. Researchers believed that they had found elevated levels of arsenic in the hair some 20 years ago. The Toronto doctors believe that the separation of elements was much less exact 20 years ago and arsenic may have been confused with antimony, common in medications during the 1800s.

UNIVERSITY OF WESTERN ONTARIO TO HOUSE UNIQUE MEDICAL CENTRE

The John P. Robarts Memorial Research Institute, a medical centre to focus on research and prevention of stroke, heart and related diseases, will be built at London's University of Western Ontario.

The Ontario government is to contribute $10-million toward the centre which it describes as unique in Canada. The government will also canvass the private sector for a matching sum of $10-million for the centre.

Robarts, premier of Ontario from 1961 to 1971, had previously represented the London area as MPP and was a former chancellor of the university. He suffered a series of strokes in August 1981 and died by his own hand in 1982.

General Awards – Science

IZAAK WALTON KILLAM MEMORIAL PRIZE

The Canada Council

The prize honours eminent Canadian scholars engaged in research in industry, government agencies or universities related to the natural sciences, medicine or engineering. Winners are chosen by the Killam Selection Committee, which comprises 13 scholars representing various academic disciplines.

1981 **Dr. Feroze Ghadially**, head of the department of pathology, University of Saskatchewan, received worldwide recognition for his contributions to the study of cancer, arthritis and the application of advanced biophysics techniques to problems of human disease. Probably the best-known pathologist working in electron microscopy, his writings have become basic text books in the field.

Dr. Raymond Lemiux, professor of organic chemistry, University of Alberta, has contributed to the development of new antibiotics through research in carbohydrate chemistry. His work on synthetic antigens is used for blood typing and grouping and in the treatment of leukemia and hemophilia.

Dr. Louis Sminiovitch, geneticist-in-chief, Hospital for Sick Children, and professor of medical genetics, University of Toronto, has an international reputation in the field of molecular and cellular genetics. He pioneered the genetic analysis of cells and researched the metastatic growth of cancer cells. He has also worked to promote public awareness of the social impacts of modern biology.

1982 **Dr. William T. Tutte**, professor of mathematics, University of Waterloo, received $50,000 for his outstanding contributions to mathematics.

Tutte is credited with making the most significant contributions to graph theory over the past 30 years, and continues to be the leading authority in the field. He has also won international acclaim for his contributions to the theory of matroids. His work led to important applications in combinatorics, geometry, linear algebra, electrical engineering, computer science and group theory in the social sciences.

1983 **Dr. Brenda Milner**, Montreal Neurological Institute, won $50,000 for her research in neuropsychology, the study of the brain and behaviour.

Milner has contributed to the study of hemispheric specialization, the effects of early brain damage on subsequent cerebral organization, and the functions of the frontal lobes of the brain.

KILLAM RESEARCH FELLOWSHIPS

The Canada Council

Awards totalling more than $1.1-million were presented to 30 Canadian scientists and scholars in the 15th annual Killam competition.

The program enables the Council to maintain valuable contact with the community of scholars. The Fellowships provide salary replacement and fringe benefits.

1983 **A.D. Bandrauk**, U. of Sherbrooke, for chemistry: the behaviour and reactions of molecules in the presence of intense lasers.

P.M. Conlon, McMaster U., for French and library science: a bibliography of all works by French writers during the Enlightenment, 1716-1789.

S.A. Cook, U. of Toronto, for computer science and mathematics: toward proving ultimate lower limits on the time and memory required for computers to solve naturally arising problems.

F.I.M. Craik, U of T, for experimental psychology: a general processing view of memory and memory disorder.

P.C. Dodwell, Queen's U., for psychology: spatial vision, pattern and recognition: the analysis of local and global processes in visual perception.

J.L. Granatstein, York U., for history: a history of Canada in its 10th decade, 1957-1967.

L.D. Hall, U. of British Columbia, for Chemistry, biochemistry, spectroscopy, anatomy: development of the medical imaging of the intact human body using positron emission tomogra-

phy and nuclear magnetic resonance spectroscopy.

M.L. Halperin, U of T, for medical sciences: control of acid secretion by the kidney; control of energy metabolism in cancer cells; textbook on regulation of energy metabolism.

R.C. Harris, UBC, for geography and history: studies of early Canadian settlement.

J.R. de J. Jackson, U of T, for English literature: the literary environment of romantic poetry.

Gabriel Kolko, York U., for history and social sciences: principal factors determining the outcome of war between technologically advanced and agrarian societies: the United States and Vietnam, 1950-1975, as a case study.

H.H. Stern, Ontario Institute for Studies in Education, for education and applied linguistics: a systematic study of language teaching methodology.

Charles Taylor, McGill U., for philosophy: the nature of the human person.

R.S.C. Wong, U. of Manitoba, for mathematics: asymptotic approximations of integrals.

HENRY MARSHALL TORY MEDAL

Royal Society of Canada

The medal was endowed by the late Henry Marshall Tory, mathematician and physicist, foundeı of the universities of British Columbia and Alberta, a prime organizer and first president of the National Research Council, a leader in the creation of Carleton College at Ottawa and its first president, and a former president of the Royal Society of Canada.

The award is given every two years for outstanding research in a branch of astronomy, chemistry, mathematics, physics or an allied science.

1981 **Alexander Edgar Douglas**, RRSC, of the National Research Council, for his outstanding work in molecular spectroscopy. Dr. Douglas has been with the NRC since 1941.

1983 **Dr. Ron J. Gillespie**, professor of chemistry, McMaster U., Hamilton, Ont. Gillespie was born and educated in London, England, and joined the staff at McMaster in 1958. He has achieved worldwide recognition for his career in inorganic chemistry. Gillespie's application of "super acid" media studies to organic systems led to discoveries of new carbonium species. This area of chemistry developed into a flourishing branch of organic chemistry of particular importance to the petrochemical industry.

STEACIE PRIZE IN THE NATURAL SCIENCES

National Research Council

The prize is named after the late Dr. Edgar Steacie, a physical chemist and former president of the National Research Council of Canada. The fund was established through contributions from friends, associates and former colleagues of Steacie. A prize of $5,000 accompanies the citation.

1982 **Dr. Brian Sykes**, professor, department of biochemistry, U. of Alberta, and member, Medical Research Council of Canada Group in Protein Structure and Functions.

Sykes' research has made notable contributions to studies of biological systems and to the development of new nuclear magnetic resonance techniques and experimental approaches.

E.W.R. STEACIE MEMORIAL FELLOWSHIPS

Natural Sciences and Engineering Research Council of Canada

The fellowships are awarded annually by the council to four of Canada's most promising researchers.

1983 **Dr. Kamilo Feher**, professor of electrical engineering at the U. of Ottawa. His work led to the discovery, development and manufacture of original telecommunications products. His achievements include development of the first hybrid digital/analog-voice-video microwave and cable system, known as Data Above Voice/Video. A consultant of Spar Aerospace, he has led research into a digital satellite earth station. At the U. of Ottawa, he developed a digital satellite and microwave communications research laboratory.

1982 **Christopher C. Coy**, St. Catharines, Ont. YSF Gold Medal (Intermediate), Science Teachers of Ontario Award, Canadian Federation of Biological Societies Award, for: Investigating field cricket pheromones.

Kathleen Leggett, Toronto, Ont. YSF Gold Medal (Senior), John Chapman Award, Joseph Kerbel Youth Science Scholarship, Canadian Society for Immunology Award, Biological Council of Canada Award, for: Red dye number 2: a study of its effects on certain living organisms and an analysis of the chemical reactions involved in the production of such effects.

Mark Yarmoshuk, St. Catharines, Ont. YSF Gold Medal, Grolier Limited and Abitibi-Price Inc. awards, for: The pill with acid improves stem cutting development.

Paul Robert Benedetti, Cambridge, Ont. YSF Gold Medal (Junior), Engineering Institute of Canada and Commodore Business Machines awards, for: Micro outbytes mech. computer.

Henry Fierz, Bath, Ont. YSF Gold Medal (Senior), Canadian Council of Professional Engineers, Northern Telecom Bell/Northern Research Scholarship, Shell Canada Award, for: Highwind surfboard.

Paul Jeffrey, Hatt, Lion's Head, Ont. YSF Gold Medal (Senior), Royal Astronomical Society, Canadian Association of Physicists, Northern Telecom/Bell Northern Scholarship, Shell Canada Award, for: Drift Interferometry.

Joseph Hugh, Pasika, Sudbury, Ont. YSF Gold Medal (Intermediate), Northern Telecom/Bell Northern Research Award, for: Circa 1700: polymer chemistry research.

Wong Albert Hung Choy, Victoria, B.C. YSF Gold Medal (Junior), Northern Telecom/Bell Northern Research Award, Optex Corporation Award, for: Electrodynamics.

Dr. Janet Rossant, associate professor of biological science, Brock University, and the department of pathology, McMaster U.

Rossant's research is in early mammalian embryogenesis and fetal maternal interactions, an important area of research in light of recent interest in human and animal in vitro fertilization and possible genetic manipulation of the fetus.

LE PRIX MARIE-VICTORIN

Ministry of Cultural Affairs, Quebec

A $15,000 bursary and a medal are awarded for work in the pure sciences (physics, chemistry, biology, the natural sciences).

1982   **Professor Camille Sandorfy**, U. of Montreal, for the advancement of physics and chemistry. Sandorfy was also awarded the Chemical Institute of Canada Medal for 1983.

PMAC MEDAL OF HONOUR

Pharmaceutical Manufacturers Association of Canada

The award recognizes contributions to the advancement of science. The medal was specially struck in gold in 1945 by the Royal Canadian Mint. It bears the likeness of the Winged Goddess of Samothrace, symbolizing our conquest of disease and death. Some notable recipients:

1945   **Sir Alexander Fleming**
1948   **Dr. Charles H. Best**
1950   **Dr. Edward C. Kendall**
1952   **Dr. T. Clarence Routley**
1955   **Sir Henry Hallett Dale**
1958   **Dr. Wilder Graves Penfield**
1964   **Dr. Ray Farquharson**
1967   **Dr. Murray L. Barr**

1973   **Dr. Gustave Gingras**

CANADA-WIDE SCIENCE FAIR

Youth Science Foundation

In 1981, 236 young Canadians from nine provinces presented science projects at the 20th Annual Canada-wide Science Fair. Nine gold medals were awarded.

1981   **Harold Yachsyn**, Edmonton, Alta. YSF Gold Medal, Queen's U. Applied Science Award, Whiteshell Nuclear Research Establishment Award, for: In situ Sonic Tar Sand Separation.

Yazim Mustapha, Winnipeg, Man. YSF Gold Medal, Canadian Federation of Biological Societies Award, Labatts Award, for: Aggressive Behaviour of Fish.

Paul R. Benedetti, Cambridge, Ont. YSF Gold Medal, Canadian Institute of Mining and Metallurgy Syncrude Canada Limited Award, World Book Childcraft, for: Basic Industrial Smart Robot.

Chris Crowe and Kathryn Tate, Sudbury, Ont. YSF Gold Medal, Canada Cement Award, Grolier Award, for: The Magnus Effect.

Simone Howden, Kingston, Ont. YSF Gold Medal, Canadian Federation of Biological Societies Award, Molson Award, for: Coordination of Different Ages.

Nancy Porter, Smiths Falls, Ont. YSF Gold Medal, Eaton Foundation Award, Optox Corporation Award, for: Synoposis of Glue Testing.

David S. Schneider, Nepean, Ont. YSF Gold Medal, Rockwell International of Canada Award, Shell Canada Award, for: The Use of Bacteriophage in Biological Insecticides.

John D. Swain, Agincourt, Ont. YSF Gold Medal, Canadian Association of Physicists Award, Shell Canada Award, for: Design of a New Gravitational Wave Detector.

John Griffioen and Jack Tu, Kingston, Ont. YSF Gold Medal, Commodore Business Machines Award, Westcoast

Transmission Award, Solar Energy Society Award, for: Phase Change Heat Storage in a Hypar Solar House.
Dr. Noël James, professor of geology, Memorial U. Internationally recognized in the field of deposition of carbonates, James studies the sedimentology, paleontology and diagenesis of modern and ancient carbonate rocks. Since these rocks contain metallic ores and are possible reservoirs for hydrocarbons, a better understanding of their history aids further mineral and oil exploration. In 1982 James won the Geological Association of Canada Past President's Medal.
Dr. Geraldine A. Kenney-Wallace, professor of chemistry, U. of Toronto. Kenney-Wallace is known internationally for her research on the physical and chemical dynamics of molecules in liquids on a time-scale of trillionths of a second. Some applications include microelectronics and optical processing for communications using molecules and their interactions to encode and decode information.

SANDFORD FLEMING MEDAL

Royal Canadian Institute

1982/83   **Lydia Dotto**, co-director of *Canadian Science News* and former science writer with *The Globe and Mail*, for making scientific and technological news understandable to the public.

The Royal Canadian Institute is Canada's oldest scientific organization. It was founded in 1849 by John Henry Lefroy and Sandford Fleming to encourage the study and exchange of scientific and cultural knowledge. The Institute continues to present weekly lectures in Toronto.

PURE SCIENCES

DISTINGUISHED SERVICE AWARD

Royal Astronomical Society of Canada

An award to members for outstanding service to a centre or to the Society.

1983   **Dr. Lloyd A. Higgs**, Penticton, B.C.
       Christopher G. Aiken, Victoria, B.C.

KEN CHILTON PRIZE

Royal Astronomical Society of Canada

Given in remembrance of Ken E. Chilton to an amateur astronomer, for astronomical work carried out or published during the year.

1981   **C. McCaw**, Vancouver, B.C.
1982   **Chris Spratt**, Victoria, B.C.

SIMON NEWCOMBE AWARD

Royal Astronomical Society of Canada

Presented for the best article on astronomy, astrophysics or space science submitted by a member of the Society during the year.

1982   **Phil Mozel**, Toronto, Ont.

GOLD MEDAL

Royal Astronomical Society of Canada

The Gold Medal was established in 1905 to encourage the study of astronomy. It is awarded to a fourth year University of Toronto Arts and Science graduate who has an overall A standing and the highest average mark in two full courses and two half courses in astronomy.

1981   **T.C. Box**
1982   **M.J. Gaspar**, Toronto, Ont.

DOROTHEA KLUMPKE-ROBERTS AWARD

Astronomical Society of the Pacific

Professor emerita Helen Sawyer Hogg, University of Toronto, was awarded the Dorothea Klumpke-Roberts Award in 1983 for her contribution to the public's understanding and appreciation of astronomy.

Hogg, famous for her studies of variable stars in globular clusters, was a professor at U of T for 40 years, and for 30 years wrote a column on astronomy for The Toronto Star. A Companion of the Order of Canada, she received the Royal Astronomical Society Distinguished Service Award in 1967, and was the first Canadian and second woman to receive the Rittenhouse Silver Medal. She also holds five honorary degrees.

The Astronomical Society of the Pacific created the award in 1974. Previous recipients include Carl Sagan, Fred Hoyle, Walter Sullivan, Isaac Asimov and Bart Bok.

FLAVELLE MEDAL

Royal Society of Canada

The medal is awarded for an outstanding contribution to biological science during the preceding two years or for significant additions to a previous outstanding contribution to biological science.

1982   **Clayton O. Person**, U. of British Columbia

ACCOLADES FOR UNIQUE BOTANY BOOK

And Some Brought Flowers: Plants in a New World, **by John Downie, Albert Charles Hamilton and Ann Revell (University of Toronto Press, 1980), is one of the handsomest, most readable botanical books ever published for the general public. With beautiful illustra-**tions and lively historical anecdotes, it achieves a much wider context than the mere naming of plants.

GEORGE LAWSON MEDAL

Canadian Botanical Association

The award recognizes contributions made by an individual to Canadian botany.

1981   **Stanley John Hughes**, Biosystematic Research Institute, Agriculture Canada, for his paper on conidiophores, conidia and classification. It formulated a new approach to the classification of the Fungi Imperfecti, once an obscure and unyielding group of fungi. He was also the first to demonstrate that the "sooty moulds" actually represented three different families belonging to different orders of the fungi. This complex of fungi had defied mycologists for about two centuries. He has been awarded the Gold Medal of the Swedish Academy of Science and been elected president of the Mycological Society of America.

1982   **Leslie Laking**, Hamilton, Ontario. Former director of the Royal Botanical Gardens, Hamilton, Ont., among Canada's finest.

A ROOT TO RICHES

Père Joseph Lafitau found the root ginseng near Montreal, while serving as a missionary at Sault-Saint-Louis (Caughnawaga) from 1712 to 1717. A profitable trade with China for the medicinal root was established (worth 20,000 pounds sterling in 1752) but died as the Canadians tried to rush the gathering and drying process and delivered poor-quality ginseng.

MARY E. ELLIOTT SERVICE AWARD

Canadian Botanical Assocation

For outstanding service to the Canadian Botanical Association and to botany in Canada.

1981 Janet R. Stein, professor of botany, U. of British Columbia.

WORLD'S TALLEST BEGONIA

Ellen Cassidy of Richmond, B.C., grew what is believed to be the world's tallest begonia plant in 1979. The plant reached 3 feet, 8 inches.

GOLD MEDAL

Canadian Society of Plant Physiologists

1982 Dr. David Canvin, Queen's U.

CANADIAN BOTANIST HONOURED

Dr. Michael Shaw, professor, University of British Columbia, was, in 1973, elected a fellow of the American Phytopathological Society. He was only the fifth Canadian scientist to be so honoured.

AWARD FOR OUTSTANDING RESEARCH/PRIX POUR L'EXCELLENCE DE LA RECHERCHE

Canadian Phytopathological Society

The award, established in 1977, is given periodically for research in plant pathology.

The Society encourages research, education and the dissemination of knowledge on all aspects of the nature, cause and control of plant diseases.

1980 Dr. William C. Broadfoot, Lethbridge, Alta., whose research in the early 1930s demonstrated the importance of microbiological antagonism in suppressing the activities of the take-all fungus (Gaeumannomyces graminis), which caused a serious root rot of wheat in western Canada.

Dr. Arthur Henry, Edmonton, Alta., whose 1930s research showed that the growth of the fungus Cochliobolus sativus, which caused a serious root rot of wheat in western Canada, was suppressed by a number of fungi and bacteria in the soil, and that changes in temperature resulted in changes in microbiological antagonism against the pathogen.

Dr. Sanford B. Guthrie, who was the first to suggest that control of a plant pathogen, Actinomyces scabies on potatoes, might be brought about by the activity of saprophytic bacteria developing in decomposing fresh organic material added to the soil.

1981 Dr. Thomas C. Vanterpool, Victoria, B.C., for his outstanding research, including the discovery of synergism between plant viruses, his extensive discoveries related to browning root rot of wheat in Saskatchewan and its control by phosphate fertilizers, and his pioneering investigations of diseases of oilseed crops.

EARLY BOTANIC NOTABLES

John Isham, a writer for the Hudson's Bay Company from 1732 to 1749, was respected by Indians and traders alike. He wrote source studies on the fur trade and the flora and fauna of the Far North. He was also a source of inspiration to his assistant, Andrew Graham, whose contributions to Canadian botany were long neglected due to the plagiarization of his written work. Only since the recent publication of his *Observations on Hudson's Bay* has Isham been recognized as the "pioneer naturalist of the North."

Archibald Menzies accompanied Captain Vancouver to the West Coast in 1790 and described many plants, including the madrona or Menzies Arbutus.

Catharine Parr Traill, Lady Dalhousie,

Elizabeth Simcoe, Susanna Moodie and Juliana Horatia Ewing all gathered specimens and wrote of Canadian plants, contributing both to natural history and the country's historical and literary heritage.

John Richardson contributed to studies of Canadian botany by describing many northern plants in his journals while accompanying Sir John Franklin's first and second expeditions to the Arctic.

Another adventurous botanist was Thomas Drummond, who joined Richardson on Franklin's second expedition. Drummond accidentally became separated from the party and was then abandoned by his guide. He spent two winter months alone in the Arctic and though it was his first encounter with such a harsh environment, he survived to continue his botanical career.

Jean-Francois Gaultier, a physician at the Hotel-Dieu and the Quebec seminary from 1742 until his death in 1756, wrote a 400-page manuscript describing plants of Canada, which was only discovered in 1951.

David Douglas, a Scotsman, was a botanist who collected specimens for the Royal Horticultural Society in the 1820s. He identified and described many new plants, including the Douglas fir. Douglas was gored to death by an enraged wild bull in the Hawaiian Islands in 1834 after a second trip to the Pacific Northwest.

In 1699 the surgeon Sieur de Diereville visited Acadia and described the flora and fauna he observed. Some 25 specimens of Acadian plants in the herbarium of the Musee de l'histoire naturelle in Paris are labelled with his name, and the honeysuckle Diervilla (Diervilla Acadensis) was named in his honour.

OUTSTANDING CONTEMPORARY CANADIAN BOTANISTS

The Canadian Botanical Association cites the following as leaders in the field:

Dr. David Canvin, Queen's U.
Dr. Michele C. Heath, U. of Toronto
Dr. Vladimir Krajina, U. of British Columbia
Dr. George F. Ledingham, U. of Regina
Dr. Rolf Sattler, McGill U.
Dr. Michael Shaw, UBC

RUTHERFORD MEMORIAL MEDAL IN CHEMISTRY

Royal Society of Canada

The medal is for outstanding research in any branch of chemistry. It commemorates Lord Rutherford of Nelson, a British scientist who was a leader in nuclear research and winner of the 1908 Nobel Prize.

1983   **Dr. Jaun C. Scaiano**, a senior research officer with the National Research Council, Ottawa. A leader in the field of photochemistry, Scaiano uses modern laser techniques to detect and study the kinetics of rapid organic reactions. His work has revolutionized and set new standards in organic chemistry. Scaiano also developed the first computerized laser photolysis system.

SAVING THE ELMS

Drs. Edward Kondo of Sault Ste. Marie, Erik Jorgensen of Willowdale, Ont., and Dibyendu N. Roy of Toronto, Ont., developed a chemical fungicide in 1975 to immunize the elm tree against Dutch elm disease.

More than 100,000 of the towering shade trees in eastern and central North America have been destroyed by the tree-killing disease carried by the European elm bark beetle.

CHEMICAL INSTITUTE OF CANADA MEDAL

Chemical Institute of Canada

Presented for outstanding contribution to chemistry or chemical engineering in Canada.

1983 **Professor Camille Sandorfy**, U. of Montreal, for his article "Chemical Spectroscopy in the Far Ultraviolet." Sandorfy was also awarded the 1982 Le Prix Marie Victorin by the province of Quebec.

MERCK SHARP AND DOHME LECTURE AWARD

Chemical Institute of Canada

Presented to a scientist under 40 for a contribution in organic chemistry or bio-chemistry while working in Canada. The winner receives $1,500 and delivers a lecture at the conference of the Institute.

1983 **R.H. Kluger**, Toronto, Ont., for "Bio-organic Approaches to Co-enzyme Mechanisms."

GENE EXPERT AT McGILL

Dr. Kelvin Ogilvie, a professor and biological engineer in the chemistry department at McGill University, is one of the world's top experts in gene splicing.

Ogilvie and a colleague designed a method to synthesize genes more efficiently, more quickly and in greater bulk than anyone else. He also helped to create a device called the "gene machine" which produces DNA fragments in an automated process.

Ogilvie was named an Upjohn Fellow in 1974, a fellow of the Chemical Institute of Canada in 1977, and he won the 1982 Steacie Memorial Award as the most promising scientist in Canada.

MONTREAL MEDAL

Chemical Institute of Canada

A medal for leadership or an outstanding contribution to chemistry or chemical engineering in Canada.

1983 **W.H. Gauvin**, Montreal, Que., for "Current Megatrends and their Portent for the Chemical Industry."

UNION CARBIDE AWARD FOR CHEMICAL EDUCATION

Chemical Institute of Canada

Presented to the person who has made outstanding contributions in Canada to education at any level in the field of chemistry or chemical engineering. A commemorative scroll and $750 are awarded. The recipient presents a lecture at the conference of the Institute.

1982 **D. Harpp**, Montreal, Que.
1983 **R.Y. Moir**, Kingston, Ont., for "The Next Two Generations of Canadians: Leaders or Slaves?"

CARBIDE WILLSON FOUNDS A CHEMICAL INDUSTRY

Thomas J. (Carbide) Willson, from Hamilton, Ont., discovered a method to produce calcium carbide and acetylene gas in 1891, and so launched Canada's chemical industry.

The Chemical Industry of Canada paid this tribute to him in 1949: "If any chemical industry can be called typically Canadian, it is probably the manufacture of calcium carbide and the chemicals derived from it through acetylene."

NORANDA LECTURE AWARD

Chemical Institute of Canada

The award is given to a scientist under 40 for outstanding contribution in physical chemistry while working in Canada.

1982　**R. LeBlanc,** Trois Rivieres, Que., for "Optical and Surface Studies of Biological Interfaces."

1983　**D.K. Bohme,** Downsview, Ont., for "Ion chemistry in the Gas Phase: Solving Chemistry without Solutions."

DUNLOP LECTURE AWARD FOR MACROMOLECULAR SCIENCE

Chemical Institute of Canada

Awarded for a distinguished contribution to macromolecular science or technology while working in Canada. The winner receives a scroll and $1000.

1983　**H.P. Schreiber,** Montreal, Que., for "Applied Polymer Sciences: Variations on a Ruminative Theme."

MASTERMINDING MODERN MATERIALS

Dr. William Chalmers, working at McGill University, discovered a process to produce acrylics in 1931, by polymerizing specific materials into a hard transparent solid. Today acrylics make up a huge part of our everyday existence.

CATALYSIS AWARD

Chemical Institute of Canada

Presented for outstanding contribution in the field of catalysis while living in Canada. The recipient presents a lecture to the Institute.

1982　**C.H. Amberg,** Ottawa, Ont.

ALCAN LECTURE AWARD

Chemical Institute of Canada

The award recognizes outstanding contribution in inorganic chemistry of electrochemistry from individuals working in Canada. The winner receives a scroll and $1000.

1982　**G. Ozin,** Toronto, Ont., for "Some Light on Taking Metal Atom Chemistry Out of the Cold."

1983　**W.R. Fawcett,** Guelph, Ont., for "The Eclectrode Position of Semi-Conducting Films and Their Use in Solar Engery Conversion."

SYNTEX AWARD IN PHYSICAL ORGANIC CHEMISTRY

Chemical Institute of Canada

The award is presented to a scientist who has made a distinguished contribution to physical organic chemistry while living in Canada. The winner presents a lecture to the Institute and receives $1,000.

1983　**K.V. Ingold,** Ottawa, Ont., "Vitamin E in Vitro and in Vivo."

NORMAN AND MARION BRIGHT MEMORIAL AWARD

Chemical Institute of Canada

The award is for outstanding contribution in Canada to the advance of chemical technology.

1983　**R. Faggiani,** Hamilton, Ont.

ENVIRONMENTAL IMPROVEMENT AWARD

Chemical Institute of Canada

The award is presented to an organization operating in Canada for a significant contribution to environmental improvement.

1981　**ERCO Industries Limited**

PURVIS MEMORIAL LECTURE

Society of Chemical Industries

Given biannually, the award commemorates the Honourable Arthur B. Purvis, a former president of CIL who was killed in a plane crash in 1941 while serving as chairman of the British Supply Council in North America.

1983   **W.J. Mandry**, chairman of the board of directors, CIL Inc.

R.S. JANE MEMORIAL LECTURE AWARD

Canadian Society for Chemical Engineering

The R.S. Jane Memorial Lecture Award honours the late Dr. Robert Stephen Jane who made an outstanding contribution to the chemical profession and the chemical industry in Canada. The annual award is for an outstanding contribution to chemical engineering or industrial chemistry in Canada. The recipient presents a lecture at the Conference of the Society and receives a scroll and $300.

1983   **E.J. Buckler**, for "Ventures and Adventures in Rubber Technology."

GETTING TO THE CORE OF IT ALL

The Vibra-Corer, developed by Fred Wink of Delta, B.C., has been used since 1980 to obtain samples of placer deposits.

Conventional drilling methods have always been inadequate for recovering certain soil samples, and after 30 years of wondering why no one had solved the problem, Wink decided to do it himself. He developed a portable, practical drill to provide soil profiles.

His invention was recently used in an extensive site investigation for a new dam in southeast Alaska. Where conventional drilling had failed to recover certain soils, particularly the sands and loose silts, the Vibra-Corer was a success.

DUNCAN R. DERRY AWARD
Geological Association of Canada

1983   **Dr. R.W. Hutchinson**, department of geology, U. of Western Ontario, London, Ont. An inspiring teacher, a gifted speaker and an enthusiast. His inspired students populate exploration companies and mineral deposit research institutions around the world. He has added significantly to the knowledge and understanding of diverse important mineral deposits and has increased efficiency in mineral discovery.

PAST-PRESIDENTS' MEDAL
Geological Association of Canada

First awarded in 1974, the medal acknowledges significant recent accomplishments in the earth sciences.

1983   **Andrew D. Miall**, for his contributions to the field of clastic sedimentology. He has advanced the understanding of its processes at every scale, from micro- to plate tectonic. His work has helped not only sedimentologists and stratigraphers, but also economic geologists dealing with placer deposits and coal and uranium occurrences. He is now editor of *Geoscience Canada*.

WRONG ROCKS

Jacques Cartier returned to France from Canada in 1542. He had with him rocks that he thought contained diamonds. The "diamonds" unfortunately were only mica. The phrase "false as the diamonds of Quebec" originates from Cartier's dreams of wealth.

LOGAN MEDAL
Geological Association of Canada

1983   **Dr. John O. Wheeler**, chief geologist to the Geological Survey of Canada, for outstanding scientific leadership in the elucidation of the tectonic evolution of the Canadian Cordillera and its mineral resources, and in the description and analysis of the regional geology and mineral resources of all of Canada. Wheeler contributed to the systematic mapping of the bedrock geology of 60,000 sq. km of the Canadian Cordillera, identified the tectonic evolution of the Whitehorse Trough and set the pattern for subsequent tectonic analysis of the region. His study of the structure of much of southeastern B.C. was a major basis for establishing the geometry and anatomy of the core zone of the southern part of the Columbian Oregon.

BANCROFT AWARD

Royal Society of Canada

The award is made every two years for publication, instruction or research in the geological and geophysical sciences that has contributed to public understanding and appreciation of the subject. A scroll and $1,000 are presented to the winner.

1982 **Dr. Christopher R. Barnes**, department of earth sciences, Memorial U., St. John's, Nfld.

CANADIAN GEOTECHNICAL PRIZE

Canadian Geotechnical Society

The prize is for the best paper of the year published in the *Canadian Geotechnical Journal*.

1982 **Dr. K.Y. Lo and C.M.K. Yuen**, for "Design of Tunnel Lining in Rock for Long-term Time Effects."

LEGGAT AWARD

Canadian Geotechnical Society

The award recognizes individual contributions to the development of theoretical and applied techniques for problems of national concern in the geotechnical field in Canada.

1982 **Donald J. Bazett**, Crippen Consultants, Vancouver, B.C.

WILLET G. MILLER MEDAL

Royal Society of Canada

The medal is given biennially for outstanding research in any branch of the earth sciences. It commemorates the late Willet G. Miller, geologist and pioneer in the development of the Ontario mining industry.

1982 **Dr. Donald Stott**, the Geological Survey of Canada. Recognized internationally, he is an outstanding geologist and a leading authority on the geology of the cretaceous and jurassic systems of Western Canada. His models for deposition of sediments are of major importance to understanding the development of the Rocky Mountains and to outlining the vast coal and petroleum deposits in the foothills and plains of Alberta and British Columbia. His achievements in research have contributed to academic knowledge as well as practical and industrial applications in the energy fields.

CANADIAN MATHEMATICS OLYMPIAD

A national mathematics competition sponsored annually by the Canadian Mathematical Society under the patronage of the Governor-General. The Olympiad, established in 1968, attracts some 300 high school students each year.

The Olympiad is designed to test ability and ingenuity. Questions are selected to test natural ability rather than specific knowledge or training.

In 1981, a Canadian team competed for the first time in the 22nd International Mathematics Olympiad, in Washington, D.C. Team members were:

David Ash, Thunder Bay, Ont.

Arthur Baragar, Edmonton, Alta.
David Bernier, Quebec, Que.
John Bowman, Edmonton, Alta.
John Chew, Toronto, Ont.
Georges Gonthier, Paris, France
Cary Timar, Toronto, Ont.
Julian West, Vancouver, B.C.

Team delegates were G.J. Butler and E. Barbeau. Team members who won individual prizes were David Ash (first), John Chew (second), Georges Gonthier, (first), Cary Timar (second) and Julian West (third).

There were five questions on the 1981 Olympiad competition paper. Students were allowed three hours to complete the paper. Question 5 was as follows (see answer below):

Eleven theatrical groups participated in a festival. Each day, some of the groups were scheduled to perform while the remaining groups joined the general audience. At the conclusion of the festival, each group had seen, during its days off, at least one performance of every other group. At least how many days did the festival last?

Let $N = (1,2, \dots ,n)$ be the days of the festival and let each group be labelled with a subset $A \subset N$ where the group A performs on day x if and only if $x \in A$. In order for two groups A and B to watch each other perform at least once, we cannot have $A = B$. Thus different groups have different labels. Moreover, we cannot have $A \subset B$ or $B \subset A$ either. We first show that $n = 6$ is sufficient. One possible labelling for the 11 groups is $(1,2)$, $(1,3)$, $(1,4)$, $(1,5)$, $(2,3)$, $(2,4)$, $(2,5)$, $(3,4)$, $(3,5)$, $(4,5)$ and (6). We now show that $n = 5$ is insufficient. The label of each group would be a subset $A \subset (1,2,3,4,5)$ and clearly $1 \leq |A| \leq 4$. Define a chain to be a sequence $A1 \subset A2 \subset A3 \subset A4$ with $|Ai| = i$ for $1 \leq i \leq 4$. The number of chains is $5 \times 4 \times 3 \times 2 = 120$. A subset of size 1 or 4 appears in $4 \times 3 \times 2 = 24$ chains while a subset of size 2 or 3 appears in $2 \times 3 \times 2 = 12$ chains. Since there are 11 groups, their labels must appear at least $11 \times 12 = 132$ times in the 120 chains. By the pigeonhole principle, two of the labels A and B appear in the same chain, violating the conditions that $A \not\subset B$ and $B \not\subset A$.

At the 1982 International Mathematics Olympiad in Budapest, Hungary, Canada placed 17th in the unofficial rankings; 119 students from 30 countries participated.

Team members were:

Todd Cardno, Hamilton, Ont.
Edward Hatton, Peterborough, Ont.
Alastair Rucklidge, Toronto, Ont.
Charles Timar, Toronto, Ont.

Team delegates were G.J. Butler and E. Barbeau. Canadian team members who received individual prizes were: Alastair Rucklidge (third) and Charles Timar (third).

In 1983, **William Rucklidge** of Toronto was not quite 17 years old when he won the Canadian Mathematics Olympiad. Rucklidge, who will be a member of the Canadian team at the 1983 International Math Olympiad in Paris, France, is carrying a family banner. His brother Alastair was the first-place winner in the 1982 Canadian Olympiad and was a member of the Canadian team in Hungary at the '82 International Math Olympiad.

CANADA'S PUZZLE-MINT

J.A.H. Hunter has been preparing his Fun with Figures column for Canadian newspapers since 1950. The column also appears in newspapers in Australia, South Africa, the U.S., the U.K. and Hong Kong.

Hunter, 81, is a former British naval officer who began publishing his column in *The Globe and Mail* when he first came to Canada. His 8,000th puzzle was published in the spring of 1983, the most ever published by a problemist. He also invented and named alphametics, puzzles where letters stand for meaningful words in a meaningful context. The alphametic today is the most popu-

lar type of simple math puzzle in the world.

He claims that math is only a hobby to him, but his recent book, *Entertaining Mathematical Teasers and How to Solve Them*, is the latest in a series of mathematical problem books designed to tease and please those with a mathematical bent.

CITATIONS

Canadian Meteorological and Oceanographic Society

The citations recognize individuals or groups who have helped to alleviate pollution by promoting environmental improvements or in developing environmental ethics.

1982 **Ross Howard**, Toronto, Ont., for his book and numerous articles in *The Toronto Star*, which have contributed significantly toward public awareness of air pollution and acidic precipitation problems.

HIGHEST TIDES

The world's greatest tides occur in the Bay of Fundy. Burncoat Head in the Minas Basin of Nova Scotia features the greatest mean spring range with 47.5 feet and an extreme range of 53.5 feet.

GRADUATE STUDENT PRIZE

Canadian Meteorological and Oceanographic Society

The prize is awarded for contributions of special merit in meteorology and/or oceanography by graduate students.

1982 **Glen B. Lesins**, Toronto, Ont., for his contributions to the design and construction of a unique pressure-controlled wind tunnel used in cloud physics research.

JEAN OF ALL SCIENCES

Jean-Francois Gaultier, a physician who came to Canada in 1742, was also an astronomer, mineralogist and noted biologist. He set up the first ever meteorological station in Canada in 1742. He kept a daily log until 1756 that was not discovered until this century.

DR. ANDREW THOMSON PRIZE IN APPLIED METEOROLOGY

Canadian Meteorological and Oceanographic Society

Awarded to a member of the Society for an outstanding contribution in the field of applied meteorology.

1982 **M.K. Thomas**, Toronto, Ont., for his contributions to applied climatology, especially his leadership and diplomacy in launching national and international climate programs, and for his many papers on the nature and value of climatology.

POWERFUL CURRENTS

The strongest currents in the world are the Natwakto Rapids in Slingsby Channel, B.C. (Lat 51° 05'N., Long. 217° 30'W.) The flow rate may reach 16.0 knots (18.4 mph).

PRESIDENT'S PRIZE

Canadian Meteorological and Oceanographic Society

The prize is awarded for a recent paper of special merit on oceanography or meteorology. The paper must have been published in *Atmosphere-Ocean* or have been presented to the Society membership and have been accepted for publication in a refereed journal.

1982 **Dr. G.J. Boer**, Downsview, Ont., for

his contributions to climate modelling and diagnostics and for his paper "Diagnostics Equations in Isobaric Co-ordinates."

ENDURING FOGS

The longest sea level fogs in the world last for weeks on the Grand Banks, Nfld. For an average of more than 120 days per year, visibility is less than 1,000 yards.

PRIZE IN APPLIED OCEANOGRAPHY

Canadian Meteorological and Oceanographic Society

The prize is awarded annually to a member or members of the Society for a significant contribution to the application of oceanography in Canada.

1982 **Dr. J.R. Wilson**, Nepean, Ont., for his dedication and expertise as director of the Marine Environmental Data Service, in particular for his central role in developing the *Canadian Wave Climate Study*, a source of accurate data for both practical and scientific uses.

CANADIANS ON TOP OF THE WORLD

Forty scientists and technicians have spent the spring of 1983 on top of the world. Under the sponsorship of the federal government, an expedition to study the Alpha Ridge was based just 400 km southwest of the North Pole. The earth scientists and oceanographers are attempting to unlock the secrets of the ridge and the Arctic Ocean.

Operating under the code name Caesar 83, the expedition also under-lines Canada's sovereignty in the Arctic, which is more often visited by research-ers from the USSR than by Canadians.

RUBE HORNSTEIN PRIZE IN OPERATIONAL METEOROLOGY

Canadian Meteorological and Oceanographic Society

Awarded for outstanding operational meteorological service in its broadest sense. The award may be granted for cu-mulative work or for a single notable achievement.

1982 **P.C. Haering**, Delta, B.C., for his outstanding work in the application of satellite data to operational meteorol-ogy.

MORLEY K. THOMAS AWARDS

Canadian Atmospheric Environment Service

March 23, 1983, was World Meteoro-logical Day, when the Canadian Atmos-pheric Environment Service paid tribute to the more than 2,000 weather observ-ers across the country. Also honoured were 33 volunteer observers who had provided continuous service for 30 years or more.

The long-serving volunteers received the Morley K. Thomas award for braving any kind of weather at least once a day to record temperature and precipitation in their backyards and then forward the information to Environment Canada.

Vernon Tuck of Grimsby, Ont., 91, is Canada's senior volunteer weather-man. The retired optometrist has been recording the weather since 1944.

HERZBERG MEDAL

Canadian Association of Physicists

Named after Gerhard Herzberg, the Canadian physicist and 1972 Nobel Prize-winner, the medal is given for outstanding research in physics in Canada, to a scientist under 38 years of age.

1983 Dr. W.G. Unruh, U. of British Columbia, Condensed matter physics

CAP MEDAL FOR ACHIEVEMENT IN PHYSICS

Canadian Association of Physicists

The medal is presented to a scientist who has had an outstanding career in physics or who has made a major contribution to the science.

1983 Dr. P.A. Egelstaff, U. of Guelph

PROCESS WITH POTENTIAL

Professor P.K. John, Phillip Tong and chemist King Wong, of the physics department of the University of Western Ontario, in collaboration with K.P. Chik, a physicist at the Chinese University of Hong Kong, have produced thin films of amorphous silicon that are photosensitive, highly stable, and have good semiconductor properties.

The process has potential for widespread applications in solar energy, optical image storage, silicon chip technology and microelectronics uses.

IAN McRAE AWARD OF MERIT

Canadian Nuclear Association

The Ian McRae Award of Merit was established in 1976 in honour of the late first president of the Canadian Nuclear Association. It is given for an outstanding nonscientific contribution to the advancement of nuclear energy in Canada.

1982 Roy F. Errington, Ottawa, Ont., for founding the Commercial Products Division of Atomic Energy of Canada Ltd., now called the Radiochemical Company. The unit started with three people in 1946 and has grown to employ 1,000 people "applying nu-

clear technology for the benefit of mankind world-wide." Errington also helped found a major medical sterilization industry and paved the way for commercial exploitation of food irradiation.

W.B. LEWIS MEDAL

Canadian Nuclear Association

The W.B. Lewis Medal was established in 1973 in honour of the former senior vice-president (science), Atomic Energy of Canada Ltd. It recognizes a Canadian scientist or engineer for competence and accomplishment in nuclear science and engineering.

1982 Ernie Siddall, Chalk River, Ont. His innovative approach to safety and risk analysis has had a significant impact on all nuclear power plant design. Siddall is also a musician and a sailor who has twice crossed the Atlantic in his own yacht.

MONUMENTAL MEASUREMENT

The National Research Council Laboratory in Ottawa and the US National Bureau of Standards Boulder Laboratories recorded the highest frequency ever directly measured in a visible yellow light at $5.20206528 \times 10^{14}$ hertz (c. 520 terahertz or million million cycles per second). The measurement was made in February 1979.

RUTHERFORD MEDAL IN PHYSICS

Royal Society of Canada

The medal is awarded for outstanding research in any branch of physics.

1983 Dr. David Rowe, professor of physics, U. of Toronto. Dr. Rowe has done significant work in theoretical nuclear physics. His recent accomplishments have been in applications of sophisticated modern techniques of Lie algebra group theory and differential geometry to nuclear modelling. Rowe's use of modern mathematics as an approach to nuclear physics has been a major contribution to the field.

CANADIAN PHYSICIST WINS TOP U.S. AWARD

Boris P. Stoicheff, professor of physics at the University of Toronto, was awarded the 1983 Frederic Ives Medal of the Optical Society of America. The award, the society's highest honour, consists of a silver medal and a citation. Stoicheff was recognized for his contributions to high resolution Raman spectroscopy, nonlinear optics and the applications of nonlinear optics to atomic and molecular spectroscopy.

Stoicheff is a fellow of the Royal Society of Canada, an officer of the Order of Canada and president of the Canadian Association of Physicists for 1983/84.

GERHARD HERZBERG AWARD

Spectroscopy Society of Canada

The award is made for outstanding contributions to the science of spectroscopy, the theory and interpretation of interactions between matter and radiation.

1982   **Dr. J.C.D. Brand**, U. of Western Ontario, for long service and many contributions to the field of spectroscopy.

ENRICO FERMI AWARD

United States Government

Wilfrid Bennett Lewis of Deep River, Ont., won the U.S. government's Enrico Fermi Award in 1982.

The award is granted for achievement in the development, use or control of atomic energy and has been presented to such notables as Edward Teller and Robert Oppenheimer, pioneer developers of the atomic bomb. Lewis is the first scientist to receive the award for work done inside Canada.

Lewis began working on atomic problems at Cambridge University in the 1930s. He worked on radar in England during the Second World War and came to Canada to be atomic energy director at the National Research Council in 1946. He was head of research for Atomic Energy Canada Ltd. from 1952 until 1963. Since then he has served as an advisor to the UN and the International Atomic Energy Agency.

Lewis' award, a gold medal and $25,000, was for his work toward the peaceful use and control of atomic energy in Canada and for promoting international control of nuclear power.

BOOST FOR BIOLOGY

Dr. James Hillier, Brampton, Ont., and Albert Prebus of Edmonton, Alta., gave biological and medical research a tremendous boost with their development of the electron microscope in the late 1930s.

CREDIT WHERE CREDIT IS DUE

"I naturally ... discovered, as we white men say when we are pointed out some geographical feature by an Indian who has been familiar with it since childhood, many lakes and small streams never before visited except by the red man."
Warburton Pike, *Barren Ground Journey*

"The task of the explorer ... was not so much to find a route as, first, to find Indians who would show him routes which they and their ancestors had used for generations and then to plot these routes on his maps and assess their value ..."
David Glover, *David Thompson's Narrative*

MASSEY MEDAL

Royal Canadian Geographical Society

The medal has been awarded annually since 1959 for achievement in the exploration, development or description of the geography of Canada. It was instituted by the late Rt. Hon. Vincent Massey, the first Canadian to hold the office of Governor-General since Confederation and also an Honorary Patron of the Society.

1983 **Willis Roberts**, Fredericton, N.B., for conceiving and establishing the Land Registration and Information Service, a system by which geographical areas are uniquely identified and computerized.

Other major winners of the Massey Medal since 1959 are as follows:

1959 **Superintendent Henry Asbjorn Larsen**, Royal Canadian Mounted Police, for his contribution to Canadian geographical knowledge while master of the patrol vessel *St. Roch*, and in recognition of the first west to east voyage through the Northwest Passage.

1962 **Dr. Diamond Jenness**, for his authoritative studies of the Canadian Indians, the Copper Eskimo and the pre-historic Old Bering Sea and Cape Dorset Eskimo cultures, based on field studies commenced with the Canadian Arctic Expedition 1913-1916 and continued as a member and as chief of the anthropological division of the National Museum of Canada.

1964 **Dr. Yves Oscar Fortier**, Geological Survey of Canada, for exploration and study of the Arctic Islands and for being first to recognize their oil-bearing potential.

1966 **Dr. Alf Erling Porsild**, National Museum of Canada, for his research on the Canadian Arctic, particularly its botany and the use of Arctic plants

for food, and for his work in the establishment of the Canadian reindeer herd.

1972 **Isobel Moira Dunbar**, Defence Research Board, for her work in arctic geography and sea ice, notably on the climatology of ice distribution and the interpretation of ice in photographs, including satellite and infrared photography.

1978 **Edward Gustav Pleva**, U. of Western Ontario, for his contribution to modern geographical education in Canada, and especially to the training of university and high school teachers from coast to coast.

1980 **Dr. Maurice Hall Haycock**, for his contribution to historical and cultural geography through his paintings of the Canadian North from Newfoundland to the Yukon to the Pole.

1981 **Dr. Raymond Thorsteinsson**, Geological Survey of Canada, for his pioneer work in exploring the geology of the Canadian North, which laid the foundation for economic development and national policies.

VIKING WINNERS, BY ACCIDENT

It is only partially recorded, but the story goes that around the year 986, Bjarni Herjulfsson, a Viking, was going from Iceland to Greenland to spend Christmas with his dad. Bjarni got lost in the fog or blown off course — either way he missed Greenland. When he finally found his way home, he told his friend Lief Eriksson that he had sighted new lands. The lands were most likely Baffin Island, the coast of Labrador and possibly Newfoundland.

Lief (the Lucky) soon followed Bjarni's route (c. 1000) and established a short-lived colony in the new lands. Eriksson named areas: Helluland (flagstoneland, probably Baffin Island), Markland (woodland, the Labrador coast) and Vinland (maybe wineland but more likely Meadowland, the Strait of Belle Isle, or Newfoundland).

Freydis Eriksson, sister of Lief, is the first known European woman to explore Canada.

GEOGRAPHIC INTRIGUE

Religious and burial artifacts of the now extinct Beothuk Indians of Newfoundland are surprisingly similar to those of ancient Egypt. It is pure speculation, but could the ancient Egyptians have found Newfoundland?

Did Irish missionaries of the sixth century sail to America in leather boats? Some contend that St. Brendan, an Irish abbot and missionary, crossed to Newfoundland in the mid-sixth century. There is more substantial evidence that Irish monks fled from the Vikings around the year 800, first from Ireland to Iceland and then from Iceland when the Norsemen arrived there about 874. The monks may have established themselves on the Strait of Belle Isle.

Sinclair, Earl of Orkney, is said to have reached Canada in 1398.

EARLY EVIDENCE

A Viking map of Iceland and Greenland (c. 1440), published by Yale University in 1965, shows a large land mass which is inscribed as "Vinland Island, discovered by Bjarni & Lief in Company."

FIRST PRIZE FOR DISCOVERING CANADA

Giovanni Caboto (John Cabot), who sailed from Bristol in 1497 on his voyage of discovery, most likely sighted the Nova Scotia and Cape Breton coasts before crossing to Newfoundland and sailing from Cape Race for England.

He described his discovery as "a very good and temperate country" and reported "Brazil wood and silks grow there. The sea is covered with fishes, which are caught not only with the net, but with baskets, a stone being tied to them in order that the baskets may sink into the water."

In 1498, on his return to England, Cabot received a reward of 10 pounds and an annual pension of 20 pounds from Henry VII for his services to the Crown.

He didn't live long enough to collect his pension, however, as he perished on his second voyage to the New World.

NEAT COUNTRY

Kanada or Kanata is an Iroquois word meaning collection of huts or lodges (nice to think that Canada means home). The Algonquin word meaning settlement is Odanah, and the Cree word Kanatan means "something that is very clean or neat."

The name Canada first appeared in Cartier's account of his second voyage.

Indians told Cartier that the St. Lawrence flowed through three countries or kingdoms: those of Saguenay, Canada and Hochelaga. They described the Saguenay River as the road to the Kingdom of Great Wealth. When he reached Ile-aux-Coudres he was told he had entered the kingdom of Canada. The area ended somewhere between present-day Trois-Rivieres and Quebec City.

SOME WINNING EXPLORERS

John Davis. The first explorer of the far northern coasts, he made three voyages, the first in 1585. He charted the outline of the whole of the southern part of Davis Strait.
Sir Frances Drake. On a two-year buccaneering jaunt, he may have sighted the B.C. coast. If he did, he was two centuries ahead of later explorers.

William Baffin. He sailed further into the North in 1615 than anyone else was to do for 200 years. He did not realize that he reached the entrance of the Northwest Passage.

Samuel de Champlain. Explorer and colonizer, he was truly the Father of New France.

Etienne Brulé. The pioneer of French exploration westward into the continent, he was likely the first European man to live with the Indians.

Henry Kelsey. He was the first European to see the buffalo, the musk-ox and the Canadian prairies.

The Family La Verendrye. Pierre Gaultier, Sieur de La Verendrye, his four elder sons and his nephew, Christophe, Sieur de La Jermeraye, dreamed of finding the Western Sea for the benefit of the French Empire in North America. They penetrated the Canadian Shield and travelled so far west as to sight the Rocky Mountains.

Captain Cook. He explored the Pacific North-West in 1778. His is the first record of a European landing on our West Coast.

CHAMPIONS OF THE BARREN LANDS

Samuel Hearne was 24 when he was sent out from Fort Prince of Wales (Churchill, Man.) to find the rumoured copper deposits of the North and to find as well the elusive route to the Orient, the Northwest Passage.

His first try, in November 1769, lasted but a month. His Indian guides had stolen his supplies and deserted him. He set out again in February 1780 but returned nine months later, his scientific instruments lost in a storm and his supplies, once again, stolen.

He left again almost immediately, setting out in December 1770 on his third attempt, but this time he had a loyal companion, Matonabbee. They were hungry for most of the winter, but he learned well the techniques of survival.

He explored an area, more than a quarter-million square miles and walked nearly 5,000 miles through rough terrain. On June 21, 1771, he reached the Arctic Circle and a month later stood under the midnight sun at the mouth of the Coppermine River. He returned to the fort on June 30, 1772. His journey had taken 18 months and 23 days.

He was the first European to come overland to the shores of the Arctic Ocean. The area he explored was so remote that others did not follow him until the 1920s.

Farley Mowat, in his book *Canada North*, describes Samuel Hearne as the "Marco Polo of the Canadian Barren Lands."

Alexander Mackenzie was the first European to cross the width of the continent north of Mexico. He claimed the Pacific Northwest for Britain and Canada, and won a knighthood and historical renown for his efforts.

In June 1789, Mackenzie, trader and partner in the North West Company, set out from the Athabaska district determined to find a route to the Pacific. With him were three Indians, one of them a guide, four Canadien voyageurs, a young German and several wives of the party members. They travelled by canoe down the Slave River, the Great Slave Lake and then the river that now bears Mackenzie's name to the Arctic Ocean. He called the river the "river of disappointment" because it did not flow to the Pacific.

In 1792, after a trip to England for better scientific instruments, he was back in the Northwest. He set out again, with another Scot, named MacKay, the crew of voyageurs, Indian guides and interpreters. After a winter at the forks of the Peace and Smoky rivers they made an assault on the Rocky Mountain barrier. They crossed at the Peace River Pass and then followed prehistoric Indian trading trails through the B.C. interior to the coast.

They went up the Parsnip River, discovered the Fraser and descended it for some 400 miles until they reached the Blackwater River, where they turned west. Here the Indians tricked Mackenzie, directing him to a snow-clogged 2,600-foot pass instead of to the easier Salmon River trail. They struggled through the rock-lined snow fields of the Mackenzie Pass, down into the Bella Coola Valley and then westward again to the Dean Channel and the sea.

Simon Fraser was the son of a Loyalist officer who died during the American Revolution. He joined the North West Company in 1792 and was sent to the Athabaska region. He was placed in charge of the area west of the Rocky Mountains in 1805, and he selected sites and founded posts that became important in the later development of the interior of B.C.

He set out in May 1808 from the junction of the Netchako and Fraser rivers with 24 men in four canoes, to explore what he thought was the Columbia River. He followed 400 miles of the river that Alexander Mackenzie had travelled earlier. He found his way around impassable rapids, made heroic portages at Black Canyon and at Hells Gate, where his men "clung like flies to the canyon walls," and then proceeded down to the widening expanse of the Fraser Valley. When he realized he could not be travelling the Columbia River, he was bitterly disappointed and ordered his expedition to turn back before reaching the mouth of the river.

David Thompson was just 14 years old when he joined the Hudson's Bay Company and was sent from England to Churchill. Later, assigned to posts on the Saskatchewan River, he learned astronomy and surveying. He began surveys and exploration for the Company in 1792, first on the Nelson River and later in the Athabaska district.

Thompson joined the North West Company in 1797 and began to survey and map countless lakes and rivers on the prairies. In 1807, he crossed the Rockies at Howse Pass and built Kootenay House, the first trading post on the Columbia River. He found the source of the Columbia, and spent the next years exploring and mapping its upper reaches. Early in 1811 he began his descent to the mouth of the mighty river. He reached the Pacific in July, only to find the Americans had claimed the lands at the mouth of the Columbia just four months earlier.

Thompson left the West in 1812 and settled in Lower Canada. Through the next two years he painstakingly prepared a map of the western territories. Remarkably precise, the map was the reference map of the West for many years.

Modern historians have called him "the greatest practical land geographer the world has produced."

SIR JOHN ROSS, SIR JAMES ROSS

Whereby they Explore the Arctic, Put a Gin Company on the Map, Survive Despite Incalculable Odds, and Locate the Magnetic Pole for the First (but not the Last) Time.

John Ross began his explorations of the Arctic in 1818 while in command of expeditions for the Royal Navy. He rediscovered Baffin Bay, which had been visited only by whalers for 200 years. He entered Lancaster Sound, sailed around, and eventually decided that it was not the Northwest Passage, although his second-in-command, Edward Parry, disagreed. On their return to England the Admiralty went with Parry, and, though Ross received a promotion,

Parry was put in command of the next official expeditions.

Ross turned to the private sector to fund another expedition of his own. Felix Booth, the gin distiller, came forth to lend his support and Ross set out in 1829 in a steam-paddle yacht named *Victory*. He took a crew of 21 that included his nephew, James Clark Ross, as his second-in-command.

Ross took the little yacht to Lancaster Sound, and this time passed through it into Prince Regent Inlet. He went on into an ice-jammed gulf, which they named the Gulf of Boothia in honour of their spirited sponsor.

There, in the Gulf of Boothia, the *Victory* was hemmed by ice, and there she stayed for three long arctic winters. Ross sent his nephew out from the *Victory*, in command of sledging parties. While the *Victory* was ice-bound, James Ross learned how the Inuit survived on a diet of fresh meat and oil, and he gathered minerals, discovered King William Island and explored and mapped Boothia and Somerset. Always mindful and their sponsor, young Ross named the northmost point of King William Island, Cape Felix. While in Boothia, James Clark Ross located the magnetic pole in 1831. (The magnetic pole wanders and was, in 1966, somewhere under Viscount Melville Sound.)

In 1832, at the end of the third winter, Ross and his crew abandoned the Victory and set out in small boats. They eventually reached Creswell Bay, with ironic consequences.

Edward Parry, who had taken over Ross's command of the Royal Navy's arctic exploration, had lost one of his two ships to the ice in 1825. Before transferring the crew to the surviving ship, he had ordered the wrecked ship's stores to be placed on the beach at Creswell Bay. It was these stores that enabled John Ross and his crew to survive their fourth winter.

In June 1833 they set out, again, in their small boats. They were picked up in August by a whaler near the mouth of Lancaster Sound. Remarkably, Ross brought all but three of his men through the ordeal and was knighted on his return to England.

GEOGRAPHIC GIANT

Geographically, Canada is the largest democracy in the world.

Applied Sciences

HONORARY MEMBER

Engineering Institute of Canada

Membership is conferred for outstanding service to the profession of engineering.

1983 **Ian D. Sinclair**, Toronto, Ont., who joins a list of such illustrious Canadians as John G. Diefenbaker, J.G. Chenevert, Maxwell Cohen, John P. Robarts, Mr. Justice Berger and Wilfrid B. Lewis.

JULIAN C. SMITH MEDAL

Engineering Institute of Canada

In memory of a late past president of the institute, the medal is awarded for achievement in the development of Canada.

1983 **Walter F. Light**, Northern Telecom Ltd., Mississauga, Ont.

RAISING THE ROOF

Engineering history was made in Montreal in 1975 when the 41,000-ton roof of the Velodrome was raised by jacks some four inches to strike its centring. It was the heaviest lift operation in the history of engineering.

SIR JOHN KENNEDY MEDAL

Engineering Institute of Canada

The medal is awarded for outstanding merit or for noteworthy contribution to the science of engineering or to the benefit of the institute.

1983 James Milton Ham, president of the U. of Toronto.

PLUMMER MEDAL

Engineering Institute of Canada

Awarded to the best paper published by the *Canadian Society for Chemical Engineering* or the *Metallurgical Society of the Canadian Institute of Mining and Metallurgy* on the application of chemical engineering to the advancement of the science and practice of metallurgy.

1981 Dr. J.R. Wynnyckyj and Professor S.K. Barua, of Waterloo.

1982 No award

SIR SANDFORD FLEMING

Sandford Fleming was born in Scotland and studied engineering before coming to Canada. He stood well over six feet, had a big voice and was known for his exuberant nature and loyalty to the British Empire. His long life was filled with accomplishment.

After qualifying as a civil engineer in Canada, he became one of the founders of the Royal Canadian Institute in 1849. In 1851 he designed Canada's first postage stamps. One of them, the Three Penny Beaver, was the first stamp issued by any government to have a picture other than the usual portrait of a monarch or head of state.

During his career Fleming was chief engineer and surveyor of railroads under construction in Ontario, Nova Scotia, New Brunswick and Newfoundland. He believed in the need for a railway to the Pacific through British territory and was appointed chief engineer of the Canadian Pacific Railway in 1871. He surveyed the prairie route of the railroad, the Yellowhead Pass and the Kicking Horse Pass.

In 1878 Fleming revolutionized the world's way of keeping time with his system of Standard Time. There was wide resistance to the idea at first, but Fleming pushed hard to get it accepted. North American railways were the first to adopt Standard Time and by 1900 it was in use throughout the world.

Fleming published a number of papers, produced the first lithographed, accurate, large-scale surveyor maps in Canada, wrote an interdenominational hymn and prayer book, and promoted and charted a submarine telegraph cable from Vancouver to Australia.

He was chancellor of Queen's University, a charter member and later president of the Royal Society of Canada and was created KCMG in 1897. He died at 87, shortly after completing work for his biography.

LEONARD MEDAL

Engineering Institute of Canada

Honouring Lieutenant Colonel Leonard, a founder of the Canadian Society of Civil Engineers, the award is for the best paper on a mining subject presented to the institute or to the Canadian Institute of Mining and Metallurgy.

1977 D.R. Piteau, D.B. Martin and G.S. Zimmer

1979-82 No award

DUGGAN MEDAL

Engineering Institute of Canada

The medal is for the best paper dealing with the use of metals for structural or mechanical purposes.

1979　**R. Bjorhovde** and **P.C. Birkemoe**, U. of Alberta
1980-82　**No award**

GZOWSKI MEDAL

Engineering Institute of Canada

Sir Casimir Gzowski, a founder of the Canadian Society of Civil Engineers, was president of the Society from 1889-1891.

The award is for the best paper on a civil engineering subject (limited to structural and bridge surveying and all heavy civil engineering construction).

1982　**William C-P Aau**, U. of Alberta
John L. Dawe, Mouth of Keswick, N.B.

RECORD-SETTING BRIDGE

The Quebec Bridge (Pont de Québec), which opened to traffic in 1917, has the world's longest cantilever span — 1,800 feet between the piers and 3,239 feet overall. Carrying a railroad track and two roadways, it was begun in 1899. During its construction, 87 lives were lost and it cost $22.5-million.

T.C. KEEFER MEDAL

Engineering Institute of Canada

The medal is for the best paper in any area of civil engineering not expressly covered by the Gzowski Medal.

1982　**S. Beltaos** and **B.G. Krishnappan**, National Water Research Institute, Burlington, Ont.

R.A. ROSS MEDAL

Engineering Institute of Canada

The medal is awarded for the best paper on electrical engineering subjects.

1982　**Dr. G.R. Slemon**, dean of applied science and engineering, U. of Toronto. **Brown Boveri**, Can. Inc., Montreal, Que.

ROBERT W. ANGUS MEDAL

Engineering Institute of Canada

The medal is awarded each year for the best paper on a mechanical engineering subject.

1982　**T.A. Brzustowski**, department of mechanical engineering, U. of Waterloo

MEN OF STEEL

Casimir Stanislaus Gzowski obtained a commission in the Imperial Russian Engineers in 1830. He took part in the Polish insurrection of 1830-31 and after being confined to military prison was shipped to the U.S. in 1833. He came to Canada in 1841 and began the work that was to make him famous. He was superintending engineer of roads and harbours in western Ontario, engineer of the harbour works at Montreal, and consulting engineer on channel improvements between Montreal and Quebec. Later he was the chief engineer of the main line of the Grand Trunk Railway between Montreal and Island Pond. He was a partner in the construction of the Grand Trunk main line from Toronto to Sarnia. One of the founders of the Candian Society of Civil Engineers, he was created KCMG in 1890.

Thomas Coltrin Keefer was born at Thorold and educated at Upper Canada College. He worked on the Erie Canal and later the Welland Canal. He did preliminary surveys for the Grand Trunk

Railway line between Montreal and Toronto and prepared plans that resulted in the Victoria Bridge on the St. Lawrence at Point St. Charles. He designed and built Montreal's first aqueduct and was chief engineer for the Ottawa Waterworks Commission and later for the Montreal Harbour Commission. He was a president of the American Society of Civil Engineers and one of the founders of the Canadian Society of Civil Engineers.

Samuel Keefer was involved in many early feats of engineering in Canada. In 1833, at the age of 30, he was responsible for the reconstruction and enlargement of the Welland Canal, for the canals upon the St. Lawrence and Richelieu rivers and for highway development from the Gaspe to Lake Huron. He built many bridges, including Canada's first suspension bridge at the Chaudiere Falls, Ottawa.

EADIE MEDAL

Royal Society of Canada

The medal is given in recognition of a major contribution to any field through engineering or applied science. It is funded by Bell Canada in honour of its past president and chairman of the board, Thomas W. Eadie.

1982/83 **Dr. Colin Campbell,** professor of electrical and computer engineering, McMaster U. Campbell's contributions to microelectronics and communications engineering include studies on techniques for microwave measurement, development of thin-film devices using dielectrics and work on lasers and masers.

Campbell's most recent contribution has been in the development of Surface Acoustic Wave (SAW) devices, which form a new class of components for communications circuitry.

His is one of the very few laboratories in Canada engaged in experimental and theoretical studies of SAW devices. Campbell's work has directly helped in the development of an industrial high technology enterprise.

SUSPENDED SUCCESS

The first truly successful railway suspension bridge in the world was the double-decker Niagara Suspension Bridge, opened in 1855. It was the first bridge built across the Niagara River.

SCHREYER AWARD/LE PRIX SCHREYER

Canada's highest award for outstanding achievement in consulting engineering.

1982 **Hatch Associates Limited,** Toronto, Ont., who were the consulting engineers for a new iron and steel complex in Trinidad and Tobago that cost nearly $500-million. The firm was responsible for the project from the first feasibility studies through to start-up.

The designers and engineers incorporated a number of new concepts and innovative features into the project, including: new static watt compensation system; a remote-controlled furnace feed system; overhead crane wheel equalization system; herringbone roof system; new modeling technique for ventilation of mill buildings; novel structural design; and an innovative underground power and fresh air supply.

HAIR-RAISING HIGHWAY

The Cariboo Road is a modern, four-lane highway that runs about 400 miles through the Fraser valley and canyon from Yale to Barkerville in B.C. The highway can be a hair-raising experience isiting motorists. The scenery is breathtaking but also distracting, as the road twists and turns on the very narrow ledges of the steep canyons. When the road was first constructed in 1865 it was considered an engineering miracle.

Construction began in 1862 when gold was discovered in the Cariboo. James Douglas, "the Father of British Columbia," employed the small corps of Royal Engineers in the territory to supervise the construction. Together with private contractors they blasted the narrow wagon trail out of the sides of the canyon.

CANADIAN ENGINEERS' GOLD MEDAL

Canadian Council of Professional Engineers

The council is a federation of Canada's 12 provincial and territorial professional engineering associations and represents 107,000 registered professional engineers. The Canadian Engineers' Gold Medal is the highest honour conferred by the profession.

1982   **Larkin Kerwin**, CC, Eng, president, National Research Council, Ottawa, Ont.

CANADIAN ENGINEERS' MERITORIOUS SERVICE AWARD

Candian Council of Professional Engineers

A bronze medal is awarded to recognize outstanding service and dedication to the Canadian engineering profession. The first award was presented in 1981.

1982   **Dr. Ralph N. McManus**. P. Eng., Alta.

GREENPEACE BATTLES TO SAVE THE EARTH

Greenpeace is audacious, swashbuckling and serious. The movement began in British Columbia in 1970 and uses direct, nonviolent action to rouse public opinion against perceived ecological marauders.

Its first efforts were in opposition to underground nuclear bomb testing at Amchitka Island in Alaska. Greenpeace now claims 35,000 members in Canada and hundreds of thousands of members worldwide with organizations in Britain, France, Germany, Holland, Australia, New Zealand, Japan, Denmark and the U.S.

Since its tactics are to arouse public awareness, Greenpeace plots nonviolent actions that will grab headlines. Greenpeace also uses more traditional methods of influencing governments, such as research and the presentation of briefs.

Some of its more daring endeavours include using high-speed inflatable craft to interfere with whaling operations, preventing sealing ships from breaking through pack ice, using skindivers to free dolphins and sending skydivers into a proposed nuclear plant site. One of its ships was rammed by a French naval vessel when Greenpeace members protested French nuclear tests and another made a daring escape from Spanish authorities after the ship was impounded for interfering in whaling operations.

In 1982 Greenpeace U.S. and Canada cooperated in an anti-acid-rain protest by occupying smokestacks simultaneously in Ohio, Indiana and Arizona. In another incident, in Ontario, three Greenpeace volunteers occupied Ontario Hydro's smokestack at Naticoke Generating Station. They were protesting the proposed sale of electricity to the U.S.A., which they said could add 100,000 metric tonnes of sulphur dioxide per year to Ontario air and kill up to 25 lakes each year. The licence to generate and sell the power to the U.S. was later denied.

Also in 1982 was a successful lobbying by Greenpeace and other environmental groups of the International Whaling Commission. Members voted 25-7 in favour of phasing out commercial whaling by 1986.

GRANDDADDY OF ACID RAIN RESEARCH

National Geographic magazine named Dr. Eville Gorham, a Canadian ecologist presently at the University of Minnesota, the "grandfather of acid rain research."
As early as the 1950s Gorham elaborated on the work of Robert Angus Smith, an Englishman who published a book in 1852 on the relationship between sooty skies and the acidity of precipitation. Gorham's work, warning of the dangers of acid rain, was ignored until the "father" of acid rain study, Swedish soil scientist Svante Oden, provoked concern in 1967.

SCIENTIFIC RESEARCH AND EDUCATION GRANTS

Canadian National Sportsmen's Fund

1983 $ 9,100   **W.T. Momot**, Lakehead U., to study the response of the walleye to intense harvest.
$13,850   **G.W. Friars**, U. of Guelph, for the determination of optimum selection criteria in sea-ranched Atlantic salmon.
$15,760   **D.E. Gaskin**, U. of Guelph, to study behavioural ecology of right whales in the Bay of Fundy.
$ 7,571   **L.C. Cwynar**, U. of Toronto, to map postglacial migration routes of trees into Southern Yukon.
$15,000   **D.H. Turpin**, Queen's U., to study inorganic carbon supply, photosynthesis and phytoplankton growth rates: the implication of acid rain.
$ 8,850   **B.M. White**, Queen's U., for the molecular tagging of snow goose colonies.
$ 3,600   **R.J. Robertson**, Queen's U., to study dominance and foraging behaviour in black-capped chickadees.
$ 6,826   **R. Boonstra**, U. of Toronto, to study microevolution in populations of meadow vole and its implications for population regulation.
$ 6,844   **H.R. MacCrimmon**, U. of Guelph, to study comparative reproductive strategies of repeat-spawning stream salmonids in allopatric and sympatric populations relative to habitat requirements, cultural impacts and interspecific compatibility.
$ 7,090   **W.R. Kaufman**, U. of Alberta, to study control of salivary gland degeneration in ixodid ticks.
$ 7,500   **F.C. Zwickel**, U. of Alberta, to study effects of removal of adult female blue grouse on behaviour and reproductive success of yearling females.
$ 5,900   **P.J. Harrison**, U. of B.C., to study biological productivity of frontal areas in British Columbia coastal waters.
$ 9,871   **G.A. Wobeser**, U. of Saskatchewan Western College of Veterinary Medicine, for a study of the development of *Clostridium botulinum* type C toxin in vertebrate carcasses as a factor in the initiation of botulism outbreaks in waterfowl.
$25,000   **E. Ishiguro, W.W.Kay, T.J. Trust**, U. of Victoria, to study virulence mechanisms and prevention of salmonid kidney disease.
$19,310   **A.R.E. Sinclair, C. Krebs,** U. of B.C., to study the impact of predation on declining populations of snowshoe hares and other vertebrates in the Kluane Region, Yukon Territories.
$16,570   **J.N.M. Smith**, U. of B.C., to study territorial behaviour and popula-

tion limitation in ducks of the genus *Bucephala*.

$13,700   J.G. Eales, U. of Manitoba, to study responses of the thyroidal system of rainbow trout to acute and chronic stressful variables with glucocorticoid and catecholamine hormones.

$16,952   D.A. Boag, U. of Alberta, for a study of post-hatch ecology of juvenile dabbling ducks with special emphasis on the northern pintail.

EDUCATION

Conservation Scholarships (*for PhD students at Canadian Universities*)

$11,000   Villis O. Nams, University of Victoria

$11,000   Kathy M. Martin, Queen's University

$11,000   Ian R. Kirkham, Dalhousie University

$11,000   Malcolm Ramsay, University of Alberta

$28,050   Terry E. Quinney, Carleton University

FOCUSSING ON FOXES

An animal common to Canada's southern prairies which virtually disappeared after the turn of the century may be restored to its natural habitat by 1984.

The swift fox, less than half the size of a red fox, is the focus of a project of the Wildlife Reserve of Western Canada and the University of Calgary.

The fox disappeared in Canada, but survived in parts of the United States and several pairs were brought to Alberta where they reproduced. Descendants of these pairs will be returned to the prairie wilds in what at first will be a controlled program. They will be released in carefully selected sites after being acclimatized and their adaptability will be monitored by small transmitters.

The program is being funded by the World Wildlife Fund and Environment Canada's wildlife service.

OUTSTANDING SERVICE AWARD 1983

International Fund for Animal Welfare

Lorne Greene, once the voice of the CBC news, and later famous as Ben Cartwright in the TV series *Bonanza*, was awarded the Outstanding Service Award for 1983. Greene received the award in recognition of his role as host of the documentary television program *New Wilderness*.

HE WON FAME BUT HE WAS NOT WHO HE SAID HE WAS

He was not, as he claimed, an Apache, born in Mexico. He was George Stansfeld Belaney, born in 1888, in England, of English parents. It is true, however, that he was welcomed as a blood brother of the Ojibwa and he was an early and serious conservationist who loved the Canadian wilderness.

He became Grey Owl, and wearing native costumes he created a romantic myth about himself as he aroused international attention as a native author and lecturer. Perhaps no one would have listened to a conservation message from George Belaney.

HEASLIP AWARDS FOR ENVIRONMENTAL STEWARDSHIP

National Survival Institute

The awards honour Marguerite and Vernon Heaslip, the founders of the institute. The award program was created to recognize outstanding contributions to the protection, enhancement or rehabilitation of the quality of our environment.

The award program is supported by

the United Nations Environment Programme and in 1982 the winners received United Nations Commemorative Medals to observe the 10th anniversay of the UN conference on the human environment.

1982 **Business**
Sonja Bata, Toronto, Ont., a member of the International Board of Directors of the World Wildlife Fund and president of World Wildlife Fund (Canada), brings awareness of worldwide conservation efforts to the international business community.

Education
Prof. Irving Fox, Westwater Research Centre, an expert in environmental planning and management, for his work to educate the public and governments on water management.

Environmental Non-Governmental Group
Tony LeSauteur, a civil servant committed to public participation in environmental planning and protection, for his leadership in public education through such groups as Québec federation de la faune, Société pour Vaincre la Pollution and STOP.

Government
Prof. Maxwell Cohen, chairman of the Canadian section of the International Joint Commission, 1974-79, for developing a public consultation program. His leadership helped to ensure the effectiveness of the IJC.

Individual
Dick and Vivian Pharis, among the founders of the Alberta Wilderness Association in 1960, for demonstrating the importance of Alberta's mountains and foothills as the source of several great rivers.

Labour
The Hon. Jay Cowan, chairman of the Occupational Health and Safety Committee of the Manitoba Federation of Labour, for playing a key role in identifying problems in the transportation of hazardous chemicals.

WILD HORSES WON'T BE DRAGGED AWAY

Herds of wild horses were saved from meat-packing plants in the spring of 1983 because of mild weather and public indignation.

The province of Alberta had planned to trap a number of the 1,550 to 2,000 horses that run free in the foothills of the Rockies.

PIMLOTT CONSERVATION AWARD

Canadian Nature Federation

The award honours the late Douglas Pimlott, a noted wildlife biologist and conservationist. It is for outstanding contribution to Canadian conservation characterized by the completion of difficult tasks of national significance. A Muskax Inuit sculpture is presented to each year's winner.

1982 **Dr. Vladimir J. Krajina**, professor emeritus of botany, U. of British Columbia. Born and educated in Czechoslovakia, Krajina was a resistance leader during the war. He fled Czechoslovakia in 1948 during the Communist takeover.

Called "the father of ecological reserves in Canada," he spearheaded efforts to obtain ecological reserve legislation in B.C. The resulting legislation, passed in 1971, has since been used as an example by seven other provinces. His work has contributed to substantial improvement in B.C.'s forest management.

In 1975, one of the largest ecological reserves, a magnificent wilderness area in the Queen Charlotte Islands was named in Krajina's honour. He was made a member of the Order of Canada in 1981.

PROFESSOR WINS SUPPORT FOR WORLD'S TURTLES

Professor Nicholas Mrosovsky of the University of Toronto launched the *Marine Turtle Newsletter* several years ago. Today the newsletter is read by about 700 scientists and conservationists in 80 countries and has aroused worldwide interest in the conservation of sea turtles, most species of which are listed by the World Wildlife fund as threatened or endangered.

SAFE, IN THEORY ANYWAY

The North West Council passed legislation to preserve the buffalo in 1877. Good intentions but ...

Peter Pond, the intrepid explorer with the North West Company, reportedly saw oil seeps in Alberta in 1778. He was the first European to do so.

PAID BACK WITH INTEREST

James Miller William, a Hamilton, Ont., carriage maker, discovered North America's first commercial oil well in June 1858.

In order to clear a debt, two brothers gave Williams a parcel of land. It was part of a petroleum-soaked property they owned in Enniskillen Township in Ontario's Lambton County.

Williams, who was experimenting with oil as a lamp fuel, at first dug down 14 feet with a spade to bring in his well. It got easier, and even more profitable, when a drill was brought in later.

ALTERNATIVE ENERGY BREAKTHROUGH

The government, private enterprise and a Nova Scotia university have worked together to make a breakthrough in Canadian alternative energy technology.

The fuel (70 per cent pulverized coal, 28 per cent water and two per cent chemical additive) is expected to provide fuel for the furnace of a major industrial plant by 1985.

The fuel will not require massive capital investment, is easily handled, cuts acid-rain-producing emissions by 60 per cent and will cost less than oil.

The development of the synthetic fuel was a joint project of the National Research Council, the federal Department of Energy Mines and Resources, Scotia Liquicoal Ltd., Halifax, N.S., the Technical University of Nova Scotia and Fluid Kinetics Inc. of Fairfield, Ohio.

The market for the fuel and its technology is expected to be used by the hundreds of electrical generating stations now fuelled by expensive oil instead of lower-cost, compatible liquid fuel.

Oilmen who have received the Order of Canada

for their contributions to the petroleum industry in Canada:

Bill Daniel, Toronto, Ont.
Carl Nickle, Alta.
S.R. (Bob) Blair, Alta.
George Govier, Alta.
Maurice Strong, Quebec
Jack Gallagher, Alta.

FIRST GUSHER

Hugh Nixon Shaw drilled and brought in Canada's first oil gusher in Petrolia, Ont., in 1862. At its peak it produced 2,000 barrels per day.

John George (Kootenay) Brown, a farmer, trapper and guide at Waterton, near Pincher Creek, Alta., used to skim globules of oil from the ground to grease his machinery. His employee Wm. Aldridge dug pits to form small oil pools and sold the oil for about $1 a barrel. He is credited as Alberta's first discoverer of oil.

GIANTS OF PETROLEUM

James (Jim) Lowry founded Home Oil in 1925 and by the end of World War II had developed it into the largest independent Canadian oil producing company.

Robt. (Bob) Arthur Brown, who became president after Lowry, made the most important oil and gas finds in Alberta, for Home.

Frank McMahon, Vancouver hotel owner and of Queen's Plate fame, developed Pacific Petroleum Ltd. He was the driving force behind West Coast Transmission, which now supplies gas to the interior of B.C. and the Pacific Northwest. He also had discoveries at Turner Valley and LeDuc.

The biggest oil field in Alberta is 'Pembina.' It was championed by Arne Nielsen, a geologist and senior executive of Mobil Oil. He converted the disbelievers.

ADEQUATE ASSETS

Petrocan, Canada's government-owned oil company, which opened shop in 1976, had assets exceeding $7-billion in the spring of 1983.

The first big gusher in Alberta was the Dingman #1 well at Turner Valley. It commenced in 1913-14.

The famous Le Duc well came in in 1947. It was drilled by Vern Hunter, known as 'Dry Hole Hunter,' because he had drilled 133 dry holes before

scoring with Le Duc. Imperial Oil, which funded the search, was understandably becoming impatient with 'Dry Hole' before the find.

CANADIAN COUP IN CHINA

Petro-Canada Exploration Ltd. and Ranger Oil (Canada) Ltd. are part of a consortium that has won a drilling licence for oil exploration off the coast of China. The license is the first ever granted by the People's Republic of China.

The drilling program is for an unspecified number of wells and will last for five to seven years. The partners receive revenue in cash or oil production surplus to China's requirements in return for financing the exploration.

FROM SEWAGE TO SOIL

Carl Klauck of Holland Landing, Ont., takes sewage sludge, supermarket garbage and pig manure and, with some help, creates potting soil.

He checks the acid balance of the organic waste, chemically adjusts it, and then feeds it to his one million little red worms. The waste, after being processed in the worms' digestive tracts, is high in nutrients and when mixed with sand and peat moss makes a perfect potting soil.

In 1977 Klauck was mentioned favourably in a U.S. environmental major report on waste management.

ENERGY CONSERVATION AND DOLLAR WINNERS

A practical application of the old adage that oil and water do not mix has led to considerable energy savings for CN Marine Inc., operator of 27 East Coast ferries.

Bilge, which was formerly dumped, is put in holding tanks. When the oil rises, the seawater is drained from the bottom of the tanks. The remaining oily fluid goes through two more filtration processes. In the end, CN Marine recovers about 110,000 gallons of fuel each year. The recovered oil is used to provide steam to heat terminal buildings at Moncton and Port aux Basques, Nfld. In winter, the steam is also used to remove ice on the vessel ramps.

CN estimates that the bilge separation saves more than $160,000 a year and solves an environmental problem.

ELECTRIC HEAT WINNING SUPPORT

Statistics Canada reported that during the 1970s homeowners moved dramatically to electric heat. Compared with only 5.7 per cent in 1971, 24.1 per cent of Canadian homes were heated electrically in 1981.

DISCOVERY GAVE BIRTH TO AN INDUSTRY

Abraham Gesner, born in 1797 at Cornwallis, N.S., was a physician, geologist, writer and scientist. In 1846 he distilled kerosene from coal and the world soon glowed by the light of the kerosene lamp. In 1854, he patented a process for distilling kerosene from petroleum and thus became the founding father of the petrochemical industry.

CANADIAN FORESTRY ACHIEVEMENT AWARD

Canadian Institute of Forestry

A gold medal is presented in recognition of superior accomplishments in scientific forestry.

1982   **Grant Lee Ainscough**, vice-president and chief forester, MacMillan Bloedel Ltd., for his pioneering development in the late 1960s of a comprehensive land use and environmental protection program for MacMillan Bloedel and for his unflagging work to improve forest management practices.

CANADIAN FORESTRY SCIENTIFIC ACHIEVEMENT AWARD

Canadian Institute of Forestry

A gold medal is presented to an individual currently active in research who makes substantial advances in the science and practice of forestry.

1982   **Dr. Louis Zsuffa**, Ontario Forest Research Centre, Maple, Ont., professor of forest genetics, faculty of forestry, U. of Toronto, for his work in the development of hybrid poplars.

Zsuffa has also received an award from the Yugoslav Council of Science and Art which presented him with its Scientific Award for achievements in poplar research in 1961. in 1967 the Yugoslav National Poplar Commission honoured him for his special contributions in advancing poplar culture.

TRUE TALES OF TALL TREES

A fir tree cut down in 1902 in Lynn Valley, North Vancouver, B.C., was reportedly 14 feet 2 inches across the butt 5 feet up from the ground and its height measured 415 feet. The yield from the single tree was almost 100,000 board feet — enough lumber to build an estimated nine modern homes. If the records are correct, it is the tallest tree ever to be accurately measured in North America.

The Kerrisdale Tree, a Douglas fir felled by loggers in Vancouver's Kerrisdale district, measured 380 feet long on the ground.

A 700-year-old Douglas fir still standing at Red Creek, B.C., measures 13 feet 1 inch in diameter at breast height and soars 241 feet into the air or about 24 storeys, even though it has lost its top. It's estimated the tree would have topped 300 feet in healthy maturity.

Cathdral Grove in MacMillan Provincial Park, B.C., is a 30-acre old-grove forest. The tallest tree in the park is 275 feet.

Nimpkish Island, B.C., has a grove of western hemlocks and western red cedars which are 200 feet plus and Douglas firs, 250 to 300 feet, which are still growing. They are Canada's tallest standing trees. Most are about 350 years old and in time could grow to 350 feet. The trees are owned by a lumbering company but ways are trying to be found to turn the area into an ecological reserve.

GOLDEN SMOKEY AWARD

U.S. Department of Agriculture, Forest Service

The Golden Smokey Bear Award is given periodically for significant contributions to the Cooperative Forest Fire Prevention Program. The award is the highest given by the U.S. agency for fire prevention.

1980 **The Canadian Forestry Association**, for its 25 years of outstanding contributions to forest fire prevention. The CFA coordinates programs such as National Forest Week, a National Forest Fire Prevention poster contest and the Smokey Bear Ranger program.

It was the first time Canada has won the award since it was established in 1958.

THE TREE TRADE

Canada is a major exporter of forest products. In 1978 exports of wood, wood products and paper amounted to $9.6-billion or 19 per cent of the value of all commodity exports.

B.C., Ontario and Quebec are the leading timber-producing provinces. In 1978, B.C. sawmills produced 66 per cent of all lumber in Canada and most of the sulphate pulp and softwood plywood. Most of the groundwood pulp and hardwood plywood came from Ontario and Quebec.

Lumbering for export began in 1765, when William Davidson of the Miramichi River in New Brunswick sold masts 100 feet high and 3 feet in diameter to the Royal Navy for $680 each.

FORESTRY CAPITAL OF CANADA

Canadian Forestry Association

Presented by Governor-General Ed Schreyer, the award commends a community for its forestry efforts.

1982 **The County of Simcoe**, Simcoe, Ont., for its continuing program of forest renewal during the last 60 years. Since 1922 Simcoe County has planted 28,000 acres on what was waste and barren countryside and has encouraged residents of the county to plant more than 45 million trees on private property in the area.

NATIONAL FORESTRY POSTER AWARD

Canadian Forestry Association

The 22nd annual Poster Contest was won by 11-year-old **Rhoda Gross**, a grade 6 student at Clearview Colony School in Pipestone, Man. Her poster *Who Protects the Heart of the Forest?* was judged the best of an estimated 80,000 posters prepared by young artists for local and regional art displays on a forestry theme.

Rhoda and her teacher, Eileen Doherty, were flown to Ottawa where she was received by the Governor-General and Mrs. Schreyer.

NATIONAL TREE FARM AWARD

Canadian Forestry Association

The award recognizes outstanding contributions to private land extension forestry in Canada.

1981 **J.F.W. Gourlay**, Mississauga, Ont., supervisor of private land forestry for the Ontario Ministry of Natural Resources, has been a strong voice for better management of privately owned forest land.

RECORD-MAKING RECORDS

Dr. A.C. Carder of Victoria, B.C., has been researching tree records for years. The 72-year-old Carder has some of the best-kept, most-extensive tall-tree records in existence.

And Randy Stoltmann, 20, of West Vancouver has taken up big trees with a passion. He spends all of his free time searching for, photographing and measuring Canada's giants.

TREES FOR TOMORROW AWARD

Canadian Forestry Association

The award is granted to an individual who has made an outstanding contribution to the conservation of Canada's forests and renewable resources.

1982 **F.L.C. Reed**, Ottawa, Ont., for his effective support and encouragement for adequate forest renewal as a private consultant and latterly as assistant deputy minister of the Canadian Forestry Service.

TREES AND TROPICS

Ken Davis, head of the nonprofit Canadian Foundation for World Development, is a champion of the United Nations' four-fold program of awareness, education, tree planting and conservation in Canada and abroad.

Aart Van Wingerden, a North Carolina nursery owner, and Davis have been experimenting with fast-growing trees in the tropics. They hope to plant 50 million trees in Haiti in the next five years.

CANADIAN LUMBERMEN'S ASSOCIATION

A wooden plaque is presented annually to an individual who has been active in the manufacturing, merchandising or technical and research branches of the Canadian lumber industry.

1982 **Robert Plunkett**, New Rochelle, N.Y., for his extensive contributions to the lumber industry and to the CLA.

PROSPECTOR OF THE YEAR AWARD

Prospectors and Developers Association

1982 **Harold and Al Musselwhite**. The Musselwhite brothers prospected together for years in Ontario, and in 1963 they struck gold. Over 10 days, they staked 18 sq. mi. of claims.

The price of gold was low at the time and the brothers could rouse no interest in their claim until 1973. Then a consortium including Imperial Oil, Dome Mines and Inco spent more than $2-million drilling the property and are investing another $40-million to complete the mine. The brothers will receive royalties after all of the development costs have been paid.

DISTINGUISHED SERVICE AWARD

Prospectors and Developers Association

1982 **Dr. Francis (Franc) Renault Joubin**, for his prime role in the discovery and development of the uranium deposits in the Blind River area of Ontario.

U OF T PROF WINS METAL MEDAL

Professor C.B. Alcock, department of metallurgy and material science, University of Toronto, was awarded the Kroll Medal and Prize for 1983/84.

The Metals Society of London, England, presents the annual award for contributions to research and development in chemical metallurgy. Alcock was also elected a fellow of the Royal Society of Canada in 1983

HUESTIS AWARD

British Columbia and Yukon Chamber of Mines

Given for excellence in prospecting and mineral exploration, the award is named after H.H. (Spud) Huestis who pioneered the exploration of low-grade copper ores in southern B.C. Huestis' determination led to the opening of the Bethlehem mines, which in turn was the stimulus for the discovery of most of Canada's copper and molybdenum reserves.

1983 **Egil Lorntzsen**, British Columbia. He began prospecting, with no formal training, in 1934 and had many successes during the nearly 50 years he scoured the province. In 1959, he staked a copper showing that is now called the Lornex Mine — the largest base metal mine in Canada.

B.C. SCIENTISTS DISCOVER METAL EXTRACTION PROCESS

Four scientists with the nonprofit B.C. Research Foundation have discovered a way to use rock-eating bacteria to extract metal from ore without polluting the environment.

Previously rock-eating bacteria had produced sulphuric acid. In the new method, found by the team under leader Al Bruunesteun, the bacteria produce sulphur from the sulphuric acid. The process, now used to concentrate copper ores, is being adapted to process nickel, zinc and gold.

SCHOLZ MEDAL

British Columbia and Yukon Chamber of Mines

Awarded annually for excellence in mineral development and engineering, the medal commemorates E.A. Scholz who played a prominent role in turning a small producer, Placer Development Ltd., into a major international corporation.

1983 **Harold Wright**, Vancouver, B.C., for his contributions to the growth of the Canadian mining industry. He and his brother developed Wright Engineers into a world-class engineering firm. A director of several mining companies, he is a former president of the Canadian Institute of Mining and Metallurgy. In 1965 he received the Gold Medal of Great Britain's Institution of Mining and Metallurgy and the Order of Canada in 1977. A Canadian Olympic sprinter in 1937, Wright was president of the Canadian Olympic Association from 1969 to 1977.

HE WON A VISIT WITH THE QUEEN

Martin Frobisher's financial backer, one Michael Lok, believed that the black ore samples Frobisher brought to England from Frobisher Bay contained gold. Accordingly he sent Frobisher back to the New World to mine the ore. There, Frobisher found plenty of the black ore, as well as trouble with the natives on Countess of Warwick Island. In a battle he and one of his men were wounded, but Frobisher returned to England with the ore and was interviewed by Queen Elizabeth I. On a third voyage, he built a stone house at Frobisher Bay and mined more ore. When he returned to England, however, he learned that all the ore was worthless and that his backer was ruined.

Later, Frobisher joined the Royal Navy and commanded one of the larger ships in the battle against the Spanish Armada. He received tremendous acclaim as a sea-going hero.

COAL AWARD

Canadian Institute of Mining and Metallurgy

The award is presented by the Coal Division of the CIM.

1983   **Alexis Ignatieff**, former deputy director, Energy Mines and Resources. Ignatieff is civil servant who worked unstintingly on behalf of Canada for mining and mineral development in this country.

BARLOW MEMORIAL MEDAL

Canadian Institute of Mining and Metallurgy

1983   **Dr. R.W. Boyle**, special projects officer, Geological Survey of Canada, for the best paper appearing in the 1982 *CIM BULLETIN*.

ARVIDA AHEAD

The aluminum smelter at Arvida, Que., is the largest aluminum smelter in the western world. Owned by the Aluminum Company of Canada, the smelter has a capacity of 475,000 tons per year.

DOFASCO AWARD

Canadian Institute of Mining and Metallurgy

For contributions to the advancement of materials engineering in Canada.

1983   **Professor J.J. Jonas**, department of mining and metallurgy, McGill U., for his contributions to hot-rolling and for his work in mechanical metallurgical education.

AIREY AWARD OF THE METALLURGICAL SOCIETY OF CIM

Canadian Institute of Mining and Metallurgy

The award is made for significant contributions to the advancement of metallurgy in Canada in the industrial field.

1983   **Dr. Herbert Veltman**, director, Sherritt Research Centre, Fort Saskatchewan, Alta., for the development of a new leach process for zinc.

ALCAN AWARD

Canadian Institute of Mining and Metallurgy

The award, established by the Aluminum Company of Canada Ltd., is for contributions to the field of metallurgy.

1983   **Professor Ernest Peters**, department of metallurgical engineering, U. of British Columbia, for his contributions to hydro metallurgy and hydro metallurgical education.

THERE'S GOLD IN THEM THAR FLOWERS

Harry Warren, geological science professor at the University of British Columbia, has been trying for many years to discover what minerals lie beneath the ground by studying the vegetation on top and he's hopeful of striking gold.

He has found that some species of cyanogenic plants absorb gold from the earth in which they grow. His evidence indicates that there are a number of types of plants and trees which may collect quantities of gold, silver, molybdenum, mercury and copper. As well, he and his researchers have developed methods of analyzing the mineral content in plants.

The technology would add another tool to the prospector's bag and would be particularly useful in parts of Canada where rugged terrain and poor transportation prohibit the use of heavy digging equipment.

Warren may expand his research to include the search for minerals in the pollen of bees.

INCO MEDAL

Canadian Institute of Mining and Metallurgy

The medal is for a practical contribution of outstanding importance to the mining and metallurgical industry in Canada.

1983 **Richard Geren**, executive vice-president, Iron Ore Co. of Canada, for support and leadership which enabled the iron ore industry to weather difficult economic times.

McPARLAND MEMORIAL MEDAL

Canadian Institute of Mining and Metallurgy

The medal is given for outstanding performance in the engineering fields of mining and for innovations in the installation or operation of mines.

1983 **V.B. (Jim) Cook**, president, V.B. Cook Co. Ltd., Thunder Bay, Ont., for

innovations and contributions to mine planning and design in Canada.

J.C. SPROULE PLAQUE

Canadian Institute of Mining and Metallurgy

The plaque is awarded for distinguished contributions to the exploration and development of Canada's mineral resources in the northern regions.

1983 **H.M. Giegrerich**, president, Cominco Alaska, Inc., for outstanding leadership on the Polaris project in the far North.

LARGEST SMELTER

The Cominco Ltd. plant at Trail, B.C., has the world's largest zinc smelter. It has the capacity to produce 295,000 tons of zinc and 900 tons of cadmium each year.

ROBERT ELVER AWARD

Canadian Institute of Mining and Metallurgy

The award recognizes a member of the Institute who has made a significant contribution to mineral economics in Canada.

1983 **Brian Mackenzie**, department of geological sciences, Queen's U., for his micro-economic theory in mineral economics and for developing a mineral economic program in Canada.

A.O. DUFRESNE AWARD

Canadian Institute of Mining and Metallurgy

The award is for innovation, research, project management, education or outstanding personal achievement contributing to exploration in the Canadian mining industry.

1983 Given posthumously to George Mannard, former president of Kidd Creek Mines, for his lifelong work in the development of Canadian ore bodies.

LARGEST MINE

The Kidd Creek Mine, Timmins, Ont., is the world's largest lead, zinc and silver mine.

BLAYLOCK MEDAL

Canadian Institute of Mining and Metallurgy

The medal is awarded to a member of the institute for distinguished service to Canada through achievement in mining, metallurgy or geology.

1983 Leo Brossard, president, Cominco Mining Co., for geological and mining development.

SANCTA BARBARA MEDAL

Canadian Institute of Mining and Metallurgy

The medal is awarded to a woman who has made a significant contribution to the welfare of a mining community in Canada. Sancta Barbara is the patron saint and protector of the mines of the world.

1983 Lillian Salton, Toronto, Ont. Now 82 years old, Salton was a pioneer wife and mother in the Canadian mining industry. She gave freely to meet the needs of others in the Canadian wilds and at mining sites abroad.

EARLIEST SMELTER

Iron was smelted in northern Newfoundland around the year 1000, probably by the Vikings.

PAST PRESIDENTS' MEMORIAL MEDAL

Canadian Institute of Mining and Metallurgy

The award is made to a person not more than 45 years of age, who has set an outstanding example to young members of the institute and to young people contemplating a career in the industry.

1983 A. (A) MacKenzie, Mira, N.S., for his innovations in electrical technology in the coal industry in Canada.

DISTINGUISHED SERVICE MEDALS

Canadian Institute of Mining and Metallurgy

The award is for distinguished or meritorious service of a nature not necessarily technical or scientific.

1983 Leslie B. English, former president, mines, Safety Appliance Co. of Canada, for his concern and involvement with mine safety in Canada.

CANADA'S FIRST AGRARIAN SYSTEM

The seignorial system existed in France until the French Revolution in 1789 and survived in Quebec until 1854. A land grant was either bestowed or sold, and provided the owner, the seignior, with rights, privileges and obligations. The terms of the grants and those which the seignior gave their tenants (habitants) differed from one to another.

Generally, a seignorial grant gave some judicial rights and by custom granted some status. The seignior had rights and privileges within the church and during public and religious ceremonies.

If the seignior had purchased his grant, he was required to pay taxes, clear land, protect his tenants and build a mill.

The habitants paid taxes in cash or kind, and gave four days work each year either to cultivate the seignior's fields or to build roads or bridges. They were also liable for military service. If an habitant sold his holding, he had to pay a tax of about one-twelfth of the sale price.

The first seignior in New France was granted to the Sieur de Poutrincourt by the Sieur de Monts. He received land at Port Royal in 1604.

The first Seignior to establish habitants was Robert Giffard who received a grant at Beauport and brought settlers in 1634.

FIRST FAIRS

The first community fair held in Canada was at Windsor, N.S., in 1765. Called the Hants Exhibition, it is thought to be the oldest permanent fair in North America, and has been held annually since 1815. In 1792, the first fair held in Upper Canada was at Niagara-on-the Lake, Ont.

The Royal Agricultural Winter Fair was first held in Toronto in November 1922. The objectives of the fair are to: establish a national and international exposition commensurate with the progress and development of Canadian agriculture; bring together the best that Canada produces in livestock and poultry, dairy products, fruit products, horticultural display, vegetables, seed grain and in production of all kinds from the land; bring to public attention the high quality and excellence of the farms of Canada.

PRINCE PAYS TRIBUTE

"Few countries owe so much to agriculture and to their farmers as Canada ... .

"The early settlers were pioneers in more ways than one. To leave home and to face unknown hazards required considerable courage and much faith. To survive the back-breaking labour and the hardships of life the year round demanded physical and moral stamina of a high order. But not content with that they designed and built machinery and equipment which their particular conditions demanded. And, of course, when they had the time, they enjoyed the traditional country sports and especially anything to do with horses.

"These things they did for themselves and for their families but very soon they became responsible for Canada's growing prosperity. The export of their surplus production made it possible for the modern industrial Canadian nation to emerge and to prosper.

"The drive and the energy which brought these early farmers success both for themselves and for their country have continued ever since. Their descendents have built great cities and thriving communities. But all the time the farmers have tried to improve their own performance....

"They have researched for a better method, more knowledge and greater productivity ... .

"We salute the farmers of Canada, backbone of the nation and food producers to the world."

His Royal Highness The Prince Philip,
Duke of Edinburgh

ROYAL AGRICULTURAL WINTER FAIR 1982

Breeding Horses

GOVERNOR-GENERAL'S CUP
Monarchy, E. Mahon and Diana Gill, Toronto, Ont.

LIEUTENANT-GOVERNOR'S CUP:
Charo, Pamela Dorion, Oakville, Ont.

ARABIANS
Stallion: **Negors Image**, Dam and Diann Nicholas, Colden, N.Y.
Mare: **Saida Sudani**, Tina and Rocco Fortura, Dearborn Heights, Mich.

THOROUGHBREDS
Stallion: **Eyes to Rule**, Sheila MacLeod, Caledon, Ont.
Mare: **Dan's Harem**, Rita Jefferies-Pleau, Puslinch, Ont.

SADDLE HORSES
Stallion: **Oshea Count**, Parkway Stables, Alma, Ont.
Mare: **Raven, Raven**, Mr. and Mrs. P.G. Mallette, Utopia, Ont.

STANDARD BREDS
Stallion: **Tijuana Taxi**, Dwyer Hill Farms, Ashton, Ont.
Mare: **Final Edition**, Donald Beisel, Woodstock, Ont.

HACKNEY PONIES
Stallion: **Clover Leaf's Radiation**, Debbie Mulcunry, Simpsonville, Ky.
Mare: **High & Mighty Favorita**, The Eponaria Stud, D.P. Hansen and El Ochsenschlager, Cold Spring, N.Y.

HACKNEY HORSES
Stallion: **Suddie Marksman**, Mr. and Mrs. R. Weaver, Peoria, Ill.
Mare: **Amazing Grace**, A.B.C. Farms, Brampton, Ont.

PALOMINOS
Stallion: **Sparkling Nuggett**, Betty Reeve, Markham, Ont.
Mare: **My Golden Opportunity**, Kathryn A. Boyd, Newmarket, Ont.

PERCHERONS
Stallion: **Confetti**, Ironwood Farms, Renfrew, Ont.
Mare: **Blackhome Connie Lyn**, Reginald Black & Sons, Moorefield, Ont.

SHETLAND PONIES
Stallion: **Ridge-Vue's Patton**, Lionel R. Purcell, Markham, Ont.
Mare: **Michigan's Winter Mist**, Murray Meadows, St. Paul's, Ont.

WELSH PONIES
Stallion: **Ardmore Afterglo**, Eric Caleca, Andover, N.J.
Mare: **Ardmore Daylight**, Mrs. D.G. Rockwell, King, Ont.

CANADIAN HUNTERS
Stallion: **Fair Swap**, Dwyer Hill Farms, Ashton, Ont.
Mare: **Coffee Break**, Hermitage Farm, Claremont, Ont.

CLYDESDALES
Stallion: **Doura Royal Scot**, Wreford Hewson, Beeton, Ont.
Mare: **Kirklandhill, Queen O'Carrick**, Wreford Hewson, Beeton, Ont.

BELGIANS
Stallion: **Masters Continue**, Carlsberg, Schomber, Ont.
Mare: **Nesbitt's Lady Jennifer**, S.G. Nesbitt & Son Ltd., Minden, Ont.

Geldings or Mares
BELGIANS
Harry V. Heck, Abingdon, Ill.

CLYDESDALES
Shantz Construction, Orangeville, Ont.

PERCHERONS
Don Robertson, Lindsay, Ont.

SEMEN SUPER SALES

Semex Canada marketed and exported boar semen to more than 20 countries in 1982. One sale to Australia was the largest sale of boar semen ever recorded.

Beef Cattle
ABERDEEN ANGUS
Grand champion bull: Ellanin Senator, Ellanvannin & Deep Down Ranch, Gormley, Ont. Grand champion female: Ellanin Etiquette 38M, Ellanvannin & Anderson Farms, Gormley, Ont.

Premier breeder and exhibitor: Prospect Farm, Arva, Ont.

CHAROLAIS

Grand champion bull: RCC Royal Express 3269, Royal Charolais Co. & Proehl Charolais, Greensburg, Penn.
Grand champion female: J Bar J Ice Maid 002, Wat-Cha Charolais & Larry Grimes, Mount Forest, Ont.
Premier breeder and exhibitor: Royal Charolais Co., Greensburg, Penn.

HEREFORDS

Grand champion bull: Gold-Bar Godfather 107H 119N, Gold-Bar Livestock, Ariss, Ont.
Grand champion female: Tara Miss Nancy 4N, Tara Cattle Farms, Gerald, Sask.
Premier breeder and exhibitor: Gold-Bar Livestock, Ariss, Ont.

LIMOUSIN

Grand Champion Bull: Nordic Night X1M 62N, Doug McAlpine, Guelph, Ont.
Grand Champion Female: Hor Mar Heloise, Cressman Cattle Co., Waterloo, Ont.
Grand champion percentage female: WLN Miss Kerri LN 78K, Mainline Limousins, Lambeth, Ont.
Premier breeder and exhibitor: Cedar Patch Acres, Alton MacKay, Listowel, Ont.

SHORTHORNS

Grand champion bull: Duncairn Columbus 9N, Duncairn Farms, Regina, Sask.
Grand champion female: H.C. Roan Duchess 12K, John Sims, Cameron, Ont.
Premier breeder and exhibitor: Mrs. S.G. Bennett, Georgetown, Ont.

SIMMENTAL

Grand champion bull: Kingfield Grand Slam, Kingfield Simmentals, King City, Ont.
Grand champion female: TLCC Magic, Cherry Lane Polled Simmentals, Puslinch, Ont.
Premier breeder and exhibitor: Cherry Lane Polled Simmentals, Puslinch, Ont.
Beef herdsman's award ($50 prize): Ron Wells and family, Crystal Brook Polled Herefords, Cargill, Ont.

Dairy Cattle

AYRSHIRES

Grand champion bull: Woodland View Polly Kelly 2 ET, Terrace Bank Farm, Howick, Que.
Grand champion female: Rosayre Kelly's Peggy, Donald S. Rose, Mountain, Ont.
Premier breeder and exhibitor: Donald S. Rose, Mountain, Ont.

BROWN SWISS

Grand champion bull: Loreldo Brutus, Loreldo Farms, Belgrave, Ont.
Grand champion female: Crikside Twinkle, Morris Grier, Woodmore, Man.
Premier breeder and exhibitor: Dun Rovin Acres Ltd., Kincardine, Ont.

GUERNSEYS

Grand champion female: Grandview TH Laughter, Bruce Telfer, Paris, Ont.
Best Group of 4: Bruce Telfer, Paris, Ont.
Premier breeder: Ralph Larmer & Sons, Blackstock, Ont.
Premier exhibitor: Kenneth A. Forster, Lyndon, Ont.

HOLSTEINS

Grand champion male: Clairbois Violyn Matt, Boisclair Ferme & Fils, Arthabaska, Que.
Grand champion female: Continental Scarlet-Red, Continental Holsteins, Leduc, Alta.
Best group of four: Bon Haven Farms, Beeton, Ont.
Premier breeder: Romandale Farms, Unionville, Ont.
Premier exhibitor: Hanover Hill Holsteins, Port Perry, Ont.

JERSEYS

Grand champion bull: Don Head Imperial Duke, W.P. Wallraff, Bowmanville, Ont.
Grand champion female: Favorite Lassie Lou, Nabholz Jerseys, West Union, Iowa.
Best group of four: R. Tenger & Son, Enniskillen, Ont.
Premier breeder and exhibitor: Brian Sales, Paris, Ont.

DUAL-PURPOSE SHORTHORNS

Grand champion bull: Valley Crest Park King, Harold Patterson, Milton, Ont.

Grand champion female: Valley Crest Alice 2, Harold Patterson, Milton, Ont.
Premier breeder and exhibitor: Harold Patterson and family, Milton, Ont.
Dairy herdsman's award ($50 prize): Shady Walnut Farms, Norwich, Ont.

Market Livestock

STEERS
Grand champion steer: Aberdeen Angus, Larry Glasman, Russell, Man.
Cross breeds and other breeds champion: Hasson Livestock, Guelph, Ont.
Aberdeen Angus champion: Larry Glasman, Russell, Man.
Hereford champion: Stewart Cattle Company, Russell, Man.
Charolais champion: William A. Scott & Sons, Drumbo, Ont.
Simmental champion: Hasson Livestock, Guelph, Ont.
Limousin champion: Brad Stewart, Russell, Man.
Maine Anjou champion: Stewart Cattle Company, Russell, Man.
Chianina champion: Earley & Bruton, Kerwood, Ont.
Champion group of 5 steers: Don Watson, Millgrove, Ont.
Champion group of 10 steers: Law & Stewart Herefords, Russell, Man.

HEIFERS — CARCASSES
Grand champion carcass: Jeff Scott, Drumbo, Ont.

QUEEN'S GUINEAS
Grand champion: John Nostadt, Maidstone, Ont.
Aberdeen Angus champion: Joe Hasson, Ariss, Ont.
Herefords and Shorthorns champion: Laurie Eedy, Denfield, Ont.
Charolais-cross champion: Gord Vessie, Glanworth, Ont.
Simmental-cross champion: Jamie Hirons, Tottenham, Ont.
Limousin-cross champion: John Nostadt, Maidstone, Ont.
Crossbreds and other breeds: Mark Toole, Newmarket, Ont.

CHIP-CHUCKING CHAMPS

Cecil Wiggins, Tim Wieczorek and Elmer MacGregor of Ottawa, Ont., are proud holders of a coveted championship title.

They stood the field and proudly threw cow chips further than any other team at the World Championship Cow Chip Throwing Contest held in Beaver, Okla., in April 1983.

Swine

DUROCS
Champion boar: Lesterosa Soggy 82P, Lesterosa Swine Ltd., Forest, Ont.
Champion gilt: Lesterosa Choice 523N, Lesterosa Swine Ltd., Forest, Ont.
Premier breeder and exhibitor: Lesterosa Swine Ltd., Forest, Ont.

HAMPSHIRES
Champion boar: Sandsdale-Lodge Jerry 24P, Andy J. Perreaux, Redvers, Sask.
Champion gilt: Sandsdale-Lodge Lass 6P, Andy J. Perreaux, Redvers, Sask.
Premier breeder and exhibitor: R.J. Robinson, Walton, Ont.

LACOMBES
Champion boar: Montville Harry 52P, Lloyd Jenkins, Montague, P.E.I.
Champion gilt: Montville Harriet 50P, Lloyd Jenkins, Montague, P.E.I.
Premier breeder and exhibitor: Lloyd Jenkins, Montague, P.E.I.

LANDRACE
Champion boar: Emerald Royal Eros 301P, Emerald Stock Farms, Balcarres, Sask.
Champion gilt: Beebe Plain Lady 334N, Beebe Plain Farms, Beebe, Que.
Premier breeder and exhibitor: Emerald Stock Farms, Balcarres, Sask.

YORKSHIRES
Champion boar: Ardyne McFlannel, William Crow, Cambridge, Ont.
Champion gilt: Rusholme Bonnie 783N, Darryl S. Mitchell, Glencoe, Ont.
Premier breeder and exhibitor: Lesterosa Swine Ltd., Forest, Ont.

Swine herdsman's award ($30): Hugh A. Hart, Gadshill, Ont.

Sheep

DORSETS
Champion ewe: Driscoll Bros. 97N, Driscoll Bros. Arthur, Ont.
Champion ram: Comfort G R 63N, G.R. Comfort, St. Anns, Ont.

HAMPSHIRES
Champion ewe: Ayre Acres 19N, Lloyd Ayre, Bowmanville, Ont.
Champion ram: Lomanco Jr 35N, Lois Laberge, Danville, Que.

LEICESTERS
Champion ewe: Eldonview 49N, Donald Grant, Woodville, Ont.
Champion ram: Stan Driscoll & Sons 5P, Stan Driscoll & Sons, Moorefield, Ont.

LINCOLNS
Champion ewe: Gardhouse 43N, William A. Gardhouse, Newmarket, Ont.
Champion ram: Gardhouse 38N, William A. Gardhouse, Newmarket, Ont.

NORTH COUNTRY CHEVIOTS
Champion ewe: Woodstock 10N, Estate of Almon Boswell, Charlottetown, P.E.I.
Champion ram: 11ABE 1-41, Theo Montminy, St. Gilles, Que.

SUFFOLKS
Champion ewe: Ayre 3N, Boyd Ayre, Hampton, Ont.
Champion ram: Hopewell 6P, Hopewell Suffolks, Elmira, Ont.

OXFORDS
Champion ewe: Kelly W. Driscoll 6N, K.W. Driscoll, Moorefield, Ont.
Champion ram: Strathearl 47N, Strathearl Farm, Rockwood, Ont.

SOUTHDOWNS
Champion ewe: Armstrong S 106N, Sheila Armstrong, St. Pauls, Ont.
Champion ram: Todd 73N, St. Helen's Farms, Lucknow, Ont.

ANY OTHER BREED
Champion ewe: Emke Bros. 34P, Emke Brothers, Elmwood, Ont.
Champion ram: Emke Bros. 25N, Emke Brothers, Elmwood, Ont.

Canadian Sheep-shearing Competition
Champion: Thomas V. Howard, Barrie, Ont.
Shepherd's Award ($30): Emke Brothers, Elmwood, Ont.

FLEECE WOOL
Range wool champion: Charles R. Clouser & Son, Nova, Ohio
Domestic and Eastern: Doug Calder, Belwood, Ont.
Grand champion fleece: Charles R. Clouser & Son, Nova, Ohio

LADIES LEAD AND WOOL CLASS:
Lisa Barr, Oxford Mills, Ont.

Live Market Lambs

PUREBRED, GRADE OR CROSSBRED MARKET LAMBS
Champion and reserve pen, 3 lambs: Dan Emke, Walkerton, Ont.
Champion and reserve wether lamb: Gerald R. Comfort, St. Anns, Ont.

Goats

ANGORA
Champion buck: Brandy Creek Rufus, Margrit Multhaupt, Valcourt, Que.
Champion doe: Brandy Creek Gesi, Margrit Multhaupt, Valcourt, Que.

DAIRY GOATS
Best doe in show (all breeds): Stony Acres Magda, Jack Kent, Caledonia, Ont.

ALPINE
Grand Champion doe: Stony Acres Magda, Jack Kent, Caledonia, Ont.

NUBIAN
Grand champion doe: Pixieland Myeshia, Jeanne Farron, Paris, Ont.

SAANEN
Grand champion doe: Stormy Monday Charity May, Ruth Mausolf, Edmonton, Alta.

TOGGENBURG

Grand champion doe: Arcadia Starlight's Carmen, Arcadia Dairy Goats, Kinburn, Ont. Dairy goat herdsman's award ($30): Wanda McCrackin, Welland, Ont.

Poultry, Waterfowl, Pigeons, Rabbits & Cavies

Best waterfowl in show: Rouen, Gordon Ridler, Guelph, Ont.
Best pigeon in show: Nun, Lloyd Foster, St. John, N.B.
Best rabbit or cavy in show: Polish Sr. Doe, Eric S. Coppock, Grassie, Ont.
Grand champion standard fowl: Plymouth Rock White, Gordon Ridler, Guelph, Ont.
Champion coloured standard poultry: Ray Watford, Richmond Hill, Ont.
Best young bird: Nun, Lloyd Foster, St. John, N.B.
Best young standard poultry: Plymouth Rock White Cockerel, Gordon Ridler, Guelph, Ont.
Champion fantail pigeon: C.F. Waite, Belleville, Ont.
Grand champion bantam: Old English black red hen, James G. McPhail, Georgetown, Ont.
Best silver laced Wyandotte: H. Volkmann, Bolton, Ont.
Championship Jersey Giant: John Tilt, Kitchener, Ont.

Foodstuffs

Best butter: Teeswater Creamery Ltd., Teeswater, Ont.
Cheddar cheese champion: Rejean Galipeau Ault Foods, Winchester, Ont.
Variety cheese champion: Fromagerie de Corneville, St. Hyacinthe, Que.

RECORD CROPS AND WHEAT SALES

Prairie farmers produced a record 45-million-ton wheat harvest in the 1982 crop year and despite a world surplus of feed grains such as wheat and barley, the Canadian Wheat Board is managing to set export records.

Halfway through the crop year, which ends July 31, 1983, the Wheat Board had sold 13.5 million metric tons, well up from 11.9 million tons for the same period a year earlier. Last year Canada set an export record of about 25 million tons.

Field Crops — World Champions

Oats: J. Wesley Yellowlees, Enniskillen, Ont.
Wheat, Canuck: J. Miklos Enterprises, Wrentham, Alta.
Barley, Ming: Don Smith (4-H), Markham, Ont.
Rye: Willi Hilgendag, Brantford, Ont.
Ear corn: Dean Todd, Flora, Ind.
Shelled corn: M.H.C. Townsend, Avondale, Harare, Zimbabwe.
Soybeans, Maple Arrow: Lorne W. Fell, Staff, Ont.
Hay: Russell Bolton, Seaforth, Ont.
Tobacco: Joe Dockx, Jr. Clear Creek, Ont.
Flax, Dufferin: Clark Frantz, Starbuck, Man.

PEDIGREED SEED

Canuck: J. Miklos Enterprises, Wrentham, Alta.
Tobin: Seidle Bros., Medstead, Sask.
Open sheaf wheat: A.B. Wylds, Ripley, Ont.
Maple syrup: Harold G. Kent, Richards Landing, Ont.

FIELD CROPS — CANADIAN CHAMPIONS

Barley, 2-rowed, Palliser: Mr. and Mrs. C. Deurloo, Granum, Alta.
Barley, 6-rowed: Don Smith, Markham, Ont.
Corn, sweet: Neil Mark, Little Britain, Ont.
Grass seeds: W.E. and M.E. Jones, Bridgenorth, England
Legume seeds, Algonquin: Steve Merkl, Brooks, Alta.
Peas, Rondo: R. Hague & Son, Madam Green Farm, Chichester, England
Wheat, spring canuck: Miklos Enterprises, Wrentham, Alta.
Wheat, winter: William C. Whitewell, Binbrook, Ont.
Christmas trees: Don Robitaille, Midland, Ont.

FIRST WATERPOWERED GRISTMILL IN NORTH AMERICA

The first crop of cultivated wheat was grown in Canada near Annapolis Royal, N.S., in 1606 and North America's first waterpowered grist mill was built nearby at Port Royal in 1607.

Champlain, assisted by Jean Poutrincourt, a French nobleman, constructed the mill at the mouth of the Le Quille River. The mill was a boon to the early settlers who had been grinding imported French wheat with handmills. Within a few years the settlers were grinding their own grown wheat.

The post was destroyed in 1613 by a British force from Virginia.

Pedigreed seeds — Canadian Champions

Pedigreed seed corn, true single cross: Maple Leaf Mills Ltd., Wallaceburg, Ont.

Pedigreed seed corn, other than single cross: M.H.C. Townsend, Harare, Zimbabwe

Pedigreed Barley, 2-rowed variety: John Holmen, Wayne, Alta.

Pedigreed barley, 6-rowed variety: William Coleman & Sons, Kippen, Ont.

Pedigreed soybeans: Henry Mergl, Maidstone, Ont.

Pedigreed white beans: Anderson Brothers, Kent Bridge, Ont.

Pedigreed flax: Loyns Seeds, Lac Vert, Sask.

Pedigreed oats: Richard J. Mueler, Barrhead, Alta.

Pedigreed hard red spring wheat: Miklos Enterprises, Wrentham, Alta.

Pedigreed soft winter wheat: Kenneth McAlpine, Ailsa Craig, Ont.

Pedigreed durum wheat: Harold T. Hierath, Milk River, Alta.

Pedigreed alfalfa seeds: Steve Merkl, Brooks, Alta.

Pedigreed birdsfoot trefoil: Alex Graham Spence, Elmvale, Ont.

Pedigreed brome grass: W.B. Fulton, Rock Ford, Alta.

Pedigreed fescue: E.S. Burlingham & Sons, Forest Grove, Ore.

Pedigreed rapeseed/canola: Seidle Brothers, Medstead, Sask.

Pedigreed Timothy seed: Ernest Kvaruberg, Calmar, Alta.

Pedigreed — any other species of grass seed: Turf Seed Inc. Hubbard, Ore. (Omega Perennial)

Pedigreed — any other species of forage legume: Frank Kastelic, Sangudo, Alta. (Aurora Alaike)

FIELD CROPS OPEN SECTION

Barley, 2-rowed: Mr. and Mrs. C. Deurloo, Granum, Alta.

Barley, 6-rowed: Ada Yellowlees, Enniskillen, Ont.

Buckwheat: W.R. Campbell, Alma, Ont.

Corn, ear, dent: Dean Todd, Flora, Ind.

Corn, shelled dent: M.H.C. Townsend, Harare, Zimbabwe

Corn, ear, sweet, over 8-rowed variety: Neil Mark, Little Britain, Ont.

Flax, linseed type: Clark Frantz, Starbuck, Man.

Lentils: Sabourin Seed Service, St. Jean Baptiste, Man.

Oats: Wesley J. Yellowlees, Enniskillen, Ont.

Peas, field, small and medium seeded varieties: R. Hague & Son, Madam Green Farm, Chichester, England

Peas, including those used principally in the green state: N. & J. Bradford, Moulton Chapel, Spalding, Lincs., England

Rye, spring or winter: Willi Hilgendag, Brantford, Ont.

Soybeans: Lorne W. Fell, Staffa, Ont.

Sunflower, small seeded varieties: Beneden Farm, Dunnville, Ont.

Wheat, hard red or white spring: J. Miklos Enterprises, Wrentham, Alta.

Wheat, hard red winter: Frank Jacobs & Son, Fox Warren, Man.

Wheat, soft red winter: Charles McCorkle, West Point, Ind.

Wheat, soft white winter: William C. Whitwell, Binbrook, Ont.

Wheat, Durum: J. Miklos Enterprises, Wrentham, Alta.

FIELD CROPS, OPEN SECTION, SMALL SEEDS

Brassica — rapeseed/canola, kale, turnip, or mustard seed: Joseph F. Graves, Port Lorne, Annapolis, N.S.

Birdsfoot trefoil: Kim Turnbull, Canfield, Ont.

Clover, red: Les Hoggard, Richardson Seed, Burnaby, B.C.

Rye grass: W.E. and M.E. Jones, Bridgenorth, Shropshire, England

Timothy: Alpherie Beaulieu, Ste. Martine, Que.

Any other species of grass seed: A.N. Dowling, Marriners Farm, Arlesford, Hants, UK

FORAGE CROPS AND SHEAVES

Hay, hand prepared — not eligible for world championship: Russell T. Bolton, Seaforth, Ont.

Hay, first cut, 85% or more alfalfa: Allan R. Palmer, Newport, N.S.

Hay, first cut at least 85% legume other than alfalfa: Allan R. Palmer, Newport, N.S.

Hay, first cut, legume and grass, at least 30% legume or grass: Douglas Livingston, Woodbridge, Ont.

Hay, first cut, at least 85% grass: Frank Kastelic, Sangudo, Alta.

Hay, second cut, 85% or more legume: Russell Bolton, Seaforth, Ont.

Sheaf, oats: Fran Wylds, Ripley, Ont.

Sheaf, wheat: A.B. Wylds, Ripley, Ont.

Sheaf, barley: Rosnor Farms, Mildmay, Ont.

Open sheaf award: A.B. Wylds, Ripley, Ont.

WHEAT, BY CORNE, IN CARROT

Luc de la Corne, the last French commander of the western posts held by the French, is said to have planted and grown wheat in the Carrot River valley of Saskatchewan about the year 1754.

Tobacco — Flue Cured

Tips: Joe Dockx Jr., Clear Creek, Ont.

Body leaf: Joe Dockx Jr., Clear Creek, Ont.

Cutter leaf: Fred Fisher, Vanessa, Ont.

Cutters: Fred Fisher, Vanessa, Ont.

Sand leaves or lugs: Fred Fisher, Vanessa, Ont.

Champion flue-cured tobaccos

Champion: Joe Dockx Jr., Clear Creek, Ont.

Burley tobacco cigarette type: George Kotulak Sr., Leamington, Ont.

4-H Champion Specials

Champion field crop exhibit: Murray Norton, Goodwood, Ont.

Best exhibit of tobacco: Clark Chernak, Simcoe, Ont.

Best Exhibits

Wheat: Murray Gervais, Dresden, Ont.

Oats: Dave Willems, Gloucester, Ont.

Barley: Don Smith, Markham, Ont.

Barley: Dale Connell, Palmerston, Ont.

White beans: William C. Fatheringham, Seaforth, Ont.

Seed potatoes: Murray Norton, Goodwood, Ont.

Corn: Brian Steven, Wyoming, Ont.

Corn: Gerard Van Arkel, Dresden, Ont.

Soybeans: Randy Molzen, Alvinston, Ont.

Hay: Daniel Proulx, Cumberland, Ont.

Hay: Joe Verudort, Elora, Ont.

Wheat, any variety: Murray Gervais, Dresden, Ont.

Oats, any variety: David Willems, Gloucester, Ont.

Barley, 6-rowed: Don Smith, Markham, Ont. (world champion)

Barley, 2-rowed: Dale Connell, Palmerston, Ont.

Potato, any variety: Murray Norton, Goodwood, Ont.

Corn, ear, dent: Brian Steven, Wyoming, Ont.

Corn, shelled, dent: Gerard Van Arkel, Dresden, Ont.

Soybeans, any variety: Randy Molzan, Alvinston, Ont.

White beans, any variety: William C. Fatheringham, Seaforth, Ont.

Flue-cured tobacco: Clark Chernak, Simcoe, Ont.

Hay, first cut, 85% or more legume: Daniel Proulx, Cumberland, Ont.

Hay, first cut, less than 85% legume: Joe Verudor, Elora, Ont.

Honey and Beeswax

Grand champion exhibitor: John Overton, Schomberg, Ont.

Best exhibit of liquid honey: Vincent Nevidon, Cambridge, Ont.

Best exhibit of granulated honey: John Overton, Schomberg, Ont.

CLASSIFICATION WINNERS

Liquid honey, white, provinces west of Ontario: Bob Lyons, Pincher Creek, Alta.

Liquid honey, white, Ontario and provinces east: Stan Coon, Etobicoke, Ont.

Liquid honey golden: Jim Pierce, Lindsay, Ont.

Liquid honey, amber: Vincent Nevidon, Cambridge, Ont.

Liquid honey, dark: Irene Giguere, St. Germain, Man.

Granulated honey: John Overton, Schomberg, Ont.

Comb honey: Irene Giguere, St. Germain, Man.

Cut comb honey: Richard Flewell, Claremont, Ont.

Chunk honey: Richard Flewell, Claremont, Ont.

Beeswax, producer's type: Irene Giguere, St. Germain, Man.

Beeswax, candles hand-dipped: Bruce W. Fallis, Winnipeg, Man.

SYRUP SAVER

Denis Desilet of the Rural Engineer Department, Laval University, developed a labour-efficient vacuum tapping system for the maple syrup industry in the late 1960s and was subsequently credited with saving the industry.

Maple Products

Champion 4-H maple syrup: Scott Shaw, Eldorado, Ont.

Sugar or butter — best exhibitor: Shaw Maple Products, Orillia, Ont.

Best Ontario maple syrup, excluding champion: Mark Lupton, Huntsville, Ont.

World champion maple syrup exhibit: Harold G. Kent, Richard's Landing, Ont.

CLASSIFICATION WINNERS

Maple syrup, Canada #1 Extra Light: Harold G. Kent, Richard's Landing, Ont.

Maple syrup, light: Mark Lupton, Huntsville, Ont.

Maple syrup, medium: Mark Lupton, Huntsville, Ont.

Maple syrup blocks (hard sugar): Shaw Maple Products & Pancake House, Orillia, Ont.

Maple sugar (creamed sugar): Mrs. Raymond Bould, Sutton, Que.

Maple butter: Mark Lupton, Huntsville, Ont.

Stirred maple sugar (crumb): Lawrence Howard, Echo Bay, Ont.

MAPLE PRODUCTS 4-H

Maple syrup, Canada #1, extra light: Scott Shaw, Eldorado, Ont.

Maple syrup, Canada #1, light: Karen Shaw, Eldorado, Ont.

Maple syrup, Canada #1 medium: Sherry Sager, Madoc, Ont.

DEVELOPING A WEED WASTER

Professor Ruben Hacham, University of Windsor, is developing a method of weed-killing that is as fast as chemical weed control but won't cause environmental damage. A tool connected to any farm tractor touches the top of a week and "whamo" — the weed is cooked and begins to wither away, almost immediately. The device receives an electric current from the tractor motor and charges 7,000 volts of electricity at low current, causing the internal cells of the weeds to burst.

The device has worked on 50 species of weeds, both annuals and perennials, and has proved efficient for clearing brush and young trees along hydro corridors. The current moves poorly through soil so nearby crop plants are unaffected. In tests, crop yields were the same as in plots treated with chemicals or cultivated.

Vegetables

Rutabagas
Grand champion exhibitor: Dale Jewell, York, P.E.I.

Carrots
Champion carrot exhibitor: Shirley Creighton, Alliston, Ont.

Onions
Citron 2: Lillie Norton, Goodwood, Ont.

Onion, globe, yellow cooking: Nick Tummers, Puslinch, Ont.

Onion, red: Karen Creighton, Alliston, Ont.

Onion, large spanish: Marvin Creighton, Hamilton, Ont.

Onion, white globe: Heather Creighton, Alliston, Ont.

Onion, flat type: Nick Tummers, Puslinch, Ont.

Champion onion exhibitor: Marvin Creighton, Hamilton, Ont.

Onions, rope, red: Heather Creighton, Alliston, Ont.

Onions, rope, yellow Spanish: Heather Creighton, Alliston, Ont.

Onions, rope, mixed: Heather Creighton, Alliston, Ont.

Parsnips: Shirley Creighton, Alliston, Ont.

Pumpkin pie: J.C. Cunningham, Georgetown, Ont.

Pumpkin, field: Beneden Farms, Dunnville, Ont.

Squash, hubbard warted or green: Wilfred Haufe, Toronto, Ont.

Squash, hubbard, blue: Geoff Tummers, Puslinch, Ont.

Squash, pepper: Beneden Farms, Dunnville, Ont.

Squash, banana: Dan Smerek, Smithville, Ont.

Squash, golden hubbard: Geoff Tummers, Puslinch, Ont.

Squash, butternut: Howard Stensson, Oakville, Ont.

Squash buttercup: Marvin Creighton, Hamilton, Ont.

Squash, collection: Nick Tummers, Puslinch, Ont.

Vegetable marrow: Lillie Norton, Goodwood, Ont.

Largest pumpkin or squash: Mathew Smerek, Niagara Falls, Ont.

Display of squash: Nick Tummers, Puslinch, Ont.

Indian corn display: Beneden Farm, Dunnville, Ont.

Champion table stock potatoes: Edwin Jewell, York, P.E.I.

Champion seed potatoes: Frank Rick, Trout Creek, Ont.

Youth Day Competition

THE JEFFREY BULL MEMORIAL TROPHY

Awarded to the team of three contestants that makes the highest aggregate score, evaluating three classes of dairy cattle, two classes of beef cattle, two classes of swine and one class of sheep.

Winners: Dale Hamilton, Janice Jeffrey, Steve English of Victoria County, 1616 points out of 1950.

Royal Agricultural Winter Fair Medals

Awarded to the highest scoring individual in each class of livestock.

Dairy: Janice Jeffrey, Lindsay, Ont.

Beef: Heather McDiarmid, Perth, Ont.

Swine: Steve English, Lindsay, Ont.

Sheep: Donna Thompson, Charlottetown, P.E.I.

ROBERT GRAHAM MEMORIAL TROPHY

Awarded to the contestant under 26 years of age who made the highest marks, judging two classes of heavy horses and two classes of light horses.

Tara McKnight, Cookstown, Ont., 264 points out of 300.

INTER-AGRICULTURAL COLLEGE LIVESTOCK EVALUATION COMPETITION

Competing are teams of four students enrolled in the second year at an agricultural school who evaluate three classes of dairy cattle, two classes of beef cattle, two classes of swine and one of sheep.

Champion: U. of Guelph, 2055 out of 2400 points.

TOP INTER-AGRICULTURAL INDIVIDUAL EVALUATOR

Don Bellamy, Centralia College, 703 out of 800 points.

OPEN JUNIOR FARMER JUDGING COMPETITION

Elgin Craig, Wellington County, 567 out of 650 points.

WORLD WHEAT BEATERS

David Fife came to Canada from Scotland in 1820. He began experiments to develop higher-yielding wheat plants on his farm near Peterborough, Ont.

He produced a variety which matured earlier and produced a higher yield than other strains, and which milled into excellent flour. His Red Fife was the most popular wheat of the period and it played a part in the development of even finer wheats.

Sir Charles E. Saunders, according to *The London Press*, "contributed more to the wealth of his country than any other man."

Saunders' father was director of Canada's first experimental farms, at Ottawa. Saunders, a graduate chemist, intended to pursue his deep love of music, but his father convinced Saunders to assist him.

His task was to produce a variety of wheat that would ripen quickly and be ready for harvest before the early frosts of the Canadian northwest descended. Methodically, he crossed and planted numerous strains. In 1904 he produced a variety which met the criteria. It was a cross of Red Fife and an Indian variety called Hard Red Calcutta. The new wheat, which Saunders named Marquis, was resistant to disease, had a high yield and was ready for harvest just 100 days after planting. Introduced in 1908, it was soon in wide use. Canada's wheat acreage was increased, as farmers were willing to settle in the northwest with a quality wheat that matured in the short growing season.

Saunders later developed Reward, Ruby and Garnet wheats, strains that were suitable for the prairies. He did not personally profit from his discoveries and retired in the 1920s to live on a small pension. He was given a larger pension after pressure was brought to bear by the farm community that had benefited from his research. He was titled in 1934 and died in 1937. He was the first fellow named by the Agricultural Institute of Canada and is in the Canadian Agricultural Hall of Fame.

AIC FELLOWSHIP AWARD
Agricultural Institute of Canada

The highest honour of the institute. Recipients are selected for professional distinction. Their services to Canadian agriculture are in scientific achievement, scholarship, leadership, breadth of knowledge and experience.

1982 **Thomas M. MacIntyre**, past president of the Nova Scotia Institute of Agrologists and the Canadian Society of Animal Science, for the development of applied research programs which have gained wide acceptance throughout the Atlantic provinces. He is author or co-author of some 35 publications on animal and poultry nutrition, and animal breeding and management.

J.E. (Ted) McCannel, senior assistant coordinator, Country Operations Grain Transportation Authority, Winnipeg, Man., for his long service to agriculture and for his contribution to the profession of agrology.

John E. Moxley, past president the Macdonald Branch of the Agricultural Institute of Canada and of the Canadian Society of Animal Science, in recognition of outstanding achievements in dairy cattle genetics and management, and the application of these to the development of a dairy cattle milk recording system. His system, now in use in Quebec, sees some 300,000 records processed each month. In 1977 l'Ordre des Agronomes du Québec made Moxley Commandeur de l'Ordre du Mérite Agronomique.

Eric D. Putt, Morden, Man., for his outstanding contribution to the agricultural economy of Canada and elsewhere through his work in sunflower research. Among his many contributions are the development of the first commercial hybrid sunflower and the identification of disease-resistant genes. In 1980 he received the V.S. Pustovit Award of the International Sunflower Association.

D. Donn Mitchell, Douglas, Man., for leadership in practical agriculture. His family farm, Klondike Farms, has grown to an 8400-acre cash crop and beef enterprise with one of the country's best known herds of polled Herefords. His other interests include Bar-Five Simmental Breeders Ltd. and Shilo Farms, a major irrigated enterprise on marginal farmland. The first chairman of the Western Canadian Grain Stabilization Fund, he has served for 20 years as director of the Royal Manitoba Winter Fair. He was one of the founding forces behind the Manitoba Bull Test Station and was named Mr. Manitoba Farmer in 1978.

Edwin Ballantyne, retired executive director of Alberta Environment;
Glenn Flaten, Saskatchewan farmer and president of the Canadian federation of Agriculture;
Mark Kilcher, retired researcher, the agriculture research station in Swift Current;
Garland Laliberte, head of agricultural engineering, University of Manitoba;
Doug McRorie, vice-president, agricultural services, the Royal Bank of Canada;
Doug Morrison, chairman of the department of animal and poultry science, University of Guelph.

A FORTUITOUS FIND, A GRAFT, A WORLD-FAMOUS APPLE

John McIntosh settled on a small farm at Dundela, near Dundas, Ont., where, in 1811, he found growing some young wild apple trees. He transplanted them close to his house and was delighted when one of the trees grew to produce a tasty apple.

An itinerant worker later showed McIntosh's son, Alan, how to graft the tree so that other trees would bear the fruit. Alan demonstrated the technique and sold branches from the tree to farmers in the area. Soon the region was known for apple orchards and the McIntosh apple was sought by growers from the Annapolis Valley to the Okanagan and beyond Canada's boundaries. Today Canada is one of the world's leading exporters of apples.

AIC FELLOWSHIPS

Agricultural Institute of Canada

The Agricultural Institute of Canada named seven new fellows in 1983: Robert Chancey, director of the agricultural research station in St. John's Nfld;

CANADIAN HOLSTEINS AGRICULTURAL AMBASSADORS

In recent years Canada has exported Holsteins to more than 60 countries; annually, some 20,000 head valued at $32-million have been exported. Semen has been exported to more than 50 countries for an annual value of more than $8-million.

One individual contract included 1,000 head of Holsteins for a Saudi Arabian "turn key" (a complete dairy complex from planning to production).

Agriculture Canada geneticist Dr. Jacques Chesnais reports that in the recent two decades average milk production per cow has increased annually by 35 kg; the cumulative benefits of genetic progress are now worth some $56-million annually. In the last 10 years the average of all artificially inseminated Holstein sires shows an improvement in their mature female offspring of 53 kg of milk.

The worldwide acceptance of the Canadian Holstein is a reflection of the achievements of the Canadian breeders and the artificial insemination industry.

CHAMPION CANADIAN PLOWMAN

Canadian Plowing Council

The Canadian plowing championships began at Coburg, Ont., in 1953 and continue to be held each year. The top two plowmen then represent Canada at the World Plowing Contest. Finalists from all parts of Canada use the same type of equipment and plow three plots within two days. The most important elements considered by the judges are straightness and uniformity of the furrow and the general appearance of the seed bed. Time is also a factor.

1981 **Robert D. Brown**, Ayr, Ont., and **John Charles Marcil**, Carignan, Que., who represented Canada at the World Championships in Tasmania.

1982 **Ken Ferguson**, Stouffville, Ont., and **Robert D. Brown**, Ayr, Ont., who represented Canada at the World Championships in Zimbabwe.

A WINNING CANADIAN FARMER

One of Canada's most successful farm operations is Cold Springs Farm at Thamesford, near London, Ont.

Under the direction of Harvey Beaty, the operation, which began with a small flock of laying hens, has grown to an agribusiness conglomerate with company divisions grossing more than $30-million annually.

There are 42 farm locations. One million turkeys are raised and many are vacuum-packed under the Cold Springs Farm label. There is a retail food store where Beaty pioneered cut-up turkey marketing in Canada. The swine divisions markets 30,000 finished hogs a year and the beef feedlots finish some 2,000 head annually. Elevators and feed complexes dry and store more than 30,000 tonnes of grain corn a year and manufacture all the feed requirements for various species of livestock and poultry.

MAN OF THE YEAR

Canadian Seed Trade Association

The award recognizes individuals whose work in science, administration or government has contributed to the advancement of Canadian agriculture by means of seed or seed-related activities.

1982 **Dr. Lorne S. Donovan**, principal research scientist and chief of the forage section of the Ottawa Research Station.
Donovan has been the premier corn breeder in Canada for several decades, and the 38 hybrids he has released to the seed industry have had an enormous impact on Canadian agriculture. The inbred lines of corn he has developed have helped introduce successful corn production to short-season areas of Canada. He has also worked on the breeding of short-season soybean crops.

CANADIAN COMBINE

Thomas Carrol of Massey-Harris developed the self-propelled combine that revolutionized wheat farming in Canada and around the world in 1938. His machine was the first to cut, thresh, clean and deliver grain in a single one-man operation.

CANADIAN AGRICULTURAL HALL OF FAME

The Hall of Fame perpetuates the memories of persons who made outstanding contributions to Canada's basic industry. Their portraits hang in the Coliseum of the Royal Agricultural Winter Fair in Toronto. Only three portraits are unveiled each year.

1982 **Roy G. Snyder**, Waterloo, Ont. As the

first full-time employee of the Waterloo Cattle Breeding Association in 1946 and its manager from 1950 to 1963, Snyder established the first artificial insemination centre in the world to adopt an all-frozen semen program.

He was instrumental in importing the first pure-bred Charolais bull and placed the first Brown Swiss bulls into artificial insemination service in Canada. He also participated in the first combined Holstein-Friesian bull purchase by the Ontario A.I. Centres.

Dr. Rene Trepanier, former deputy minister of agriculture for Quebec. He established the Quebec Artificial Insemination Centre, introduced calhood vaccination to the province, and introduced more aggressive apple-marketing programs. He was influential in the establishment of the Veterinary School at St. Hyacinthe and was awarded an honorary doctorate in veterinary medicine by the University of Montreal.

He is noted as a breeder and importer of Ayrshire cattle and Belgian horses.

1983 Sydney Blewett Williams, president, Hays and Williams Enterprises Ltd., Calgary, Alta. He provided strong leadership in the establishment of the Federal Task Force on Agriculture, 1967 to 1969, the Canadian Dairy Commission, the Farm Products Marketing Agencies Act, CanFarm and the Small Farm Development Program, as deputy minister of agriculture from 1967 to 1975.

SOME WINNERS IN CANADA'S AGRICULTURAL HALL OF FAME

Alexander J. McPhail, whose efforts led to the formation of the Saskatchewan Wheat Pool.

Dr. E. Cora Hind, a reporter on the Winnipeg *Free Press* who had an uncanny ability to forecast wheat production. Her predictions were used by the trade for 29 years in preference to all others.

Dr. John H. Wesson was a mover in a campaign that joined farm organizations together into the Canadian Federation of Agriculture.

Alexander M. Stewart, who won the world's oat championship at the Chicago International in 1937 and went on to produce, process and merchandise pedigreed seed. He introduced many varieties that influenced Canada's agricultural economy.

Senator Patrick Burns, a pioneer rancher and meat packer who is credited with doing more to develop the beef cattle industry in Western Canada than any other person. He was one of the founders of the Calgary Stampede.

Alfred Bagg had the distinction of having the first accredited Jersey herd in Canada.

Joseph E. Brethour recognized that fat-hog production had no future in Canada, concentrated on the production of a bacon-type hog and became the founder of the modern Yorkshire.

Cecil Ivor Delworth, a practical horticulturalist and plant breeder, developed many techniques now used by greenhouse owners and flower producers throughout the world.

Harvey Farrington established the first cheese factory in Canada at Norwich Ont., in 1894. In its second year of operations, the factory's total output, 10 tons, was shipped to Great Britain, thus pioneering the export of Canadian cheese to the UK.

Dr. William Richard Graham played a leading role in developing the OAC strain of Barred Plymouth Rocks. He was a co-founder of the Poultry Science Association, and a prime mover in the World Poultry Science Association, the sponsor of world poultry conferences.

During the First World War he was largely responsible for Canada's adoption of national grades for eggs and poultry.

Dr. H. H. Hannam was dedicated to the belief that food is a powerful factor in the cause of peace and pushed hard for a world food bank. He saw his dream come true when the UN voted a large sum for the establishment of a world food bank. He was president of the Canadian Federation of Agriculture from 1943 until his death in 1963.

William Weld began publishing the *Farmer's Advocate* in 1866. He promoted many progressive ideas, including soil and water conservation, forest protection and the establishment of the Ontario Agricultural College.

Dr. Kenneth F. Wells has received international acclaim representing Canada in all parts of the world on behalf of animal health. A landmark of his distinguished career was the eradication program which successfully eliminated an outbreak of foot and mouth disease in Saskatchewan due to the establishment of the Canadian maximum security quarantine system. He also founded the Western College of Veterinary Medicine at the University of Saskatchewan.

Humanities and Canadian Life

KINETTE PUBLIC SPEAKING TROPHY

Association of Kinsmen Clubs

1982   Gail Holden, Winnipeg, Man.

FOUNDING MEMBER PUBLIC SPEAKING TROPHY

1982   Gord Jamieson, Simcoe, Ont.

KINSMAN OF THE YEAR

1982   Phil Wright, Fort St. John, B.C.

B'NAI BRITH CANADA AWARDS

B'Nai Brith Canada

As Canadian Jewry's largest service organization, B'nai Brith Lodges offer social programming for the aged, the handicapped, the retarded, the emotionally disturbed and the needy.

Twenty thousand families across Canada are represented in B'nai Brith, which grants two awards annually to outstanding Canadians for their achievements in the field of humanitarian concerns and in the business world.

HUMANITARIAN AWARD (YOUTH SERVICES)

1982   Harry (Red) Foster, Toronto, Ont., a former athlete, retired advertising executive, mainstay of Canadian Associations for the Retarded and founder of the Special Olympics.

1983   George A. Cohon, president, McDonald's Restaurants of Canada Ltd., one of a group who saved Toronto's Santa Claus Parade, and a worker on behalf of children's charities such as Big Brothers and Ronald McDonald Houses.

HALL HONOURED

TV star Monty Hall, Canadian by birth, received the 1983 Beth Sholom Brotherhood Humanitarian Award for his work on behalf of Variety Villages in Canada and around the world.

HONOURS AND AWARDS

Boy Scouts of Canada

Scouting in Canada began in 1908, a year after R.S.S. Baden-Powell started the movement in England. The aim of Boy Scouts of Canada is to help boys develop as resourceful and responsible members of the community by providing opportunities for their intellectual, physical, social and spiritual growth.

JACK CORNWELL DECORATION

John Travers Cornwell, a London, England, boy scout, at the age of 16 served as a Boy (1st class) on Board H.M.S. *Chester* at the Battle of Jutland in 1916. Mortally wounded early in the action, he remained at his post, surrounded by the dead and dying, awaiting orders until the end of the action. Transferred to hospital, he died a few days later. He was posthumously awarded the Victoria Cross, and to perpetuate his memory, the Jack Cornwell Decoration was instituted.

1982 Cub **James Andrew Siteman**, 9, Sydney Forks, N.S., (the posthumous award was accepted by Scout Elliot Siteman) for his courage and determination to do his best, despite suffering physical, emotional pain and a severe health problem.

HIGHEST SCOUTING HONOURS AND AWARDS

Silver Cross

For gallantry, with considerable risk.

Brian Dean, Saint John, N.B.
Carl Urquhart, Fredericton, N.B.

Bronze Cross

For gallantry with moderate risk.

Patrol Leader **Gordon Ihumatak**, 15, Coppermine, N.W.T.
Ian Arthur Sparshu, 14, Mill Bay, B.C.

Medal for Meritorious Conduct

For especially meritorious conduct not involving heroism or risk of life.

1st Devon Scout Troop, Devon, Alta.
Beaver Leader **Julie Gaal**, Penticton, B.C.
Scout Patrol Leader **Philip Stephen Gerard**, 13, Duncan, B.C.
Scouter-in-Training **Karl Lloyd Hartlen**, 16, North Sydney, N.S.
Scout **John Christopher Ovas**, 12 Toronto, Ont.
Scout Richard **James Ovas**, 14, Toronto, Ont.
Scout **Gary Rose**, 13, Thamesville, Ont.

Certificate for Meritorious Conduct

For meritorious acts worthy of recorded commendation but which do not justify a medal or a bar.

1st Devon Scout Troop, Devon, Alta.
Scouter-in-Training **Peter William Cseppento**, 16, Castlegar, B.C.

Cub **Barclay Dammann**, 8, Swanhills, Alta.
Patrol Leader **Brian Materi**, 12, Edson, Alta.
Cub **Luke Nishenapaise**, 9, Wunnimin Lake, Ont.
Scout **Kevin Sampson**, 16, Toronto, Ont.
Cub **Bradley Stansfeld-Jones**, 10, Coquitlam, B.C.
Cub **Jeffery William Yanko**, 10, Calgary, Alta.

Certificate for Gallantry

For gallantry, with slight risk and worthy of recorded commendation.

Scout **Raymond Marcel Bourget**, 17, Yellowknife, N.W.T.

Silver Fox

For service to scouting in the international field, performed by persons who are not members of Boy Scouts of Canada.

Robert Crause Baden-Powell, Surrey, England.

Silver Wolf

For service to scouting — normally of national importance.

His Excellency Governor-General **Edward Schreyer**, Ottawa, Ont.
Gordon W. Crane, North Vancouver, B.C.
Donovan F. Miller, Vancouver, B.C.
J. Percy Ross, Ottawa, Ont.
Helen I. Smith, Oakville, Ont.
Hubert Roy, Whitehead, Pointe Claire, Que.

Bar to the Silver Acorn

For continued service to scouting.

George A. Clements, Yarmouth, N.S.
Abram Y. Goss, Saint John, N.B.
Richard A. Norman, Kitchener, Ont.
Gordon H. McConnell, Kitchener, Ont.

Silver Acorn

For service to scouting.

John F. Adams, Burnaby, B.C.
Donald F. Brown, Digby, N.S.
G. Raymond Bryson, London, Ont.
Robert S. Buckley, Dorval, Que.
Charles W. Burchell, Dartmouth, N.S.
Murray G. Carpenter, McLean, Sask.

George A. Clements, Yarmouth, N.S.
Gerard DeCoene, Langton, Ont.
John F. Funnell, Winnipeg, Man.
Waldo E. Goodman, New Glasgow, N.S.
Carl Goodspeed, Rothesay, N.B.
Robert Grant, Cambridge, Ont.
Walter T. Harpur, Willowdale, Ont.
Bernard C. Haysom, Regina, Sask.
Marguerite Hobley, Thunder Bay, Ont.
Ronald Iles, Ottawa, Ont.
Howard A. Jackson, Midland, Ont.
William I. Lewis, Brockville, Ont.
Bernard Mason, Wolfville, N.S.
Robert Matthews, Westmount, Que.
Paul K. Mengelberg, Longlac, Ont.
Robert H. Morrow, Grand Falls, Nfld.
Graham R. Norman, Sherwood Park, Alta.
Orville J. O'Brien, Ottawa, Ont.
Jim Oxley, Moose Jaw, Sask.
Ralph Ross, Lachine, Que.
Reverend Ralph K.M. Rowe, Wunnumin Lake, Ont.
David H. Searle, Yellowknife, N.W.T.
Donald Scott, Hants County, N.S.
Ruth Shergold, Vancouver, B.C.
Todd Smith, New Glasgow, N.S.
Robert Steadman, Pointe Claire, Que.
The Honourable Gordon A. Winter, St. John's, Nfld.
Wilfred S. Wootton, Vancouver, B.C.

VANIER AWARDS

Canada Jaycees

Inspired by the late Governor-General Vanier, the awards are made annually to Canadians, 19 to 40, from all walks of life, who exemplify a Jaycee ideal that "the earth's great treasure lies in human personality and service to humanity is the best work of life."

1983 **Donna** and **Emerson Coish**, Wabush, Nfld., who have worked for years to assist the mentally handicapped gain acceptance in society.
Donald Grant Devine, premier of Saskatchewan, for his achievements in agriculture, law, community service and public service.
Dianne Lynn Dupui, Toronto, Ont., for her inspirational work with mentally handicapped young people. Her

Famous People Players Theatre, employing the handicapped as puppeteers, has achieved international fame, including an appearance at the White House.
David Sheldon Fraser, Halifax, N.S., a sportsman who works with disabled athletes, especially the blind.
Gina Osborne, Brampton, Ont. Osborne and her husband, Ray, have 14 "special needs" children. The children, aged 3 to 17, are, except for one, adopted. The family is multiracial, two children are blind, two are without their full limbs, two are deaf and others suffer from fetal alcohol syndrome, spina-bifida and mental retardation.

AWARD OF MERIT

Consumers' Association of Canada.

In recognition of outstanding service to the consumer movement. Originating in 1977, this award is not necessarily granted on an annual basis.

The association provides consumers with information that helps maintain a decent standard of living and allows the views of consumers to be heard by governments, trade and industry. Through its battles, the CAC has helped to achieve the mandatory use of protective hockey helmets; restriction in the use of DDT and other long-life pesticides; and increased the labelling of precaution information on over-the-counter drugs. The association has some 170,000 members.

1981 **Helen Anderson**, Islington, Ont.
Ethel Marliss, Edmonton, Alta.

WONDERFUL WINNERS

Aden Bowman Collegiate in Saskatoon, Sask. is the Canadian school that has collected the most money for UNICEF over the years through the Halloween collection by children. From 1962 to

1982 the students of the collegiate collected $100,250.76 on behalf of children around the world.

Jean Arnold Tory, a member of the Order of Canada and a tireless worker for Canadian service agencies, founded UNICEF Canada in Toronto in 1955 when she floated a trial balloon for UNICEF on Hallowe'en. The success of the Toronto experiment, where children collected pennies on behalf of other children, led to the formation of a Canada-wide UNICEF committee.

R.M. TAYLOR MEDAL

Canadian Cancer Society/National Cancer Institute of Canada.

Recognition is given for achievement in the cancer field — in science, patient care, public education or public service. The R.M. Taylor Medal is the most prestigious award of the society.

1982 **Ruth Hartman Frankel,** CC, Toronto, Ont. The medal presented to Frankel is another in a long list of presentations honouring her for her volunteer efforts on behalf of cancer patients the world over. She was a B'nai B'rith Woman of the Year in the 1960s and in 1969 was made a Companion of the Order of Canada. She has been honoured by the League of Friends in England and by the U.S. National Institute of Social Sciences. France presented her with the Pierre and Marie Curie Medal on behalf of the Ligue Nationale Francais Contre Le Cancer and Poland awarded her a commemoration medal on the 25th anniversary of the Marie Sklodowska (Curie) Institute. In 1981, the Ontario Medical Association awarded her the Centennial Medal for tangible achievement.

HUMAN RELATIONS AWARD

Canadian Council of Christians and Jews

The Council promotes human relations and interreligious dialogue. The Human Relations Award is presented to prominent citizens who have fostered good human relations in Canada.

1981 **Anthony Crittin**, chairman, Commercial Life Assurance Co., Toronto, Ont.
Alfred Powis, chairman, Noranda Mines Ltd., Toronto
Rabbi Erwin Schild, Adath Israel Synagogue, Toronto
Melvyn Dobrin, president, Steinberg's Ltd., Montreal, Que.
Conrad Harrington, chancellor, McGill University, Montreal
Paul Lacoste, rector, University of Montreal, Montreal
Anthony G. Anselmo, president, Safeway Stores Ltd., Calgary, Alta.
Lil Faider, Calgary
Rabbi Lewis Ginsberg, Calgary
R.J. (Larry) Hegan, Calgary
1982 **Cardinal Gerald Emmett Carter**, Archdiocese, Toronto.
The Salvation Army in Canada
Metropolitan Toronto Chairman, **Paul Godfrey**

AWARD FOR THEME SONG

In 1982 a special presentation was made to Murray McLauchlan for his song *If the Wind Could Blow My Troubles Away*. The song was used as the theme song for the International Year of Disabled Persons by Canada, the USA and the United Nations.

AWARD OF MERIT

Canadian Council of the Blind

The highest award of the council, it recognizes outstanding work on behalf of blind Canadians.

1982 **Edna Marie Mulrooney**, St. John's, Nfld., in recognition of a life of service which earned the love and respect of blind persons throughout Newfoundland and Labrador.

BOOK OF FAME CITATION

The book contains the names and citations of outstanding blind Canadians as selected yearly by the council. Winners are presented with a framed copy of the appropriate page of the book.

1982 **Edward William Barfoot**, Brandon, Man. Among other achievements, Lewis devised the game "Showdown" for blind people which does not require sighted assistance. It is being considered for inclusion in the 1984 Disabled Olympics.
Edna Velzora Parkin, Saint John, N.B.
Pearl Ashton, London, Ont.

CANADIAN FRIENDSHIP AWARD

American Legion

A medal bearing the seal of the American Legion is presented to war veterans who are members of veterans' organizations in Canada. It recognizes outstanding service in veterans' affairs and the perpetuation of the spirit of international goodwill and comradeship between the Canadian and American Legions.

1982 **Bartholomew (Bart) Watkins**, Glace Bay, N.S.
Len Whitechurch, Elie, Man.
E.W. Swinn, Winnipeg, Man.
Demi Stewart, Saskatoon, Sask.
Alex Shaw, Lethbridge, Alta.
H. Robertson, Toronto, Ont.
Al Pratt, Vancouver, B.C.
Nick Ponych, Lethbridge, Alta.
Thomas G. Pascoe, Calgary, Alta.
Weston E. Nutbrown, Lennoxville, Que.
Terry Murphy, Richmond, B.C.
Cy Morton, Vancouver, B.C.
J.D. Moore, Montreal North, Que.
Joseph A. Montsion, Winnipeg, Man.
Neil McKinnon, Barrie, Ont.
Ken McKay, Saskatoon, Sask.
Don McCrady, Vancouver, B.C.
Archie MacKay, Vancouver, B.C.
H. LaFortune, Simcoe, Ont.
Gordon Kerr, Burnaby, B.C.
Hartwell Illsey, Vancouver, B.C.

Elsie Gray, Halifax, N.S.
Don Gray, La Prairie, Man.
Lou Gobel, Calgary, Alta.
Henry G. Ford, Belleville, Ont.
Jean Crimes, Edmonton, Alta.
Clifford Cooper, Richmond, B.C.
Ernie Cleveland, Saskatoon, Sask.
John Clarke, Vancouver, B.C.
Harold Caudle, Toronto, Ont.
Cliff Barnes, Thunder Bay, Ont.
Arthur Lyle Steele, Regina, Sask.
R.J. "Jim" Foote, Edmonton, Alta.
Hayden P. Marcelle, Thunder Bay, Ont.
Harry M. Sample, Thunder Bay, Ont.
Don Sarkissian, Nanaimo, B.C.
Jack Storie, Windsor, Ont.
Issie I. Rynd, Chomedey, Que.

JOHN MORGAN WINS LENIN PEACE PRIZE

John Morgan of Toronto is one of four people worldwide to receive the 1982 Lenin Peace Prize. The award is for "outstanding services performed in the struggle for strengthening and preserving peace." Morgan, a retired Unitarian minister, was born in Indiana but became a Canadian citizen in 1966. An outspoken minister, he is currently president of the Canadian Peace Congress.

SENIORS ALIVE

Canadian Institute of Religion and Gerontology

The Institute is an interfaith organization devoted to the spiritual well-being of older people. It concerns itself with the rapidly expanding population of seniors, the erosion of human rights for senior citizens and the multiplying problems which are confronting expanding years of life.

Seniors Alive is an award given to a person who continues to serve beyond retirement age.

1981 Senator **David Arnold Croll**

Lotta Dempsey Ham, journalist
Rev. Dr. Harold Vaughan
Lawrence Crawford
1982   Jack Lerette, Toronto, Ont.
Stella Annie Burry, St. John's Nfld.

SPIRITUAL WELL-BEING AWARD

The award commemorated the year of
the World Assembly on Aging.

1982   Maude Fields, Toronto, Ont. Fields,
96, is still serving St. Basil's Church as
Sacristan, caring for her 92-year-old
husband, managing her home and
getting about the city on her own. She
says: "I have seen all stages of life
in my work for my Church. I have
seen marriages, babies born and baptized, death and burial. I have found
that life is very good."
Sister St. Michael Guinan, director of
the Institute, is a noted sociologist
and gerontologist. Her academic cre-
dentials and her contributions to education are outstanding. She is listed
in at least 12 Who's Who publications
starting with The World Who's Who
of Women, the International Who's
Who in Community Service and the
Who's Who in America.

ARTHUR NAPIER MAGILL AWARD

Canadian National Institute for the Blind

The only national honour the CNIB presents, the award is given to a person
who has made an effective contribution
to the blind in Canada.

1982   David S. Lloyd, Toronto, Ont. Upon
his retirement in 1967, David Lloyd
became associated with a small group
of amateur radio operators who were
training blind people at CNIB headquarters. He formed the Amateur
Radio Club of CNIB and was its chairman for nine years. He travelled
across the country setting up provincial
organizations and helped raise more
than $25,000 for the CNIB amateur
radio clubs. Through his efforts there

are now more than 150 licensed
blind radio hams in Canada, each
sponsored by a sighted licensed radio
operator.
In 1970 he received international
recognition when he became the first
Canadian to receive the Christopher
Columbus Gold Medal from the International Institute of Communications in
Genoa, Italy. Lloyd is also a member
of the Order of Canada.

PROGRESS AWARD

Canadian Progress Club

"It's great to be a Canadian/Soyons fiers
d'etre Canadiens," expresses the philosophy of this service organization and
which in 1981 raised about $1-million
for community projects. The award is
presented to a Canadian who has made
a contribution to Canadian or international society as a whole.

1982   Rev. Dr. Robert L. Rumball. The
former CFL player is a minister of the
United Church whose lifelong work is
ministry to the deaf. Through his
efforts Mission Churches, schools and
other institutions have been established for the deaf in Canada and in
other countries.
He is a member of the Order of
Canada and in 1978 was awarded the
Lions Club International Humanitarian
Award. In 1980, he was awarded
the Paul Harris Fellowship by Rotary
Clubs International, an award which
provides a needy student with scholarship assistance for university studies.
The Ontario Community Centre for the
Deaf was recently renamed in his
honour.

NEW CHAIR DEVELOPED

It's not a wheelchair, it's not a car, its
an OC3 Flyer. The OC3 Flyer is a vehicle with a state-of-the-art computerized
feedback system, electronic controls,
front-wheel drive and electro-

magnetic brakes and it travels at speeds up to four miles an hour.

The chair, now in production by Everest & Jennings, Can. Ltd., promises a new kind of freedom for disabled people.

The chair was initially designed by Scott Walter of the Ontario Crippled Children's Centre, who made 10 or 12 chairs for children at the centre a few years ago. Dr. Morris Milner of McMaster Hospital joined the project to help get production of units on a mass level. The OC3 Flyer can be adapted to fit different needs and will be used by the disabled throughout the world.

The Canadian research and development of the chair was sponsored by the Shriners.

C. DOUGLAS TAYLOR AWARD

Canadian Rehabilitation Council for the Disabled

The award honours the late Douglas Taylor, founding president of the Canadian Council for Crippled Children. It is presented to a person, who has demonstrated distinguished leadership in the development of services to the disabled in Canada.

1981   **Mira Ashby**, Toronto, Ont., whose efforts stimulated interest in the rehabilitation of brain-injured persons. She established Ashby House, a centre for the treatment of brain-injured people that has become a world model, and she initiated an educational program for social workers, physicians and allied health professional staff interested in the field. She has done more to stimulate, publicize and educate on behalf of the brain-injured adult than any other individual.

1982   **Robert Faser**, Grimsby, Ont.

1983   **Ralph Long**, Vancouver, B.C.

MAJOR AWARDS

Canadian Rehabilitation Council for the Disabled

Ability Fund Award

Presented to an individual or organization for outstanding service to disabled people through the National Ability Fund Campaign.

1982   **Canadian Association of Broadcasters**, Ottawa, Ont.

CRCD Award

Given to a disabled person who through his or her own efforts has successfully established himself or herself and inspired others to do likewise.

1983   **Dorothy Aldridge**, Toronto, Ont.
       Archie Neil Chisholm, Sydney, N.S.

Keith S. Armstrong Award

Conferred from time to time on an individual professionally employed in the voluntary field relating to rehabilitation and who has over time provided exceptional service to the physically handicapped.

1983   **Dr. Sidney Dinsdale**, Ottawa, Ont.

Easter Seal Award

Presented to an individual or organization who has rendered outstanding service to crippled children through the Easter Seal campaign.

1983   **Terry Vollum**, Toronto, Ont.

Reader's Digest Award

Given to an organization, agency or institution which over the three preceding years has significantly contributed to the development of services for the rehabilitation of the disabled.

1983   **Saskatchewan Council for Crippled Children and Adults**, Saskatoon, Sask.

Walter Dinsdale Award

A new award presented to an individual or organization for the development of technical aids for the benefit of disabled people

1983   **Edward H. Snell**, CET, mobility technologist, Rehabilitation Engineering Department of the Ontario Crippled Children's Centre, Toronto Ont.

HIGHEST HONOUR GOES TO A CANADIAN

The International Red Cross awarded its highest honour, the Henry Dunant Medal, to George Aitken of West Vancouver, B.C., in 1979. Aitken was only the second Canadian to receive the medal.

In 1948, while Aitken was president of the Manitoba Division of the Canadian Red Cross, he mounted a large-scale relief operation for a major flood disaster. He was instrumental in developing a contingency relief plan which later became the basis for the dramatic relief work during the Manitoba floods of 1950.

He continued his work with the Red Cross and later distinguished himself internationally by setting up a financial system for the League of Red Cross Societies.

DISTINGUISHED SERVICE AWARD

Canadian Red Cross Society

The award is given for outstanding service to the Canadian Red Cross.

1983   **Norman McKee**, Kitchener, Ont.

THE RED CROSS SYMBOL IN CANADA

Father Lacombe, the outstanding missionary of the late 19th century, was respected by both the Cree and Blackfoot nations, though they were traditional enemies.

While at the Mission of Sainte Anne in 1860 he received a Blackfoot chief: "In the name of the tribe he asked that a priest should be sent among his people. The Chief promised that the missionary would be unmolested, and that while he was with them, they would not make war upon their Cree enemies. He wanted the priest to carry a white flag bearing a Red Cross as a sign easily recognized and to be respected by all" — Katherine Hughes in *Father Lacombe, the Blackrobe Voyageur*

The red cross was not officially adopted until 1864 by the International Red Cross at Geneva.

DUKE OF EDINBURGH'S AWARD IN CANADA

Operated throughout the world under a variety of titles, the award program is a challenge from Prince Philip to all young people between the ages of 14 and 25. It offers them opportunities to broaden their interests and experiences under adult guidance and assessment through participation in a balanced program of practical, cultural and adventurous activities. There are three awards: bronze (age 14 and over), silver (age 15 and over) and gold (over 16).

To qualify, a young person must satisfy the requirements of the four sections of the program: service, expeditions, skills and fitness. The award itself consists of a lapel pin or brooch and a certificate.

More than 25,000 young Canadians are participating in the award program through organized groups such as guiding, scouting, cadets, church, school and youth clubs or as individuals.

1982 Gold Award Achievers

British Columbia
Stephen M. Allen, Prince George

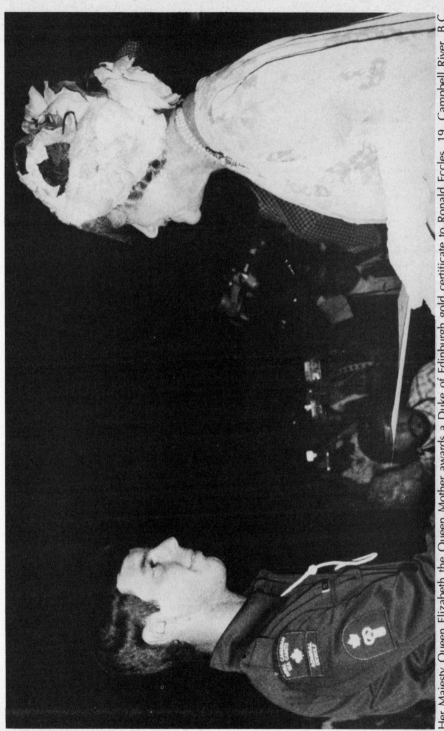

Her Majesty Queen Elizabeth the Queen Mother awards a Duke of Edinburgh gold certificate to Ronald Eccles, 19, Campbell River, B.C.

Brad A. Audette, Campbell River
Catherine E. Carter, Vancouver
Sarah E. Clay, Vancouver
Elizabeth A. Cloakey, Vancouver
Andrew Digney, Burnaby
Trish H. Dundas, Vancouver
Wendy P. Eeles, Burnaby
Robert Emery, Victoria
Alice L. Garry, Vancouver
Robert Goral, Maple Ridge
Deborah J. Helsdon, Surrey
Norman Howe, Vancouver
Karen Janke, Maple Ridge
Kathleen A. Jeffrey, Vancouver
Karen E. Johnson, Victoria
Albert P. Joseph, New Westminster
Ashley R. Knightley, Victoria
Lisa M. Kozlik, Maple Ridge
Rob. V. Kragelj, Campbell River
Susan Larson, Victoria
Sarah E. Lehman, Vancouver
Kirk D. Lewis, Sidney
Jane K. Little, Vancouver
Jennifer L. Ludlow, Victoria
Kenneth E. Lutz, Victoria
Hilary D. Macdonald, Vancouver
Stephen J. Malins, Sidney
Heather E. McClelland, Sidney
Nicola-Jane McNeill, Vancouver
Heather L. Michaud, Kelowna
Harold P. Miller, Victoria
Megan N. O'Keefe, Vancouver
Brian Olsen, Richmond
Sarah J. Pendleton, Vancouver
Karin Pfeiffer, Victoria
John W. Pollitt, Vancouver
Mark W. Poppleton, Victoria
Claire C. Quérée, Vancouver
Caroline S.A. Rigg, Vancouver
Sara C. Rigsby, Quesnel
P. Mark Sandercock, Duncan
R. Michael Sandercock, Duncan
Rhonda M. Saunders, Sidney
Tricia M. Schulte, Vancouver
David Scott, Burnaby
Nicola C. Scudder, Vancouver
Jennifer M. Selman, Vancouver
Diane M. Senez, Chilliwack
Leonard W. Seymour, Sidney
Michael J. Seymour, Sidney
Scott Sheppard, Vancouver
Paula E. Silvester, Victoria
Alison Sinclair, Vancouver
Craig R. Smith, Salmon Arm

Belinda L. Storey, Fernie
Peter J. Tremblay, Prince George
Konia J. Trouton, Vancouver
Timothy R. Wait, Saanichton
Rachel J. Walker, Vancouver
Charles Brennan West, Maple Ridge
Russ G. White, Williams Lake
Amanda L. Wilkinson, Vancouver
Robert A. Williams, Vancouver
Randall M. Wingfield, Victoria
Peggy V. Wright, Duncan

CROSS-COUNTRY CONSCIOUSNESS RAISING

Mike Flynn, a 32-year-old Niagara Falls social worker, cycled 3,800 miles across Canada, through the winter, on behalf of the Kidney Foundation. He used snow chains on his bicycle tires as he battled high winds and snowstorms on his two-month endeavour.

While he raised money on behalf of the foundation, he felt his greatest accomplishment was to raise Canadian awareness of the Kidney Foundation.

Alberta
Matthew E. Campbell, Black Diamond
Patricia J. Grimley, Hinton
Paul A. Grimley, Hinton
Michael S. Hagans, Edmonton
Patrick M. Hort, Canora
Perry S. Murray, Edmonton
Janet L. Paterson, Lethbridge
Grant W.A. Smith, Edmonton
Tracy D. Stevenson, Breton
Michael K. Stiles, Medley
Lawrence A. White, Edmonton
Saskatchewan
Leanne Creek, Regina
Mary Ferguson, Regina
Bernhard May, Regina
Hope McWhirter, Regina
Thomas J. Morrison, Regina
Roberta Wesley, Edgeley
Manitoba
Sharon E. Hendricks, Winnipeg
Quebec
Armen Antaby, Montreal
Vicki M. Becker, Pierrefonds

Alain Busque, St. Joseph de Beauce
Terry Constantakis, Laval
Diane Gagne, Ste-Foy
Michael C.N. Hope, Westmount
Dany Jacques, Ste. Marie de Beauce
Sylvain Lastere, Laval
Marie-Claude LaChance, Ste. Marie de Beauce
Ian Parris, Laval
Dominique Pouliot, St-Isidore
Gregory E. Waugh, Montreal

MUSIC FOR CYSTIC FIBROSIS

Kevin Denbok, 17, of Collingwood, Ont., is a special winner. As a young boy he had dreams about growing up and making an album. Last year his dream came true when he recorded an album of original songs.

The financial support to make the record was given by "friends" and one of Canada's foremost musical directors agreed to produce the album and waive his usual $7,000 to $8,000 fee. And the director arranged for free studio time and convinced a recording engineer to contribute his skills to the project.

Kevin obviously has a golden tongue — he also has cystic fibrosis. His album, which could have gone for commercial release, is being distributed independently across Canada and all the profits go to the Canadian Cystic Fibrosis Foundation. By April 1983, Canadian Kinsmen Clubs had sold almost 30,000 copies of the album.

Ontario
Dave C. Anderson, Sarnia
Christine Arsenault, Milton
Peter Askew, London
Janice F. Bango, Sault Ste. Marie
Stephen A. Baker, Kitchener
Karen L. Ball, Sault Ste. Marie
Randal Barker, Lakefield
Brian D. Bond, Willowdale
Denise E. Bourgeois, Sault Ste. Marie

Suzanne C. Bourgeois, Ottawa
Leigh Bowie, Ottawa
Darryl T. Boyling, Sault Ste. Marie
David A. Brain, Sault Ste. Marie
Stewart B. Brannen, Sault Ste. Marie
Kim M. Brier, Sault Ste. Marie
Todd Brough, Picton
Leslie A. Buchanan, Sault Ste. Marie
Ronald M. Burgess, Hamilton
Michel J. Burrowes, Malton
Elizabeth S. Campbell, Sault Ste. Marie
Christopher C. Capon, Willowdale
Anthony Castle, Mississauga
Christine E. Chamberlain, Toronto
Andrew W. Chester, Brighton
Brenda F. Chisholm, Oakville
Jack Colakoglu, Cambridge
Susan L. Cousins, Windsor
Stephen E. Dawson, Haliburton
Margaret A. Demerchant, Kitchener
Ian K. Duquemin, St. Catharines
David F. Eastcott, Peterborough
Tim Fenton, Picton
Gordon A. Fiddler, Sandy Lake
Kevin S. Finley, Scarborough
Katherine E. Fischer, Stratford
Paul Fleet, London
Alastair D. Foreman, Kingston
Terri-Lyn A. Fowlie, Oshawa
Charles E. Frosst, St. Catharines
Kevin G. Gable, Freelton
Chris Giffin, Picton
Scott J. Gooch, Orono
Mark S. Greenfield, Milton
Tom G. Greenfield, Milton
Ashok Gupta, Pickering
Andreas Hagens, Sault Ste. Marie
Brad T. Hampson, Ottawa
Rodney R. Hardman, Oakville
Michael P. Hassall, Bramalea
D. Jordan Hatherley, Sault Ste. Marie
Anna-Marie L. Hosking, Port Hope
Anthony R. Hueton, Oakville
Jocelyn T.W. Hummel, Toronto
Gregory W. Jenson, Toronto
Andrew J. Jones, Omemee
Katharine A. Jorna, Stratford
Susan E. Jorna, Stratford
David R. Justice, Oakville
Kristal Kaulbach, Mississauga
Elizabeth A. Kelly, Blackstock
Lisa J. Kertesz, Mississauga
Laura A. Kilmer, Rexdale
James A. King, Kingsville

Ronald A. LaSalle, Kilbride
Roger T. Litwiller, Kitchener
Richard F. Luden, Windsor
Dorothy L. MacDougall, Chatham
Ian P. MacKinnon, Agincourt
Shawn McManus, London
Thomas Mifek, London
Susanne G. Noecker, New Hamburg
Robert S. Paquin, Cornwall
Andrew D.C. Paterson, Agincourt
Robert A.H. Paterson, Agincourt
John M. Peltier, Mississauga
Jacqueline A. Pepper, London
James D. Piecowye, MB, Ajax
James L. Proudlove, Stratford
Nelson A. Proulx, Sault Ste. Marie
Linda D. Rees, Willowdale
Meredith A. Roberts, Toronto
Sara L. Rowland, Toronto
Ian P. Rutherford, Willowdale
William Sarantakos, Willowdale
Kelly M. Saunders, London
Harry A. Schonert, Willowdale
Paul Shaw, London
Paula M. Shewchuk, Sault Ste. Marie
Aldyn A. Smith, Brampton
George Smola, Agincourt
Janice L. Somers, London
Earla C. Sproule, Sault Ste. Marie
William Stonehill, London
Pam Storozuk, Sault Ste. Marie
Patti J. Storozuk, Sault Ste. Marie
M. Elizabeth K. Stuart, Toronto
Andrew G. Thexton, Peterborough
Barry C. Thirnbeck, Amherstview
Beverly D. Thomson, Toronto
Hans U. Von Sallwurk, Oshawa
Timothy J. Wakfer, London
Jeannette D. Wannamaker, Strathroy
N.J. Grant Wardlaw, Orangeville
Martha A.E. Webb, Mississauga
Charlene P. Wight, Ottawa
Kelly M.E. Wright, Sault Ste. Marie
L. James Young, Mississauga.

NURSE WINS NIGHTINGALE MEDAL

Elizabeth Lowe of Renforth, N.B., was recently awarded the Florence Nightingale Medal from the International Committee of the Red Cross. The medal is awarded every two years for outstanding service in peace and war. Lowe was the only Canadian to receive the 1983 award.

As a lieutenant nursing sister with the Royal Canadian Army Corps in the Second World War, she was with the first contingent of nurses to enter Sicily in 1943. At the risk of losing her own life to sniper fire and shelling, Lowe assisted the wounded in an overcrowded Syracuse hospital which had been abandoned by the retreating German forces.

Lowe has worked for the Canadian Red Cross since 1956, as director of Nursing Services, New Brunswick Division, and since 1977 as director of health services for that division. She retired in 1981.

New Brunswick
J. Beth Baldwin, Saint John
Sophie M. Bernard, Moncton
J. Bruce Cochrane, Salisbury
Bradley C. Daniels, Fredericton
Kevin Fletcher, Fredericton
Carl A. A. Gaudet, Saint John
Victor A. Griffiths, Burtts Corner
Karen F. Hatt, Saint John
Ken Hurley, Harvey Station
Denis LeBlanc, Moncton
Lisa A. MacDonald, Saint John
Paula M. McFarlane, Nelson-Miramichi
Douglas J. Melia, Moncton
Lila J. Mitton, Moncton
Eric Neilsen, Harvey Station
Jeannette Savoie, Néguac
Kelley A. Shannon, Saint John
Michael G. Trenholm, Port Elgin
Deborah G.A. (Leavitt) Wright, Saint John
Prince Edward Island
Catherine G. Campbell, Sherwood
George F. Collard, West Covehead
Glen S. Collard, West Covehead
Peter J. Creelman, Summerside
Patricia A. Dalton, Sherwood
Sandra Livingstone, Cornwall
Newfoundland
Carolyn R. Bennett, Grand Falls
Violet D. Jackson, Grand Falls
Sherry A. Parmiter, Point Leamington

Craig W. Ryan, Stephenville
Heather A. Templeton, St. John's

CANADA'S FIRST HOSPITAL BENEFACTOR

The Duchess d'Aiguillon, a powerful lady in the Court of Louis XIII and a niece of Cardinal Richelieu, responded to Jesuit appeals and provided money for a much needed hospital at Quebec. She obtained the money for L'Hotel-Dieu by means of a lien "taken on the coaches and carriages of Soissons" and made a contract with the Hospitaliers of L'Hotel-Dieu de Dieppe in Normandy in 1637 to build and staff the hospital. In 1640 she provided an additional 40,000 livres for the hospital.

Nova Scotia
Angela R. Adams, Springhill
Willard J. Buchanan, Liverpool
John C. Caldwell, Liverpool
Lloyd A. Dawe, North Sydney
Monica Fricker, Neil's Harbour
Adel D. Gilbert, Springhill
Donna M. Hillier, North Sydney
David J. Jessome, Florence
Denise A. Jessome, Florence
Anthony M. Keating, Brooklyn
Nancy E. Lake, Bridgewater
Gwen MacDonald, Iona
Cathy MacDougall, Iona
Cheryl MacNeil, Iona
Deborah MacNeil, Iona
Janet MacNeil, Christmas Island
Jill L. Maddison, Springhill
Estelle McRitchie, Little Narrows
Hubert J. Mertens, North Sydney
Shelley Murphy, Iona
Bruce E.W. Oliver, Port Hastings
Anita L. Park, Thorburn
Donna R. Park, Thorburn
Sherri I. Park, Thorburn
Anne Marie Quinn, Christmas Island
Ian H. Scully, Thorburn
Deborah L. Weagle, Bridgewater
Burton W. Wentzell, Milton

SPREADING THE WEALTH

Thomas Bell, chairman of Abitibi-Price, Inc., was named philanthropist of the year in 1982 by the National Society for Fund-Raising Executives. He was cited for his ability to extract money from others for a good cause, and the fund-raising executives are the people who should know just how good he is.

In 1966, he was chairman of a campaign that raised $12-million for Toronto's Hospital for Sick Children, and he has contributed to the drive to raise $13.5-million for the Toronto General's renewal fund.

The Fund Raiser's society also named actor Don Harron as volunteer of the year for his fund-raising work on behalf of OXFAM, the Kidney Foundation, Help the Aged International, the United Way and the University of Toronto.

AWARDS OF VALOUR AND FORTITUDE

Girl Guides of Canada/Guides Du Canada

1982   Marnie Essery, patrol leader, Sooke, B.C.
Cheryl Thompson, lone cadet, Prince Albert, Sask.

RECOGNITION OF SERVICE

Medal of Merit

1982   Margaret Hennig, Langley, B.C.
Norma Johnson, Marathon, Ont.
Diana Leins, Creston, B.C.

LIFESTYLE AWARDS

Health and Welfare Canada

The Lifestyle Award is presented by the Minister of Health to individuals who have made, on a voluntary basis, a remarkable and continuing contribution in promoting health and social services in their communities. Winners receive a medal, a pin, a mounted plaque and a copy of their citation.

1983   **Elizabeth (Leitch) Saxon**, Corner Brook, Nfld.
Milton B. Fitzpatrick, Charlottetown, P.E.I.
John C. Bullen, Beresford, N.B.
Paul Berthou, Longueuil, Que.
Roger and **Madeleine Couillard**, Dollard-des-Ormeaux, Que.
Kathleen Elizabeth Wilson, Huntingdon, Que.
Ruth Burrows, Belleville, Ont.
James T. Jenkinson, Mississauga, Ont.
Glenyce Henshaw, Ottawa Ont.
Dorothy Maye, Uxbridge, Ont.
William J. Neil, Winnipeg, Man.
Beatrice Mary Johnston, Regina, Sask.
Elizabeth Mary Marin, Weyburn, Sask.
Heather Amy Morrison, Vancouver, B.C.
Hulda Roddan, Surrey, B.C.

BIKERS JOIN THE FIGHT

Engines roared one day in May 1982 in Ontario as 2,000 motorcyclists took to their bikes to raise money for the fight against retinitis pigmentosa, a disease that affects children and young adults causing a deterioration of the retina that can lead to blindness.

The ride was organized by the Ontario Road Riders Association and together the bikers raised $55,000.

OCCUPATIONAL SAFETY AND HEALTH ACHIEVEMENT AWARD

Canada Safety Council

The award provides a visible form of recognition to individuals for outstanding contribution to the prevention of death, injury and disease in the workplace in Canada.

1982   **Henry E. Weisbach**, Toronto, formerly of the Ontario Federation of Labour, was instrumental in bringing together persons of diverse opinions and philosophy and so assisted in the establishment of the joint labour/ management cooperative concept in the field of health and safety in Canada.

DANNY KAYE AWARD

UNICEF Canada

The award was created to honour Danny Kaye, the irrepressible and irresistible entertainer who has given his unique contributions and tireless effort to bring joy to the children of the world. Danny Kaye was the first recipient of the UNICEF Canada award.

1982   **Will Millar** of the Irish Rovers

SPECIAL RECOGNITION AWARD

Presented on behalf of UNICEF volunteers across Canada.

1983   **Mrs. Graydon D. Saunders**, Kitchener, Ont., a UNICEF supporter for 28 years.

MOTHER OF THE YEAR

A Canadian who is a 52-year-old mother of five, and whose contralto voice moves people around the world to tears, has been named Spiritual Mother of the Year by Pioneer Women Na'amat, the women's labour Zionist organization of Canada.

Maureen Forrester received the 1983 award for her work on behalf of crippled and battered children and those afflicted with cystic fibrosis.

CANADA PEACE AWARD

World Federalists of Canada

"Every day it becomes more imperative that we honour those among us who have the courage and the competence to lead us and our governments so skillfully ... We know that at best these awards may be little more than gestures of genuine goodwill ... small tokens of great concern for first things first" — Richard Pilant, WFC.

1972	Lester B. Pearson
1973	Norman Z. Alcock
1973	Maurice F. Strong
1974	Hanna Newcombe
1974	Deganaweda
1975	Hugh L. Keenleyside
1976	Paul Gerin-Lajoie
1976	George Ignatieff
1978	William Epstein
1979	Cyrus and Ann Eaton
1981	John Peters Humphrey, professor, faculty of law, McGill University. Humphrey was director of the Human Rights Division of the UN for 20 years. He was instrumental in setting up Amnesty International Canada and the Canadian Human Rights Foundation.

WILDER PENFIELD AWARD

Vanier Institute of the Family

From time to time the Vanier Institute of the Family grants the award to a person who has demonstrated "wisdom and leadership in the evolution of human society." The award commemorates Dr. Wilder Penfield, a world-renowned Canadian neurosurgeon and the institute's first president.

1972	Dr. Margaret Mead, American anthropologist
1977	E. Friedrich Schumacher, British economist
1979	Dr. René Dubos, American microbiologist and philosopher
1980	Mr. Justice Emmett M. Hall, former member of the Supreme Court of Canada

WORKING FOR THE FAMILY

"A familial society is one in which the quality of a person's immediate rela-tions — at home, at work, at study, at play — are perceived as fundamental to the quality of the society and its institutions ... It is a society in which caring and sharing begin in the family, are lived in the community with others, and are even extended to the whole world."

That unattributed statement can be found on the pamphlet of the Vanier Institute of the Family. The statement would seem to embody the philosophy of the late Governor-General George P. Vanier and Madame Vanier, who founded the Institute in 1965 with a mandate to promote the well-being of families.

The late Governor-General and Madame Vanier, who had four sons and one daughter, spent much of their lives in the service of Canada and the Canadian people; he as a soldier, lawyer and diplomat, she as a voice for public causes. In Government House they spoke with graciousness on behalf of unity both in the family and in the nation.

The Governor-General died in 1967 and in 1972 Madame Vanier moved to France to join her son, Jean, and assist him at the headquarters of l'Arche, a group that works to help the mentally handicapped.

CANADIAN AWARDS 1983

Diefenbaker Foundation

Carl O. Nickle, once an avowed supporter of western separatism, was named along with fellow Calgarian Harry Cohen as recipient of the 1983 Canadian Award by the John G. Diefenbaker Memorial Foundation.

The awards are presented to "Canadians who have in some way made their community, their province, their country a better place to live and have contributed to the social, cultural, political or historic enrichment of Canada."

Nickle, an oil man and philanthropist, has also been a broadcaster, a publisher and an MP. In 1981 he publicly supported the West-Fed Association, a western separatist party. Cohen is a film distributor.

Recipients receive statuettes of the former Conservative prime minister.

THE FIRST MASS

The first record of a mass said in Canada is found in an account of the Cartier voyage of 1534.

"And afterwards, that is to say on Saturday, August 14, the day and feast of the Assumption of Our Lady, we set forth together from the harbour of Blanc Savalon, after hearing Mass ..."

PILGRIMS PASS OVER CANADA

According to a story in *Our Heritage* published in Kingston, Ont., January 28, 1967, George Johnson, an English separatist, and three companions searched Canada for a suitable site for a pilgrim settlement in 1597. The English government offered to release imprisoned separatists if they would settle in Canada.

Johnson's account states that a ship set forth in 1597 for Ramea, an island in the Gulf of St. Lawrence. They encountered difficulties off the coast of Newfoundland and all the settlers' provisions were lost. A search was made, according to the account, for another site but dissension amongst the pilgrims brought them back to Southampton in 1603.

AWARD CONFERRED ON CHRETIEN

The Christian Culture Award presented annually by Assumption University of the University of Windsor, Ont., was bestowed in 1983 on Canada's Minister of Energy Jean Chretien. Previous notables who have received the award include Malcolm Muggeridge, the late Marshall McLuhan, and the late William Kurelek.

FIRST BAPTISM

The abbé Jessé Fléché, a priest from the diocese of Langres, France, arrived at Port Royal, N.S., in February 1610. On June 24 of the following year he baptized the Indian Chief Membertou.

Membertou was described as the "greatest, most renowned and most formidable savage within the memory of men; grave and reserved; feeling a proper sense of dignity for his position as commander." Fléché returned to France in July, claiming to have baptized about 100 Indians.

BROTHERS WHO SERVED OTHERS

Paul-Émile Cardinal Léger was named Cardinal in 1953 by Pope Pius XII. He was only the sixth Canadian to reach that high office of the Catholic Church. Yet in 1967 he asked the Pope to relieve him of his archbishopric because he felt compelled to devote himself to the care of lepers in Africa.

Légér received the Royal Bank of Canada award in 1969 for his service to humanity. He returned to Montreal in 1980 and has since suffered periodic illness.

His brother Jules Léger was a distinguished Canadian diplomat who became the Governor-General of Canada in 1974.

EARLY MISSIONARIES INTREPID EXPLORERS

Father Le Caron preceded Champlain into Central Ontario when he entered Huronia in the summer of 1615.

Father John de Quen discovered Lake St. John when he ascended the Saguenay River to make a sick call to the Porcupine Indians.

The Jesuits went from Tadoussac on the St. Lawrence clear up to Hudson's Bay and east almost to the Labrador coast line. Father Charles Albane explored the overland route to Hudson Bay and actually reached it on July 1, 1671.

ANGLICANS IN THE NEW WORLD

Anglican clergyman Erasmus Stourton arrived in Newfoundland in 1627. The following year Sir George Calvert, a Catholic, brought out two priests to serve the colony, angering Stourton. The subsequent quarrel resulted in his banishment at Calvert's order. When he returned to England, the Anglican priest protested in vain to the authorities.

CANADIAN MOTHER PLEADS FOR PEACE AT UN

Ruth Klassen is a 55-year-old mother of three teenage sons who has devoted her time and energy to the peace movement in Canada. In June 1982, she addressed the United Nations General Assembly's special session on disarmament.

The wife of a University of Waterloo history professor, she taught an annual seminar at Carleton University on global peace and war issues for five years. She is a co-director of the Peace Research Institute, an affiliate of the Canadian Peace Research Institute.

COMMITTED TO HIS FAITH

Edgar Bronfman of Montreal and New York is chairman and chief executive officer of the Seagram empire. Deeply committed to the Judaic faith, he is president of the World Jewish Congress.

The congress plays an important role in the Jewish world by seeking to relieve anti-Semitism and taking a persuasive role in issues such as the plight of Russian jews.

A CHAPEL, A SISTERHOOD AND A SAINTHOOD

Marguerite Bourgeoys was brought to Ville-Marie in 1653 to teach French and Indian children. In 1657 she urged the settlers to build the first Notre Dame-de-Bon-Secours Chapel. The present chapel is located on the site of the original one in Old Montreal.

In 1658 she opened a school for day students, then returned to France to gather assistance. She returned to Montreal with three companions and a servant and together they founded a religious order, the Sisters of the Congregation de Notre Dame. The order is an uncloistered teaching order of nuns that has spread throughout the continent.

The nuns opened a boarding school and gave instruction in a number of small schools as well. The Ferme St. Gabriel on Point St. Charles is a stone house that Bourgeoys erected in 1698. Today it is the "home farm" of the order.

Marguerite Bourgeoys was canonized in 1982.

CANADIANS BLESSED

In May 1982 two Canadians were named by the Pope as blessed — the first major step to sainthood.

Brother Andre Bessette (1845-1936), known as "a man of miracles," was born at Gregoire d'Iberville, Que., the eighth of 10 children. Orphaned early in life he suffered poverty and ill health.

He devoted his entire adult life to the service of the church and was from 1909 until his death the curator of St. Joseph's oratory near Montreal. He was noted for his great works in spreading the word of God and as a witness for Christ.

Mother Marie Rose established Canada's first Marian teaching institute for young people. Born Eulalie Durocher, she founded the Sisters of the Holy Names of Jesus and Mary at Longueuil in 1844 and was the institute's first mother superior. She died in 1849 at the age of 38.

FIRST BISHOP

Canada's first Bishop was Francois-Xavier de Laval de Montigny. A Jesuit, he was consecrated Bishop of Quebec in 1674.

An aristocrat, he was an important member of Quebec's governing council. He fought against state interference in ecclesiastical affairs and was especially vigorous in opposing the sale of liquor to Indians.

He organized the parish clergy, founded a seminary to educate native clergy and established a bond between the papacy and the Church in new France.

MILESTONES

The Church of England built its first church in North America in St. John's, Nfld., in 1720. The present Anglican Cathedral was later constructed on the same site.

The oldest protestant church on the Canadian mainland is at Halifax. It is St. Paul's Anglican Church and was erected in 1750, the year Halifax was founded. There is a royal pew in the church which was curtained to give privacy to Prince Edward who was the commander of the British military forces in North America. He was Queen Victoria's father.

The first Anglican Bishop to be appointed outside of Great Britain was Charles Inglis. He was appointed Bishop for Nova Scotia and Quebec in 1787.

PRESBYTERIAN ELECT MODERATOR

Rev. Donald C. MacDonald was elected Moderator-designate of the 109th General Assembly of the Presbyterian Church in Canada in the spring of 1983. Rev. Macdonald, 67, is a Nova Scotian who was ordained in 1942. He became executive officer of the church in 1970 after serving pastorates in the Maritimes.

The first General Assembly of the Presbyterian Church of Canada was in 1870. The first Lutheran Church in Canada was erected in Halifax in 1761. The Salvation Army's first service in Canada was held in London, Ont., in August 1883.

EDUCATION

CANADA'S FIRST INSTITUTE OF HIGHER LEARNING

The Quebec Seminary was founded in 1663 by Bishop Laval in order to educate native clergy.

The first Canadian-born person to earn a Bachelor of Arts degree in Canada, probably from the Seminary, was a Huron Indian named Louis Vincent Sabatannen.

The seminary established Laval University in 1852.

THE RHODES SCHOLARSHIPS

The Rhodes Scholarship Trust

Cecil Rhodes, in his will, listed the qualities he was seeking in scholars: literary and scholastic attainments, success in outdoor sports, qualities of truth, courage, devotion to duty, sympathy for and protection of the weak, kindliness, unselfishness and instincts to lead and take an interest in one's contemporaries.

A Rhodes Scholarship is tenable at the University of Oxford, usually for a period of two years. It covers academic and living expenses and is presently valued at about 6,000 pounds per year.

SCHOLARS MAKE HISTORY

In 1977, women were admitted for the first time into the community of Rhodes Scholars.

The first Canadian female winners of the Rhodes Scholarship were:

Eileen Gillese, Alberta
Melanie Dobson, New Brunswick
Mary Sheppard, Newfoundland
Jessie Sloan, Ontario.

Rhodes Scholars 1981

William H. Devlin	Newfoundland
Bruce W. MacDougall	Maritimes
Andrew D. Lynk	Maritimes
G. Mark Crawford	British Columbia
Thomas E. Patterson	Western Region
Gregor W. Smith	Western Region
Charalee F. Graydon	Western Region
Pierre Legrand, Jr.	Quebec
Jean-François Garneau	Quebec
Helene J. Grafstein	Ontario
Laurence S. Grafstein	Ontario

Rhodes Scholars 1982

Alex Cameron	Maritimes
Keith Collins	Maritimes
Catherine Craig	Newfoundland
Timothy Endicott	Ontario
Andrew Nevin	Ontario
William Hinz	Quebec
Pierre Piché	Quebec
Paul Vogt	Western Region
Jeff Telgarsky	Western Region
Keith Krause	Western Region
Peter Goddard	British Columbia

CLASS OF '06

Poet and lawyer Marc Lescarbot, a member of the settlement at Port Royal, N.S., began teaching a class of Micmac Indians in 1606.

SPECIAL RECOGNITION AWARD

Canadian Teachers' Federation Awards

Given annually for distinguished service to education or the teaching profession.

1981   **Brother Augustus F. Brennan**, BSc, MSc, St. John's, Nfld.,
       W. Robert Gordon, BA, B.Ed, M.Ed, Winnipeg, Man.
1982   **Dr. S.C.T. Clarke**, University of Alberta.
1983   **Dr. Sherburne McCurdy**, former president and executive secretary of the Newfoundland Teachers' Association and former president of the Canadian Teachers' Federation. Since 1971 he has been president of the Alberta College, Edmonton, Alta.

HILLROY FELLOWSHIP AWARDS FOR OUTSTANDING MERIT

An annual cash award to teachers for innovative ideas that improve the quality of teaching and learning in the classroom. The late Roy C. Hill, whose firm had prospered by selling stationery to schools, established the fellowship. The awards are cash prizes and are not intended to finance specific projects.

1981 $7,000   **Susan Rona** and **Ivan A. Smith**, Que., for "An Alternative Program for High School Dropouts."

1982 $7,000 **Rita M. Hlady**, Sask., for "A Futures Studies Curriculum for Gifted Students in Grades 7 and 8."

$5,000 **Raffaella Montemurro** and **Joan M. Dutton**, Alta., for "Thematic Teaching in an Arts Core Program."

1983 $5,500 **Colleen Politano**, B.C., for "Instructing Wilderness Survival to Kindergarten Children."

$3,500 **Gary Merritt**, Ont., for "Computer Teaching Strategies with School-Wide Application."

$3,500 **Ronald Lancaster**, Ont. "Enthusiasm is Caught — Not Taught."

$3,500 **S. Christie**, N.S. "Freedom — An Original Play about Nova Scotia's Black Loyalists: developed by Grades 11 and 12 students to promote racial and cultural understanding."

Founded in 1920, the Federation represents 220,000 teachers from 14 provincial and territorial teacher organizations.

LITERACY GRADUALLY WINNING IN CANADA

In 1971, 33.3 per cent of the population had less than Grade 9 education. That statistic has since substantially decreased. The 1981 census showed 21.9 per cent or 4 million Canadians had less than a Grade 9 education.

Grade 9 is the level of education considered necessary for people "to function in our word-oriented society" according to Statistics Canada.

SIR ARTHUR SIMS SCHOLARSHIP

The Royal Society of Canada

An award for outstanding merit and promise in any subject of the human-ities, social sciences, or natural sciences. It is open to graduates of Canadian universities who are British subjects. Awarded biennially, the scholarship of 650 pounds is to encourage Canadian students to undertake postgraduate work in Great Britain.

1982 **Christine M. Stevenson**, Ottawa, Ont., to attend Courtauld Institute of Art, University of London.

SOME CHAMPION CANADIAN EDUCATORS

Egerton Ryerson

An advocate of equal rights for all religious denominations, he became the first principal of Victoria College at Cobourg, Ont., in 1841. As chief superintendent of education in Canada West from 1844, he laid the groundwork for Ontario's education system and in 1848 he began publishing the *Journal of Education*, which he edited until 1876.

Monsignor Moses Michael Coady

Coady pioneered adult education among the fishermen of the Maritimes. He won a Carnegie Award for Adult Education in 1936 and was vice-president of the American Association for Adult Education in 1944-45 and president of the Canadian Association for Adult Education in 1949-51.

Rt. Rev. Athol Murray

Founder and president of Notre Dame College at Wilcox, Sask. He established the school in 1927 for boys who couldn't normally afford such an education. His students became known for both leadership and athletic skills.

Canon Lionel Groulx

Teacher of humanities at the Seminary at Valleyfield he was the first professor

of Canadian history at the University of Montreal, 1915-48. While he did not directly espouse separatism, he was a nationalist and a teacher with a voice who urged French Canadians to fight to the last for their culture.

E.A. (Ned) Corbett

An advocate of adult education, he founded Banff School of Fine Arts in 1933.

POLYSAR AWARD

The Chemical Institute of Canada

Awarded for chemical science teaching in community colleges and CEGEPs. Sponsored by Polysar Ltd., the award is a scroll and $500.

1980	D.L. Thorn
	G.W. Rayner-Canham
1981	R. Palepu
	G. Roy

FIRST DEGREES TO WOMEN

Mount Allison University was the first Canadian University to grant degrees to women.

The first woman in Canada to receive a degree was Grace Anne Lockhart, who was awarded a Bachelor of Science in 1875.

THE MILNER MEMORIAL AWARD

Canadian Association of University Teachers Awards

Granted in honour of James Milner, whose services to the cause of academic freedom deserve the greatest recognition that the CAUT can give.

For distinguished contribution to the cause, or for actions undertaken, or for writings which contribute to academic freedom in the Canadian community.

1971	Mr. Justice Bora Laskin
1973	Professor J. Percy Smith
1974	Professor Harry S. Crowe
1980	Professor Archie Malloch

J.H. STEWART REID MEMORIAL FELLOWSHIP

A fellowship of $5,000 is granted for one year to a student who has completed at least one full academic year of graduate work. The fellowship is for any field of study and is tenable at any Canadian university.

1982/83 **Rocco Fondacaro**, who is completing his PhD in social psychology at the University of Western Ontario, London, Ont.

FUR FORTUNE FOUNDS McGILL

Montreal fur trader James McGill left 10,000 pounds in his will for the founding of McGill University. McGill died in 1813 but subsequent litigation delayed the opening of the university until 1828.

McGill, a partner-trader in the North West Company, was married to a French-Canadian and a member of the Beaver Club, a convivial association organized by the elite of the fur trade to keep good relations with the French fur traders. Membership was limited at first to those traders who had actually wintered in the "pays en haut." The club met for meetings in various taverns from 1785-1804 and from 1807-24.

OUTSTANDING ACHIEVEMENT AWARD

Canadian Council for Exceptional Children Awards

Presented for outstanding contribution to the well-being of exceptional children and youth.

1982 **Professor Howard Stutt**, chairman,

department of educational psychology and counselling, McGill University

SPECIAL EDUCATION POLICIES AWARD

Presented annually to a school board or a publicly supported policy-making body for its comprehensive special education policies, consistent with the policies of the Council for Exceptional Children.

1982   Kent County, Ont., Board of Education

JOAN KERSHAW PUBLICATION AWARD

An award presented to a person or group who has published an article, report or book concerned with exceptional children.

1982   Southern Manitoba Chapter #367 of the Canadian Council for Exceptional Children for the publication *The Positive Path*.

FIRST CANADIAN CONVENT AND SCHOOL FOR GIRLS

A convent and a boarding school for the daughters of settlers and for Indian girls was founded at Quebec by Marie de l'Incarnation, in 1639.

Marie Guyart Martin was a widow who took her final vows in the Ursuline Order in France before coming to Quebec.

She founded the first Ursuline Order in North America and is revered as a mystic as well as a missionary. Her letters were published in Paris in 1861 and 1876, and historians refer to her as one of the "more remarkable women in Canadian history."

CERTIFICATE OF HONOUR

Canadian Association of Principals

A salute to those approximately 1,500 students who received from the Canadian Association of Principals the "Certificate of Honour."

The certificate is awarded by school principals to students who show social and civic responsibility and high contribution to the school community.

DONALD FORSTER WINS PRESIDENCY AT U OF T

Donald Forster will assume the presidency of the University of Toronto, Canada's largest, in September 1983. In 1982 it granted 9,700 degrees and certificates. It has a staff of 7,800 on three campuses teaching 2,500 courses to 58,000 students. Its libraries contain more than 5 million volumes.

Forster is a bachelor with a background in administration, economics and political science. He was born in Toronto and was previously president of the University of Guelph.

SAMUEL R. LAYOCK MEMORIAL AWARD

Canadian Home and School and Parent-Teacher Federation

Samuel R. Laycock, a classicist, psychologist, educator, author, lecturer and university dean, was known for his leadership in the education of exceptional children. He was a founder of the Canadian Mental Health Association and for 14 years conducted a CBC radio program, *School for Parents*.

The award is presented annually to an educator who works well with children; takes an interest in the education of all children and enlists the cooperation of parents and other teachers; shows leadership, inspires others to achieve and has made a contribution to relations between school and home.

1981 **Wanda A. Eddingfield**, Swift Current, Sask., in recognition of 50 years of devotion to education and young people.

1982 **Thomas Charles Wilkinson**, Charlottetown, P.E.I., active at all levels of home and school, is a past president of the national association. He has worked to promote parental participation in the education of their children and to create greater understanding between parents and teachers.

FIRST SCHOOL

The first residential boys' school in British North America was opened at Windsor, N.S., in 1788. It was the forerunner of King's College.

R.W.B. JACKSON AWARD

Canadian Educational Research Association.

The award honours the late R.W.B. Jackson who was a leading figure in educational research in Canada.

The award is for the best research, based on articles published in the *Canadian Journal of Education/Revue Canadienne de l'Education*.

1981 **Drs. W. Todd Rogers** and **Bryan R. Clarke**, University of British Columbia, Vancouver, B.C.

R. TAIT McKENZIE AWARDS OF HONOUR

Canadian Association for Health, Physical Education and Recreation

Canadian born and educated, R. Tait McKenzie became the first professor of physical education at the University of Pennsylvania in 1905. Throughout his career, he was a leader and innovator

in the field. A legendary figure, he was an anatomist, author, craftsman, gymnast, musician, physician, sculptor and teacher. His summer home and studio at Almonte, Ont., still stands in the Mill of Kintail Conservation area.

1982 **F.M. Van Wagner**, McGill U., educator, conservationist and instigator in the founding of the Quebec Basketball Referees Association, the Quebec Camping Association, the Quebec Physical Education Association.
George A. Wearring, U. of Western Ontario. His special interest is the health aspect of human motor performance in sport, exercise and play.
James F. Leys, Almonte, Ont., for preserving and restoring the Mill at Kintail and for recovering McKenzie's sculptures and returning them to the Mill on behalf of the Canadian people.

CITATION FOR OUTSTANDING ACHIEVEMENT

Canadian Parks/Recreation Association

For work that has enhanced the public image or further developed the body of knowledge in parks and recreation to the benefit of Canadian citizens.

1982 **Howard Nixon**, Saskatoon, Sask. Educator, coach, government advisor, and organizer of programs from the local to the Olympic level.
Robert E. Secord, assistant deputy minister, Recreation Division, Ontario Ministry of Tourism and Recreation, for his administration and organization of sports and leisure bodies and programs.

AWARDS OF MERIT

Canadian Parks/Recreation Association

1982 **Neil Balkwill**, Regina, Sask.
Margo Fournier, Prince Albert, Sask.
Lt. Col. E.B. McCorkell, Saskatoon, Sask.

Emile St. Amand, Saskatoon, Sask.
Gus Vickers, Lunenburg, N.S.

SALUTE THE MODERN CUSTODIANS OF KNOWLEDGE

The modern librarian collects, sorts, stores and distributes information in time-honoured fashion, but is meeting, as well, the challenge of technological revolution and unprecedented demands in the new information age.

In 1971, Canada's public libraries contained an average of 37,700 volumes. In 1974, Canadians borrowed more than 99 million volumes from public libraries. In 1978, operating costs for Canada's 2,829 public libraries were over $226-million. In 1982, the Canadian Library Association had 5,000 members representing public, business, institutional, medical and special libraries.

In 1982, Canadian librarians circulated general and specific reference materials, books, magazines, films, video tapes, audio records and tapes, talking books, braille books, toys, prints, slides and pictures, multilingual material, micro-film copies and computer print-outs.

OUTSTANDING SERVICE TO LIBRARIANSHIP AWARD

Canadian Library Association

For outstanding service in Canadian librarianship that contributes to the development of library service in Canada.

1982　**Bruce Braden Peel**, former university librarian at the University of Alberta, a past president of the CLA, and past president of the Bibliographical Society of Canada.
　　Robert Harold Blackburn, chief librarian of the University of Toronto Library for 27 years, who oversaw the opening of the Sigmund Samuel Wing, the Thomas Fisher Rare Book Library and the John P. Robarts Library.

AWARD FOR SPECIAL LIBRARIANSHIP

Canadian Library Association

1982　**Susan Klement**, Toronto, Ont.

MARGARET B. SCOTT AWARD OF MERIT

Canadian Library Association

Awarded annually for outstanding contribution to Canadian school librarianship.

1982　**Art Forgay**, Regina, Sask.

CLA DAFOE SCHOLARSHIP

Canadian Library Association

1982　$1,750　**Patricia Bellamy** of Vancouver, B.C., who is specializing in reference work and library administration.

HOWARD V. PHALIN WORLD BOOK GRADUATE SCHOLARSHIP IN LIBRARY SCIENCE

1982　$2,500　**Margaret Taylor**, Ottawa, Ont., a specialist in the use of videotex systems in health sciences information and public health education programs.

H.W. WILSON COMPANY SCHOLARSHIP

1982　$2,000　**Gloria Anderson**, Ottawa, Ont.

FIRST LENDING LIBRARY

Poet and lawyer Marc Lescarbot, a member of the settlement of Port Royal, N.S., loaned books from his own collection more than 300 years ago.

CHILDREN'S SERVICE AWARDS

1982　**Joanna Von Levetzow**, Toronto, Ont. A social worker and volunteer she founded and was the first volunteer director in 1975 of the Canadian Association of Toy Libraries. Under her direction Canada developed one of the world's best developed systems of toy libraries. There were 12 such libraries in the country in 1975 and in 1982 there were 150.

Mary J. Wright, London, Ont., professor emerita, University of Western Ontario. During the 1960s, as chairman of the department of psychology, Professor Wright founded the first Laboratory of Pre-School Studies. Much of her life has been given to the concerns of young children as a member of organizations, a teacher, researcher and author.

MUSEUMS PROUDLY DISPLAY OUR HERITAGE

The National Museums of Canada is a cultural chain linking the country. In the National Capital Region, the National Gallery of Canada, the National Museum of Man (including the Canadian War Museum), the National Museum of Natural Sciences and the National Museum of Science and Technology (including the National Aeronautical Collection) maintain extensive permanent collections which reflect Canada's natural and human history. Another 21 Associate Museums and 25 National Exhibition Centres complete the network. These, with travelling laboratories and exhibitions, loan and exchange program allow all Canadians to share in the diversity of our collected national heritage.

AWARDS OF MERIT

Canadian Museums Association/ Association Des Musées Canadiens

1982 **Ruth Whitehead**, curatorial assistant, Nova Scotia Museum, for excellent interpretation and use of Micmac cultural material for education and community development.

René Ribes, conservateur, Musée d'archéologie, University of Quebec, for his contribution to museology and research of Canadian prehistory.

Johane La Rochelle, directeur, Musée du Bas St-Laurent, Que. The achievement of a major event in Eastern Quebec, "Le tour des arts" brought together artists from the region of La Pocatiere and the Iles of Madeleine.

Population of Haute-Beauce, Que., with special mention to Pierre Mayrand, for their cooperation and understanding in working to enshrine their culture in museum displays.

Michel St-Jean, designer, National Museums of Canada, Ont., for excellence in exhibit design of a new exhibition hall of plant life at the National Museum of Natural Sciences.

Dorothy Burnham, research associate, Royal Ontario Museum, for her pioneering work in researching Canadian textiles.

Katharine Brett, curator emeritus, Royal Ontario Museum, for her pioneering research and writing in the curatorial field of textiles and costumes.

Wyn Van Slyck, president, Dugald Costume Collection Inc., for almost 30 years of contributing her time, money, and massive efforts to the collection, interpretation, documentation and preservation of one of the finest costume collections in Western Canada.

Carl Noonan, head, preparation department, Winnipeg Art Gallery, Man., for his unique contribution in combining the conservation needs of art work with the aesthetics of effective display.

Bob Broadland, Bakerville Restoration Fund co-ordinator, Heritage Conservation Branch, B.C., for public relations, and dedication to the advancement of museums across Canada.

1983 **Rupert Batten**, preparator, Newfoundland Museum, for his contribution to the preservation of traditional Newfoundland furniture.

Jules Bélanger, président, La Société

219

historique de la Gaspésie, for having started both the creation of the Gaspé Regional Museum and the founding of the Gaspé Historical Society.

B.C. Provincial Museum's Occupational Health and Safety Committee, for outstanding public and worker safety achievements.

M. Yvon Forgues, directeur-général, Musée Régional de Mines et des Arts de Malartic, Qué., for efficient and original administration.

Stanley W. Gorham, acting head of Natural Science Department and curator of Vertebrate Zoology, new Brunswick Museum, for contributions to the field of natural sciences.

Guelph Civic Museum, Guelph, Ont., for excellence in a community museum.

Jean-Pierre Hardy, Recherchiste, Musée national de l'Homme, Ottawa, Ont., for contributions to the history of the working class.

Saskatchewan Western Development Museum, Saskatoon, Sask., for the Colony Trek project.

Henry Isaak, curator, Morden and District Museum, Morden, Man., for dedicated service and initiative.

Edward J. Longard, chief curator of exhibits, Nova Scotia Museum, for establishing exhibit presentations at the Nova Scotia Museum and the Maritime Museum of the Atlantic and for assisting many local museums.

Walter Peddle, education officer, Newfoundland Museum, for contributing to the preservation of traditional Newfoundland furniture.

Pratt & Whitney Aircraft du Canada Ltée, Longueuil, Que., for the restoration of "La Maison marsil" and the voluntary involvement of 500 company employees in creating a museum.

MANIA FOR MUSEUMS

55 million people visited 708 museums in Canada in 1978. Presumably Canadians are the most museum-going people in the world, or a percentage of our museum visitors are tourists.

A LIVING MUSEUM

A living museum is under construction near Sudbury, Ont. Science North, scheduled to open in 1984, will focus on the science and resources of the Canadian North. It will be a hands-on centre, with scientists working in laboratories and exhibits that people can touch. The building, designed by Raymond Moriyama, is in the shape of a snowflake.

GLENBOW MUSEUM ACQUISITIONS SOCIETY GOLD MEDAL

Glenbow Museum, Calgary, Alta.

The medal sculpted by Dora de Pedery-Hunt portrays a settlers' cart in a prairie field ringed by mountains (from a Glenbow exhibit). The medal is awarded occasionally for outstanding contributions to the museum.

The first Glenbow Museum Acquisitions Society Gold Medal was presented in 1982 to **Mrs. Eric L. Harvie**, whose late husband, an oilman and Alberta rancher, founded the Glenbow Museum in 1957.

The second medal was awarded on the same occasion in 1982 to **Premier Peter Lougheed** of Alberta.

THE MOUNTIES

A poem published in the Saskatchewan *Herald*, **September 1878, praised the North West Mounted Police, formed in 1873.**

Oh! let the prairies echo with
The ever-welcome sound,
Ring out the boots and saddles,
Its stinging notes resound.

Our horses toss their bridled heads,
And chafe against the reins,
Ring out, ring out the marching call
For the Riders of the Plains.

POLICE AND THE WEST

The peaceful settlement of the Canadian West and the early history of the Royal Canadian Mounted Police are intertwined.

The territories under the control of the Hudson's Bay Company were purchased by the Dominion of Canada in 1870. The government soon felt the need of an official presence in the vast unsettled land.

The North West Mounted Police, a semi-military force of 300 men, was created in 1873. By July of 1874, the force under Commissioner French and Assistant Commissioner Macleod were leaving the Red River settlement of Fort Dufferin on the "Great March West." The trek was through the prairies to the Rockies. Their objectives were to deal with American whiskey traders who were causing Indian unrest; to gain the respect and confidence of the Indian nations; to protect settlers; and to maintain law and order.

Through the early years they took control of the entire West. They gained the confidence of the Indians and helped them settle on reservations. They dealt with labour unrest on the CPR line under construction, fought in the Northwest Rebellion, provided medical treatment, recorded vital statistics, collected custom dues, delivered mail and acted as Indian agents.

Rapid settlement began in 1896 and brought additional responsibilities. Members of the force became land agents, immigration officers, agricultural experts and welfare officers while maintaining their other duties.

The NWMP was also the only police force in the North. They maintained law and order during the Klondike Gold Rush and later played an important part opening up the Arctic frontier.

In 1904, the prefix "Royal" was granted by King Edward VII and the force was known as the Royal North-West Mounted Police until 1920 when the Mounted Police absorbed the Dominion Police and took the responsibility of enforcing federal law throughout Canada. The new name of the force was the Royal Canadian Mounted Police.

SOME AWARD-WINNING MEMBERS OF THE RCMP

Sgt. W.W. Patton, Royal Life Saving Society, Certificate of Thanks
Sgt. R.A. Cameron, Royal Life Saving Society, Certificate of Thanks
Cst. P.D. Kelly, Royal Life Saving Award
CPl. D.J. Ray, Royal Life Saving Award
Sgt. J.J.A. Mundle, Order of Canada
Cpl. W.R. Mossman, Serving Brother of St. John
S/Sgt. P.T. Walsh, Serving Brother of St. John
Cst. C.N. Duncan, Medal of Bravery
Cst. E.B.R. Rebier, United Nations Silver Medal

COMMISSIONER'S COMMENDATION

For excellent service to certain cases.

S/Sgt T.G. Bomba
Cst. T.R. Hansen
Cpl. William J. Jack
Cpl. D.E. Massey
Cst. B.G. Shannon
Cst. R.C. Phillips
Cst. J.D. Presley

Between 1981 and April 1983, 238 members of the RCMP received Long Service Silver Medals, representing 30 years of service. Members of the force receiving Long Service Medals Gold for 35 years of service:

C/Supt's. W.J. Hunter
M.T. Fox
Commr. R.H. Simmonds

LAW AND ORDER

Four Peel County, Ont., detectives achieved a Canadian first when they 'raised' the palm print of a murderer from the body of his victim. The print, admitted as evidence, led to the conviction of the murderer.

Det. Sgts. Haslett and Fernandes, Dets. Brown and Hancock used a slow, methodical photographic process to raise the print.

Constance Glube was named Chief Justice of the Supreme Court of Nova Scotia's trial division in 1982. She is Canada's first woman Chief Justice.

Walter Surma Tarnopolsky, a leading civil rights advocate, was appointed to the Ontario Court of Appeal in 1983, that province's highest court.

Tarnopolsky, 50, is a former president of the Canadian Civil Liberties Association and served as chairman of the civil liberties section of the Canadian Bar Association. He has served on the Canadian Human Rights Commission and has taught at the law schools of the University of Saskatchewan, the University of Windsor, Osgoode Hall, York University and Ottawa University. He fought for and helped achieve changes in a number of provisions of Canada's new Charter of Rights.

The son of emigre farmers, Tarnopolsky was born in Gronlid, Sask. He studied at the University of Saskatchewan, New York's Columbia University and at the London School of Economics.

One day she was Bertha Wilson, the next she was Mme. Justice Wilson, the first woman to be appointed to the Supreme Court of Canada. Appointed in 1982, she upheld the majority judgments of the court in some eight cases and dissented from the majority on two in her first year on the bench of the highest court of the land.

CANADIAN BANKS' LAW ENFORCEMENT AWARDS

Canadian Bankers' Association

Gold medals and citations are awarded annually for outstanding police action on behalf of a chartered bank.

One hundred and five Canadian policemen have received the Canadian Banks' Law Enforcement Award since its inception in 1971.

1982 **Montreal Urban Community Police Department**
Sergeant Detectives A. Savard and **P. Tétrault** for action following an armed robbery at a branch of the National Bank of Canada.
Constable Robert Gauthier, for his action following an armed robbery of the National Bank of Canada. After robbing the bank, a gunman was walking towards the alley behind the branch where his accomplice was waiting at the wheel of a stolen van. Gauthier, directing traffic at the intersection, noticed the branch manager signalling to him and took up pursuit. Once in the alley, the officer came face-to-face with the guman. Identifying himself, Gauthier ordered the suspect to stop. The bandit, disregarding the command, drew a gun from a briefcase he was carrying and fired at the officer.

During the chase, the suspect fired a second time at Gauthier. At one point the men found themselves on either side of the waiting van. The suspect fired a third shot at Gauthier who returned fire for the first time, through a window of the van. Several more shots were exchanged.

Undeterred by two gunshot wounds,

the suspect continued to run, eventually commandeering a taxi on a nearby street. Despite the extreme risk, Gauthier approached the taxi and with complete disregard for his own safety disarmed the dangerous suspect and arrested him.

Constable Raymond Ducharme, for his action following an armed robbery of the National Bank of Canada.

Ottawa Police Force

Constable Iain MacFarlane, for preventing an armed robbery at a branch of the Bank of Montreal.

Ontario Provincial Police (Brighton Detachment)

Constable Ray McNicol, for his action following an armed robbery at a Toronto branch of the Canadian Imperial Bank of Commerce.

Edmonton Police Department

Detective R.K. Kirkhope and **Constables J. Ewatski, R.J. Stewart** and **B.J. Murdoch**, for their actions following an armed robbery at a branch of the Toronto Dominion Bank.

FIRST COURT OF LAW

Sir Richard Whitbourne was sent to Newfoundland by the British admiralty as commissioner to inquire into disputes and disorder among the fishermen. There was considerable friction between the colonists and those who wanted Newfoundland to remain a fishing station only.

Whitbourne was a seaman and later a commander in the Royal Navy. He had considerable Newfoundland experience and was an advocate of colonization. He was empowered to hold vice-admiralty courts in 1615.

BUSY LAWYER

Gerald Gregory Brodsky is a 42-year-old Winnipeg lawyer who has defended 160 murder cases since he was called to the bar in 1963; that's about one case every 42 days. Seven of the cases ended in conviction. Of the remainder about half ended in acquittal, and about half ended with the jury returning lesser verdicts.

His philosophy when he started in practice was "to take those cases nobody wanted, the cases that couldn't be won. The reason for doing that was that you couldn't be criticized for losing and if you won, you were a hero."

Jeff Lyons, QC, has a reputation as a winning consumer lawyer. The lawyer who represents the little guy, he has taken on some of the giants of the country in class-action suits.

After a suit against Ford, which was settled out of court for about $10-million, all of the car companies in North America embarked on a rust prevention program that today offers a five-year perforation guarantee.

The first parking ticket handed out in Canada was issued in Toronto in 1907. And they're still at it.

FIRST INUIT LAWYER

Keeviak became Canada's first Inuit lawyer at the age of 47 when he was called to the Alberta Bar in February 1983.

Keeviak, whose non-Inuit name is David Ward, is a former Golden Gloves boxer, football player, city alderman and broadcaster.

He was born in Chesterfield Inlet on the west shore of Hudson Bay but has lived in Edmonton since he was a small boy. He graduated from the University of British Columbia with a law degree in 1981.

MALONEY WINS AWARD

Arthur Edward Martin Maloney, a noted Canadian lawyer, received the John

Howard Society of Ontario Award in 1982. Maloney received the award "for his leadership in the campaign to abolish the death penalty in Canada and his humanitarian principles and practice through his illustrious career as a lawyer, parliamentarian and Ontario's first ombudsman."

The first woman called to the British Columbia bar was Mabel Pennery French in 1912.

FIRST JUDGE IN B.C.

Matthew Begbie was appointed as the first judge in the new colony of British Columbia in 1858. He arrived from Britain just as gold seekers from the U.S. were beginning to flow into the B.C. mainland to prospect in the Fraser River Gold Rush.

In the California gold rush, miners had established their own law and imposed their own justice. Begbie, together with James Douglas, imposed British authority and British justice and they maintained law and order. He was known as the Hanging Judge.

Begbie was born in Scotland in 1819 and educated at Cambridge. He was appointed chief justice of British Columbia in 1870 and had authority over the courts on Vancouver Island and on the mainland. He was knighted in 1874 and died in Victoria in 1894.

VISCOUNT BENNETT FELLOWSHIPS

Canadian Bar Association

The awards presented by the law association are for graduate level studies and are worth $12,000 and $7,000 respectively. The winners were selected from 30 candidates.

1982 **David Lepofsky**, Toronto, Ont., who

achieved an outstanding academic record and excelled in community projects despite being handicapped by blindness. He graduated from Osgoode Hall Law School with honours, one of eleven students in a class of 309 to achieve this distinction.
Robert Richards, Ottawa, Ont.

FIRST RECORDED CANADIAN STING

Donnacona, the Indian chief who was kidnapped and taken to France by Cartier, wanted to return home to his people.

Cannily, he told the French everything they wanted to hear — of the kingdom of Saguenay; of its gold and jewels and of the cinnamon, cloves and oranges which grew there.

He was an effective story teller and later a Spanish spy at the French court reported to his own court, "The King of France says the Indian King told him there is a large city called Sagana, where there are many mines of gold and silver in great abundance, and men who dress and wear shoes as we do; and there is an abundance of cloves, nutmeg and pepper."

Perhaps the French were trying to rouse the envy of the Spanish. Nevertheless an expedition was sent to the New World in 1541 with orders to find, conquer and loot the kingdom.

As for Donnacona, he died of smallpox in France before the expedition was sent to Canada.

FELLOWSHIPS IN LEGAL JOURNALISM

Canadian Bar Association

The Louis St. Laurent Fellowships in legal journalism are offered annually to help working journalists become familiar with the legal systems in Canada. Each award is worth up to $24,000 per annum plus transportation and book expenses.

1982/83   Pamela Fayerman, Winnipeg *Free Press*. A "courts beat" reporter for the *Free Press*, Pamela Fayerman attends law school at Queen's University.
Heather Matheson, CBC Producer, Montreal, Que. The producer of the CBC's *Cross-Country Checkup* attends McGill University.

TOLERANCE AND BIGOTRY

"If there be any man to be found in Canada who from any narrow, any selfish, any exclusive, any bigoted, or any fanatical sentiment would yield for a single moment to a disposition to advance his own race, religion or sect at the sacrifice of the interest and the conscience of others ... I ask such a one if he is prepared to re-open a war of races, and a war of creeds, because he wishes to deny to a small and helpless Roman Catholic minority in the province of Manitoba the rights which the Imperial statute and the law under which Manitoba came into the union have guaranteed to them ...

He may regard, as many do regard, that this is a question of separate schools, and that he is opposed to separate schools ... It is not a question of separate schools, it is a question of the constitution of the country. The progress and the prosperity and the future development of Canada depend upon that constitution being sacredly maintained."

Sir Charles Tupper defending in Parliament the Conservative government's move to restore Manitoba Catholics' education rights in 1896. They were abolished by the provincial Liberal government in 1890.

QUEEN'S COUNSEL APPOINTMENTS

On December 31, 1982, The Hon. Mark MacGuigan announced the appointment of 28 Queen's Counsel.

Ivan John Cable, senior partner of the law firm Cable, Vail, Coscoe, and Morris of Whitehorse, Yukon Territory
Georges Clermont, vice-president, Corporate and Legal Affairs, Canada Post Corporation
Jean-Claude Delorme, President, Teleglobe Canada
Gerald Donegan, general counsel, Vancouver Regional Office, Department of Justice
Reginald L. Evans, general counsel, Department of Justice
Claude Foisy, former vice-chairman, Canada Labour Relations Board
The Hon. John A. Fraser, MP for Vancouver South
David G. Frayer, general counsel, Winnipeg regional office, Department of Justice
Alphonse Giard, counsel, Law Department, Canadian National
Ross Goodwin, senior partner of the law firm Goodwin, de Blois, of Québec
The Hon. J. Robert Howie, MP for York-Sunbury
Lawson A.W. Hunter, assistant deputy minister, Bureau of Competition Policy, and director of investigation and research, Department of Consumer and Corporate Affairs
Marcus L. Jewett, general counsel, Constitutional and International Law, Department of Justice
Brigadier General F. Karwandy, Judge Advocate General, Department of National Defence
Wilfrid Lefebvre, general counsel, Tax Litigation Section, Department of Justice
Louise Lemelin, commissioner, Law Reform Commission of Canada.
Gilles Marceau, MP for Jonquière
Gerald H. McCracken, senior counsel, criminal prosecutions section, Toronto, Department of Justice
The Hon. Joan Neiman, senator, Ottawa
Michael B. Philips, senior departmental assistant, Office of the Secretary of State, External Affairs
Daniel C. Préfontaine, general counsel, policy

planning and criminal law amendments section, Department of Justice
Barbara J. Reed, counsel, Privy Council Office, Ottawa
Michel Robert, senior partner of the law firm Robert, Dansereau, Barre, Marchessault & Lauzon, of Montreal.
W. Kenneth Robinson, MP for Etobicoke-Lakeshore
H.B. Shaffer, counsel, legislation section, Department of Justice
Stephen J. Skelly, Assistant Deputy Minister, legal services, Department of Justice
Edward R. Sojonky, senior counsel, civil litigation section, Department of Justice
Walter S. Tarnopolsky, Professor of Law, University of Ottawa

---

Ten of Canada's 16 prime ministers have been lawyers.

FREEDOM FINALLY WON

Donald Marshall, 29, of Halifax, was convicted of murder in 1971 and served 11 years in Dorchester Penitentiary.

The young man always protested his innocence and finally, in the spring of 1983, the courts agreed with him after hearing that there was enough evidence to charge another man with the murder. Donald Marshall had finally won his freedom.

ANIMALS

1982 STOCK OF THE YEAR

Canadian Professional Rodeo Association

Saddle bronc
G10 Guilty Cat. In 1982 he was out 13 times, bucked off eight riders and was ridden five times with cowboys winning 1st or 2nd place.
Bareback horse of the year
3C Three Cheers for Velvet. A son of the famous bucking mare, Three Bars, Cheers has been best bareback horse at Calgary and second at the National Finals Rodeo.
Bull
XI Charles Manson. Five year old XI Charles Manson is a black bull whose riders usually mark in the high 80s. He was top bull at the 81 STampede.
Calf Roping Horse
Yankee. This 13-year-old palamino gelding won the title in 1980, and carried his rider Bill Reeder, of Cardston, Alta., to 2nd place at the 1982 Canadian Rodeo Finals.
Steer Wrestling Horse
Twist. Twist has won the title for three of the past four years. Ken Guenthner rode him to the 1981 Canadian Steer Wrestling Championship. Together they won the Calgary Stampede's $50,000 steer-wrestling title.

PEAK PEKINGESE

Champion St. Aubrey Dragonora of Elsdon, a Pekingese owned by Anne Snelling of Ottawa, won the best in show ribbon at the Westminster Kennel Club show in New York City, February, 1982.

TOP DOGS

Dogs in Canada Magazine

The top ten — all breeds
Owners of the dogs are presented with a certificate honouring their dog's achievements in Canadian show rings during the year.

These are the winning dogs in Canadian competition, and are not necessarily the top ten dogs in Canada (every boy and girl knows his or her dog is the best).

1982 1 English Setter, **Fantail's Sunshine Man**, 19,930 points
2 Bouvier des Flandres, **Glen Miller's Beau Geste**, 9,128
3 Shih Tzu, **Samalee's Reflection of Baron**, 8,850

4 German Shepherd Dog, **Lido von Vellmar**, 7,734

5 Shih Tzu, **Shente's Brandy Alexander**, 6,941

6 Maltese, **Revlo's Ringo Star of Midway**, 6,460

7 West Highland White Terrier, **Whitebrier Jeronimo**, 5,915

8 Afghan Hound, **Persia's Jake Logan**, 5,837

9 Doberman Pinscher, **Freespirit's Apollo**, 5,447

10 Great Dane, **Zingara's Zsultan Khayam**, 5,032

TOP DOGS THROUGH THE YEARS

1963 **(Can. & Am.) Loramar's I'm a Dandy**, toy poodle

1964 (Can. & Eng.) **Stoney Gap Sugar Candy of Mahnraf**, West Highland White Terrier

1965 (Can. & Eng.) **Outdoor's Navarmy Bonanza**, bulldog

1966 (Can. & Am.) **Ja-Mar's Avenger of Arbor**, German shepherd

1967 (Can. Am., Eng. & Bda.) **Tophill Orsino**, Miniature poodle

1968 (Can. Am., Eng. & Bda.) **Tophill Orsino**, miniature poodle

1969 (Can. & Am.) **Scher-Khoun's Shadrack**, boxer

1970 (Can. & Am.) **Scher-Khoun's Shadrack**, boxer

1971 (Can. Am. & Bda.) **Lullhaven's Snowmist Ensign**, samoyed

1972 (Can. & Am.) **Davos Baroness Zareba**, Great Dane

1973 **Ambassadeur**, St. Bernard

1974 (Can. Am. & Bda.) **Sir Lancelot of Barvan**, Old English sheepdog

1975 (Can. & Am.) **Mi-Tu's Han Su Shang**, chow chow

1976 (Can. Am. & Bda.) **Mephisto's Soldier of Fortune**, boxer

1977 (Can. & Am.) **Kishniga's Desert Song**, borzoi

1978 **Hornblower's Long John Silver**, Newfoundland

1979 **Haviland's Count Royal**, boxer

1980 **Le Dauphin of Limberlost**; great pyrenees

1981 (Can. Am. & Bda.) **Storybook's Marauder**, English setter

CATS CROSSING

The first cats to cross the Atlantic by raft were Guiton and Puce, who essayed the daring voyage from Halifax to Falmouth, England (accompanied by their owners), in 1956.

HEAVIEST LOAD

In July, 1973, a 162-pound Newfoundland named Bonzo Bear dragged a 4,400-pound weight a distance of 15 feet. It was the heaviest recorded load pulled by dog power.

CHAMPION CHICKENS

The Starcross, a breed of chicken developed by Donald Shaver of Galt, Ont., averages a record-cracking 288 eggs a month.

CANADIAN NATIONAL RETRIEVER CHAMPIONSHIP

National Retriever Club of Canada

1982 **Piper's Pacer**, 5-year-old black Labrador male owned by Mr. and Mrs. Roy McFall, Anchorage, Alaska. Piper's Pacer is recognized as the best field dog in North America. He holds the Amateur Field Championship and Field Championship titles in the U.S. as well as the Amateur Field Championship and Field Championship titles in Canada.

JUMBO TRAIN WRECK

Jumbo, the largest elephant ever held in captivity, was dispatched to his maker by a rapidly moving railroad train in St. Thomas, Ont., on September 15, 1885. The seven-ton behemoth which, it is said, liked to knock back whisky and beer with his faithful keeper, was the property of circus magnate Phineas T. Barnum. After Jumbo's demise, the ever-resourceful Barnum built two special wagons to display the remains. (P.S. The train was derailed.)

RALSTON PURINA ANIMAL HALL OF FAME

Ralston Purina Canada

Every year, hundreds of pet animals in Canada show extraordinary intelligence in helping to save human lives. Fires in the home continue to be the most common event in which pet dogs and cats give warning, wakening the families in time to escape.

The 1983 members are honoured for the part they played in other unusual and high risk situations.

Framed portraits with citations and the equivalent of a year's supply of pet food and accompanying gifts are presented to the owners at the Canadian National Sportsmen's Show.

1983 **Maude**, N.S. German Shepherd owned by Deborah Johnston and Bernard Chisholm.
Maude saved Debbie Chisholm, 3, from drowning in the frigid waters of Pictou harbour when the little girl slipped away from her family home. Maude leaped into the harbour and pulled the child out, blue with cold. Maude is recognized for her intelligence and action. **Dixie**, Bramalea, Ont., Beagle owned by Lloyd Viney.
Dixie is credited with discovering a dangerous explosive device hidden in a tree in a small park near his home. Peel Regional Police officers responded to his owner's call and removed the explosives for examination and evidence.
Dixie is honoured for his persistence in scenting out the dangerous device and preventing potential tragedy.

MORE HEROES FROM THE PURINA ANIMAL HALL OF FAME.

Pat, a black Labrador Retriever owned by Tom Murphy of Kingston, Ont., saved Mur-

phy's live by towing him with a rope attached to an oarless boat for 3 $1/2$ hours in strong winds and rough water on the St. Lawrence River. Pat was inducted in the Hall of Fame in 1968.

Baby, of St. Boniface, Man. a deaf-mute cat, saved the life of its owner when he suffered a heart attack. The cat managed to waken the owner's wife by throwing herself on the sleeping woman until she rose, and discovered her collapsed husband in another room. Baby was inducted into the Hall of Fame in 1974.

Indian Red, Morgan/Quarter Horse, Newmarket, Ont. The first horse to be honoured in the Animal Hall of Fame. He drew attention to a helpless 77-year-old woman who had collapsed and was lying snow-covered in a ditch on a country road at night.

COMPOUND FOR CAREFREE CATS

Dr. Andrew Frazer of Saskatoon, Sask., developed a compound in 1979 which is now being researched by the Ontario Humane Society and the Animal Welfare Foundation in Canada. The compound, if successful, would render house cats sterile with a simple injection. If the birth-control vaccine (still a few years away) works, the number of homeless cats would be substantially reduced.

POLICE SERVICE DOGS GET THEIR MAN

The RCMP Dog Service was initiated in 1935 with the purchase of Black Lux who was teamed with Constable W.H. Billington. The force has its own breeding program and uses German Shepherds, generally male, for field service. In 1978 service dogs were called to assist in 10,318 cases and by 1980 there were some 70 PSD teams stationed across the country.

Police Service Dogs have been used

Maude, a German Shepherd, owned by Deborah Johnston, 1, saved Debbie Chisholm, 3, from drowning in Pictou harbour, N.S.

Dixie, a Beagle owned by Lloyd Viney, discovered dangerous explosive devices.

successfully to search for missing children, the mentally ill and for lost hunters, in avalanche rescue missions and in the search for explosives and drugs. They have found missing articles, uncovered evidence, helped with crowd control and assisted in the apprehension of criminals.

In one case in 1976, PDS Smokey and his master constable Jean of Dorval, Que., took just a few hours to uncover 20 to 25 boxes of deteriorating negatives that were creating a harmful and highly explosive gas in the National Library at Ottawa. The noxious boxes were among 10,000 others, packed floor to ceiling making a human search costly and difficult.

Two years earlier, PDS Pax with Constable Gillette helped to uncover dynamite and other explosives that were intended for use in a planned jail break at Archambault penitentiary in Quebec. In 1977, the same team rescued an injured hunter who was lost in the woods near Beauleau Lake, B.C. Blowing snow had obliterated the hunter's tracks and he had wandered in circles leaving confusing cross scents. Pax, working through the dense bush and over windfalls and rock slides, found the hunter in just over an hour and probably saved his life.

In 1977, PSD Major II and Corporal Barter were tracking an escaped convict on mountainous terrain along the Fraser River. Major was unleashed, went ahead, and was momentarily out of sight on a steep embankment when he was stabbed by the convict. He fell to the ground but before he could be reached, he rose and, bleeding heavily, continued to pursue the suspect. Barter followed the trail of blood and found Major standing over the escapee. Suffering from a 3 $1/2$-inch knife would that had severed the jugular vein as well as a large throat nerve, Major was not expected to recover. He was transferred by helicopter to a veterinary hospital for surgery, and lived to return to full duty just two weeks after the operation.

FIRST GUN FIRED IN BATTLE IN CANADA

In 1609 Samuel de Champlain agreed to help the Huron, the Montagnais and Algonquin Indians against the Iroquois. He accompanied the Indians, who were to become allies of the French, on a foray. The foray gave him a chance to explore what are now the Richelieu River and Lake Champlain.

The party came upon the Iroquois at Fort Ticonderoga at Crown Point near Lake Champlain. There was a brief skirmish but the Iroquois fled when Champlain fired his harquebus, a heavy matchlock gun mounted on a stand.

CONTEST FOR THE CONTINENT

In the expeditions to the east coast of North America the European powers did not find the easy plunder they had discovered in Central America, and the inhospitable land would not provide easy settlement.

But the nation that found a fast route to the rich markets of Asia and controlled that route would be ahead of its rivals, so the search for the Northwest Passage went on. The Europeans were hungry for the fish of the Grand Banks and the beaver furs which fishermen and independent traders were bringing to Europe. There was wealth to be extracted from the new lands and the rivalry intensified.

France established settlements in Acadia and the St. Lawrence valley to exploit the fur trade and then penetrated westward toward the Rockies and southward to the centre of the continent to the Gulf of Mexico.

In the east, the English and the Dutch

were establishing colonies down the Atlantic seaboard. (The Dutch who were settling in the Hudson Valley, retired from the contest in 1674 when New Netherlands [New York] was ceded to Britain. To the north of the French after 1670, there were the Hudson's Bay Company lands, and France and England each claimed parts of Newfoundland's coastline.

When England and France were at peace in Europe the North American contest was generally held to skirmishes, which were often blamed on the Indians. When there was war in Europe, there was also war in America.

Between 1689 and 1713 there were a series of wars between the English and the French, with only one five-year period of peace. In North America victory was generally with the French, but in Europe the tide went with the English and in 1713 France surrendered all her claims to Hudson Bay, Newfoundland and Acadia.

Still the struggle for the continent went on, culminating with the Seven Years' War and English domination. The English broke through the French defences at Louisbourg in 1758 and in 1759 they took Quebec, but still the French fought back, finally capitulating to England in Montreal in 1760.

In 1763, the Treaty of Paris gave all of France's holdings on the continent to the British save for the islands of St. Pierre and Miquelon which, to this day, remain French possessions.

"LE CID CANADIEN," HERO OF NEW FRANCE

"Le Cid Canadien," Pierre le Moyne d'Iberville, born in Canada in 1661, is a legendary figure from Quebec's past.

In 1686 he went with an overland expedition from new France (Quebec) to James Bay. The expeditionary force captured the three Hudson's Bay Posts on the Bay and d'Iberville was put in charge of the forts. The next year he captured a British sloop that arrived in James Bay and sailed her to Quebec.

He convinced the French that Quebec could best protect its holdings from the sea and was given command of three ships. He began the vigorous defence of Quebec that was to make him its hero.

Sailing the Atlantic coast from Hudson Bay to the state of Maine, he harried and captured British ships and attacked British settlements.

He was commander of an expedition to establish the first French posts in Louisiana and was made its governor in 1703. Then in 1706, he was ordered to conquer the West Indies. He captured the islands of St. Christopher and Nevis for the French, but died of yellow fever before reaching Havana.

In 1953 a large, powerful ice-breaker and supply ship went into service on Canada's Arctic patrol; she was named the *D'Iberville* in honour of the romantic son of New France.

WOLFE AND MONTCALM, HEROES OF THE DECISIVE BATTLE FOR CANADA

France and Britain had been struggling for control of North America for 200 years. That struggle climaxed in 1758 when the forces of the two powers met on the Plains of Abraham.

The French troops were led by the Marquis de Montcalm de Saint-Servan, a brilliant general who had been severely handicapped by corrupt civil authorities in Quebec and a jealous and uncooperative governor. Montcalm knew that Quebec needed defence installations placed on the St. Lawrence and ordered batteries built. The civil authorities ignored or delayed his orders and the installations which would likely have changed the outcome of the battle were never built. Montcalm secured the southern borders of the colony but was forced to withdraw his troops to Quebec when supplies and reinforcements were not forthcoming.

The British began choking off New France in 1757 as they set up naval blocades of French ports and sent naval squadrons to intercept French troop ships.

Then Britain sent large numbers of troops and naval vessels to North America.

In 1758 the British broke the French control of the Ohio Valley and cut French communication to the west, then destroyed the French stronghold at Louisbourg with a land and naval bombardment that lasted eight days. The young brigadier who directed the assault at Louisbourg was James Wolfe. Still the British tightened the knot, capturing forts Niagara, Carillon and St. Frederic.

With Louisbourg destroyed, the British controlled the St. Lawrence. They ordered Wolfe to attack Quebec and gave him the support of a fleet and the temporary rank of major-general.

The British placed Quebec City under siege and bombarded it throughout the summer of 1758. Montcalm, high above the river, would not surrender.

On the night of September 12, the fleet, with Wolfe's troops aboard, slipped unnoticed up the river past Quebec to Anse de Foulon (Wolfe's Cove). Early the next morning, the British troops quietly scaled the steep cliffs and assembled on the Plains of Abraham, taking the French utterly by surprise. Montcalm was forced to march his troops from east of Quebec, through the city and out onto the Plains, where the battle was joined.

During the battle Wolfe was killed and Montcalm fatally wounded. The French at Quebec surrendered on September 18. But the war elsewhere went on.

While the British force spent a miserable winter in Quebec, the remaining French forces were regrouping. In the spring the French moved from Montreal toward Quebec, defeated the British at Ste. Foy and then beseiged Quebec.

Both armies waited: the British inside Quebec and the French outside. They waited for the spring, and for ships to come up the St. Lawrence carrying supplies and reinforcements.

The British naval blockade held and the first ships to come up the river were British, forcing the French to withdraw.

In September 1759 the British marched into Montreal and the war in North America was over, three years before the war in Europe ended.

At the Peace of Paris in 1763, the French surrendered the St. Lawrence region, apparently without regret.

Voltaire, the leading French intellectual of the time, was pleased that the French had not given up valuable holdings such as the sugar islands in the Caribbean. All they had lost, he said, "were a few acres of snow."

THE HEAD OF CHATEAUGUAY

Charles-Michel d'Irumberry de Salaberry, born at Beauport, Que., in 1778, was a professional soldier. In 1812, he was commissioned to raise the Canadian Voltigeurs, a mostly French-Canadian force.

In the fall of 1813 an American army began to advance on Montreal. De Salaberry and his troops met the Americans at Chateauguay, just 15 miles from Montreal.

Deploying his troops skillfully, de Salaberry tricked the Americans into believing that his army was of significant size and after a brief encounter the American force withdrew.

De Salaberry was made a Companion of the Bath in 1817 and in 1818 was appointed to the legislative council of Lower Canada.

JOSEPH BRANT

Joseph Brant was born in 1742 on the banks of the Ohio River and educated in a private school. He was a hereditary chief of the Mohawk Indians and his Indian name was Thayendanega.

He became the principal chief of the Six Nations and as an ally of the British led the Iroquois against the French in the Seven Years War. He again came to the aid of the British during the suppression of the Indian uprising in 1763. During the American Revolution he led the Six Nations as a support force for the British against the Americans.

He brought the Six Nations to what is now Ontario in 1784. Some of his people settled on a reserve at Grand River, others went to a reserve near Kingston and some to the Bay of Quinte.

CHECKING SPANISH EXPANSIONISM

In 1789 the Spanish dispatched Estevan Jose Martinez to establish a Spanish settlement at Nootka Sound on Vancouver Island. Once there, Martinez seized British trading ships but left American ships unmolested.

Britain threatened war with Spain over the incident. In 1790 Spain agreed to restore British property and agreed that the Pacific coast was open to British subjects except within 10 miles of Spanish settlements. While Spain did not withdraw from Nootka until 1795, the British checked Spanish expansionism on the North West coast.

YOU'VE GOT IT PONTIAC

Pontiac is a heroic Indian figure. He was chief of the Ottawas and led a confederation of Indian nations against the British in 1763.

The Indian tribes who were loyal to the French resented British traders and feared the loss of their lands to settlers.

Pontiac forced a confederacy of most of the tribes from the head of Lake Superior southward almost to the Gulf of Mexico. Senecas, Ottawas, Potawatomis, Hurons, Kickapoos, Mascouten, Chippewas and Wyandots all banded together to drive the British from their frontiers.

The confederation captured 10 of the 14 British garrisoned forts in the huge region and Pontiac himself held Detroit in siege from July to October of 1763.

It took the British months to quell the uprising and five years passed before the Indians accepted a peace treaty.

SIR ISAAC BROCK, "SAVIOUR OF CANADA"

Isaac Brock was commander of the armed forces in Upper Canada when the War of 1812 began. His direction of 1600 British regular troops and a small militia force against the Americans early in the war convinced Upper Canadians that defence against the U.S. was possible.

In Upper Canada a large part of the population was composed of former Americans and some of them were encouraging surrender before the fighting began.

Lower Canada was resolute against the Yanks. The French-Canadians were not republicans and proved to be extremely loyal to their recent conquerors. The Assembly there voted greater financial support for the war than any other British colony in North America.

Since the Atlantic provinces were protected by the might of Britain's navy and Quebec was well defended, it became clear that the continentalist Americans would attack between the Niagara Peninsula and Detroit.

The Americans were convinced they couldn't lose; how could they with 7-million citizens versus Canada's 700,000?

Brock struck first, taking a small American garrison at Michilimackina, then forced back an American attack and brought about the surrender of that force at Detroit. he repulsed another American invasion at the Battle of Queenston Heights, but was killed in the action and died without knowing he had been recently knighted.

The war dragged on with the British (Canadian) forces actually gaining American territory. Later, at the peace negotiations, Britain and the U.S. agreed to go back to pre-war boundary lines.

Canada would likely not have become a nation but for the resolve of the people, and General Brock who helped strengthen that resolve.

HEROINE OF 1812

Laura Secord came to Upper Canada with her Loyalist parents from Massachusetts, and her husband James Secord served with the militia.

When the Americans crossed into the Niagara Peninsula in June of 1813, she overheard American soldiers who billeted in her home speaking of an upcoming attack at Beaver Dam.

Determined to warn the militia commander, she walked some 19 miles to deliver her message. The commander had already been forewarned of the attack by Indian scouts but did not tell the heroic woman that her trek had been unnecessary.

On June 24, Indian allies led by John

Brant defeated the Americans at Beaver Dam, and today Laura Secord remains a recognized heroine.

"Here (near Beaver Dam), I found all the Indians encamped; by moonlight the scene was terrifying, and to those accustomed to such scenes, might be considered grand ... the Indians they all rose, and, with some yells, said "Woman", which made me tremble. I cannot express the awful feeling it gave me; but I did not lose my presence of mind. I was determined to persevere. The chief at first objected to let me pass, but finally consented to accompany me to FitzGibbon's (the commander's) station ...
I then told him what I had come for ... that the Americans intended to make an attack upon the troops under his command. Benefiting by this information, Capt. FitzGibbon formed his plans accordingly, and captured about 500 American infantry."
Laura Secord, *The Anglo-American Magazine,* November 1853.

TORONTO, THE WHITE HOUSE AND FRANKLIN D. ROOSEVELT

During the War of 1812 an American force landed at York (Toronto), then the capital of Upper Canada. The invaders not only set the town ablaze, but got the mace that symbolized the authority of the Upper Candian legislature and carried it to Washington.

In 1814 a British Force got its own back when soldiers set fire to the White House, destroying the interior and scorching the exterior. (White paint applied to the exterior to hide the scorching in 1817 encouraged the use of the name "White House.")

The Mace was not returned until 1934, however, when Franklin D. Roosevelt, the late president of the United

States, visited Toronto and brought it back.

nerable to attack from the south, and nudged the province into Confederation.

TECUMSEH, INDIAN HERO

Tecumseh was a chief of the Shawnee. He was born near present-day Springfield, Ohio, in 1768. Fearing the incursion of white settlers, he formed a confederacy of tribes that he hoped could peacefully resist largescale settlement in Indian territory. The confederacy however was smashed by the American army at Tippecanoe in 1811. He joined the British in the War of 1812 and was made a brigadier-general in charge of Indian troops.

He cut the supply lines of an American force that had entered Canada which was a factor in their subsequent withdrawal. He commanded Indians at the successful seige of Detroit, under Brock. He and his men were with the British in several other battles through the war. He was killed in 1813 at the Battle of Moraviantown on the Thomas River (near present-day London).

A FENIAN BATTLE SONG (1866)

We are a Fenian brotherhood, skilled
  in the arts of war,
And we're going to fight for Ireland
  and the land that we adore;
Many battles have we won, along
  with the boys in blue,
And we'll go to capture Canada,
  for we've nothing else to do.

The Fenians were an Irish republican movement. The American Fenians recruited Civil War veterans to form an army to attack and capture Canada. Their dreams of forming an Independent Irish Republic in North America were unrealized. But the confusion, pain and death they caused showed the people of New Brunswick that they were vul-

FIRST TROOPS OVERSEAS

A contingent of Canadian civilian voyageurs who were expert in boat building and river travel were sent to Africa in 1884 to serve in the relief of Khartoum. They were the first officially recognized contingent of Canadian troops to serve in an overseas war.

IN FLANDERS FIELDS — MOST FAMOUS CANADIAN POEM

In Flanders fields the poppies blow
Between the crosses row on row,
  That mark our place; and in the sky
  The larks, still bravely singing, fly
Scarce heard amid the guns below.

We are the Dead. Short days ago
We lived, felt dawn, saw sunset glow,
  Loved and were loved, and now we lie
  In Flanders fields.

Take up our quarrel with the foe;
To you from failing hands we throw
  The torch; be yours to hold it high.
  If ye break faith with us who die
We shall not sleep, though poppies grow
  In Flanders fields.

John McCrae (1872-1918) was a Canadian poet who died of pneumonia in a hospital in Boulogne, France, where he was a medical officer during World War One. The poem was first published in Punch, the British magazine, in 1915.

THE VICTORIA CROSS

The highest military decoration for bravery in the Commonwealth is the Victoria Cross. The medal is a bronze cross pattee suspended from a dull crimson ribbon (formerly the ribbon was blue for the navy and red for the army). The decoration bears the words: "For Valour" and, in relief, the Royal crest.

The decoration was founded by Queen Victoria in 1856 to reward those men who displayed outstanding gallantry in the Crimean War.

Since the award was initiated, 94 Canadians or foreign nationals serving in Canadian units have received the award, 69 of them in the First World War.

Most VC winners were volunteer soldiers, and they came from all ranks and from many branches of the armed service. The sole criterion for the award is supreme bravery.

Editor's note: due to space limitations *Prudential's Book of Canadian Winners and Heroes* can only list the recipients of the Victoria Cross without the accompanying citations.

The editors have, however, selected a limited number of citations to include only as examples of the courage displayed by all the VC winners. We refer the interested reader to the book *Valiant Men* by John Swettenham.

Alexander Robert Dunn

VC: Balaclava, October 25, 1854
Born: York, Upper Canada, September 15, 1883
Unit: 11th (Prince Albert's Own) Regiment of (Light) Dragoons (Hussars), (British Army)
Died: Senafe, Abyssinia, January 25, 1868

Dun's bravery in the Crimean War made him Canada's first VC recipient.
"[During the Charge of the Light Brigade at Balaclava] Lieutenant Alexander Dunn ... one of the handsomest men of his day, and also ... one of the finest swordsmen and horsemen in the Army, won the Victoria Cross; having emptied his revolver at the Russians he flung it at them and resorted to his sabre, which he used to such good effect (Dunn stood six feet three and used a sword much longer than regulations permitted) that he saved Sergeant Bentley's life by cutting down several Russians who were attacking him."

The 11th Hussars

[He then saved another life by] cutting down

a Russian Hussar, who was attacking Private Levett, 11th Hussars.

London Gazette, February 24, 1857

Herbert Taylor Reade

VC: Delhi, India, September 14, 1857
Born: Perth, Upper Canada, September 2, 1828
Unit: 61st (South Gloucestershire) Regiment of Foot, (British Army).
Died: Bath, England, June 23, 1897

"[During the Indian Mutiny, Surgeon Reade] ministering to the wounded up and down [the] tortuous alleys of Delhi, ... was never far from the rebels.

"He ... was tending the wounds of a number of men when a large party of mutineers ... levelled a murderous fire on the men below ...

"He shouted for volunteers and a party of about 10 men ... followed him ...

"The young Canadian pursued and cut down the enemy ... Of the leader and his 10, only three returned whole ...

"But this was only one act of bravery ... The mutineers had mounted several cannon ... Leading his entire regiment, Reade dashed for these batteries, and a sanguinary melee ensured.

"Reade fought bitterly around the guns. With a Sergeant ... he spiked one, a feat which won him the plaudits of all who had followed this intrepid fighting surgeon.

"With the fall of the Magazine the way was now cleared for the complete occupation of Delhi."

From Canada's Second Victoria Cross

William Hall

VC: Lucknow, India, November 16, 1857
Born: Horton Bluff, N.S., April 28, 1827
Unit: Royal Navy (HMS *Shannon*), Naval Brigade
Died: Avonport, N.S. August 25, 1904

Hall, son of an escaped American slave, was the first black to ever win the VC, and the first Canadian sailor to win it.

Campbell Mellis Douglas

VC: Island of Little Andaman, May 7, 1867, during the Burma Campaign

Born: Quebec City, August 5, 1840
Unit: 24th (2nd Warwickshire) Regiment of Foot, (British Army)
Died: Wells, Somerset, December 31, 1909

Hampden Zane Churchill

VC: Leliefontein, Komati River, November 7, 1900, during the South African War
Born: Toronto, November 19, 1867
Unit: The Royal Canadian Dragoons
Died: Toronto, July 13, 1913

Arthur Herbert Lindsay Richardson

VC: Wolve Spruit, Standerton, July 5, 1900
Born: Southport, near Liverpool, England, 1873
Unit: Strathcona's Horse
Died: Liverpool, December 15, 1932

Richard Ernest William Turner

VC: Leliefontein, Komati River, November 7, 1900
Born: Quebec City, July 25, 1871
Unit: The Royal Canadian Dragoons
Died: Quebec City, June 19, 1961

"The guns were in grave danger of being captured. Lieutenant Turner galloped up and shouted, 'Dismount and hold back the enemy!' I remember him distinctly saying 'Never let it be said the Canadians had let their guns be taken!' ... Again Lieutenant Turner galloped up, now seriously wounded in the neck and his arm shattered ... But the important thing was, the guns of D battery had not been captured; they had been saved by the stubborn resistance of the RCD."
Trooper A. E. Hilder, RCD

Edward James Gibson Holland

VC: Leliefontein, Komati River, November 7, 1900
Born: Ottawa, February 2, 1878
Unit: The Royal Canadian Dragoons
Died: Cobalt, Ontario, June 18, 1948

Michael O'Leary

VC: Cuinchy, France, February 1, 1915
Born: Macroom, Ireland, September 29, 1889
Unit: 1st Battalion, The Irish Guards (British Army)
Died: London, England, August 2, 1961

"On the last day of January the Germans attempted a surprise against the trenches neighbouring those of the Irish Guards. The position was lost, and had to be retaken ... The morning ... broke fine and clear, and simultaneously a storm of shot and shell descended on the German trenches which were marked down for recapture ... O'Leary ... marked down the spot where a German machine gun was to be found ... and it was a matter of life and death to perhaps hundreds of his comrades that he should reach it in time to prevent its being brought into action. He put on his best pace, and within a few seconds found himself in a corner of the German trench on the way to his goal. Immediately ahead of him was a barricade ... but to O'Leary ... it was no obstacle, and its five defenders quickly paid with their lives. ... Leaving his five victims, O'Leary started off to cover the 80 yards that still separated him from the second barricade, where the German machine gun was hidden. He was literally now racing with death ... At every moment he expected to hear the sharp burr of the gun in action. A patch of boggy ground prevented a direct approach to the barricade, and it was with veritable anguish that he realized the necessity of the detour by a railway line. ... A few seconds passed, and then, the Germans working feverishly to remount their machine gun and bring it into action ... perceived ... O'Leary, a few yards on their right with his rifle levelled at them. The officer in charge had no time to realize that his finger was on the button before death squared his account. Two other reports followed in quick succession, and two other figures fell to the ground with barely a sound. The two survivors ... threw up their hands. With his two captives before him, the gallant Irishman returned in triumph, while his comrades swept the enemy out of the trenches, and completed one of the most successful local actions we have ever undertaken."
The Victoria Cross

Fred Fisher

VC: St. Julien, Belgium, April 23, 1915 (Posthumous)
Born: St. Catharines, Ont., August 3, 1894
Unit: 13th Battalion, Canadian Expeditionary Force

Died: April 23, 1915

Frederick William Hall

VC: Ypres, Belgium, April 24, 1915 (Posthumous)
Born: Kilkenny, Ireland, February 21, 1885
Unit: 8th Battalion, CEF.
Died: April 24, 1915

Edward Donald Bellew

VC: Near Keerselaere, Belgium, April 24, 1915
Born: Bombay, India, October 28, 1882
Unit: 7th Battalion, CEF
Died: Kamloops, B.C. February 1, 1961

Francis Alexander Caron Scrimger

VC: Ypres, April 25, 1915
Born: Montreal, February 10, 1881
Service: Canadian Army Medical Corps (Attached to 14th Battalion, CEF)
Died: Montreal, February 13, 1937

Frederick William Campbell

VC: Givenchy, France, June 15, 1915 (Posthumous)
Born: Mount Forest, Ont., June 15, 1867
Unit: 1st Battalion, CEF
Died: June 19, 1915

Leo Clark

VC: Pozières, France, September 9, 1916
Born: Waterdown, Ont., December 1, 1892
Unit: 2nd Battalion, CEF
Died: October 19, 1916

John Chipman Kerr

VC: Courcelette, France, September 16, 1916
Born: Fox River, N.S., January 11, 1887
Unit: 49 Battalion, CEF
Died: Port Moody, B.C., February 19, 1963

"[Kerr] advanced about 30 yards into the hostile position before a sentry took alarm and hurled a grenade. [He] saw the grenade coming and ... attempted to protect himself with his arm. He was partially successful ... for ... the bomb ... did no more than blow off the upper joint of his right fore-finger and wound him slightly in the right side.

"The exchange of bombs between the defenders and attackers now became general. ... Good throwing was done by our men ... but Kerr felt that the affair promised to settle into a stationary action unless something new and sudden happened. So he clambered out of the trench ... and moved along the parados until he came into close contact with, and full view of the enemy. ... Despite loss of blood, he was still full of enterprise and fight. He tossed [his] grenades among the crowded defenders beneath him and then opened fire into them with his rifle. ...

"While Kerr pumped lead into the massed enemy beneath his feet he directed the fire of his bombers so effectively, by voice and gesture, that the defenders were forced back to the shelter of the nearest bay. He immediately jumped down into the trench and went after them, with all the Canadian bombers and bayonet-men at his heels. A dug-out was reached ... Kerr went on alone, rounded a bay and once again joined battle with the defenders of the trench. But the spirit of combat, even of resistance, had gone out of them. Up went their hands!

"Before having his wounds dressed, Private Kerr escorted the 62 Germans across open ground, under heavy fire, to a support trench.
Thirty Canadian VCs.

James Cleland Richardson

VC: The Somme, France, October 8, 1916 (Posthumous)
Born: Bellshill, Lanark, Scotland, November 25, 1895
Unit: 16th Battalion, CEF Piper
Died: October 8, 1916

Frederick Maurice Watson Harvey

VC: Guyencourt, France, March 27, 1917
Born: Athboy, County Meath, Ireland, September 1, 1888
Unit: Lord Strathcona's Horse (Royal Canadians), CEF

Thain Wendell MacDowell

VC: Vimy Ridge, France, April 9, 1917
Born: Lachute, Quebec, September 16, 1890
Unit: 38th Battalion, CEF
Died: Nassau, Bahamas, March 29, 1960

William Johnstone Milne

VC: Vimy Ridge, April 9, 1917 (Posthumous)
Born: Wishaw, Scotland, December 21, 1892
Unit: 16th Battalion, CEF
Died: April 9, 1917

Ellis Wellwood Sifton

VC: Vimy Ridge, April 9, 1917 (Posthumous)
Born: Wallacetown, Ont., October 12, 1891
Unit: 18th Battalion, CEF
Died: April 9, 1917

John George Pattison

VC: Vimy Ridge, April 10, 1917
Born: Woolwich, England, September 8, 1875
Unit: 50th Battalion, CEF
Died: June 3, 1917

"[Sometimes, as at Vimy, a company finds itself held] before an embattled fortification whose point of vantage covers the whole local zone of attack ... On that April afternoon the 50th Battn. encountered just such a check. ... Each time they had been beaten back with heavy losses. ... Another attack was organized, with no more success than the last; and then, as so often occurs, a critical situation was relieved by the clearheaded bravery of a single soldier. Private Pattison, an engineer from Calgary, proceeded to deal with the situation. He advanced single-handed towards the machine gun post in a series of short rapid dashes, taking cover on the way in available shell-holes while deciding his next point of vantage. In a few moments he had reached a shell-hole within 30 yards of the vital strong-point. He stood up in full view of the machine gunners and under their point-blank fire threw three bombs with such good aim that the guns were put out of action and the crews temporarily demoralized. This was Pattison's opportunity, and he took it without hesitation. As his last bomb exploded amidst the Germans he rushed across the intervening space, and in a moment was using his bayonet upon the ... enemy. He had killed them all before his companions had caught him up. Twenty minutes later all objectives were gained and the Canadians busy consolidating the captured line. Pattison

came unscathed through the day's fighting and ... the following day; but he never wore his VC He was killed in June."
Thirty Canadian VCs.

Robert Grierson Combe

VC: Acheville, France, May 3, 1917 (Posthumous)
Born: Aberdeen, Scotland, August 5, 1880
Unit: 27th Battalion, CEF
Died: May 3, 1917

William Avery Bishop

VC: Near Cambrai, France, June 2, 1917
Born: Owen Sound, Ont., February 8, 1894
Unit: Royal Flying Corps
Died: Palm Beach Florida, September 11, 1956

"["Billy" Bishop flew with the Royal Flying Corps and was the greatest Commonwealth "ace" of the war. In all, he scored 72 victories over enemy aircraft. He won the Victoria Cross on June 2, 1917, when he crossed the enemy lines alone and attacked a German aerodrome 12 miles behind the front. Four aircraft rose to meet him but Bishop shot three down, one after the other, then emptied his Lewis gun at the fourth machine before escaping to his station.]

"At the age of 24, Bishop had won almost all the coveted awards of war service. ... His late Majesty King George personally pinned the medals on Bishop at Buckingham Palace and told him he was the only man who had received the Victoria Cross, the Military Cross and the Distinguished Service Order at the same time.
The Legionary, March 1940

Harry Brown

VC: Hill 70 (near Lens, France), August 16, 1917 (Posthumous)
Born: Ganonoque, Ont., May 11, 1898
Unit: 10th Battalion, CEF
Died: August 17, 1917

Michael James O'Rourke

VC: Hill 70, August 15-18, 1917
Born: Limerick, Ireland, March 19, 1878
Unit: 7th Battalion, CEF
Died: December 6, 1957

Frederick Hobson

VC: Hill 70, August 18, 1917 (Posthumous)
Born: London, England, September 23, 1875
Unit: 20th Battalion, CEF
Died: August 18, 1917

Okill Massey Learmonth

VC: Hill 70, August 18, 1917 (Posthumous)
Born: Quebec City, February 22, 1894
Service: 2nd Battalion, CEF
Died: August 19, 1917

"When a portion of the company recoiled from the massive assault, the Company Commander [Major Learmonth] leaped in and himself bombed the attacking Germans. ... he was wounded as ... he stood like some flaxen-haired Ajax defying the fires of the enemy. In spite of his wound, he remained. A second time Learmonth was hit. ... The men saw their Company Commander, sorely stricken but still full of fight; and the spectacle inspired them. Wave after wave of the enemy launched the most violent assaults against No. 3 Company, to no purpose. ... For a third time Major Learmonth was wounded. ... He asked to be laid in the trench where ... he continued to direct the resistance. ...

"The time came ... when Learmonth could carry on no longer. Not, however, until he had turned over his command, complete in all details, to Lieut. Hugh Smith, did he consent to be carried out. On his way he insisted on being borne to Battalion Headquarters where, although it was quite apparent that he was dying, he gave to Major Vanderwater a comprehensive verbal report on the whole of the morning's operations."

History of the 2nd Canadian Battalion

Robert Hanna

VC: Hill 70, August 21, 1917
Born: Kilkeel, County Down, Ireland, August 6, 1887
Unit: 29th Battalion, CEF
Died: Mount Lehman, B.C. June 15, 1967

Filip Konowal

VC: Hill 70, August 22-24, 1917
Born: Kedeski, Russia, March 25, 1887
Unit: 47th Battalion, CEF
Died: Ottawa, June 3, 1959

Philip Eric Bent

VC: Polygon Wood, Belgium, October 10, 1917 (Posthumous)
Born: Halifax, N.S. January 3, 1891
Unit: The Leicestershire Regiment (British Army)
Died: October 10, 1917

Thomas William Holmes

VC: Passchendaele, Belgium, October 26, 1917
Born: Montreal, August 17, 1898
Unit: 4th Canadian Mounted Rifles Battalion, CEF
Died: Toronto, January 4, 1950

Robert Shankland

VC: Passchendaele, October 26, 1917
Born: Ayr, Scotland, October 10, 1887
Unit: 43rd Battalion, CEF
Died: Vancouver, January 20, 1968

"By coincidence three VC winners — Segeant-Major F.W. Hall, Corporal Leo Clarke and Lieutenant Shankland — all lived on Pine Street, Winnipeg, which was later renamed Valour Road."

The Legionary, November, 1965.

Christopher Patrick John O'Kelly

VC: Passchendaele, October 26, 1917
Born: Winnipeg, November 18, 1895
Unit: 52nd Battalion, CEF
Died: Lac Seul, Ontario, November 15, 1922

Alan Arnett McLeod

VC: Albert (Somme), France, march 27, 1918
Born: Stonewall, Man., April 20, 1899
Service: Royal Flying Corps
Died: Winnipeg, November 6, 1918

"[2nd Lieutenant Alan McLeod won the V.C. at 18 years of age when flying a slow, two-seater, Armstrong Whitworth bomber-reconnaissance machine which had "the aerodynamics of a cow." He and his observer, Lieutenant Hammond, were attacked by a fast German fighter which they shot down. Seven more Fokker triplanes descended: Hammond shot one down.]

"We jumped up to about five or six thousand feet [McLeod wrote to his parents], and foolishly stayed to scrap with them ... we fought for a while ... Then they got us. By this time I had a few bullets in me, and they were beginning to hurt, when our machine burst into flames."

Letter dated April 8, 1918

"[The entire floor of the aircraft fell out. McLeod climbed on to the wing, controlled the aircraft from there, and managed to flatten out for a crash landing while Hammond climbed out on the edge of the rear cockpit and perched there; from that position he shot down a third Fokker which had approached too close to the stricken aircraft.]

"The story of two men, coming down in flames, flying and fighting with the bottom literally ripped out of their plane — the pilot perched on the wing root with his hand on the control column, the observer sitting on the edge of the cockpit and somehow managing to fire his gun — became part of the tradition of the service."

Knights of the Air

"[They landed in No Man's Land, where the bombs and ammunition started to explode. McLeod, with five wounds, dragged his companion, clear; but he was hit once more and collapsed from loss of blood. South African troops evacuated them from the front line after dark.]"

Edmund De Wind

VC: Near Grougie, France, March 21, 1918 (Posthumous)
Born: Comber, County Down, Ireland, December 11, 1883
Unit: 31st Battalion, CEF, later 15th Battalion, Royal Irish Rifles (British Army)
Died: March 21, 1918

Harcus Strachan

VC: Masnières, France, November 20, 1917
Born: Borrowstounness, Scotland, November 7, 1889
Unit: Fort Garry Horse, CEF

"For most conspicuous bravery and leadership during operations.

"He took command of the squadron of his regiment when the squadron leader ... was killed. Lt. Strachan led the squadron through

the enemy line of machine-gun posts, and then, with the surviving men, led the charge on the enemy battery, killing seven of the gunners with his sword."

London Gazette, December 18, 1917

"The men went forward at the gallop to an objective dear to any cavalryman's heart. A battery of field guns lay before them. A good horse, firm ground and guns to be taken — a cavalryman wants no more. The Canadians charged down upon them, and in a moment were among the guns, riding the gunners down or sabring them as they stood. ... There was a brief mêlée of plunging horses and stumbling artillerymen. Then the business was finished."

The Victoria Cross

"All the gunners having been killed and the battery silenced, he rallied his men and fought his way back at night through the enemy's line, bringing all unwounded men safely in, together with 15 prisoners.

"The operation — which resulted in the silencing of an enemy battery, the killing of the whole battery personnel and many infantry, and the cutting of three main lines of telephone communication two miles in rear of the enemy's front line — was only rendered possible by the outstanding gallantry and fearless leading of this officer."

London Gazette, December 18, 1917

James Peter Robertson

VC: Passchendaele, November 6, 1917 (Posthumous)
Born: Albion Mines, Pictou, Nova Scotia, October 26, 1883
Unit: 27th Battalion, CEF
Died: November 6, 1917

Colin Fraser Barron

VC: Passchendaele, November 6, 1917
Born: Baldavie, Renfrewshire, Scotland, September 20, 1893
Unit: 3rd Battalion, CEF
Died: Toronto, August 15, 1958

George Randolph Pearkes

VC: Passchendaele, October 30-31, 1917
Born: Watford, Hertfordshire, England, February 26, 1888

Unit: 5th Canadian Mounted Rifles Battalion, CEF

"[Pearkes was hit by shrapnel and knocked down. He describes his feelings at the time:] I thought 'Now I've got it!' There seemed to be a little uncertainty among the men alongside me, whether they should go on when I'd been hit. For a moment, I had visions of going back wounded and I said to myself: 'This can't be. I've got to go on for a while anyway, wounded or not.' So I clambered to my feet and I found a stiffness in my left thigh but I was able to move forward ... then the rest of the company all came forward. [After seizing the objectives, and holding them against counter-attacks throughout the day, the survivors (who were by then reduced to a mere handful) were relieved when darkness made it possible. One of them, A.C. Philps, wrote to Pearkes' biographer:] 'I would have followed him through hell if I had to.' "
Information supplied by Dr. R.H. Roy, biographer of General Pearkes

Cecil John Kinross

VC: Passchendaele, October 30, 1917
Born: Uxbridge, Middlesex, England, February 17, 1896
Unit: 49th Battalion, CEF
Died: Lougheed, Alberta, June 21, 1957

Hugh MacKenzie

VC: Passchendaele, October 30, 1917 (Posthumous)
Born: Liverpool, England, December 5, 1885
Unit: 7th Canadian Machine Gun Company, CEF
Died: October 30, 1917

George Harry Mullin

VC: Passchendaele, October 30, 1917
Born: Portland, Ore. August 15, 1892
Unit: Princess Patricia's Canadian Light Infantry, CEF
Died: Regina, Saskatchewan, April 5, 1963

Gordon Muriel Flowerdew

VC: Bois de Moreuil, France, March 30, 1918 (Posthumous)
Born: Billingford, Norfolk, England, January 2, 1885

Unit: Lord Strathcona's Horse (Royal Canadians), CEF
Died: March 31, 1918

George Burdon McKean

VC: Gavrelle Sector (near Vimy Ridge), April 27-28, 1918
Born: Wellington, Durham, England, July 4, 1888
Unit: 14th Battalion, CEF
Died: England, November 28, 1926

Rowland Richard Louis Bourke

VC: Ostend, Belgium, May 10, 1918
Born: London, England, November 28, 1885
Service: Royal Naval Volunteer Reserve
Died: Esquimalt, B.C., August 29, 1958

"[Bourke tried to enlist in the Canadian services when war broke out, but was rejected because of defective eyesight. After joining the Royal Naval Volunteer Reserve in England he commanded a motor launch during a naval attempt to block the port of Ostend, then used by the Germans, in May, 1918. After the raid Bourke searched the smoke-filled harbour for British survivors and, despite machine-gun bursts at close range and heavy shellfire, rescued one officer and two seamen. His launch was hit in 55 places, two of the crew killed and others wounded. Bourke, however, brought her out at reduced speed. He turned the survivors over to a monitor which took his launch in tow.]"
Based on the *London Gazette*, August 28, 1918

Joseph Kaeble

VC: Neuville-Vitasse, France, June 8-9, 1918 (Posthumous)
Born: St. Moise, Quebec, May 5, 1893
Unit: 22nd Battalion, CEF
Died: June 9, 1918

John Bernard Croak

VC: Amiens, France, August 8, 1918 (Posthumous)
Born: Little Bay, Newfoundland, May 18, 1892
Unit: 13th Battalion, CEF
Died: August 8, 1918

Herman James Good

VC: Near Amiens, August 8, 1918
Born: South Bathurst, N.B. November 29, 1887
Unit: 13th Battalion, CEF
Died: Bathurst, N.B., April18, 1969

Harry Garnet Bedford Miner

VC: Demuin, France, August 8, 1918 (Post-humous)
Born: Cedar Springs, Ont., June 24, 1891
Unit: 58th Battalion, CEF
Died: August 8, 1918

Jean Brillant

VC: Méharicourt (near Amiens), August 8-9, 1918 (Posthumous)
Born: Assametquaghan, Que., March 15, 1890
Unit: 22nd Battalion, CEF
Died: August 10, 1918

"On the first day of operations shortly after the attack had begun, his company left flank was held up by an enemy machine-gun. Lt. Brillant rushed and captured the machine-gun, personally killing two of the enemy crew. Whilst doing this, he was wounded, but refused to leave his command.

Later on the same day, his company was held up by heavy machine-gun fire. He reconnoitred the ground personally, organised a party of two platoons and rushed straight for the machine-gun nest. Here 150 enemy and 15 machine-guns were captured, Lt. Brillant personally killing five of the enemy, and being wounded a second time. He had this wound dressed immediately, and again refused to leave his company.

Subsequently this gallant officer detected a field gun firing on his men over open sights. He immediately organised and led a rushing party towards the gun. After progressing about 600 yards, he was again seriously wounded. In spite of this third wound, he continued to advance for some 200 yards more."
London Gazette, September 27, 1918

"Je suis fini, ... dit le blessé, 'prends charge de la compagnie, car je sais que ça ne sera pas long.' "
Histoire du 22e Batallion canadien-français

"[He then fell unconscious from exhaustion and loss of blood, dying on the following day.]"

Raphael Louis Zengel

VC: Amiens, August 9, 1918
Born: Faribault, Minn., November 11, 1894
Unit: 5th Battalion, CEF

Alexander Picton Brereton

VC: Amiens, August 9, 1918
Born: Oak River, Man. November 13, 1892
Unit: 8th Battalion, CEF

Frederick George Coppins

VC: Hackett Wood (Hatchet Wood), Amiens, August 9, 1918
Born: London, England, October 25, 1889
Unit: 8th Battalion, CEF

James Edward Tait

VC: Amiens, August 8-11, 1918 (Posthumous)
Born: Dumfries, Scotland, May 27, 1886
Unit: 78th Battalion, CEF
Died: August 11, 1918

Thomas Dinesen

VC: Parvillers (near Amiens), August 12, 1918
Born: Rungsted, Denmark, August 9, 1892
Unit: 42nd Battalion, CEF

Robert Spall

VC: Parvillers, August 12-13, 1918 (Posthumous)
Born: Ealing, Essex, England, March 5, 1890
Unit: Princess Patricia's Canadian Light Infantry, CEF
Died: August 13, 1918

Charles Smith Rutherford

VC: Monchy-le-Preux, France, August 26, 1918
Born: Colborne, Ont., January 9, 1892
Unit: 5th Canadian Mounted Rifles Battalion, CEF

William Hew Clark-Kennedy

VC: Wancourt, France, August 27-28, 1918

Born: Dunskay, Ayrshire, Scotland, March 3, 1880
Unit: 24th Battalion, CEF
Died: October 25, 1961

Claude Joseph Patrick Nunney

VC: Drocourt-Quéant Line, France, September 1-2, 1918 (Posthumous)
Born: Hastings, England, December 24, 1892
Unit: 38th Battalion, CEF
Died: September 18, 1918

Arthur George Knight

VC: Villers-lez-Cagnicourt (near Arras, France), September 2, 1918 (Posthumous)
Born: Hayward's Heath, Sussex, England, June 26, 1886
Unit: 10th Battalion, CEF
Died: September 3, 1918

William Henry Metcalf

VC: Arras, September 2, 1918
Born: Waite Township, Me., January 2, 1885
Unit: 16th Battalion, CEF
Died: Lewiston, Maine, August 8, 1968

Cyrus Wesley Peck

VC: Villers-lez-Cagnicourt, September 2, 1918
Born: Hopewell Hill, N.B., April 26, 1871
Unit: 16th Battalion, CEF
Died: Sidney, B.C., September 27, 1956

Bellenden Seymour Hutcheson

VC: Drocourt-Quéant Support Line, France, September 2, 1918
Born: Mount Carmel, Ill. December 16, 1883
Service: Canadian Army Medical Corps (attached 75th Battalion, CEF)
Died: Cairo, Illinois, April 9, 1954

John Francis Young

VC: Dury-Arras Sector, September 2, 1918
Born: Kidderminster, England, January 14, 1895
Unit: 87th Battalion CEF
Died: Ste. Agathe, Quebec, November 7, 1929

Walter Leigh Rayfield

VC: Arras, September 2-4, 1918
Born: Richmond-on-Thames, England, October 7, 1881
Unit: 7th Battalion, CEF
Died: Toronto, February 19, 1949

George Fraser Kerr

VC: Bourlon Wood (near Cambrai, France), September 27, 1918
Born: Deseronto, Ont., June 8, 1894
Unit: 3rd Battalion, CEF
Died: Toronto, December 8, 1928

Graham Thomson Lyall

VC: Bourlon Wood, September 27, 1918
Born: Manchester, England, March 8, 1892
Unit: 102nd Battalion, CEF
Died: Mersa Matruh, Egypt (serving in British Army), November 28, 1941

Samuel Lewis Honey

VC: Bourlon Wood, September 27-30, 1918 (Posthumous)
Born: Conn., Ont., February 9, 1894
Unit: 78th Battalion, CEF
Died: September 30, 1918

Milton Fowler Gregg

VC: Near Cambrai, September 27-October 1, 1918
Born: Mountain Dale, N.B., April 10, 1892
Unit: The Royal Canadian Regiment

John MacGregor

VC: Near Cambai, September 29-October 3, 1918
Born: Cawdor, Nairnshire, Scotland, February 11, 1888
Unit: 2nd Canadian Mounted Rifles Battalion, CEF
Died: Powell River, B.C., June 9, 1952

William Merrifield

VC: Abancourt, France, October 1, 1918
Born: Brentwood, England, October 9, 1890
Unit: 4th Battalion, CEF
Died: Toronto, August 8, 1943

Wallace Lloyd Algie

VC: North-east of Cambrai, October 11, 1918 (Posthumous)
Born: Alton, Ont., June 10, 1891
Unit: 20th Battalion, CEF
Died: October 11, 1918

Thomas Ricketts

VC: Ledeghem, Belgium, October 14, 1918
Born: Middle Arm, White Bay, Nfld., April 15, 1901
Unit: 1st Battalion, The Royal Newfoundland Regiment
Died: St. John's, February 10, 1967

"In the platoon's Lewis gun detachment was a young soldier ... Private Thomas Ricketts, who was only 17 years old. Two years previously he had advanced his age to 18 in order to join the Regiment. ...

"King George introduced the youthful Ricketts to Princess Mary and others [at the investiture] saying: 'This is the youngest VC in my army.' "

The Fighting Newfoundlander

"The attack was temporarily held up by heavy hostile fire and the platoon to which he belonged suffered severe casualties from the fire of a battery at point-blank range.

"Pte. Ricketts at once volunteered to go forward with his section commander and a Lewis gun to attempt to outflank the battery. Advancing by short rushes under heavy fire from enemy machine guns with the hostile battery, their ammunition was exhausted when still 300 yards from the battery. The enemy, seeing an opportunity to get their field guns away, began to bring up their gun teams. Pte. Ricketts, at once realising the situation, doubled back 100 yards under the heaviest machine-gun fire, procured further ammunition, and dashed back again to the Lewis gun, and by very accurate fire drove the enemy and the gun teams into a farm.

"His platoon then advanced without casualties, and captured the four field guns, four machine guns and eight prisoners."

"A fifth field gun was subsequently intercepted by fire and captured."

London Gazette, January 6, 1919

William George Barker

VC: Forêt de Mormal, France, October 27, 1918

Born: Dauphin, Man., November 3, 1894
Service: Royal Air Force
Died: Killed in flying accident near Ottawa, March 1, 1930

" 'The spectacle of this attack was the most magnificent encounter of any sort which I ever witnessed. The ancient performances of the gladiators in the Roman arenas were far outclassed in the epic character of the successive engagements in which enemy machines, one after the other, were taken on and eliminated. ... The hoarse shout, or rather the prolonged roar, which greeted the triumph of the British fighter, and which echoed across the battlefront, was never matched in Rome, nor do I think anywhere else.'

"The writer was General Andrew McNaughton, then ... Brigadier-General commanding the Canadian Corps Heavy Artillery. From his advanced headquarters in the Valenciennes area he had witnessed one of the most spectacular air battles of all time. The pilot of the British fighter turned out to be a Canadian. ...

"Major Barker had first attacked a German two-seater high above its own lines, causing it to break up in the air. He afterwards came under a series of attacks, at different levels, by Fokker D VII fighters. Three times he was wounded — first in one leg and then the other, and subsequently in one arm. Twice he fainted and spun down out of control, recovering only to find himself surrounded by Fokkers. Nevertheless he sent three of his opponents down in flames. He finally crash-landed his machine, a Sopwith 'Snipe,' in the British lines. ...

"The fuselage is on display at the Canadian War Museum. The War Museum also holds a portrait of Barker ... and a black and white watercolour painting by R.W. Bradford depicting Barker's great air battle.

"Major Barker ... was now awarded the Victoria Cross, the citation for which concludes: 'This combat, in which Major Barker destroyed four enemy machines ... brought his total successes up to 50 enemy machines destroyed.' "

Major Barker and his Sopwith Snipe

Hugh Cairns

VC: Valenciennes, Nobember 1, 1918
      (Posthumous)
Born: Ashington, Northumberland, England,
      December 4, 1896
Unit: 46th Battalion, CEF
Died: November 2, 1918

John Robert Osborn

VC: Hong Kong, December 19, 1941 (Post-
      humous)
Born: Norfolk, England, January 2, 1899
Unit: 1st Battalion, The Winnipeg Grenadiers
Died: December 19, 1941

A Company of the Winnipeg Grenadiers ... became divided during an attack on Mount Butler ... A part ... led by Company Sergeant-Major Osborn captured the hill at the point of the bayonet and held it for three hours when ... the position became untenable ... With no consideration for his own safety he assisted and directed stragglers to the new Company position exposing himself to heavy enemy fire to cover their retirement. ...

"The Company was ... completely surrounded by the enemy who were able to approach to within grenade throwing distance of the slight depression which the Company were holding. Several enemy grenades were thrown which ... Osborn picked up and threw back. The enemy threw a grenade which landed in a position where it was impossible to pick it up and return it in time. Shouting a warning to his comrades this gallant Warrant Officer threw himself on the grenade which exploded killing him instantly."

Canada Gazette, April 6, 1946

The British named a barracks after Osborn, at Hong Kong.

Charles Cecil Ingersoll Merritt

VC: Dieppe, August 19, 1942
Born: Vancouver, November 10, 1908
Unit: The South Saskatchewan Regiment

John Wier Foote

VC: Dieppe, August 19, 1942
Born: Madoc, Ontario, May 5, 1904
Service: Canadian Chaplain Services, at-
         tached to The Royal Hamilton Light
         Infantry

"[The Reverend John Foote was the first member of the Canadian Chaplain Services ever to win the Victoria Cross.]

"Gallantry was shown in no sudden blaze of violent action but coolly and calmly through eight hours of the gruelling, terrible battle of Dieppe, in which he '... exposed himself to an inferno of fire and saved many lives by his gallant efforts ... his example inspired all around him. Those who observed him state that the calmness of this heroic man as he walked about, collecting the wounded on the fireswept beach, will never be forgotten.

"Then, at the end of his trial by fire, he climbed from the landing craft that was to have taken him to safety, and walked courageously into the German positions, that he might be taken prisoner and so minister to those men whose fate for the next three years was to be barbed wire and chains.

The Legionary, March, 1946

Frederick Thornton Peters

VC: Oran, North Africa, November 8, 1942
Born: Charlottetown, P.E.I., September 17,
      1889
Service: Royal Navy
Died: November 11, 1943

"[H.M.S. Walney and H.M.S. Hartland were two ex-American coastguard ships that were lost in a gallant attempt to force the boom defences in the harbour of Oran during the landings on the North African coast.] Captain Peters led his force through the boom towards the jetty in the face of point-blank fire from shore batteries, a Destroyer and a Cruiser. Blinded in one eye, he alone of the 17 officers and men on the bridge survived. The Walney reached the jetty disabled and ablaze, and went down with her colours flying."

London Gazette, May 18, 1943

Paul Triquet

VC: Casa Berardi, Italy, December 14,
      1943
Born: Cabano, Quebec, April 2, 1910
Service: Royal 22e Régiment

"The capture of the key road junction on the main Ortona-Orsogna lateral was entirely dependent on securing the hamlet of Casa Berardi ... Captain Triquet's company ... with the support of a squadron of a Canadian armoured regiment, was given the task of crossing the gully and securing Casa Berardi ... The gully was held in strength and on approaching it the force came under heavy fire from machine guns and mortars. All the company officers and 50 per cent of the men were killed or wounded. Showing superb contempt for the enemy, Captain Triquet went round reorganizing the remainder and encouraging them with the words 'Never mind them, they can't shoot. ... There are enemy in front of us, behind us, and on our flanks, there is only one safe place, that is on the objective.' ... [He] dashed forward and with his men following him, broke through the enemy resistance. In this action four tanks were destroyed and several enemy machine gun posts silenced. ...

"Captain Triquet and his company, in close co-operation with the tanks, forced their way on until a position was reached on the outskirts of Casa Berardi. By this time the strength of the company was reduced to two sergeants and 15 men. In expectation of a counter attack, Captain Triquet at once set about organizing his handful of men into a defensive perimeter around the remaining tanks and passed the *mot d'ordre* 'Ils ne passeront pas.' A German counter attack supported by tanks developed almost immediately. Captain Triquet ... was everywhere encouraging his men and directing the defence, and by using whatever weapons were to hand personally accounted for several of the enemy. This and subsequent attacks were beaten off with heavy losses and Captain Triquet and his small force held out against overwhelming odds until the remainder of the battalion took Casa Berardi and relieved them the next day."

Canada Gazette, March 11, 1944

Charles Ferguson Hoey

VC: Maungdaw, Burma, February 16, 1944 (Posthumous)
Born: Duncan, B.C., March 29, 1914
Unit: 1st Battalion, The Lincolnshire Regiment
Died: February 16, 1944

John Keefer Mahony

VC: Melfa River, Italy, May 24, 1944
Born: New Westminster, B.C., June 30, 1911

Unit: The Westminster Regiment (Motor)

Andrew Charles Mynarski

VC: Over Cambrai, June 12, 1944 (Posthumous)
Born: Winnipeg, October 14, 1916
Service: Royal Canadian Air Force
Died: June 12, 1944

"Pilot Officer Mynarski was the mid-upper gunner of a Lancaster aircraft detailed to attack a target at Cambrai in France, on the night of 12th June, 1944. The aircraft was attacked from below and astern by an enemy fighter ... Fire broke out ... and the captain ordered the crew to abandon the aircraft ... Mynarski left his turret and went towards the escape hatch. He then saw that the rear gunner was still in his turret and apparently unable to leave it ...

"Without hesitation ... Mynarski made his way through the flames in an endeavour to reach the rear turret and release the gunner. Whilst so doing, his parachute and his clothing, up to the waist, were set on fire. All his efforts to move the turret and free the gunner were in vain. Eventually the rear gunner clearly indicated that he should try to save his own life. Pilot Officer Mynarski reluctantly went back through the flames to the escape hatch. There, as a last gesture to the trapped gunner, he turned towards him, stood to attention in his flaming clothes and saluted, before he jumped out of the aircraft. ... He was found eventually by the French, but was so severely burnt that he died from his injuries."

London Gazette, October 11, 1946

The rear gunner miraculously survived the crash.

David Ernest Hornell

VC: Shetland Islands, June 24, 1944 (Posthumous)
Born: Mimico, Ont., January 26, 1910
Service: Royal Canadian Air Forces
Died: June 25, 1944

"Flight Lieutenant Hornell was captain and first air pilot of a twin-engined amphibian aircraft engaged on an anti-submarine patrol in northern waters. The patrol had lasted some hours when a fully-surfaced U-boat was sighted. ... The U-boat opened up with anti-aircraft fire which became increasingly fierce and accurate. ... He brought his aircraft down very low and released his depth charges in a perfect straddle. The bows of the U-boat were lifted out of the water; it sank and members of the crew were seen in the sea.

"Flight Lieutenant Hornell contrived, by superhuman efforts at the controls, to gain a little height ... fire in the starboard wing had grown more intense and the vibration had increased. Then the burning engine fell off. ... With the utmost coolness, the captain took his aircraft into the wind and, despite the manifold dangers, brought it safely down on the heavy swell. Badly damaged and blazing furiously, the aircraft rapidly settled.

"After ordeal by fire came ordeal by water. There was only one serviceable dinghy and this could not hold all the crew. So they took turns in the water, holding on to the sides. ... The survivors were finally rescued after they had been in the water for 21 hours. By this time ... Hornell was blinded and completely exhausted. He died shortly after being picked up."

London Gazette, July 28, 1944

Ian Willoughby Bazalgette

VC: Trossy St. Maximin, France, August 4, 1944 (Posthumous)
Born: Calgary, October 19, 1918
Service: Royal Air Force

David Vivian Currie

VC: St. Lambert-sur-Dives, France, August 18, 1944
Born: Sutherland, Sask., July 8, 1912
Unit: 29th Armoured Reconnaissance Regiment (The South Alberta Regiment)

"Major Currie first attacked and seized the village [St. Lambert-sur-Dives] which was a key point of the Chambois-Trun escape route for the remnants of two German armies cut off in the Falaise pocket. He held it through three days and nights of continuous fighting hurling back repeated enemy attempts to force a breakthrough. His strategy was successful in blocking the German escape route. ... [He] took his tiny force of tanks, anti-tank guns and infantry and thrust them in

the path of vastly superior forces and firepower. ...

"When two of his tanks were knocked out he went on foot through many enemy outposts successfully to extricate the crews of his disabled tanks. ...

"Says the citation:

" 'Throughout the operations the casualties to Major Currie's force were heavy. However, he never considered the possibility of failure or allowed it to enter the minds of his men. In the words of one of his non-commissioned officers 'We knew at one stage that it was going to be a fight to the finish, but he was so cool about it, it was impossible for us to get excited.'

"In a final assault, Major Currie's little band destroyed seven enemy tanks, twelve 88-millimeter guns and 40 vehicles, killed 300 Germans, wounded 500 and captured 1100 more. He then ordered an attack and completed the capture of the village."

The Legionary, January 1945

Ernest Alvia Smith

VC: Savio River, Italy, October 21-22, 1944
Born: New Westminster, B.C., May 3, 1914
Unit: The Seaforth Highlanders of Canada

Aubrey Cosens

VC: Mooshof, Germany, February 25-26, 1945 (Posthumous)
Born: Latchford, Ont., May 21, 1921
Unit: The Queen's Own Rifles of Canada

Frederick Albert Tilston

VC: The Hochwald, Germany, March 1, 1945
Born: Toronto, June 11, 1906
Unit: The Essex Scottish Regiment

"On the western edge of the Hochwald one man epitomized the spirit which finally won the forest and the route across the Rhine. He is Freddie Tilston, the man who 'never would make an officer.'

"It's his first attack as a company commander and his last. Across 500 yards of open ground with no tank support, Major Tilston leads his company just behind the creeping barrage. He is wounded, for the first time, in the head. Into enemy trenches he charges, firing his Sten from the hip. His left platoon comes under heavy fire. He dashes forward and silences the machine gun with a grenade.

"He approaches the wood. Flying steel smashes into his hip and he falls. he waves his men on, then struggles to his feet and catches up.

"His wounds are forgotten as he leads the sadly depleted company into hand to hand fighting with the enemy. ...

"Fred Tilston consolidates his position ... then stumbles from platoon to platoon urging his men to hold the vicious counter attacks which slash into grenade-throwing distance.

"His ammunition runs low and ... [Tilston] crosses the bullet-swept ground to the company on the left to replenish the supply of grenades and bullets. Six times he lurches across the deadly killing ground; but this was no ordinary man the enemy soldiers squinted at through their sights. He just couldn't be killed or stopped.

"But on his last trip he is hit again, in the other leg. this time he stays on the ground. ... His concern was not for his shattered legs, but only to pass on the plan and to urge his men to hold.

"And as medical assistance finally came, his only words were: 'We held.' "

The Legionary, March 1955

Frederick George Topham

VC: East of the Rhine, March 24, 1945
Born: Toronto, August 10, 1917
Unit: 1st Canadian Parachute Battalion

"[Corporal Topham, a medical orderly, parachuted with his battalion on to a strongly defended area east of the Rhine.]

"During this fighting ... Topham won the fourth Victoria Cross awarded to a Canadian during the campaign. As he treated casualties after the drop, Topham heard a cry for help from a wounded man in the open. The recommendation for the decoration continues:

'Two medical orderlies from a field ambulance went out to this man in succession but both were killed as they knelt beside the casualty. Without hesitation and on his own initiative Corporal Topham went forward through intense fire to replace the orderlies who had been killed before his eyes. As he worked on the wounded man, he was himself shot through the nose. Inspite of severe bleeding and intense pain he never

faltered in his task. Having completed immediate first aid, he carried the wounded man steadily and slowly back through continuous fire to the shelter of the woods.'

"Refusing assistance for his own wound, he continued to perform his duties for two hours, until all casualties had been evacuated from the area. Then, having successfully resisted orders for his own removal, he rescued three men from a burning carrier at great risk from exploding ammunition. His heroic conduct serves to emphasize the great debt owed by the Army to its medical services."

The Victory Campaign

Robert Hampton Gray

VC: Onagawa Wan, Japan, August 9, 1945
      (Posthumous)
Born: Trail, B.C., November 2, 1917
Service: Royal Canadian Naval Volunteer
         Reserve (attached to the Fleet Air
         Arm of the Royal Navy)

"On August 9 — the day the A-bomb was dropped on Nagasaki — the Corsairs roared off again for Japan. As they approached Onagawa Wan, smudges of flak told the pilots it would be a difficult target.

"Fire from the enemy anti-aircraft guns was intense at the Corsairs peeled off to attack warships in the bay. Gray drew a bead on a destroyer and swung onto an attacking course. His aircraft was immediately coned by fire from ship and shore. Shells and tracer ripped the diving aircraft. Flame and smoke plumed out behind. But Gray held his course. As the plane dived closer through the punishing flak, Gray's wingmates sensed what was happening.

"It was a matter of split-seconds and courage now. Would the plane hold together long enough? The wounded Corsair screamed to within 150 feet of the destroyer ... 100 feet ... 75 feet ... Gray was now beyond the limits of ordinary courage. He could have dropped his bombs from a safer height and preserved a bit of precious altitude.

"Even with a badly damaged aircraft, at some point on the run he made his decision. If he released his bombs and pulled up, he might make it back to the carrier. At worst, it would probably mean a ditching. But he didn't pull up. He dived to within 50 feet of the enemy destroyer before dropping bombs.

One struck directly amid-ships. A second bomb either hit the target or exploded ... alongside. The destroyer sank almost immediately."

Valour Unlimited

THE GEORGE CROSS

The George Cross was instituted by King George VI in 1940. The decoration is the second-highest award for bravery in the Commonwealth. The award is presented for "acts of the greatest heroism or of the most conspicuous courage in circumstances of extreme danger" to civilians and members of the armed forces.

The decoration is a silver cross which bears a representation of Saint George slaying the dragon and the words: "For Gallantry." The ribbon is garter blue.

Ernest Ralph Clyde Frost

GC: R.A.F. Station, West Raynham, England March 12, 1940
Born: Three Rivers, Que., July 22, 1917
Service: Royal Air Force and Royal Canadian Air Force
Died: Sarnia, Ontario, July 28, 1969

John MacMillan Stevenson Patton

GC: Weybridge, Surrey, England, September 21, 1940
Born: Warwick, Bermuda, August 29, 1915
Unit: 1st Battalion, Royal Canadian Engineers

James Hendry

GC: Loch Laggan, Scotland, June 13, 1941 (Posthumous)
Born: Falkirk, Scotland, December 20, 1911
Unit: No 1 Tunnelling Company, RCE

Karl Mander Gravell

GC: Simons Valley, Alberta, November 10, 1941 (Posthumous)
Born: Norrköping, Sweden, September 27, 1922
Service: Royal Canadian Air Force
Died: November 10, 1941

Gordon Lowe Bastian

GC: 500 miles off Brest, France, March 30, 1943
Born: Barry, Wales, March 30, 1902. First came to Canada in 1927.
Service: Merchant Navy (British)

"The ship in which Mr. Bastian was serving was torpedoed and sustained severe damage. Mr. Bastian was on watch in the engine-room when the ship was struck. He at once shut off the engines. He then remembered that two firemen were on watch in the stoke-hold. The engine-room was in darkness and water was already pouring into it. Although there was grave risk of disastrous flooding in opening the watertight door between the stokehead and engine-room, Mr. Bastian did not hesitate but groped his way to the door and opened it. The two firemen were swept into the engine-room with the inrush of water. One man had a broken arm and injured feet and the other was badly bruised and shaken. Mr. Bastian made efforts to hold them both but lost one, so he dragged the other to the escape ladder and helped him on deck. He then returned for the other and helped him to safety. The more seriously injured man had practically to be lifted up the ladder by Mr. Bastian, who was himself half choked by cordite fumes.

"Second Engine Officer Bastian took a very great risk in opening the watertight door into the already flooded and darkened engine-room of the sinking ship and both men undoubtedly owe their lives to his exceptional bravery, strength and presence of mind."

London Gazette, August 17, 1043

Kenneth Gerald Spooner

GC: Over Lake Erie, May 14, 1943 (Posthumous)
Born: Smiths Falls, Ont., May 24, 1922
Service: Royal Canadian Air Force
Died: May 14, 1943

John Rennie

GC: Slough, England, October 29, 1943 (Posthumous)
Born: Aberdeen, Scotland, December 13, 1920
Service: The Argyll and Sutherland Highlanders of Canada

Died: October 29, 1943

Arthur Dwight Ross

GC: R.A.F. Station Tholthorpe, Yorkshire, England, June 28, 1944
Born: Winnipeg, March 18, 1907
Service: Royal Canadian Air Force

"[Air Commodore Ross] was about to enter the debriefing room [when] there was a great yellow flash on the airfield. Running to the scene Ross found that an Alouette Squadron aircraft, returning from the operation on three engines, had crashed into another aircraft ... loaded with bombs. By the time he arrived both aircraft were burning fiercely with gas tanks and bombs in imminent danger of exploding.

"A/C Ross immediately took charge, assisted by Flight Sergeant J.R. St. Germain, the bomb aimer of another aircraft, Corporal M. Marquet and leading Aircraftmen M.M. McKenzie and R.R. Wolfe. A/C Ross and Marquet had just extricated the pilot when ten 500-pound bombs exploded. The rescuers were hurled to the ground. Undeterred by the flames which were now rapdily approaching the tail, the Air Commodore, assisted by St. Germain, McKenzie and Wolfe, turned his attention to the imprisoned rear gunner of the Alouette. ... Finally St. Germain and Marquet had to break the steel supports of the turret to extricate the gunner. Just then another bomb explosion threw the rescuers to the ground again. St. Germain, rising quickly, covered one of the victims with his own body to protect him. The Air Commodore was struck by flying debris and lost his right hand.

"Turning the further rescues over to his assistants Ross walked to the ambulance. ... In the meantime Marquet, seeing that the burning petrol endangered two aircraft, supervised their removal while Mckenzie and Wolfe continued their efforts to extinguish the fire. The entire crew of the Alouette aircraft was saved. Of the rescuers, McKenzie and Wolfe were injured as well as Ross. For their deeds in this incident St. Germain and Marquet received the George Medal. McKenzie and Wolfe were awarded the British Empire Medal."

The Dangerous Sky

Roderick Borden Gray

GC: Atlantic Ocean, August 27, 1944 (Posthumous)
Born: Sault Ste. Marie, Ont., October 2, 1917
Service: Royal Canadian Air Force

"[Flying Officer Gray was the navigator of a Coastal Command Wellington bomber that had spotted a German U-boat in the Atlantic. The bomber attacked, straddled the submarine with depth charges, but was itself set on fire by gunfire and crashed into the sea. Two of the crew were trapped in the aircraft but Gray and three others managed to extricate themselves. A survivor, Warrant Officer Gordon S. Bulley, reports:]

"When I got to the surface I saw Cy [Gray] had managed to escape with a dinghy only large enough to hold one man. ... Then we ... heard the skipper calling for help ... He had been badly wounded. He couldn't move his right side. His left hand was badly smashed and his face was cut. Cy was also seriously injured and he told us he was sure his leg had been broken. For my own part I was quite OK. ...

"Not long after we got the skipper into the dinghy we heard cries for help coming from the other air gunner, F/Sgt. Ford. Cy and I both swam around and finally located him in the darkness. He had a broken arm and could not swim. We hauled him into the dinghy and put him on top of the skipper. ... Cy and I clung to the dinghy until dawn. ...

"[Gray's companions begged him to get in but he refused. Knowing that the dinghy was already overloaded, he remained in the water clinging to the side.]

"When dawn finally broke Cy showed no sign of life. We tried to shake him and immediately realized he was dead. There was nothing for us to do but cut him loose from the dinghy.

"[During the afternoon a Sunderland flying boat rescued the three survivors.]"

The Legionary, May 1945

Arthur Richard Cecil Butson

GC: Grahamland, Antarctica, July 27, 1947
Born: Hankow, China, October 24, 1922
Came to Canada in 1952.

TOMMY PRINCE

Prince was decorated twice by George VI for valour in the Second World War, and in the Korean War he received 10 medals, including the U.S. Silver Cross and the Military Medal.

The grandson of Saulteaux chief Pagius, Prince died at the age of 62 in Winnipeg. He was Canada's most decorated Indian.

CANADIAN WAR HEROES BEHIND ENEMY LINES

Canadians Behind Enemy Lines, by Roy MacLaren (published in 1981), is an account of Canadian war heroes whose stories have never been told or have been, for the most part, forgotten.

Hundreds of Canadians served behind enemy lines in Europe and Asia, but few came home.

Gustave Bieler, a Montreal school teacher was the first of many bilingual French-Canadians who parachuted into enemy territory as saboteurs during the Second World War.

Bieler was badly injured on the drop in November 1942 and spent weeks recuperating under an assumed name in a Paris hospital. Later, still badly crippled, he began recruiting workers to sabotage railway lines in the area. His 25 sabotage teams managed in one month in 1943 to cut the Cologne-Maris line 13 times. They destroyed one troop train and derailed 20 others.

He was captured in 1944, and was interrogated and tortured by the Gestapo for three months before being sent to a concentration camp. Again, he was tortured and starved, yet when he faced a German firing squad in September 1944, his courage moved the Germans to accord him a guard of honour.

Canadians fought behind the lines in the Pacific war as well. Henry Fung, 19, from Vancouver, and Charlie Chang of Toronto were with four or five Chinese Canadian volunteers (despite the fact that Chinese Canadians were not permitted to vote until 1947) who were dropped in the Malayan jungles where they recruited guerrillas to fight against the Japanese.

HEROIC CANADIAN BATTLES OF THE FIRST WORLD WAR

The Second Battle at Ypres, 1915

The Canadian 1st Contingent held off an attack by some of Germany's best troops despite suffering the first gas attack in modern warfare.

Vimy Ridge, 1917

All four divisions of the Canadian Corps fought brilliantly to capture an enemy position considered impregnable.

Moreuil wood, 1918

The Canadian Cavalry Brigade fought courageously and slowed down the German offensive.

Heroic Canadian Battles of The Second World War

Two thousand unseasoned and ill-equipped troops were sent to Hong Kong in 1941. They held out against the Japanese for more than two weeks. When they surrendered, more than a third of the troops had been killed or wounded. The survivors were imprisoned, in terrible conditions, for more than three and a half years. Five hundred and fifty-seven of the men who left Vancouver in 1941 did not return.

Dieppe, 1942

Often called a rehearsal for D-day, the Dieppe landing had been revealed earlier to the Germans. Thus, in the first amphibious operation in the European war, Canadian soldiers came under heavy fire as they hit the beach in front of the town. Of the 4,963 Canadian soldiers in the raid, 907 were killed and 1,946 were captured.

Ortona, 1954

The battle for Ortona, Sicily, in 1943 was fought against elite German paratroopers in dirty house-to-house combat. The Canadians took the port in December, and went on to help break through enemy lines at the Liri Valley and the Foglia River.

D-Day, 1944

Fifteen thousand Canadian troops landed with the Allies on the beaches of Normandy in June 1944 and were the first of the allied troops to meet their planned objective.

Schedlt Estuary, 1944-45

The 1st Canadian Army fought its way through the coastal towns of France, Belgium, Holland and Germany, and after a long and extremely bitter struggle cleared the Germans out of the Schedlt Estuary, and opened a supply route permitting the Allies to make the final onslaught on Nazi Germany.

ORDER OF MILITARY MERIT

Government of Canada

The Queen is the Sovereign of the Order which was created on July 1, 1972, to recognize meritorious service and devotion to duty by members of the Canadian Forces. The Order has three grades of membership: Commander (CMM), Officer (OMM), and Member (MMM).

Commander of Military Merit

1982 **Brigadier-General Blake Baile**, CD, Trail, B.C. Baile began his military career in 1947 and served with the Seaforth Highlanders before transferring to the Regular force in 1950.

Assigned to the 2nd Battalion, the Royal Canadian Regiment (RCR), he served in Korea, London (Ont.), and the Federal Republic of Germany. From 1966 to 1968 he commanded RCR in Soest, Germany, after which he became an assistant chief of staff at the Allied Command Europe Mobile Force at Seckenheim. Following a number of staff appointments, he was promoted to his present rank in 1976 and appointed commander of the Canadian Contingent, United Nations, Middle East. In August 1980, he assumed command of Northern Region with headquarters in Yellowknife, N.W.T.

Commodore Constantine Cotaras, CD, Vancouver, B.C. joined the Royal Canadian Navy, University Naval Training Division, in 1948, graduated from Royal Roads in 1950, and from the Royal Naval College, Greenwich, England in 1953. He served aboard minesweepers and destroyers before being appointed to command the minesweeper HMCS *Miramichi* in 1961. Following staff appointments, he took command of the destroyer escort HMCS *Ottawa* and later, the hydrofoil HMCS *Bras D'Or*. He attended the U.S. Naval War College before taking command of the destroyer escort HMCS *Yukon*. In 1976 he was named commander, Fifth Canadian Destroyer Squadron, at Halifax. Promoted to his present rank in 1977, he became chief of staff, sea, and later chief of staff, plans and operations, at Maritime Command Headquarters in Halifax. In 1981 he was appointed commandant of the Canadian Forces College, Toronto.

Major-General William George Paisley, CD, Nipawin, Sask. Paisley enrolled in the Royal Canadian Air Force in 1947. Trained as a pilot, he served in Chatham, N.B., Odiham, England, Bagotville, Que., Zweibrucken, Federal Republic of Germany, and Metz, France. In 1964, he was appointed commanding officer of 6 Strike and Reconnaissance Operational Training Unit, at Cold Lake, Alta. After attending the United States Air Warfare College he returned to Zweibrucken to assume command of 430 Fighter Squadron. In 1977, he was promoted brigadier-general and took command of 1 Canadian Air Group with headquarters in Lahr, Germany. In 1980, he was named chief of staff, operations, at Air Command Headquarters, in Winnipeg. Major-General Paisley was promoted to his present rank in July, 1982, and named commander of the Fighter Group as well as commander of the 22nd NORAD Region, both located at CFB North Bay, Ont.

Officer of Military Merit

Lieutenant-Colonel Robert Paul Alden, CD, of Saint John, N.B., 4 Canadian Mechanized Brigade Group, Lahr, Federal Republic of Germany.

Lieutenant-Colonel Edward Norman Berntson, CD, of Glen Ewen, Sask., CFB Comox, B.C.

Captain (N) Donald George MacPhail Chown, CD, of Kingston, Ont., HMCS *Cataraqui*, Kingston, Ont.

Major Terrence Jude Christopher, CD, of Sydney, N.S., Directorate Personnel Selection, Research and Second Careers, National Defence Headquarters, Ottawa.

Lieutenant-Colonel (retired) John Edward Dardier, CD, of Ottawa.

Captain (N) (retired) David Redford Donaldson, CD, of Ottawa.

Major Joseph Robert Russell Doyon, CD, of Kirkland Lake, Ont., Cobat Training Centre, Artillery School, Gagetown, N.B.

Major Dawson Wray Einarson, CD, of Capreol, Ont., The Princess of Wales Own Regiment, Kingston, Ont.

Major Hugh Lloyd King, CD, of St. Lambert, Que., Air Transport Group, CFB Trenton, Ont.

Chief Petty Officer 1st Class Frederick Gilbert McKee, MMM, CD, of Montreal, Canadian Forces Chief Warrant Officer, National Defence Headquarters, Ottawa. This is a promotion within the Order.

Lieutenant-Governor (retired) Harold Edward Miskiman, CD, of Toronto.

Commander Lawrence Edward Murray, CD,

of Stratford, Ont., Maritime Command Headquarters, Halifax.

Lieutenant-Colonel James Lee Senecal, CD, of Edmonton, CFB Gagetown, N.B.

Lieutenant-Colonel Guy Claude Tousignant, CD, of Sherbrooke, Que., Director Procurement and Supply Services, at NDHQ, Ottawa.

Lieutenant-Colonel Ronald Edward Werry, CD, of Winnipeg, The Royal Winnipeg Rifles, Winnipeg.

Colonel Michael Marko Zrymiak, CD, of Glenavon, Sask., Air Reserve Group Headquarters, CFB Winnipeg.

Thirty-four members of the Canadian Regular and Reserve Forces were appointed Members (MMM) of the Order of Military Merit in 1982.

CHIEF OF THE DEFENCE STAFF COMMENDATION

National Defence, Canada

The Chief of the Defence Staff Commendation may be awarded to any member of the Canadian Forces who has performed a deed or activity that is considered beyond the demands of normal duty. It may also be awarded to a member of the armed forces of a country other than Canada for an achievement of meritorious service that is of benefit to Canada and the Canadian Forces.

The commendation is a framed, gold-embossed scroll. The symbol for the Commendation is worn below the button on the left breast pocket of the CF uniform and is a gold bar with three maple leaves.

1982   **Major Michael Eric Hugh Pinfold**, CD
      Captain James Hugh Carnegie, CD
      Captain James Frederick Cottingham
      Captain Nigel Field
      Captain Allan Donald MacQuarrie, CD
      Captain Harvey Paul Richard Smith, CD
      Lieutenant David William Amberley
      Lieutenant Charles Cue, CD
      Lieutenant Benjamin Alexander Leveille

Master Warrant Officer Jacques Renaudin, CD
Warrant Officer Robert Leroy Foston, CD
Petty Officer 1st Class Charles Frederick Wilson, CD
Sergeant Steven F. MacLean, CD
Petty Officer 2nd Class William Lawrence McGuire, CD
Sergeant John Mount
Sergeant William David Townsend, CD
Petty Officer 2nd Class Jules Joseph Verhaeghe, CD
Master Corporal Paul D'Amours, CD
Master Corporal David William Hutchinson, CD
Master Corporal Marcel Richard L'Archeveque, CD
Master Corporal Anthony B. Martin
Master Corporal Brian Neil McMillan, CD
Master Corporal Joseph Donald Rogers, CD
Master Corporal James Paul West, CD
Corporal Jean Savard
Trooper Jacques M.J. Hébert.
Lieutenant-Commander (USN) David Charles Cradduck

SPY SIGNALLED OUTBREAK OF WAR

Eric Curwain, who settled in Toronto following the Second World War, was the secret agent who, while hidden beneath the rafters of the British Embassy in Warsaw in September 1939, sent the Morse code message of the German attack on Poland that signalled the outbreak of the war.

Years later, in Port Credit, Ont., Curwain recalled, "It was on the basis of that message that Britain declared war."

Curwain, who entered the British secret service in 1938, was born in Cambridge, England. He fled Poland following the Nazi invasion. Later he came to Canada using the alias Bill Simpson and found amateur radio operators who were trained at the Allied espionage base, Camp X, near Oshawa. He was in Hungary at the end of the war.

He taught languages in Ontario after the war and did public relations work. He retired in 1970 and died in 1983.

BATTLE OF BRITAIN, 1940

Hundreds of Canadians, including a single poorly equipped RCAF squadron, fought in the skies over England in the Battle of Britain in 1940, and struck a devastating blow to the Nazi Luftwaffe.

BATTLE OF THE ATLANTIC, 1939-45

The people at home built the ships and the men of the Royal Canadian Navy and the Canadian Merchant Marine sailed them in gradually larger and larger convoys. Without the supplies from North America there would have been no allied victory over Germany. They fought the storms of the North Atlantic and the German submarine fleet.

MORE FAMOUS CANADIAN COMMANDING OFFICERS

Colonel John Butler, a United Empire Loyalist, formed Butler's Rangers and fought against American forces in Maryland, Kentucky, and along the Mohawk Trail. The Rangers captured Daniel Boone at Blue Licks, in 1782. Butler was a cousin of George Washington.

Lieutenant-Colonel George T. Dennison, a veteran of the Fenian Raids, wrote a book, *Modern Cavalry*, published in 1868, considered one of the best on cavalry tactics.

General J.A. Dextrase, CBE, CMM, DSO, CD., commanded the Fusiliers Mont-Royal in Europe in 1944. A brilliant tactician, he was recalled from private life to command the 2nd Battalion, Royal 22nd Regiment, in Korea. He was the first French-Canadian to be named Chief of the General Staff.

Lieutenant-General Sir Arthur Currie was a lieutenant-colonel in 1914 who in 1916 became Commander of the Canadian Corps. He was the only militia officer ever to command a Canadian force in a major war.

Lieutenant-General Guy Granville Simmonds CB, CBE, DSO, CD. Considered by many as the most outstanding Canadian General in the Second World War, he was Chief of the General Staff from 1951 to 1955.

REGIMENT CELEBRATES CENTENNIAL

The Royal Canadian Regiment, Canada's senior regular infantry regiment, marked its centennial in 1983.

The regiment, whose colonel-in-chief is Prince Philip, served in the Riel rebellion, the Trail of '98, the Klondike gold rush, the Boer War, the First World War, the Second World War and Korea.

THE QUIET CANADIAN: SIR WILLIAM STEPHENSON, INTREPID

Sir William Stephenson, Military Cross, Distinguished Flying Cross, 1914-1915 Star, General Service Medal, World War I Victory Medal (British); Commander of the Legion of Honour, Croix de Guerre with Palms (French); Croix de Guerre with Palms (Belgian); Presidential Medal for Merit (first non-American to receive this decoration) and the Badge of Knighthood (British).

Williamson, "the Quiet Canadian" who was also called "Intrepid," grew up in Winnipeg and in 1914 joined the Royal Canadian Engineers. Crippled by a gas attack, he transferred to the Royal Flying School, and shot down 26 aircraft. He was captured in 1918 but escaped to the Allied lines.

Between the wars he became an extremely successful scientist and industrialist. He realized early the horrific threat of the Nazis and began to devote more and more of his time and energy to working against them. In 1940 he was entrusted with a grave responsibility by Winston Churchill when he undertook to establish a worldwide intelligence network for the Allies and maintain a secret liaison between Churchill and Roosevelt. His contribution to the war effort may never be fully disclosed. The book *A Man Called Intrepid*, by Toronto author William Stevenson, is a stimulating account of the hidden story.

"It is difficult for laymen to comprehend how one shadowy figure, through undercover operations, could have exercised on the fate of the Western world an influence so indispensable to its survival. Was this not genius?" — General Sir Colin Gubbins, KCMG, DSO, MC.

A SOLDIER FOR PEACE

Lieutenant-General E.L.M. (Tommy) Burns is one of the most distinguished generals in Canadian history.

He served in both world wars, was Deputy Minister of Veteran Affairs, a Special Advisor to the Department of External Affairs and was then seconded to the United Nations.

He served as Chief of Staff of the Truce Supervision Organization in Palestine from 1954 to 1956 and was on the scene when the Suez Crisis broke out in 1956. He commanded the UN Emergency Force in the Suez from 1956 until 1959 demonstrating his skill as a negotiator with national and local authorities in the area.

In 1960 General Burns became Canada's principal disarmament negotiator and became a passionate champion of arms control and peace.

In 1981 he said: "Unlimited expenditure and research to create a magic weapon system that will bring superiority in a nuclear-armed world will only increase the danger of a holocaust." Take it from an old soldier.

OUTSTANDING CADET AWARDS

Army Cadet League of Canada

Air Canada Award

Presented to the two outstanding male cadets attending the Cadet Leadership and Challenge Course at the national Army Cadet Camp at Banff, Alta. The winners receive an all-expenses-paid trip to Barbados from Air Canada and the Army Cadet League of Canada.

1982   **Simon Asselin**, 2623 South Shore Cadet Corps, St-Hubert, Que.
Richard Doyon, 2625 Corps de Cadets, St-Georges de Beauce, Que.

CP Air Award

Presented to the two outstanding cadets graduating from the Cadet Parachutist Course at the Canadian Airborne Centre, Edmonton, Alta. Winners receive an all-expenses-paid trip to any point served by CP Air on its Canadian network from CP Air and the Army Cadet League of Canada.

1982   **Kevin Hayes**, 1856 Moose Jaw Schools Cadet Corps, Moose Jaw, Sask.
Mike Sox, 2313 South Alberta Light Horse Cadet Corps, Medicine Hat, Alta.

Centennial Award

Presented to the outstanding female cadet attending the Cadet Leadership and Challenge Course at the National Army Cadet Camp, Banff, Alta. The winner receives an all-expenses-paid trip for two to Disneyworld Florida, sponsored by the Army Cadet League of Canada.

1982   **Cadet Leslie McMillen**, 2360 Cameron Highlanders, Ottawa Cadet Corps.

GUARDING THEIR TITLE

The Royalaires Colour Guard of Edmonton, Alta., in competition at the Colour Guard Olympics, were consistently the highest-scoring Canadian unit in the competition until 1981. They regained their title in 1983.

INNIS-GERLIN MEDAL

Royal Society of Canada

The award is for distinguished and sustained contribution to the literature of the social sciences in honour of economic historian Harold Innis, FRSC (1894-1952), and sociologist Leon Gerin, FRSC (1863-1951), who were distinguished men of Canadian letters and were presidents of the society during 1946-47 and 1933-34 respectively.

Dr. Malcolm C. Urquhart, FRSC, Professor of Economics, Queen's University, Kingston, Ont. Dr. Urquhart is a leading scholar in the development of an empirical basis for the study of Canadian economic history. His skill ranges from economic theory to statistical analysis to historical perspective.

A major work, *The Historical Statistics of Canada from 1959 to 1965*, provided Canadian scholars with a new access to historical material. As director of the Institute for Economic Research (1960-66) he also contributed to the development of a professional approach to economics in Canada. Currently he heads a major project estimating Canada's national income from 1870 to 1926.

PRIX LEON-GERIN

Royal Society of Canada

Awarded to a Canadian domiciled in Quebec for works in the human sciences (moral science, philosophy, psychology, social sciences and/or the law). The winner receives an engraved medal and $15,000.

1982 Jacques Henripin, the University of Montreal. To honour a researcher who has devoted more than 30 years to the study of the behaviour and needs of Quebec society. He is a pioneering authority of demographic research in Quebec.

JOHN KENNETH GALBRAITH

John Kenneth Galbraith was born in 1908 and raised in Elgin County, Ont. He is an internationally recognized economist. He studied at the Ontario Agricultural College before moving to the United States to continue his studies.

After teaching economics at Harvard he served various administrations of the American government except for the five years he was editor of *Fortune* magazine. He was the United States Ambassador to India from 1961 to '63.

The author of several books, he has influenced economists and economic attitudes of government leaders including those in Canada.

THESIS WINS ATTENTION IN U.K.

A novel scientific study of mistresses, undertaken as a PhD thesis by Edna Salamon, daughter of a Winnipeg cattle dealer, has won attention in the U.K. The press, the BBC and publishers have all been interested in her work. She has even been offered jobs in the U.S.

Salamon, who has an honours degree in criminology from the University of Manitoba, prepared her thesis for a doctorate at the London School of Economics. She credits her hairdresser, however, for helping her formulate the idea for the study. She also believes that people responded to her openly because she is Canadian. "Everybody thinks of Canadians as living in igloos, right? Consequently you can ask the most inane questions and they just attribute it to being Canadian. You know: 'Oh, you're unsophisticated.' They talked more than they might have with a more polished person."

NORTHROP FRYE

Herman Northrop Frye was born in Sherbrooke, Que., in 1912. He was educated at Moncton, B.C., and at the University of Toronto, before being ordained into the United Church. He returned after a short time in Saskatchewan to academic studies in 1936, attending Oxford and then again the University of Toronto.

He joined the English department of Victoria College at U of T in 1939, became principal of the college in 1959, and was named University Professor in the University of Toronto in 1966.

He was the editor-in-chief of *Canadian Forum* for several years and for 10 years he wrote the section on English Canadian poetry for *Letters in Canada*, an annual survey of Canadian writing. Dr. Frye has taught full terms at Harvard, Princeton, Columbia, Berkeley, Cornell and Oxford and has lectured around the world. His books include: *Fearful Symmetry: A Study of William Blake; Anatomy of Criticism: Four Essays; Fables of Identity; The Stubborn Structure; The Critical Path; Creation and Recreation.* His most recent book, *The Great Code,* published in 1982, is a major work which examines the influence of the Bible on the imaginative tradition of Western literature, and the interaction between Biblical and secular knowledge.

Professor Frye holds 30 honorary degrees and is esteemed throughout the world as scholar, teacher and literary critic. He is an intellectual giant of Canadian letters.

AN EARLY CONFEDERACY

The league of Five Nations was a confederation of Iroquois tribes: the Mohawks, Oneidas, Onondagas, Cayugas and Senecas. The federation was formed about 1500 by Dekanawida, a chief from the area around present-day Kingston, and Hiawatha, a Mohawk (not Longfellow's Hiawatha). They called the confederation the Longhouse.

The elders of the tribes gathered at the Longhouse and voted on issues that were critical to the tribes.

In 1722 the Tuscaroras were brought into the league, which became known as the Six Nations.

THE ACADIANS: THEIR EXPULSION, SURVIVAL AND RETURN

Acadia (Nova Scotia) was a French colony until the Treaty of Utrecht ceded the colony to Great Britain in 1713.

When British rule began, there were about 1,600 Acadian families farming, as their forefathers had done, in the Annapolis Valley along the Fundy coast. They had developed a method of diking the marshlands and were prospering. They were also a peaceful people who wished only to keep their language, their faith and customs.

By 1750 their population had grown to somewhere between 12,000 and 15,000.

Most Acadians wished to remain neutral between the British and the French. British officials were suspicious of them, however, as they had refused on several occasions to take an oath of allegiance to Britain.

In 1755, the British and French were again at war. The British became fearful that the Acadians would side with the French and take up arms against them, and so they expelled them from their homeland.

It was a monumental tragedy for the Acadians. They were forced to leave their possessions, their homes and their lands. There was no provision for their maintenance and in the confusion that arose as they were being forced aboard ships, many families were permanently separated.

In 1758, a second expulsion was forced by the British. The plan was to deport the Acadians to the English colonies along the Atlantic seaboard, and some Acadians did make their homes in these colonies. Others went to Louisiana, some ended up in France, still others escaped, fleeing to Quebec, P.E.I. or to the St. John River.

In 1763, 350 Acadian families were exiled to St. Pierre and Miquelon, the French Islands in the Gulf of St. Lawrence.

While some Acadians did make new homes in the British American colonies, many tried to return to their homes in Nova Scotia. They returned slowly, often at great cost and suffering. The British, no longer fearing attacks by the French, allowed them to stay, but their lands were gone, taken over by new Loyalist settlers.

The Acadians had to start over, on the St. John River, in Cape Breton or on Prince Edward Island.

The township of Clare in Nova Scotia was laid out for them in 1768 and later 16,000 acres were set out for them on the Dadawaska River in New Brunswick.

Today, the descendents of these determined Canadians still retain the Acadian culture.

THE FOUNDING OF THE EMPIRE: HAPPY BIRTHDAY NEWFOUNDLAND

Sir Humphrey Gilbert, a half-brother of Sir Walter Raleigh, took formal possession of Newfoundland, and all lands 200 leagues to the north and to the south, in St. John's harbour on August 5, 1583. Thus, Newfoundland became Britain's first colony.

Gilbert sailed to England after only 17 days and was lost at sea.

BRITISH GOVERNORS HELP FRENCH-CANADIAN SURVIVE

James Murray became the first British military governor of Quebec following the fall of New France and its first civil governor in 1764.

Though the French dreaded military oppression, Murray's government exercised authority with unusual restraint and the daily life of the colony was able to continue much as before.

Murray himself admired the French Canadians and was sympathetic to the problems they faced with British law. He even opposed the election of a House of Assembly, since most of the population was Roman Catholic and British law at the time excluded Roman Catholics from public office. Rather than let government fall into the hands of the small minority of English-speaking people in Quebec, he instituted rule by governor and council.

During his time, the rebuilding of Quebec City was begun, the newspaper the *Quebec Gazette* was founded, the economy improved and a conciliatory man, Jean Briand, installed as Bishop of Quebec. Unfortunately for nearly everyone concerned, Murray was recalled to England in 1766 to answer charges that he was too sympathetic to the French Canadians and unfair to the small

number of English in the colony, most of whom were merchants.

Colonel Guy Carleton, the first Lord Dorchester, was appointed lieutenant-governor and commander-in-chief of Quebec in 1766. He became the second civil governor of Quebec in 1768.

Carleton realized that Quebec "must to the end of time be peopled by the Canadian [French-Canadian] race." He was primarily responsible for the passing of the Quebec Act in 1774. The act gave Roman Catholics in Canada civil equality and "the free exercise" of the Roman Catholic religion was confirmed. This was remarkable as Catholic emancipation did not take place in England until 1829.

French civil law was reintroduced, while criminal cases were heard in accordance with British law. Seigneurial dues were continued and the right of the Catholic Church to tithe was permitted. While the last clauses caused habitants some dismay, the rest of the act returned the colony to a way of life that resembled pre-war New France.

The British had originally intended to "anglicize" the colony and to assimilate the Canadians. The Quebec Act helped to ensure the survival of the French-Canadian people and perhaps even of Canada, as the French-Canadians remained loyal to the British in the War of 1812 against the Americans.

ENGLISH CANADA FOUNDED BY THE LOYALISTS

United Empire Loyalists were those people living in British North America who did not agree absolutely with the aims of the American revolution. Persecuted and driven out of the American colonies, they fled by the thousands to British-held New York, while a small number came north and established a Loyalist settlement at Niagara.

At war's end, the British ceded New York to the Americans and began to transport the Loyalists to Canada. They went to Nova Scotia, New Brunswick, Quebec and Ontario.

They were given land grants and were promised assistance for three years. For some settlers the first years were exceedingly hard as the essentials promised were not always forthcoming.

More than 40,000 Loyalists came to Canada. Those who settled outside of Quebec strengthened British holdings and are the foundation of English-speaking Canada.

In Quebec, the Loyalist influence far outweighed their numbers as the French-Canadian majority began to be treated as the minority. The coming of the Loyalists to Quebec was of greater importance to Quebec than the defeat of the French or the military occupation that followed the defeat.

Today there are more than 3.5-million Canadians whose ancestors were United Empire Loyalists.

PHILANTHROPIST BEGINS SETTLEMENT

Thomas Douglas Selkirk, the fifth Earl of Selkirk, was, by all accounts, a man who felt deep concern for his impoverished Scottish countrymen. Between 1803 and 1809 he arranged the passage and settlement of many families to P.E.I. and Upper Canada.

He wanted to etablish Scottish settlements in the uncolonized regions of the West, and managed to buy a controlling interest in the Hudson's Bay Company.

His plan for a Red River colony was not strictly altruistic. The Hudson's Bay Company had been slow to enter the West. Its more aggressive Canadian rival, the North West Company, had ignored the Hudson's Bay Company

charter and taken over most of the fur trade by opening up new trade routes in the West.

Selkirk's scheme would directly challenge the North West Company by providing cheap provisions and labour for the HBC posts and making good the Company's claim to the soil under the charter. The Hudson's Bay Company sold Selkirk 116,000 square miles in the valley of the Red and Assiniboine rivers for the grand sum of 10 shillings.

The first 70 settlers reached the Red River near Winnipeg in 1812 after travelling 730 miles overland from Hudson Bay in just 55 days. Others followed in the next thee years and an agricultural community of some 200 was established in the area that the North West Company used as a supply base.

The Metis, who had been supplying the Nor'west traders with pemmican, also considered the area as their own. Settlement would interfere with the buffalo hunt and cut off their pemmican trade with the North West Company. Conflict was inevitable and the "Pemmican War" erupted.

The North West Company attempted to disperse the settlers and posts belonging to both companies were attacked or seized. An encounter of Metis and Nor'west traders with 26 settlers and the local HBC governor, Robert Semple, ended with the deaths of Semple and 20 of the settlers after shooting broke out. In 1816, Selkirk himself came to Canada to take command of Swiss and German mercenaries hired to battle the Metis and Canadians. In 1817 the British governor-in-chief imposed government authority; peace was made and charges were brought against the participants. The war moved into the law courts. There were delays, changes of venue, prisoners escaped, others were released. Selkirk was fined 2,000 pounds for his part in the affair, his health was ruined and he died in 1820, a disappointed man.

The North West Company was also exhausted, its profits depleted. In 1821, it agreed to a merger with the Hudson's Bay Company. The Montreal fur trade ended and the voyageurs disappeared. The empire of the Hudson's Bay Company extended from the boundary of Labrador to the Pacific and from the lower reaches of the Mackenzie River to the American passes over the Rockies, a continental domain it held for nearly half a century.

In 1836 Lord Selkirk's Red River Colony was reestablished by the company. It prospered and the settlement of the West finally began.

SIR JAMES DOUGLAS, THE FATHER OF BRITISH COLUMBIA

Douglas was born in British Guiana and educated in Scotland. He joined the North West Company in 1819 and after that company merged with the Hudson's Bay Company he was sent west.

He founded Fort Connolly in the B.C. north, explored the southern tip of Vancouver Island and in 1843 established Fort Victoria. He became governor of Vancouver Island in 1851.

The first settlers were mainly British and the colony grew slowly. Then in 1858 everything changed. Gold was discovered in the Fraser River and suddenly gold seekers and adventurers, mostly from the United States, were inundating Victoria and the Fraser Valley. In the first season some 25,000 men arrived, mainly from California, and more followed as gold was found up the Fraser River and in the Cariboo. Victoria quickly changed from a sleepy fur-trading outpost into a northern San Francisco.

Douglas was alarmed. The HBC and Britain had been driven out of the territory south of the 49th parallel by waves of covered-wagon settlers. Douglas resolved that there should be no further retreat.

He did not have legal jurisdiction over the mainland but he acted as though he did. He quickly imposed his authority in the name of the British government, kept order and thus prevented the absorption by the United States of a vital part of Canada.

A few months later he became the first governor of the colony of British Columbia. He was created a Knight Commander of the Bath in 1863 and retired the following year. He lived his last years in Victoria.

CONGRATULATIONS FROM THE QUEEN

Her Majesty the Queen sent 2,283 messages in 1982 to Canadians celebrating their 60th wedding anniversaries and up.

The Governor-General sent 7,601 congratulatory certificates to Canadians celebrating their 50th to 59th anniversaries in 1982.

Her Majesty the Queen sent messages of congratulations to 802 Canadians who celebrated their 100th birthdays and up in 1982.

The Governor-General sent 7,601 congratulatory certificates to Canadians celebrating their 90th to 99th birthdays in 1982.

CANADA'S OLDEST CITIZEN?

David Trumble was born December 15, 1867, the year in which Canada became a nation. He is 115 years old and he lives in an old folks' home in Cannifton, Ont.

He was married four times, and has 18 children and at least 100 grandchildren.

Trumble, who worked as a farm labourer at 96, published a book when he was 109 and could walk eight miles a day when he was 114. He didn't stop smoking until he was 100 years old and drove a car until he was 104.

RURAL GROWTH OUTSTRIPS URBAN

The 1970s became the first decade in Canadian history to record a faster growth rate for rural areas than urban areas, according to Statistics Canada.

Since 1976, the rural population has grown by 8.9 per cent to 6 million people — almost double the urban growth rate of 5 per cent, according to the 1981 census. And for the first time since the 1930s the agricultural labour force did not shrink in size but remained stable with 481,275 workers. The number of agricultural workers as a percentage of the total labour force, however, shrank to 4 per cent in 1981 from 5.6 per cent in 1971, with Alberta reporting the greatest decline.

Who says you can't keep your children down on the farm?

CANADA GROWING

On January 1, 1983, there were 240,500 more people living in Canada than there were a year earlier, according to Statistics Canada. The population of the country was about 24,739,400.

CANADIANS FLUSH

Most housing units in Canada have indoor plumbing and more than half a million homes have at least three bath or powder rooms, according to the 1981 census. Extra bedrooms were especially popular in B.C. (12 per cent of homes) and Alberta (11.4 per cent of homes.)

However, Canadians from 111,605 homes (including 11 per cent of homes in the Northwest Territories) must still brave the cold when nature calls, as their homes have no indoor plumbing at all.

TRUE LOVE LASTS

Jean Cummings and Jack Mowers intended to marry in Scotland 40 years ago, but because of the war they lost contact with each other. They were married at last, in Vancouver, in April 1983.

SECRET BUT STEADY

On Valentine's Day, 1983, Torontonian Meryl Dunsmore, a 72-year-old grandmother, received for the 56th year in a row a valentine card signed, as always, "Your Secret Admirer." She received the first card when she was fresh out of high school and since then the cards have been mailed from all over the world.

TEMPERANCE AND PROHIBITION

The first public temperance meeting held in Canada was in Montreal in 1829.

STRANGE TALE OF HEROIC SURVIVAL

A startling story is told of Marguerite de La Roque, who was likely the daughter or niece of Jean-Francois de Roberval.

Roberval had attempted to found a colony near Cap Rouge in the St. Lawrence River valley in 1542. Despotic and possibly mad, he ruled the colony in a tyranically harsh manner. Not surprisingly the colony failed and he decided to return with the survivors to France.

But Marguerite had displeased Roberval and he put her, along with her maid and lover, ashore on an island off Quebec in the Gulf of St. Lawrence before sailing home. Marguerite's maid and lover perished on the island, as did the child she delivered there. Marguerite survived, and two years after being abandoned she was discovered by fishermen who took her back to France.

TEENAGE HEROINE

Madeleine de Jarret Verchères lived with her parents, her two younger brothers, a servant and two soldiers in the family seigniorial fort, named Fort Dangerous, on the St.Lawrence River. Her parents were away from home on October 22, 1692, the day on which the Iroquois attacked the fort.

Madeleine was only 14 years old, but she was spirited and determined. She rallied, and pointed out that they might be able to convince the Indians that there was a full garrison within the seigniory, if they fired what guns they had systematically. Together they kept up the regular fire and together they held the Indians from attacking for eight days, when relief came.

Madeleine was not a once-in-a-lifetime heroine; later, in 1722, she saved the life of her husband Pierre-Thomas Tarieu de la Pérade when he was attacked by an Indian.

CANADA'S FIRST FARM FAMILY

Louis Hébert, an apothecary, was with the first settlers in Acadia in 1604. Later, he cultivated a garden at Port Royal.

In 1617, he brought his wife and three children from France to settle in Quebec. They were Canada's first farm family.

Hébert was granted 10 acres of land at Sault au Matelot, now a part of Quebec City. He cleared the land with hand tools and his son-in-law is believed to have been the first habitant to use a plough on Canadian soil. Hébert grew corn, planted orchards and vineyards and tended vegetable gardens.

He acted as apothecary and attorney while his wife tended the sick in the settlement and taught Indian children in her home.

Hébert died in Quebec in 1627. In 1628, when the small colony was close to starvation, David Kirke forced its surrender and removed the colony to England. Madame Hébert and the family of her son-in-law refused to leave.

The Héberts were true settlers and many Quebec families are descended from them. Champlain wrote of the Hébert family: "The only family that established and maintained itself was that of the late Hébert; but it was not without a struggle that he was able to hold his ground, for the Company (of New France) constrained and compelled him to submit to many unlawful conditions in regard to the corn he raised each year, preventing him from selling it to anyone, or exchanging it with anyone, except the Company, and then at a price fixed by themselves. That was not the way to create a great desire on the part of anyone to go and people a country, when a man cannot have any free enjoyment of its returns."

Voyages, Vol. 5, 1632

AN ISLAND NAMED FOR A BRIDE

Samuel de Champlain was 40 when he was married in France during the winter of 1609/10. His bridge was Hélène Boullé. She was a true child bride as she was only 12 years old.

Champlain named Saint Helen's Island, across from Montreal, in her honour in 1611.

Hélène Boullé lived with Champlain in Quebec from 1620 until 1624. Some accounts say that she retired to a convent after his death in 1635.

CANADA'S FIRST BRIDE SERVICE

They were called the filles du roi, because they were orphan girls from good French families who were made wards of the state and raised in charity institutions.

The young women were sent to New France from 1665 to 1671 to be brides for settlers and regimental soldiers who wanted to settle in New France at the end of their tour of duty.

A man could ask for the hand of any girl and if she liked what she saw, and accepted his proposal, she was granted a royal dowry. A usual dowry might include, an ox, a cow, two chickens, two pigs, two barrels of salt meat and eleven crowns.

The women were carefully chaperoned on the voyage, and upon arrival in new France Marguerite Bougeoys, founder the Sisters of the Congregation of Notre-Dame, took the responsibility of protecting them.

INTERNATIONAL ATTENTION FOR CANADIAN NATIVE WOMEN'S RIGHTS

Sandra Lovelace lost her status rights when she married a non-Indian.

In 1977 she took her battle for her Indian status into the courts of the United Nations. She alleged that Canada had violated an international covenant on civil and political rights through the Indian Act.

In July 1981, the UN Human Rights Committee found Canada in breach of an article of the covenant because Sandra Lovelace was not allowed to be recognized as a member of her band and to enjoy her culture in the community of the band.

Behind the issue is the fear that non-Indian men may eventually gain control over the reserves if equal status is allowed.

Thanks to Lovelace, however, the issue won't just go away.

SAMSON INDIANS HAVE WON A BONANZA

The Samson Indian reserve near Hobbema, Alta., is home to Canada's wealthiest Indians. An oil-rich band, every Samson baby is born a millionaire. The band, along with three others, was able to strike a land deal with the government at the turn of the century that allowed them to maintain mineral rights. Samson residents receive monthly dividend cheques and don't pay income tax.

NATIVE OF CANADA'S NORTH CROSSES THE ATLANTIC

Martin Frobisher, on his first attempt to discover the Northwest Passage in 1576, first met the Inuit in Frobisher Bay. He traded with them until five men in his only long boat went ashore and disappeared. He was not able to examine the shoreline without a boat. When a man in a kayak approached his ship he took "with main force boate and al ... out of the Sea" and returned to England with his unfortunate captive.

Watercolour drawings by the artist John White possibly executed on the return voyage to England are in the British Museum.

The victim purportedly died of a cold in England.

VIKING BABY BORN IN CANADA

Snorri was the son of Thorfinnr Thordardson who, about 1003-10, went with 60 men and five women to found a colony, most likely in present-day Newfoundland. The settlement was abandoned after three years because of disturbances with the natives.

Snorri was born at the settlement. Among his descendants were several bishops of Iceland. His great grandmother, Auda the Deep-Minded, is said to be an ancestor of Queen Elizabeth II.
Our Heritage, published in Kingston,
1967

The first recorded birth of a European child in North America was a son of Nicholas Guy born on March 27, 1613, at Cooper's Cover (now Cupids) on Conception Bay, in Newfoundland.

Guy was with 30 colonists who tried to establish a settlement chartered by the London and Bristol Company in 1610. Guy later became mayor of Bristol. The settlers were unable to defend themselves against plundering fishermen and pirates and abandoned the first British attempt at colonization.

ENGLISH CHILDREN BROUGHT TO CANADA

Some 30,000 homeless English children were brought to Canada over a period of 60 years and placed in foster homes under a program initiated by Dr. Thomas J. Barnado in the 1860s.

PREHISTORIC EVIDENCE

A bone scraper or fleshing tool found in the Old Crow Flats area in northern Yukon is the earliest evidence of man on Canadian territory. Found July 1966 by Peter Lord (working with C.R. Haring-ton), it was carbon dated to about 5,000 B.C.

BRITISH COLUMBIA

Frances Barkley was the first white woman in British Columbia. She arrived at Nootka on Vancouver Island in 1787.

HAPPY CANADIANS

A Gallup poll released in January 1983 revealed that Canadians are among the happiest people in the world.

The survey was part of a worldwide study of values and beliefs, conducted for the Centre for Applied Research in the Apostolate, a Catholic research organization. (The survey used a sample of all Canadians, not just Catholics.)

According to the poll, 95 per cent of Canadians say they are either very happy or quite happy. If the results are true, we are happier than people in the U.S., Europe and Japan.

In France people said they were dissatisfied with their jobs, while the Italians seemed to be the most religious but also the loneliest and the Americans the most patriotic.

The survey also indicated that Canadians are smug, law-abiding, and cautious with confidence in the police, the church, the legal system, the armed forces and education. There was even less confidence in the civil service, the press, Parliament and labour unions.

According to data analysts, the average Canadian is purposeful, comfort-oriented, gregarious and values family life.

GETTING THE GNP INTO SHAPE

Canadians are into fitness. And while working out in the living room or running in the park is not costly, experts estimate that Canadians are now spending $500-million a year on fitness programs.

CANADA'S ORIGINAL DINNER CLUB

The Ordre de Bon Temps or the Order of Good Cheer was North America's first and probably most exclusive association. It was formed amongst the men of Port Royal under the leadership of Samuel de Champlain, during the long winter of 1606/07. A chain known as "the collar of the day" was worn by the steward of the day (the members took turns). The steward hunted for food and in the evening, carrying a staff in his hand and a napkin on his shoulder, he led the ceremonial procession of men bearing the meal to the table. Entertainment generally followed dinner.

The Ordre de Bon Temps of Quebec formed by the Quebec government in 1946 was so named to honour the association at Port Royal.

WORLD CULINARY OLYMPICS, 1984, FRANKFURT, GERMANY

Canadian Federation of Chefs de Cuisine

The Canadian Culinary Olympic Team for 1984, as chosen by the Canadian Federation of Chefs de Cuisine, includes some of the finest chefs in the nation.

Georges A. Chauvet, director of public relations and intergovernment liaison for Canadian teams.
Henri Dane, team manager
Huber Scheck, team captain
Gerhard Pichler, team member
Tony Murakami, team member
Josef Erni, team member

NAT BAILEY SCHOLARSHIPS
Canadian Restaurant Association Foundation

The late Nat Bailey's hamburger and sauce made his chain of Vancouver White Spot drive-in restaurants famous.

Two annual scholarships of $2,000 and $1,000 are awarded to secondary school graduates who enroll in a four-year degree course in hotel and food administration at a Canadian university, who have shown outstanding academic achievement, leadership and interest in Canada's food service industry.

1982 **David R. DeClark**, Chatham, Ont.
  Sandra D. Lennon, Oakville, Ont.
1983 **George Kibedi**. An economist, professor and author, Kibedi is executive director of the Ontario Hostelry Institute, professor and director of tourism management studies in the Canadian School of Management, Master of Business Administration Program, Toronto.
  John J. Leon. President of Colonel Sanders Kentucky Fried Chicken Ltd., Leon is one of the original members of the University of Guelph's Policy Advisory Board which was set up to establish the advanced management program for the hospitality industry.
  Z. Paul Mastalir. Head of the culinary arts department of Southern Alberta Institute of Technology, past president of both the Calgary Academy of Chefs and the Canadian Federation of Chefs de Cuisine, and manager of the Alberta team of chefs for the 1984 Culinary Olympics.

JACK C. SIM "MAN OF THE YEAR" AWARD
Canadian Restaurant Association

This award was endowed in 1980 by the late Jack C. Sim, past national president of the Canadian Restaurant and Foodservices Association and founder and past president of the CRA Foundation. It is the highest honour conferred by the CRA Foundation.

1983   George D. Bedell, Guelph, Ont.

THE BIG CHEESE

The world's largest cheese was produced in Perth, Ont., in 1893. It measured 28 feet around, weighed 11 tons and stood six feet all. It would have taken a determined cheese fancier, eating a pound a day, 423 years to clean the cheese board. The cheese travelled on two flatbed railway cars to Chicago, where it drew marvelling crowds at the World's Fair before it fell through the pavilion floor.

GROCER OF THE YEAR AWARD

Canadian Federation of Independent Grocers

James Penner of Steinbach, Man., was named Grocer of the Year in April 1983. His company, Penner Foods Ltd., is a four-supermarket company which has doubled its annual sales to $30-million in the past four years.

HONOUR AWARD

Canadian Home Economics Association

The CHEA is a professional association for graduates of consumer and family studies, foods and nutrition, home economics and human ecology. The award honours the attainment of high professional standards through continuing research and education among home economists.

1982   Emmie Ducie Oddie, Tregarva, Sask.

HOME ECONOMIST WINS ORDER OF CANADA

Dietitian and home economist Dr. Margaret McCready of Toronto was appointed a Member of the Order of Canada in 1981.

A PhD graduate of the University of Aberdeen, Dr. McCready was director of household science at McGill and later dean of Macdonald Institute at the University of Guelph. After her retirement from Guelph she spent two years as chairman of the department of home science, University of Ghana.

McCready was president of the Canadian Home Economics Association from 1948-50. She was active in the formation of the Consumers Association of Canada, the Vanier Institute for the Family and the Freedom From Hunger Campaign, and was a member of the Ontario Advisory Council on Senior Citizens and the Committee on Living and Learning in Retirement.

COFFEE FOR THE EIGHTIES

The *International Coffee & Cocoa Magazine* recognized Mother Parker's Mississauga Coffee facility in 1981 as the most modern coffee plant in North America.

The company, which is 100 per cent Canadian owned, has a complete green coffee handling system, roasting, blending, grinding and storage system and is completely automated and computerized.

CANADIAN COOKS BUY CANADIAN COOKBOOKS, LOTS OF THEM

The bestselling Canadian Cookbooks of 1982 according to the Cookbook Store in Toronto, Ont.:

Harrowsmith Cookbook, Harrowsmith Magazine

Winter Entertaining and *Summer Entertaining*, The Georgian Bay Gourmets (Ann Connell, Joan Leavens, Helen De Carli, Mary Hunt)

Food That Really Schmecks, Edna Staebler

What's Cooking with Ruth Fremes (three volumes)

Muffins, Joan and Marilyn

Muffin Mania, Cathy Prange

101 Marvelous Muffins, Adelle Marks

Mad About Muffins, Angela Clubb

Choice Cooking, The Canadian Diabetic Association

Classic Canadian Cooking, Elizabeth Baird

Summer Berries, Elizabeth Baird

Company's Coming: *Delicious Squares, Casseroles*, Jean Pare

The Best of Bridge and *Enjoy, More from the Best of Bridge*, A Calgary Bridge Club

The Polish Touch, Marie Curie Sklowdowska Association

GARGANTUAN OMELETTE

Students at Conestoga College in Kitchener, Ont., cooked the world's largest ever omelette on June 29, 1978.

The omelette used 12,432 eggs and was cooked in a custom made pan measuring 30 by 10 feet.

NORTH AMERICA'S FIRST CONVENIENCE FOOD

Peter Pond was a fur trader with the North West Company who dreamed of reaching the Pacific coast. He is thought to have gone as far as Great Slave Lake in 1778, and the only reason he made it that far is because of pemmican.

Made by the Plains Indians, pemmican consisted of pellets of dried meat pounded into a paste and mixed with fat and sometimes berries and then pressed into cakes. It was highly nutritious, portable and kept indefinitely. It allowed fur traders and explorers to travel even when fresh food was unavailable.

On Pond's suggestion the North West Company supplied pemmican to its agents, a major factor in the company's rapid expansion into the West.

Pemmican is still being used today as a survival food, and is commercially manufactured for hunters and others going into the wilderness.

EARLE WILLARD McHENRY AWARD

Canadian Society for Nutritional Sciences

The award, made available by Canada Packers Limited, is given for distinguished service in the field of nutrition. It consists of $1,000 and a scroll.

1982   Dr. J. Alexander Campbell, Ottawa, Ont.

THESE CAKE CHEFS THINK REALLY BIG!

Roy Butterworth and Frank Brennan baked and constructed what was the world's tallest recorded free-standing wedding cake for the incorporation of Bedford, N.S., on May 1, 1980. The cake of 48 tiers was 32 feet, six inches tall.

In April 1983, Butterworth, who is chef of Halifax's Lord Nelson Hotel, assisted Maurice Olaizola in the creation that really took the cake. Built in a Quebec suburban shopping centre, the 1,000-pound giant had 50 layers and towered 35 feet. It required 600 pounds of basic batter to which were added 1,800 eggs, 300 pounds of sugar and 150 pounds of butter and margarine.

Olaizola is chief chef at the Chateau Frontenac in Quebec.

CHAMPION OF SWEETS

Arthur Ganong of St. Stephen, N.B., was one smart, sweet man. He created the chocolate bar, the lollipop and the heart-shaped box of chocolates for Valentine's Day. The Ganong confectionery firm continues to thrive in New Brunswick on chocolate production.

WISER'S DE LUXE CULINARY CLASSIC

Wiser's Distillery Limited, and endorsed by the Canadian Federation of Chefs de Cuisine

The Culinary Classic is a competition open to professional chefs, sous chefs, pastry chefs, apprentice chefs and chefs-in-training. Organized by the Federation of Chefs de Cuisine, the competition is based entirely on original creations.

Appetizer/Hors d'oeuvre National Winners
1982 **Josef Erni**, Hilton Harbour Castle, Toronto, Ont. For *le petit savarin de cresson aux queues de langoustines et goujonnettes de sole.*
Regional Winners
Yoshitaka Chubachi, sous chef, Westin Hotel, Winnipeg, Man.
Camille Calender, Centre d'Accueil Le Mainbourg, Montreal, Que.
Richard Bergeron, chef, Residence of the Delegate General of Quebec, New York, N.Y.
Fish/Seafood national Winner
1982 **Josef Erni**, Hilton Harbour Castle, Toronto, Ont. For *le pavé de l'omble de l'arctique soufflé a la mousseline de truite au fine champagne.*
Regional Winners
Anton Walker, sous chef, Westin Bayshore, Vancouver, B.C.
Zdravko Kalabric, chef, Restaurant Chemin du Roy, Repentigny, Que.
Poultry/Game National Winners
1982 **Madhu P. Sharma**, Loews Westbury Hotel, Toronto, Ont. For *poitrine de poulet "couronne de luxe."*
Regional Winners
Charles Ramseyer, chef saucier, Four Seasons Hotel, Vancouver, B.C.
Slimane Alaoui, chef de partie, four Seasons Hotel, Ottawa, Ont.

Robert Cholette, Tele-Metropole Inc., Montreal, Que.
Meat Dish National Winners
1982 **Hneri Varaud**, Rene Varaud Restaurant, Montreal, Que. For *poêlée de ris de veau au cognac, sa beuchelle de blancs de cailles et de langoustines aux morilles embeurrée d'artichauts aux nouilles fraîches.*
Regional Winners
Donald E. Bottcher, chef, Oak Bay Beach Hotel, Victoria, B.C.
Kerry Sear, executive chef, Delta Ottawa, Ottawa, Ont.
Dessert National Winners
1982 **Robert Long**, Windsor Board of Education, Windsor, Ont. For maple cranberry mousse "Maple Syrup mousse."
Regional Winners
Klaus Hoffman, chef training, Red River Community College, Winnipeg, Man.
Richard Bergeron, chef, Residence of the Delegate General of Quebec, New York, N.Y.

TASTE OF CANADA '83 FIRST NATIONAL CULINARY COMPETITION

Ontario Hostelry Institute, George Brown College and the Ontario Restaurant and Food Service Association

Taste of Canada '83 was the first national competition for culinary students. Five major culinary colleges were represented by 100 competitors at the 10-day event held in Toronto.

The judges were world-renowned chefs from Europe, the UK, the USA and Canada.

GRAND PRIZE WINNERS

Wisers Deluxe Culinary Classic Grand Student Award

Akinkuono Adejumke, Southern Alberta Institute of Technology

George Brown Alumni Association Award

Maria Mercedes, George Brown College

CFSEA George Brown Junior Branch Award
Pastry Chefs Guild of Ontario Award

Debbie Platnick, Northern A.I. of T.

Students chosen to accompany the Canadian team to the 1984 World Culinary Olympics in Frankfurt, West Germany

Shaun Plausini,
Robert Church, SAIT.

CATEGORY WINNERS

Cocktail Hors d'Oeurvre
Peter Schellenberg, Red River Community College
Cold Buffet Platter-Meat
AkinkuoNo Adejumke, SAIT
Cold Buffet Platter-Seafood
David Correa, GBC
Hot Food Served Cold
Robert Church, SAIT
Individual Entrées
Shaun Plausini, GBC
Special Occasion Cakes
Debbie Platnick, NAIT
Petits Fours Friandises
Debbie Platnick, NAIT
Desserts
Kathy Harold, Georgian College
Puff Pastry and Danish
Kathy Harold, GC

ELECTRICAL EATS

The Windsor Hotel in Ottawa served the world's first electrically cooked meal in 1892. It was prepared on an apparatus invented by Thomas Ahearn.

CANADIAN HOTELS JOIN ELITE GROUP

Five Canadian hotels are members of the exclusive international hotel organization, Relais et Châteaux.

Founded in Paris in 1954, Relais et Châteaux has about 300 members in 20 countries. To qualify, establishments must have fewer than 100 rooms and be exceptional in character, courtesy, comfort, cuisine and calm. The hotels generally emphasize luxury and haute cuisine.

Last year 32 new members were admitted to the chain while 15 establishments were dropped. Nine Canadian hotels applied for membership and one Canadian hotel is a continuing member.

Continuing member: **Hotel Spainière**, Val David, Que.
New members: **The Windsor Arms** Hotel, Toronto, Ont.
The **Millcroft Inn**, Alton, Ont.
Le **Manoir des Erables**, Montmagny, Que.
l'**Hostellerie les Trois Tilleuls**, St. Marc-sur-Richelieu, Que.

SO LONG TO THE FOOT-LONG

The world's largest hotdog was prepared by Hygrade Ltd. in Montreal. It made its appearance at Olympic Stadium in August 1977. The weiner weighed 171 pounds, eight ounces and measured nine feet, three inches in length. The bun weighed 40 pounds, and the food company estimated that the hotdog equalled 2,063 standard hotdogs.

FIRST RESIDENT PRESIDENT

Hans Bueschkens of Windsor, Ont., is the first Canadian to hold the prestigious post of president of the World Association of Cooks Societies. The Society has more than 100,000 members in 30 countries.

FIRST HONEY MONEY

Commercial honey production began in Canada when the Langstroth bee hive was brought to Ontario and Quebec in 1860.

BARNES LABEL STILL STICKING AROUND

Canada's oldest operating winery is Barnes Wines near St. Catharines, Ont., founded by George Barnes in 1873.

EXTRACT WITH IMPACT

Bovril, a hot drink made from beef extract, was first created for shivering Montrealers attending a mid-winter ice carnival around the turn of the century. The new drink was not quite to the taste of Montrealers but it travelled well, first to London and then around the world and came back to Canada — a hit.

CANADA'S BEST-SELLING WINE A WEST-COAST WHITE

A medium-dry white wine, produced by Calona Wines Ltd., in Kelowna, B.C., outsold French and Italian imports in 1982. The Rhine-style wine is called Schloss Laderheim and the 750-mL bottle sells for under $5.

MARQUIS DE JOUENNES TROPHY

Opimian Society of Canada

The Opimian Society, a nonprofit wine-importing club with some 10,000 members across Canada, holds an annual competition to find the Canadian who tastes best. Preliminary rounds are held in major Canadian cities with the third and final round held during a weekend of sybaritic wining and dining in an elegant and formal atmosphere. The 1982 championship took place at Toronto's King Edward and Four Seasons Yorkville hotels.

The competition is formidable. Finalists blind taste wines and then answer questions within a set time. The test covers areas such as residual sugar, country of origin, grape varieties, regions within countries and latitude of regions.

The winner receives the title, the Marquis de Jouennes Trophy and a keeper trophy, an all-expenses-paid trip to various destinations and a case of assorted table wines.

1980   Conrad Porth, Lloydminster, Alta.
1981   Vern Christensen, Toronto, Ont.
1982   Gene Russell, Weston, Ont., (first woman champion) and Freddie Grimwood, Montreal, Que.

C'EST SI BON! THE FRENCH LIKE A CANADIAN WINE

The Burgundy region of France produces some of the finest wines in the world but wine buyers from that region have given their endorsement to a Canadian red.

The House of Chauvenet of Nuits St. Georges in Burgundy purchased 650 cases of 1980 Marechal Foch in 1982 from Inniskillin Wines of Niagara-on-the-Lake, Ont.

The wine is made from a hybrid American and French grape and is currently being quaffed by restaurant patrons in France.

CANADIAN GRAND PRIX MARTINI COMPETITION

Martini and Rossi through its agent McGuinness Distillers Ltd.

Sixteen bartenders competed at the second annual Canadian Grand Prix Martini competition held in Toronto in 1982.

Contestants drew to see what type of drink they were to concoct. There were 12 varieties of cocktail, each containing vermouth. The winning bartender, who must be under 28 years of age, is flown to Torino, Italy, for the International Grand Prix Martini contest.

The winner in both 1981 and 1982 was **Rick Thompson** of London, Ont.

Since Thompson was 27 at the time of the Canadian event, he was ineligible for the international competition. Runner-up Kathy Sartor of Toronto competed in his place.

Thompson's winning drink was a perfect Manhattan: one ounce of rye, half an ounce of sweet vermouth, half an ounce of dry vermouth stirred, strained and served in a cocktail glass with a twist of lemon.

FEWER CANADIANS DRINK BUT ENJOY IT MORE

A Gallup poll conducted in March 1983 indicated that 73 per cent of Canadian 18 years of age and older admit to having at least an occasional drink of beer, wine or liquor. That's down from 77 per cent in 1982 and 78 per cent in 1978. (In 1943, only 59 per cent admitted to the use of alcohol.)

While fewer Canadians are drinking, those who do are drinking more. Figures from the Brewers Association of Canada show an increase in the number of drinks taken by the average Canadian each week. The number of drinks per week per capita for wine rose to 1.35 in 1982 from 0.94 in 1976. For spirits, it increased to 3.68 from 3.59. The figure dropped slightly for beer.

Poll results show the heaviest users are aged 18 to 29 and the lightest are 50 or older.

BEER EMPLOYS THOUSANDS

The Canadian beer industry employs 1.5 per cent of the country's labour force.

Canada's 38 breweries employ some 12,000 people and another 160,000 people such as farmers, bottlers, carton makers and truckers are directly involved in the production and distribution of Canadian beer. Their salaries, wages and commissions and employee benefits total more than $550-million and the purchase of domestic materials and supplies exceeds $430-million.

CANADA'S WINNINGEST BEER FAMILY

"Industria et Spe," that is, "by means of industry and hope," is the motto of the Molson family. It describes the successful course of the family whose fortune is founded on beer after two hundred years in Canada.

John Molson left England for Montreal in 1782 at the age of 19. Described as a "youth of considerable consequence and breeding," he was determined to stay in Canada, and used a portion of his inheritance to enter a partnership in a small brewery. In 1786, when legally of age and in possession of all of his inheritance, he bought out his partner and became the sole owner of the brewery. Part of the Molson Breweries today remains on the same site.

He was the first of his family to "enter into trade" and while he was in good part a selftaught brewer, his timing was propitious and his product well received. Within a few years he expanded the brewery, and invested in a foundry, a cooperage and in lumber and land. In 1807 he commissioned the construction of Canada's first steamship, the *Accommodation* and Canada's first organized steamship line, the St. lawrence Steamboat Company, was often called the Molson Line. In 1837 he opened the private Molson Bank. It was chartered in 1855 and by 1925, when it amalgamated with the Bank of Montreal, it had 125 branches from Quebec to B.C. John Molson was also the major shareholder in Canada's first railroad, the Champlain and St. Lawrence.

Molson died in 1836, but the Molson family has continued to flourish through depressions, wars and social change. Its beer is world-famous and its companies hold an important place in Canadian commerce.

CUTTING THE MUSTARD

Stephen Sandler, a 20-year-old student at Toronto's Ryerson Polytechnical Institute is producing a first-class Russian-style mustard that gourmet shops can't keep in stock.

Stephen uses his great-grandmother's recipe and calls his mustard Sandler's, naturally. It's outselling other hot and sweet mustards in gourmet shops across the city.

WELL, WELL-TRAVELLED

John Hathaway of Vancouver is probably Canada's most well-travelled man. He covered 50,600 miles while visiting every continent from Nov. 10, 1974 to Oct. 6, 1976.

SHE MUST HAVE BEEN PICKLED TINK TO WIN

Pat Donahue ate 91 pickled onions (total weight 30 oz.) in 1 min., 8 sec. in Victoria, B.C., on March 9, 1978, to win her way into the *Guiness Book of World Records*.

OLYMPIC PERFORMANCE

During the Montreal Olympics in 1976 the McDonalds outlet at the corner of Atwater and St. Catharine streets sold

$74,000 worth of hamburgers in just two weeks, setting a North American record. Canadians are the world's most frequent (per capita) marchers through golden arches. Annual sales per location average some $860,000, as opposed to $130,000 in the USA where it all started.

JAMES BURRITT MEMORIAL AWARD

Alliance of Canadian Travel Associations

An essay competition open to travel agents.

1983   Katie Irwin, Linkletter Travel, Summerside, P.E.I., won the first annual award for her essay "Tourism and What it Means to Canada."

FOUR SEASONS GETS TOP RATING

The *Institutional Investor*, an American business magazine, asked 100 prominent bankers in 1982 to rate the hotels where they do business. The bankers took into account opulence and extra touches such as flowers and free shoe shines when they made their ratings.

From the results of the poll the magazine rated Toronto's Four Seasons Hotel as number one in Canada and 24th in the world. The only other Canadian hotel mentioned was Montreal's Ritz-Carlton, which ranked 35th in the world.

The bankers' favourite was the Oriental Hotel in Bangkok.

RECORD PRICE FOR A CANADIAN COIN

The 1911 silver dollar pattern was auctioned by the late Frank Rose as part of the sale of the legendary collection of John McKay-Clements, on May 15,

1976, at a Toronto hotel. The final bid was for $110,000.

Frank Rose was a leader in Canadian coin circles. he was a co-founder of the country's first numismatic and philatelic newspaper, *Canadian Coin and Stamp World*, and was one of the founders of the Torex coin show. A coin dealer, he was also known as an auctioneer and writer.

PLAYING CARD MONEY IN THE NEW WORLD

In 1685 there was a constant shortage of French currency in New France. merchants were demanding payment for supplies and would not be put off until a money supply was sent from France. Finally the governor issued the first uniquely Canadian currency when he cut playing cards into quarters, signed each portion and affixed the treasurer's seal. Playing card money remained in general currency until the fall of Quebec in 1759. What bits that have survived are now on display at the Bank of Canada's Currency Museum in Ottawa.

FRED BOWMAN NUMISMATIC AWARD

Canadian Numismatic Research Society

The award is for the best numismatic article on a Canadian subject involving original research. There is no restriction on where the article may be published. Fellows of the Society are not eligible.

1981 **R.C. Bell**, for a series "Commercial Coins of the West," which appeared in the CN Journal.
1982 No award given.

BIRDER EXTRAORDINAIRE

There are 9,021 known species of birds in the world, with previously unknown species being found at the rate of one or two per year in the distant deep jungles. Norman Chesterfield a 69-year-old mink rancher from Wheatley, Ont., has seen more than 5,500 of them — more species than any other person in the world.

Yet Chesterfield didn't start bird listing until he was 40 years old. In the 25 years it took him to gain his crown, he visited more than 100 countries. He believes that he may be the only person so far to have sighted members of all 109 bird families in the Western Hemisphere. Of the 154 families of birds in the world, Chesterfield has seen representatives of 144. In 1982, when he became the world's leading bird lister, he had spotted 5,556 birds.

CANADIAN COLLECTOR HONOURED

Vincent Graves Green, the sole Canadian member of London's Roll of Distinguished Philatelists and the dean of Canadian philately, was given a 90th birthday celebration in the spring of 1983.

At the dinner in Green's honour, seven rare wines bottled in 1893, the year of his birth, were served. The clarets, ports and cognac included a Chateau Lafitte and an Armagnac Chateau de Percenade.

Few philatelic honours have escaped Vincent Greene. When he sold his collection he endowed the Vincent G. Greene Philatelic Research Foundation, whose purpose is to promote the academic study of Canadian Philately and Postal History.

MAIL SERVICE MILESTONES

The first postal route in the Colony of Canada was established in 1763 but the first Canadian postage stamp did not come into being until 1851. It depicted a beaver in its natural habitat and was designed by Sandford Fleming, surveyor, engineer and author of the system of Standard Time.

Canada was the first country to use a pictorial design and to use adhesive on the back of stamps. It was also the first to issue a multi-coloured stamp and a Christmas stamp.

The Canadian Philatelic Association was formed in 1887. Its initial convention held at Toronto in 1887 and Henry Hechler was elected its first president.

Hechler was born in Germany in 1853. Following service in the Franco-Prussian War he emigrated to Halifax, N.S., in 1871, where he established a tobacco-liquor-stamp business that eventually dealt in almost everything from buttons to real estate. He published the *Philatelic Courier*, thought to be the first Canadian stamp journal published on a regular basis. As Officer Commanding the 63rd Rifles of Halifax, he led a group of volunteers as part of the government forces in the Riel Uprising of 1885. he died in 1928.

Following a period of inactivity, the CPA was reactivated in 1923 as the Canadian Philatelic Society. The first president was Fred Jarrett of Toronto. He published the *Standard British North America Catalogue* in 1928 which established him as the Father of Canadian Philately. Also the speed typing champion of the world for several years, Jarrett was made a member of the Order of Canada for his contribution to Canadian philately.

In 1959, the Society was renamed the Royal Philatelic Society of Canada.

NOTABLE STAMP COLLECTIONS AND DEALERS

The collection of G.E. Wellburn of British Columbia inspired many to form collections of the early stamps and postal history of Western Canada.

Charles de Volpe of Quebec and Dr. C.M. Jephcott were both collectors who specialized in the early stamps of Canada.

Early dealers could not afford a full-time stamp business and usually engaged in stamp commerce on a part-time basis. A notable exception was Eli Marks who formed the Marks Stamp Company in Toronto in the late 1800s. One of his first employees was Leslie A. Davenport, who was a professional philatelist in Canada for 75 years.

One of the first Canadians to auction stamps and related material full time was J.N. Sissons. In his business life he auctioned most of the major Canadian philatelic items that became available. Today his catalogues are considered valuable reference material for researchers.

Canada has been host to three international stamp exhibitions, in 1951, 1978 and in 1982. The 1982 exhibition was known as CANADA '82 and was the first international youth exhibition held in the western hemisphere.

Source: F.G. Stulberg, Toronto, Ont.

CHAMBER POT CHAMP

Len Yeck of Brantford, Ont., has a unique collection of 140 chamber pots. Ninety of them hang on his living-room wall and another 15 are displayed on the walls of his basement.

The pots are generally between 50 and 100 years old, come in all shapes and sizes, and some have been used by famous people.

Yeck, an auctioneer, began collecting the pots when they were left unsold in an auction sale.

BELL'S BOOK COLLECTION BEST

The greatest private collector of books in Canada's history was Andrew James

Bell. Bell was born in Ottawa in 1856 and started collecting books when he was in his early 20s. By the 1930s he had more than 30,000 volumes in the library of his Toronto home, and among them many of the world's rarest books.

Bell died in 1932 and left his library to Victoria College at the University of Toronto. He had taught at the college for more than half a century, and since his only income was his modest university salary he bought his books shrewdly.

After his death it was discovered that he had acquired the finest collection in Canada and one of the five best on the continent of the works of the Renaissance writer Desiderius Erasmus.

BEATING THE ODDS

Dr. William Ziemba is a member of the commerce faculty of the University of British Columbia. He has developed computer systems for beating the odds at race tracks and in lotteries. After working for four years on a system to win at the race tracks he now can win $200 to $300 routinely on the ponies. He gives seminars on the mathematics of betting and in the summer of '82 he was asked by the federal justice department to be a witness against a Quebec lottery. Using a computer system, he was able to predict the outcome of 13 weekend games in the National Hockey League.

Ziemba is not interested in betting on the horses full-time, and says he would never try programming the National Football League because the point spread system is too sophisticated.

CHEWED OUT?

Susie Presutti, 22, of Vaughan, Ont., has been weaving a gum-wrapper chain since 1973. The chain was measured at 145 feet in the spring of 1983. That's a lot of chew and a lot of bubbles.

A CAPITAL COLLECTION

Angelo Savelli, a Hamilton, Ont., steelworker, has a collection of bubble-gum cards and sport pictures estimated to be worth $350,000.

A collector's collector, his interest began in 1949 when he was 11 years old. His collection, one of the world's finest, covers just about every sport there is.

Savelli, who has been a steelworker for 28 years, says he often went without coffee and doughnuts at work so he'd have more money to spend on his collection. Those small sacrifices have paid off in a solid investment.

BURGEONING BUREAUCRACY

The first bureaucracy in Canada began in New France in 1621 when a code of laws and a registry of marriages, births and deaths were instituted at Quebec.

The registry, which spanned three centuries, did not include the Indian population. Canada, however, was the first country to have such a continuous record.

The first Dominion census was carried out in 1871. It recorded 2,110,000 English and 1,082,000 French Canadians.

CANADA'S FIRST VISIONARY CIVIL SERVANT

Jean Talon, a former chief commissary of the French Army, became Canada's first chief civil servant in 1665. He was known as the "Great Intendant."

He was in charge of justice, police

and finance and was responsible for the entire civil administration of the colony.

During his terms in office, Talon encouraged immigration, built three model villages near Quebec, and advocated early marriage and a high birth rate. By 1672, when he left Quebec, the population of the colony had doubled to nearly 8,000.

He encouraged diverse agriculture. As well as food products, he asked farmers to grow hemp for the shipbuilding industry, hops for the brewery he had built, and hemp and flax for spinning and weaving. He subsidized lumbering and fishing and sent out an expedition to search for copper.

He was a vigourous, energetic and far-sighted man, but his efforts irritated both the governor and the private traders. His successors were not able to follow his version and after his departure immigration slowed and the colony returned to a dependence on the fur-trade and agriculture.

THE FIRST MAJOR CANADIAN BUREAUCRATIC BUNGLE AND ITS CONSEQUENCE

Medard Chaouart, Sieur des Groseillier and his brother-in-law Pierre Esprit Radisson asked the governor of New France, Sieur d'Argenson, in 1679 for permission to undertake a fur-trading expedition. The request was denied.

Des Groseillier, who had been successful in convincing the Hurons to continue the fur trade even after their defeat by the Iroquois, ignored the ruling and he and Radisson set out for Lake Superior. While they were on this journey, they probably realized that a water route must connect Lake Superior and Hudson Bay.

They returned to Quebec the next year by way of the Ottawa River, laden with prime furs. One report says they required 300 Indian paddlers in 60 canoes to transport their cargo.

When they arrived in Quebec, Des Groseillier was imprisoned for a short time on a charge of illicit trading and both men were fined so severely that most of their profits evaporated. The traders were embittered and infuriated. They had reopened the fur trade for the French and their reward was insult and the confiscation of their fortunes.

Des Groseillier went to France, to try and redeem his money and to interest the French in opening a fur trade in Hudson Bay. He was unsuccessful on both counts. He returned to Quebec and tried again for redress. Finding none, he and Radisson went to Boston and from there to England where they were received at the court of Charles II.

The brothers-in-law aroused the imagination of the English court with their scheme of a fur trade to Hudson Bay. Backed by courtiers and merchant investors, they set out in 1668 on a successful fur trade expedition to the Bay. In 1670, their investors were granted a royal Charter and the Hudson's Bay Company was established.

Eventually, France, with the British to the north and south of its territory, was squeezed out of North America. Thus did the French governors' ruling contribute to the loss of an empire. Bureaucrats beware.

ONLY ODIUM FOR OTTAWA

Queen Victoria picked Ottawa as the permanent capital of the Province of Canada in 1857, when the politicians were unable to agree on a permanent seat of government.

The American press noted at the time that Ottawa was safe "because invading soldiers would get lost looking for it in the bush."

In 1860, the *London Times* said, "that

nothing could ever develop on the remote and unpromising site" and "as for the buildings already begun, they might serve as lunatic asylums, whenever the town is sufficiently prosperous to require them for that purpose." Essayist Goldwin Smith described Ottawa as "a sub-arctic lumber village converted by royal mandate into a political cockpit."

WORLD'S LONGEST SLED-DOG MAIL RUN

Gene Dubois of Dawson City completed the world's longest sled-dog mail run in 1983 when he mushed from Dawson City across northern Canada to Quebec City. The journey took six months but Dubois was only a week off his target of the opening of the Quebec Carnival.

AN UNCONVENTIONAL COUPLE

Sylvia Ostry of Winnipeg is the head of the economics and statistics department of the Organization for Economic Co-operation and Development in Paris. She is the former chairman of the Economic Council of Canada.

Her husband, Bernard, meanwhile, is the consummate public servant as Ontario's deputy minister of industry and trade. In 1951 he worked with Krishna Mennon, India's speical envoy to the United Nations. Ostry helped draft a peace plan that brought about the end of the Korean War and then helped to bring together a voting bloc that gave the plan the votes it needed to pass the UN general assembly.

Lester Pearson reportedly told UN officials in a private speech that the peace plan was the work of "a young genius who's a Canadian."

RESPECT FOR SAUVE

Jeanne Sauve, the first woman Speaker of the House of Commons, has earned the respect of the house and of the nation for her quiet determination, wit and grace.

RESPONSIBLE GOVERNMENT REALIZED

Louis-Hippolyte Lafontaine, leader of the French-Canadian reformers, and Robert Baldwin, leader of the reform movement in Upper Canada, joined forces in the House of Assembly to fight for responsible government.

Their goal was achieved in 1848. Lafontaine, Baldwin and their reform members formed a government they called the "Great Ministry." They enacted legislation which reformed the municpal and judicial systems, gave government support to the construction of needed railroads, and secularized King's College at the University of Toronto, while firmly establishing the supremacy of Parliament in Canada.

Throughout it all Lafontaine refused to speak English in the Assembly. His stubbornness paid off when the British government repealed that part of the Act of Union that prohibited the use of French for the official proceedings of the legislature.

In 1854 Baldwin gave his blessing to a coalition which formed the liberal-conservative party, a party that was to develop into the Conservative Party.

CONFEDERATION WON WITH CHAMPAGNE

George Brown in a letter to his wife in 1864, gave a description of the luncheon that followed the Charlottetown conference:

"When the Conference adjourned, we all proceeded on board our steamer and the members were entertained at luncheon in princely style. Cartier and I made eloquent speeches — of course — and whether as the result of our eloquence or of the goodness of our champagne, the ice became completely broken, the tongues of the delegates wagged merrily, and the banns of matrimony between all the Provinces of British North American having been formally proclaimed and all manner of persons duly warned — to speak or forever after to hold their tongues — no man appeared to forbid the banns and the union was thereupon formally completed and proclaimed."

CELEBRATED DIVERSITY

George-Etienne Cartier was a dynamic spokesman for Quebec and Confederation.

He had a vision of the new nation as a diversity of races ... In our own federation we should have Catholic and Protestant, English, French, Irish and Scotch and each by his efforts and his success would increase the prosperity and the glory of the new confederacy."

SIR OLIVER MOWAT, CHAMPION OF THE PROVINCES

Mowat, a lawyer and politician, supported Confederation. Unlike John A. Macdonald, however, he was not a centralist and at the Quebec Confederation Conference he spoke for and won rights for the provinces.

Later, as Liberal premier of Ontario, he battled with Macdonald over federal and provincial rights. He took his case to the Privy Council in London where he won an extension of provincial boundaries, provincial control of the waterways, provincial control of liquor licences and the appointment of Queen's Counsel as well as the right to collect duties and assessments.

He was premier of Ontario for 24 years and died in office in 1903.

A FIRST FOR FAIRCLOUGH

Ellen Fairclough of Hamilton, Ont., became Canada's first woman cabinet member when John Diefenbaker appointed her secretary of state in 1957. Later she became minister of immigration and postmaster general.

PREMIERS TO PRIME MINISTERS

Canada has had 16 prime ministers in the 115 years since Confederation, but only two have risen from the ranks of provincial premiers.

Sir John Thompson was premier of Nova Scotia in 1882 and became prime minister in 1892. He fell ill while dining with Queen Victoria at Windsor Castle in 1893 and died in England.

Sir Charles Tupper was premier of Nova Scotia before Confederation and became prime minister in 1896. Three months after he took office, there was a general election and the government of Sir Wilfrid Laurier was elected.

NELLIE McCLUNG IN MANITOBA

Nellie McClung was an early protagonist for women's rights in Canada. She was a practical activist and with her workers scoured Manitoba to collect 44,000 signatures on a suffrage petition. Women were enfranchised in Manitoba in 1916 as a result of the feminist movement.

PARLIAMENTARY PREMIERE

Agnes MacPhail was the first woman to be elected to the Parliament of Canada. MacPhail was a 31-year-old schoolteacher who was supported by Ontario farmers. She sat with the new Progressives.

WINNING VOTE FOR WOMEN

Idola Saint-Jean was born in Montreal in 1880. A French language teacher, she was an early activist for women's suffrage and women's rights in the province of Quebec. The fight was hard. Quebec women were not equal before the law, they could not control their own finances and they could not vote in provincial elections. She founded "l'Alliance canadienne pour le vote des femmes du Quebec" and in 1930 she upset many traditional-minded citizens when she ran in the federal election. Saint-Jean was subjected to rudeness and indignity, but women received the right to vote in Quebec in 1940.

POLITICAL EXPORT MAKES P.M.

Andrew Bonar Law, born in New Brunswick in 1858, became prime minister of Great Britain in 1922. He was the only Canadian-born person to hold that office.

ELECTION A COMMONWEALTH FIRST

Louise McKinney, born in Frankville, Ont., in 1868, became the first female member of a British Commonwealth legislature when she was elected to the Alberta legislature in 1917. She helped strengthen prohibition and improve conditions for women and immigrants. She worked for the Women's Christian Temperance Union and women's suffrage and was convinced that once women had the vote many of the evils of society would be eliminated. She was defeated in 1921 but continued working for the WCTU and women's rights and was active in the formation of the United Church.

CLAIROL FASHION AWARDS

Clairol Canada

To qualify for the award, designers must have between two and five years experience and must work under their own label or create a line for a manufacturer. The collection must sell at a retail level.

There were 105 applications from across Canada and there were nine finalists. A jury of six fashion experts selected the winner at a gala in Montreal. The winner received a silver trophy designed by sculptor Colin Gibson and a $3,000 cash award.

1983 **Paddye Mann**, 30, a boutique owner, Pakenham, Ont.
Finalists
Albert Shu, Vancouver
Carolyn Sandstrom, Calgary
Shelly Widmeyer Walsh, Toronto
Tam Southam, Toronto
Judi Fried, Montreal
Claude Gagnon, Montreal
Kentsou, Montreal
Catherine Arsenault Toth, Halifax

SEAL OF ACHIEVEMENT AWARD

For outstanding contribution to the fashion industry in Canada as chosen by the fashion press of Canada.

1983 **Alfred Sung**, Toronto. The 34-year-old designer was born in Hong Kong and after training in Paris and New York, he moved to Toronto. His ready-to-wear collection is sold in his own boutique in Toronto and in department and specialty stores across North America.

DESIGNS FOR DIANA

Donald Campbell is a fashion designer with a salon in Knightsbridge, London. His dresses are worn by some of London's most elegant people including Diana, Princess of Wales.

Campbell, the son of a United Church

minister, was born in Cobourg, Ont. He studied fashion design at Ryerson Polytechnical Institute in Toronto and worked in the Toronto dress trade for several years before moving to London in the mid-50s.

MISS CANADA AND MISS UNIVERSE

Miss Canada Pageant

Miss Canada was crowned in November 1982, before 35 other contestants and a national television audience. Miss Canada then went to the Miss Universe contest and was named the most beautiful woman in the world.

1982 **Karen Baldwin**, London, Ont. Karen is 19 years old and five-foot-nine inches tall. She has brown hair and green eyes. She enjoys sports, especially swimming, and likes to cook, read and dance. She plans to attend university to study business administration and hopes for a career in fashion or advertising.

MISS TEEN CANADA 1983

Miss Teen Canada Pageant

1983 **Lori Dawn Assheton-Smith**, Edmonton, Alta., was crowned Miss Teen Canada 1983 before a national TV audience by Emily Sertic, Miss Teen Canada 1982 (also from Edmonton) in March 1983.

The 1983 Queen, who is 16 years old, is five feet, six and one half inches tall. She has light brown hair and blue eyes. She attends high school, plays the piano, skis and plans to study business administration at university.

A NATION OF CLOCK WATCHERS?

According to market research gathered for TMX Canada Inc., Canadians purchased nearly six million watches in 1982. The average price of a watch is $42 in 1982, but Canadians bought bargain basement digitals at $4.98 and uniquely designed gold and gem creations in the million-dollar range — still a lot cheaper than a watch which sold to an anonymous buyer for $8.4 million in Tokyo in 1981.

CANADIAN HAIRSTYLING CHAMPIONSHIP

Allied Beauty Association

Contestants from across Canada compete in the event which is judged on workmanship and suitability for day and evening styles. The winner receives a trophy, a cash prize of $1,000 and represents Canada at international competitions.

1983 **Aldo Di Tacchio**, Toronto, Ont.
Provincial champions
June Laxton, Clearbrooke, B.C.
Debra Jauch, Edmonton, Alta.
Lori Hrychuk, Saskatoon, Sask.
Carole Foerster, Winnipeg, Man.
Andre Guimond, Trois Rivieres, Que.
Ian Smith, Halifax, N.S.

DESIGNERS HONOURED

Five Canadian jewelry designers who work in gold were honoured in April 1983 by the Canadian Gold Information Centre when they, and a display of their work, were presented at the first Gold Jewelry Design forum in Toronto. The designers and craftsmen were:

Ivan Kotulsky, Toronto
Madeleine Dansereau, Montreal
Ludwig Nickel, Winnipeg
Michael Kwong, Bermark Jewellery Ltd.
Donald Spratling, French Jewellery Co. of Canada.

MISS RODEO CANADA

Canadian Professional Rodeo Association

The Miss Rodeo Canada pageant is held in conjunction with the Canadian Finals

Rodeo. Contestants are judged on horsemanship, rodeo knowledge, public speaking, off-stage presentation, personal appearance as well as personality and poise.

The winner wears a coveted 10K white gold crown, receives a wardrobe and a silver and gold buckle, and promotes the Rodeo Association through the next rodeo season.

1983 **Kathy Cornelson**, Eastend, Sask. Cornelson, the 1982 Miss Rodeo Shaunavon, competed with 10 other young ladies for the Miss Rodeo Canada title. She has won awards in youth cutting, barrel racing and pole bending. One of her goals is to teach handicapped children and adults to work with and ride horses.

SAVED MANITOBA MUSKRATS

Tom Lamb, born in 1898 in northern Manitoba to an independent fur trader, was a teamster, a trapper, a cattle rancher, a conservationist and bush pilot. His action filled life is the subject of a book *The Last Great Frontiersman* by Leland Stowe published in 1983.

Among other exploits, Lamb is credited with saving the Manitoba fur industry. During the Depression, surveys showed that there were only 26,000 muskrats left in the province, though at the turn of the century Manitoba had sold more than 850,000 of the pelts. Lamb learned that a drop in marsh water levels had hindered the muskrats ability to find winter food. He was able to get some marsh land set aside and built dams to raise the water levels. In three years he had turned the industry around.

FABULOUR FUR FAIR

The largest fur fair ever held in North America was held in May 1983 in Montreal. There were more than 175 exhibitors from Canada, Austria, England, Finland, France, Germany, Hong Kong, Japan, Italy and the U.S., showing their wares to some 400 buyers from around the world. The annual show in Frankfurt, West-Germany, is the only show larger.

NOVA SCOTIA GIANTS

Angus MacAskill was born in 1825 in Scotland and was brought as an infant to Cape Breton Island. He was the world's tallest recorded "true" giant. At maturity he was seven feet, nine inches tall and weighed in at 400 pounds.

He toured with Tom Thumb in a travelling show and then returned home and invested his savings in a general store and some farms. According to legend he lifted a 2,100-pound anchor, a feat which caused him fatal injury. He died in 1863 at St. Ann's.

Anna Hanen Swan (1846-88), of Nova Scotia, stood seven feet, 5 1/2 inches when she was measured in London in 1871. Her husband Martin van Buren Bates, from Kentucky, was seven feet, 2 1/2 inches tall. Thus they were the tallest married couple known.

SURE TOUCH

Lou Myles of Toronto is tailor to the internationally known singer Vic Damone. Damone, 54, has made the 10-best-dressed-men's list of the Custom Tailors Guild of America for eight years.

Percy Williams, 20, wins the gold medal at the Olympic Games, Amsterdam, 1928.
(From the Prudential *Great Moments in Sport Collection*). Artist — Tom Hodgson

Athletics & Recreation

SPORTS

CANADIAN SUMMER OLYMPIC MEDALISTS FROM 1896

1896 Athens
Canada not represented

1900 Paris
George Orton (competed for USA), 2,500 m steeplechase, gold
400 m hurdles, bronze

1904 St. Louis
Etienne Desmarteau, 56-pound weight throw, gold
Argonaut Rowing Club, Toronto, eights, silver
Galt Football Club, soccer, gold
George S. Lyon, golf, gold
Shamrock Club, Wpg., lacrosse, gold

1908 London
Robert Kerr, 100 m, bronze, 200 m, gold
Ed Archibald, pole vault, bronze
Calvin Bricker, long jump, bronze
Garfield MacDonald, triple jump, silver
Con Walsh, hammer throw, bronze
Argonaut Rowing Club, Toronto, eights, tie bronze
Aubert Côté, wrestling, freestyle, bantamweight, bronze
F.P. Toms, N.B. Jackes, rowing, coxless pairs, bronze
W. Morton, W. Anderson, W. Andrews, F. McCarthy, cycling, 4000 m team pursuit, bronze
Walter Henry Ewing, shooting, clay pigeon, individual, gold
George Beattie, shooting, clay pigeon, individual, silver
Walter Henry Ewing, George Beattie, A.W. Westover, Mylie E. Fletcher,

George L. Vivian, D. McMackon, shooting, clay pigeon, team, silver
Patrick Brennan, Ernest Hamilton, Clarence McKerrow, Angus Dillon, Thomas Gorman, Henry Hoobin, George H. Rennie, George H. Campbell, John Broderick, Alexander Turnbull, I. Duckett, Frank Dixon, lacrosse, team, gold
William A. Smith, Charles Robert Crowe, B.M. Williams, D. McInnis, W.M. Eastcott, shooting, military rifle, team, bronze

1912 Stockholm
George Goulding, 10,000 m walk, gold
William Hapeny, pole vault, tie bronze
Calvin Bricker, long jump, silver
Duncan Gillis, hammer throw, silver
Frank Lukeman, pentathlon, bronze
George Hodgson, swimming, 400 m freestyle, gold, 1500 m freestyle, gold
Everard Butler, rowing, single sculls, tie bronze

1920 Antwerp
Earl Thomson, 110 m hurdles, gold
George Vernot, swimming, 400 m freestyle, bronze, 1500 m freestyle, silver
Chris Graham, boxing, bantamweight, silver
Chris Newton, boxing, lightweight, bronze
Bert Schneider, boxing, welterweight, gold
George Prud'homme, boxing, middleweight, silver
Moe Herscovitch, boxing, middleweight, bronze

1924 Paris

Douglas Lewis, boxing, welterweight, bronze

Colin Finlayson, William Wood, George Mackay, Archibald Black, rowing, coxless fours, silver

Arthur Bell, Robert Hunter, Harold B. Little, Norman Taylor, John Smith, L. William Wallace, William Langford, Warren B. Snyder, J. Campbell (cox), rowing, eights, silver

Samuel G. Vance, George Beattie, James Montgomery, William Barnes, John Black, Samuel Newton, shooting, clay pigeon, team, silver

1928 Amsterdam

Percy Williams, 100 m, gold, 200 m, gold

James Ball, 400 m, silver

Alexander Wilson, Philip Edwards, Stanley Glover, James Ball, 4 x 400 m relay, bronze

Fanny Rosenfeld, 100 m, silver

Ethel Smith, 100 m, bronze

Fanny Rosenfeld, Florence Bell, Ethel Smith, Myrtle Cook, 4 x 100 m relay, gold

Ethel Catherwood, high jump, gold

Munro Bourne, Garnet Ault, James Thompson, Walter Spence, swimming, 4 x 200 m freestyle relay, bronze

Jack Guest, Joseph Wright, rowing, double sculls, silver

Frederick Hedges, Herbert Richardson, Edgar Norris, Frank Fiddes, Jack Murdock, William Ross, John Hand, Athol Meech, John Donnelly (cox), rowing, eights, bronze

Raymond Smillie, boxing, welterweight, bronze

James Trifunov, wrestling, freestyle, bantamweight, bronze

Maurice Letchford, wrestling, freestyle, welterweight, bronze

Donald P. Stockton, wrestling, freestyle, middleweight, silver

1932 Los Angeles

Alexander Wilson, 400 m, bronze, 800 m, silver

Philip Edwards, 800 m, bronze, 1500 m, bronze

Raymond Lewis, James Ball, Philip

Edwards, Alexander Wilson, 4 x 400 m relay, bronze

Duncan McNaughton, high jump, gold

Hilda Strike, 100 m, silver

Eva Dawes, high jump, bronze

Mildred Frizzell, Mary Frizzell, Hilda Strike, Lillian Palmer, 4 x 100 m relay, silver

Noel de Mille, Charles Pratt, rowing, double sculls, bronze

Albert Taylor, Donald Boal, William Thoburn, Cedric Liddell, Harry Fry, Stanley Stanyar, Joseph Harris, Earl Eastwood, George MacDonald (cox), rowing, eights, bronze

Horace Gwynne, boxing, bantamweight, gold

Daniel McDonald, wrestling, freestyle, welterweight, silver

Philip Rogers, Gerald Wilson, Gardner Boultbee, Kenneth Glass, yachting, 6 m class, bronze

Ronald Maitland, Ernest Cribb, Harry Jones, Peter Gordon, Hubert Wallace, George Gyles, yachting, 8 m class, silver

Tait McKenzie, olympic art, medals, bronze

1936 Berlin

Philip Edwards, 800 m, bronze

John Loaring, 400 m hurdles, silver

Elizabeth Taylor, 80 m hurdles, bronze

Mildred Dolson, Dorothy Brookshaw, Hilda Cameron, Eileen Meagher, 4 x 100 m relay, bronze

Joseph Schleimer, wrestling, freestyle, welterweight, bronze

Francis Amyot, canoeing, singles, 1000 m, gold

Frank Saker, Harvey Charters, canoeing, pairs, 1000 m, bronze

Frank Saker, Harvey Charters, canoeing, pairs, 10,000 m, silver

James Stewart, Gordon Aitchison, Ian Allison, Charles Chapman, Douglas Peden, Malcolm Wiseman, Arthur Chapman, Edward Dawson, Norman Dawson, Don Gray, Irving Meretsky, Stanley Nantais, Robert Osborne, Tom Pendlebury, P.P. McCallum, basketball, silver

1948 London

Viola Myers, Diane Foster, Nancy

Mackay, Patricia Jones, 4 x 100 m relay, bronze

Douglas Bennett, canoeing, singles, 1000 m, silver

Norman Lane, canoeing, singles, 10,000 m, bronze

Jean Weinzweig, Olympic art, composition for one instrument, silver

1952 Helsinki

Gerard Gratton, weightlifting, middleweight, silver

George Genereux, shooting, clay pigeon, gold

Kenneth Lane, Donald Hawgood, canoeing, pairs, 10,000 m, silver

1956 Melbourne

Irene MacDonald, diving, springboard, bronze

Donald Arnold, Lorne Loomer, Walter D'Hondt, Archibald McKinnon, rowing, coxless fours, gold

Lawrence West, Donald Pretty, Richard McClure, Douglas McDonald, David Helliwell, Philp Kueber, William McKerlich, Robert Wilson, Carlton Ogawa (cox), rowing, eights, silver

Gerald Ouellette, shooting, small bore rifle, prone, gold

Gilmour Boa, shooting, small bore rifle, prone, bronze

1956 Stockholm

John Rumble, Brian Herbinson, Jim Elder, equestrian, three-day event, team, bronze

1960 Rome

Donald Arnold, John Leckie, William McKerlich, Walter D'Hondt, Lorne Loomer, Archibald MacKinnon, Nelson Kuhn, Glen Mervyn, Sohen Biln (cox), rowing, eights, silver

1964 Tokyo

Harry Jerome, 100 m, bronze

William Crothers, 800 m, silver

Roger Jackson, George Hungerford, rowing, coxless pairs, gold

Douglas Rogers, judo, heavyweight, silver

1968 Mexico

Ralph Hutton, swimming, 400 m freestyle, silver

Elaine Tanner, swimming, 100 m backstroke, silver, 200 m backstroke, silver

Elaine Tanner, Marilyn Corson, Angela Coughlan, swimming, 4 x 100 m freestyle relay, bronze

James Day, Jim Elder, Tom Gayford, equestrian, Grand Prix jumping, team, gold

1972 Munich

Leslie Cliff, swimming, 400 m individual medley, silver

Donna Marie Gurr, swimming, 200 m backstroke, bronze

Bruce Robertson, swimming, 100 m butterfly, silver

Erik Fish, Bill Mahony, Bruce Robertson, Bob Kasting, swimming, 4 x 100 m medley relay, bronze

David Miller, John Ekels, Paul Coté, yachting, soling class, bronze

1976 Montreal

Greg Joy, high jump, silver

John Wood, canoe, 500 m C-1, silver

Michel Vaillancourt, equestrian, Grand Prix jump, silver

Cheryl Gibson, swimming, 400 m individual medley, silver

Stephen Pickell, Shannon Smith, Clay Evans, Gary McDonald, swimming, 4 x 100 m relay, silver

Nancy Garapick, swimming, 100 m backstroke and 200 m backstroke, two bronze

Becky Smith, swimming, 100 m, individual medley, bronze

Shannon Smith, swimming, 400 m freestyle, bronze

Gail Amundrud, Barbara Clark, Becky Smith, Anne Jardin, swimming, 4 x 100 m free relay, bronze

Wendy Hogg, Robin Corsiglia, Susan Sloan, Anne Jardin, swimming, 4 x 100 m medley relay, bronze

CANADIAN WINTER OLYMPIC MEDALISTS, FROM 1920

1920 Antwerp

Winnipeg Falcons: R. Benson, O. Benson, W. Byron, F. Frederickson, C. Frederickson, M. Goodman, M. Halderson, K. Johansson, A. Woodman, ice hockey, gold

1924 Chamonix

Toronto Granites: J. Cameron, E. Collett, A. McCaffrey, D. Munro, W.

Ramsay, C. Slater, R. Smith, H. Watson, H. McMunn, ice hockey, gold

1928 St. Moritz
U. of T. Grads, Dr. J. Sullivan, R. Taylor, J.C. Porter, L. Hudson, R. Plaxton, D. Trottier, N. Mueller, H. Plaxton, F. Sullivan, F. Fisher, Bert Plaxton, C.Delahay, G. Gordon, ice hockey, gold

1932 Lake Placid
Montgomery Wilson, figure skating—men, bronze
Alex Hurd, speed skating—men's 500 m, bronze
Alex Hurd, speed skating—men's 1,500 m, silver
William Logan, speed skating—men's 1,500 m, bronze
William Logan, speed skating—men's 5,000 m, bronze
Frank Stack, speed skating—men's 10,000 m, bronze
Jean Wilson, speed skating—ladies' 500 m, gold
Hattie Donaldson, speed skating—ladies' 1,000 m, silver
Jean Wilson, speed skating—ladies' 1,500 m, silver
Winnipeg Monarchs: W. Cockburn, C. Crowley, A. Duncanson, G. Carbutt, R. Hinkel, V. Lingquist, H. Malloy, W. Monson, K. Moore, R. Rivers, H. Simpson, H. Sutherland, S. Wagner, S. Wise, F. Wooley, ice hockey, gold

1936 Garmisch-Partenkirchen
Port Arthur: D. Moore, W. Nash, H. Murray, F.F. Deacon, D. Neville, K. Farmer, H. Farquharson, R. Milson Pudas (coach), A. Sinclair, W. Thompson, W. Kitchen, ice hockey, silver

1948 St. Moritz
Barbara Ann Scott, figure skating, ladies, gold
S. Morrow, W. Diestelmeyer, figure skating, pairs, bronze
R.C.A.F. Flyers: M. Dowey, B. Dunster, J. Lecompte, H. Laperrière, W. Halder, G. Mara, R. Schroeter, T. Hibbert, A. Renaud, O. Gravelle, P. Guzzo, ice hockey, gold

1952 Oslo
G. Audley, speed skating—men's 500 m, bronze
Edmonton Mercurys: R. Hansch, E. Paterson, J. Davies, R. Myers, A. Purvis, D. Miller, W. Dawe, D. Gauf, R. Watt, G. Abel, R. Dickson, L. Hommes (coach), F. Sullivan, L. Secco, W. Gibson, G. Robertson, T. Pollock, ice hockey, gold

1956 Cortina D'Ampezzo
Lucille Wheeler, alpine skiing, ladies' downhill, bronze
F. Dafoe, N. Bowden, figure skating, pairs, silver
Kitchener-Waterloo: D. Brodeur, C. Brooker, K. Laufman, D. Rope, R. White, A. Hurst, J. Logan, W. Colvin, B. Klinck, H. Lee, G. Scholes, K. Woodall, F. Martin, J. Horne, P. Knox, J. McKenzie, G. Théberge, B. Bauer, ice hockey, bronze

1960 Squaw Valley
Anne Heggtveit, alpine skiing, ladies' slalom, gold
D. Jackson, figure skating, men, bronze
B. Wagner, B. Paul, figure skating, pairs, gold
Kitchener-Waterloo: R. Attersley, M. Benoit, J. Connelly, J. Douglas, F. Etcher, R. Forhan, D. Head, H. Hurley, K. Laufman, F. Martin, R. McKnight, C. Pennington, D. Rope, R. Rousseau, G. Samonlenko, H. Sinden, D. Sly, R. Bauer, ice hockey, silver

1964 Innsbruck
V.S. Emery, J. Emery, D. Anakin, P. Kirby, bobsleigh, 4-man, gold
Petra Burka, figure skating, ladies, bronze
D. Wilkes, G. Revell, figure skating, pairs, silver

1968 Grenoble
Nancy Greene, alpine skiing, ladies' giant slalom, gold
Nancy Greene, alpine skiing, ladies' slalom, silver
Canada: R. Bourbonnais, K. Broderick, P. Conlin, B. Glennie, T. Hargreaves, F. Huck, J. McLeod (coach), M. Johnston, G. Pinder, W. MacMillan, S. Monteith, M. Mott, T.

O'Malley, D. O'Shea, B. Mackenzie, H. Pinder, R. Cadieux, W. Stephenson, G. Dineen, ice hockey, bronze

1972 Sapporo
Karen Magnussen, figure skating, women, silver

1976 Innsbruck
Kathy Kreiner, alpine skiing, ladies' giant slalom, gold
Cathy Priestner, speed skating, ladies' 500 m, silver
Toller Cranston, figure skating, men's, bronze

1980 Lake Placid
Gaetan Boucher, speed skating, 1000 m men, silver
Steve Podborski, alpine ski, downhill — men, silver

RECENT CANADIAN WINNERS IN INTERNATIONAL AMATEUR SPORT COMPETITION

Alpine Ski

1976 Kathy Kreiner, Olympic gold, giant slalom
1980 Steve Podborski, Olympic bronze, downhill
1981 Steve Podborski, World Cup silver, downhill

Archery

1974 Lucille Lessard, World champion, field

Athletics

1976 Greg Joy, Olympic silver, high jump
1978 Carmen Ionesco, Commonwealth, gold, discus
Diane Jones-Konihowski, Commonwealth, gold, pentathlon
Claude Ferragne, Commonwealth, gold, high jump
Bruce Simpson, Commonwealth, gold, pole vault
Borys Chambul, Commonwealth, gold, discus
Phil Olsen, Commonwealth, gold, javelin
1979 Diane Jones-Konihowski, Pan Am, gold, pentathlon
Scott Neilson, Pan Am, gold, hammer throw

Bruce Simpson, Pan Am, gold, pole vault
Debbie Brill, World Cup, gold, high jump
1981 Marita Payne, World Cup, bronze, 4 x 400 m relay
Charmaine Crooks, World Cup, bronze, 4 x 400 m relay

Bowling

1980 Jean Gordon, World champion, ten pin

Boxing

1978 Kelly Perlette, Commonwealth, gold, 71 kg
Roger Fortin, Commonwealth, gold, 81 kg

Canoe

1981 Larry Cain, World champion, 500 m C1, 1000 m C1

Curling

1980 Rick Folk, Ron Mills, Jim Wilson, Tom Wilson, World champions

Cycling

1978 Jocelyn Lovell, World championships, silver, 1 km
Jocelyn Lovell, Commonwealth, gold, time trial
Jocelyn Lovell, Commonwealth, gold, tandem sprint
Jocelyn Lovell, Commonwealth, gold, 10 mile
Gord Singleton, Commonwealth, gold, tandem sprint
1979 Gord Singleton, Pan Am, gold, 1 km
Gord Singleton, Pan Am, gold, time trial
Claude Langlois, Pan Am, gold, 4000 m individual pursuit
Gord Singleton, World championships, silver, sprint

Diving

1978 Janet Nutter, Commonwealth, gold, 3 m
Linda Cuthbert, Commonwealth, gold, 10 m

Equestrian

1976 **Michel Vaillancourt**, Olympic, silver, jumping
1978 **Liz Ashton, Juliette Bishop, Mark Ishoy, Cathy Wedge**, World champions, 3 day event

Figure Skating

1973 **Karen Magnussen**, World champion
1976 **Toller Cranston**, Olympic, bronze

Gymnastics

1978 **Monica Goermann, Sherry Hawco, Karen Kelsall, Elfie Schlegel**, Commonwealth, team gold
Elfie Schlegel, Commonwealth, gold
Jean Choquette, Nigel Rothwell, Owen Walstrom, Philip Delesalle, Commonwealth, team gold
1979 **Carmen Alie, Diana Carnegie, Shannon Fleming, Monica Goermann, Sherry Hawco, Elfie Schlegel, Ellen Stewart**, Pan Am, team gold
Monica Goermann, Pan Am, gold, overall
Monica Goermann, Pan Am, gold, uneven bars
Sherry Hawco, Pan Am, gold, balance beam

Judo

1979 **Brad Farrow**, Pan Am, gold, 65 kg
Louis Jani, Pan Am, gold, 80 kg
1981 **Phil Takahashi**, World championships, bronze, 60 kg
Kevin Doherty, World championships, bronze, 78 kg

Lacrosse

1978 **John Mouradian, Bob Burke, Tim Barrie, Pat Differ, John Grant, Carm Collins, Brian Jones, Steve Mastine, Tim Briscoe, Jim Calder, Jim Wasson, Sandy Lynch, Mike French, Murray Cawker, Fred Greenwood, Bob Flintoff, Dave Huntley, Dave Durante, Stan Cockerton, Jim Branton, Ted Greves, Doug Hayes, Dan Wilson**, World champions, field
1980 **Mario Govorchin, Greg Thomas, Jim Attchison, Moe Jodoin, Kevin Parsons, Mat Aiken, Fred Klomp, Rico**

Bellusci, Gary Lindsay, Dave Cochrane, Ray Mathison, Randy Delmonico, Wayne McAuley, Gord Quilty, Rhys Parsons, Frank Nielsen, Randy Bryan, Dan Wilson, Mike Reelie, Tim Kelly, John Lewis, Mark Valastin, World champions, box

Ladies Golf

1978 **Cathy Sherk**, World champion

Parachuting

1980 **Kathy Cox**, World champion, accuracy
1981 **Kelly Dunn, Claude Marchand, Graham Taylor, Mark Vincent**, World championship, silver, 4-way team
Eric Bradley, Vincent Brouillet, Kelly Dunn, Rob Laidlaw, Lawrence McLeod, Claude Marchand, Karen Opleta, Graham Taylor, Mark Vincent, Mike Zahar, World championship, silver, 8-way team

Rowing

1979 **Bruce Ford, Pat Walter**, Pan Am, double sculls
Brian Dick, Tim Storm, Pan Am, pairs without cox
1981 **Betty Craig, Tricia Smith**, World championships, silver, pairs

Shooting

1978 **Yvon Trempe**, Commonwealth, gold, free pistol
Jules Sobrian, Commonwealth, gold, rapid fire pistol
John Primrose, Commonwealth, gold, trap
Desmond Vamplew, Commonwealth, gold, full bore rifle
1979 **Guy Lorion**, Pan Am, gold, air rifle
Tom Guinn, Ed Jans, Art Tomsett, Bud Wolochow, Pan Am, gold, team free pistol
Susan Nattrass, World champion, trap

Softball

1976 **Ken Bate, Randy Benn, Bob Burrows, Lyall Cornett, Wayne Forland, Bob Holness, Bill James, Stan Kern, Pete Landers, Jim McMillan, Dave Ruthowsky, Peter Songhurst, Harvey Stevenson, Mike Taafe, Reg Under-**

wood, Carl Walker, World champions, three-way tie

1979 **Randy Benn, Cliff Bishop, Warren Campbell, Dennis Eckert, Alden Govenlock, John Green, Rob Guenter, Mike Henderson, Bob Holness, Sonny Phillips, Dave Ruthowski, Mark Smith, Reg Underwood, Carl Walker, Bob Walton, Dave Williams, Dave Wilson**, Pan Am, gold

Speed Skating

1976 **Cathy Priestner**, Olympic, silver, 500 m
1977 **Sylvia Burka**, World champion, overall
1978 **Sylvie Daigle**, World champion, indoor 500 m
1980 **Gaetan Boucher**, World champion, indoor overall
Gaetan Boucher, Olympic, silver, 1000 m

Swimming

1973 **Bruce Robertson**, World champion, 100 m butterfly
1975 **Nancy Garapick**, World championships, bronze, 100 m backstroke
Nancy Garapick, World championships, bronze, 200 m backstroke
1976 **Cheryl Gibson**, Olympic, silver, 400 m individual medley
Stephen Pickell, Graham Smith, Clay Evans, Gary McDonald, Olympic, silver, 4 x 100 m medley relay
Becky Smith, Olympic, bronze, 400 m individual medley
Shannon Smith, Olympic, bronze, 400 m freestyle
Nancy Garapick, Olympic, bronze, 100 m backstroke
Nancy Garapick, Olympic, bronze, 200 m backstroke
Gail Amundrud, Barbara Clark, Becky Smith, Anne Jardin, Olympic, bronze, 4 x 100 m freestyle relay
Wendy Hogg, Robin Corsiglia, Susan Sloan, Anne Jardin, Olympic, bronze, 4 x 100 m medley relay
1978 **Carol Klimpel**, Commonwealth, gold, 100 m freestyle
Wendy Quirk, Commonwealth, gold, 100 m butterfly

Cheryl Gibson, Commonwealth, gold, 200 m backstroke
Lisa Borsholt, Commonwealth, gold, 200 m breaststroke
Robin Corsiglia, Commonwealth, gold, 100 m breaststroke
Graham Smith, Commonwealth, gold, 200 m breaststroke
Graham Smith, Commonwealth, gold, 100 m breaststroke
Graham Smith, Commonwealth, gold, 200 m individual medley
Graham Smith, Commonwealth, gold, 400 m individual medley
Dan Thompson, Commonwealth, gold, 100 m butterfly
George Nagy, Commonwealth, gold, 200 m butterfly
Graham Smith, World champion, 200 m individual medley
1979 **Anne Gagnon**, Pan Am, gold, 200 m breaststroke

Synchronized Swimming

1978 **Helen Vanderburg**, World champion, solo
Helen Vanderburg, Michelle Calkins, World champions, duet
1979 **Helen Vanderburg**, Pan Am, gold, solo
Helen Vanderburg, Kelly Kryzcka, Pan Am, gold, duet

Water Ski

1979 **Joel McClintock**, World champion, overall
Pat Messner, World champion, slalom

Weightlifting

1978 **Michel Mercier**, Commonwealth, gold, 60 kg
Russ Prior, Commonwealth, gold, 110 kg
Marc Cardinal, Commonwealth, gold, +110 kg
1979 **Terry Hadlow**, Pan Am, gold, 90 kg snatch

Wheelchair

1980 **Mel Fitzgerald**, Disabled Olympics, 800 m, 1500 m

Wrestling

1978 **Ray Takahashi**, Commonwealth, gold, 52 kg
 Egon Beiler, Commonwealth, gold, 62 kg
 Richard Deschatelets, Commonwealth, gold, 82 kg
 Steve Daniar, Commonwealth, gold, 90 kg
 Wyatt Wishart, Commonwealth, gold, 100 kg
 Bob Gibbons, Commonwealth, gold, +100 kg
1979 **Doug Yeats**, Pan Am, gold, 62 kg Greco Roman
 Howard Stupp, Pan Am, gold, 68 kg Greco Roman

Yachting

1979 **Terry Neilson**, Pan Am, gold, laser
1980 **Glen Dexter, Andreas Josenhans**, World champions, soling
 Sandy MacMillan, World champion, soling
1980 **Terry McLaughlin, Evert Bastet**, World champions, Flying Dutchman

VII PAN AMERICAN GAMES (1979), SAN JUAN, PUERTO RICO

Canadian Medal Winners

Archery

Daniel Desnoyers, Loretteville, Que., **Stan Siatkowski**, Toronto, Ont., **Chris Smith**, Harvey Station, N.B., silver
Linda Kazienko, Scarboro, Ont., **Joan McDonald**, Toronto, Ont., **Marie-Claude Pitre**, Carignan, Que., silver
Joan McDonald, Toronto, Ont., bronze
Stan Siatkowski, Toronto, Ont., bronze

Women's Athletics

Diane Jones-Konihowski, Edmonton, Alta., pentathlon, gold
Angella Taylor, Toronto, Ont., 200 m, silver
Sharon Lane, Ancaster, Ont., 100 m hurdles, silver
Angella Taylor, Toronto, Ont., 100 m, bronze
Penny Werthner-Bales, Ottawa, Ont., 1500 m, bronze
Geri Fitch, Toronto, Ont., 3000 m, bronze

Jill Ross, London, Ont., pentathlon, bronze
Carmen Ionesco, St. Bruno, Que., discus, bronze
Carmen Ionesco, St. Bruno, Que., shot put, bronze
Debbie Brill, Aldergrove, B.C., high jump, bronze
Anne Mackie-Morelli, Vancouver, B.C., **Marita Payne**, Toronto, Ont., **Micheline Racette**, Montreal, Que., **Janette Wood**, Oakville, Ont., 4 x 400 m relay, bronze

Men's Athletics

Scott Neilson, New Westminster, B.C., hammer throw, gold
Bruce Simpson, Agincourt, Ont., pole vault, gold
Bishop Dolegiewicz, Toronto, Ont., shot put, silver
Richard Hughson, Waterloo, Ont., marathon, bronze
Zenon Smiechowski, Grande Prairie, Alta., decathlon, bronze
Milt Ottey, Toronto, Ont., high jump, bronze
Bruno Pauletto, Sept Isles, Que., shot put, bronze

Women's Basketball

Candace Clarkson, Brantford, Ont., **Chris Critelli**, St. Catharines, Ont., **Denise Dignard**, Port Cartier, Que., **Sharon Douglas**, Regina, Sask., **Holly Jackson-Pedersen**, Calgary, Alta., **Alison Lang**, Saskatoon, Sask., **Dori McPhail**, Brandon, Man., **Debbie Steele**, Shuvenacadie, N.S., **Sylvia Sweeney**, Montreal, Que., **Carol Turney**, Victoria, B.C., **Debbie Huband**, Ottawa, Ont., **Bev Smith**, Salmon Arm, B.C., bronze

Boxing

Ian Clyde, Ottawa, Ont., 51 kg, bronze
Pat Fennell, Campbellford, Ont., 81 kg, bronze

Cycling

Gord Singleton, Niagara Falls, Ont., sprint, gold
Gord Singleton, Niagara Falls, Ont., 1 km time trial, gold
Claude Langlois, Montreal, Que., 4000 m individual pursuit, gold
Eon D'Ornellas, Oshawa, Ont., **Pierre Harvey**, Rimouski, Que., **Normand St. Au-**

bin, Roxboro, Que., **Bernard Willock**, Victoria, B.C., 100 km team time trial, bronze

Diving

Janet Nutter, Toronto, Ont., 3 m, bronze
Linda Cuthbert, Toronto, Ont., 10 m, bronze

Equestrian

Terry Leibel, Toronto, Ont., **Ian Millar**, Perth, Ont., **John Simpson**, Cochrane, Alta., **Michel Vaillancourt**, Hudson, Que., team jumping, silver
Ian Millar, Perth, Ont., individual jumping, bronze

Women's Fencing

Patty Balz, King City, Ont., **Karen Bergenstein**, Fonthill, Ont., **Chantal Gilbert-Payer**, Quebec, Que., **Louise Marie Leblanc**, Ottawa, Ont., **Jacynthe Poirier**, Chibougamou, Que., foil team, silver

Field Hockey

Julian Austin, Westhill, Ont., **Paramjit Bahia**, Richmond, B.C., **Dave Bissett**, Vancouver, B.C., **Bubli Chohan**, Vancouver, B.C., **Sarbjit Dusang**, Vancouver, B.C., **Bruce Eede**, Hamilton, Ont., **Alan Hobkirk**, Vancouver, B.C., **Fred Hoos**, Richmond, B.C., **Hash Kanjee**, Vancouver, B.C., **Steve Lewis**, Delta, B.C., **Peter Motzek**, Delta, B.C., **Michael Paget**, Victoria, B.C., **Mohinder Pal**, Willowdale, Ont., **Reg Plummer**, Vancouver, B.C., **Doug Pready**, Grand Forks, B.C., **Kelvin Wood**, Calgary, Alta., silver

Women's Gymnastics

Carmen Alie, Montreal, Que., **Diana Carnegie**, Rexdale, Ont., **Shannon Fleming**, Etobicoke, Ont., **Monica Goermann**, Winnipeg, Man., **Sherry Hawco**, Cambridge, Ont., **Elfie Schlegel**, Etobicoke, Ont., **Ellen Stewart**, Mississauga, Ont., gold
Monica Goermann, Winnipeg, Man., allround, gold
Sherry Hawco, Cambridge, Ont., balance beam, gold
Monica Goermann, Winnipeg, Man., uneven bars, gold
Elfie Schlegel, Etobicoke, Ont., uneven bars, silver
Elfie Schlegel, Etobicoke, Ont., vault, silver

Monica Goermann, Winnipeg, Man., floor exercises, silver
Elfie Schlegel, Etobicoke, Ont., all-round, bronze
Monica Goermann, Winnipeg, Man., balance beam, bronze

Men's Gymnastics

Jean Choquette, Montreal, Que., **Pierre Clavel**, Montreal, Que., **Marc Epprecht**, Cambridge, Ont., **Warren Long**, Victoria, B.C., **Nigel Rothwell**, Windsor, Ont., **Owen Walstrom**, Vancouver, B.C., silver
Warren Long, Victoria, B.C., floor exercises, silver
Warren Long, Victoria, B.C., vault, silver
Warren Long, Victoria, B.C., all-round, bronze
Warren Long, Victoria, B.C., horizontal bar, bronze
Jean Choquette, Montreal, Que., pommel horse, bronze
Pierre Clavel, Montreal, Que., rings, bronze

Judo

Brad Farrow, Delta, B.C., 65 kg, gold
Louis Jani, Montreal, Que., 80 kg, gold
Kevin Doherty, Thunder Bay, Ont., 71 kg, silver
Phil Takahashi, Ottawa, Ont., 60 kg, bronze
Joe Meli, Lethbridge, Alta., open, bronze

Rollerskating

Sylvie Gingras, Granby, Que., ladies' singles, bronze
Guy Aubin, Montreal, Que., men's singles, bronze
Guy Aubin, Montreal, Que., **Sylvie Gingras**, Granby, Que., pairs, bronze
Lori Beal, Agincourt, Ont., **Robert Dalgliesh**, Burlington, Ont., free dance, bronze

Rowing

Bruce Ford, Victoria, B.C., **Pat Walker**, Victoria, B.C., double scull, gold
Brian Dick, St. Catharines, Ont., **Tim Storm**, St. Catharines, Ont., pairs without cox, gold
Phil Monckton, Ottawa, Ont., single scull, silver
Bob Cherwinski, Hamilton, Ont., **Doug Turton**, Hamilton, Ont., **Carl Zintel**, Hamilton, Ont., **Mel Laforme**, Hamilton, Ont.,

Miles Cohen, Hamilton, Ont., four with cox, silver

Fred Withers, White Rock, B.C., **John Richardson**, W. Vancouver, B.C., **Robin Catherall**, Vancouver, B.C., **Marius Felix**, Victoria, B.C., **Rob Hartvickson**, Vancouver, B.C., **Dave Wilkinson**, Cobble Hill, B.C., **Greg Hood**, Rossland, B.C., **David Orr**, Vancouver, B.C., **Mike Conway**, Vancouver, B.C., eight with cox, silver

Shooting

Guy Lorion Jr., Longueuil, Que., air rifle, gold

Tom Guinn, South Woodslee, Ont., team free pistol, gold

Ed Jans, Calgary, Alta., **Art Tomsett**, Victoria, B.C., **Bud Wolochow**, Richmond, B.C., team free pistol, gold

Hans Adlhoch, Longueuil, Que., **Guy Lorion**, Longueuil, Que., **Alfons Mayer**, Kitchener, Ont., **Arne Sorensen**, Calgary, Alta., 3 position rifle team, silver

Edward Jans, Calgary, Alta., **Jules Sobrian**, Omemee, Ont., **Robert Zimmer**, Regina, Sask., **Steven Kelly**, Ottawa, Ont., centre fire team, silver

John Cowan, Niagara Falls, Ont., **Jim Kagan**, Edmonton, Alta., **George Leary**, Gormley, Ont., **John Primrose**, Edmonton, Alta., bronze

George Leary, Gormley, Ont., trap, bronze

Guy Lorion, Longueuil, Que., 3 position rifle, bronze

Alfons Mayer, Kitchener, Ont., prone rifle, bronze

Kurt Mitchell, Calgary, Alta., air rifle, bronze

Tom Guinn, S. Woodslee, Ont., individual free pistol, bronze

Men's Softball

Randy Benn, Victoria, B.C., **Cliff Bishop**, Winnipeg, Man., **Warren Campbell**, Victoria, B.C., **Dennis Eckert**, Victoria, B.C., **Alden Govenlock**, Sooke, B.C., **John Green**, Victoria, B.C., **Rob Guenter**, Saskatoon, Sask., **Mike Henderson**, Brookfield, N.S., **Bob Holness**, Victoria, B.C., **Sonny Phillips**, Tracy, N.B., **Dave Ruthowski**, Victoria, B.C., **Mark Smith**, Victoria, B.C., **Reg Underwood**, Victoria, B.C., **Carl Walker**, Victoria, B.C., **Bob Walton**, Victo-

ria, B.C., **Dave Williams**, Victoria, B.C., **Dave Wilson**, Victoria, B.C., gold

Women's Swimming

Anne Gagnon, Beauport, Que., 200 m breaststroke, gold

Joanne Bedard, Ste. Foy, Que., 200 m breaststroke, silver

Cheryl Gibson, Edmonton, Alta., 100 m backstroke, silver

Cheryl Gibson, Edmonton, Alta., 200 m backstroke, silver

Nancy Garapick, Halifax, N.S., 200 m individual medley, silver

Gail Amundrud, Vancouver, B.C., **Anne Jardin**, Pointe Claire, Que., **Carol Klimpel**, Scarborough, Ont., **Wendy Quirk**, Pointe Claire, Que., 4 x 100 m freestyle, silver

Gail Amundrud, Vancouver, B.C., **Anne Gagnon**, Beauport, Que., **Nancy Garapick**, Halifax, N.S., **Cheryl Gibson**, Edmonton, Alta., 4 x 100 m medley relay, silver

Anne Gagnon, Beauport, Que., 100 m breaststroke, bronze

Gail Amundrud, Vancouver, B.C., 100 m freestyle, bronze

Gail Amundrud, Vancouver, B.C., 200 m freestyle, bronze

Wendy Quirk, Pointe Claire, Que., 400 m freestyle, bronze

Barbara Shockey, Saskatoon, Sask., 800 m freestyle, bronze

Nancy Garapick, Halifax, N.S., 100 m butterfly, bronze

Nancy Garapick, Halifax, N.S., 200 m butterfly, bronze

Nancy Garapick, Halifax, N.S., 400 m individual medley, bronze

Men's Swimming

Dan Thompson, Toronto, Ont., 100 m butterfly, silver

George Nagy, Toronto, Ont., 200 m butterfly, silver

Graham Smith, Edmonton, Alta., 200 m individual medley, silver

Bill Sawchuk, Thunder Bay, Ont., 400 m individual medley, silver

Bill Sawchuk, Thunder Bay, Ont., **Alan Swanston**, Rockwood, Ont., **Peter Szmidt**, Pointe Claire, Que., **Graham Welbourn**, Claresholm, Alta., 4 x 100 m freestyle relay, silver

Stephen Pickell, Vancouver, B.C., **Bill Saw-**

chuk, Thunder Bay, Ont., **Graham Smith**, Edmonton, Alta., **Dan Thompson**, Toronto, Ont., 4 x 100 m medley relay, silver

Graham Smith, Edmonton, Alta., 100 m breaststroke, bronze

Stephen Pickell, Vancouver, B.C., 100 m backstroke, bronze

Clay Evans, Vancouver, B.C., 100 m butterfly, bronze

Bill Sawchuk, Thunder Bay, Ont., 200 m butterfly, bronze

Peter Szmidt, Pointe Claire, Que., 400 m freestyle, bronze

Alex Baumann, Sudbury, Ont., 400 m individual medley, bronze

Rob Baylis, N. Vancouver, B.C., **Bill Sawchuk**, Thunder Bay, Ont., **Peter Szmidt**, Pointe Claire, Que., **Graham Welbourn**, Claresholm, Alta., 4 x 200 m freestyle, bronze

Synchronized Swimming

Helen Vanderburg, Calgary, Alta., solo, gold

Kelly Kryczka, Calgary, Alta., **Helen Vanderburg**, Calgary, Alta., duet, gold

Janet Arnold, Kim Birnie, Sharon Hambrook, Beth Irwin, Raphaela Jablonca, Kelly Kryczka, Leslie Ringrose, Helen Vanderburg, all of Calgary, Alta., team, silver

Tennis

Nicole Marois, Hélene Pelletier, Quebec, Que., women's doubles, silver

Men's Volleyball

Richard Bacon, Stelio de Rocco, Paul Gratton, Dean Hitchcock, Tom Jones, Mark Kolodzeij, Al Kostiuk, Richard McDonald, Don Saxton, Al Taylor, all of Calgary, Alta., **Charles Parkinson**, Winnipeg, Man., **James Helmer**, Ottawa, Ont., bronze

Water Polo

René Bol, Ottawa, Ont., **Dominique Dion**, Quebec, Que., **George Gross, Jr.**, Ottawa, Ont., **Alex Juhasz**, Ottawa, Ont., **Mark Lawrence**, Burnaby, B.C., **Guy Leclerc**, Hull, Que., **Bill Meyer**, Ottawa, Ont., **Paul Pottier**, Dundas, Ont., **Ron Schaefer**, Coquitlam, B.C., **Pat Simmons**, Ottawa, Ont., **Gaetan Turcotte**, Quebec, Que., bronze

Weightlifting

Terry Hadlow, Elliott Lake, Ont., 90 kg snatch, gold

Terry Hadlow, Elliott Lake, Ont., 90 kg overall, silver

Marc Cardinal, Ottawa, Ont., super heavy snatch, silver

Marc Cardinal, Ottawa, Ont., super heavy jerk, silver

Marc Cardinal, Ottawa, Ont., super heavy overall, silver

Eric Rogers, Edmonton, Alta., 75 kg jerk, silver

Eric Rogers, Edmonton, Alta., 75 kg overall, silver

Jacques Giasson, LaSarre, Que., 67.5 kg snatch, silver

Michel Mercier, LaSarre, Que., 60 kg snatch, bronze

Gary Bratty, Stoney Creek, Ont., 67.5 jerk, bronze

Jacques Giasson, LaSarre, Que., 67.5 overall, bronze

Terry Hadlow, Elliott Lake, Ont., 90 kg jerk, bronze

Greco-Roman Wrestling

Doug Yeats, Montreal, Que., 62 kg, gold

Howard Stupp, Laval, Que., 68 kg, gold

Brian Renken, Thunder Bay, Ont., 74 kg, bronze

Louis Santerre, Montreal, Que., 82 kg, bronze

Steve Daniar, Thunder Bay, Ont., 90 kg, bronze

Freestyle Wrestling

Clark Davis, Vancouver, B.C., 82 kg, silver

John Park, Parry Sound, Ont., 62 kg, bronze

Egon Beiler, Kitchener, Ont., 68 kg, bronze

Marc Mongeon, Kitchener, Ont., 74 kg, bronze

Richard Deschatelets, St. Johns, Nfld., 90 kg, bronze

Mike Kappel, Niagara Falls, Ont., 100 kg, bronze

Wyatt Wishart, Thunder Bay, Ont., 100 kg, bronze

Yachting

Terry Neilson, Toronto, Ont., laser, gold

Gil Mercier, Pointe Claire, Que., **Peter Jones**,

Toronto, Ont., **Gord Crothers**, Kingston, Ont., lightning, silver

Jerry Roufs, Montreal, Que., **Charles Robitaille**, Quebec, Que., 470, bronze

Jim Beatty, Toronto, Ont., **John Dakin**, Toronto, Ont., **John Wood**, Toronto, Ont., soling, bronze

CARDED ATHLETES

The government of Canada, recognizing that many other nations support their top athletes financially, finally established an assistance program through Sport Canada. That agency, on the advice of the voluntary national sport governing bodies, provides direct assistance to athletes. The goal is to allow athletes to devote themselves full time to developing skills, and later provides help for development of their after-sport careers. Athletes receive "A", "B" or "C" cards, which indicate level of skill. "A" carded student athletes, for example, can get up to $220 a month living and training allowance ($385 if self-supporting), $1,200 a year for "high performance assistance" for such things as travel to international competitions and tuition fees. "B" carded athletes receive less, as do "C" carded. The list below shows "A", "B", "C" and uncarded athletes of merit, together with abbreviated performance records. They are the cream of the crop.

"A" CARDED ATHLETES

Todd Brooker, 23, Paris, Ont. Alpine skier Brooker follows a family tradition of athletic excellence: his father was a member of Canada's Olympic hockey team in 1956. Brooker competes in slalom, giant slalom and downhill events.

Early competitive history
1975 Junior National Championships
      downhill, 1
      giant slalom, 3
      slalom, 2
Recent performance:

1983 Val D'Isere, France
      downhill, DNF
      Kitzbuhel, Austria,
      downhill, 17, 2:08:69
      Kitzbuhel, Austria,
      downhill, 1, 2:01.96
      Sarajevo, Yugoslavia
      downhill, 14
      St. Anton, Austria
      downhill, 15,2:06.40
      National Championships
      downhill, 2, 1:51.00
      Aspen, USA
      downhill, 1, 1:47.87
      Lake Louise
      downhill, DNF

Steve Podborski, 26, Don Mills, Ont. Alpine skier Podborski has been voted athlete of the month three times (December 1980, January 1981 and March 1982) by the Sports Federation of Canada. He was selected Ontario amateur athlete of the year (1980 and 1981) and was ranked the top downhiller in the world for 1980/81 by the Federation Internationale de Ski. He was awarded the John Semmelink Trophy by the Canadian Ski Association (June 1981) and was the first North American male skier to win a World Cup championship (1981). Podborski received the Norton Crowe award for male athlete in both 1981 and 1982. In 1983, Podborski received an excellence award from the government of Ontario.

Early competitive history
1976 Cortina, Italy,
      downhill, 6
      Val D'Isere, France,
      giant slalom, 36
      giant slalom, DNF
      Val Gardena, Italy
      downhill, 18
      downhill, 27
Recent performances

1983 Val D'Isere, France
      downhill DNF
      Val D'Isere, France
      downhill, 34, 2:02;31
      Kitzbuhel, Austria,
      downhill, 2, 2:06.79
      Kitzbuhel, Austria
      downhill, 9, 2:03.20

Serajevo, Yugoslavia
downhill, 2
St. Anton, Austria
downhill, 4, 2:05.08

National Championships
downhill, 1, 1:50.64

Debbie Brill, 30, Burnaby, B.C. Highjumper
Debbie Brill was named B.C. athlete of the
decade in 1980. She is a two-time winner of
the Jack W. Davies trophy, three-time winner
of the Fred N.A. Rowell trophy, won the
Myrtle Cook Trophy in 1967, and is eight-
time winner of the Dr. Calvin D. Bricker
Memorial Trophy. In 1979 she set a Commonwealth record (1.96 m) and was a member of the 1980 Canadian Olympic team.
She was named the outstanding female athlete
of 1980 by the B.C. Track and Field Association. Brill took a year's maternity leave in
1981 to have Neil Bogard Ray Brill, born August 1, 1981. Her world indoor best (1.99
m) was at the Edmonton *Journal* Invitational
in 1982. In 1982 she was inducted into
the Canadian Amateur Sports Hall of Fame.
Brill was co-winner of the Bobbi Rosenfeld
award for Canada's female athlete of the year,
1971.

Early competitive history
1969 Pacific Conference Games,
      high jump, 1, 1.71 m
1970 Commonwealth Games
      high jump, 1, 1.78 m
1971 Pan-Am Games
      high jump, 1, 1.85 m
1972 Olympic Games
      high jump, 8, 1.82 m

Recent performances
1982 National Outdoor Championships
      high jump 1, 1.84 m

      Commonwealth Games
      high jump, 1, 1.88 m

Mark McKoy, 22, Scarborough, Ont. Sprinter
Mark McKoy specializes in 110m hurdles.
He was chosen outstanding male athlete at the
1982 Senior National Outdoor Championships and set a Commonwealth and Commonwealth Games record in 1982. He
finished third at the International Superstars
Competition in Hong Kong, November 1982

and set a Canadian senior record and world
best in the 4x200 m relay at the '83 National
Indoor Championships.

Early competitive history:
1980 Olympic Alternative — West Germany
      100m, 11, 14.64
      Olympic Alternative — Philadelphia
      100 m, 8, 14.42
1981 Pacific Conference Games
      110 m hurdles, 6, 14.31
      4 × 100 m relay, 1, 39.6

Recent performances
1983 *Toronto Star* invitational
      50 yd hurdles, 2, 6.04
      Ontario Championships
      50 m hurdles, 1, 6.54
      National Indoor Championships
      4x200 m relay, 1, 1:23.97
      50 m hurdles, 1, 6.58
      OUAA Championships
      60m hurdles, 1, 7.83
      CIAU Championships
      60m hurdles, 1, 7.83

Milt Ottey, 23, Toronto, Ont. High jumper
Milt Ottey was a member of the 1980 Canadian Olympic team. He set Canadian and
Commonwealth records (2.30 m) at the Western Athletics Conference competition, May
1982, and was runner-up for the Norton
Crowe award for male athlete of the year in
1982. He was chosen the top jumper in
the world in 1982 by *Track and Field News*
magazine and was named Ontario athlete
of the year in 1982. He has won CTFA awards
for '82: Jack W. Davies (top athlete), Cal D.
Bricker Memorial (jumps), F.N.A. Rowell
(field).

Early competitive history
1978 Canada-France Junior Dual Meet
      high jump, 4
      Canada-Mexico Junior Dual Meet
      high jump, 2
      National Indoor Championships
      high jump, 5, 2.05 m
1979 Canada-USSR Dual Meet
      high jump, 3, 2.14 m
      Mansfield Relays
      high jump, 1, 2.11 m
      National Outdoor Championships
      high jump, 1, 2.08 m

Recent Performance
1982 European Tour — West Berlin
high jump, 1, 2.30 m
Eight Nation Invitational Meet
high jump, 1, 2.24 m
Commonwealth Games
high jump, 1, 2.31 m
1983 Ottawa Int'l Indoor Games
high jump, 1, 2.31 m
Sunkist Invitational
high jump, 1, 2.26 m

Angella Taylor, 25, Toronto, Ont. Sprinter
Angella Taylor competes in the 100m, 200m,
400m and 50m. She was a member of the
1980 Canadian Olympic team and was named
Ontario athlete of the year that year by the
Ontario Sportswriters and Sportscasters Association. She was named female athlete of
1980 by the Sports Federation of Canada and
named outstanding female athlete of the
year at the 1981 CIAU Championships. She
was chosen outstanding female athlete at
the 1982 Senior National Outdoor Championships and has set Senior Canadian, Commonwealth and Commonwealth Games records
at the '82 Commonwealth games. She received the 1982 Velma Springstead Trophy
for female athlete of the year and was the
1983 winner of the Excellence Award from
the government of Ontario.

Early competitive history
1978 Colgate Games
100 m, 3
Etobicoke Guardian Games
100 m, 4, 12.45
National Championships
200 m, 2, 23.87
1979 Canada-Germany Dual Meet
100 m, 3, 11.69
Canada-Italy Dual Meet
200 m, 3, 23.64
Canada-USSR Dual Meet
400 m, 3, 56.56
National Outdoor Championships
100 m, 1, 11.49
200 m, 1, 23.43

Recent performance
1982 Eight Nation Invitational Meet
100 m, 2, 11.08
200 m, 1, 22.73
4x100 m relay, 3, 44.03

Commonwealth Games
100 m, 1, 11.00
200 m, 3, 22.48
4x100 m relay, 2, 43.66
4x400 m relay, 1, 3:27.70
1983 Sherbrooke Mondo Invitational
200 m, 1, 23.72
50 m, 4, 6.48
Milrose Games
60yd, 4, 6.90
Toronto Star Invitational
50yd, 2, 5.87
National Indoor Championships
200 m, 1, 23.59

Willie Dewit, 23, Grande Prairie, Alta. Boxer
Dewit's event is the 81kg heavyweight. He
was named Alberta "Golden Boy" for 1981
and selected Canada's "best prospect" in
the same year. In 1980 he received an award
for outstanding service to amateur boxing
in Canada from the president of CABA. He
was the first Canadian ever to win the North
American Heavyweight Boxing Championship, June 1982, and was named Canada's
athlete of the month for June 1982 by the
Sports Federation of Canada.

Early competitive history
1979 Alberta Championships
+81kg heavyweight, 1
B.C. Golden Gloves
+ 81kg heavyweight, 2
1980 Alberta Championships
+81kg heavyweight, 1
Alberta Golden Gloves
+81kg heavyweight, 2
B.C. Golden Gloves
+81kg heavyweight, 1

Recent performances
1982 North American Championships
91kg heavyweight, 1
Commonwealth Games
91kg heavyweight, 1
Canada vs. Italy
+91kg Super Heavy, Lost
1983 World Championships
91kg heavyweight, 1

Shawn O'Sullivan, 21, Toronto, Ont. Boxer
O'Sullivan's event is the 71kg light-middle-
weight. He was winner of the outstanding
boxer award at the 1981 New Zealand Games

and winner of the outstanding fighter award at the 1980 Finland International Competition. In 1980 he received an award for outstanding service to amateur boxing in Canada. He defeated Armando Martinez of Cuba, the 1980 World and Olympic Champion, at the 1981 Cordova Cardin Tournament and received an award for best bout of the tournament. He was named athlete of the month for November 1981 by the Sports Federation of Canada and won the Viscount Alexander Trophy for male athlete of the year in 1981. He received a world champion award from the government of Canada at the 1982 Tribute to the Champions and won gold at the 1981 World Cup — the first world/Olympic medal for Canada since Horace (Lefty) Gwynne's gold in the 1932 Olympics. In January 1983, he received an Excellence Award from the government of Ontario.

Early competitive history
1978   Ontario Golden Gloves
       57kg featherweight, 1
       Quebec Golden Gloves
       57kg featherweight, 1
       Ontario Championships
       54kg bantamweight, 1
       Junior National Championships
       57kg featherweight, 1

Recent performances
1982   Commonwealth Games
       71kg lt. middleweight, 1
       Canada vs. Italy
       71kg lt. middleweight, Won
1983   World Championships
       71kg lt. middleweight, 1

Hugh Fisher, 28, Burnaby, B.C. competes in the kayak. He was a member of the 1980 Canadian Olympic team and in 1979 and 1980 was World Champion in the outrigger.

Early competitive history
1976   Olympic Games
       k-4 1000 m, 10
       National Championships
       k-2 500 m, 1
       k-4 500 m, 1
       k-1 500 m, 2

Recent performances
1982   World Championships
       k-2 1000 m, 2, 3:37.45

World Championships
k-2 10,000 m, 10, 41:02.26
k-2 500 m, 9, 1:44.56
National Championships
c-2 500 m, 2 (jr), 2:00.887
c-4 1000 m, 1(jr), 4:37.958
National Championships
k2 500 m, 1, 1:39.275
K-4 1000 m, 1, 3:16.537
K-1 500 m, 3, 1:48.776.

Alwyn Morris, 25, Caughnawaga, Que., competes in the kayak and was a member of the 1980 Canadian Olympic team. In 1977 he won the Tom Longboat award for top North American Indian Athlete.

Early competitive history
1977   National Championships
       k-1 100 m, 1(jr), 4:08.3
       k-1 500 m, 1(jr)
       k-1 500 m, 7(sr)
1978   Continental Cup
       k-4 500 m, 3
1979   Continental Cup
       k-1 1000 m, 1, 4:05.6
       k-2 500 m, 3, 1:45.8
       k-4 1000 m, 4, 3:23.6

Recent performances
1982   Tata Regatta
       k-2 500 m, 1, 1:35.7
       Nottinghamshire Int'l Regatta
       k-2 1000 m, 4, 3:29.84
       World Championships
       k-2 1000 m, 2, 3:37.45
       k-1 10,000 m, 8, 45:12.67
       k-2 500 m, 9, 1:44.56
       National Championships
       k-1 1000 m, 1, 3:54.022
       k-2 1000 m, 4, 3:41.326
       k-2 500 m, 7, 1:49.738
       k-4 1000m, 4, 3:29.229
       k-1 500 m, 2, 1:47.812

Jim Elder, 49, Aurora, Ont. Equestrian jumper Jim Elder was a member of the 1980 Canadian Olympic team and was inducted into the Canadian Amateur Sports Hall of Fame in 1970.

Early competitive history
1956   Olympic Games
       three day event, 3

1959 Pan-Am Games
three day event, 1
1967 Pan-Am Games
prix des nations, 3
1968 Olympic Games
prix des nations, 1
1969 Royal Winter Fair
prix des nations, 1
1970 World Championships
prix des nations, 1
1971 Pan-Am Games
prix des nations, 1

Recent performances
1982 Velodrome Horse Show, Montreal
grand prix, 1
grand prix, 6
World Championships
Nation's Cup, 5

Michel Vaillancourt, 29, Calgary, Alta.
Equestrian jumper Michel Vaillancourt was a
member of the 1980 Canadian Olympic
team and won the 1976 Martini & Rossi
horseman of the year award.

Early competitive history
1972 Ottawa Winter Fair
puissance, 1
1975 Aurora Horse Show
grand prix, 2
Hamilton Horse Show
grand prix, 2
Pan-Am Games
team, 3

Recent performances
1980 Vancouver Int'l Horse Show
grand prix, 6
1982 Northlands Horse Show
grand prix, 1
Spruce Meadows Horse Show
world cup (Prelim), 1

Marie-Claude Asselin, 21, Ste-Agathe, Que.
Freestyle skier Asselin competes in aerials,
ballet and moguls. She received the sport excellence award from the government of Canada at the 1982 Tribute to the Champions
and was named freestyle's best French-Canadian amateur athlete in 1979 by sports writers
across Canada. She was women's aerial
World Cup champion in 1981, 1982 and
1983 and women's combined World Cup
champion in 1981 and 1982. In the 1982

World Cup standings, she was 1st in combined, 4th in moguls, 6th in ballet and 1st in
aerials. In the 1981 World Cup standings,
she was 1st in combined, 4th in moguls, 4th
in ballet, 1st in aerials. Asselin won the
Elaine Tanner Trophy for female athlete (under
20) of the year 1982.

Early competitive history
1977 Junior National Championships
combined, 1
1978 Junior National Championships
combined, 1
North American Championships
combined, 1

Recent performances
1983 Ravascletto Italy (WC)
aerials, 1
ballet, 7
combined, 1
moguls, 5
Squaw Valley, USA (WC)
aerials, 1
ballet, 4
combined, 1
moguls, 9
Angel Fire, USA (WC)
aerials, 1
ballet, 10
combined, 2
moguls, 2

Peter Judge, 25, Canmore, Alta. Freestyle
skier Judge competes in aerials, ballet and
moguls. In the 1981 World Cup standings, he
was 2nd in combined, 14th in moguls, 10th
in ballet and 10th in aerials. In the 1982
World Cup standings, he was 2nd in combined, 11th in moguls, 9th in ballet and 10th
in aerials. In the 1980 World Cup standings,
he was 9th combined.

Early competitive history
1976 National Championships
combined, 3
moguls, 2
1978 World Cup
combined, 4

Recent performances
1983 Squaw Valley USA (WC)
aerials, 6
ballet, 1
combined, 1

moguls, 7
Angel Fire, USA (WC)
aerials, 4
ballet, 12
combined, 6
moguls, 19

Paul Martini, 22, Woodbridge, Ont. Figure skater Martini competes in the pairs with partner Barbara Underhill. The two were named athletes of the month for November 1982 by the Sports Federation of Canada.

Early competitive history
1978 Ennia Challenge
      pairs, 5
      Grand Prix International
      pairs, 1
      Junior National Championships
      pairs, 1
      Junior World Championships
      pairs, 1

Recent performances
1982 World Championships
      pairs, 4
      NHK Trophy
      pairs, 1
      National Championships
      pairs, 1
      World Championships
      pairs, 3

Brian Orser, 21, Penetanguishene, Ont. Figure skater Orser competes in the singles.

Early competitive history
1975 Canada Games
      singles, 1
1977 Novice National Championships
      singles, 1
1978 Junior National Championships
      singles, 3
      Junior World Championships
      singles, 4
1979 Junior National Championships
      singles, 1

Recent performances
1982 World Championships
      singles 4
      St. Ivel Ice International
      singles, 1
      Skate Canada
      Singles, 2

1983 National Championships
      singles 1
      World Championships
      singles, 3

Barbara Underhill, 20, Oshawa, Ont. Figure skater Underhill competes in the pairs with partner Paul Martini. They were named athletes of the month for November 1982 by the Sports Federation of Canada.

Early competitive history
1978 Ennia Challenge
      pairs, 5
      Grand Prix International
      pairs, 1
      Junior National Championships
      pairs, 1
      Junior World Championships
      pairs 1
      Nebelhorn Trophy
      pairs, 1

Recent performances
1982 World Championships
      pairs, 4
      NHK Trophy
      pairs, 1
1983 National Championships
      pairs 1
      World Championships
      pairs, 3

Betty Craig, 26, Brockville, Ont. Sweep rower Betty Craig was a member of the 1980 Canadian Olympic team and received a sport excellence award from the government of Canada at the 1982 Tribute to the Champions.

Early competitive history
1975 National Championships
      pair without cox, 2
      four with coxswain, 4
      eight with coxswain, 1
1976 Olympic Games
      pair without cox, 5

Recent performances
1981 World Championships
      pair without cox, 2, 3:45.77
1982 Canadian Henley Championships
      pair without cox, 1
      four with cox, 1
      World Championships
      pair without cox, 3, 3:35.93

Janice Mason, 23, Victoria, B.C. Sculler
Janice Mason was a member of the 1980
Canadian Olympic team.

Early competitive history
1978 Canadian Henley Championships
      single scull, 4
      double scull, 3
      Jr. double scull, 1

Recent performances
1981 Canadian Henley Championships
      eight with coxswain, 1, 3:08.29
1982 Canadian Henley Championships
      four with coxswain, 1
      World Championships
      double scull, 3, 3:26.49

Lisa Roy, 24, Victoria, B.C. Sculler Lisa Roy
was a member of the 1980 Canadian Olympic
team.

Early competitive history
1978 Canadian Henley Championships
      double scull, 3
      jr pair with cox, 1
      National Championships
      pair with coxswain, 2
      pair with coxswain, 3
      four with coxswain, 1

Recent performances
1981 English Henley Regatta
      pair without cox, 1
      Canadian Henley Championships
      double scull, 1, 3:20.78
1982 Canadian Henley Championships
      four with coxswain, 1
      World Championships
      double scull, 3, 3:26.49.

Tricia Smith, 26, Vancouver, B.C. Sculler
Tricia Smith was a member of the 1980 Canadian Olympic team and received a sport
excellence award from the government of
Canada at the 1982 Tribute to the Champions.

Early competitive history
1974 National Championships
      four with cox, 1
1975 Canadian Henley Championships
      four with cox, 4
      National Championships
      four with cox, 1
      eight with cox, 1

1976 Olympic Games
      pair without cox, 5

Recent performances
1981 World Championships
      pair without cox, 2, 3:45.77
1982 Candian Henley Championships
      pair without cox, 1
      four with coxswain, 1
      National Championships
      pair without cox, 1
      World Championships
      pair without cox, 3, 3:35.93.

Tim Storm, 27, St. Catharines, Ont. Sculler
Tim Storm has represented Canada at two
World Championships.

Early competitive history
1973 Junior National Championships
      eight with coxswain, 1
1974 Junior National Championships
      four with coxswain, 1
1975 Canadian Henley Championships
      jr four sculls, 1

Recent performances
1981 Canadian Henley Championships
      jr double scull, 1
      Canadian Henley Championships
      double scull, 2
1982 Canadian Henley Championships
      four sculls, 1
      World Championships
      double scull, 4, 6:29.47

Susan Nattrass, 32, Edmonton, Alta. Trap
shooter Nattrass was inducted into Canada's
Sports Hall of Fame in 1977 and in the same
year was Canadian woman athlete of the
year (co-winner) and Ontario athlete of the
year. She is a six-time world trapshooting
champion and was the first woman to compete in the Olympic trapshooting event. She
was captain of the women's all-American
trapshooting team 1973-1978 and had the top
women's all-round standing for North America 1973-1977. She was a member of the
Canadian international trapshooting team from
1969 to 1982 and became an officer of the
Order of Canada in 1981. She was named
athlete of the month for October 1981 by the
Sports Federation of Canada and won the
Velma Springstead Trophy for female athlete
of the year 1981, and the Lou Marsh trophy as

Canada's athlete of the same year. Among her other honours, she received the world champion award from the government of Canada at the 1982 Tribute to the Champions.

Early competitive history
1974   World Championships
       trap, 1, 143/150 (world record)
1975   World Championships
       trap, 1, 188/200 (world record)
1976   Benito Juarez International
       trap, 1
       Olympic Games
       trap, 25
1977   World Championships
       trap, 1, 192/200 (world record)
1978   World Championships
       trap, 1, 195/200 (world record)

Recent performances
1981   Championship of the Americas
       trap, 2, 190/200
1982   Grand Prix of Great Britain
       trap, 1, 135
       World Championships
       trap, 2, 186

Patrick Vamplew, 30, Toronto, Ont. Vamplew competes in rifle. He won the 1982 Golden Anniversary Award from the Shooting Federation of Canada for outstanding contributions to the sport.

Early competitive history
1977   Benito Juarez International
       small bore 3 positions, 24, 1094
       Dom of Can. Rifle Assoc. CHPS.
       small bore air rifle, 1, 389/400
       National Championships
       small bore prone, 1, 880/950
1982   Commonwealth Games
       full bore rifle, 5 (team), 558
       World Championships
       small bore prone, 6 (tie), 595

Horst Bulau, 20, Ottawa, Ont. Ski jumper Bulau was named athlete of the month for March 1981, January 1982 and January 1983 by the Sports Federation of Canada. He was third overall in World Cup standings in 1980/81 and 1981/82 and second overall in World Cup standings in 1982/83. He received a sport excellence award from the government of Canada at the 1982 Tribute to the Champions and won the John Semmelink Memorial Award

for 1978/79. He received an excellence award from the government of Ontario in 1983.

Early competitive history
1978   Junior National Championships
       90m, 1
       National Championships
       90m, 3

Recent performances, World Cup
1983   Falun, Sweden
       70m, 1
       Falun, Sweden
       90m, 8
       Lahti, Finland
       70m, 1
       Lahti, Finland
       90m, 1
       Baerum, Norway
       90m, 3
       Oslo, Norway
       90m, 2
       Planica, Yugoslavia
       70m, 5
       Planica, Yugoslavia
       90m, 2

Gaetan Boucher, 25, Quebec, Que. Speed skater Boucher was the 1977 Quebec athlete of the year, French-Canadian athlete of the year, and junior Canadian athlete of the year. In 1980 he was the Canadian Sports Award's athlete of the month for February, and in both 1980 and 1982 was French-Canadian athlete of the year. He was named athlete of the month for December 1981 by the Sports Federation of Canada. He received the Dick Ellis Memorial Trophy for team of the year 1981 (short track relay) and was 1980 winner of Cassa's skater of the year award. From 1976 to '82 he won the Thompson Trophy for fastest Canadian in 500m and he received a sport excellence award from the government of Canada at the 1982 Tribute to the Champions. Boucher was the first Canadian male to win an Olympic medal (1980-1000m) since Gordon Audley's bronze in 500m in 1952.

Early competitive history
1974   Junior National Championships
       all around, 1
1975   Junior World Championships
       1500m, 29, 2:17.55
       3000m, 33, 4:59.49
       500m, 12, 42.71

Recent performances
1982 Golden Skates Competition
        all-round (sprint), 1, 150.680
        National Indoor Team Trials
        all-round, 2, 636
        North American Indoor Chps.
        all-round, 1
        World Short-Track Championships
        all-round, 2
        Berlin Sprints
        all-round (sprint), 2, 155.450
        Season Opener
        3000m, 3
        1500m, 1
        5000m, 9
        all-round, 20
1983 World Outdoor Championships
        1500m, 12, 2:01.08
        500m, 4, 39.24
        5000m, 27, 7:33.73
        all-round, 22
        World Sprint Championships
        All-round (sprint), 17

Sylvie Daigle, 21, Sherbrooke, Que. Speed skater Daigle was the Sports Federation of Canada's junior female athlete of the year in 1979 and in 1981 she received the Thompson Trophy for fastest Canadian in 500m.

Early competitive history
1979 Canada Games
        1000m, 1, 1:36.09
        1500m, 1, 2:34.19
        500m, 1, 47.12
        Jr. Canada vs. USA Meet
        1000m, 1,
        500m, 1

Recent performances
1983 World Sprint Championships
        all-round (sprint), 21
        World Short-Track Championships
        1500m, 1
        500m, 1, 49.54
        500 (semi), 1, 49.49 (world record)
        World Short-Track Championships
        1000m, 1, 1:43.66 (world record)
        3000m, 1, 6:10.88
        all-round, 1.

Louis Grenier, 22, Quebec, Que. Speed skater Grenier has represented Canada at five world championships. His sister Natalie is

also a member of the National Speed Skating Team.

Early competitive history
1972 National Indoor Championships
        all-round, 1
1973 National Indoor Championships
        all-round, 1
1979 North American Indoor Chps.
        all-round, 1

Recent performances
1982 North American Indoor Chps.
        all-round, 3
        World Short-Track Championships
        all-round, 3
1983 World Short-Track Championships
        1500m, 3
        500m, 1, 45.37 (world record)
        1000m, 1, 1:39.21
        3000m, 1, 5:33.33
        all-round, 1.

Alex Baumann, 19, Sudbury, Ont. Swimmer Alex Baumann won the top performance award in the Four-Nation Cup, August 1980. He was a member of the 1980 Canadian Olympic team and has set Canadian, Commonwealth and world records. He received a world champion award from the government of Canada at the 1982 Tribute to the Champions and was Ontario amateur athlete of the year in 1981. He was named athlete of the month for July 1981 and October 1982 by the Sports Federation of Canada. In 1983 he won an excellence award from the government of Ontario.

Early competitive history
1978 Coca Cola Meet
        400m individual medley, 5, 4:47.9
        Canada vs. US Meet
        1500m freestyle, 5, 16:16.16
        Darmstadt International Meet
        200m individual medley, 1, 2:16.39
        Florida Tour
        1500m freestyle 1, 17:11.17

Recent performances
1983 West Germany International Meet
        400m individual medley, 1, 4:17.51
        100m freestyle, 4, 50.95
        200m individual medley, 1, 2:00.66
        Winter National (Short Course)

200m freestyle, 2, 1:47.58
100m freestyle, 1, 49.61 (Can. senior record)
400m individual medley, 1, 4:13.55
200m individual medley, 1, 1:58.96 (multiple records)
4x100m freestyle relay, 1, 48.96, (Can. senior record)
4x100m freestyle relay, 1 (heat), 49.2 (Can. senior record)
50m freestyle, 1 (tied), 23.19

Victor Davis, 19, Guelph, Ont. Swimmer Victor Davis was named athlete of the month (August 1982) by the Sports Federation of Canada and won an Ontario excellence award in 1983. He was named male swimmer of the year for 1982 by the Canadian Amateur Swimming Association and named male swimmer of the year for 1982 by the Aquatic Federation of Canada.

Early competitive history
1980 Winter National (Short Course)
       100m breaststroke, 4, 1:05.02
       200m breaststroke, 4, 2:20.47
       Summer National Championships
       200m breaststroke, 11, 2:28.21
       100m breaststroke, 10, 1:08.29
       Canada Cup
       100m breaststroke, 2, 1:04.52
       200m breaststroke, 3, 2:20.32
1981 New Zealand Games
       200m breaststroke, 1, 2:22.14
       100m breaststroke, 1, 1:06.10

Recent performances
1982 Commonwealth Games
       200m breaststroke, 1, 2:16.25 (Comm. Games record)
       200m individual medley 4, 2:07.44
1983 Swedish Swim Games
       100m breaststroke, 4, 1:06.59
       200m breaststroke, 1, 2:19.09
       200m butterfly, 5, 2:07.58
       200m individual medley, 6, 2:12.84
       West Germany International Meet
       200m breaststroke, 2, 2:15.05
       100m breaststroke, 5, 1:04.30
       Winter National (Short Course)
       200m butterfly, 1, 1:58.49
       100m breaststroke, 1, 1:02.11
       400m individual medley, 3, 4:22.24
       200m individual medley, 2, 2:02.95
       200m breaststroke, 1, 2:12. 04

Cameron Henning, 22, Edmonton, Alta. Henning was a member of the 1980 Canadian Olympic swim team.

Early competitive history
1976 Summer National Championships
       200m backstroke, 21, 2:17.80
1977 Summer National Championships
       100m backstroke, 9, 1:01.60
       200m backstroke, 9, 2:10.50

Recent performances
1982 Commonwealth Games
       200m backstroke, 1, 2:02.88 (Comm. Games record)
1983 CIAU Championships
       400m freestyle, 1, 3:51.99
       Winter National (Short Course)
       200m backstroke, 3, 1:59.96
       1500m freestyle, 4, 15:37.10.

Anne Ottenbrite, 17, Whitby, Ont. Ottenbrite swam to Commonwealth and Commonwealth Games records at the 1982 Commonwealth Games. She was named female swimmer of the year 1982 by the Canadian Amateur Swimming Association.

Early competitive history
1981 Summer National Championships
       100m breaststroke, 5, 1:14.66
       Canada Games
       100m breaststroke, 1, 1:13.19
       200m breaststroke, 1, 2:37.72
       Canada Cup
       100m breaststroke, 1, 1:12.99
       200m breaststroke, 1, 2:34.51

Recent performances
1982 Commonwealth Games
       200m breaststroke, 1, 2:32.07 (multiple records)
       100m breaststroke, 1 (heat), 1:11.74 (Comm. Games record)
       100m breaststroke, 2, 1:11.99
       4x100m medley relay, 1, 4:14.33 (Comm. Games record)
1983 Winter National (Short Course)
       100m breaststroke, 2, 1:09.98
       200m individual medley, 7, 2:20.69
       200m breaststroke, 1, 2:28.95 (Can. senior record).

Peter Szmidt, 22, Pointe Claire, Que. Swimmer Szmidt was named athlete of the month

(July 1980) by the Sports Federation of Canada and was a member of the 1980 Canadian Olympic team. He was named aquatic athlete of 1980 by the Aquatic Federation of Canada.

Early competitive history
1975   Summer National Championships
       1500m freestyle, 8, 17:10.34
1976   Dolphin Swim Meet
       1500m freestyle, 9, 16:57.24
       400m freestyle, 9, 4:13.75
       Olympic Trials
       1500m freestyle, 8, 16:40.95
       200m freestyle, 15, 1:59.86
       400m freestyle, 24 (heat) 4:21.89

Recent performances
1982   Commonwealth games
       4x100m freestyle relay, 3, 3:27.74
       200m freestyle, 2, 1:51.65
       400m freestyle, 2, 3:53.74
1983   CIAU Championships
       400m freestyle, 2, 3:54.02
       200m freestyle, 2, 1:51.68
       1500m freestyle, 2, 15:28.50
       Winter National (Short Course)
       200m freestyle, 1, 1:47.52 (Can. senior record)
       400m freestyle, 1, 3:49.11
       1500m freestyle, 1, 15:17.57

Dan Thompson, 27, Toronto, Ont. Thompson was a member of the 1980 Canadian Olympic swim team.

Early competitive history
1975   Summer National Championships
       100m butterfly, 8, 59.42
       World trials
       100m butterfly, 9, 58.64
1976   Olympic Trials
       100m butterfly, 6, 57.71

Recent performances
1982   World Trials
       100m butterfly, 1, 55.00
       100m freestyle, 16, 55.52
       World Championships
       100m butterfly, 9, 55.28
       4x100m medley relay, 4, 3:46.08
       Commonwealth Games
       100m butterfly, 1, 54.71 (multiple records)
1983   Winter National (Short Course)

100m butterfly, 1, 53.17 (multiple records)

Mike West, 19, Waterloo,Ont. West is the current Canadian record holder 100m backstroke.

Early competitive history
1980   Winter National (Short Course)
       100m backstroke, 14, 1:00.85
       Summer National Championships
       100m backstroke, 9, 1:00.14
       Canada Cup
       200m backstroke, 10, 2:09.84
       100m backstroke, 8, 1:00.17
1981   Canada Cup
       100m backstroke, 3, 59.52

Recent performances
1983   Swedish Swim Games
       100m backstroke, 2, 57.99
       200m backstroke, 5, 2:06.49
       West Germany International Meet
       100m backstroke, 5, 57.60
       200m backstroke, 3, 2:03.05
       50m backstroke, 4 (tie), 26.92
       Winter National (Short Course)
       100m backstroke, 1, 54.71 (Can. senior record)
       200m backstroke, 1, 1:58.66. (Can. senior record).

Janet Arnold, 22, Calgary, Alta. Synchronized swimmer.

Early competitive history
1975   Junior National Championships
       duet, 8
       figures, 9
       team, 1

Recent performances
1982   World Championships
       figures, 12
       team, 1
1983   Pan Pacifics
       team, 1

Sue Clarke, 22, Calgary, Alta. Synchronized Swimmer.

Early competitive history
1977   Junior National Championships
       duet, 2
       figures, 5

solo, 4
team, 4

Recent performances
1982 World Championships
figures, 21
team, 1
1983 Pan Pacifics
team, 1

SHARON HAMBROOK, 20, Calgary, Alta.
Synchro swimmer Hambrook and partner
Kelly Kryczka were named athletes of the
month (July 1982) by the Sports Federation of
Canada, and picked swimmers of the year
for 1982 by the Aquatic Federation of Canada.

Early competitive history
1977 Junior National Championships
figures, 3
solo, 7
team, 1

Recent performances
1982 World Championships
figures, 2
duet, 1
team, 1
1983 Pan Pacifics
duet, 1
solo, 1
team, 1

Kelly Kryczka, 22, Calgary, Alta. Synchro
swimmer Kryczka and Sharon Hambrook were
named athletes of the month (July 1982) by
the Sports Federation of Canada, and were
picked swimmers of the year 1982 by the
Aquatic Federation of Canada.

Early competitive history
1979 Pan American Games
duet, 1
team, 2
National Championships
duet, 1
solo, 4
team, 2

Recent performances
1982 World Championships
figures, 4
solo, 2
duet, 1
team, 1

1983 Pan Pacifics
duet, 1
team, 1

Chantal Laviolette, 20, Montreal, Que. Synchronized swimming.

Early competitive history
1977 Canada-Mexico International
team, 1
1979 Central Division Chps.
duet, 1
Junior National Championships
duet, 1
figures, 1
solo, 1

Recent performances
1982 National Championships
figures, 10
solo, 5
duet, 9
World Championships
figures, 14
team, 1

Penny Vilagos, 20, Montreal, Que. Synchronized swimming.

Early competitive history
1977 Central Division Chps.
duet, 1
figures, 2
solo, 2
team, 2

Recent performances
1982 National Championships
figures, 4
solo, 4
duet, 2
World Championships
figures, 9
team, 1

Vicky Vilagos, 20, Montreal, Que. Synchronized swimming.

Early competitive history
1977 Central Division Chps.
duet, 1
figures, 1
solo, 1
team, 2

Recent performances

1982 National Championships
figures, 3
solo, 3
duet, 2
World Championships
figures, 5
team, 1

Carolyn Waldo, 19, Beaconsfield, Que. Synchronized swimming.

Early competitive history
1979 Central Division Chps.
duet 1
Junior National Championships
duet 1
Quebec Championships
duet 1

Recent performances
1982 National Championships
figures, 8
solo, 8
duet, 7
World Championships
figures, 3
team, 1

Clark Davis, 26, Clemen Sport, N.S. Wrestler Davis won a silver at the 1982 Worlds. It was the first Olympic/World medal for Canada since Joseph Schleimer's bronze at the 1936 Olympics. He was named Quebec's outstanding athlete of 1982 at the 10th Annual Quebec Sports Award banquet.

Early competitive history
1976 Junior National Championships
82kg freestyle, 1
82kg Greco Roman, 1
Pan American Jr Championships
82kg freestyle, 1
90 kg Greco Roman, 1

Recent performances
1982 World Championships
90kg freestyle, 2
Commonwealth Games
90kg freestyle, 1
1983 World Cup
90kg freestyle, 1

Evert Bastet, 33, Hudson, Que. Bastet was a member of the 1980 Canadian Olympic

yachting team. He sails a Flying Dutchman with Terry McLaughlin.

Early competitive history
1967 World Championships
Flying Dutchman, 5
1968 Olympic Games
Flying Dutchman, spare
1970 US National Championships
Flying Dutchman, 1
1971 Sport
Flying Dutchman, 1
1972 Olympic Games
Flying Dutchman, 14

Recent performances
1982 North American Championships
Flying Dutchman, 6
1983 World Championships
Flying Dutchman, 3

Terry McLaughlin, 27, Toronto, Ont. McLaughlin was a member of the 1980 Canadian Olympic yachting team.

Early competitive history
1974 National Championships
470, 3
1976 Olympic Trials
Flying Dutchman, 1
1977 US National Championships
Flying Dutchman, 5

Recent performances
1982 Pre Olympic Regatta
Flying Dutchman, 6
North American Championships
Flying Dutchman, 6
1983 World Championships
Flying Dutchman, 3

Terry Neilson, 25, Toronto, Ont. Yachtsman Neilson won a world champion award from the government of Canada at the 1982 Tribute to the Champions. He was runner-up for the Norton Crowe award for male athlete of the year 1982 and won an excellence award from the government of Ontario in 1983.

Early competitive history
1978 National Championships
Laser, 1
1979 European Championships
Laser, 1
national Championships

Laser, 1
US National Championships
Laser, 2

Recent performances
1982 Cork
Finn, 6
Gold Cup
Finn, 5
European Championships
Finn, 39

Andrew Roy, 25, Ottawa, Ont. Yachtsman Andrew Roy received a sport excellence award from the government of Canada at the 1982 Tribute to the Champions.

Early competitive history
1979 National Championships
Laser, 2

Recent performances
1982 World Championships
Laser, 2
North American Championships
Laser, 3

"B" CARDED ATHLETES

Laurie Graham, 23, Inglewood, Ont. Skier Graham received a sport excellence award from the government of Canada at the 1982 Tribute to the Champions.

Early competitive history
1977 (EC) Flaine, France
downhill, 15
(EC) Bettmeralp, Switzerland
giant slalom, 28

Recent performances
1983 Federation Internationale de ski
slalom, 2, 1:35.91
Norther American Ski Trophy Series
downhill, 1, 1:37.65
National Championships
downhill, 3, 1:36.11
(WC) Mont Tremblant
downhill, 1, 1:32.53

Charmaine Crooks, 22, Toronto, Ont. Sprinter Crooks was a member of the 1980 Canadian Olympic track and field team. She received a sport excellence award from the government of

Canada at the 1982 Tribute to the Champions.

Early competitive history
1979 Junior National Championships
200m, 2, 24.44
400m, 1, 54.4
National Outdoor Championships
400m, 1, 53.12

Recent performances
1982 Buchanan Invitational
400m, 1, 53.22
Commonwealth Games
400m, 7, (53.16)
4x400m relay, 1, 3:27.70.

Jillian Richardson, 18, Calgary, Alta. Sprinter Richardson specializes in the 200m and 400m events.

Early competitive history
1980 Junior National Indoor Champs
200m, 1, 25.55
Colgate Games
200m, 3, 25.00
400m, 5, 55.69

Recent performances
1982 European Tour—Viareggio, Italy
400m, 1, 53.45
European Tour—Nice, France
400m, 3, 53.0
European Tour—Brussels, Belgium
400m, 5, 53.82
Commonwealth Games
4x400m relay, 1, 3:27.70
1983 National Indoor Championships
200m 3, 24.48 (Can. junior record)
400m, 1, 53.0 (Can. junior record)

Alain Laroche, 20, Lac Beauport, Que. Free-style skier Laroche placed 4th in combined, 20th in moguls, 10th in ballet and 12th in aerials in the 1982 World Cup standings.

Early competitive history
1978 Junior National Championships
aerials, 8
ballet, 2
combined, 2
moguls, 4

Recent performances
1983 World Cup Angel Fire, USA
aerials, 1

ballet, 13
combined, 2
moguls, 7

Jean Choquette, 27, Montreal, Que. Choquette was a member of 1980 Canadian Olympic gymnastic team.

Early competitive history
1975 **Pan American Games**
all round, 16
1976 **Junior National Championships**
all round, 1
1977 **National Championships**
all around, 3
World University Games
all around, 40.

Recent performances
1982 **National Championships**
all around, 5, 109.45
horizontal bar, 1, 19.350
parallel bars, 3, 18.325
pommel horse, 1, 18.775
rings, 3, 18.675

Elfie Schlegel, 19, Etobicoke, Ont. Schlegel was a member of 1980 Canadian Olympic gymnastics team.

Early competitive history
1977 **Chunichi Cup**
all around, 4
Empire Cup
all around, 3
Moscow International Meet
all around, 13
Recent performances
1982 **Tokyo Elite International Meet**
beam, 9, 8.85
vault, 7, 9.025

Pat Walter, 24, Victoria, B.C. Sculler Walter was a member of the 1980 Canadian Olympic rowing team.

Early competitive history
1975 **Canadian Henley Championships**
double scull, 4
1977 **National Championships**
single scull, 1, 7:30.00
1978 **British Columbia Championships**
single scull, 1, 7:10.00
double scull, 1, 6:36.00

Recent performances
1982 **World Championships**
single scull, 7, 7:07.04

Alfons Mayer, 45, Kitchener, Ont. Mayer was a member of the 1980 Canadian Olympic shooting team. He won the 1982 Golden Anniversary Award from the Shooting Federation of Canada for outstanding contributions to the sport.

Early competitive history
1967 **Pan American Games**
small bore prone, 1, 598/600
(world record)
1968 **Olympic Games**
small bore 3 positions, 38, 1127
small bore prone, 42, 591/600
1971 **Pan American Games**
small bore prone, 3, 592/600

Recent performances
1982 **World Championships**
small bore air rifle, elim.
300m free rifle prone, elim.
small bore prone, 10 (tie), 594
small bore 3 positions, 41 (tie), 1133

John Primrose, 43, Edmonton, Alta. Primrose has won the Canadian trapshooting championship 10 times. He was inducted into the Canadian Amateur Sports Hall of Fame in 1975 and won the 1982 Golden Anniversary Award from the Shooting Federation of Canada for outstanding contributions to the sport.

Early competitive history
1962 **World Championships**
trap, 38, 281/300
1965 **World Championships**
trap, 24
1966 **World Championships**
trap, 9, 288/300

Recent performances
1982 **National Team Trials**
trap, 1, 287
Commonwealth Games
trap, 4 team, 182
trap, 5, 187
World Championships
trap, 9 (team), 567
trap, 14 (tie), 195

Kathy Bald, 20, Etobicoke, Ont. Swimmer.

Early competitive history
1980   Winter National (Short Course)
       100m breaststroke, 8, 1:14.81
       200m individual medley, 2, 2:20.39
       Summer National Championships
       50m freestyle, 13, 27.72
       200m individual medley, 4, 2:21.29
       100m breaststroke, 14, 1:17.00

Recent performances
1983   West Germany International Meet
       100m breaststroke, 2, 1:10.03 (Can.
       senior record)
       200m individual medley, 2, 2:16.90
         200m breaststroke, 2, 2:30.65
       (Can. senior record)
       50m breaststroke, 2, 33:02
       Winter National (Short Course)
       200m freestyle, 4, 2:02.37
       100m breaststroke, 1, 1:09.73 (Can.
       senior record)
       100m freestyle, 2, 56.62
       200m individual medley, 2, 2:16.29
       200m breaststroke, 3, 2:31.48

Cheryl Gibson, 24, Edmonton, Alta. Swimmer
Gibson won the top performance award in
the Four-Nation Cup, August 1980. She was a
member of the 1980 Canadian Olympic
team.

Early competitive history
1975   Pan American Games
       100m backstroke, 4, 1:07.33
       200m backstroke, 3, 2:22.68
       200m butterfly, 2, 2:21.95
       200m individual medley, 3, 2:24.22
       400m individual medley, 2, 5:06.87

Recent performances
1982   Commonwealth Games
       200m individual medley, 2, 2:19.91
       100m backstroke, 4, 1:04.15
       4x100m medley relay, 1, 4:14.33
         (Comm. Games record)
       200m backstroke, 3, 2:15.87
       400m individual medley, 4, 4:57.56

Russ Prior, 34, Winnipeg, Man. Weightlifter
Prior has set Canadian, Commonwealth,
Commonwealth Games and Pan American
records during his career. He was a member
of the 1980 Canadian Olympic team.

Early competitive history

1966   Canada vs USA
       82.5kg, 1
       National Teenage Championships
       75kg, 6
1967   Intermediate National Chps.
       82.5kg, 2

Recent performances
1981   Pan American Championships
       +110kg, 2, 367.5kg
1982   National Championships
       +110kg, 1, 360kg

Ray Takahashi, 25, Nepean, Ont. Takahashi
was named most outstanding Canadian wrestler of 1980 and was a member of the 1980
Canadian Olympic team.

Early competitive history
1975   Pre Olympic Meet
       48kg freestyle, 2
1976   Junior National Championships
       52kg freestyle, 1
       Pan American Jr Championships
       52kg Greco Roman, 1

Recent performances
1982   World Championships
       52kg freestyle, 7
       Commonwealth Games
       52kg freestyle, 2
       Canada Cup
       52kg freestyle, 3

"C" CARDED ATHLETES

Carmen Ionesco, 32, St. Bruno, Que. Ionesco's events are discus and shot put. She was a
member of the 1980 Canadian Olympic
team and was the 1979 Canadian record-
holder in discus (62.74m) and shot put
(17.17m). She was ranked the number one
shot putter and discus thrower in Canada for
1975, 1976, 1978, 1979 and 1980.

Early competitive history
1972   Olympic Games
       discus, 7, 60.74m
1973   National Championships
       discus, 1
       shot put, 1

Recent performances
1982   National Outdoor Championships
       discus, 1, 55.18m

shot put, 1, 16.55m
Eight Nation Invitational Meet
discus, 3, 55.98m
Commonwealth Games
discus, 4, 54.52m
shot put, 6, 15.80m

Diane Jones-Konihowski, 32, Edmonton, Alta.
Jones-Konihowski's event is the heptathlon.
In 1980 she set the New Zealand pentathlon
record (4332). She won the 1978 Velma
Springstead Award, the 1978 Bobbi Rosenfeld
Award and held the 1977 Canadian record
in shot put (16.14m), as well as the 1977
Canadian record in 50m hurdles (7.25 seconds). In 1975 she set a world indoor record
(4540) and Canadian pentathlon record
(4673). She was Canadian Pentathlon Champion 1969 to 1970 and 1972 to 1978. She
was a member of the 1980 Canadian Olympic
team.

Early competitive history
1969 Pan Pacific Games
      high jump, 2, 1.70m
1970 Commonwealth Games
      pentathlon, 8, 4388
      World University Games
      pentathlon, 8
1972 Olympic Games
      pentathlon, 10, 4359

Recent performances
1982 Colgate Games
      shot put, 3, 13.52m
1983 National Indoor Championships
      high jump, 5, 1.65m

Greg Joy, 27, Toronto, Ont. Joy was the 1976
Olympic silver medalist in high jump (2.23m)
and set a world record (2.31m) in 1978.

Early competitive history
1974 National Championships
      high jump, 2, 2.10m
1976 NCAA Championships
      high jump, 1
1976 Olympic Games
      high jump, 2, 2.23m

Recent performances
1983 National Indoor Championships
      high jump, 1, 2.18m
      OUAA Championships
      high jump, 1, 2.24m

CIAU Championships
high jump, 1, 2.20m

Molly Killingbeck, 24, Scarborough, Ont.
Sprinter Killingbeck's events are the 200m and
400m.

Early competitive history
1978 National Championships
      200m
1979 National Outdoor Championships
      200m, 4
1980 National Indoor Championships
      200m, 1, 24.46
      400m, 1, 54.80

Recent performances
1982 Commonwealth Games
      4x100m relay, 2, 43.66
      4x400m relay, 1, 3:27.70
1983 Sherbrooke Mondo Invitational
      50m, 3, 6.47
      600m, 1, 1.27.41 (Can. senior record)
      Toronto Star Invitational
      50 yd, 4, 5.98
      National Indoor Championships
      200m 2, 23.80
      400m, 2, 53.4

Phil Olsen, 26, Nanaimo, B.C. Javelin
thrower Olsen held the 1976 Commonwealth
record and junior world record at the qualifying round of the Montreal Olympics (87.72m).
He was a member of the 1980 Canadian
Olympic team and has been a member of the
Canadian national team since 1973.

Early competitive history
1973 Canada Games
      javelin 1, 68.38m
1975 NCAA Championships
      javelin, 7
1975 Pan American Games
      javelin, 5, 77.60m
1976 NCAA Championships
      javelin, 1, 83.26m
1976 Olympic Games
      javelin, 11, 77.70m

Recent performances
1982 National Outdoor Championships
      javelin, 1, 82.34m
      Eight Nation Invitational Meet
      javelin, 4, 82.92m
      Commonwealth Games

javelin, 4, 77.96m

Bruno Pauletto, 29, Sept-Iles, Que. Pauletto's event is shot put. He was a member of the 1980 Canadian Olympic track and field team.

Early competitive history
1977 **Pan Pacific Games**
shot put, 2, 18.43m
World Cup
shot put, 5, 18.30m
World University Games
shot put, 4, 18.20m
1978 **Commonwealth Games**
shot put, 2, 19.33m

Recent performances
1982 **National Outdoor Championships**
shot put, 2, 19.05m
Commonwealth Games
shot put, 1, 19.55m

Claire Backhouse, 25, Vancouver, B.C. Badminton.

Early competitive history
1976 **Junior National Championships**
doubles, 1
1977 **Junior National Championships**
mixed doubles, 1
Mexico Open
doubles, 1
singles, 2

Recent performances
1982 **Commonwealth Games**
doubles, 1
Canadian Open
doubles, 2
mixed doubles, 2
singles, qtr.
1983 **Swedish Open**
doubles, 3rd round
mixed doubles, 2nd round
singles, 1st round
All-England Championships
doubles, 1st round
mixed doubles, 2nd round
singles, 3rd round

Claude Langlois, 28, Montreal, Que. Langlois was a member of the 1980 Canadian Olympic cycling team.

Early competitive history

1978 **Quebec Championships**
men's 4000m ind. pursuit, 1
1978 **National Championships**
men's 4000m team pursuit, 1
1979 **Pan American Games**
men's 4000m ind. pursuit, 1

Recent performances
1981 **National Championships**
1000m time trial, 3
points race, 4
men's 4000m ind. pursuit, 5
men's 4000m team pursuit, 2

Jocelyn Lovell, 33, Toronto, Ont. Lovell has been Canadian cycling champion 40 times. He was named Canadian athlete of the year in 1975.

Early competitive history
1967 **Pan American Games**
1000m, time trial, 4, 1:12.81
1968 **Olympic Games**
1000m time trial, 7, 1:05.18
1969 **World Championships**
1000m time trial, 9, 1:09.22
1970 **Commonwealth Games**
10 mile, 1
1000m time trial, 3
men's tandem sprint, 2

Recent performances
1982 **National Championships**
1000m time trial, 1, 1:08.38
men's 4000m team pursuit, 1, 4:43.79
World Championships
1000m time trial, 7, 1:09.30
Commonwealth Games
1000m time trial, 6, 1:09.11

Cynthia Neale, 31, King, Ont. Neale was a member of the 1980 Canadian Olympic equestrian team. She captured the first European Grand Prix victory by a Candian Horse and rider. In 1978 and 1979 she won the Martini & Rossi Horsewoman of the Year Award.

Early competitive history
1971 **Pan American Games**
team, 1
1972 **Olympic Games**
team, 6
1974 **National Championships**
Prix St Georges, 3

Recent performances
1982 World Championships
      Grand Prix, 32 (team), 7

Monica Goermann, 19, Winnipeg, Man.
Goermann was a member of the 1980 Canadian Olympic gymnastics team.

Early competitive history
1976 Junior National Championships
      all around, 18
1977 Junior National Championships
      all around, 2
1978 Commonwealth Games
      all around, 2
1979 Pan American Games
      all around, 1
      beam, 3
      floor exercise, 2
      team, 1
      uneven bars, 1

Recent performances
1981 Great Britain vs Canada
      floor exercise, 1 tie, 9.55
      National Championships
      all-round, 15, 36.05

Sherry Hawco, 19, Cambridge, Ont. Hawco
was a member of the 1980 Canadian Olympic gymnastics team.

Early competitive history
1977 National Championships
      all around, 3
1978 Commonwealth Games
      all around, 2
      team, 1
Recent performances
1981 Great Britain vs Canada
      all around, 2, 37.65
      beam, 1 tie, 9.4
      uneven bars, 2, 9.5
      vault, 2, 9.6
      National Championships
      all around, 1, 73.25
      beam, 4, 17.150
      floor exercise, 7, 17.050
      uneven bars, 3, 17.975

Brad Farrow, 27, Delta, B.C. Farrow was a
member of the 1980 Canadian Olympic judo
team and a member of the 1982/83 national
team.

Early competitive history
1973 National Championships
      -65kg, 5
1974 Pan American Championships
      -65kg, 5

Recent performances
1982 National Championships
      -65kg, 1
      World University Championships
      -65kg, 3

Louis Jani, 26, Montreal, Que. Jani was a
member of the 1980 Canadian Olympic judo
team and is a member of the 1982/83 national team.

Early competitive history
1977 British Open
      -86kg, 3
      National Championships
      -86kg, 1

Recent performances
1982 National Championship
      -86kg, 1
      World University Championships
      -86kg, 3
      Pan American Championships
      -86kg, 1
      Kano Cup
      -86kg, 2
1983 Hungarian Cup
      -86kg, 2

Bruce Ford, 29, Victoria, B.C. Sculler Ford
was a member of the 1980 Canadian Olympic
rowing team.

Early competitive history
1977 Canadian Henley Championships
      double scull, 4
      jr single scull, 1

Recent performances
1980 English Henley Regatta
      double scull, 1, 7:27.00
      Head of the Charles
      double scull, 1

Fred Altmann, 48, Toronto, Ont. Skeet shooting.

Early competitive history
1976 Benito Juarez International

314

skeet, 7, 190/200
1977 European Grand Prix
skeet, 7
National championships
skeet, 2, 379/400
World Championships
skeet, 16

Recent performances
1982 Benito Juarez International
skeet, 5 team, 405
skeet, 6, 189
National Team Trials
skeet, 3
Commonwealth Games
skeet, 1 team, 191
skeet, 9, 187
World Championships
skeet, 43 (tied), 192

Tom Guinn, 39, Font Hill, Ont. Guinn was a member of the 1980 Canadian Olympic shooting team. He won the 1982 Golden Anniversary Award from the Shooting Federation of Canada for outstanding contributions to the sport.

Early competitive history
1974 World Championships
free pistol, 31
1975 Pan American Games
free pistol, 5
1976 Benito juarez International
air pistol, 2
free pistol, 8

Recent performances
1982 Commonwealth Games
free pistol, 4 team, 1071
air pistol, 3 team, 1125
free pistol, 1, 553
air pistol, 3, 571
free pistol, 19 (tie), 553
air pistol, 53 (tie), 564

Guy Lorion, Jr., 30, Longueuil, Que. Lorion won the 1982 Golden Anniversary Award from the Shooting Federation of Canada for outstanding contributions to the sport.

Early competitive history
1976 National Championships
small bore 3 positions, 2, 2278
1977 Benito Juarez International
small bore 3 positions, 8, 1136

team, 3, 4512

Recent performances
1982 Commonwealth Games
small bore air rifle, 5 team, 1116
small bore 3 positions, 2 team, 2279
small bore air rifle, 5, 565
small bore 3 positions, 3, 1144
1982 World Championships
small bore air rifle, elim.
small bore 3 positions, 38 (tie), 1135

J. Francois Senecal, 22, Laval, Que. Senecal won the 1982 Golden Anniversary Award from the Shooting Federation of Canada for outstanding contributions to the sport.

Early competitive history
1978 National Championships
small bore 3 positions, 1 jr.
small bore prone, 1 jr.
1979 Benito Juarez International
small bore 3 positions, 2 juv.
small bore prone, 1 juv.

Recent performances
1982 National Championships
small bore 3 positions, 7, 2275
small bore air rifle, 1, 574
small bore prone, 7, 2366
British National Championships
small bore 3 positions, 3
Commonwealth Games
small bore air rifle, 5 team, 1116
small bore 3 positions, 2 team, 2279
small bore air rifle, 1, 574
small bore 3 positions, 8, 1123

Michelle Macpherson, 17, Agincourt, Ont. Swimmer.

Early competitive history
1979 Canada Cup
100m butterfly, 8, 1:08.12
400m, individual medley, 8, 5:17.76
Summer National Championships
100m butterfly, 16, 1:06.67
200m individual medley, 13, 2:27.83
400m individual medley, 14, 5:13.77

Recent performances
1982 Commonwealth Games
100m butterfly, 3, 1:01.93
4x100m medley relay, 1, 4:14.33
(Comm. Games record)

400m individual medley, 3, 4:55.09
1983 Winter National (Short Course)
100m backstroke, 6, 1:05.77
400m individual medley, 2, 4:49.57
200m backstroke, 4, 2:19.52
200m individual medley, 3, 2:18.23
100m butterfly, 2, 1:01.31

Michel Mercier, 29, La Sarre, Que. Weight-lifting.

Early competitive history
1973 Quebec Championships
60kg, 1
1974 National Championships
60kg, 2
1975 Canada Games
60kg, 1, 207.5 kg

Recent performances
1982 National Championships
67.5kg, 2, 277.5 kg

Richard Deschatelets, 29, Sturgeon Falls, Ont. Wrestling.

Early competitive history
1972 Junior European Championships
82kg freestyle, 6
1973 Junior National Championships
82kg freestyle, 1
1973 Junior World Championships
74kg freestyle, 3
1974 CIAU Championships
82 kg freestyle, 2

Recent performances
1982 World Cup
100kg freestyle, 3
US National Championships
100kg freestyle, 3
National Championships
100kg freestyle, 1
Romanian International
100kg freestyle, 5
Commonwealth Games
100kg freestyle, 1
Canada Cup
100kg freestyle, 4

Chris Rinke, 23, Port Coquitlam, B.C. Wrestling.

Early competitive history
1978 Junior National Championships

74kg freestyle, 7
1979 Junior National Championships
74kg freestyle, 1
Pan American Jr Championships
74kg freestyle, 3

Recent performances
1982 World Cup
82kg freestyle, 3
National Championships
82kg freestyle, 2
Commonwealth Games
82kg freestyle, 1
1983 World Cup
82kg freestyle, 3

Bob Robinson, 25, Montreal, Que. Wrestling.

Early competitive history
1976 Junior National Championships
52kg freestyle, 3
52kg Greco Roman, 1
1977 Junior National Championships
57kg Greco Roman, 2

Recent performances
1982 World Cup
62kg freestyle, 3
National Championships
62kg freestyle, 1
Commonwealth Games
62kg freestyle, 1
Canada Cup
62kg freestyle, 4
1983 World Cup
62kg freestyle, 4

Doug Yeats, 26, Montreal, Que. Yeats was a member of the 1980 Canadian Olympic wrestling team.

Early competitive history
1975 Pre Olympic Meet
62kg Greco Roman, 4
1976 Olympic Games
57kg Greco Roman, 12
1977 Junior National Championships
62kg freestyle, 2

Recent performances
1982 US National Championships
68kg Greco Roman, 1
Concord International
68kg Greco Roman, 3
World Championships

68kg Greco Roman, 9

UNCARDED ATHLETES

Ken Read, 28, Calgary, Alta. Downhill skier Read was the 1979 Sports Federation of Canada's outstanding male athlete and the 1978 winner of the Lou Marsh Trophy for Canada's athlete of the year. He was named athlete of the month (January 1980) by the Sports Federation of Canada and received the John Semmelink Memorial Award for 1979/80.

Early competitive history
1975 National Championships
downhill, 1
(WC) Val d'Isere, France
downhill, 1
1976 Olympic Games
downhill, 5
National Championships
downhill, 1

Recent performances
1983 (WC) Val D'Isere, France
downhill, 4, 1:59.56
(WC) Val D'Isere, France
downhill, 2, 1:59.32
(WC) Kitzbuhel, Austria
downhill, 13 (tie), 2:08.41
(WC) Kitzbuhel, Austria
downhill, 3, 2:02.47
(WC) Sarajevo, Yugoslavia
downhill, 5
(WC) St. Anton, Austria
downhill, DNF
National Championships
downhill, 3, 1:51.65
(WC) Aspen, USA
downhill, 11, 1:49.38
(WC) Lake Louise
downhill, DNF

Borys Chambul, 30, Toronto, Ont. Chambul was a member of the 1980 Canadian Olympic track and field team (discus). His best throw was in 1981 (62.74m) at Birchmont, Ont. He held the NCAA record in discus (65.40m) from 1976 to 1981. He has held both Canadian and Commonwealth records.

Early competitive history
1975 World University Games

discus, 5, 55.60m
1976 NCAA Championships
discus, 1, 61.64m
National Championships
discus, 1, 56.30m

Recent performances
1982 Can/Yug Dual Meet
discus, 1, 60.42m
National Outdoor Championships
discus, 1, 58.76m

Bruce Simpson, 33, Agincourt, Ont. Pole vaulter Simpson was an alternate team member for the 1981 World Cup.

Early competitive history
1970 Commonwealth Games
pole vault, 5, 4.60m
1971 Pan American Games
pole vault, 3, 5.00m
1972 Olympic Games
pole vault, 5

Recent performances
1982 Edmonton *Journal* Invitational
pole vault, 2, 5.20m
Toronto Star Invitational
pole vault, 6, 5.20m
National Outdoor Championships
pole vault, 1, 5.15m
Commonwealth Games
pole vault, 4, 5.10m

Johanne Falardeau, 22, Quebec, Que. Badminton.

Early competitive history
1976 Junior National Championship
doubles, 3
mixed doubles, 1
singles, 3

Recent performances
1982 National Championships
doubles, semi
mixed doubles, qtr
singles, 1
Commonwealth Games
team, 2
mixed doubles, 3rd round
singles qtr
doubles, 1
Canadian Open
doubles, 2

mixed doubles, qtr
singles, semi
1983 **All-England Championships**
doubles, 1st round
mixed doubles, 2nd round,
singles, 3rd round

Craig Clow, 27, Montreal, Que. Freestyle skier Clow was men's aerial World Cup champion in 1982 and in the 1981 world cup stood 4th in aerials. In the 1982 world cup standings he was 18th combined and 1st in aerials.

Early competitive history
1980 (WC) **Poconos, USA**
aerials, 1
(WC) **Blackcomb, Canada**
aerials, 1
(WC) **Mont Ste Anne, Canada**
aerials, 1

Recent performances
1983 (WC) **Ravascletto, Italy**
aerials, 2
moguls, 15
(WC) **Squaw Valley USA**
aerials, 3
(WC) **Angel Fire, USA**
aerials, 9

Bill Keenan, 26, Calgary, Alta. Freestyle skier Keenan stood 5th in moguls at the 1981 World Cup. In the 1982 World Cup standings he was 23rd combined, 3rd in moguls, and 44th in aerials. In the 1983 men's moguls, he was World Cup champion.

Early competitive history
1980 (WC) **Oberjoch, Germany**
moguls, 3
1981 (WC) **Livigno, Italy**
moguls, 1
(WC) **Oberjoch, Germany**
Moguls, 3

Recent performances
1983 (WC) **Livigno, Italy**
moguls, 1
(WC) **Ravascletto, Italy**
moguls, 1
(WC) **Squaw Valley, USA**
moguls, 3
(WC) **Angel Fire, USA**
moguls, 1

Brian Pockar, 24, Calgary, Alta. Figure skater Pockar received a Sport Excellence Award from the government of Canada at the 1982 Tribute to the Champions.

Early competitive history
1971 **Canada Games**
singles, 4
1972 **Novice National Championships**
singles, 10
1974 **Junior National Championships**
singles, 3

Recent performances
1982 **National Championships**
singles, 2
World Championships
singles, 3

Nigel Rothwell, 26, Windsor, Ont. Gymnastics.

Early competitive history
1975 **Pan American Games**
all around, 25
1977 **National Championships**
all around, 5
World University Games
all around, 43

Recent performances
1982 **National Championships**
all-around, 7, 109.15
floor exercise, 4, 18.000
horizontal bar, 5, 18.325
parallel bars, 2, 18.375
rings, 5, 18.300
vault, 2, 18.425

Brian Gabriel, 27, Kitchener, Ont. Gabriel was a member of the 1980 Canadian Olympic shooting team.

Early competitive history
1979 **National Team Trials**
skeet, 3
1980 **Benito Juarez International**
team, 2, 417
skeet, 22, 175

Recent performances
1982 **Benito Juarez International**
skeet, 15, 179
skeet, 5 team, 405
National Team Trials
skeet, 1

Commonwealth Games
skeet, 1 team, 191
skeet, 4, 191

Ed Jans, 37, Calgary, Alta. Jans was a member of the 1980 Canadian Olympic shooting team. He won the 1982 Golden Anniversary Award from the shooting Fed. of Can. for outstanding contributions to the sport.

Early competitive history
1971   **Pan American Games**
       free pistol, 4, 540/600
1972   **Olympic Games**
       free pistrol, 30, 542/600
1975   **Benito Juarez International**
       free pistol, 3, team placing

Recent performances
1982   **National Championships**
       air pistol, 26, 548
       centre fire, 19, 572
       free pistol, 13, 527
       rapid fire, 3, 576
       standard pistol, 3, 568
       Commonwealth Games
       free pistol, 4 team, 1071
       rapid fire, 7 team, 1132
       free pistol, 16, 519
       rapid fire, 19, 554

Art Tomsett, 55, Victoria, B.C. Tomsett won the 1982 Golden Anniversary Award from the Shooting Fed. of Can. for outstanding contributions to the sport.

Early competitive history
1977   **Benito Juarez International**
       air pistol, 14, 371/400
       centre fire, 26, 561/600
       standard pistol, 17, 546/600
1978   **National Championships**
       free pistol, 4

Recent performances
1982   **National Championships**
       air pistol, 24, 549
       free pistol, 12, 529

Lisa Borsholt, 21, North Vancouver, B.C.
Early competitive history
1975   **Summer National Championships**
       100m breaststroke, 4, 1:17.69
       200m breaststroke, 4, 2:44.85
       World Trials

100m breaststroke, 4, 1:17.03
200m breaststroke, 3, 2:45.42
Recent performances
1982   **World Trials**
       200m breaststroke, 2, 2:38.91
       100m breaststroke, 3, 1:13.62
       Commonwealth Trials
       100m breaststroke, 3, 1:13.85
       200m breaststroke, 4, 2:39.07
       100m breaststroke, 4, 1:13.86

Nancy Garapick, 22, Halifax, N.S., was a member of the 1980 Canadian Olympic swim team. She was named athlete of the week (November 29, 1982) by the Canadian Inter-university Athletic Union and won the Bobbi Rosenfeld Award for Canada's female athlete of the year 1975. On April 27, 1975, she set a world record in 200m backstroke (2:16.33) at the Eastern Championships in Brantford, Ont.

Early competitive history
1974   **Summer National Championships**
       100m backstroke, 3, 1:08.10
       200m backstroke, 3, 2:24.88
1975   **Summer National Championships**
       100m backstroke, 1, 1:05.10
       200m backstroke, 1, 2:18.74
       200m individual medley, 5, 2:28.47
       400m individual medley, 7, 5:11.70

Recent performances
1983   **CIAU Championships**
       200m individual medley, 1, 2:17.21
       200m freestyle, 1, 2:02.80
       200m backstroke, 1, 2:18.48

Carol Klimpel, 20, Scarborough, Ont., has set Canadian and Commonwealth swimming records and was a member of the 1980 Canadian Olympic team.

Early competitive history
1977   **Canada Games**
       100m freestyle, 3, 59.96
       Summer National Championships
       100m freestyle, 9
       Winter National (Short Course)
       100m freestyle, 9
1978   **Commonwealth Games**
       100m freestyle, 1
       4x100m freestyle relay, 1, 3:50.28
       (Comm. Games record)

4x100m medley relay, 1, 4:15.26
(Comm. Games record)

Recent performances
1982 World Trials
100m freestyle, 2, 57.81
World Championships
100m freestyle, 12, 57.82
4x100m freestyle relay, 5, 3:51.22
1983 US International (Short Course)
50m freestyle, 8, 26.53

Maureen New, 20, Edmonton, Alta.

Early competitive history
1979 Winter National (Short Course)
100m backstroke, 14, 1:07.00
200m backstroke, 11, 2:22.24
1980 Winter National (Short Course)
100m backstroke, 13, 1:07.02
200m backstroke, 11, 2:22.24

Recent performances
1982 Commonwealth Games
100m freestyle, 5, 58.32
4x100m medley relay, 1, 4:14.33
(Comm. Games record)
1983 Winter National (Short Course)
100m freestyle, 5, 57.00
50m freestyle, 5, 26.48

Graham Smith, 25, Edmonton, Alta. has set
both Commonwealth and Commonwealth
Games records and was a member of the
1980 Canadian Olympic team. He won a
Sport Excellence Award from the government
of Canada at the 1982 Tribute to the Champions.

Early competitive history
1973 Summer National Championships
100m breaststroke, 3, 1:09.44
200m breaststroke, 5, 2:34.33
1974 Summer National Championships
100m breaststroke, 1, 1:08.04
200m breaststroke, 1, 2:29.28

Recent performances
1981 Canada Cup
100m breaststroke, 2, 1:04.08
200m individual medley, 1, 2:06.60
1982 CIAU Championships
100m breaststroke, 1, 1:02.50 (meet
record)

200m breaststroke, 1, 2:17.35 (meet
record)
200m individual medley, 1, 2:03.84

Jay Tapp, 24, Winnipeg, Man., swimmer
Early competitive history
1977 Summer National Championships
100m backstroke, 9, 1:01.78
200m backstroke, 11, 2:12.69
1978 Canada-USSR Dual Meet
100m backstroke, 3, 59.87
100m freestyle, 3, 53.43
4x100m freestyle relay, 1, (Commonwealth record

Recent performances
1981 Canada Cup
100m backstroke, 5, 59.69
1982 CIAU Championships
100m backstroke, 1, 58.87

Chun Hon Chan, 48, Montreal, Que.
Early competitive history
1961 National Championships
52kg, 1
1962 Commonwealth Games
52kg, 5
1962 National Championships
52kg, 1

Recent performances
1980 National Championships
52kg, 1
1981 National Championships
52kg, 2, 172.5 kg
1982 National Championships
56kg, 4, 180 kg

Terry Hadlow, 26, Elliot Lake, Ont., was a
member of the 1980 Canadian Olympic team.
He set a Canadian senior record at snatch
(157.5kg) at the 1982 Ontario Championships.

Early competitive history
1974 National Championships
67.5kg, 10
1975 Canada Games
67.5kg, 1, 220 kg
1975 National Championships
75kg, 5

Recent performances
1981 Pan American Championships

100kg, 3, 317.5 kg
1982 Ontario Championships
100kg, 2, 335kg
Pan American Championships
90kg, 4, 320 kg

Wyatt Wishart, 25, Thunder Bay, Ont.
Early competitive history
1976 Pan American Jr Championships
100kg freestyle, 1
100kg Greco Roman, 1
1977 Chicago International
100kg freestyle, 2
Junior World Championships
90kg freestyle, 3

Recent performances
1982 World Cup
+100kg freestyle, 3
National Championships
+100kg freestyle, 1
Commonwealth Games
+100kg freestyle, 1

73rd CANADIAN OPEN CHAMPIONSHIP

Glen Abbey Golf Club, Oakville, Ont.
July 29-August 1, 1982

1 **Bruce Lietzke**, Afton, OK
Score: 277
Earnings: $76,500
2 **Hal Sutton**, Shreveport, LA
Score: 279
Earnings: $45,900
3 **Charles Coody**, Abilene, TX
Score: 280
Earnings: $24,650
4 **Tommy Valentine**, Gainesville, GA
Score: 280
Earnings: $24,650.

1982 SENIOR GOLF CHAMPIONSHIP OF CANADA

Royal Canadian Golf Association

Mayfair Golf and Country Club and Highlands Golf Club, Edmonton, Alta.
July 14-16, 1982

1 **Arnold Baker**, Lennoxville, Que.
2 **Edward Ervasti**, London, Ont.
3 **Bob Harvey**, Weston, Ont.

39TH CANADIAN JUNIOR CHAMPIONSHIP FOR THE PEPSI-COLA SILVER CUP (17 AND 18 YEARS OF AGE)

Royal Canadian Golf Association

Club De Golf Beauce, Ste-Marie De Beauce, Que. August 25-28, 1982

1 **Jack Kay**, Don Mills, Ont.
2 **Jamie Harper**, Nanaimo, B.C.
3 **Scott Kraemer**, West Vancouver, B.C.

13TH CANADIAN JUVENILE CHAMPIONSHIP FOR THE JACK BAILEY TROPHY

Royal Canadian Golf Association

Club De Golf Beauce, Ste-Marie De Beauce, Que., August 25-28, 1982

1 **John Fram**, Jr., Sidney, B.C.
2 **Francois Hurtubise**, Candiac, Que.
3 **John Moore**, Moncton, N.B.

78TH CANADIAN AMATEUR GOLF CHAMPIONSHIP FOR THE EARL GREY CUP

Royal Canadian Golf Association

Kanawaki Golf Club, Caughnawaga, Que., August 18-21, 1982

1 **Doug Roxburgh**, Vancouver, B.C.
2 **Stu Hamilton**, Brampton, Ont.
3 **Brian Christie**, Jr., Pitt Meadows, B.C.

OLDEST CLUB

The Royal Montreal Golf Club, founded in 1873, is the oldest golf club in North America.

LADIES GOLF TEAM ARE WINNERS

1982's top Canadian amateur women were:

Marlene Streit, Stouffville, Ont.
Mary Ann Hayward, Beaconsfield, Que.
Dawn Coe, Lake Cowichen, B.C.

Cheryll Gibb, Ambersburg, Ont.
Patty Grant, Kamloops, B.C.

CLUBS FOR CONNOISSEURS

John Saksun Jr., of Etobicoke, Ont., has designed a set of golf clubs that are so carefully made that they among the best clubs produced anywhere in the world.

Jon Gustin, the pro at the Country Club of Birmingham, Ala., said, "There is no golf equipment made as well. The only ones I've seen come as close is a set of 1953 Spalding Synchrodyne ... Believe me, no golf equipment in the world is made with such precision, such sophistication."

The clubs, which sell under the trade name Accuform, retail in Toronto for more than $1,000.

KITCHENER GOLFER A MASTER

Kitchner's Gary Cowan has competed in the Masters golf tournament eight times, more than any other Canadian. As well, Cowan is the only foreigner who has won the U.S. Amateur twice. His first appearance was in 1962 and his last was in 1973, and he was the low amateur in 1964.

CANADIAN AMATEUR FOOTBALL CHAMPIONS

Canadian Amateur Football Association

Canadian Junior Football Champions
1982   Renfrew Trojans, B.C.

Canadian Interuniversity Athletic Union Champions
1982   UBC Thunderbirds, B.C.

Canadian Senior Touch Football Champions
1982   Montreal Phoenix, Que.

Canadian Women's Touch Football Champions
1982   Ottawa Reflections, Ont.

1982/83 Junior Achievers

Most Valuable Player: Offence
Ron Almeda, London Beefeaters, London, Ont.

Most Valuable Player: Defence
Larry Wruck, Saskatoon Hilltops, Saskatoon, Sask.

THE PEARSON CUP

Major League Championship of Canada

Awarded to the winner of the annual baseball game between the Toronto Blue Jays and the Montreal Expos. The tournament began in 1978 and has since raised $238,000 for amateur baseball in Canada.

1983   Toronto Blue Jays
1982   Montreal Expos

SOFTBALL CANADA

1982 Canadian National Softball Champions, Fast Pitch

Senior Men's National Champion
Victoria Budgets, B.C.
Senior Ladies' National Champion
Vancouver Alpha Sports, B.C.
Junior Men's National Champion
Halifax Fisherman's Market, N.S.
Junior Ladies' National Champion
Edmonton Jolane Transport, Alta.
Midget Boys' National Champion
Napanee Legionaires, Ont.
Midget Girls' National Champion
Markham Ballentine's Broncos, Ont.

1982 Canadian National Softball Champions, Slow Pitch

Senior Men's National Champion
Burnaby Labatt's Batts, B.C.

CANADIANS MAKE ALL-STARS

Three Canadian baseball palyers were picked for the 10-man world all-star team in September 1982. The team was selected at the end of the World Baseball Championships in Seoul, Korea.

Doug McPhail, an Edmonton schoolteacher with a .415 batting average, was named the best centrefielder.

Rod Heisler of Moose Jaw, Sask., was chosen as the best lefthanded pitcher. He had a 3-0 record and 2.35 ERA in four starts.

Larry Downes of Niagara-on-the-Lake, Ont., the team catcher, had a 1.000 fielding percentage and a .412 batting average.

The players were the first Canadians ever chosen to the world select team. Canada finished fifth in the 10-nation tournament.

WOMEN'S FIELD HOCKEY TEAM SURPRISES, HAPPILY

Canada's 10th ranked field hockey team won the silver medal in World Cup play at Kuala Lumpur, in April 1983. Previously, Canada had never finished higher than fifth in international women's field hockey competitions.

The team finished first in its six-team pool and then defeated Australia in the semi-finals, before losing 4-2 to a larger and more powerful Netherlands team.

Darlene Stoyko of Mississauga, Ont., and Jean Gourlay, of Thornhill, Ont., were named as tournament all-stars and the Canadian team won the fair play award.

CANADIAN LACROSSE ASSOCIATION

1982 National Championship Winners

Bantam
1   Burlington, Ont.

2   London, Ont.
3   Kincardine, Ont.
Midget
1   Peterborough U.E. Petes, Ont.
2   Huntsville O.P.P. Hawkes, Ont.
3   Niagara-on-the-Lake Warriors, Ont.
Intermediate
1   No Competition Held
2   Gold Bar Miners, Edmonton, Alta.
Founders
Gold, Owen Sound Signmen, Ont.
Silver, Delta Islanders, B.C.
Bronze, Baie Comeau Tomahawks, Que.
Presidents
Gold, Orangeville, Ont.
Silver, Six Nations, Ont.
Bronze, Nanaimo, B.C.
Minto Cup
Peterborough James Gang, Ont.
Mann Cup
Peterborough Lakers, Ont.

CANADIAN RUGBY UNION

National Championship
1982   Ontario
National Junior Championships (John Deere Trophy)
1982   British Columbia
Canada Junior vs Japan National High Schools' Team
1982   British Columbia
Can-Am Match
1982   Canada and USA tied 3-3

BALMY BEACHERS BEST IN BAHAMAS

The Balmy Beach Rugby Club of Toronto was the champion club at the Freeport International Rugby Festival in April, 1983. The team defeated teams from England, the Bahamas and Montreal to win the championship.

CANADIAN CRICKET ASSOCIATION

1982 "Gopaulsingh" Trophy

The 1982 men's under 25 tournament was held in Ottawa with competitors from Ontario, Quebec, British Columbia, Manitoba and Alberta.

1982 Ontario "A" Cricket-Team: Paul Prashad, Martin Prashad, Rawley Cottle, Imtiaz Kirmani, Pat Hindrichsen, Danny Singh, Rajaindra Singh, Pat Clarke, Colin Nibbs, Loncoln Pantlitz, Richard Burke, Karam Singh

1982 CANADIAN LAWN BOWLING CHAMPIONSHIPS

Men's Singles
Gold, British Columbia: **Robert Walker**
Silver, Ontario: **Bill Clendinning**
Bronze, Saskatchewan: **Keith Roney**
Men's Pairs
Gold, Ontario: **John Bush, David Houtby**
Silver, British Columbia: **Brain Taylor, John Bell**
Bronze, Alberta: **David Christie, Harold McFadden**
Men's Fours
Gold, Ontario: **Wilfred Wright, Richard Klemmer, Brad Flemming, Wayne Wright** (S)
Silver, British Columbia: **Dave Dundalf, Manuel Valoma, Lou Sousae, Dave Brown** (S)
Bronze, Nova Scotia: **Cecil Bruce, Sid Currie, Fred Hollett, Don Purcell** (S)
Ladies' Singles
Gold, Quebec: **Dorothy Randle**
Silver, Prince Edward Island: **Shirley James**
Bronze, Alberta: **Peggy Sung**
Ladies Pairs
Gold, British Columbia: **Ruth Fouts, Kathleen Finch**
Silver, Alberta: **Christine Adams, Tina Reimer**
Bronze, Manitoba: **Bea Gavenor, Elaine Jones**
Ladies' Triples
Gold, Ontario: **Shirley Otis, Norma Grant, Lynda Robbins** (S)
Silver, British Columbia: **Margaret Veitch, Alice Duncalf, Dorothy Macey** (S)
Bronze, Saskatchewan: **Rosemary Woldie, Jean Pope, Jean Black** (S)

DCRA RIFLE MATCHES

Dominion of Canada Rifle Association

Target Rifle Individual

Des Burke Target Rifle Award
1982 J.C. Roy, Quebec

Governor-General's Prize
1982 R.G. Best, British Columbia
Tess Spencer (Women)
1982 C.L. Cresswell, Ontario

Target Rifle Aggregates

Canadian Open Target Rifle Champion
1982 R.G. Best, British Columbia
Canadian Target Rifle (Bisley Aggregate)
1982 R.G. Best, British Columbia
MacDonald Stewart Grand Aggregate
1982 A. Marion, Quebec
Polar Bear
1982 R.G. Best, British Columbia
Samuel de Champlain Aggregate
1982 R.G. Best, British Columbia

International Team Matches

Palma Match
1982 Canada

Interprovincial Team Matches

London Merchants Cup
1982 Quebec
MacDonald Stewart Aggregate Team Match
1982 British Columbia
Provincial Team Match
1982 Atlantic Region

DOMINION OF CANADA RIFLE ASSOCIATION

Candian Winners at the Commonwealth Games, Brisbane, October 1982

Individual Results

Free Pistol
T. Guinn
Air rifle
J.F Senecal

SHARP SHOOTING

Susan Nattrass and Pat White, both of Edmonton, took gold and silver medals in the women's trapshooting event in Mexico City at the Benito Juarez shooting competition in April 1983. George Leary of Toronto won the open competition. Nattrass, six-time world women's

champion, broke 166 of 200 clay birds to win. Leary shot 193 of 200 for his victory, then teamed with Edmonton shooters John Primrose and Fred White for a 415 team total and a bronze medal.

TEAM EFFORT

Three Canadians combined for a silver medal in the air-rifle event of the Benito Juarez shooting competition at Mexico City, finishing just behind West Germany. Guy Lorion, Jr., of Longueuil, Que., Jean-Francois Senecal of Laval, Que., and Bob Cheyne of Port Moody, B.C., scored a combined 1,711 points in the event, compared with 1,724 for the German team. Canada had a full 23-member team at the competition, which is rated second in importance only to the world championship.

CANADIAN NATIONAL RACQUETBALL CHAMPIONSHIPS

Canadian Racquetball Association

Men's Open
1982   Lindsay Myers, Vancouver, B.C.
Senior
1982   Bill Condratow, B.C.
Masters
1982   Ronald Thompson, Saskatchewan
Golden Masters
1982   Finton Kilbride, Ontario
Junior Boys (under 19)
1982   Allen Lee, Ontario
Junior Boys (Under 16)
1982   Brian Wilkie, Saskatchewan.
Men's Open Doubles
1982   Wayne Bowes, Edmonton, Alta. Bob Daku, Lethbridge, Alta.
Men's Senior Doubles
1982   Bill Condratow, Rick Barker, B.C.
Women's Open
1982   Heather McKay, Ontario
Women's Senior
1982   Laverne Dzuren, Alberta
Junior Girls (Under 19)
1982   Lisa Devine, P.E.I.

Junior Girls (Under 16)
1982   Crystal Fried, Alberta, B.C.
Women's Open Doubles
1982   Heather Stupp, Dena Rassenti, Quebec

RACQUETBALL VICTORY

Heather McKay of Toronto took a straight-set victory to win the women's pro division of the 1982 $40,000 Pony Racquetball Championships. McKay defeated No. 1-ranked Lynn Adams of the U.S. to earn $7,000.

CANADIAN SQUASH CHAMPIONSHIPS 1981/82

Canadian Squash Racquets Association

Hardball

Men's Amateur
John Nimick, Haverford, PA.
35 and Over
Tom Poor, Boston, Mass.
40 and Over
Andy Pastor, Toronto, Ont.
45 and Over
Gerry Shugar, Toronto, Ont.
50 and over
Neil Desaulniers, Montreal, Que.

Junior Hardball Championships

Boys Under 19
Alex Doucas, Montreal, Que.
Boys Under 16
Russell Ball, Philadelphia, PA.
Boys Under 14
Jamie Moore, Sarnia, Ont.
Boys Under 12
Sunil Desai, Brooklyn, N.Y.
Doubles Championship
D. Hetherington and J. Gillespie, Toronto, Ont.
Veterans Doubles
Bart McGuire and John Murphy, New York, N.Y.
Senior Doubles
Jim Bentley and Bill Bewley, Toronto, Ont.
Mixed Doubles

Vic Harding and Barbara Savage, Toronto, Ont.

Softball

Men's Amateur
Doug Whittaker, Toronto, Ont.
35 and Over
Bob Puddicombe, Vancouver, B.C.
40 and Over
Christopher Pickwoad, Montreal.
45 and Over
Warren Reynolds, Weston, Ont.
50 and Over
John Thissen, Ottawa, Ont.
Women's
Joyce Maycock, Vancouver, B.C.
Women's Veterans
Kathy Lundmark, Calgary, Alta.

Junior Softball Championships

Boys Under 19
Alex Doucas, Montreal, Que.
Girls Under 19
Diana Edge, Ottawa, Ont.
Boys Under 16
Gary Waite, Sarnia, Ont.
Girls Under 16
Whitney Stewart, Rochester, N.Y.
Boys Under 14
Sabir Butt, Toronto, Ont.
Girls Under 14
Jennifer Beck, Calgary, Alta.
Boys Under 12
Ric Hartunian, Bramalea, Ont.
Girls Under 12
Lori Coleman, Ajax, Ont.

1982 Lapham Cup

Men's hardball singles team match.
Canada beat the U.S.A. II matches to 4.

Canadian Team Members
Jay Gillespie, Toronto, Ont.
Paul Deratnay, Toronto, Ont.
Gerry Shugar, Toronto, Ont.
David Hetherington, Toronto, Ont.
Peter Frost, Toronto, Ont.
Bob Smart, London, Ont.
John Boynton, Toronto, Ont.
Neil Desaulniers, Montreal, Que.
Jim Bentley, Toronto, Ont.
John Fuller, Toronto, Ont.
Hugh Murray, Hamilton, Ont.

Bill Bewley, Toronto, Ont.
Gary Kritz, Kitchener, Ont.
Lorne Webster, Montreal, Que.
Jeff Williams, Montreal, Que.

1982 Grant Trophy

Men's doubles team match
Canada beat the U.S.A. 6 matches to 5.

Canadian Team Members
Jay Gillespie and Dave Heatherington, Toronto, Ont.
Terry Reidel and Bill Herzog, Kitchener, Ont.
Gary Kritz, Kitchener, Ont., and Paul Deratnay, Toronto, Ont.
John Fuller, Toronto, Ont., and Neil Desaulniers, Montreal, Que.
Bill Bewley and Jim Bentley, Toronto, Ont.
Barry Grant and Peter Frost, Toronto, Ont.
Gerry Shugar, Toronto, Ont., and Hugh Murray, Hamilton, Ont.
John Boynton, Toronto, Ont. and Bob Smart, London, Ont.
Don Ayer, Kitchener, Ont., and Jim Shaw, London, Ont.
Lorne Webster and Jeff Williams, Montreal, Que.
Ernie Whelpton and Bill Richards, Toronto, Ont.

CANADIAN UNIVERSITY CHAMPIONSHIPS 1981/82

Canadian Squash Racquets Association

Harald Martin Trophy (Ontario Universities Athletic Association Men's Softball Championships)
University of Toronto, lead by Alan Grant and Taylor Fawcett
Molson's Trophy (Ontario Universities Athletic Association Men's Softball Championships)
York University, Douglas Whittaker
U.S. Intercollegiate Hardball Championships
The University of Toronto tied with Yale for 3rd place behind Harvard and Princeton. Vic Wagner, of Ottawa, playing for Yale, won the individual event and the Poole Trophy, thus emulating the feats of other Canadians Peter Landry (1947), John Smith Chapman (1958), Phil Mohtadi (1976) and Mike Desaulniers (1977, 1978 and 1980).

Dr. Labib North American Student Hardball Squash Championship
McGill University, Jill Samis
Can-Am Team Event, Hardball
York University, Yeo-women
Can-Am Team Event, Softball
Queen's University
Manta-Can Am Invitational
York University, Jo-Ann Beckwith
OWIAA Team Championships
University of Toronto, Lead by Patti Hogan and Anne Green

SQUASH

Mark Talbott, a Toronto-based American, captured the Canadian Pro Squash Title. Talbott made it 16 wins out of 17 tournaments by downing Clive Caldwell of Toronto in the final of the Canadian pro championship at Toronto's Skyline Club in April, 1983.

"THE CONQUEROR OF THE WORLD"

The Mennen Cup
Pakistan's Jahangir Khan, 19, whose name, Jahangir, translates as "conqueror of the world," won the Mennen Cup hardball squash tournament in Toronto in 1983.

TABLE TENNIS STARS

Zoran Kosanovic, 26, and Errol Caetano, 28, both of Toronto, won the doubles finals of the 1982 Norwich Union Canadian Open in Toronto. Ottawa's Mariann Domonko's blanked Sook Kim of Korea, 3-0, to capture the women's singles title.

TENNIS CANADA AWARDS 1982

Female Player of the Year
Marjorie Blackwood, Ottawa, Ont.
Male Player of the Year

Rejean Genois, Laval, Que.
Most Improved Female Player
Carling Bassett, Toronto, Ont.
Most Improved Male Player
Bill Cowan, Toronto, Ont.
Coach of the year
Louis Cayer, Montreal, Que.
Journalist of the Year
Gilles Blanchard, *La Presse*, Montreal, Que.
Tennis Canada's Executive of the Year
Roy Mansell, Toronto, Ont.

1982 CANADIAN TENNIS CHAMPIONS

Tennis Canada

Open

Player's International
Men's Singles
Vitas Gerulaitis
Men's Doubles
Steve Denton and **Mark Edmondson**
Player's Challenge
Women's Singles
Martina Navratilova
Women's Doubles
Martina Navratilova and **Candy Reynolds**

Closed

Men's Singles
Glenn Michibata
Women's Singles
Carling Bassett
Men's Doubles
John Picken and **Robert Bettauer**
Women's Doubles
Carling Bassett and **Angela Walker**

Junior

Under 18
Boy's Singles
Hatem McDadi
Girls' Singles
Suzie Hatch
Boys' Doubles
Grant Connell and **Dale Willard**
Girls' Singles
Suzie Hatch and **Monica Kowalewski**
Under 16
Boys' Singles
Andrew Sznajder
Girls' Singles

Rene Simpson
Boys' Doubles
Richard Robert and **Chris Smith**
Girls' Doubles
Rene Simpson and **Kim Ferguson**
Under 14
Boys' Singles
Lorne Goldberg
Girls' Singles
Carol Culik
Boys' Doubles
Lorne Goldberg and **Jean Francois Mathieu**
Girls' Doubles
Helen Kelesi and **Michelle Bogaard**
Under 12
Boys' Singles
Darren Goldberg
Girls' Singles
Maureen Drake
Boys' Doubles
Eric Godin and **Philipe Leblanc**
Girls' Doubles
Maureen Drake and **Jacqueline Cernik**

Veterans

Mens' Over 35
Singles
J.C. Gosselin
Doubles
Chauncey Steele and **Paul Sullivan**
Mens' Over 45
Singles
Lorne Main
Doubles
Ken Binns and **Kevin Parker**
Mens' Over 55
Singles
Jacques Giguere
Doubles
Art Jeffrey and **Jack Pedlar**
Mens' Over 60
Singles
Jan Rubes
Doubles
George Robinson and **Ellis Tarshis**
Mens' Over 65
Singles
Joey Richman
Doubles
Chet Coleman and **Tom Harvey**
Women Over 40
Singles
Enid Jackson

Doubles
Enid Jackson and **Sally Hemeon**
Womens' Over 50
Singles
Hana Brabenec
Doubles
Hana Brabenec and **Sally Sutton**

JUNIOR TENNIS

1983 junior tennis team:
Helen Kelesi, Richmond, B.C.
Andrew Sznajder, 15, Toronto, Ont.
Jana Klepac, 17, Marathon, Ont.
Grant Connell, 17, Vancouver, B.C.

CARLING BASSETT RISING FAST

Carling Bassett, 15, of Toronto is the sensation of the 1983 Canadian tennis season.

She won the Ginny tournament of Central Pennsylvania in February 1983, and that was only her third tournament as a professional. By the end of April, Carling had moved from 167th spot on the WTA computer to 22nd in the world and it took her just 10 months to plow through the rankings. She moved from 34th to 22nd in April when she advanced to the finals of a tournament at Amelia Island, Fla., and pushed Chris Evert Lloyd to three sets before losing.

In June she reached a high point for Canadian tennis when she advanced to the quarter-finals of the women's singles at Wimbledon. While she lost to Andrea Jaeger in the semi-finals she showed enough poise and skill to make believers of the whole tennis world.

FAST CANADIANS

No human on earth, without the help of an engine, can go faster than a speed skier. There are only some 200 daredevils in the world who streak down near vertical high-altitude slopes, and Canadian Terry Watts, a B.C. gold miner, is among them.

Watts was clocked at 125.954 mph at the world speed skiing championships in France in 1983. Watts, Kent Wills and Phil Graves, all of Vancouver, placed in the top 10 at the International Speed Skiing Championships held at the 13,000-foot level of Velocity Peak in Colorado on a run 3/5th of a mile long.

1982 SHELL CUP CANADIAN SENIOR CROSS COUNTRY SKI CHAMPIONSHIPS

Canadian Ski Association

Womens' 10 km
Shirley Firth, Northwest Territories, 38 min., 31 sec.
Mens' 30 km
Doug Gudwer, British Columbia, 1 hr., 40 min., 5 sec.
Womens' 5 km
Shirley Firth, Northwest Territories, 16 min., 19 sec.
Mens' 15 km
Pierre Harvey, Quebec, 46 min., 56 sec.
Womens' 17 km
Shirley Firth, Northwest Territories, 59 min., 41 sec.
Mens' 25.5 km
Pierre Harvey, Quebec, 1 hr., 18 min., 35 sec.
Women's Shell Cup Winner
Shirly Firth, Northwest Territories
Mens' Shell Cup Winner
Pierre Harvey, Quebec
Men's 5 km. (15 and under)
Brian Rasmussen, British Columbia, 14 min., 49 sec.
Men's 10 km (16 and 17)
Darren Derochie, Ontario, 27 min.
Men's 10 km (18 and 19)
Jocelyn Vezina, Quebec, 26 min., 23 sec.
Women's 2.5 km (15 and under)
Kjerstein Baldwin, Manitoba, 7 min., 40 sec.
Women's 7.5 km (16 and 17)
Mary Stockdale, Saskatchewan, 23 min., 32 sec.
Women's 10 km (18 and 19)

Marie-Andree Masson, Quebec, 29 min., 48 sec.
Men's 3 × 7.5 km relay
British Columbia: **Kurt Tuggle, Louis Helbig, Eric Gaarder**, 1 hr., 1 min., 10 sec.
Women's 3 × 5 km Relay
Quebec: **Suzie Desharnais, Jose Bertrand, Marie-Andree Masson**, 59 min., 32 sec.

1982 CANADIAN WINTER GAMES

Northern Ontario Ski Division Cross Country of the Canadian Ski Association

Women's 5 km
Jean McAllister, Ottawa, Ont., 18 min., 27 sec.
Women's 10 km
Jean McAllister, Ottawa, Ont., 36 min., 58 sec.
Men's 15 km
David Lumb, Ontario, 50 min., 25 sec.
Men's 10 km
Yves Bilodeau, Quebec, 32 min., 3 sec.
Men's 3 × 10 km relay
Ontario:
Wayne Dustin, Dave Beedell, David Lumb, 1 hr., 35 min., 37 sec.
Women's 3 × 5 km relay
Ontario:
Kelly Rogers, Lise Melocke, Jean McAllister, 56 min., 17 sec.
Men's 7.5 km (15 and under)
James Haddon, Ottawa, Ont., 24 min., 4 sec.
Men's 7.5 km (16 and 17)
Eric Harnula, Alberta, 23 min., 58 sec.
Men's 15 km (18 and 19)
Frank Ferrari, Ontario, 49 min., 17 sec.
Women's 5 km (15 and under)
Kjerstein Balwin, Manitoba, 20 min., 38 sec.
Women's 5 km (16 and 17)
Mary Stockdale, Saskatchewan, 19 min., 40 sec.
Women's 5 km (18 and 19)
Marie-Andree Masson, Quebec, 19 min., 22 sec.

1982 SHELL CUP

Canadian Ski Association

Senior Men
Pierre Harvey, Stoneham, Que.

Senior Women
Shirley Firth, Inuvik, N.W.T.
Junior Men (18 and 19)
James Haddon, Deep River, Ont.
Junior Women (18 and 19)
Kjerstin Baldwin, Winnipeg, Man.
Junior Men (16 and 17)
Frank Ferrari, Timmins, Ont.
Junior Women (16 and 17)
Marie Andree Masson, Victoriaville, Que.
Junior Men (15 and under)
Dennis Lawrence, Regina, Sask.
Junior Women (15 and under)
Mary Stockdale, Saskatoon, Sask.

ONTARIO SNOWMOBILE RACING FEDERATION

1981/82 Season Winners

Overall Eastern Pro Series Formula Champion
Peter Vandolder, Annan, Ont.
Sno Pro Competition
1   **Brad Hulings**, Grand Rapids, Mich.
2   **Gary Vessair**, Honey Harbour, Ont.
3   **Jacques Villeneuve**, St. Cuthbert, Que.
Mod II Class
1   **Howard Gifford**, Sudbury, Ont.
2   **Gaye Pirie**, Pakenham, Ont.
.3   **Deryle Ladd**, Oshawa, Ont.
Mod III Class
1   **Howard Gifford**, Sudbury, Ont.
2   **Harold Lemke**, Belleville, Ont.
3   **Gaye Pirie**, Pakenham, Ont.
Super Mod I Class
1   **Peter Vandolder**, Annan, Ont.
2   **Terry Gobbo**, Coniston, Ont.
3   **Joe Clarke**, Kingston, Ont.
Super Mod II Class
1   **Brad Hulings**, Grand Rapids, Mich.
2   **Jim Dimmerman**, White Bear Lake, Man.
3   **Larry Van Dyke**, Stouffville, Ont.
Pro Stock Class
1   **Ken Avann**, Keswick, Ont.
2   **Mike Hession**, Milton, Ont.
3   **Ted Harshman**, Sauble River, Ont.
Sprint 540
1   **Andy Vandolder**, Annan, Ont.
2   **Jim Dimmerman**, White Bear Lake, Man.
3   **Frenchy Cloutier**, Timmins, Ont.
Mod Division
1   **Howard Gifford**, Sudbury, Ont.

2   **Harold Lemke**, Belleville, Ont.
3   **Gaye Pirie**, Pakenham, Ont.
Super Mod Division
1   **Peter Vandolder**, Annan, Ont.
2   **Larry Van Dyke**, Stouffville, Ont.
3   **Michael David**, Campbellcroft, Ont.
Pro Stock Division (Top 5)
1   **Grant McKinlay**, Whitby, Ont.
2   **Ted Harshman**, Sauble River, Ont.
3   **Mike Hession**, Milton, Ont.
4   **Ken Avann**, Keswick, Ont.
5   **Gilles Larochelle**, Cloyne, Ont.
Formula Division (Top 5)
1   **Gary Vessair**, Honey Harbour, Ont.
2   **Peter Vandolder**, Annan, Ont.
3   **Bruce Vessair**, Honey Harbour, Ont.
4   **Larry Van Dyke**, Stouffville, Ont.
5   **Jim Dimmerman**, White Bear Lake, Man.

NANCY GREENE'S FLAWLESS RUN

Nancy Greene was Queen of the Slopes when she won the women's giant slalom at the 1968 Winter Olympics in Grenoble, France, by a healthy 2.63 seconds over the classy international field of 48 skiers from 18 nations. Her time was a sensational 1 minute, 51.97 seconds, through 58 gates on the icy 1,610-metre course. It was the second medal of the games for the 24-year-old Rossland, B.C., girl as she reached a peak in a skiing career that spanned three Olympics.

In 1960 Nancy had watched another Canadian, Anne Heggtveit of Ottawa, win the gold medal in the same race. Nancy, then 16, promised herself that one day she would win the gold.

Two weeks before her victory at Grenoble, Nancy suffered a bad ankle injury raising doubts that she would be able to compete in the Olympics. Then she was distressed by her position in the downhill, as dirt, imbedded in her freshly waxed skis, left her back in 10th position. She brightened when two steady, controlled runs in the slalom brought her a silver medal. She was ready for the giant slalom.

On the epic day she flashed out of the starting gate and carved a run which was flawless. She said after the race,

Nancy Greene's electrifying performance in Grenoble won a gold medal at the Olympics

Barbara Ann Scott was the toast of Canada after winning an Olympic gold at St. Moritz, Switzerland. (From the Prudential *Great Moments in Sport Collection*). Artist — Don Anderson

"There wasn't a move I made that I would change if I had to ski the giant slalom again."

WORLD'S LONGEST SKI MARATHON

Heinz Neiderhauser of White Lake, Ont., finished first in the 1983 two-day Canadian cross-country ski marathon. He skied the 100 miles from Lachute, Que., to Ottawa in only 14 hours, over the bronze coureur-de-bois category.

Eleven-year-old Christopher Blanchard of Pointe Claire, Que., was the youngest skier to complete the full course.

VICTORY FLIGHT

Horst Bulau, 20, of Ottawa won the Shell Canadian 90-metre ski-jumping championships in February 1983. He flew 117 and 109.5 metres successively to record 251.1 points and claim the national championship. On the previous day Bulau took the 70-metre title with jumps of 98.5 and 90.5 metres for 279 points, to sweep the competition.

SLED CHAMPION

Miroslav Zajonc, 22, formerly of Czechoslovakia, is now a landed immigrant living in Toronto. In February, 1983, Zajonc competed with the Canadian luge team and won the world championship title for the one-man sled at Lake Placid, N.Y. The Canadian team is hopeful that he will be granted early citizenship and be able to compete in the '84 Winter Olympics for Canada.

HERMAN "JACK RABBIT" SMITH-JOHANNSEN

Herman Johannsen was born in 1875, in Norway where he skied from a very young age. He graduated from the University of Berlin as an Engineer in 1899, but his footloose spirit brought him to America, where he got a job selling heavy machinery. In Canada, in 1902, the Grand Trunk Railway was being pushed through Northern Ontario and Quebec and, in winter, Johannsen was able to reach the remote job sites on his skies. With a change of socks, a gun, a bedroll and his sales brochures, on a sleigh pulled by a dog, he would spend days or even weeks in the countryside, taking orders for his company. According to one legend, the Cree Indians he met in the bush knew him as "Okamacum Wapooes" or "Chief Jack Rabbit."

He was wiped out in the Crash of '29 at the age of 54. During the Depression, he moved his family to the Laurentians. "Jack Rabbit" hunted and fished and made his living with his skills as a skier and woodsman. Instrumental in the development of skiing in Canada, he built jumps and laid out hills and trails all over the Eastern Townships, the Laurentians and Ontario. In the early 1930s, he blazed and later cut the "Maple Leaf Trail" from Shawbridge to Mont Tremblant, winding through 90 miles of beautiful scenery and carefully avoiding any hill too steep or any climb too long. In 1932, he was the coach of the Canadian Olympic ski team. In 1967, he created the Canadian Ski Marathon and in 1972 was awarded the Order of Canada by the Governor-General.

At 107, he is an inspiration to Canadians who have learned the simple pleasures of cross country touring on skis. The great adventurer Lowell Thomas credits "Jack Rabbit" for giving a big push to skiing in America through the instruction he gave to people in Lake Placid and the Adirondacks and for laying out the trails in the Laurentians.

In the 1940s, he was called in to consult on the proposed trails on

Jack Rabbit
Father of Skiing

Whiteface Mountain in Lake Placid. For the 1980 Olympics, "Jack Rabbit's" headings on Whiteface were transformed into some of the premier Alpine race courses in the world. He is a member of Canada's Sports Hall of Fame.

SPORTS FEDERATION OF CANADA

1982 Canadian Sports Awards

Canadian Press Awards

Bobbi Rosenfeld Award (Female Athlete of the Year)
Gerry Sorensen, Kimberley, B.C. Skiing
Lionel Conacher Award (Male Athlete of the Year)
Wayne Gretzky, Brantford, Ont. Hockey
Velma Springstead Trophy (Female Athlete of the Year)
Angella Taylor, Downsview, Ont. Track and field running
Norton Crowe Award (Male Athlete of the Year)
Steve Podborski, Don Mills, Ont. Downhill skiing
Elaine Tanner Trophy (Female Athlete of the Year Under 20)
Marie-Claude Asselin, Ste. Agathe, Que. Freestyle skiing
Viscount Alexander Trophy (Male Athlete of the Year Under 20)
Gordon Kluzak, Climax, Sask. Hockey
Dick Ellis Memorial Trophy (Team of the Year)
The Canadian Junior Hockey Team
Coach: Dave King, Saskatoon, Sask.
Captain: Troy Murray, South Porcupine, Ont.

SPORTS FEDERATION OF CANADA

1982 Athlete of the Month Award

January
Horst Bulau, Ottawa, Ont. Ski jump
February
Wayne Gretzky, Brantford, Ont. Hockey
March
Steve Podborski, Don Mills, Ont. Downhill skiing
April
Al Hackner, Thunder Bay, Ont. Curling

May
Alex Stoeda, Coquitlam, B.C. Race cycling
June
Willie deWit, Grand Prairie, Alta. Heavyweight boxing
July
Kelly Kryczka, Calgary, Alta.
Sharon Hambrook, Calgary, Alta. Synchronized swimming.
August
Victor Davis, Waterloo, Ont. Swimming
September
Mariann Domonkos, Chateauguay, Que. Table tennis
October
Alex Baumann, Sudbury, Ont. Swimming
November
Barbara Underhill and **Paul Martini**. Figure skating
December
Carling Bassett, Toronto, Ont. Tennis.

TOP TRIATHLETE

Canadian Runner, in April 1983, named **Rocky Phillips, 29, of Toronto as Canada's top triathlete.**

The triathlete must swim a 2.4-mile ocean course, then bicycle 112 miles and then run a hot-weather marathon. Phillips was the top Canadian in the October, 1982, Hawaiian Ironman Triathlon. His time was 10 hours, 46 minutes and 38 seconds.

HARRY JEROME AWARDS

Black Business Association

The award honours the memory and athletic achievement of Harry Jerome, Canada's most outstanding sprinter of the 1960s. Jerome died in Vancouver in December 1982 at the age of 42.

The awards were presented in March 1983 to **Angella Taylor, Milt Ottey** and **Mark McKoy** of Toronto. They were all gold medallists in track and field events at the Commonwealth Games. Other award winners were silver medallist sprinters **Ben Johnson, Desai Williams** and **Toni Sharpe**.

CANADIANS RUNNING

Jacqueline Gareau of St. Bruno-de-Montarville, Que., finished first in the women's division of the 1980 Boston Marathon, ahead of Rosie Ruiz, the New York subway racer.

In 1983 Gareau finished the grueling marathon in a personal best time of 2 hours, 29 minutes, 23 seconds, finishing second in the women's division of the race.

David Edge of Lancaster, Ont., was the top Canadian man in the 1983 marathon. He finished in 2:11.03.

JUMPING INTO THE NEWS

Milt Ottey of Toronto set a Canadian and Commonwealth record in June 1982 when he cleared 2.32 metres (seven feet, 7 1/4 inches) at the National Collegiate Athletic Association track and field meet in Provo, Utah. Ottey is closing in on the world record of 2.37 metres.

Ottey was selected as the number one high jumper in the world for 1982 by *Tack and Field News* magazine, a Los Angeles publication. Ottey is the first Canadian to achieve the magazine's number one ranking in a field event.

In previous years the magazine named three other Canadians as number one in track events: Harry Jerome (200 metres), Bill Crothers (800 metres) and Jerome Drayton (marathon).

PEERLESS IN PENTATHLON

Dave Steen of Toronto shattered a world indoor pentathlon record in February 1983. He scored 4,104 points in a competition at Toronto's Maple Leaf Gardens, bettering the previous mark of

4,100 set by England's Daley Thompson in 1981.

BEST EVER FINISH BY A CANADIAN

Alison Wiley of Toronto finished second in the World Cross-Country Running Championships held March 19, at Gateshead, England. His performance was the best ever by a Canadian at the Senior world championships. He finished only eight seconds after the first place finisher Grete Waltz of Norway.

CANADIAN INTERUNIVERSITY ATHLETIC UNION

CIAU Champions

Basketball

W.P. McGee Trophy (Men's basketball champions)
1981/82 Victoria
Mike Moser Memorial Trophy (Outstanding male basketball player)
1981/82 Karl Tilleman,Calgary
1981/82 All-Canadian Team
Dave Coulthard, York
John Hatch, St. Francis
Gerald Kazanowski, Victoria
Eli Pasquale, Victoria
Karl Tilleman, Calgary
Lee Davis, St. Mary's
Jude Kelly, Brandon
Stan Korosec, Windsor
Gary McKeigan, Concordia
Murray Redekop, Saskatchewan
Coach Stuart W. Aberdeen Memorial Trophy (Men's basketball coach of the year)
1981/82 Ken Shields, Victoria
Bronze Baby (Women's basketball champions)
1981/82 Victoria
Nan Copp Award (Outstanding female basketball player)
1981/82 Luanne Hebb, Victoria
1981/82 All-Canadian Women's Team
Andrea Blackwell, Bishop's
Luanne Hebb, Victoria
Janis Paskevich, Calgary
Donna Posnick, Winnipeg

Barb Tucker, Laurentian
Sheila Brennan, Saskatchewan
Cheryl Kryluk, Winnipeg
Linda Marquis, McGill
Joanne McLean, New Brunswick
Lynn Polson, Bishop's

Cross Country

Men's National Championship
1981/82 Queen's
Women's National Championship
1981/82 Western

Field Hockey

Women's National Championship
1981/82 Toronto

Football

Vanier Cup (Men's football champions)
1981/82 Acadia
Robert L. Stanfield Trophy (Winners of Atlantic Bowl Football Game)
1981/82 Acadia
Forest City Bowl/Western Bowl Trophy (Winners of Forest City Bowl/Western Bowl game)
1981/82 Alberta
Ted Morris Trophy (Most valuable player of the Vanier Cup game)
1981/82 Steve Repic, Acadia
Hec Creighton Trophy (Outstanding football player)
1982/83 Rick Nizch, Ottawa
J.P. Metras Trophy (Outstanding lineman)
1982/83 Peter Langford, Guelph
President's Trophy (Outstanding defensive player)
1982/83 Mike Emery, British Columbia
Don Loney Trophy (Most valuable player of the Atlantic Bowl game)
1981/82 Larry Priestnall, Acadia
M.L. Van Vliet Trophy (Most valuable player of the central [Western] Bowl game)
1981/82 Greg Marshall, Western
Peter Gorman Trophy (Outstanding freshman football player)
1982/83 Mike Fabilli, Ottawa
Frank Tindall Trophy (Football coach of the year)
1981/82 John Huard, Acadia
1981/82 All-Canadian Team
Offensive Team
Dan Feraday, Toronto
Glenn Steel, British Columbia

Greg Marshall, Western
Tom McCartney, Queen's
Gerald Prud'homme, Concordia
Mark Magee, Toronto
Mike Hudson, Guelph
Percy Gendall, Alberta
Jeff Arp, Western
Kevin Dalliday, Carleton
Tony Grassa, St. Francis Xavier
Jeff Hale, Guelph
Defensive Team
Jason Riley, British Columbia
Chris Rhora, Acadia
John Celestino, Windsor
Mark Joncas, McGill
Kevin Ford, Western
Mark Chouinard, McGill
Stuart MacLean, Acadia
Mike Every, British Columbia
Ron Poulton, McGill
Glenn Music, Alberta
Barry Quarrell, Wilfrid Laurier
Tom Johnson, Acadia

Gymnastics

Men's National Championship
1981/82 York
Top All-Round Male Gymnast
1981/82 Dan Gaudet, York
Men's Coach of the Year
1981/82 Masaaki Naosaki, York
Women's National Championship
1981/82 Manitoba
Top All-Round Female Gymnast
1981/82 Patti Sakaki, British Columbia
Women's Coach of the Year
1981/82 David Johns, Manitoba

Ice Hockey

University Cup-Men's Hockey Champions
1981/82 Moncton
Senator Joseph A. Sullivan Trophy (Outstanding hockey player)
1981/82 Paul Stothart, Queen's
Gruen Award (Most valuable player of hockey championship tournament)
1981/82 Alain Grenier, Moncton
Coach of the Year
1981/82 Reg Higgs, Regina
All-Canadian Men's Team 1981/82
Goal
Ron Patterson, British Columbia
Mark Locken, St. Mary's

Russ Jackson, the greatest Canadian-born quarterback in history, threw a record four touchdown passes in Ottawa's 29-11 Grey Cup victory over Saskatchewan, Nov. 29, 1969. (From the Prudential *Great Moments in Sport Collection*). Artist — Gerald Sevier

Defence
Serge Turcotte, Laval
Tim Wicijowski, Regina
Ken Johnston, Dalhousie
Rich Mastroluisi, McMaster
Forward
Bill Holowaty, British Columbia
Paul Stothart, Queen's
Brian Gualazzi, Dalhousie
Tim Morrison, Brandon
Ron Davidson, Queen's
Larry Ell, Regina
National Hockey Championships
1981/82 Moncton

Soccer

Sam Davidson Memorial Trophy (Soccer champions)
1981/82 McGill
Coach of the Year
1981/82 Greg Zorbas, Laurentian
1981/82 All-Canadian Team
First Team
Tom Abbott, Waterloo
Geoff Agostini, St. Mary's
Rudy Bartholomew, Alberta
Larry Courvoisier, New Brunswick
Barry Hackett, Laurentian
Brian Decarie, McGill
Scott Fraser, Wilfrid Laurier
Tim Heaney, Concordia
Gary Palenz, Prince Edward Island
Ross Webb, St. Mary's
Frank Woods, Victoria
Second Team
Doug Adlen, Victoria
Keith Bridge, Laurentian
Harry Christakis, Wilfrid Laurier
Tim Duru, Alberta
Scott Fisher, Alberta
Mark Olivieri, Alberta
Peter Pinheiro, Laurentian
Paul Scholz, Wilfrid Laurier
Al Sigurdson, British Columbia
Dan Sudeyko, British Columbia
Joe Turpin, New Brunswick

Swimming and Diving

Nelson C. Hart Trophy (Highest point score by a university in the men's swimming and diving championship)
1981/82 Calgary
Outstanding Male Swimmer

1981/82 Graham Smith, Calgary
Outstanding Male Diver
1981/82 Randy Sageman, Toronto
Coach of the Year
Swimming
1981/82 Derek Snelling, Calgary
Diving
1981/82 Skip Phoenix, Toronto
1981/82 Men's National Champions:
Calgary
Event Winners 1981/82
100 m backstroke, **Jay Tapp**, Calgary
200 m backstroke, **Frank Kennedy**, Acadia
100 m breaststroke, **Graham Smith**, Calgary
200 m breaststroke, **Graham Smith**, Calgary
100 m butterfly, **Dave Churchill**, Toronto
200 m butterfly, **Claus Bredschneider**, Toronto
200 m I.M., **Graham Smith**, Calgary
400 m I.M., **Brian Johnson**, Calgary
50 m freestyle, **Dan Friegang**, Calgary
100 m freestyle, **Dan Friegang**, Calgary
200 m freestyle, **Eugene Gyorfi**, Calgary
400 m freestyle, **Eugene Gyorfi**, Calgary
1500 m freestyle, **Eugene Gyorfi**, Calgary
800 m free relay, **Calgary: Brian Johnson, John Scott, Dan Friegang, Eugene Gyorfi**
400 m medley relay, **Calgary: Jay Tapp, Graham Smith, Brian Armstead, Dan Friegang**
1 m diving, **Randy Sageman**, Toronto
3 m diving, **John Nash**, Carleton
Women's Swimming and Diving Champions:
1981/82 Toronto
Outstanding Female Diver
1981/82 Eniko Kiefer, McGill
Outstanding Female Swimmer
1981/82 Lisa Dixon, Calgary
Coach of the Year
Swimming
1981/82 Jack Kelso, British Columbia
Diving
1981/82 Don Lieberman, British Columbia
1981/82 Women's National Champions:
Toronto
Event Winners
100 m backstroke, **Lisa Dixon**, Calgary
200 m backstroke, **Lisa Dixon**, Calgary
100 m breaststroke, **Judy Garay**, Toronto
200 m breaststroke, **Kathy Richardson**, Brock
100 m butterfly, **Lori O'Hara**, Toronto
200 m butterfly, **Lori O'hara**, Toronto
200 m I.M., **Lisa Dixon**, Calgary
400 m I.M., **Kathy Richardson**, Brock

50 m freestyle, **Ronda Thomasson**, British Columbia
100 m freestyle, **Ronda Thomasson**, British Columbia
200 m freestyle, **Ronda Thomasson**, British Columbia
400 m freestyle, **Susan Mason**, Dalhousie
800 m freestyle, **Maxine Charles**, Calgary
800 m free relay, **Calgary: Lisa Dixon, Maxine Charles, Chandra Abdurahman, Helen Mc-Henry**,
400 m medley relay, Toronto: **Brenda Barnes, Judy Garay, Lori O'Hara, Kathy Becker**
l m diving, **Eniko Keifer**, McGill
3 m diving, **Eniko Keifer**, McGill
CIAU Swimming and Diving Records
100 m back, F **Wendy Hogg**, British Columbia (1979), 1:05.08
M **Graham Smith**, Calgary, (1981), 57.42
200 m back, F **Wendy Hogg**, British Columbia (1979), 2:21.50
M **Graham Smith**, Calgary (1981), 2:06.05
100 m breast, **Judy Garay**, Toronto (1982), 1:13.73
M **Graham Smith**, Calgary (1981), 1:02.50
200 m breast, F **Kathy Richardson**, Brock (1982), 2:35.99
M **Graham Smith**, Calgary (1981), 2:17.35
100 m fly, F **Debbie Armstead**, Calgary (1981), 1:02.39
M **Dan Thompson**, Toronto (1980), 54.10
200 m, F **Debbie Armstead**, Calgary, (1981), 2:18.52
M **Claus Bradschneider**, Toronto (1981), 2:00.90
200 m I.M., F **Becky Smith**, Lakehead (1979), 2:19.92
M **Graham Smith**, Calgary (1981), 2:03.44
400 m, I.M. **Kathy Richardson**, Brock (1982), 4:55.98
M **Brian Johnson**, Calgary (1981), 4:27.37
50 m free, F **Lori Scott**, Windsor (1980), 26.68
M **Gary McDonald**, York (1978), 22.84
100 m free, F **Kelly Neuler**, Laurentian (1981), 58.04
M **Mike Olson**, Calgary (1981), 50.29
200 m free, F **Leslie Brafield**, Toronto (1981), 2:03.90
M **Mike Olson**, Calgary (1981), 1:50.12
400 m free, F **Debbie Armstead**, Calgary, (1981), 4:20.85
M **Mike Olson**, Calgary (1981), 3:53.08

800 m free, F **Liz McKinnon**, Lakehead (1978), 8:58.47
1500 free, M **Eugene Gyorfi**, Calgary (1982), 15:31.62
400 m free relay, F **Calgary: Chandra Abdurahman, Anne Harrison, Debbie Armstead, Bonnie Robertson**, (1982), 3:59.28
M **British Columbia: Tyler Cant, Mike Ball, Kevin Stapleton, Mike Blondal**, (1982), 3:28.23
800 m free relay, F **Calgary: Lisa Dixon, Debbie Armstead, Bonnie Robertson, Anne Harrison**, (1982), 8:40.20
M **Calgary: Brian Johnson, John Scott, Dan Friegang, Eugene Gyorfi**, (1982), 7:32.71
400 m medley relay, F **Toronto: Brenda Barnes, Judy Garay, Lori O'Hara, Kathy Becker**, (1982), 4:30.13
M **Calgary: Jay Tapp, Graham Smith, Brian Armstead, Dan Freigang**, (1982), 3:49.17
1 m diving, F **Eniko Keifer**, McGill (1982), 422.15
M **Randy Sageman**, Toronto (1981), 537.10
3 m diving, F **Eniko Keifer**, McGill (1982), 454.30
M **Mike Mourant**, Calgary (1981), 591.25

Track and Field

Men's National Championship
1981/82 Toronto
Outstanding Male Athlete of the Meet
1981/82 Ian Newhouse, Alberta
1981/82 Men's National Championship
Event Winners
60 m, **Tony Sharpe**, York
300 m, **Tony Sharpe**, York
600 m, **Ian Newhouse**, Alberta
1000 m, **Simon Hoogewarf**, British Columbia
1500 m, **Dave Campbell**, Victoria
5000 m, **Randy Cox**, Victoria
60 m hurdles, **Mark McKoy**, York
4x400 m relay, **Manitoba: Dan Moroz, Andre Smith, Roger Lourenzo, Cal Langford**
4 x 800 m relay, **British Columbia: Jason Gray, Ian Gillespie, Frances Ward, Simon Hoogewarf**
distance medley relay, **Victoria: Dave Campbell, Randy Cox, Brad Brohman, Steve Guille**
high jump, **Rob Pitter**, Toronto
pole vault, **Dave Parker**, British Columbia
long jump, **Dave Steen**, Toronto
triple jump, **Dave Binder**, Toronto
shot put, **Frank Balkovik**, Toronto.

Women's National Championship
1981/82 Western
Outstanding Female Athlete of the Meet
1981/82 Sandy Gilkes, Manitoba
Event Winners
60 m, **Sandy Gilkes**, Manitoba
300 m, **Sandy Gilkes**, Manitoba
600 m, **Giselle Plantz**, Western
1000 m, **Christine Slythe**, Sherbrooke
1500 m, **Debbie Scott**, Victoria
3000 m, **Debbie Scott**, Victoria
60 m hurdles, **Jill Ross-Giffen**, Toronto
4x200 m relay, **Manitoba: Sandy Gilkes, Tanya Brothers, Cheril Croxford, C. Cooke**
4 x 400 m relay, **Manitoba: Sandy Gilkes, Tanya Brothers, C. Cooke, Nancy Rettie**
4 x 800 m relay, **Saskatchewan: Theresa Hlady, Lesio Pillopow, Leila Preston, Beverly Britton**
High jump, **Alison Armstrong**, Western
Long jump, **Jill Ross-Giffen**, Toronto
Shot put, **Melody Torcolacci**, Queen's

Volleyball

Tantramar Trophy (Men's Volleyball Champions)
1981/82 Calgary
Men's Volleyball Coach of the Year
1981/82 Mike Burchuk, Winnipeg
1981/82 Men's All-Canadian Team
Mark Kolodziej, Calgary
Doug Kozak, Manitoba
Brian Newman, Calgary
Paul Paquin, Manitoba
Dave Slokar, Victoria
Rod Walsh, Dalhousie
Rod Bolianaz, Winnipeg
Dave Chambers, York
Olav Jurgensen, Winnipeg
Neil Klassen, Winnipeg
Phil Perrin, Dalhousie
Brad Willock, British Columbia
1981/82 Male Player of the year
Mark Kolodziej, Calgary
Women's Volleyball Champions
1981/82 Dalhousie
Women's Volleyball Coach of the Year
1981/82 Garth Pischke, Manitoba
1981/82 Women's All-Canadian Team
Karin Maessen, Dalhousie
Ruth Klassen, Winnipeg
Andree Ledoux, Laval
Bonnie MacRae, Calgary

Joyce Senyk, Saskatchewan
Lyn Tremblay, Laval
Rachel Belliveau, Sherbrooke
Karen Fraser, Dalhousie
Denise Guay, Laval
Donna Kastelie, York
Sue Rendell, Memorial
Maria Taylor, York
1981/82 Female Player of the Year
Karin Maessen, Dalhousie

Wrestling

Men's Wrestling Championship
1981/82 Guelph
Outstanding Male Wrestler
1981/82 Mark Jodoin, Lakehead
Wrestling Coach of the Year
1981/82 Londo Iacovelli, Guelph

L.B. (Mike) Pearson Award

Awarded by the CIAU to a Canadian citizen who has participated in interuniversity athletics and pursued the ideals and purposes of interuniversity athletics and amateur sport.

1980   The Right Honourable Roland Michener

Austin-Matthews Award

The recipients are chosen for their outstanding contribution to the development of interuniversity sport in Canada.

1981   **Elizabeth Chard**

National Champions

Men's Basketball
1982 Dawson College, Quebec
Women's Basketball
1982 Vancouver Community College, British Columbia.
Men's Volleyball
1982 Sheridan College, Ontario
Women's Volleyball
1982 College Jonquiere, Quebec
Men's Hockey
1982   St. Hyacinthe, Quebec

Badminton

1982 Men's Singles
Serge Lebel, Canador College, Ontario.
1982 Women's Singles

Linda Loignon, College Ste. Foy, Quebec.
1982 Men's Doubles
Jean Bussieres and Jocelyn Pelletier, F.X.
Garneau, Quebec.
1982 Women's Doubles
Chantale Rioux and Joanne Boucher, F.X.
Garneau, Quebec.
1982 Mixed Doubles
Elizabeth Houde and Rejean Bedard, Ste.
Foy, Quebec.

VII PAN AMERICAN WHEELCHAIR GAMES, HALIFAX, N.S.

Canada finished 2nd behind the U.S.A.
1982 **Rick Hansen**, Vancouver, B.C., 5
     golds
     800 m race for Class 4 men, 2:12.6,
     beating the previous world record
     of 2:25.80
     Mel Fitzgerald, St. John's, Nfld., for a
     world record in the 800m Class 5 &
     6 men, winning time 2:12.9
     Dan Westley, Surrey, B.C., for 400 m
     final, won in record time

CANADIAN WHEELCHAIR SPORTS ASSOCIATION

Canadian Medalists at the 1982 Pan-Am Games

Archery

Male Paraplegic (Double Fita)
Brian Ward, 3
Female Paraplegic (Advanced Metric)
Joan Lewis, 2
Male Paraplegic (Short Metric)
Gaetan Bertrand, 1

Women's Basketball

Silver Medal Canadian Team
**Sarah Baker, Diane Earl, Elaine Ell, Lola
Graha, Darlene Jackman, Joanne McDonald,
Diane Pidskalny, Marg Prevost, Lucie Raiche,
Irene Wownuk-Wilson
Joanne Skillen**, coach

Men's Basketball

Silver Medal Canadian team
**Flo Aukera, John Boyko, Murray Brown,
Peter Collistro, Rick Hansen, Braden Hirsch,
John Lundie, Reg McClellar, Ron Minor,
Roy Sherman, John Stubbert**

Brent Patterson, coach
Doug Wright, coach

Field

Women's Discus (Class 1A)
Martha Gustafson, 1
Women's Discus (Class 1B)
Barb Kvale, 3
Women's Discus (Class 5 to 6)
Diane Pidskalny, 1
Women's Club (Class 1A)
Martha Gustafson, 2
Men's Club (Class 1A)
Jerry Terwin, 3
Men's Discus (Class 1A)
Jerry Terwin, 2
Men's Discus (Class 2)
Brian Halliday, 3
Men's Discus (Class 3)
Walter Dann, 3
Women's Javelin (Class 5)
Diane Pidskalny, 2
Men's Javelin (Class 2)
Clarence Bastarache, 2

Swimming

Women's 100 m Breaststroke (Class 5$
Donna Daisley-Harrison, 1
Men's 25 m Breaststroke (Class 1B)
Mark Burger, 2
Men's 100 m Breaststroke (Class 5)
Jeff Standfield, 1
Men's 100 m Breaststroke (Class 4)
Bob Coakley, 2
Men's 100 m Breaststroke (Class 6)
Gary Collins-Simpson, 1, North Vancouver,
B.C. World Record
Women's 100 m Backstroke (Class 5)
Donna Daisley-Harrison, 1
Men's 25 m Backstroke (Class 1B)
Mark Burger, 3
Men's 100 m Backstroke (Class 4)
Jeff Standfield, 3
Men's 100 m Backstroke (Class 6)
Gary Collins-Simpson, 1, World Record
Women's 25 m Butterfly (Class 2)
Josée Faucher, 1, Que. World Record
Women's 50 m Butterfly (Class 4)
Irene Wownuk-Wilson, 2
Women's 100 m Butterfly (Class 5)
Donna Daisley-Harrison, 1
Men's 25 m Butterfly (Class 1B)
Mark Burger, 1

Men's 100 m Butterfly (Class 6)
Gary Collins-Simpson, 1, World Record
Women's 25 m Freestyle (Class 1A)
Martha Gustafson, 1
Men's 25 m Freestyle (Class 1A)
Jerry Terwin, 2
Men's 25 m Freestyle (Class 1B)
Mark Burger, 1
Women's 50 m Freestyle (Class 2)
Josee Faucher, 1, World Record
Men's 50 m Freestyle (Class 3)
Ron Van Ellswick, 2
Women's 100 m Freestyle (Class 4)
Irene Wownuk-Wilson, 2
Women's 100 m Freestyle (Class 5)
Donna Daisley-Harrison, 1
Men's 100 m Freestyle (Class 1B)
Mark Burger, 2
Men's 100 m Freestyle (Class 6)
Gary Collins-Simpson, 1, World Record
Women's 200 m Freestyle (Class 2)
Josee Faucher, 1

1982 ARCTIC WINTER GAMES

The 1982 Arctic Winter Games were held in Fairbanks, Alaska, and involved nearly 1,000 athletes and coaches from Alaska, the Yukon and the Northwest Territories.

The games were initiated in 1970 to provide northern athletes with increased opportunities for training and competition.

The seventh biennial games included 15 sports categories from basketball to snowshoeing.

The final standings of the 1982 games were:

Alaska 61 gold, 47 silver, 41 bronze, Total 149
Yukon 38 gold, 49 silver, 32 bronze, Total 119
Northwest 19 gold, 21 silver, 41 bronze, Total 81

NORTHERN ATHLETES

Arctic sports, are perhaps the most unusual competitions in the Winter Games. They were developed over the years by Alaskan and Canadian Eskimos. Traditionally, the sports involved friend against friend, neighbour against neighbour, father against son in friendly competition. The events test stamina, strength and endurance — the same skills required for survival. Records of the events have only been kept for a quarter of a century, and some say that present-day achievements, although impressive, probably don't meet those of the athletes of long ago.

Northwest's Tim Angotingoak and Alaska's Lady Laraux set world records in the two-foot high kick (7-foot-9) and women's one-foot high kick (6-9), respectively. Arctic Winter Games records were bettered in four events during the three-day competition, which drew some of the largest crowds of the games.

Northwest's Allen Anavilok was the only double gold uluist in arctic sports as he captured the men's kneel jump and rope gymnastics competitions while setting games records in both events. Alaska's Ike Towarak set a games record while winning the men's one-foot high kick and Northwest's Tony Klegenberg set a games record while winning the one-hand reach.

Other gold uluists were Northwest's Jerry Cockney in the airplane event and Yukon's Jucelyn McIntyre in the women's kneel jump.

Women's One-Foot High Kick
1. **Laraux** (A), 6-9 (new world record)
2. **Pickett** (A), 6-8
3. **McIntyre** (Y), 6-6
Men's One-Foot High Kick
Towarak (A), 8-10 (new Arctic Winter Games record)
2. **Angotingora** (NWT), 8-8
3. **Klenverg** (NWT), 8-4
Airplane
1. **Cockney** (NWT), 131-7
2. **Helm** (Y), 104-11
3. **Anailok** (NWT) 100-0
Women's Kneel Jump

1. **McIntyre** (Y), 38 inches
2. **Laraux**, (A), 37 1/4
3. **Pickett** (A), 29 3/4
Men's Kneel Jump
1. **Anavilok** (NWT) 60 inches (New AWG record)
2. **Klengenberg** (NWT), 56 1/2
3. **Cockney** (NWT) 54 1/2
One-Hand Reach
1. **T. Klengenberg** (NWT), 5-4 1/2 (new AWG record)
2. **Adam** (NWT), 5-0
3. **Arey** (Y), 5-0
Rope Gymnastics
1. **Anavilok** (NWT), 22
2 **Reggie Joule** (A), 19
3. **Danny Hatogina** (NWT), 18
Two-Foot High Kick
1. **Angotingoak** (NWT), 7-9 (world record)
2. **Tony Klengenberg** (NWT), 7-4
3. **Charles Komeak**, NWT, 7-2

SPECIAL OLYMPICS — TRUE ACHIEVEMENT

In a world where too often the mentally handicapped are told that they can't achieve, the Special Olympics are helping prove otherwise. Physical training and athletic competition enhance physical, emotional and intellectual development and strengthen motivation, confidence and self-esteem for everyone, including the mentally handicapped.

There are now well over 17,000 mentally handicapped Canadians participating in sports and recreation programs, and each one of them is proving that he or she can achieve.

The Special Olympics were originally conceived by Dr. Frank Hayden, professor at McMaster University at Hamilton, Ont. The first games were in the U.S. in 1968 and were sponsored by the Joseph P. Kennedy Foundation. Harry (Red) Foster and the Canadian Association for the Mentally Retarded brought the Special Olympics to Canada in 1969. The program has spread throughout Canada and today there are games held at the local level and right up to international competitions.

The official sports of the Special Olympics are: bowling, one-metre diving, floor hockey, skating (speed and figure), swimming, track and field, soccer, wheelchair track events, alpine skiing and cross-country skiing. The games are held every four years and in 1981 there were more than 225 gold medalists.

Athletes who won four or more gold medals at the Special Olympics 1981:

Randy Akeson, 21, Ont., **Clarence Bates**, 19, Ont., **Jennifer Anderson**, 11, N.B., **Chris Aucin**, 13, B.C., **Jim Boughner**, 14, Ont., **Terri Clements**, 12, P.E.I., **Gerald De Gar**, 29, B.C., **Craig Gough**, Alta., **Jeff Henshaw**, 11, N.S., **Barbi Jollymore**, 18, N.S., **Carol Kelly**, 13, N.S., **Allande Leblanc**, 30, N.B., **Norman Linnell**, 16, Sask., **Tracy Miller**, 15, Ont., **Colleen Moorman**, 20, Ont., **Vangie Moulton**, 15, Ont., Theresa Roberts, 41, Ont., **Rolly Scott**, 15, Ont., **David Sephton**, 25, B.C.

GAMES FOR THE PHYSICALLY DISABLED

Canadian Federation of Sport Organization for the Disabled

The following results include the athletes of the Canadian Blind Sports Association, Canadian Wheelchair Sports Association and the Canadian Amputee Association.

1981 Gold Medalists
British Columbia
Amputee
Gary Simpson-Collins, 400m free, 100 m breast, 200 m I.M., 100 m fly, 100 m back
Karen Austrom, 50 m back
Blind
Crystal Wilson, 3000 m walk, lawn bowling
Mike Mansfield, long jump
Gordon Grenon, 100 m fly, 200 m free, 100 m free, 200 m i.m., 200 m breast, 400 m i.m.
Yvette Michell, 100 m breast, 200 m free, 100 m free, 200 m i.m.

Donna Lyn Marleau, 50 m free, 100 m fly, 100 m back, 200 m breast, 100 m breast
Lisa Bentz, 200 m back, 50 m back, 100 m free
Pierre Morten, wrestling
Pat York, 100 m breast, 1500 m run, 400 m run, 60 m relay
Wheelchair
Jeff Stanfield, 100 m back, 100 m free, 200 m i.m., 100 m breast, 25 m fly
Denis Day, slalom
Noor Jamal, table tennis, table tennis dbls, table tennis dbls.
Marg Prevost, table tennis, table tennis
Julien Wedge, murderball, 4 x 200 m relay
Tim Frick, murderball
Gordon Hogg, table tennis
Peter Brooks, 10,000 m run, 5,000 m run
Dan Westley, 1000 m run, 1,500 m run, 5,000 m run, 100 m run, 800 m run
Lenny Marriot, weightlifting l.w.
Peter Steel, shot put, javelin, discus
Diane Rakiecki, 100 m run, 200 m run
Gary A. Reid, murderball
Merle Smith, murderball, 100 m run
Glen Walter, 400 m run, 4 x 200 m relay, murderball
Bruce Teichman, 4 x 200 m relay, 400 m run, 100 m run, murderball, 200 m run
Jan Van Derest, murderball, 200 m run
Dan Neff, 100 m run, 4 x 200 m relay, 200 m run, murderball
Ken Bartel, murderball
Alberta
Amputee
Daniel Leonard, 100 m run, 50 m free, shot put, javelin, discus
Brenda Martel, shot put, volleyball, long jump, discus
Karen Gillis, volleyball
Dan Palamareck, shot put
Loretta Faris, table tennis
Crystal Leary, 50 m free
Daryl Johnson, shot put, discus
Nancy M. Anderson, long jump
Wheelchair
Bob Coakley, 100 m back, 50 m fly, 100 m fly, 200 m i.m., 100 m breast
Duncan Campbell, 4 x 100 m relay, table tennis, slalom
Dan Palamarek, 4 x 100 m relay, slalom
Mark Burger, 4 x 100 m relay, 25 m back, 25 m breast, 25 m free

Ron Payette, 1500 m run, 400 m run, 100 m run, discus
Terry Gehlert, 200 m run, 100 m run, 4 x 100 m relay
Blind
Jim Visser, 100 m back, 200 m breast
Andrea Rossi, 200 m back, 400 m free, 100 m fly, 100 m back, 200 m breast, 400 i.m.
Eva Sageri, 50 m free, 100 m breast, 200 m free, 100 m free
Scott Herron, 200 m back, 100 m back, 400 m i.m.
Jean Paquette, 400 m run, 60 m run, 200 m run, 800 m run
Saskatchewan
Amputee
Joe Harrison, 100 m run, javelin, volleyball, 200 m run, discus
Wheelchair
Barbara Ann Kuale, discus, slalom, 100 m run, 200 m run
Alan Jackson, archery (50m), 50 m back
Shawn Konowski, discus
Mervin Figley, table tennis
Braden Hirsch, shot put, javelin
Richard Schell, billiard (para), air pistol, air rifle
Manitoba
Amputee
Arnold Boldt, long jump, high jump, volleyball
Tim McIssac, 400 m free, 100 m fly, 50 m free, 100 m breast, 100 m free, 200 m i.m., 200 m free
Charles Pond, wrestling
John Knight, javelin, shot put
Wheelchair
Paul Lejeune, table tennis, javelin
Jerry Terwin, club throw, table tennis, discus, 25 m free, 25 m back
Diane Pidskalny, shot put, javelin, slalom, table tennis, discus, table tennis
Ontario
Amputee
Cheril Barrer, 100 m run, 400 m run, high jump
Jacki Mitchell, 400 m free, 100 m back, 100 m breast, 100 m free
Ed Doerbson, 100 m free
Denis LaPalme, 100 m back, 100 m breast, 100 m free, 200 m i.m.
Corky Lessard, 50 m back, 50 m free, 3 x 50 m i.m.
Marjorie Seagant, 50 m free, 50 m breast

Jeff Williams, 50 m free, 3 x 50 m i.m. 1,500 m run
Hans Noe, 100 m breast
Jeff Teisson, 100 m run, 50 m free, 50 m breast, 400 m run, 200 m run
Tom Callahan, 100 m run, 400 m run
Danny O'Connor, long jump, high jump
Ann Farrell, 100 m run, 400 m run, javelin, 800 m run
Leslie Kinstler, 100 m run, high jump
Magella Belanger, 100 m run, 400 m run, long jump, 200 m run
Giselle Marie Cole, 100 m run, 400 m run, 200 m run
Mark Ludbrook, 50 m free
Billy Patterson, shot put
Mike Johnson, shot put
Peter Palubicki, discus, heavyweight, shot put, javelin
Stephaine Balta, shot put, javelin, discus
Tom Collins, 200 m run
Blind
Greg Thompson, 4 x 100 m relay
Betty Merret, 100 m run, 400 m run, triple jump, high jump, 200 m run
Rick Broderick, lawn bowling, 50 m free, 1500 m run, 400 m run, 100 m run
Alan Farough, 400 m free, 200 m back, 4 x 100m relay wrestling, 400 m med relay
Kim Kilpatrick, 4 x 100 m relay
Sarah Thompson, 3,000 m walk, 100 m run
John Baxter, discus
Craig McFarlane, wrestling, 200 m run
Barbara Smith, discus, lawn bowling, shot put
Andre Mainville, 800 m run, 1500 m run, 100 m run, 400 m run
Rod Barkley, 800 m run
Gordon Hope, wrestling
Bruce Vandermolen, 400 m med. relay, 50 m free, 4 x 100 m. relay, wrestling, 100 m breast
Rebecca Redmile, 400 m i.m., 4 x 100m free rel.
Wendy Gipps, 400 m free, 400 m med rel., 4 x 100 m free rel., 200 m free
Brian Arthur, 4 x 100 m free rel., 200 m breast
Tami Boccaccio, 4 x 100 m free rel., 400 m med. rel.
Dave Smith, wrestling, 5000m run
Robert Fenton, 200 m breast, 200 m free, 400 m med. rel.
Ray Quesnel, shot put

Melanie Marsden, 3000 m run
Robert Peeling, high jump
Wheelchair
Angela Ieriti, 1500m, 400 m, 100 m, 4 x 100m rel., 800 m
Paul Clark, 1500m, 400 m, 100 m, 200 m, 800 m, 4 x 400 m. rel.
Ron Robillard, 4 x 400 m rel.
Doug Staniszewski, 500 m, 200 m
Les Sam, slalom
Chris Stoddart, 100 m run, 200 m run, 4 x 400 m rel.
Betty Higgens, javelin
Lola Graham, javelin, slalom
Joanne Francis, shot put, javelin, 200 m run, 100 m run, 4 x 400 m rel.
Brian Halliday, shot put, discus
Greg Way, javelin
I. Wilson-Wounuk, 100 m back, 200 m i.m., 100 m breast, 25 m fly, 100 m free
Brenda Eakins, 4 x 400 m rel.
Segrid Voth, 100 m back, 50 m fly, 100 m free, 200 m i.m., 100 m breast
Ted Inman, table tennis
Joseph Ross, table tennis, billiards (quad)
Carol Dobson, javelin
Cindy Trottier, discus, slalom, shot put, club throw
Don Bell, javelin
Dan Alton, 100 m back
Tom Hainey, 100 m fly, 100m back, 200m breast, 100m free
Tom Baratte, slalom
Yvonne Green, 25m fly, 100m, 50m breast, 50m free
Ron VanElswyk, 100m free, 50m free, 1500m
Heather William, 3000m, 4 x 400m rel.
Tim Haslam, 400m, 200m, 4 x 400m rel.
Quebec
Amputee
Josce lake, 100m back, 100m breast, 100m free
Denny Quennville, volleyball, 100m fly, 100m free
Christian Potvin, shot put, volleyball
Blind
Mario Caron, discus, triple jump, 4 x 200 m relay
Aurele Gregoire, discus, long jump, 1500m, 400m, javelin, shot put
Nicole Charron, discus, long jump, javelin, shot put
Danielle Lessard, javelin

Yvan Bourdeau, long jump, triple jump, 60 m, 4 x 200m rel.
Gilles Marois, javelin, pentathalon, 4 x 200 m rel.
Pierre Lambart, 4 x 200 m rel.
Wheelchair
Josee Faucher, 50 m back, 25 m fly, 50 m breast, 50 m free
Bruno Charlot, slalom
Andre Viger, 1,000 m, 1,500 m, 5,000 m, 400 m, 800 m
Gaetan Bertrand, archery
New Brunswick
Wheelchair
Fred Edney, discus, table tennis, shot put, table tennis
Lynn Allen Richard, table tennis, table tennis
Brian Mills, table tennis
Clarence Bastarache, table tennis, table tennis, 50 m breast, javelin
Lucie Raiche, discus, shot put, 1500 m, 400 m, 800 m
Jake Donahue, shot put
Nova Scotia
Wheelchair
Brian Ward, archery (90m)
Dan Walter, shot put
Prince Edward Island
Amputee
Allison McNally, volleyball
Keith W. Coffin, archery (90m), javelin, discus
Margie Savidant, 3 x 50 m i.m., volleyball
Pat Griffin, discus, volleyball, air pistol
Dale Murphy, volleyball
Blind
Philip Bower, lawn bowling, triple jump
Carol Schuman, long jump, 1500 m, 800 m
Thomas Kay, 800 m
Wheelchair
Susan Buchan, table tennis

BEATS ALL DESPITE HANDICAP

Madeline McNeil, 29, of Kingston, has had just 10 per cent vision since birth and in the last year has lost her sight completely. She also has a 251 average in five-pin bowling, curls and is a dart champion. In May 1982, playing in a darts tournament at Branch 9 of the Royal Canadian Legion in Kingston, she threw the needed double-one that gave her team the B-Section runner's-up championship. Her skill won her an interview on the U.S. television show *That's Incredible*.

THORBURN ON CUE

Cliff (the Grinder) Thorburn, of Canada, became the first player in world professional snooker championships to ever compile a maximum break of 147.

He was competing in the World Championships, at Sheffield, England, in April 1983. Thorburn had achieved 20 maximum scores through his career, but none had been achieved in tournament play.

Thorburn, 35, won the world individual snooker championship in 1980 and led Canada to the 1983 world team title.

MAJOR CANADIAN ACHIEVEMENTS IN MEN'S SNOOKER

1923 **Conrad Stanbury**, Winnipeg, Man. First professional in world to make run of over 100 (125).

1935 **Con Stanbury**, first Canadian to compete in world championship.

1944 **Vic Kireluk**, Oshawa, Ont., first Canadian to make 147 run in snooker.

1947 **Leo Levitt**, Montreal, Que. Second Canadian to make 147 run at snooker.

1950 **George Chenier**, Hull, Que. World record run of 144.

1963 **George Chenier**, First player to run 150 and out in world straight pool championships.

1978 **Bernie Mikkelsen**, Calgary, Alta. First Canadian to make 147 run in competition.

1980 **Cliff Thorburn**, Victoria, B.C. World champion. (First champion not from the British Isles.)

1980 **Cliff Thorburn** has 20 runs of 147 — the most by any player in world.

1980 **Canadian Team: Cliff Thorburn; Kirk Stevens**, Scarborough, Ont.; **Bill Werbeniuk**, Winnipeg, Man. Runner-up, world team championship.

1981   Cliff Thorburn and Natalie Stelmach, Sudbury, Ont., world mixed pairs champions.

1982   Jim Bear, Vancouver, B.C. runner-up in 1982 world amateur snooker championship. Calgary.

SNOOKER AND BILLIARDS

Men's Championships

Amateur Billiards
1981   Robert Chaperon, Sudbury, Ont.
Amateur Snooker
1982   Brian McConnell, Regina, Sask.
1983   Alain Robidoux, St. Jerome, Que.
Professional Snooker
1980   Cliff Thorburn, (not challenged since)
Open Snooker Championship
1983   Title Holder: Cliff Thornburn
North American Snooker Championship
1983   Title Holder: Bill Werbeniuk
World Team Championships (England)
1982   Champions Cliff Thorburn
        Kirk Stevens
        Bill Werbeniuk

Women's Championships

1982   Susan LeMaich, Hamilton, Ont.

Runs in Snooker by Women

1977   First century run by a woman: Natalie Stelmach, Sudbury, Ont., 109
1981   Sue LeMaich, Hamilton, 102, 109, 102, 108
1982   Sue LeMaich, Hamilton, 112
        Most century runs by a woman (world record). Highest run in competition in the world (85).

CANADIAN CHAMPIONSHIPS

Chess Federation of Canada

Men
1982   Kevin Spraggett
Women
1982   Nava Shternberg,, Toronto, Ont.
Junior
1982   Doug Bailey

CHESS MEDAL

Canada's only medal in world team chess competitions was a bronze won when a Canadian team finished third at the World Students' Team Championships in Puerto Rico in 1971.

CANADIAN PAIR, MIXED BRIDGE CHAMPIONS OF THE WORLD

Dianna Gordon and George Mittleman of Toronto defeated 450 couples from 60 countries at the Biarritz World Bridge Olympiad, in October 1982, at Biarritz, France. They are the only Canadians ever to win a world title. They have been playing bridge together since they met in an Ottawa tournament in 1970.

NATIONAL CHAMPIONSHIP RECORDS

Canadian Tenpin Federation, Inc.

Women 20 Game
1981   Wendy Zielonka, Hamilton, Ont.
Women 10 Game
1981   Lorna Pollock, Victoria, B.C.
Women Single Game
1981   Wendy Zielonka, Hamilton, Ont.

Record Canadian Scores

Individual Three-Game Series — Women
1982   Tina Chang, Victoria, B.C. - 735
Four-Woman Team Single Game
1981   Arcadettes, London, Ont. - 822: M. Hunter, L. Black, J. Galloway, R. Kibler

1981 FIQ American Zone Championships — Winnipeg, Canada

Women's Singles
Silver, Simone Hindmarsh, Canada, 1145
Women's 3-Player Team
Gold, Lorna Pollock, Canada, 1080
Simone Hindmarsh, Canada, 1156

Joanne Walker, Canada, 1126
Women's 5-Player Team
Bronze, Joanne Walker, Canada, 1100
Cathy Townsend, Canada, 1028
Lorna Pollock, Canada, 1050
Simone Hindmarsh, Canada, 991
Wendy Zielonka, Canada, 1023
Men's 2-Player Team
Gold, Bob Puttick, Canada, 1312, Don Wira, Canada, 1133
Men's 5-Player Team
Bronze, Steve Lee, Canada, 1160, Don Wira, Canada, 1217, Rick Hughes, Canada, 470, Ed Maurer, Canada, 552, Dan Russo, Canada, 1154, Bob Puttick, Canada, 1186
Men's Individual
Silver, Bob Puttick, Canada, 3077

TILLEMAN TOPS IN COLLEGE BASKETBALL

Karl Tilleman of the University of Calgary Dinosaurs won the Mike Moser Memorial Trophy as this country's most outstanding university basketball player in both 1982 and 1983. He and David Coulthard of York University are the only two-time winners.

The 22-year-old point guard, who stands 6-foot-2, scored an average of 34.9 points per game in the 1982/83 season. He shot 53 per cent from the floor and 83 per cent from the line and averaged just over five rebounds a game.

BOXING

World amateur champions Shawn O'Sullivan and Willie DeWit led Canada to a sweep of an international boxing card in Halifax in April 1983, each scoring technical knockouts. Middleweight O'Sullivan, of Toronto, was fighting the flu, but stopped Reggie Boya of Philadelphia in the second round of a fight in the 156-pound class. Heavyweight DeWit of Grande Prairie, Alberta, also won in the second round, over Leland Hardy of Philadelphia in the 201-pound class.

LIGHTWEIGHT BOXING CHAMP

Toronto's Nicky Furlano won a unanimous 12-round decision over Louis Loy to capture the North American Boxing Council's lightweight championship in 1983. Furlano came back to win after Loy knocked him to the canvas in the opening round for a standing eight count.

HANDBALL WINNERS

John Phillips of the Toronto Firefighters Club captured the Canadian national handball championship over Gerrard Caya of Montreal, 21-16, 21-5, in the 1982 tournament final at Saint John, N.B. Harold McLean, also of Toronto, defeated Lee Hardy, 21-18, 21-6, to take the Golden Masters title.

1982 CANADIAN WINDSURFING CHAMPIONSHIPS

Canadian Windsurfer Class Association

Men's Champion
Derek Wullf, Toronto, Ont.
Women's Champion
Karen Morch, Toronto, Ont.
There were 270 competitors in the 1982 Championships, held at Kingston, Ont.

Raines Koby, Toronto, the 1981 Canadian Men's Champion, competed in the 1982 Mistral World Championships in the Canary Islands and won the World Title.

CARLING O'KEEFE WORLD CHAMPIONSHIP BATHTUB RACE

Loyal Nanaimo Bathtub Society

The 16th annual Nanaimo to Vancouver Bathtub race was held in July, 1982.
1st: Brian Ranger, Nanaimo, B.C., 1:50.43

2nd: **Tim Denbigh**, Nanaimo, B.C., 1:54.14
3rd: **Steve Frankson**, Nanaimo, B.C., 1:54.24

The '82 season was the last for 6 h.p. engines. The Loyal Society has permitted 7.5 or 8 h.p. motors in the '83 engines.

CANOEING

Nancy Olmsted of North Bay, Ont., and **Hugh Fisher** of Burnaby, B.C., won individual events and Canada took four first-place medals at a 13-country canoeing competition in Vichy, France, in June 1982.

Olmsted finished first in the junior women's 500 metre K-1 event. Fisher took the men's 500-metre K-1.

Barb Olmsted, North Bay, Ont., **Sue Holloway**, Ottawa, Ont, **Alexandra Barre**, Quebec City and **Lucy Guay**, Montreal, won the senior women's 500-metre K-4.

Nancy Olmsted teamed with a French canoeist to win the K-2 500-metre race.

Other members of the team placed well with five second places and three third places.

THE CALDER CLELAND MEMORIAL TROPHY

Canadian Secondary School Rowing Association and the St. Catharines Rowing Club

The trophy is awarded annually to the winners of the High School Championship Eight Race, but nobody gets to take it home anymore. The trophy was presented to rowing in 1945 by the late William B. Cleland in memory of his youngest son who was killed while serving with the RCAF. Cleland is thought to have found the trophy in an antique shop while on a trip to England. It has a positive evaluation on today's market of in excess of $1,000,000.

The trophy is an Omar Khayyam wine jug with a legend on a silver plaque:

"This wine jug, a creation of the Goldsmiths and Silversmiths of England, was presented by the guild to the Princess Eugenie upon her accession to the Throne of France in 1853, as Empress of Napoleon III.

Oarsmen unaware of its value have left it teetering on the water's edge, standing unguarded in front of grandstands, decorating high school lobbies, and allowed it to be carried off across the country and into the U.S. by victorious high school rowers. Today, the trophy remains with its custodians, for safekeeping.

1982 Brentwood College, Vancouver Island, B.C.

LOSING CANADIAN CREW WINS SPECIAL MEDAL

The eight-oared crew of the Toronto Argonauts received a citation and medals at the 1912 Olympics in Sweden for losing a rowing event.

The Argonauts were beaten by inches after a tremendous duel with the English Leanders. After the race it was shown that the course laid out on the river at Stockholm had been measured on a band that gave the English crew a length or more of an advantage.

Asked if he wished to protest, the Canadian coach replied that "the Leanders had rowed well and had won, and such mishaps were not to be cried about by sportsmen." This view so impressed the King of Sweden that he had a special set of medals struck which were presented to the Argonaut eight.

BROTHERS HELP BEAT CAMBRIDGE

Toronto rowers **Mark and Mike Evans** were in the crew of the Oxford eight that defeated the Cambridge eight for the eighth consecutive year in April 1983, on the River Thames.

The Oxford crew finished the seven-kilometre race 4 1/4 lengths ahead of their annual rivals. After 129 annual contests there have been 60 Oxford wins, 68 Cambridge wins and one dead heat.

The Evans brothers, who are twins, rowed in the sixth and seventh seats.

BLUENOSE, UNDEFEATED CHAMPION OF THE NORTH ATLANTIC

Following the First World War, Eastern fishermen became contemptuous of the expensive yachts that were built only to race and could not sail in heavy winds. They wanted races between real sail carriers and real sailors. In 1920 the International Fishermen's Trophy Race came into being. Under the rules the vessels had to meet the general specifications of a fishing schooner and must have spent at least one fishing season on the banks.

The *Bluenose* was designed and built to meet the challenge by marine architect William Roue and shipbuilders Smith and Rhuland of Lunenburg, N.S. She was launched in 1921.

Her captain was Angus Walters who took her on her maiden voyage to fish the Grand Banks.

The *Bluenose* won the International Fisherman's Trophy in 1922, 1923, 1931 and 1938, meeting all challenges for the trophy.

The *Bluenose* visited the 1933 Chicago World's Fair and took part in the Silver Jubilee of George V in England, but when the Second World War broke out she was tied up until 1942, then sold to a West Indies trading company. Captain Walters tried in vain to raise money to keep her in Canada but she

went to the Caribbean to work as a freighter.

The *Bluenose* was wrecked off the coast of Haiti in 1946.

The representation of the famous ship on the obverse of the Canadian ten-cent coin was sculpted by Emanuel Hahn and has been on the coin since 1937. *Bluenose II*, a replica of the famous schooner, was built and launched at Lunenburg in 1963.

SURE SOLING

Hans Fogh, 44, a Toronto sail manufacturer, and John Kerr, 31, a Toronto publisher, won the 1982 European Open Soling Championship in Drago Denmark in April 1982. The third member of their crew was Dane Paul Jenson, who replaced regular team member Steve Calder for the European challenge.

Skipper Fogh and his crew sailed ahead of 64 other boats from 22 countries to win the coveted European trophy.

FIRST SOLO SAILING

Captain Joshua Slocum set out in April 1895 from Yarmouth, N.S., in his 36-foot sloop, the *Spray*. He was the first man to sail around the world alone. He sailed 46,000 miles and returned to Nova Scotia in July 1898.

CANADIAN WHITE WATER ASSOCIATION

1982 National Championships

Slalom
K-I Men
1. **Stan Woods**, British Columbia
K-I Women
1. **Claudia Kerckoff**, Ontario
K-I Junior
1. **Karl Strasser**, Ontario
C-I Men

The Bluenose, after five hours on the trecherous Atlantic Ocean, beat the U.S. to win the International Challenge Race, Oct. 29, 1923. (From the Prudential *Great Moments in Sport Collection*). Artist — Franklin Arbuckle

1. **Mark Heard**, British Columbia
C-2 Men
1. **Dale O'Brien** and **Darryl O'Brien**, Alberta
Wild Water
K-l Men
1. **Robin Lang**, New Brunswick
K-l Women
1. **Morna Fraser**, British Columbia
K-l Junior
1.**Martin Illing**, Ontario
C-l Men
1. **Don Cohen**, British Columbia
C-2 Men
1. **Dale O'Brien** and **Darryl O'Brien**, Alberta

1982 Pan American International

West River, Vermont, Slalom
C-2 Men
Chuck Lee and **Rick Lidstone**, Alberta, placed second.
West River, Vermont, Wild Water
K-l Men
Robin Lang, New Brunswick, placed second.
K-l Women
Morna Fraser, British Columbia, placed first.
Sheila Taylor, Alberta, placed third.
Minden, Ontario, slalom
C-2 MEN
Chuck Lee/Rick Lidstone, Alberta, lst
Minden, Ontario, Wild Water
K-l Men
Robin Lang, New Brunswick, lst
Al Crane, 3rd
K-l WOMEN
Morna Fraser , B.C., lst
Sheila Taylor, Alberta, 3rd
C-l MEN
Pat Vicars, 3rd
Overall Series Winners
Wild Water
K-l Women
Morna Fraser, British Columbia
Slalom
C-2 Men
Chuck Lee and **Rick Lidstone**, Alberta

THE ESSO CUP

Imperial Oil Limited and the Canadian Amateur Swimming Association

The Esso Cup was established in 1980 as part of Imperial Oil's support of Cana-

dian amateur swimming. The cup is awarded to an athlete for the most outstanding swim in an invitational meet. Swimmers compete against other world times.
1982
Victor Davis, Waterloo, Ont., 100m breaststroke

ICE CANOE RACE

Carnaval De Quebec

The race is a tradition of the Quebec Carnival and is held during carnival week in early February each year. Each team has five oarsmen who struggle through ice and over ice and row on open water as they vie against each other for the trophy and the $1,200 first-place prize money.

The teams start the race at the entrance to Louise Basin, across the river, and proceed in a north-south direction toward the quay at Levis, touch the quay and then go to Queen's wharf at Quebec and from there return to the entrance of the Louise Basin, Port of Quebec.
CLASS "A" (professional)
1 **Andre Gaze**, Montmagny, Que., 40:30
2 **Guy Gilbert**, St. Foy, Que.
3 **Albert Lebel**, Montmagny, Que.
Class "B" (amateur)
1 **Paul Begin**, Lauzon, Que., 56:37
2 **Richard Begin**, Lauzon, Que.
3 **Michel Roy**, Quebec, Que.

SKATING TO A BRONZE

Barbara Underhill of Oshawa, Ont., and **Paul Martini** of Woodbridge, Ont., skated a near perfect short program at the world figure-skating championships in Helsinki in March 1983 to take third place in the pairs event behind East Germany and the Soviet Union. Their marks ranged from 5.3 to 5.7 for technical merit and from 5.4 to 5.9 for artistic impression. Then the pair went on to skate another dazzling performance in their free-skating program. They were given 5.6s 5.7s and 5.8s for technical merit and three 5.9s, four 5.7s and two 5.8s for artistic impression. Their medal was the first bronze won by a Canadian pair since Debbi Wilkes and Guy Revell finished third in West Germany in 1964.

INTERNATIONAL ICE HOCKEY FEDERATION WORLD JUNIOR HOCKEY CHAMPIONSHIP

Canada's National Junior Hockey Team won the IIHF World Junior Cup Trophy for the first time ever in 1982.

PEE WEE HOCKEY SHORTS

1982 Esso Challenge Cup (Annual International Pee Wee Hockey Tournament)

1982 **Toronto Marlboroughs**
The Air Canada Cup for supremacy in midget hockey in Canada in 1983 was won by the **Regina Pat Canadians**.
The **North York Rangers** won the Centennial Cup for the best of Junior "A" play in Canada in 1982/83.

The Allan Cup was won by the **Cambridge Hornets** in the 1982/83 season. The Allan Cup represents the best in Senior Amateur hockey in Canada.

Ontario defeated Alberta to win the 1982/83 Women's National Hockey Championships.

CANADIAN AMATEUR HOCKEY ASSOCIATION

1981/82 Champions

Western Canada Purolator Cup (Bantam)
Yorkton Terriers
Loblaw Cup (All-Ontario Bantam)
Toronto Young Nats
Atlantic Canada Purolator Cup (Bantam)
Fredericton Caps
Air Canada Cup (Midget)
Burnaby Winter Club
Colonel Sanders Cup (Juvenile)
North Shore Winter Club
Centennial Cup (Junior "A")
Prince Albert Raiders
Memorial Cup (Major Junior)
Kitchener Rangers
Hardy Cup (Intermediate)
Georgetown Raiders
Allan Cup (Senior)
Cranbrook Royals

CANADA'S OLYMPIC HOCKEY TEAM SUMMARY

YEAR	CANADA'S STANDING	GOLD MEDALISTS	SITE
1980	6th	United States	Lake Placid, N.Y.
1976	Did not compete	Soviet Union	Innsbruck, Austria
1972	Did not compete	Soviet Union	Sapporo, Japan
1968	3rd	Soviet Union	Grenoble, France
1964	4th	Soviet Union	Innsbruck, Austria
1960	2nd	United States	Squaw Valley, Colorado
1956	3rd	Soviet Union	Cortina-D'Ampezzo, Italy
1952	1st	Edmonton Mercurys	Oslo, Norway
1948	1st	RCAF Flyers	St. Moritz, Switzerland
1936	2nd	Great Britain	Garmisch-Partenkirchen, Germany
1932	1st	The Winnipegs	Lake Placid, N.Y.
1928	1st	U. of T. Grads	St. Moritz, Switzerland
1924	1st	Toronto Granites	Chamonix, France

WORLD HOCKEY CHAMPIONSHIPS

Canada has won 19 World Hockey Championships, including five gold medals in Olympic competition (1924, 1928, 1932, 1948 and 1952). The first world championship was won by the Winnipeg Falcons in 1920. Other winning years for Canada were 1930, 1931,

1934, 1935, 1937, 1938, 1939, 1950, 1951, 1958, 1959 and 1961.

1983 **U.S.S.R.**, gold
      Czechoslovakia, silver
      Canada, bronze

CANADA CUP

The Canada Cup was first contested in 1976 and brought together the Soviet Union, Czechoslovakia, Sweden, Finland, the United States and Canada. Team Canada finished in first place after round robin play, with four wins and one loss (to Czechoslovakia), then beat the second-place Czechs in a best-of-three final two games straight.

The same six countries played in the 1981 Canada Cup and once again Team Canada finished first after the round robin, with four wins and one tie. But after winning its semi final over the United States (4-1), Canada lost to the Soviets (8-1) in the final in Montreal.

RINGETTE CANADA

NATIONAL RINGETTE CHAMPIONSHIPS

1983 Juniors (14 and under)
      Waterloo, Ont.
      Belles (17 and under)
      Winnipeg, Man.
      Debs (18 and over)
      Winnipeg, Man.
1982 Juniors (14 and under)
      Sudbury, Ont.
      Belles (17 and under)
      Gloucester, Ont.
      Debs (18 and over)
      Winnipeg, Man.

DAIGLE WINS FIVE

Sylvie Daigle of Sherbrooke, Que., set a world best in Kobe, Japan, for the women's 3,000 metres at the international short-track speed skating competition for the Daiei Cup. Daigle, 19, also became the first skater to win all five individual titles in the world short track championships.

BASE CLINCHES BONSPIEL

John Base skipped his Canadian crew to a 7-2 victory in eight ends over Norway to clinch the 1983 World Junior Curling Championships. The bonspiel was held at Medicine Hat, Alta. It was Canada's first junior championship since 1978.

1982 CANADIAN AND WORLD CURLING CHAMPIONS

Canadian Curling Association

World Curling Championships
Air Canada Silver Broom
Al Hackner, Canada
World Junior Championships, Uniroyal World
Soren Grahw, Sweden
Ladies World Curling
Marianne Jorgensen , Denmark
Canadian Championship, Labatt Brier
Al Hackner, North Ontario
Canadian Ladies Championships
Colleen Jones, Nova Scotia
Canadian Mixed Championships
Glen Pierce, Ontario
Canadian Jr. Men's
John Base, Ont.
Canadian Jr. Women's
Sandra Plut, British Columbia
Canadian Sr. Men's
Lloyd Gunnlaugson, Manitoba
Canadian Sr. Ladies'
Verda Kempton, Nova Scotia

CURLING SHORTS

Manitoba held the Canadian senior men's curling championship in 1983 at the championship event in Sarnia, Ont. It finished with a 9-2 record.

Ontario's rink under skip **Alison Goring** won the Canadian 1983 junior women's curling championships in Calgary.

The 1983 world curling championships were won by **Canada** in Regina in April 1983. **Ed Werenich** and his rink from Toronto Avonlea, who won the

Canadian curling championship in March, defeated West Germany 7-4 to win the Air Canada Silver Broom.

CHAMPION QUACKS

The Dominion calling championships were held in September 1982 at the Ontario Hunting Show in Toronto. Ten-year-old **Jason King** of Ajax, Ont., won the Canadian junior goose-calling championship.

Ray Baldakin of Toronto, Ont., won the Molson Canadian goose-calling championship.

Earl Newhall of Orillia, Ont., won the duck-calling competition for the third time.

Owen Scott of Kettleby, Ont., was named the nation's champion moose caller.

CANADIAN CASTING FEDERATION

Canadian Championships

Events - Accuracy
Men's 1/4 -oz. Plug
1982 **Ross MacSporran**
Women's 1/4-oz. Plug
1982 **Brenda MacSporran**
Men's 3/8-oz. Plug
1982 **Charlie Phillips**
Women's 3/8-oz. Plug
1982 **Brenda MacSporran**
Men's 5/8-oz. Plug
1982 **Jim Roszell**
Women's 5/8-oz. Plug
1982 **Brenda MacSporran**
Men's Dry Fly
1982 **Charlie Phillips**
Women's Dry Fly
1982 **Brenda MacSporran**
Men's Trout Fly
1982 **Charlie Phillips**
Women's Trout Fly
1982 **Brenda MacSporran**
Men's Bass Bug
1982 **Pete Edwards**
Women's Bass Bug
1982 **Brenda MacSporran**

Events - Distance
7.5 gm. Distance
1982 **Jim Roszell**
Two-Hand Spinning Distance
1982 **Norm Wallachy**
One-Hand 5/8-oz. Distance
1982 **Gord Deval**
Two-Hand Fly Distance
1982 **Jim Roszell**
One-Hand Fly Distance
1982 **Jim Roszell**
Angler's Fly Distance
1982 **Norm Wallachy**

1982 World Championships

Karlova Vary, Czechoslovakia
Women's Accuracy Skish
Gold **Brenda MacSporran**
The 1981 games were held in California.
Canada won 9 gold medals.

NATIONAL RALLY CHAMPIONSHIP OF CANADA

Final Standings

Pos.	Driver/Hometown	Car	Points
1.	Randy Black/Mississauga, Ont.	Datsun	169
2.	Taisto Heinonen/Surrey, B.C.	Toyota	140
3.	Bjorn Anderson/London, Ont.	Toyota	110

Production Class

Pos.	Driver/Hometown	Car	Points
1.	Niall Leslie/Mississauga, Ont.	Datsun (B)	82
2.	Bo Skowronnek/Saskatoon, Sask.	Volvo (B)	69
3.	Walter Boyce/Munster, Ont.	Lada (A)	60

CRC CHEMICALS TRANS-AM

Final Standings

Pos.	Driver/Hometown	Car	Points
1.	Eppie Wietzes/Willowdale, Ont.	Corvette	179
2.	Bob Tullius/Herndon, Va.	Jaguar XJS	126
3.	Phil Currin/Gainesville, Ga.	Corvette	91

CAN-AM CHALLENGE

Under-two-litre

Pos.	Driver/Hometown	Car	Points
1.	Jim Trueman/Amlin, Ohio	Ralt RT-2	740
2.	Richard Guider/Ben Lomond, Calif.	Cicale Ralt	600
3.	John Graham/Willowdale, Ont.	Chevron	270

NORTH AMERICAN FORMULA ATLANTIC CHAMPIONSHIP

Final Standings

Pos.	Driver/Hometwon	Car	Points
1.	Jacques Villeneuve/St. Cuthbert, Que.	March 81A	166
2.	Rogelio Rodriguez/Mexico City, Mexico	Ralt RT-4	130
3.	Whitney Ganz/Laguna Niguel, Calif.	Ralt RT-4	124

MOLYSLIP ENDURANCE SERIES

Final Standings

Pos.	Class	Driver/Hometown	Car	Points
1.	A	Jacques Bienvenue/St. Jean Baptiste, Que.	Porsche 911SC	95
	A	Marc Dancose/St. Laurent, Que.	Porsche 911SC	95
3.	A	Jean-Michel Centeno/Toronto, Ont.	Porsche RSR	72

NATIONAL AUTO SLALOM CHAMPIONSHIPS

Provisional Overall Results

Pos.	Class	Driver/Hometown	Car	Margin
1.	DI	Vern Lhotzky/ Vancouver, B.C.	MGB	−5.295
2.	EI	George Sheppard/ Halifax, N.S.	Datsun 510	−3.420
3.	CI	Stu Rulka/Burnaby, B.C.	Morgan 4/4	−3.210

Women's

Pos.	Class	Driver/Hometown	Car	Margin
1.	CS	Debbie Parker/ Bedford, N.S.	Honda Prelude	−0.264
2.	AS	Wanda Angelomatis/Vancouver, B.C.	Lotus Europa S2	−0.003
3.	AP	Brenda Smetaniuk/ Mississauga, Ont.	Cooper S	+0.487

CANADIAN ROAD RACE OF CHAMPIONS

Final Standings

Formula Vee

Pos.	Driver/Hometown	Car	Laps
1.	Andy Chong/Thornhill, Ont.	Olympus	20
2.	Andy Wietzes/Thornhill, Ont.	Lynx	17
3.	Tom Allen/Lethbridge, Alta.	Zink C-5	15

C Sports Racing

Pos.	Driver/Hometown	Car	Laps
1.	Jim Cooke/Lighthouse Cove, Ont.	Lola T492	25
2.	Barrie Bratt/Regina, Sask.	Johnston JM2	24
3.	Alan Downing/Saskatoon, Sask.	Lotus 23	24

Honda/BF Goodrich

Pos.	Driver/Hometown	Car	Laps
1.	Stuart Poppe/Scarborough, Ont.	Honda Civic	20
2.	Ron Lauzon/Timmins, Ont.	Honda Civic	20
3.	John DeMaria/Woodbridge, Ont.	Honda Civic	20

GT-3

Pos.	Driver/Hometown	Car	Laps
1.	Lew Mackenzie/Mississauga, Ont.	MG Midget	25
2.	Rick Horton/Calgary, Alta.	Datsun B210	25
3.	Peter Holm/Winnipeg, Man.	Fiat X 1/9	25

GT-2

Pos.	Driver/Hometown	Car	Laps
1.	Tom Jones/Thunder Bay, Ont.	VW Scirocco	25
2.	Ken Staples/Edmonton, Alta	Alfa Romeo	25
3.	Jim King/Winnipeg, Man.	VW Rabbit	25

GT-1

Pos.	Driver/Hometown	Car	Laps
1.	Tom Jones/Thunder Bay, Ont.	Mustang	25
2.	Rod harris/Fargo, N.D.	Camaro	25
3.	Pierre Guyon/Calgary, Alta.	Corvette	24

Paul Henderson's goal with seconds to go in the final game of the first Canada-Russia series left an indelible image on the minds of Canadians. (From the Prudential *Great Moments in Sport Collection*). Artist —

Formula Ford

Pos.	Driver/Hometown	Car	Laps
1.	Scott Goodyear/Willowdale, Ont.	STP Special	25
2.	Michael Clifford/N. Vancouver, B.C.	Van Diemen RF81	25
3.	Gord Cullen/Thornhill, Ont.	Crossle	25

CANADIAN BOATING FEDERATION

1982 Trophies

Cruising
Esso Novice Cup
P. Tomlinson, *Playmate*, Toronto Humber Yacht Club
Junior Esso Trophy
R. Gilpin, *Endless Love*, Toronto Humber Yacht Club
Esso Trophy
J. Mumford, *McQuarrie*, National Yacht Club
R. Gilpin, *Endless Love*, Toronto Humber Yacht Club
G. Gibson, *Lodesman*, National Yacht Club
Schenley Contest,
Predicted Log
J. Mumford, *McQuarrie* National Yacht Club
N. White, *Fore Sure*, Mimico Cruising Club
R. Gilpin, *Endless Love*, Toronto Humber Yacht Club
Cruising Division High Point
McQuarrie, John Mumford, National Yacht Club
Perpetual Trophies
Formula Outboard, Frank Dashwood Trophy
Ted Abel
Stock Outboard, George Ian Barrie Memorial
G. Lafrance (7472)
Wallace Wood Trophy
Ted Abel (4168)
McKay - Wood Trophy (Rookie of the Year)
George Boulter
H.J. McFarland Trophy
Peter McIlmoyle
Racing Inboard
Canadian Schenley Gold Helmet Award
H. Richardson
Gulf Oil Canada Ltd.
R. Gauvin
Miss Supertest Trophy
A. Kachmarik
Gimbrone Award (International)
R. Theoret/Guy Lafleur
Laberge/Beauchemin (National)
R. Theoret/Guy Lafleur
Ronald G. Robinson
Donated by Mrs. Tannis Moriarty (Robinson)
Olga and Doug Overbury
Speed Records
5 Mile Competition, Valleyfield, Que.

SPEED RECORDS
5 MILE COMPETITION, VALLEYFIELD, QUE.

CLASS	OWNER	DRIVER	BOAT NAME	SPEED
S L	**Fraser Baikie**	SAME	*Coca Cola*	82.229
MOD 50	**Tom Henderson**	SAME	*Mile Maker*	72.493
360	**Marvin R. Morton**	Pat O'Connor	*Hot Ticket*	102.857
F L	**Ted Gryguc**	SAME		66.667

WEBSTER MEMORIAL TROPHY

Royal Canadian Flying Club

In honour of the late **John Webster**, the trophy is for the best amateur pilot in Canada. The Royal Canadian Flying Club selects the winner, who receives $200 and a free pass anywhere Air Canada flies.

1982   Brian Shury, Regina, Sask.

A.D. McLEAN AWARD

For outstanding contributions to Flying Clubs in Canada.

1982   Cortlandt B. Macdonell, Calgary, Alta.

GOVERNOR-GENERAL'S SHIELD

Awarded to the top private pilot graduate from among all RCFCA member clubs. The winner receives $500 for advanced flying training.

1982   James Moshonsky, Thunder Bay, Ont.

DENNIS K. YORATH TROPHY

To the manager of an RCFCA club who makes the most productive use of his or her club.

Donald McClure, the winner in both 1981 and 1982, has won this award 16 times.

TRIBUTE TO THE TEAM THAT PUT CANADA ON THE TOP OF THE WORLD

The Sports Federation of Canada honoured the first Canadian team to conquer Mount Everest.

Canadian Team Members 1982:
Laurie Skreslet, Calgary, Alta.
Bill March, Calgary, Alta.
Lloyd Gallagher, Canmore, Alta.
John Amatt, Canmore, Alta.
Dwayne Congdon, Invermere, BC.
Dave Read, Calgary, Alta.
Peter Spear, Calgary, Alta.
Alan Burgess, Katmandu, Nepal
Steven Bezruchka, Seattle, Wash.
Pat Morrow, Kimberley, B.C.
Gordon Smith, Golden, B.C.

CANADIAN ORIENTEERING CHAMPIONSHIPS

Canadian Orienteering Federation

Bill Anderson, Ontario
Mike Green, Ontario
Ted De St. Croix, Ontario
1982 North American Championships
Justin Howell, Ontario, Kirsten Forsyth, Manitoba, Bren and Nancy Baldock, Ontario, Linda Heron, New Brunswick, Marie Skwarek, Manitoba, Miles Hicklin, Ontario, Pat De St. Croix, Ontario, Mike Waddington, Ontario, Alison Sokol, Ontario, P. Howell, Ontario, Gillian Bailey, Ontario, Dick De St. Croix, Ontario, Pam James, Nova Scotia, John Crowley, British Columbia, Marion Loewen, Quebec, Alan Stanley, Ontario, Raelene Robertson, Alberta, Gord Hunter, Ontario, Magali Robert, Ontario, Francis Falardeau, Ontario, Sue Jaenen, Ont., Nancy Lee, Ont.

SPORTS SHORTS

Basketball was invented by the Canadian-born James A. Naismith in 1891, while teaching physical education in Springfield, Mass. He set out to combine various features of soccer, football and field hockey, but his choice of nine men per side was entirely arbitrary, since his class that year happened to number 18.

The world's fastest snowshoer is the French-Canadian Richard Lemay. In 1973, at a competition in New Hampshire, he registered an all-time record for the mile of 6 minutes, 23.8 seconds. At that amazing rate, he could cover the distance from Winnipeg to Montreal in eight days flat.

The world's first stampede was held in Raymond, in 1902. The term was coined by Raymond Knight, after whom the town was named.

The French-Canadian strongman Louis Cyr may well have been the mightiest human being of all time. Richard Fox, an American promotor, offered $5,000 to anyone who could match his extraordinary strength, but Cyr remained unbeaten. Challenged by the Marquis of Queensberry to pit himself against two horses tied to either arm, he held them to a standstill, and claimed one as his prize. Cyr could sustain a 550-pound weight on one finger, and, in 1895, lifted the greatest mass ever raised in single competition — a platform containing 18 men with a combined weight of 4,337 pounds.

MAN OF THE YEAR

1982 Jockey Club Sovereign Awards

The distinctive green and white silks of **Jean Louis Levesque** have played a major role in Canadian racing over the past 15 years.

In five of those years, horses racing in Levesque's silks, with the green maple leaf front and back, have been named Canada's horse of the year. The great racemare, Fanfreluche was the first Levesque colourbearer to be voted best of the year, in 1970. Two years later, in 1972, it was La Prevoyante, an outstanding filly who also gave Levesque his first Eclipse Award for she was also voted the champion two-year-old filly in all North America. Then came his L'Enjoleur, voted Canada's best in both 1974 and 1975, who gave Levesque his first trip to the winner's circle to receive the historic Queen's Plate trophy. In 1977, Canada's horse of the year was L'Alezane, another great runner owned by Jean Louis Levesque. Bred by E.P. Taylor, L'Alezane was purchased by Levesque for $101,000 at the Saratoga Sales and went on to win eight of her 11 starts at stakes races in both Canada and the United States.

HORSE OF THE YEAR

1982 Jockey Club Sovereign Awards Champion Older Horse or Gelding & Champion Grass Horse

Frost King, the gelded son of Ruritania, has won 23 of his 43 lifetime starts. His 1982 season began with five consecutive wins, all in stakes races. Bred by Ted Smith of Toronto, Ont., Frost King is trained by Bill Marko and owned by both Smith and Marko. With career earnings of $949,132, he is the second leading money-winning Canadian-bred of all time behind Glorious Song ($1,004,534).

1982 Racing Record

Starts	1st	2nd	3rd	Earnings
17	12	1	1	$427,303

Champion Two-Year-Old Colt or Gelding

When **Sunny's Halo** won Canada's most important juvenile test, the $162,790 Coronation Futurity at Woodbine, by seven-and-a-half lengths, he was recording his third consecutive win in a stakes race during the fall of 1982. The Halo colt out of Mostly Sunny by Sunny, had previously had little trouble winning

both the Swynford Stakes and the open Grey Stakes, now rated an International Grade III event. Of Sunny's Halo's 11 starts as a two-year-old, four were in important U.S. stakes. He won the 1983 Kentucky Derby.

1982 Racing Record

Starts	1st	2nd	3rd	Earnings
11	5	2	1	$232,805

Champion Two-Year-Old Filly

By Irish Stronghold out of the Northern Dancer mare Nightlight, **Candle Bright** won four of her six starts as a two-year-old including three stakes races — Shady Well, Nandi and Ontario Debutante, the latter a Canadian Grade III event.

Candle Bright was bred by the Kinghaven Farms of D.G. Willmot.

1982 Racing Record

Starts	1st	2nd	3rd	Earnings
6	4	-	-	$140,490

Champion Three-year-old Filly & Champion Sprinter

Rick Kennedy's filly **Avowal**, bred by the late Roy Kennedy, won six of her nine starts in 1982 and finished out of the money only twice. After two complete seasons, the daughter of L'Enjoleur out of Well in Hand, a daughter of the great Bold Ruler, Avowal has an enviable record of winning nine of her 17 lifetime starts for earnings of $359,355.

1982 Racing Record

Starts	1st	2nd	3rd	Earnings
9	6	-	1	$297,547

Champion Three-Year-Old Colt or Gelding

From the first crop of the French-bred Blushing Groom, **Runaway Groom** was consigned to the Kentucky yearling sales by breeder George Gardiner of Toronto. Albert Coppola of Mclean, Va., bought the colt for $39,000.

With only four starts to his credit and never having raced further than seven furlongs, Runaway Groom was entered in the mile-and-a-quarter Queen's Plate, where he finished second to Son of Briartic. He went on to win the next two jewels in Canada's Triple Crown, the Prince of Wales at Fort Erie and the Breeders' Stakes at Woodbine, both at a mile and a half of turf.

His most impressive race of the year, came in the Travers Stakes at Saratoga (Int. Grade 1) in which Runaway Groom closed strongly to defeat the winners of the Kentucky Derby, Preakness and Belmont Stakes - Gato Del Sol, Aloma's Ruler and Conquistador Cielo.

1982 Racing Record

Starts	1st	2nd	3rd	Earnings
12	6	4	-	$268,312

Champion Older Mare

Eternal Search continued her winning ways in 1982, taking seven races, six of them stakes. Eternal Search is by Northern Answer out of the Ruritania mare, Bon Debarras.

1982 Racing Record

Starts	1st	2nd	3rd	Earnings
13	7	1	-	$246,838

OUTSTANDING JOCKEY

Jockey Club Sovereign Awards

The regular rider for horse of the year Frost King, **Lloyd Duffy** has proven he can win the big races with all the pressure and problems of being on the favorite, carrying top weight, and negotiating through large fields of horses. Duffy was voted his Sovereign Award by his fellow riders in the Jockey's Benefit Association of Canada.

OUTSTANDING APPRENTICE JOCKEY

Jockey Club Sovereign Awards

Richard Dos Ramos, a Sovereign Award winner in 1981 as Canada's outstanding apprentice jockey, has been voted the award again for 1982 by his fellow jockeys in the Jockey's Benefit Association of Canada.

The consecutive award became possible when a serious leg injury and a winter off prompted officials to extend Dos Ramos' apprentice period well into the 1982 season. The 19-year-old native of Trinidad continued to show outstanding riding ability.

JOE PERLOVE TROPHY

Jockey Club Sovereign Awards

The Joe Perlove Trophy is presented annually to the leading race-winning jockey in Canada. Designed by renowned artist Duncan Macpherson, the trophy honours the pupular *Toronto Star* sportswriter who died in 1965.

Don Seymour rode 194 horses to victory in Canada last year, the highest number of winners of any jockey in the country. The Ontario-born rider rode most of his winners in Alberta.

TRAINER OF THE YEAR

Jockey Club Sovereign Awards

Horses trained by **Bill Marko** won more purse money in 1981 and 1982 than those saddled by any other trainer in Canada. In 1982, Marko-trained horses won $825,000 in purses. The leader was Frost King, who accounted for about half the total with seven stakes victories. In addition Marko's Fraud Squad won the New Providence Stakes and four of his two-year-olds were stakes placed.

Marko's best two-year-old of 1982 was Rising Young Star, second to champion Sunny's Halo in the important Coronation Futurity (Can. Grade 1).

Marko was voted his Sovereign Award as outstanding trainer of 1982 by the Horsemen's Benevolent and Protective Association.

OUTSTANDING OWNER OF THE YEAR & OUTSTANDING BREEDER OF THE YEAR

Jockey Club Sovereign Awards

For the first time since the inception of the Sovereign Awards program, **D.G.**

Winner	Class	Owner
Armbro Bala,	Two-year-old Pacing filly,	Armstrong Brothers
Ralph Hanover,	Two-year-old pacing colt,	Pointsetta Stable
Addore,	Three-year-old pacing filly,	Mel Barr Stable
Cam Fella,	Three-year-old pacing colt,	N. Clements, N. Faulkner
Fan Hanover,	Aged pacing mare,	Dr. J. Glen Brown
Willow Wiper,	Aged pacing horse,	Bob Hamather
Armbro Blush,	Two-year-old trotting filly,	Armstrong Brothers
Turmeric,	Two-year-old trotting colt,	Ron MacLellan
Turkish Harem,	Three-year-old trotting filly,	Gratien Deschenes
Armbro Acadian,	Three-year-old trotting colt,	Don Armstrong
Delmegan,	Aged trotting mare,	Armstrong Brothers
Sokeys J J,	Aged trotting horse,	David Dubuc
Cam Fella,	Horse-of-the-year,	N. Clements, N. Faulkner

Driver of the Year

Pat Crowe was voted driver of the year for his skill with the horse of the year, Cam Fella.

Non-Driver Achievement Award

Cliff Chapman Jr. received the non-driver achievement for his versatile contributions to the standardbred sport.

JOHN J. MOONEY AWARD

Racetracks of Canada Inc.

Presented annually for outstanding contributions to Canadian horse racing.
1982 **Honourable Eugene Whelan,**Canada's Minister of Agriculture. Whelan's "new initiatives package" gave to rac-

(Bud) Willmot has been named both outstanding owner of the year and outstanding breeder of the year. Willmot's Kinghaven Farms was the leading money-winning stable on the Ontario circuit with earnings of $729,738. His stable has won the Queen's Plate with Steady Growth, the Canadian Derby with Wing Span and the Quebec Derby with Green Belt.

1982 CANADIAN TROTTING ASSOCIATION

Divisional Awards

ing both Intertrack Wagering and Telephone Account Betting as well as restructuring of the commission rates.

ROYAL HORSE SHOW CHAMPIONS 1982

Hunter Pony, 13 hands and under - **FindelinNarcissus** owned by Miss Sophie McCall, Montreal, Quebec.
Hunter pony, over 13 hands - **Nikita Korsay** owned by Buckhaven Farm, Keswick, Ont.
Junior Hunter - **Brass Note** owned by Kristi Knowles, St. Catharines, Ontario
Junior Jumper - **Jackie Blue** owned by Harold Chopping, Newmarket, Ontario
Hackney Horse - **Hurstwood Toreador** owned by James Harvey, Kingston, Ontario
Hackney Pony - **Rag-A-Muffin** owned by A.B.C. Farms, Brampton, Ontario

Roadster - **Page Boy** owned by Mr. and Mrs. John L. Sheridan, Sterling, Ontario
Conformation Hunter - **Gabriel** owned by Mr. John Lenehan, Buffalo, New York
Amateur Owner Hunter - **The Madd Hatter** owned by Miss Stephanie Stephens, Burlington, Ontario
Regular Working Hunter - **Bold Comment** owned by Dr. Daphne Bell, Kettleby, Ontario
Open Jumper - **Echo de Cavron** owned by Jan Vanden Berg, Brewster, New York
International Classes
International Welcome Competition - **Michel Robert** of France riding *Gazelle D'Elle*
Rothmans International Competition - **Walter Gabathuler** of Switzerland riding *Beethoven II*
Rothmans Scurry Competition - **Norman Dello Joio** of the United States riding *Johnny's Pocket*
Johnston & Daniel Competition - **Frederic Cottier** of France riding *Flambeau C*
Prix des Nations - International Carlsberg Cup - Swiss Equestrian Team consisting of **Markus Fuchs** riding *Insolvent;* **Phillipe Guerdat** riding *Liberty;* **Walter Gabathuler** riding *Bethoven II;* and **Thomas Fuchs** riding *Willora Carpets.*
Mercedes-Benz Challenge Relay- A team consisting of **Walter Gabathuler** of Switzerland riding *Silver Bird III* and **Phillipe Guerdat** of Switzerland riding *Liberty.*
The George Weston Limited Jumping Competition - **Michael Grinyer** riding *Prowler.*
Schickedanz Brothers Power and Speed - **Walter Gabathuler** of Switzerland riding *Silver Bird III.*
Burka International Fault and Out Competition - **Patrick Caron** of France riding *Heur De Bratand/Malesan.*
Canadian Club Puissance - **Walter Gabathuler** of Switzerland riding *Beethoven II.*

CANADIAN CHAMPION BARREL RACER

Elaine Watt, Raymond, Alta.

CANADIAN COWBOY WINS INTERNATIONAL AWARD

Tom Eirikson, bronc rider, steer wrestler and calf roper from Innisfail, Alta., won the 1982 Linderman Award, an

O.M. Fuller Memorial Speed Competition - **Patrick Caron** of France riding *Heur De Bratand/Malesan.*
McKee International Stake Trophy - **Mark Leone** of the United Stataes riding *Tim.*
World Cup Grand Prix - Rothmans - **Frederic Cottier** of France riding *Flambeau C.*
O'Keefe International Team Championship Trophy - **France.**
Lt. Col. Stuart C. Bate Trophy for Leading Rider - **Frederic Cottier** of France.
Chairman's Leading Rider Award over the fall indoor circuit (sponsored by Mr. Moffat Dunlap) - **Katie Monahan** of the United States.

1982 MAJOR EVENT CHAMPIONS

Canadian Professional Rodeo Association

Cowboy of the Year Award (C.N. Woodward Award)
Jim Freeman, Olds, Alta.

All Around Champion

Mel Coleman, Pierceland, Sask.

Saddle Bronc Champion

Big Bull Mel Hyland, Langley, B.C.

Bull-riding Champion

Brian (Jenner) Abely, Jenner, Alta.

Bareback Champion

Steve Dunham, Turner Valley, Alta.

Calf-Roping Champion

Larry Robinson, Innisfail, Alta.

Steer-Wrestling Champion

Blaine Pederson, Amisk, Alta.
American prize that has gone to only one other Canadian, Kenny McLean, who won the buckle in 1967 and 1969.

The award commemorates Bill Linderman, one of the first cowboys elected to the Prorodeo Hall of Champions, who was also an executive with the Professional Rodeo Cowboy Association.

Eirikson won the Canadian Professional Rodeo Association central circuit calf-roping championships, and in 1980

and 1981 he was the Canadian All Around Champion. On the PRCA 1982 circuit, Eirikson won $23,856.88 in bronc riding, calf roping and steer wrestling.

DOG SLEDDING

The 1,688-kilometre IDITAROD race from Anchorage to Nome is the world's longest sled-dog race. An annual event, it offers a $24,000 first prize. **"Cowboy" Larry Smith** of Dawson City has run the race four times, finishing 14th, 4th and 28th in his first three tries. In 1983 he led the pack for most of the race and finished third after 12 days, 20 hours and 19 minutes on the trail.

CANADA'S SPORTS HALL OF FAME

Canada's Sports Hall of Fame has more than 300 members. They are honoured for outstanding achievements in sport in Canada.

Three new members were inducted in 1983:

Gerry Sorensen, Kimberley, B.C. She is the First Canadian woman to win a world downhill championship, winning at Grindewald, Switzerland, followed by a victory in Haus, Austria, in February 1982.

Egon Beiler, Kitchener, Ont. Beiler retired from competition in 1981. He competed primarily in the 60-kilogram division and was a world-class wrestler for a decade.

Ian Hume, Melbourne, Que. He was a top Canadian high jumper from 1938 to 1950 and at the age of 40 he competed in the 1954 British Empire Games. He was also active as a coach, manager and administrator.

Lionel Pretoria (The Big Train) Conacher

Lionel Conacher, born in Toronto, Ont., in 1901, excelled at hockey, football, lacrosse, boxing, track and field, swimming and rowing. He played for the Argonaut Grey Cup team of 1921, and for the Toronto Maple Leafs baseball team that won the Triple A championship in 1926. In 1921 he helped Toronto win the Ontario Lacrosse Association senior title and also helped Aura Lee defeat the Toronto Granites for the Sportsman Cup in hockey.

He played professional hockey for the Pittsburgh Pirates, New York Americans, Montreal Maroons and Chicago Black Hawks. He played on two Stanley Cup teams : Chicago in 1933-34 and Montreal in 1934-35. He was named to the second all-star NHL team twice and the first team once. He spent 11 seasons in the NHL as a defenceman, scoring 80 goals and earning 105 assists.

Conacher played in the International Lacrosse (Pro) League with the Montreal Maroons, boxed four rounds with Jack Dempsey, was Canadian light-heavyweight boxing champ, and also coached Chicago and the Maroons in the NHL. He was termed one of pro hockey's finest defencemen. In later life, Conacher became an MP, and died in 1954 of a heart attack during a Parliament Hill, Ottawa, charity softball game.

Lionel Conacher, Canada's athlete of the half-century, stars in first East-West Grey Cup championship, Dec. 3, 1921 (from the Prudential *Great Moments in Canadian Sport Collection*). Artist — Tom McNeely